COMPUTATIONAL SIMULATIONS AND APPLICATIONS

Edited by **Jianping Zhu**

Computational Simulations and Applications
Edited by Jianping Zhu

Published by InTech
Janeza Trdine 9, 51000 Rijeka, Croatia

Publishing Process Manager Ana Nikolic

Technical Editor Teodora Smiljanic

Cover Designer InTech Design Team

Additional hard copies can be obtained from orders@intechopen.com

Computational Simulations and Applications, Edited by Jianping Zhu
p. cm.
ISBN 978-953-307-430-6

For EU product safety concerns:
IN TECH d.o.o., Prolaz Marije Krucifikse Kozulić 3, 51000 Rijeka, Croatia,
info@intechopen.com or visit our website at intechopen.com.

Meet the editor

Dr. Jianping Zhu received his Ph.D. in applied mathematics from the State University of New York at Stony Brook in 1990. He was on the faculty of the Department of Mathematics and Statistics at Mississippi State University from 1990 to 2001, and was chair of the Department of Theoretical and Applied Mathematics at the University of Akron from 2001 – 2005. Since 2005, he has been chair of the Department of Mathematics at the University of Texas at Arlington. His research interests are in the areas of numerical algorithms, computational simulations, and scientific computing. He received the second place award in the 1990 IBM Supercomputing Competition and the Intel Research Fellowship Award in 1992. He has written one book, edited two books, published over 80 refereed papers, and made 120 conference and colloquium presentations in 21 countries. He also served on the editorial boards of six international journals and numerous conference organizing committees. Over the last two decades, his research and education projects have been funded by over $6 million in grants from the USA federal agencies and industrial partners.

Contents

Preface

Over the last half a century, the rapid integration of mathematical modeling, computing technology, and real-life applications has made computational simulation a powerful tool for researchers to study complex phenomena in the nature and the society around us. Along with theory and experiment, computational simulation has now become the third pillar for the foundation of scientific exploration. In many circumstances, computational simulations enable researchers to study complex problems in greater detail with better understanding than theory or experiments, such as in the study of protein dynamics. In other circumstances, computational simulations allow researchers to explore numerous different scenarios much more quickly and cost-effectively than experiments, such as in optimal design of modern aircrafts or screening of potential drug molecules.

One of the main challenges facing researchers in the field of computational simulations is the highly interdisciplinary nature of the field, which typically involves complex real-world application problems, mathematical models describing those problems, appropriate numerical solution algorithms for solving those model equations, and necessary computer hardware and software to carry out simulations. Successful computational simulation projects often require team-efforts and knowledge in mathematical modeling, computer programming, and specific application problems being studied.

The purpose of this book is to highlight the interdisciplinary nature of computational simulations and to introduce researchers and graduate students who are interested in computational simulations to a broad range of applications, with a particular emphasis on those involving computational fluid dynamics (CFD) simulations. The book is divided into three parts:

- Part I covers some basic research topics and development in numerical solution algorithms for computational fluid dynamics, including Reynolds stress transport modeling and central difference schemes for convection-diffusion equations (chapter 1 – 4), and flow simulations involving simple geometries such as a flat plate or a vertical channel (chapter 5 – 8).

- Part II covers a variety of important applications in which CFD simulations play a crucial role, including combustion process and automobile engine design (chapter

9 – 12), fluid heat exchange (chapter 13 – 14), airborne contaminant dispersion over buildings and atmospheric flow around a re-entry capsule (chapter 15 – 16), gas-solid two phase flow in long pipes (chapter 17), free surface flow around a ship hull (chapter 18), and hydrodynamic analysis of electrochemical cells (chapter 19).

- Part III covers applications of non-CFD based computational simulations, including atmospheric optical communications (chapter 20), environmental studies involving climate system simulations, porous media flow, and combustion (chapter 21 – 23), solidification (chapter 24), and sound field simulations for optimal acoustic effects (chapter 25).

I am grateful to InTech for the opportunity to serve as the editor for this book, and I wish to sincerely thank all contributing authors around the world for their diligence in following editorial guidelines, their willingness to support open access publications, and their valuable technical contributions that made this book possible. Special thanks are due to Ms. Ana Nikolic, Mr. Zeljko Spalj, and the technical staff at InTech for their editorial efforts, detailed reviews, and professional assistance. I also would like to thank the University of Texas at Arlington for supporting my participation in this book project. Without the support from the authors, InTech staff, and the University, this book could not have become a reality.

Jianping Zhu, Ph.D.
Professor and Chair
Department of Mathematics
The University of Texas at Arlington
Arlington, Texas,
USA

Part 1

Research and Numerical Algorithms in Computational Fluid Dynamics Simulations

1

Reynolds Stress Transport Modelling

Sharaf F. Al-Sharif
Center of Excellence in Desalination Technology, King Abdulaziz University, Jeddah Saudi Arabia

1. Introduction

The Reynolds–averaged Navier–Stokes (RANS) approach is the most commonly employed approach in CFD for industrial applications, and is likely to continue to be so for the foreseeable future. The need to handle complex wall-bounded flows, and the need to evaluate large numbers of design variations usually prohibits high-fidelity approaches such as direct numerical simulation (DNS), and large-eddy simulation (LES). The application of Reynolds–averaging to the equations of motion introduces a set of unclosed terms, the *Reynolds Stresses*, into the mean flow momentum equations, and turbulence models are needed to provide closure of these terms before the set of equations can be solved. Within the framework of RANS approaches, a hierarchy of modelling schemes exists based on the level of sophistication in which these unclosed terms are modelled. In Reynolds stress transport (RST) modelling, rather than assuming a direct (linear or non–linear) link between the Reynolds stresses and mean strain, a separate transport equation for each of the stress components is solved. This in principle provides a number of advantages over other RANS models, which will be reviewed here.

This chapter aims to provide a general introduction and overview of Reynolds Stress transport modelling. The first section will provide a brief historical background on the development of this class of models. Next, the theoretical background and rationale underlying the most common modelling practises within this framework are presented. This is followed by a discussion of some numerical implementation issues specific to RST modelling within the context of the finite volume method. Finally the chapter is closed with some concluding remarks.

2. Development of RST modelling

Early work leading to the development of Reynold-stress transport (RST) modelling was mainly theoretical, due to the relative complexity of this level of modelling compared to the available computational capabilities of the time. Chou (1945) constructed a formal solution to the fluctuating pressure Poisson equation that is the basis for current models of the pressure–strain-rate correlation. Later Rotta (1951), laid the foundation for Reynolds stress transport modelling by being the first to develop a closed model of all the terms in the exact equation (Speziale, 1991). Because of limited computational capability at the time, successful computations were not carried out until several decades later (Speziale, 1991). Another important development came when the continuum mechanics community speculated on the potential similarity between turbulent flow and the flow of non-Newtonian fluids (Gatski,

2004). This meant that tensor representation results from the continuum mechanics literature could be used to formulate expressions for the Reynolds-stress tensor, as first proposed by Rivlin (1957). These ideas were then expanded by Crow (1968; 1967), and Lumley (1967; 1970). Computational work accelerated in the 1970's with the works of Daly & Harlow (1970), Reynolds (1970), Donaldson (1971), Naot et al. (1972), Hanjalić & Launder (1972), and Lumley & Khajeh-Nouri (1974). In a landmark paper, Launder, Reece & Rodi (1975), developed a hierarchy of Reynolds-stress transport models by consolidating the work of various separate groups into a unified framework. They were able to successfully apply the models to a variety of free-shear and wall-bounded flows of practical interest (Launder et al., 1975). Their model, particularly the simple version (the 'Basic' model), has since been one of the most widely used RST models in engineering applications because of the combined advantage of being simple in form, yet retaining the ability to overcome many of the weaknesses of eddy-viscosity formulations (Hanjalić & Jakirlić, 2002).

Later Schumann (1977) introduced the concept of *realisability* as a constraint to guide model formulation. By this it is meant that models should be designed to prevent certain unphysical solutions, such as negative normal stress components, or a stress tensor that violates the Cauchy-Schwartz inequality. Lumley (1978) extensively discussed the significance and implementation of realisability requirements. He devised and used anisotropy invariant maps, or 'Lumley triangles', to illustrate the limiting states of turbulence with respect to values of the second and third invariants of the Reynolds-stress anisotropy tensor. Lumley pointed out that to prevent a negative normal stress component from arising during computations, the time derivative of the component must be made to vanish at the instant when the component itself vanishes, thereby preventing a negative value to arise as time progresses. Such a situation can arise near a wall or a free-surface, where the interface-normal component decays much faster than the other components as the interface is approached, thus approaching a *two-component* limit. Shih & Lumley (1985) later used these arguments to devise a realisable model for the pressure–strain-rate correlation. Their model, however, did not perform well in simple shear flows, and higher order corrections were later added to achieve better agreement with these flows (Craft & Launder, 2002). Speziale (1985; 1987) used arguments of material-frame indifference in the limit of two-dimensional turbulence to develop a model for the rapid pressure–strain-rate correlation. Speziale et al. (1991) later considered the simplest topologically equivalent form (returning the same equilibrium states) to that of the Speziale (1987) model, to arrive at a more simplified, similarly performing version (Speziale et al., 1991). This latter model is also in relatively common use in engineering RST computations.

The UMIST group, starting with the work of Fu et al. (1987), Fu (1988), Craft et al. (1989), and Craft (1991) developed a model also based on ensuring realizability in the two-component limit, but using an approach slightly different from that used by Shih & Lumley. This model (the 'TCL' model, in what follows) uses a cubic expansion of the rapid pressure–strain-rate correlation in k and a_{ij}. It was shown to achieve significant improvements over previous models in a wide range of flows.

3. Modelling practises

In this section the basic equations for the mean flow of incompressible fluids are presented, along with the equations for the relevant turbulence statistics. At the level of Reynolds stress transport modelling, the Reynolds averaged Navier–Stokes (RANS) equations are solved, along with separate equations for each independent component of the Reynolds stress tensor, as well as a transport equation for the scalar rate of dissipation of turbulent kinetic energy.

The modelling approach used for the various terms appearing in the exact Reynolds stress transport equation are briefly reviewed.

3.1 Basic equations of turbulent flow

Turbulent flows are characterised by highly fluctuating velocity, pressure, and other field variables. One approach for dealing with this fluctuating nature of the flow, the one most widely used by engineers, is to work with an averaged form of the basic equations. In *Reynolds averaging* the instantaneous flow variables are decomposed into an average quantity and a fluctuation. Thus,

$$\begin{aligned}\widetilde{U}_i &= U_i + u_i \\ \widetilde{P} &= P + p\,,\end{aligned} \tag{1}$$

where capital letters denote averaged quantities, and small letters denote purely fluctuating quantities. The averaging can be either over time or over a repeated realisation of an experiment with the same nominal conditions. The latter, *ensemble* averaging, will be implied in the following, to allow for temporal variations of mean quantities. When this decomposition is substituted into the Navier Stokes equations for incompressible flow, and the result is ensemble averaged, one obtains the Reynolds-averaged Navier-Stokes (RANS) equations

$$\frac{\partial U_i}{\partial t} + U_j\frac{\partial U_i}{\partial x_j} = -\frac{1}{\rho}\frac{\partial P}{\partial x_i} + \nu\frac{\partial^2 U_i}{\partial x_j^2} - \frac{\partial \overline{u_i u_j}}{\partial x_j}\,. \tag{2}$$

When the decomposition is substituted into the continuity equation for incompressible flow, and averaging is applied, one obtains for the mean flow

$$\frac{\partial U_i}{\partial x_i} = 0\,. \tag{3}$$

If this is subtracted from the instantaneous continuity equation, the continuity condition for the fluctuating velocity is obtained

$$\frac{\partial u_i}{\partial x_i} = 0\,, \tag{4}$$

meaning that both the mean and fluctuating velocity fields are individually divergence free. The last term in the RANS equation (2) contains the Reynolds stress tensor $\overline{u_i u_j}$. Thus the averaging process introduced a new unknown tensor term, and the set of equations is no longer closed. This is called the *closure* problem of averaging approaches. The task of turbulence modelling is to construct appropriate models for these stresses that relate them to the mean flow quantities, and thus to construct a closed set of equations allowing numerical solutions to be obtained. An additional implied objective in the engineering context is for the models to be as computationally inexpensive as possible while being able to reproduce the behaviour and phenomena of relevance to the problem in question, at the required level of accuracy.

A transport equation for the fluctuating velocity can be obtained by subtracting the RANS equation (2) from the Navier-Stokes equation. Using the divergence-free property of the fluctuating field, the result can be written as

$$\frac{\overline{D}u_i}{\overline{D}t} = -\frac{1}{\rho}\frac{\partial p}{\partial x_i} - u_j\frac{\partial U_i}{\partial x_j} - \frac{\partial}{\partial x_j}\left[u_i u_j - \overline{u_i u_j} - \nu\frac{\partial u_i}{\partial x_j}\right] \tag{5}$$

The operator $\overline{\mathrm{D}}/\overline{D}t$ is used to denote the material derivative following the mean flow

$$\frac{\overline{D}}{\overline{D}t} = \frac{\partial}{\partial t} + U_j \frac{\partial}{\partial x_j} \,. \tag{6}$$

Since this interpretation will be used exclusively here, the over-bar on this mean-flow material derivative will subsequently be dropped. An exact equation for the Reynolds stresses can be obtained by using (5) to construct

$$\frac{\mathrm{D}\overline{u_i u_j}}{\mathrm{D}t} = \overline{u_j \frac{\mathrm{D}u_i}{\mathrm{D}t} + u_i \frac{\mathrm{D}u_j}{\mathrm{D}t}} \,,$$

where it has been assumed that averaging and taking the material derivative (6) commute. The result is

$$\begin{aligned} \frac{\mathrm{D}\overline{u_i u_j}}{\mathrm{D}t} &= -\left(\overline{u_i u_k} \frac{\partial U_j}{\partial x_k} + \overline{u_j u_k} \frac{\partial U_i}{\partial x_k} \right) \\ &+ \overline{\frac{p}{\rho} \left(\frac{\partial u_i}{\partial x_j} + \frac{\partial u_j}{\partial x_i} \right)} \\ &+ \frac{\partial}{\partial x_k} \left[\nu \frac{\partial \overline{u_i u_j}}{\partial x_k} - \overline{u_i u_j u_k} - \overline{\frac{p}{\rho} (u_i \delta_{jk} + u_j \delta_{ik})} \right] \\ &- 2\nu \overline{\frac{\partial u_i}{\partial x_k} \frac{\partial u_j}{\partial x_k}} \,. \end{aligned} \tag{7}$$

The first term on the right hand side above is the production rate of Reynolds stresses by mean velocity gradients. This term is closed at the RST level since it is given in terms of quantities that are being solved for at this level. All the remaining terms in the equation, except for viscous diffusion, require modelling. The second term is a correlation between the fluctuating pressure and the fluctuating strain rate. From continuity this term is traceless, so it does not contribute directly to the kinetic energy of the turbulence. Its effect is to redistribute the energy between the stress components, so it plays a very important role in determining the degree of anisotropy of the stresses. Accordingly, it has received much attention from researchers, and continues to do so. The third term in (7) is a combination of several diffusion terms, all having the effect of spatial redistribution of the Reynolds stresses. Finally, the last term is the dissipation rate of Reynolds stresses by viscous action at the smallest scales of turbulence. Since the smallest scales of motion are assumed to be isotropic, the dissipation rate tensor is frequently modelled as $\varepsilon_{ij} = \frac{2}{3}\varepsilon\,\delta_{ij}$, where ε is the scalar dissipation rate of turbulent kinetic energy. This approximation is not applicable near walls or free surfaces, where the dissipation tensor becomes markedly anisotropic. Equation (7) can be written in short form as

$$\frac{\mathrm{D}\overline{u_i u_j}}{\mathrm{D}t} = P_{ij} + \phi_{ij} + \mathcal{D}_{ij} - \varepsilon_{ij} \,, \tag{8}$$

where it is understood that each term above defines the notation for the corresponding term in (7).

An equation for the kinetic energy associated with the turbulent fluctuations, $k = \frac{\overline{u_i u_i}}{2}$, can be obtained by taking half the contraction of (7). The resulting equation is

$$\frac{\mathrm{D}k}{\mathrm{D}t} = -\overline{u_i u_k}\frac{\partial U_i}{\partial x_k} + \frac{\partial}{\partial x_k}\left[\nu\frac{\partial k}{\partial x_k} - \overline{u_i u_i u_k} - \frac{1}{\rho}\overline{p u_i}\delta_{ik}\right] - \nu\overline{\frac{\partial u_i}{\partial x_k}\frac{\partial u_i}{\partial x_k}}\,. \qquad (9)$$

In short form, this can be written

$$\frac{\mathrm{D}k}{\mathrm{D}t} = P_K + \mathcal{D} - \varepsilon \qquad (10)$$

The first term on the right hand side of (9) is the production of turbulent kinetic energy by mean velocity gradients. The next term is the diffusion of turbulent kinetic energy by various mechanisms. Finally, the last term is the scalar dissipation rate of turbulent kinetic energy. The short form (10) defines the notation that will be used in the following for the respective terms in (9). It is often convenient to work with the deviatoric Reynolds stress anisotropy tensor a_{ij} defined as,

$$a_{ij} = \frac{\overline{u_i u_j}}{k} - \frac{2}{3}\delta_{ij}\,. \qquad (11)$$

3.2 Pressure–strain rate correlation

Modelling of the pressure–strain rate correlation is to a large extent guided by consideration of the exact equation for it. An equation for the fluctuating pressure can be obtained by taking the divergence of (5), and invoking continuity (4). This gives

$$\frac{1}{\rho}\frac{\partial^2 p}{\partial x_k \partial x_k} = -2\frac{\partial U_i}{\partial x_j}\frac{\partial u_j}{\partial x_i} - \frac{\partial^2}{\partial x_i \partial x_j}(u_i u_j - \overline{u_i u_j}) \qquad (12)$$

A formal solution to this Poisson equation can be constructed using the method of Green's functions, as first demonstrated by Chou (1945). The Green's function of the Laplacian operator is

$$g(\mathbf{x}|\mathbf{x}') = \frac{-1}{4\pi|\mathbf{x}-\mathbf{x}'|}\,.$$

The fluctuating pressure is thus given by

$$\frac{p}{\rho} = \frac{1}{4\pi}\iiint_V \left[-2\frac{\partial U_i}{\partial x'_j}\frac{\partial u_j}{\partial x'_i} - \frac{\partial^2}{\partial x'_i \partial x'_j}(u_i u_j - \overline{u_i u_j})\right]_{\mathbf{x}',t}\frac{\mathrm{d}\mathbf{x}'}{|\mathbf{x}-\mathbf{x}'|} + \text{Surface integral.} \qquad (13)$$

It can be seen from this equation that the fluctuating pressure can be decomposed into three components (Pope, 2000), corresponding to the three terms appearing on the right-hand side of (13). The first term is linear in the turbulent fluctuations, and responds directly to changes in mean velocity gradient. It is thus called the *rapid* pressure, p^r. The second is a turbulence-turbulence interaction term, that does not respond directly to changes in the mean flow, but through the turbulent cascade process, and is thus called the *slow* pressure, p^s. The last term is the solution to the homogeneous (Laplace) equation and satisfies appropriate boundary conditions that ensure the superposition of the three parts, p, satisfies its own boundary conditions (Pope, 2000). This final term is only significant close to a wall or a free surface, and, since the emphasis here is on modelling regions away from walls, it will be neglected. Wall effects on ϕ_{ij} are considered in Section 3.3.

Based on the above decomposition, the pressure–strain rate correlation can similarly be decomposed into rapid, slow, and *wall influence* terms. The rapid part can be constructed as follows

$$\phi^r_{ij} = \overline{\frac{p^r}{\rho}\left(\frac{\partial u_i}{\partial x_j} + \frac{\partial u_j}{\partial x_i}\right)} \tag{14}$$

$$\begin{aligned}\frac{p^r}{\rho}\left(\frac{\partial u_i}{\partial x_j}\right) &= \frac{1}{2\pi}\iiint_{-\infty}^{\infty}\left(\frac{\partial U_k}{\partial x'_l}\frac{\partial u_l}{\partial x'_k}\right)_{\mathbf{x}',t}\left(\frac{\partial u_i}{\partial x_j}\right)_{\mathbf{x},t}\frac{d\mathbf{x}'}{|\mathbf{x}-\mathbf{x}'|}\\ &= \frac{1}{2\pi}\frac{\partial U_k}{\partial x_l}\iiint_{-\infty}^{\infty}\frac{\partial^2}{\partial x_j \partial x'_k}(u_i(\mathbf{x})u_l(\mathbf{x}'))\frac{d\mathbf{x}'}{|\mathbf{x}-\mathbf{x}'|}.\end{aligned} \tag{15}$$

In taking $\frac{\partial U_k}{\partial x'_l}$ outside the integral it is assumed that this term is reasonably constant over the volume integral. In homogeneous flows, that is of course exact, but is an approximation in inhomogeneous ones. One can thus write:

$$\phi^r = \frac{\partial U_k}{\partial x_l}\left(\mathcal{M}_{iljk} + \mathcal{M}_{jlik}\right), \tag{16}$$

where the fourth rank tensor $\mathcal{M}_{iljk}$ is given by

$$\mathcal{M}_{iljk} = \frac{-1}{2\pi}\iiint_{\infty}^{\infty}\frac{\partial^2 \overline{u_i(\mathbf{x})u_l(\mathbf{x}+\mathbf{r})}}{\partial r_j \partial r_k}\frac{d\mathbf{r}}{|\mathbf{r}|}, \tag{17}$$

using $\mathbf{r} = \mathbf{x}' - \mathbf{x}$ for the separation distance. The $\mathcal{M}_{iljk}$ tensor is symmetric in the first two indices, and in the last two

$$\mathcal{M}_{iljk} = \mathcal{M}_{lijk} = \mathcal{M}_{ilkj}. \tag{18}$$

The divergence-free velocity condition means that contraction over the middle indices results in the quantity vanishing:

$$\mathcal{M}_{ijjk} = 0, \tag{19}$$

and contraction over the last two indices can be shown to yield (twice) the Reynolds stress tensor

$$\mathcal{M}_{ilkk} = 2\,\overline{u_i u_l}\,. \tag{20}$$

The last of these kinematic conditions (20) suggested to workers that the $\mathcal{M}$ tensor could be modelled as a function of the Reynolds stresses (Launder et al., 1975). The approach taken was to model $\mathcal{M}$ as a polynomial function in the stresses. The most general fourth-rank tensor linear in the Reynolds stresses satisfying the symmetry conditions (18) is

$$\begin{aligned}\mathcal{M}_{ijkl} =& \alpha\delta_{kl}\overline{u_i u_j} + \beta(\delta_{ik}\overline{u_j u_l} + \delta_{il}\overline{u_j u_k} + \delta_{jk}\overline{u_i u_l} + \delta_{jl}\overline{u_i u_k})\\ &+\gamma\delta_{ij}\overline{u_k u_l} + [\eta\delta_{ij}\delta_{kl} + v(\delta_{ik}\delta_{jl} + \delta_{il}\delta_{jk})]k,\end{aligned} \tag{21}$$

where the coefficients $\alpha, \beta, \gamma, \eta, v$ are constants (or functions of the invariants of a_{ij}). The continuity condition (19), and the normalisation condition (20) can be used to reduce the number of undetermined constants to one. When this is done, and the resulting modelled $\mathcal{M}_{ijkl}$ is substituted into (16) the resulting linear rapid pressure–strain rate model is

$$\phi^r_{ij} = -\frac{\gamma+8}{11}(P_{ij} - 2/3P\delta_{ij}) - \frac{30\gamma-2}{55}k\left(\frac{\partial U_i}{\partial x_j} + \frac{\partial U_j}{\partial x_i}\right) - \frac{(8\gamma-2)}{11}(D_{ij} - 2/3D\delta_{ij}), \tag{22}$$

where D_{ij} is given by

$$D_{ij} = -\overline{u_i u_k}\frac{\partial U_k}{\partial x_j} - \overline{u_j u_k}\frac{\partial U_k}{\partial x_i}, \tag{23}$$

and $D = D_{ii}/2$. This is the first of the two Launder-Reece-Rodi (LRR) models in Launder et al. (1975), called the *Quasi-Isotropic* model (LRR-QI). A simplified version of (22) was also suggested in Launder et al. (1975) by observing that the dominant term in this equation is the first one appearing on the right hand side. The model thus obtained, first proposed by Naot et al. (1972), is sometimes termed the *isotropization of production* model (LRR-IP),

$$\phi^r_{ij} = -c_2(P_{ij} - \tfrac{2}{3}P\,\delta_{ij}). \tag{24}$$

Various other models have been proposed following similar lines of reasoning, in which $\mathcal{M}$ is modelled as a tensor-polynomial function of the Reynolds stress tensor or, equivalently, expressed in terms of k and a_{ij}

$$\mathcal{M} = \mathcal{M}(k, \mathbf{a})\,. \tag{25}$$

It is worth pointing out at this stage that there is an intrinsic weakness in all such models of the form (25). The tensor $\mathcal{M}$, as defined by (17), contains two kinds of directional information – the direction of the energetic velocity components, and the direction of variation or dependence of the two-point correlation (Pope, 2000). Only the former type of information is contained in the Reynolds stress tensor, so two fields having the same Reynolds stresses can have different $\mathcal{M}$ tensors. More explicitly put, the evolution of the Reynolds stresses is not uniquely determined by the Reynolds stresses (Pope, 2000). This is an intrinsic limitation in RST modelling, that is difficult to overcome without significantly complicating the modelling approach and/or computational cost (Johansson & Hallbäck, 1994; Kassinos & Reynolds, 1994). This limitation is known to cause poor results in flows where the velocity gradient has a strong rotational component, such as in pure (or dominant) rotation, and in high shear rate flows (Johansson & Hallbäck, 1994). However, in many other flows, including ones with significant rotational effects, RST models have been shown to produce very good results.
As for the slow pressure–strain-rate term, ϕ^s_{ij}, it is difficult to extract anything from the exact expression, pertaining to the non-linear turbulence–turbulence interaction part of (13). Most early models followed Rotta's (1951) linear return to isotropy model for the slow term

$$\phi^s_{ij} = -C_1 \varepsilon a_{ij}\,. \tag{26}$$

This model is motivated by the decay of homogeneous anisotropic turbulence in the absence of mean velocity gradients. It is generally observed that in such cases turbulence progressively tends towards an isotropic state, hence the negative sign in (26).
Experimental evidence shows that the return-to-isotropy process is in fact non-linear in a_{ij} (Chung & Kim, 1995). When plotted on anisotropy invariant maps, the paths taken during return-to-isotropy experiments are not straight lines, and have different behaviour depending on the sign of the third invariant (Pope, 2000). It is also found that the rate of return is highly dependent on the Reynolds number. A number of nonlinear models for the slow pressure strain term have been suggested in the literature.

3.3 Wall effects on ϕ_{ij}

The presence of a wall alters pressure fluctuations by viscous effect through the no-slip condition, and by inviscid effect through the impermeability condition. DNS results show that the viscous effect is confined to a region within $y^+ \approx 15$ from the wall (Mansour et al., 1988). The inviscid wall-blocking effect on the other hand is significant where the distance from the wall is of the same order as the turbulent length scale. Wall blocking causes two opposing effects; *wall reflection* of the fluctuating pressure field increases the energy-redistributing pressure fluctuations, which pushes turbulence towards isotropy, while it also causes selective damping of the wall-normal fluctuating velocity component in turbulent eddies, thereby increasing anisotropy. The latter effect dominates, and turbulence anisotropy near a wall is higher than that in a free shear flow at a similar rate of shear. To account for this, Gibson & Launder (1978) proposed two additive corrections to ϕ_{ij} using the unit normal vector to the wall, n_i. The first, based on the proposal of Shir (1973), is an additive correction to the slow part

$$\phi_{ij}^{s,w} = C_1^w \frac{\varepsilon}{k}\left(\overline{u_k u_m} n_k n_m \delta_{ij} - \tfrac{3}{2}\overline{u_i u_k} n_k n_j - \tfrac{3}{2}\overline{u_j u_k} n_k n_i\right) f_w \tag{27}$$

and the second, is a correction to the rapid part

$$\phi_{ij}^{r,w} = C_2^w \left(\phi_{km}^r n_k n_m \delta_{ij} - \tfrac{3}{2}\phi_{ik}^r n_k n_j - \tfrac{3}{2}\phi_{jk}^r n_k n_i\right) f_w \tag{28}$$

where $C_1^w = 0.5$, $C_2^w = 0.3$, and $f_w = 0.4k^{3/2}/(\varepsilon x_n)$ is a damping function based on the ratio of the turbulence length scale to the normal distance to the wall, x_n.

3.4 Modelling dissipation

While modelling of the turbulent kinetic energy, and of the pressure–strain rate correlation, has been to at least some degree guided by consideration of their exact equations, the same is not true for the standard dissipation rate model (Pope, 2000). Dissipation of turbulent kinetic energy is associated with the smallest scales of the fluctuating field, while the kinetic energy itself is mostly contained in the largest scales of fluctuations. The exact dissipation rate equation is comprised of a large number of terms that are all related to dissipative-scale processes, and all but one of the source-terms require modelling. It is thus not a useful starting point for modelling the dissipation rate. Instead the more empirical approach taken is motivated by the spectral energy transfer view of dissipation. The kinetic energy of the larger energy containing eddies is transferred by vortex-stretching in the presence of mean velocity gradients to smaller eddies, and the same process occurs at the 'next' smaller scales, and so on to the smallest dissipative scales, where kinetic energy is finally converted to heat by viscous (molecular) action. If the molecular viscosity is somehow changed, all that happens is that the size of the dissipative scales change to accommodate the rate of energy they receive, but the rate itself is not affected. Thus even though the *mechanism* of dissipation is governed by processes that occur at the smallest scales, dissipation can also be viewed as an energy-transfer rate that readjusts itself with the amount of energy it receives. In this sense, the amount (as opposed to the mechanism) of dissipation is in fact determined by the energy in larger scales. Under the assumption of spectral equilibrium, the transfer rate of energy across the spectrum of turbulence scales is constant and determined by the rate of energy input. Based on this assumption, and the preceding arguments, the conventional equation for dissipation is assumed to be of the form

$$\frac{D\varepsilon}{Dt} = C_{\varepsilon 1}\frac{\varepsilon}{k}P + \mathcal{D}_\varepsilon - C_{\varepsilon 2}\frac{\varepsilon^2}{k}, \tag{29}$$

where $\mathcal{D}_\varepsilon$ is the diffusion of ε. The modelled production term above reflects the assumed direct link between a single rate of transfer of energy across the spectrum and production of energy at the large scales. This assumption is an obvious weakness in the model when the turbulence is not in equilibrium, as when unsteady solutions are sought, or where the time-scale of the mean flow is of the same order or smaller than the characteristic time-scale of turbulence. In such cases the small-scale turbulence may not have enough time to adjust to the large-scale scale variations, and the instantaneous link implied by the production term in (29) is questionable.

The destruction term in (29) is motivated by consideration of the decay of homogeneous isotropic turbulence in the absence of production (Pope, 2000). In such a flow one expects that the turbulence will decay in a self-similar form in which the rates of decay of k and ε are proportional

$$\frac{k/\frac{dk}{dt}}{\varepsilon/\frac{d\varepsilon}{dt}} = \frac{-k/\varepsilon}{\varepsilon/\frac{d\varepsilon}{dt}} = C$$

If this proportionality constant is labelled $C_{\varepsilon 2}$, the following destruction term is implied

$$\frac{d\varepsilon}{dt} = -C_{\varepsilon 2}\frac{\varepsilon^2}{k} \tag{30}$$

3.5 Diffusion modelling

There are three diffusive transport terms on the right hand side of (7). The first is the viscous diffusion term

$$V_{ij} = \nu\frac{\partial^2\overline{u_i u_j}}{\partial x_k \partial x_k} \tag{31}$$

which is closed and does not require modelling. The following two terms are the pressure diffusion and turbulent convection, respectively. Most commonly these are modelled together as a combined turbulent diffusion term, T_{ij}, using the generalised gradient diffusion hypothesis (GGDH) of Daly & Harlow (1970),

$$T_{ij} = \frac{\partial}{\partial x_l}\left(C_s\frac{\varepsilon}{k}\overline{u_l u_k}\frac{\partial\overline{u_i u_j}}{\partial x_k}\right) \tag{32}$$

where C_s is typically 0.22.

A deficiency of this model is that it does not preserve the symmetry under cyclic permutation of indices that is exhibited by the triple velocity moments $\overline{u_i u_j u_k}$. This is only significant when the triple moments and pressure diffusion are modelled separately. In such case an improved model that has been suggested by Hanjalić & Launder (1972) is often used,

$$\overline{u_i u_j u_k} = -C_s\frac{k}{\varepsilon}\left(\overline{u_i u_l}\frac{\partial\overline{u_j u_k}}{\partial x_l} + \overline{u_j u_l}\frac{\partial\overline{u_k u_i}}{\partial x_l} + \overline{u_k u_l}\frac{\partial\overline{u_i u_j}}{\partial x_l}\right). \tag{33}$$

More elaborate models exist in the literature, as in (Craft, 1998) for example, but the models mentioned above are the ones more commonly used.

3.6 Accounting for low-Re effects

Viscous effects on turbulence properties and their implications on modelling are considered next. The absence of viscous terms in the equation for fluctuating pressure (12) suggests that viscous effects on the fluctuating pressure will be of secondary importance compared to the inviscid effects due to impermeability, considered in section 3.3. The focus of the discussion is thus directed to the dissipation rate tensor, and the transport equation for the scalar dissipation rate. When discussing low-Re effects, reference is frequently made to the turbulent Reynolds number, $\mathrm{Re_t}$, defined as

$$\mathrm{Re_t} = \frac{k^2}{\nu\varepsilon}. \tag{34}$$

As previously mentioned, at high Reynolds numbers the dissipation rate tensor is assumed to be isotropic, $\varepsilon_{ij} = \frac{2}{3}\varepsilon\,\delta_{ij}$. This, however, will cease to be true near a wall where the high anisotropy of the turbulence is expected to be increasingly felt at the smaller scales as the wall is approached. The simplest model accounting for this effect is that of Rotta (1951), which is based on the idea that the anisotropy of the dissipation rate tensor is similar to the stress anisotropy, thus

$$\varepsilon_{ij} = \frac{\overline{u_i u_j}}{k}\varepsilon. \tag{35}$$

This model was used by Hanjalić & Launder (1976) to give the following blending approximation for the dissipation rate tensor

$$\varepsilon_{ij} = \frac{2}{3}\varepsilon\left[(1-f_s)\,\delta_{ij} + f_s\frac{3}{2}\frac{\overline{u_i u_j}}{k}\right], \tag{36}$$

where f_s is a function of $\mathrm{Re_t}$ whose value ranges from 1 to 0 as $\mathrm{Re_t}$ ranges from 0 to ∞, ensuring the desired behaviour of ε_{ij} in these limits. The near-wall model (35) is the simplest form accounting for near-wall anisotropy of the dissipation tensor. Launder & Reynolds (1983) have shown that this form does not give the correct near-wall asymptotic behaviour of the individual tensor elements, which are rather given by

$$\begin{aligned} \frac{\varepsilon_{ij}}{\varepsilon} &= \frac{\overline{u_i u_j}}{k}, \quad i \neq 2, j \neq 2 \\ \frac{\varepsilon_{12}}{\varepsilon} &= 2\frac{\overline{u_i u_2}}{k}, \quad i \neq 2 \\ \frac{\varepsilon_{22}}{\varepsilon} &= 4\frac{\overline{u_2 u_2}}{k}. \end{aligned} \tag{37}$$

What is needed then is a term to replace the Rotta model in (36) which yields the correct asymptotic behaviour described by (37), and which contracts to 2ε. One possible form that satisfies these requirements is

$$\varepsilon^*_{ij} = \frac{\varepsilon/k\left(\overline{u_i u_j} + \overline{u_i u_k}\,n_j\,n_k + \overline{u_j u_k}\,n_i\,n_k + \overline{u_k u_l}\,n_k\,n_l\,\delta_{ij}\right)}{\left(1 + \frac{5}{2}n_p n_q \overline{u_p u_q}/k\right)}, \tag{38}$$

where n_i represents a component of the wall-normal unit vector (Pope, 2000). The use of the wall vector in a model is undesirable because of the ambiguity it introduces in complex geometries. One way to avoid it is based on the observation that the quantity $\nabla k^{1/2}$, evaluated near a wall, is a vector that points in the wall-normal direction. Thus

$$\vec{n} = \frac{\nabla k^{1/2}}{|\nabla k^{1/2}|}, \tag{39}$$

and using the value of the dissipation at the wall for a wall with $\vec{n} = (0, 1, 0)$,

$$|\nabla k^{1/2}|_{x_2=0} = \left(\frac{\partial k^{1/2}}{\partial x_2} \frac{\partial k^{1/2}}{\partial x_2} \right)^{1/2}_{x_2=0} = \sqrt{\frac{\varepsilon}{2\nu}}. \tag{40}$$

Quantities of the form $n_i n_j$ appearing in (38) can therefore be replaced by

$$n_i n_j = \frac{2\nu}{\varepsilon} \frac{\partial k^{1/2}}{\partial x_i} \frac{\partial k^{1/2}}{\partial x_j}. \tag{41}$$

Following Hanjalić & Launder (1976), when considering the implications of Low-Re effects on dissipation rate modelling, it is instructive to consider the exact transport equation for the energy dissipation rate. This is given by (Daly & Harlow, 1970)

$$\begin{aligned} \frac{\mathrm{D}\varepsilon}{\mathrm{D}t} = & -2\nu \overline{\frac{\partial u_i}{\partial x_k} \frac{\partial u_i}{\partial x_l} \frac{\partial u_k}{\partial x_l}} - 2\overline{\left(\nu \frac{\partial^2 u_i}{\partial x_k \partial x_l} \right)^2} - \frac{\partial}{\partial x_k} \left[\overline{u_k \varepsilon} + \frac{2\nu}{\rho} \overline{\frac{\partial u_k}{\partial x_l} \frac{\partial p}{\partial x}} - \nu \frac{\partial \varepsilon}{\partial x_k} \right] \\ & -2\nu \left(\overline{\frac{\partial u_i}{\partial x_l} \frac{\partial u_l}{\partial x_i}} + \overline{\frac{\partial u_l}{\partial x_i} \frac{\partial u_l}{\partial x_k}} \right) \frac{\partial U_i}{\partial x_k} - 2\nu \overline{u_k \frac{\partial u_i}{\partial x_l}} \frac{\partial^2 U_i}{\partial x_k \partial x_l}. \end{aligned} \tag{42}$$

All the terms on the right hand side above are unclosed, with the exception of viscous diffusion. The first two terms on the right hand side of (42) are the dominant ones in high Re flows. Respectively they represent generation and destruction of ε. The third term, which represents a combination of diffusive processes, can be of the same order as the difference of the first two, and must therefore be retained. These three terms are modelled by the three terms that typically appear in high-Re ε transport models, as in section 3.4. The fourth and fifth terms are respectively of order $\mathrm{Re_t}^{1/2}$ and $\mathrm{Re_t}$ smaller than the other terms (Hanjalić & Launder, 1976), and are thus neglected in high-Re model versions. In low-Re models these terms need to be reconsidered and accounted for if necessary. The last term is often modelled as

$$-2\nu \overline{u_k \frac{\partial u_i}{\partial x_l}} \frac{\partial^2 U_i}{\partial x_k \partial x_l} = C_{\varepsilon 3} \nu \frac{k \overline{u_j u_k}}{\varepsilon} \left(\frac{\partial^2 U_i}{\partial x_j \partial x_l} \right) \left(\frac{\partial^2 U_i}{\partial x_k \partial x_l} \right). \tag{43}$$

This term is present in several Low-Re models developed by the Manchester group. As for the fourth term, initial proposals meant to account for it by allowing the coefficient of the production and destruction terms, $C_{\varepsilon 1}$and $C_{\varepsilon 2}$, to be functions of $\mathrm{Re_t}$. Similarly, possible viscous effects on the diffusion terms were to be accounted for by allowing the term C_ε to depend on $\mathrm{Re_t}$ (Hanjalić & Launder, 1976). However, computations revealed that adding the term in (43) alone was sufficient in producing good agreement between computed energy profiles and available data to within experimental accuracy. Thus dependence of the coefficients $C_{\varepsilon 1}$, $C_{\varepsilon 2}$, C_ε on the turbulence Reynolds number is often (not always) abandoned. Finally the viscous diffusion term, neglected in high-Re models, is retained in its exact form.

3.7 The Launder–Reece–Rodi models

In their seminal 1975 paper, Launder, Reece & Rodi laid out a hierarchy of RST models based on arguments presented in section 3.2. Two rapid pressure-strain rate models were proposed. The first is the quasi-isotropic model (LRR-QI), which has the most general linear tensorial form satisfying the required symmetry conditions, and is given by

$$\phi^r_{ij} = -C_2(P_{ij} - \tfrac{2}{3}\delta_{ij}\,P_K) - C_3(D_{ij} - \tfrac{2}{3}\delta_{ij}\,P_K) - 2C_4 k\,S_{ij}, \tag{44}$$

where S_{ij} is the mean strain rate tensor, defined as:

$$S_{ij} = \frac{1}{2}\left(\frac{\partial U_i}{\partial x_j} + \frac{\partial U_j}{\partial x_i}\right), \tag{45}$$

and the coefficients have the following values

$$C_2 = 0.764, \quad C_3 = 0.182, \quad C_4 = 0.109\,. \tag{46}$$

The second rapid pressure-strain rate model is the isotropization of production model (LRR-IP), which is also referred to as the 'Basic' model, and simply retains the first term of the QI model and neglects the other two. Thus,

$$\phi^r_{ij} = -C_2(P_{ij} - \tfrac{2}{3}\delta_{ij}\,P_K), \tag{47}$$

where the coefficient C_2 is now set at 0.6. Both models use the Rotta return-to-isotropy model for the slow pressure-strain rate term,

$$\phi^s_{ij} = -C_1\varepsilon a_{ij}\,, \tag{48}$$

but the coefficient C_1 is 1.5 for the QI model and 1.8 for the IP model.
In the original proposal turbulent diffusion T_{ij} is modelled using (33) for the triple velocity moments (pressure diffusion is usually neglected). In many later implementations this is replaced by the simpler GGDH. Thus the models can be written as

$$\frac{D\overline{u_i u_j}}{Dt} = P_{ij} - C_1\varepsilon a_{ij} + \phi^r_{ij} + \phi^{s,w}_{ij} + \phi^{r,w}_{ij} + \frac{\partial}{\partial x_l}\left(C_s\frac{\varepsilon}{k}\overline{u_l u_k}\frac{\partial\overline{u_i u_j}}{\partial x_k}\right) - \tfrac{2}{3}\delta_{ij}\varepsilon \tag{49}$$

where ϕ^r_{ij} is replaced by either the QI or IP models, and the wall-reflection terms $\phi^{s,w}_{ij}, \phi^{r,w}_{ij}$ are given by (27) and (28), respectively. Since these models are intended as high Re models, the viscous diffusion term is neglected and an isotropic dissipation rate tensor is assumed.
Finally, closure is completed with the standard high-Re dissipation rate equation, given by

$$\frac{D\varepsilon}{Dt} = C_{\varepsilon 1}\frac{\varepsilon}{k}P_K - C_{\varepsilon 2}\frac{\varepsilon^2}{k} + \frac{\partial}{\partial x_k}\left(C_\varepsilon\frac{k}{\varepsilon}\overline{u_k u_l}\frac{\partial\varepsilon}{\partial x_l}\right), \tag{50}$$

where

$$C_{\varepsilon 1} = 1.44, \quad C_{\varepsilon 2} = 1.92, \quad C_\varepsilon = 0.15. \tag{51}$$

The Shima low-Re model

In its original form, the Launder & Shima (1989) model is a low-Re version of the Basic model that uses wall reflection terms and includes Re_t-based damping coefficients to return the correct near-wall behaviour. Shima (1998) later proposed a low-Re model, based on the QI pressure-strain rate model, that does away with the wall reflection terms in the interest of more general applicability to complex geometries. The model admittedly gives stress anisotropy results in steady channel flow that are inferior to his previous low-Re formulation, but this is a compromise made in order to discard the wall reflection terms with their associated difficulties related to complex geometries. The pressure-strain rate coefficients are no longer constant, and are given by the following expressions:

$$C_1 = 1 + 2.45 A_2^{0.25} A^{0.75} [1 - \exp(-49A^2)] \times \{1 - \exp[-(Re_t/60)^2]\} \tag{52a}$$

$$C_2 = 0.7A \tag{52b}$$

$$C_3 = 0.3A^{0.5} \tag{52c}$$

$$C_4 = 0.65A(0.23C_1 + C_2 - 1) + 1.3A_2^{0.25} C_3 \tag{52d}$$

where A_2, A_3 are the second and third invariants of the stress anisotropy tensor:

$$A_2 = a_{ij}a_{ji} \quad A_3 = a_{ij}a_{jk}a_{ki} \,. \tag{53}$$

and A is the 'flatness' parameter first defined by Lumley (1978),

$$A = 1 - \tfrac{9}{8}(A_2 - A_3). \tag{54}$$

Turbulent diffusion, comprising the triple velocity correlation and the pressure velocity correlation, is modelled using the simple gradient diffusion of Daly & Harlow (1970)

$$T_{ij} = \frac{\partial}{\partial x_k}\left(C_s \frac{k}{\varepsilon} \overline{u_k u_l} \frac{\partial \overline{u_i u_j}}{\partial x_l} \right) \tag{55}$$

where $C_s = 0.22$.
The dissipation equation is given by

$$\frac{D\varepsilon}{Dt} = C_{\varepsilon 1}\frac{\varepsilon}{k}P - C_{\varepsilon 2}\frac{\varepsilon\tilde{\varepsilon}}{k} + \frac{\partial}{\partial x_k}\left(C_\varepsilon \frac{k}{\varepsilon}\overline{u_k u_l}\frac{\partial \varepsilon}{\partial x_l} + \nu \frac{\partial \varepsilon}{\partial x_k} \right). \tag{56}$$

where $\tilde{\varepsilon}$ is the homogeneous dissipation rate, defined as:

$$\tilde{\varepsilon} = \varepsilon - 2\nu \left(\frac{\partial k^{1/2}}{\partial x_i} \right)^2 . \tag{57}$$

The coefficients $C_{\varepsilon 2}$,C_ε retain their typical values 1.92, 0.15 respectively, but $C_{\varepsilon 1}$ is prescribed as:

$$C_{\varepsilon 1} = 1.44 + \beta_1 + \beta_2 \,, \tag{58a}$$

$$\beta_1 = 0.25A\min(\lambda/2.5 - 1,\, 0) - 1.4A\min(P/\varepsilon - 1,\, 0) \,, \tag{58b}$$

$$\beta_2 = 1.0A\lambda^2 \max(\lambda/2.5 - 1,\, 0) \,, \tag{58c}$$

$$\lambda = \min(\lambda^*,\, 4) \,, \tag{58d}$$

$$\lambda^* = \left[\frac{\partial}{\partial x_i}\left(\frac{k^{1.5}}{\varepsilon}\right) \frac{\partial}{\partial x_i}\left(\frac{k^{1.5}}{\varepsilon}\right) \right] . \tag{58e}$$

3.8 The Speziale–Sarkar–Gatski model

Speziale et al. (1991) developed a pressure-strain rate model that is quadratic in a_{ij} by first considering the most general form for ϕ_{ij} (slow and rapid) that is linear in the mean strain and rotation tensors and quadratic in a_{ij}. Then they obtained their model by considering the simplest subset of that general form that has an equivalent structural equilibrium in plane homogeneous flows. The resulting model has a rapid part that is linear in a_{ij}, and a quadratic slow part, given by

$$\begin{aligned}\phi_{ij} = &- (2d_1\varepsilon + d_1^* P_\kappa)\frac{a_{ij}}{2} + \frac{d_2}{4}\varepsilon(a_{ik}a_{kj} - \tfrac{1}{3}a_{kl}a_{kl}\delta_{ij}) \\ &+ \left(d_3 - d_3^*\frac{\sqrt{A_2}}{2}\right)kS_{ij} + \frac{d_4}{2}k(a_{ik}S_{jk} + a_{jk}S_{ik} - \tfrac{2}{3}a_{kl}S_{kl}\delta_{ij}) \\ &+ \frac{d_5}{2}k(a_{ik}\Omega_{jk} + a_{jk}\Omega_{ik}),\end{aligned} \tag{59}$$

where Ω_{ij} is the mean vorticity tensor defined as:

$$\Omega_{ij} = \frac{1}{2}\left(\frac{\partial U_i}{\partial x_j} - \frac{\partial U_j}{\partial x_i}\right), \tag{60}$$

and the coefficients have the following values

$$d_1 = 1.7, \quad d_1^* = 1.8, \quad d_2 = 4.2, \quad d_3 = \tfrac{4}{5}, \quad d_3^* = 1.3, \quad d_4 = 1.25, \quad d_5 = 0.4. \tag{61}$$

The rapid part of the SSG model, aside from the nonlinear dependence on A_2 in third term of (59), is tensorially equivalent to the QI model.
Diffusion is modelled using the GGDH, and the standard high-Re version of the ε equation (50) is used, but the coefficient $C_{\varepsilon 2}$ is assigned the slightly lower value of 1.83.

3.9 The Hanjalić–Jakirlić low-Re model

Jakirlić & Hanjalić (1995) developed a low-Re RSTM that is based on the LRR-IP model, and the Gibson & Launder (1978) wall corrections (27) and (28), making modifications to handle Low-Re and near-wall effects. The modifications are expressed in terms of $\mathrm{Re_t}$, the stress anisotropy invariants, A_2, A_3, in addition to invariants of the stress dissipation rate anisotropy tensor, E_2, E_3, defined as:

$$E_2 = e_{ij}e_{ji} \quad E_3 = e_{ij}e_{jk}e_{ki}, \tag{62}$$

$$e_{ij} = \frac{\varepsilon_{ij}}{\varepsilon} - \frac{2}{3}\delta_{ij}. \tag{63}$$

A 'flatness' parameter based on the stress dissipation rate anisotropy invariants is also used:

$$E = 1 - \frac{9}{8}(E_2 - E_3). \tag{64}$$

The modelled RST equation is given by:

$$\begin{aligned}\frac{D\overline{u_i u_j}}{Dt} =& P_{ij} - C_1\varepsilon a_{ij} - C_2\left(P_{ij} - \frac{2}{3}\delta_{ij}P_\kappa\right) + \phi_{ij}^{s,w} + \phi_{ij}^{r,w} \\ &+ \frac{\partial}{\partial x_l}\left(C_s\frac{\varepsilon}{k}\overline{u_l u_k}\frac{\partial\overline{u_i u_j}}{\partial x_k}\right) - \varepsilon_{ij}.\end{aligned} \tag{65}$$

The coefficients are specified by:

$$C_1 = C + \sqrt{A}E^2, \quad C = 2.5AF^{1/4}f, \quad F = \min(0.6,\, A_2)\,, \tag{66}$$

$$C_2 = 0.8\sqrt{A}\,, \tag{67}$$

$$f = \min\left[\left(\frac{\mathrm{Re}_t}{150}\right)^{3/2}, 1\right], \tag{68}$$

$$C_2^w = \max(1 - 0.7C, 0.3), \quad C_2^w = \min(A, 0.3)\,. \tag{69}$$

The damping coefficient appearing in the wall correction terms (27) and (28) is given by:

$$f_w = \min\left[\frac{k^{3/2}}{2.5\varepsilon x_n}, 1.4\right]. \tag{70}$$

The modelled dissipation rate transport equation is given by:

$$\begin{aligned} \frac{\mathrm{D}\varepsilon}{\mathrm{D}t} &= C_{\varepsilon 1}\frac{\varepsilon}{k}P_\kappa - C_{\varepsilon 2}f_\varepsilon\frac{\varepsilon\tilde{\varepsilon}}{k} + \frac{\partial}{\partial x_k}\left(C_\varepsilon\frac{k}{\varepsilon}\overline{u_k u_l}\frac{\partial\varepsilon}{\partial x_l} + \nu\frac{\partial\tilde{\varepsilon}}{\partial x_k}\right) \\ &+ C_{\varepsilon 3}\,\nu\frac{k}{\varepsilon}\,\overline{u_i u_j}\,\frac{\partial^2 U_k}{\partial x_i \partial x_l}\frac{\partial^2 U_k}{\partial x_j \partial x_l} - C_{\varepsilon 4}f_4 k\,\Omega_k\,\Omega_k + S_l. \end{aligned} \tag{71}$$

The coefficients have the following specified values:

$$C_{\varepsilon 1} = 2.6 \quad C_{\varepsilon 2} = 1.92 \quad C_{\varepsilon 3} = 0.25 \quad C_{\varepsilon 4} = 0.1 \quad C_\varepsilon = 0.18\,, \tag{72}$$

and

$$f_\varepsilon = 1 - \frac{C_{\varepsilon 2} - 1.4}{C_{\varepsilon 2}}\exp\left[-\left(\frac{\mathrm{Re}_t}{6}\right)^2\right]. \tag{73}$$

The length-scale growth correction, S_l, is given by:

$$S_l = \max\left\{\left[\left(\frac{1}{C_l}\frac{\partial l}{\partial x_n}\right)^2 - 1\right]\left(\frac{1}{C_l}\frac{\partial l}{\partial x_n}\right)^2, 0\right\}\frac{\tilde{\varepsilon}\varepsilon}{k}A\,, \tag{74}$$

where $l = k^{3/2}/\varepsilon$, and $C_l = 2.5$.
The anisotropic stress dissipation rate tensor is modelled as:

$$\varepsilon_{ij} = f_s\varepsilon_{ij}^* + (1 - f_s)\frac{2}{3}\delta_{ij}\varepsilon, \tag{75}$$

where ε_{ij}^* is given by:

$$\varepsilon_{ij}^* = \frac{\varepsilon}{k}\frac{\overline{u_i u_j} + (\overline{u_i u_k}\,n_j\,n_k + \overline{u_j u_k}\,n_i\,n_k + \overline{u_k u_l}\,n_k\,n_l\,n_i\,n_j)f_d}{1 + \frac{3}{2}n_p n_q\frac{\overline{u_p u_q}}{k}f_d}, \tag{76}$$

$$f_s = 1 - \sqrt{A}E^2, \quad f_d = (1 + 0.1\mathrm{Re}_t)^{-1}. \tag{77}$$

3.10 The Two-Component-Limit model

Researchers at UMIST, starting with the work of Fu et al. (1987), and Craft et al. (1989), developed a stress transport model that satisfies the constraint of realizability in the limit of two component turbulence. An outline of the derivation of the model is presented in Craft & Launder (2002). Using similar arguments as in (21), but retaining up to cubic terms in a_{ij}, and using the additional constraint of realizability, the following model for ϕ^r_{ij} was obtained

$$\begin{aligned}
\phi^r_{ij} = & -0.6\left(P_{ij} - 2/3\delta_{ij}P\right) + 0.6a_{ij}P \\
& -0.2\left\{\frac{\overline{u_k u_j}\,\overline{u_l u_i}}{k}\left[\frac{\partial U_k}{\partial x_l} + \frac{\partial U_l}{\partial x_k}\right] - \frac{\overline{u_l u_k}}{k}\left[\overline{u_i u_k}\frac{\partial U_j}{\partial x_l} + \overline{u_j u_k}\frac{\partial U_i}{\partial x_l}\right]\right\} \\
& -c_2\left\{A_2(P_{ij} - D_{ij}) + 3a_{mi}a_{nj}(P_{mn} - D_{mn})\right\} \\
& +c_2'\left\{\left(\frac{7}{15} - \frac{A_2}{4}\right)(P_{ij} - 2/3\delta_{ij}P)\right. \\
& +0.2[a_{ij} - 1/2(a_{ik}a_{kj} - 1/3\delta_{ij}A_2]P - 0.05a_{ij}a_{lk}P_{kl} \\
& +0.1\left[\frac{\overline{u_i u_m}}{k}P_{mj} + \frac{\overline{u_j u_m}}{k}P_{mi} - 2/3\,\delta_{ij}\frac{\overline{u_l u_m}}{k}P_{ml}\right] \\
& +0.1\left[\frac{\overline{u_l u_i}\,\overline{u_k u_j}}{k^2} - 1/3\,\delta_{ij}\frac{\overline{u_l u_m}\,\overline{u_k u_m}}{k^2}\right]\cdot\left[6D_{lk} + 13k\left(\frac{\partial U_l}{\partial x_k} + \frac{\partial U_k}{\partial x_l}\right)\right] \\
& \left. +0.2\frac{\overline{u_l u_i}\,\overline{u_k u_j}}{k^2}(D_{lk} - P_{lk})\right\}
\end{aligned} \tag{78}$$

where A_2 is the second invariant of the stress anisotropy tensor defined in (53). In the earliest, high-Re, version of the model the recommended values of the coefficients, C_2, C_2', are

$$C_2 = 0.55, \quad C_2' = 0.6\,.$$

As for the slow pressure–strain-rate term, a second-order expression in a_{ij} is used, where the coefficients are allowed to depend on the stress anisotropy invariants in such a way as to satisfy realizability (Craft & Launder, 2002). Dependency on the third invariant, A_3, is introduced through the flatness parameter, A, defined in (54). The flatness parameter becomes zero when one stress component vanishes; thus using the form

$$\phi^s_{ij} = -C_1\varepsilon[a_{ij} + c_1'(a_{ij}a_{jk} - \tfrac{1}{3}A_2\delta_{ij})] - f_A'\varepsilon a_{ij}\,, \tag{79}$$

where the coefficients are given by

$$C_1 = 3.1(A_2A)^{1/2} \quad C_1' = 1.1 \quad f_A' = A^{1/2}\,,$$

ensures that ϕ^s_{ij} drops to zero when the turbulence is two-component.

Low-Re TCL model

A low-Re version of the TCL model was presented by Craft (1998). This version adopts a slightly different decomposition of the velocity-pressure gradient correlation Π_{ij} (which appears in the exact RST equation *before* it is decomposed, as in (7)). The alternate decomposition was found to be more appropriate when modelling inhomogeneous flows. Where this correlation is typically decomposed into the pressure–strain-rate correlation and pressure diffusion, an alternative decomposition is obtained by defining:

$$\phi^*_{ij} = \Pi_{ij} - \tfrac{1}{3}\delta_{ij}\Pi_{kk}\,. \tag{80}$$

Constructing ϕ^*_{ij} in this way ensures that it is redistributive in nature, since it is traceless and thus cannot contribute to the level of kinetic energy. This redistributive quantity is modelled as

$$\phi^*_{ij} = \phi^{*,s}_{ij} + \phi^{*,r}_{ij} + \phi^{\text{inh},s}_{ij} + \phi^{\text{inh},r}_{ij}\,. \tag{81}$$

The quantities $\phi^{*,s}_{ij}, \phi^{*,r}_{ij}$ have the same form as their homogeneous counterparts (79) and (78), respectively, but the coefficients C_1, C_2 and C'_2 are prescribed by

$$C_1 = 3.1 f_A f_{\text{Re}_t} A_2^{1/2}\,, \tag{82a}$$

$$C_2 = \min\left\{0.55\left[1-\exp\left(\frac{-A^{1.5}\text{Re}_t}{100}\right)\right],\ \frac{3.2A}{1+S^*}\right\}, \tag{82b}$$

$$C'_2 = \min(0.6, A) + \frac{3.5(S^*-\Omega^*)}{3+S^*+\Omega^*} - 2S_I\,, \tag{82c}$$

where

$$f'_A = \sqrt{A} f_{\text{Re}_t} + A(1-f_{\text{Re}_t})\,, \tag{83}$$

$$f_{\text{Re}_t} = \min[(\text{Re}_t/160)^2, 1]\,, \tag{84}$$

$$f_A == \begin{cases} (A/14)^{1/2} & A < 0.05 \\ A/0.8367 & 0.05 < A < 0.7 \\ A^{1/2} & A > 0.7\,, \end{cases} \tag{85}$$

$$S^* = Sk/\varepsilon, \quad \Omega^* = \Omega k/\varepsilon, \tag{86}$$

$$S = (2S_{ij}S_{ji})^{1/2}, \quad \Omega = (2\Omega_{ij}\Omega_{ji})^{1/2}, \tag{87}$$

$$S_I = \frac{2\sqrt{2}S_{ij}S_{jk}S_{ki}}{(S_{lm}S_{ml})^{3/2}}, \tag{88}$$

and

$$S_{ij} = \frac{1}{2}\left(\frac{\partial U_i}{\partial x_j} + \frac{\partial U_j}{\partial x_i}\right), \Omega_{ij} = \frac{1}{2}\left(\frac{\partial U_i}{\partial x_j} - \frac{\partial U_j}{\partial x_i}\right). \tag{89}$$

The inhomogeneous corrections are independent of the wall-normal vector, and are given by

$$\begin{aligned}\phi_{ij}^{\text{inh},s} =& f_{w1}\frac{\varepsilon}{k}(\overline{u_l u_k} d_l^A \delta_{ij} - \tfrac{3}{2}\overline{u_i u_k} d_j^A - \tfrac{3}{2}\overline{u_j u_k} d_i^A) d_k^A \\ &+ f_{w2}\frac{\varepsilon}{k^2}\overline{u_l u_n}(\overline{u_n u_k} d_k^A \delta_{ij} - \tfrac{3}{2}\overline{u_i u_n} d_j^A - \tfrac{3}{2}\overline{u_j u_n} d_i^A) d_l^A \\ &+ f_{w3}\nu\left(a_{il}\frac{\partial\sqrt{k}}{\partial x_l}\frac{\partial\sqrt{k}}{\partial x_j} + a_{jl}\frac{\partial\sqrt{k}}{\partial x_l}\frac{\partial\sqrt{k}}{\partial x_i} - \frac{2}{3}a_{nl}\frac{\partial\sqrt{k}}{\partial x_l}\frac{\partial\sqrt{k}}{\partial x_n}\delta_{ij} - \frac{4}{3}a_{ij}\frac{\partial\sqrt{k}}{\partial x_l}\frac{\partial\sqrt{k}}{\partial x_l}\right) \\ &+ f'_{w1}\frac{k^2}{\varepsilon}\left(\overline{u_k u_l}\frac{\partial\sqrt{A}}{\partial x_k}\frac{\partial\sqrt{A}}{\partial x_l}\delta_{ij} - \frac{3}{2}\overline{u_i u_k}\frac{\partial\sqrt{A}}{\partial x_k}\frac{\partial\sqrt{A}}{\partial x_j} - \frac{3}{2}\overline{u_j u_k}\frac{\partial\sqrt{A}}{\partial x_k}\frac{\partial\sqrt{A}}{\partial x_i}\right),\end{aligned} \tag{90}$$

$$\phi_{ij}^{\text{inh},r} = f_I k \frac{\partial U_l}{\partial x_n} d_l d_n (d_i d_j - \tfrac{1}{3} d_k d_k \delta_{ij}), \tag{91}$$

where the 'normalised length-scale gradients', d_i, d_i^A, introduced by Craft & Launder (1996), are used indicate the direction of strong inhomogeneity, when present, without the use of a wall-normal vector. These are defined by

$$d_i = \frac{N_i}{0.5 + (N_k N_k)^{0.5}}, \quad \text{where} \quad N_i = \frac{\partial(k^{1.5}/\varepsilon)}{\partial x_i}, \tag{92a}$$

$$d_i^A = \frac{N_i^A}{0.5 + (N_k^A N_k^A)^{0.5}}, \quad \text{where} \quad N_i^A = \frac{\partial(k^{1.5}A^{0.5}/\varepsilon)}{\partial x_i}. \tag{92b}$$

The coefficients appearing in the inhomogeneous corrections are given by:

$$f_{w1} = 0.4 + 1.6\min\left\{1, \max\left[0, 1 - \frac{\text{Re}_t - 55}{20}\right]\right\}, \tag{93}$$

$$f_{w2} = 0.1 + 0.8A_2\min\left\{1, \max\left[0, 1 - \frac{\text{Re}_t - 50}{85}\right]\right\}, \tag{94}$$

$$f_{w3} = 2.5\sqrt{A}, \tag{95}$$

$$f'_{w1} = 0.22, \tag{96}$$

$$f_I = 2.5 f_A. \tag{97}$$

As discussed in Section 3.6, the dissipation tensor near a wall or free surface is anisotropic, and the low-Re TCL accordingly prescribes the following anisotropic model for the dissipation rate tensor,

$$\varepsilon_{ij} = (1 - f_\varepsilon)\frac{\varepsilon'_{ij} + \varepsilon''_{ij} + \varepsilon'''_{ij}}{D} + \tfrac{2}{3} f_\varepsilon \varepsilon \delta_{ij}, \tag{98}$$

where

$$
\begin{aligned}
\varepsilon'_{ij} =& \varepsilon \frac{\overline{u_i u_j}}{k} + 2\nu \frac{\overline{u_l u_n}}{k} \frac{\partial \sqrt{k}}{\partial x_l} \frac{\partial \sqrt{k}}{\partial x_n} \delta_{ij} \\
&+ 2\nu \frac{\overline{u_l u_i}}{k} \frac{\partial \sqrt{k}}{\partial x_j} \frac{\partial \sqrt{k}}{\partial x_l} + 2\nu \frac{\overline{u_l u_j}}{k} \frac{\partial \sqrt{k}}{\partial x_i} \frac{\partial \sqrt{k}}{\partial x_l}, \\
\varepsilon''_{ij} =& \varepsilon \left(2 \frac{\overline{u_l u_k}}{k} d_l^A d_k^A \delta_{ij} - \frac{\overline{u_l u_i}}{k} d_l^A d_j^A - \frac{\overline{u_l u_j}}{k} d_l^A d_i^A \right), \\
\varepsilon'''_{ij} =& C_{\varepsilon s} \nu k \left(\frac{\partial \sqrt{A}}{\partial x_k} \frac{\partial \sqrt{A}}{\partial x_k} \delta_{ij} + 2 \frac{\partial \sqrt{A}}{\partial x_i} \frac{\partial \sqrt{A}}{\partial x_j} \right), \\
D =& \frac{\varepsilon'_{kk} + \varepsilon''_{kk} + \varepsilon'''_{kk}}{2\varepsilon},
\end{aligned}
\tag{99}
$$

and the coefficients are taken as $f_\varepsilon = A^{3/2}$, $C_{\varepsilon s} = 0.2$. The term ε'_{ij} is similar in nature to the model in (38), and its purpose is to ensure the correct wall-limiting behaviour of ε_{ij}, as discussed in Section 3.6. The term ε''_{ij} serves the specific purpose of producing the dip in ε_{12} near $y/\delta = 0.1$ observed in DNS studies of plane channel flow, and finally the term ε'''_{ij} improves the behaviour of ε_{ij} at a free surface where there is strong inhomogeneity even without significant viscous effects (Craft & Launder, 1996).

Dissipation rate equation

Early high-Re implementations of the TCL model used the same transport equation for the scalar dissipation rate (50) as in the LRR models. In later versions of the TCL model (Batten et al., 1999; Craft, 1998), an equation for the homogeneous dissipation rate,

$$
\tilde{\varepsilon} = \varepsilon - 2\nu \left(\frac{\partial k^{1/2}}{\partial x_i} \right)^2,
\tag{100}
$$

is solved, which takes the form

$$
\begin{aligned}
\frac{\mathrm{D}\tilde{\varepsilon}}{\mathrm{D}t} =& C_{\varepsilon 1} \frac{\tilde{\varepsilon}}{k} P_K - C_{\varepsilon 2} \frac{\tilde{\varepsilon}^2}{k} - C'_{\varepsilon 2} \frac{(\varepsilon - \tilde{\varepsilon})\tilde{\varepsilon}}{k} + \frac{\partial}{\partial x_k} \left(C_\varepsilon \frac{k}{\varepsilon} \overline{u_k u_l} \frac{\partial \tilde{\varepsilon}}{\partial x_l} + \nu \frac{\partial \tilde{\varepsilon}}{\partial x_k} \right) \\
&+ C_{\varepsilon 3}\, \nu \frac{k}{\varepsilon} \overline{u_i u_j} \frac{\partial^2 U_k}{\partial x_i \partial x_l} \frac{\partial^2 U_k}{\partial x_j \partial x_l} + Y_E.
\end{aligned}
\tag{101}
$$

The term Y_E is a length-scale correction based on the proposal of Iacovides & Raisee (1997), and is given by

$$
Y_E = C_{\varepsilon l} \frac{\tilde{\varepsilon}^2}{k} \max[F(F+1)^2, 0],
\tag{102}
$$

and F in turn is given by

$$
F = \left(\frac{\partial l}{\partial x_j} \frac{\partial l}{\partial x_j} \right) - C_l \{ [1 - \exp(-B_\varepsilon \mathrm{Re_t})] + B_\varepsilon C_l \mathrm{Re_t} \exp(-B_\varepsilon \mathrm{Re_t}) \},
\tag{103}
$$

$$
l = k^{3/2}/\varepsilon, \quad B_\varepsilon = 0.1069, \quad C_l = 2.55.
\tag{104}
$$

The remaining coefficients are given by

$$\begin{aligned} C_{\varepsilon 1} &= 1.0, \quad C_{\varepsilon 2} = \frac{1.92}{1+0.7A_d\sqrt{A_2}}, \quad A_d = \max(A, 0.25), \\ C'_{\varepsilon 2} &= 1.0, \quad C_{\varepsilon 3} = 0.875, \\ C_{\varepsilon l} &= 0.5, \quad C_{\varepsilon} = 0.15. \end{aligned} \tag{105}$$

4. Numerical issues specific to RST modelling

There are a number of numerical difficulties associated with the use of RST models that are not present when using eddy viscosity formulations. In particular, the use of RST models results in relatively large source terms that increase the stiffness of the algebraic equation system, in addition to the fact that the equation set becomes highly non-linear and strongly coupled (Leschziner & Lien, 2002; Lien & Leschziner, 1994). When using a collocated grid, there is also the issue of odd-even decoupling of the velocities and the Reynolds stresses.

The use of an eddy-viscosity approach adds to the momentum equations a momentum diffusion term that can be treated implicitly, thus enhancing stability. Since no such term is present in RST model equations, one approach to improve stability when applying RST models is to add and subtract a gradient-diffusion term based on an effective viscosity, ν_{eff}. Considering the stress term $\overline{u^2}$, for example, one may write

$$\overline{u^2} = \left(\overline{u^2} + \nu_{\text{eff}}\frac{\partial U}{\partial x}\right) - \nu_{\text{eff}}\frac{\partial U}{\partial x},$$

allowing the unbracketed term to be treated implicitly in the U-momentum equation.

Since the effective viscosity does not affect the final converged solution, it is not uniquely specified. One would, in general, simply be trying to significantly reduce the residual stress term that must be treated explicitly in the source term. One way to specify the effective viscosity is by reference to a simplified form of the Basic Reynolds stress model equations. What is needed is to construct a relation between $\overline{u^2}$ and $\frac{\partial U}{\partial x}$, between $\overline{v^2}$ and $\frac{\partial V}{\partial x}$, and so on. Take $\overline{u^2}$ for example, and start by assuming its transport equation is source dominated:

$$P_{11} + \phi_{11} - \frac{2}{3}\varepsilon\delta_{ij} = 0\,. \tag{106}$$

Substituting for ϕ_{11} from the Basic model,

$$P_{11} - C_1\varepsilon\left(\frac{u^2}{k} - \frac{2}{3}\right) - C_2\left[P_{11} - \frac{1}{3}(P_{11} + P_{22} + P_{33})\right] - \frac{2}{3}\varepsilon\delta_{ij} = 0\,. \tag{107}$$

This leads to

$$-2\overline{u^2}\frac{\partial U}{\partial x}\left(1 - \frac{2}{3}C_2\right) - C_1\frac{\varepsilon}{k}\overline{u^2} + \left(\text{other terms not containing } \overline{u^2} \text{ or } \frac{\partial U}{\partial x}\right) = 0\,, \tag{108}$$

or

$$\overline{u^2} = \frac{(2 - \frac{4}{3}C_2)\overline{u^2}}{C_1}\frac{k}{\varepsilon}\frac{\partial U}{\partial x} + \text{O.T.} \tag{109}$$

Thus a suitable choice for ν_{11} is

$$\nu_{11} = \frac{2 - \frac{4}{3}C_2}{C_1}\frac{k}{\varepsilon}\overline{u^2}. \tag{110}$$

Similar consideration of the $\overline{v^2}$ transport equation leads to the specification

$$\nu_{22} = \frac{2 - \frac{4}{3}C_2}{C_1}\frac{k}{\varepsilon}\overline{v^2}, \tag{111}$$

and relating the shear stress $\overline{uv}$ to $\frac{\partial U}{\partial y}$ leads to the following specification for ν_{12}

$$\nu_{12} = \frac{1 - C_2}{C_1}\frac{k}{\varepsilon}\overline{v^2}. \tag{112}$$

Maintaining the required coupling between the velocity and Reynolds stress components can be accomplished through a Rhie-Chow-type interpolation (Leschziner & Lien, 2002):

$$\overline{u_P^2} = \underbrace{\frac{1}{a_P}\Big(\sum_i a_i \overline{u_i^2} + S_u\Big) + \frac{S_u}{a_P}}_{H_P/a_p} + \nu_{11}^P \frac{(U_w - U_e)_P}{\Delta x}. \tag{113}$$

Similarly,

$$\overline{u_E^2} = \frac{H_E}{a_E} + \nu_{11}^E \frac{(U_w - U_e)_E}{\Delta x}, \qquad \overline{u_e^2} = \frac{H_e}{a_e} + \nu_{11}^e \frac{(U_P - U_E)}{\Delta x}.$$

Using linear interpolation for ν_{11}^e and H_e/a_e, one obtains for the value at face e:

$$\begin{aligned}\overline{u_e^2} = &\underbrace{\tfrac{1}{2}(\overline{u_P^2} + \overline{u_E^2})}_{\text{linear interpolation}} \\ &\underbrace{+ \frac{1}{2\Delta x}\left\{ [\nu_{11}^P + \nu_{11}^E](U_P - U_E) - \nu_{11}^P (U_w - U_e)_P - \nu_{11}^E (U_w - U_e)_E \right\}}_{\text{velocity smoothing}}.\end{aligned} \tag{114}$$

Similar expressions can be constructed for the remaining faces, and for the remaining stress terms.

5. Concluding remarks

This chapter has provided an introduction to the subject of Reynolds stress transport modelling. A brief historical account of the development of this class of RANS models was presented. This was followed by an account of the theoretical background, assumptions, approximations, as well as the rationale behind the most commonly adopted RST modelling practises. Finally, some numerical implementation issues specific to RST models were briefly discussed.

The account served to illustrate areas of strength of this class of RANS models, such as the exact form of the stress production terms, and the abandoning of the incorrectly assumed direct link between stress and strain that characterises eddy–viscosity formulations. The presentation also serves to illustrate some inherent weaknesses of present RST models, which might also be thought of as areas for potential improvement. These weaknesses are a natural result of the complexity of turbulent phenomena, and of the persistent *closure* problem—transport equations for any level of statistical moments will always contain unclosed higher moment terms.

The realizability constraint is ultimately a kinematic constraint that serves to prevent certain un-physical results. Aside from that, it does not prescribe any particular dynamic *stimulus–response* type of link between the strain field and inter-component redistribution processes. Therefore there is no reason to expect that redistributive models, in the form of tensor polynomial expansions in stress anisotropy and velocity gradient, satisfying such constraints should return the correct response to all possible strain fields and histories, particularly ones far removed from those for which the models were calibrated.

This does not diminish the value of RST models, but rather serves to emphasise the importance of testing and validation in order to understand the limits of validity and accuracy for intended applications. As discussed earlier, there is always a trade-off between accuracy and computational cost, and the need for reliable RANS models for many types engineering simulations is not likely to be replaced by LES or DNS in the near future. More importantly, these arguments emphasise the need to strive for a deeper and more general understanding of the complex turbulent phenomena described by the unclosed terms in the transport equations, with the aim of building better models.

6. References

Batten, P., Craft, T. J., Leschziner, M. A. & Loyau, H. (1999). Reynolds-stress-transport modelling for compressible aerodynamic applications, *AIAA Journal* 37(7): 785–797.

Chou, P. Y. (1945). On velocity correlations and the solutions of the equations of turbulence fluctuation, *Quart. Appl. Math.* 3: 38–54.

Chung, M. K. & Kim, S. K. (1995). A nonlinear return-to-isotropy model with reynolds number and anisotropy dependency, *Physics of Fluids* 7: 1425–1436.

Craft, T. (1991). *Second-moment modelling of turbulent scalar transport*, PhD thesis, Faculty of Technolgy, University of Manchester.

Craft, T. J. (1998). Developments in a low-reynolds-number second moment closure and it's application to separating and reattaching flows, *International Journal of Heat and Fluid Flow* 19: 541–548.

Craft, T. J., Fu, S., Launder, B. E. & Tselepidakis, D. P. (1989). Developments in modelling the turbulent second-moment pressure correlations, *Technical Report TFD/89/1*, Dept. of Mech. Eng., UMIST.

Craft, T. J. & Launder, B. E. (1996). A reynolds stress closure designed for complex geometries, *International Journal of Heat and Fluid Flow* 17(3): 245–254.

Craft, T. J. & Launder, B. E. (2002). Closure modelling near the two-component limit, *in* B. Launder & N. Sandham (eds), *Closure Strategies for Turbulent and Transitional Flows*, Cambridge University Press.

Crow, S. (1968). Visco-elastic properties of fine-grained incompressible turbulence, *Journal of Fluid Mechanics* 33: 1–20.

Crow, S. C. (1967). Visco-elastic character of fine-grained isotropic turbulence, *Physics of Fluids* 10: 1587–1589.

Daly, B. J. & Harlow, F. H. (1970). Transport equations in turbulence, *Physics of Fluids* 13: 2634–2649.

Donaldson, C. d. (1971). A progress report on an attempt to construct an invariant model of turbulent shear flows, *Proc. AGARD Conf. on Turbulent Shear Flows*, number 1 in *B*, London.

Fu, S. (1988). *Computational modelling of turbulent swirling flows with second-moment closures*, PhD thesis, Faculty of Technology, University of Manchester.

Fu, S., Launder, B. E. & Tselepidkis, D. P. (1987). Accomodating the effect of high strain rates in modelling the pressure-strain correlation, *Technical Report TFD/87/5*, Dept. of Mech. Eng., UMIST.

Gatski, T. B. (2004). Constitutive equations for turbuelnt flows, *Theoret. Comput. Fluid Dynamics* 18: 345–369.

Gibson, M. M. & Launder, B. E. (1978). Ground effects on pressure fluctuations in the atmospheric boundary layer, *Journal of Fluid Mechanics* 86(03): 491–511.

Hanjalić, K. & Jakirlić, S. (2002). Second-moment turbulence closure modelling, *in* B. Launder & N. Sandham (eds), *Closure Strategies for Turbulent and Transitional Flows*, Cambridge University Press.

Hanjalić, K. & Launder, B. E. (1972). A reynolds stress model of turbulence and it's application to thin shear flows, *Journal of Fluid Mechanics* 52(4): 609–638.

Hanjalić, K. & Launder, B. E. (1976). Contribution towards a reynolds-stress closure for low-reynolds number turbulence, *Journal of Fluid Mechanics* 74: 593–610.

Iacovides, H. & Raisee, M. (1997). Computation of flow and heat transfer in 2d rib roughened passges, *in* K. Hanjalić & T. Peeters (eds), *Proceedings of the Second International Symposium on Turbulence, Heat and Mass Transfer*, Delft.

Jakirlić, S. & Hanjalić, K. (1995). A second-moment closure for non-equilibrium and separating high- and low-re number flows, *Proceedings of the* 10th *Symposium on Turbulent Shear Flows*, Vol. 3, The Pennsylvania State University, Pennsylvania, pp. 23–25–23–30.

Johansson, A. V. & Hallbäck, M. (1994). Modelling of rapid pressure–strain in reynolds-stress closures, *Journal of Fluid Mechanics* 269: 143–168.

Kassinos, S. C. & Reynolds, W. C. (1994). A structure-based model for the rapid distortion of homogeneous turbulence, *Technical Report TF-61*, Mech. Eng. Dept., Stanford University.

Launder, B. E. & Reynolds, W. C. (1983). Asymptotic near-wall stress dissipation rates in a turbulent flow, *Physics of Fluids* 26(5): 1157–1158.

Launder, B., Reece, G. & Rodi, W. (1975). Progress in the development of a reynolds-stress turbulence closure, *Journal of Fluid Mechanics* 68(3): 537–566.

Launder, B. & Shima, N. (1989). Second-moment closure for the near-wall sublayer: development and appilication, *AIAA Journal* 27: 1319–1325.

Leschziner, M. A. & Lien, F. S. (2002). Numerical aspects of applying second-moment closure to complex flows, *in* B. Launder & N. Sandham (eds), *Closure Strategies for Turbulent and Transitional Flows*, Cambridge University Press.

Lien, F. S. & Leschziner, M. a. (1994). Upstream monotonic interpolation for scalar transport with application to complex turbulent flows, *International Journal for Numerical Methods in Fluids* 19: 527–548.

Lumley, J. (1967). Rational approach to relations between motions of differing scales in turbulent flows, *Physics of Fluids* 10: 1405–1408.

Lumley, J. & Khajeh-Nouri, B. (1974). Computational modelling of turbulent transport, *Adv. Geophys.* 18Aa: 169–192.

Lumley, J. L. (1970). Toward a turbulent constitutive relation, *Journal of Fluid Mechanics* 41: 413–434.

Lumley, J. L. (1978). Computational modelling of turbulent flows, *Adv. Appl. Mech.* 18: 123–176.

Mansour, N. N., Kim, J. & Moin, P. (1988). Reynolds-stress and dissipation-rate budgets in a turbulent channel flow, *Journal of Fluid Mechanics* 194: 15–44.

Naot, D., Shavit, A. & Wolfshtein, M. (1972). Prediction of flow in square section ducts, *Technical Report 154*, Mech. Eng. Dept., Technion, Haifa.

Pope, S. B. (2000). *Turbulent flows*, Cambridge University Press.

Reynolds, W. C. (1970). Computation of turbulent flows—state-of-the-art, *Technical Report MD-27*, Mech. Eng. Dept., Stanford University.

Rivlin, R. (1957). The relation between the flow of non-newtonian fluids and turbulent newtonian fluids, *Quart. Appl. Math.* 15: 212–215.

Rotta, J. C. (1951). Statistiche theorie nichthomogener turbulenz, *Z. Phys.* 129: 547–572.

Schumann, U. (1977). Realizability of reynolds-stress turbulence models, *Physics of Fluids* 20: 721–725.

Shih, T. S. & Lumley, J. L. (1985). Modelling of pressure correlation terms in reynolds-stress and scalar flux equations, *Technical Report FDA-85-3*, Cornell University, Ithaca, N.Y.

Shima, N. (1998). Low-reynolds-number second-moment closure without wall-reflection redistribution terms, *International Journal of Heat and Fluid Flow* 19: 549–555.

Shir, C. C. (1973). A preliminary numerical study of atmospheric turbulent flows in the idealized planetary boundary layer, *Journal of Atmospheric Science* 30: 1327–1339.

Speziale, C. G. (1985). Modelling the pressure gradient-velocity correlation of turbulence, *Physics of Fluids* 28: 69–71.

Speziale, C. G. (1987). Second-order closure models for rotating turbulent flows, *Quarterly of Applied Mathematics* 45: 721–733.

Speziale, C. G. (1991). Analytical methods for the development of reynolds-stress closures in turbulence, *Annual Review of Fluid Mechanics* 23: 107–157.

Speziale, C., Sarkar, S. & Gatski, T. (1991). Modelling the pressure-strain correlation of turbulence: an invariant dynamical systems approach, *Journal of Fluid Mechanics* 227: 245–272.

2

Study of Some Key Issues for Applying LES to Real Engineering Problems

Xiaolong Yang
Hunan University
China

1. Introduction

Most of nature and industry flows are turbulence. There are three kinds of numerical simulation methods for turbulent flows (Lesieur 1990; Pope 2000; Sagaut 2000, 2006): direct numerical simulation (DNS), Reynolds-averaged Navier-Stokes equations (RANS) and large eddy simulation (LES). DNS is a straightforward way to simulate turbulent flows. Full Navier-Stokes equations are discretized and solved numerically without any model, empirical parameter or approximation. Theoretically speaking, results of DNS exactly reflect the real flow and the whole range of turbulence scales are computed. With DNS, people can compute and visualize any quantity of interest, including some that are too difficult or impossible to be measured by experiments. But as we all know the computation cost is very high. For high Reynolds number flow, even modern computer technology can not satisfy the computation requirement.

In RANS, the flow quantities are decomposed into two parts: the average or mean term and the fluctuating term by applying Reynolds averaging. The effect of the fluctuating quantities on the mean flow quantities is described by the so called Reynolds stress tensor, which is must be modelled in terms of the mean velocities. Typical models can be grouped loosely into three categories: algebraic models, one-equation models and two-equation models. RANS is simple and robust. It is widely used in engineering problem. The general limitation of RANS is the fact that the model must represent a very wide range of scales. While the small scales tend to be universal, and depend on viscosity, the larger scales depend largely on flow condition and boundaries. So there is no one universal model for all flows. For different flows, the model must be modified to obtain good results. Another issue is that usually a time averaging is adopted in RANS. So RANS has difficult to handle unsteady flows.

In LES, a filter is applied to separate the large scales from small scales. Then only the large, energy carrying scales (or called resolved scales) of turbulence are computed exactly by solving the governing equations. While the small, fluctuating scales are modelled, which is also called subgrid scales (SGS). Compared to RANS, LES has several advantages: 1) LES can capture the large scales directly which are the main energy container of turbulence and response for the momentum and energy transfer. 2) The dissipation of turbulence energy is believed to be done by small scales. Since small scales are thought to be homogenous, universal, and less affected by flow and boundary conditions, the SGS model can be simple and requires fewer *ad hoc* parameters when it is applied to different flows. This is the big advantage of LES over RANS. That also is the reason why simple Smagrinsky model can obtain reasonable results in different flows. 3) LES can solve the unsteady flow directly. In additional, LES requires much less computation resource when compared to DNS because only large scales are computed.

Although LES has some advantages, for a long time RANS methods were used almost exclusively for the analysis of turbulent flows for practical engineering problems. LES has largely been used to study simple turbulent flows(Mahesh et al 2004; Georgiadis 2008; Bouffanais 2010). The primary reason is the computational cost. Until recently, the field of LES is attracting more and more people's attention. Not only its own scientific researcher who is applying LES to study the turbulence, but more industrial partners and engineers have started implementing LES to study real complex flows. There are two main reasons: 1) the urgent requirements from industry. the characteristics of lots nature or real engineering flows are determined by unsteady large scale motion, such as the external flow around ground vehicle, high attack angle airfoil flow etc. RANS models usually have difficult to handle such flows. But in order to improve the performance of airplane, to reduce the drag and noise around vehicle, we have to investigate such flow in depth. (2) rapid increases in computing power, memory, and storage, plus high efficient and high order computation algorithm. Indeed in the past few years applying LES to real engineering flows has becomes a research *hot spot*, such as LES of airfoil (Mary&Sagaut 2001; Dahlstrom&Davidson 2003; Mellen et al 2003), ground vehicle (McCallen *et al.* 2006; Kitoh *et al.* 2009; Krajnovic&Davidson 2005; Rodi 2006; Tsubokura *et al.* 2009; Minguez *et al.* 2008), combustion and reacting flows (Moin 2002), weather forecasting etc. But the application of LES is still limited. There are some key issues needed to solved before LES can be successfully applied to real engineering turbulence(Georgiadis 2008; Bouffanais 2010), such as the suitable SGS model, the choice of filter, the wall model, the transition model, the effect of numerical errors and the interactions between these issues. However as Bouffanais (Bouffanais 2010) pointed out that despite the numerous challenges still facing LES, one can fairly admit that LES has become one of the most promising and successful methodology available to simulate industrial turbulent flows.

In this chapter, three key issues of LES are discussed briefly: the SGS model, the filter and the numerical errors. First, the SGS model is the most important item in LES and has been extensive studied. There are thousand of different models which have been proposed during the past. But most of them are limited to simple geometry and have difficult to be applied to engineering problems. Right now the most widely used SGS models in complicated turbulence are still the simple Smagrinsky model (Smagorinsky 1963) and the so called the monotone integrated LES (MILES) model. So a simple, robust, efficient and can handling complicated geometry SGS model is what we need. The second problem is the choice of filter. In simple geometry, usually a smooth filter is adopted which is defined continuous in the whole domain. But in complicated geometry, only local discrete filter can be used. Obvious the order of filtering will be decreased. Its effect on SGS model and final simulation result need to be investigated. The third is the numerical errors of different discretization schemes. The effect of numerical errors on LES is a delicate issue and has been ignored for a long time because in simple geometry very high order can be achieved by pseudo-spectral mothod or other algorithm. But for complex problem, usually only second order can be achieved. The interaction between numerical scheme and SGS model is complicated. A first extensive theoretical analysis of numerical errors in LES has been proposed by Ghosal (Ghosal 1996) and later Chow and Moin (Chow and Moin 2003). They believed that 2nd order discretization scheme is not suitable for LES because it introduces errors larger than the SGS term. High order schemes are necessary. By applying the eddy-damped quasi-normal Markovian (EDQNM) theory to LES, a so called dynamic error analysis has been performed by Park and Mahesh (Park and Mahesh 2007) Their results show that low order scheme is acceptable for LES. The study of Yang and Fu (Yang and Fu 2008) show that there are complicated interactions between SGS model and numerical errors. A good SGS model can not only represent the effect of small scales to large scales, but also can dump the unphysical energy introduced by numerical scheme. So by careful designed SGS model, low order discretization scheme can also obtain reasonable result. Fauconnier *et al* (Fauconnier *et al* 2009) also point out that low-order methods may have advantages over high order scheme because the dissipation error of SGS model can cancel part of the numerical errors resulting in a reduction of the total errors on some quantities. Of course the disadvantage is that the accuracy of small scales is not controlled. So the best is high order scheme plus high accurate SGS model.

2. Governing equations and numerical methods

In Large Eddy Simulation (LES) a filtering operation is applied to separate the large scales from the small scales (Leonard 1974). In general, a filtered variable can be written as

$$\bar{f}(x) = \int_D f(x')G(x,x';\bar{\Delta})dx' \tag{2.1}$$

where G is the filter kernel and D is the filtering domain. The filter is characterized by a filter width $\bar{\Delta}$. The corresponding wave number $k_c = \pi/\bar{\Delta}$ is called as the filter cut-off wave number.

For our study, the fluid is assumed to be incompressible; the viscosity is constant; there are no body forces; and the flow is initially homogenous, isotropic, i.e. there are no mean velocity gradients. So the incompressible Navier-Stokes equations after applying a low-pass filter can be written as

$$\frac{\partial \bar{u}_i}{\partial t} + \frac{\partial \overline{u_i u_j}}{\partial x_j} = -\frac{1}{\rho}\frac{\partial \bar{P}}{\partial x_i} + \frac{\partial}{\partial x_j}\left[\nu\left(\frac{\partial \bar{u}_i}{\partial x_j} + \frac{\partial \bar{u}_j}{\partial x_i}\right)\right] - \frac{\partial \tau_{ij}}{\partial x_j}\ \frac{\partial \bar{u}_i}{\partial x_i}. \tag{2.2}$$

Above equations are also called the incompressible LES equations. The u, P, ρ, ν are the velocity, pressure, density and kinematic viscosity, respectively. τ_{ij} is the subgrid stress (SGS) tensor

$$\tau_{ij} = \overline{u_i u_j} - \bar{u}_i\, \bar{u}_j\,. \tag{2.3}$$

It represents the effect of the unresolved (small) scales. It is the only unclosed term in the above LES equations (2.2) and should be parameterized in terms of the resolved (large) scales.

In order to isolate other effects, the simplest homogenous, isotropic turbulence is chose as our simulation case. The advantage is that we can obtain the statistical quantities of this turbulence easily in spectral space, such s energy spectrum, total kinetic energy etc. So in such case it is convenience to write the governing equations in spectral space. Note the continuity equation can be combined with the pressure term through the projecting operation (Lesieur 1990). So the governing equation in spectral space can be simplified as

$$\left(\frac{\partial}{\partial t}+\upsilon k^2\right)\hat{u}_i(\mathbf{k},t)=-P_{im}(\mathbf{k})ik_j\widehat{u_j u_m}(\mathbf{k})\,. \tag{2.4}$$

where '$\wedge$' means the Fourier transform, the tensor $P_{im}(\mathbf{k})=\delta_{im}-k_i k_m/k^2$ is called the projection operator, which ensures the continuity equation automatically satisfied. And the $k=|\mathbf{k}|$.

For spatial discretization, a computation method similar to Rogallo's (Rogallo 1981) is adapted here. For the viscous term in the left hand side of equation (2.4), Rogallo proposed an integrated factor method which can solve it analytically.

$$\frac{\partial}{\partial t}\left[e^{\upsilon k^2 t}\hat{u}_i(\mathbf{k},t)\right]=-e^{\upsilon k^2 t}P_{im}(\mathbf{k})N_m(\mathbf{k})\,. \tag{2.5}$$

So the only term needed to be discretized is the nonlinear term in the right hand side, $N_m(\mathbf{k})=ik_j\widehat{u_j u_m}(\mathbf{k})$, which usually is solved by high order spectral scheme. But for engineering problem, spectral method is not available at most cases. Finite difference scheme or finite volume scheme is used instead. Among them, Padé compact scheme is widely adapted due to its flexibility in handling complex geometry and to obtaining high order. For one dimensional derivative, the Padé scheme proposed by Lele (Lele 1992) can be expressed as

$$\alpha f_{i-1}'+f_i'+\alpha f_{i+1}'=a\frac{f_{i+1}-f_{i-1}}{2\Delta}+b\frac{f_{i+2}-f_{i-2}}{4\Delta}\,. \tag{2.6}$$

Different coefficient defines different order of compact scheme. The highest order is 6th for 3 point stencil. The parameters of Lele (Lele 1992) are shown in Table 2.1.

Scheme	α	a	b	Order
Padé2	0	1	0	2
Padé4	1/4	3/2	0	4
Padé6	1/3	14/9	1/9	6

Table 2.1. Parameters for Padé compact scheme.

For the temporal advancement of the nonlinear term, an explicit second-order Runge-Kutta scheme, also known as predictor-corrector scheme, is used. It's simple and efficient. Briefly, equation (2.5) with only nonlinear term on the right hand side can be seen as the following form

$$\frac{\partial}{\partial t}u=N \tag{2.7}$$

where N represents the nonlinear term. By applying second-order R-K scheme to above equations, we get

$$\frac{u^* - u^n}{\Delta t} = N^n \tag{2.8}$$

$$\frac{u^{n+1} - u^n}{\Delta t} = \frac{1}{2}\left(N^n + N^*\right) \tag{2.9}$$

where n and n+1 represent the different time steps, and * represent the middle step variable. Eq. (2.8) is also called the predictor step and Eq. (2.9) is called the corrector step.

3. SGS model

In LES, only the large, energy carrying scales of turbulence are computed exactly. Specify in LES equation (2.2), the large scales are the filtered velocities, $\overline{u}_i$, which are also called the resolved scales. The small ones, u_i', (unresolved, or subgrid scales) have been removed from the equation and needed to be modelled, i.e. τ_{ij} in equation (2.2).
The SGS model is the key issue in LES. Since only large scales are resolved in LES, the energy transfer from large scales to small scales is cut off. The energy will accumulate at the cut-off wave number and lead to the unphysical solution. So the main role of SGS model is to provide necessary small scales dissipation and thus remove the accumulated energy. There are many different approaches for the modelling of the SGS stress tensor. Traditionally they are divided into three main categories: eddy viscosity models, similarity models and mixed models. Discussion of standard LES models can be found in some review paper, such as Piomelli (Piomelli 1999), Mathew (Mathew 2010) etc. Below we only discuss the eddy viscosity model briefly.
The eddy viscosity models assume:

$$\tau_{ij} = \overline{u_i u_j} - \overline{u}_i \overline{u}_j = -2\upsilon_t \overline{S}_{ij} + 1/3\delta_{ij}\tau_{kk} \tag{3.1}$$

which relate the SGS stresses to the large scale strain-rate tensor S_{ij}, where S_{ij} is

$$s_{ij} = \frac{1}{2}\left(\frac{\partial u_i}{\partial x_j} + \frac{\partial u_j}{\partial x_i}\right) \tag{3.2}$$

and ν_t is the eddy viscosity. Like RANS, equation (3.1) was developed by analogizing to the molecular viscosity. So different eddy viscosity models are actually different methods to calculate the ν_t.
The Smagorinsky model (Smagorinsky 1963) is perhaps the most successful SGS eddy viscosity models, which takes eddy viscosity proportional to the product of Δ^2 and $|\overline{s}|$,

$$\nu_t = (C_s\Delta)^2 |\overline{s}| \tag{3.3}$$

where C_s is called the Smagorinsky constant, Δ is the grid size and $|\overline{s}| = \left(2\overline{s}_{ij}\overline{s}_{ij}\right)^{1/2}$ is the magnitude of the strain-rate tensor. By choosing different C_s for various flows, Smagorinsky model has been used with considerable success. For isotropic decaying turbulence, the value of the Smagorinsky constant is taken to be around 0.18~0.23 (Lilly (Lilly 1996)), but in shear flow or near boundaries, C_s must be decreased and values 0.06~0.1 are preferred (Piomelli *et al.* (Piomelli *et al.*1988)).

Smagorinsky model can properly account for the global energy transfer. It is simple and robust, which make it the most widely used SGS model. But the modeled SGS quantities correlate poorly with the actual SGS quantities obtained from DNS. Moreover it is an absolutely dissipative model and tends to overestimate the SGS dissipation. It only allows one way energy flux, i.e. from large scales to small ones, and it fails to predict the inverse energy transfer from the subgrid scales to the resolved scales (backscatter) which is found in most flows. Many *ad hoc* corrections and variation of eddy viscosity models are proposed to solve the difficulties mentioned above. Among them the dynamic model of Germano *et al.* (Germano *et al.*1991) and its variations are the most attractive ones. The dynamic model calculates the eddy viscosity dynamically and obtains good results in different turbulence. But it still has some problems when applied to complex engineering flows.

3.1 Velocity Estimation Model (VEM)

To construct a reasonable and reliable SGS model, to properly predict the interactions between large scales and small scales is the key, which means we need to know more detailed information about the nonlinear interactions between large and small scales. Fortunately during the last several years there are many investigations in a variety of turbulent flows, including isotropic and channel flow, at low Reynolds numbers using direct numerical simulation databases and experimental measurements (Zhou 1993; Hartel *et al.* 1994; Domaradzki & Rogallo 1990). Their studies show that the large scales contain enough information. Many of the observed features of the exact SGS interactions can be inferred from the dynamics of the resolved scales alone. Thus it implies a possible way to improving SGS model, i.e. to estimate the small scales from large scales by using the observed properties of the nonlinear interactions. Based on that concept, Domaradzki *et al* (Domaradzki & Saiki 1997; Domaradzki et al 2002) develop the velocity estimation model in both spectral and physical space. Stolz and Adam also proposed similar model called deconvolution model (Stolz 1999).

The velocity estimation model is based on two observations: first, the dynamics of small scales are strongly determined by the large, energy carrying eddies; second, the contribution of small scales to large scales are mostly contained within wavenumbers that are twice that of the cutoff wavenumber, k_c. These two observations rely on the properties of nonlinear interactions in turbulent flows and have been elucidated by a large number of theoretical, numerical and experimental investigations (Zhou 1993; Domaradzki & Rogallo 1990; Domaradzki & Saiki 1997; Domaradzki et al 2002). Basically these studies showed that most of the subgrid scale transfer happens in the range of $0.5k_c \sim k_c$ and is determined by scales in the range of $k_c \sim 2k_c$. This implies that only a limited range of wavenumbers needs to be considered. Especially in VEM the modes beyond $2k_c$ are ignored. With a proper estimation of the velocity field the subgrid scale stress tensor could be determined directly from the resolved scales and provides enough dissipation for LES.

The eddy viscosity models basically try to solve the imaginary υ_t by related to the large scale strain-rate tensor. If we know the full velocity field of the turbulence flow, the τ_{ij} can be calculated directly from the definition equation (2.3) and do not need any assumption. Since the velocity in LES is the filtered velocity, a simple way to recover the full velocity is defiltering, i.e., an inversion of the filtering operation (2.1). Such a procedure is also called deconvolution. But the defiltered velocity does not contain any small scales information.

Domaradzki *et al* (Domaradzki & Saiki 1997; Domaradzki et al 2002) proposed a method to estimate the small scales. This is the basic idea of the velocity estimation model. In order to describe the different velocities, we use u to present the full, unfiltered turbulence velocity; $\overline{u}$ means the filtered velocity; and u' is the small scale velocity. And the relation among them is

$$u = \overline{u} + u' \tag{3.4}$$

VEM contains two steps: First is the defiltering operation, i.e. try to recover the full velocity u from the filtered velocity $\overline{u}$

$$u \approx G^{-1}\overline{u}\ , \tag{3.5}$$

which is inverse operation of (2.1). Bertero and Boccacci (Bertero & Boccacci 1998) give a detailed discussion about it. Since any filtering will loss part of original information, the defiltering can not recover the full velocity according to Riemann-Lebesgue theory. Only some very special filtering function and variables can return to its original state. Most results of defiltering can only be approximate. The velocity u in equation (3.5) actually only contains large scales information, so we denote it by $\tilde{u}^0$. If we using tophat filter and the filtering size is twice as the grid size, then the filtering operation can be expressed as

$$\overline{u} = au_{i-1} + bu_i + cu_{i+1}\ , \tag{3.6}$$

and a, b, c are constants. Then the defiltering operation is

$$a\tilde{u}_{i-1}^0 + b\tilde{u}_i^0 + c\tilde{u}_{i+1}^0 = \overline{u}\ . \tag{3.7}$$

By defiltering, the large scales $\tilde{u}^0$ is closed to the original u, but there is no small scales. If we approximate the u using $\tilde{u}^0$, i.e. let $u \approx \tilde{u}^0$. And then calculate the SGS tensor τ directly from the definition $\tau = \overline{\tilde{u}^0\tilde{u}^0} - \overline{\tilde{u}^0}\ \overline{\tilde{u}^0}$. Through practice, it is found that if the Reynolds number is not too high, the result is good enough. But if the Re number is high, the error is somehow too large. The information of the small scales is needed. The second step of VEM is to estimate the small scales. For full developed turbulence, the small scales are thought to be homogeneous, so a simplified way to estimate small scales can be described as

$$u' = \theta N'\ . \tag{3.8}$$

where N' is the growth rate of subgrid scales due to the nonlinear interactions among resolved scales and θ is the time scale related to the eddy turn-over time. The detailed description of the full process can be found in paper (Domaradzki & Saiki 1997; Domaradzki et al 2002). Thus the final velocity can be expressed as

$$u \approx \tilde{u} = \tilde{u}^0 + u'\ . \tag{3.9}$$

Correspondingly, the SGS stress tensor is

$$\tau = \overline{\tilde{u}\tilde{u}} - \overline{\tilde{u}}\ \overline{\tilde{u}}\ . \tag{3.10}$$

The energy spectral of full (DNS), filtered, defiltered and estimated velocity are shown in Fig. 3.1

VEM was implemented in both spectral and physical space. It was applied to different flows, such as homogenous tubulence, incompressible channel flow, Rayleigh-Bénard convection flow, and obtained quite good results. But the disadvantage of VEM is that the procedure it uses is quite complicated and need much more CPU time than Smagorinsky model.

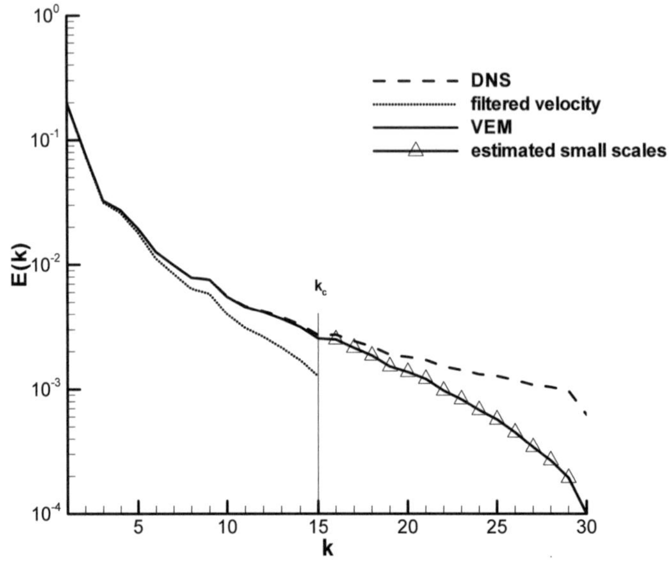

Fig. 3.1. Sketch of energy spectral for full (DNS), filtered, defiltered and estimated velocity.

3.2 Truncated Navier–Stokes (TNS) equations approach

As we can see, the traditional eddy viscosity models use the filtered velocity to calculate τ_{ij}, while the VEM tries to recover the full velocity from the filtered velocity and then use it to calculate τ_{ij}. So one may think: if we can get the full velocity from the experiment data or DNS directly, can we just skip the filtering and defiltering steps? Based on that concept, Domaradzki *et al* (Domaradzki et al 2002; Domaradzki & Yang 2004) developed a new TNS approach from VEM model. TNS uses the full velocity. It actually solves the N-S equations directly instead of LES equations. So it does not have the SGS term. Due to limitation of grid, it is an under-resolved DNS run. According to the energy transfer theory, the energy will accumulate at high modes. A mechanism is needed to provide necessary dissipation to remove the accumulated energy, such as filtering /truncation. A similar model in engine application is the MILES model, which depends on numerical scheme to provide implicit dissipation.

TNS model is still based on the same two observations of energy transfer as VEM. The large energy carrying eddies can determine the dynamics of the small scales; in return, the contribution of the small scales to the large scales are mostly contained within wavenumber range between the cutoff wavenumber, k_c, and $2k_c$. Correspondingly, a scale decomposition is performed in TNS as shown in Fig. 3.2: a range of physical (large) scales up to the traditional LES wave number cutoff k_c, and a range of modeled (SGS or estimated) scales between k_c and $2k_c$. The nonlinear interaction between the low wavenumber modes $k<k_c$ and

the high wavenumber modes $k_c<k<2k_c$ provides a natural dissipation mechanism for the large scales, which also automatically includes the effect of reversing energy (backscatter). The energy accumulated at the subgrid scales $k_c<k<2k_c$ is removed by truncation (filtering) at prescribed time intervals. In the physical space, the explanation for TNS is also straightforward. In the traditional LES, the mesh size is $\Delta_{LES} = \pi/k_c$, denoted as a coarse mesh; while the TNS operates on a fine mesh with the size of $\Delta_{TNS} = \pi/2k_c = \Delta_{LES}/2$. Instead of solving the LES equations on the coarse mesh, full Navier-Stokes equations are solved on the fine mesh with a corresponding filtering operation in physical space. It should be noticed that the filtering time interval plays a critical role in TNS. In order to avoid under-dissipating or over-dissipating, appropriate interval must be carefully chosen (Domaradzki & Yang 2004). The suitable interval depends on the filter type, grid resolution and flow condition.

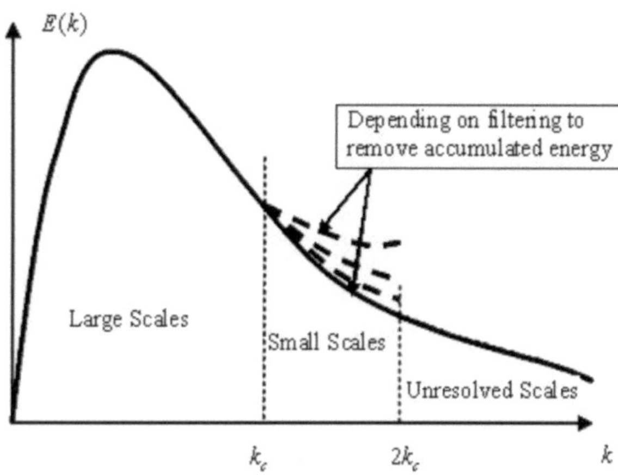

Fig. 3.2. The sketch of TNS in spectral space.

Compared to other LES models, TNS does not have the closure problem because it has no SGS term in the equation. It satisfies the Galilean transformation properties of the Navier-Stokes equations. It is easy to implement with fewer empirical parameters and can be easily extended to other types of turbulence without too much modification. When the explicit filtering is used, the TNS model also shows its advantages over the other models. For instance, as mentioned by Lund (Lund 1997), adaptation of the second explicit filtering leads the SGS term actually to be

$$\tau_{ij} = \overline{u_i u_j} - \overline{\overline{u}_i \overline{u}_j} . \quad (3.11)$$

This is not Galilean invariant in most cases. In TNS, this problem is naturally avoided since no such term exists.

TNS was tested in several different turbulent flows. Here only the results of the simplest homogeneous, isotropic decaying turbulence are discussed. For this simple flow there are lot of DNS and experiment data which can be used to test LES model. Here the DNS data of Horiuti (Horiuti 1999) is used, which have a resolution of 256^3. The initial condition for LES is obtained from DNS by truncating the full 256^3 DNS field to 32^3 in spectral space, see Fig.

5.1. Notice the energy at the cutoff k_c=15 may not be small enough compared to the energy peak. Usually for LES models in order to get good results, the energy at cutoff should be two orders of magnitude less than the energy peak. The initial parameters are summarized in Table 3.1

υ	E_0	ε	L	λ	Re_L	Re_λ	t_{ett}
1/720	0.686	0.152	0.51	0.24	245	118	0.68

Table 3.1. Initial parameters.

Fig. 3.3 shows the initial and final energy spectrum for TNS and DNS results. Note that in order to compare the results of other LES models are also presented, including Smagorinsky model and Chollet-Lesieur (C-L) eddy viscosity model (Chollet & Lesieur 1981). The C-L model in spectral space can be expressed as

$$\mu_t(k) = \upsilon^*(k / k_c)\left[E(k_c) / k_c\right]^{1/2}. \tag{3.12}$$

ν^* is the normalized eddy viscosity, which is defined as

$$\upsilon^*(k / k_c) = Ko^{-3/2}\left[0.441 + 15.2\exp(-3.03k_c / k)\right]. \tag{3.13}$$

where Ko is the Kolmogoroff constant, and is usually set to 1.4.

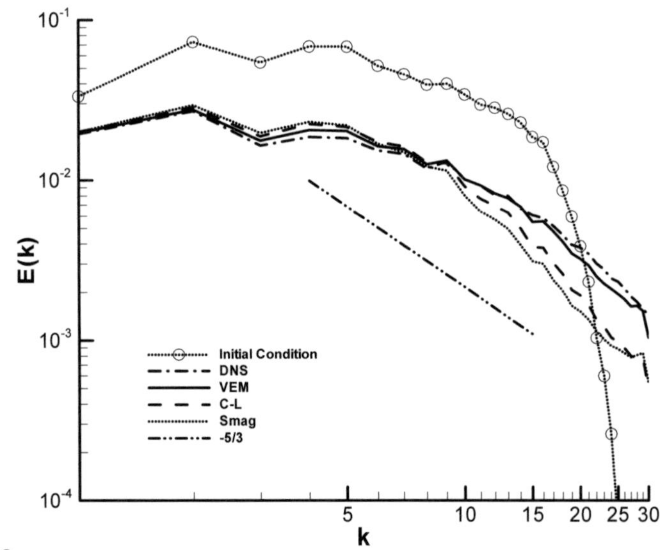

s

Fig. 3.3. Initial and final energy spectrum for DNS, LES and TNS.

As we can see from Fig. 3.3, all models obtain reasonable results compared to DNS, especially at low modes they match each other quite well. However at high modes TNS spectrum matches the result of DNS best, and the $k^{-5/3}$ spectral form is preserved. For Smagrinsky model, as indicated by many studies, the dissipation is overestimated and biggest. C-L shows good results but not as good as TNS. Fig. 3.4 shows the history of normalized energy decay for all models. Note here we simply divide the energy $E(t)$ by the initial total energy $E(0)$ to get normalized energy. Again TNS gets the best results while the Smagrinsky model shows too much dissipation.

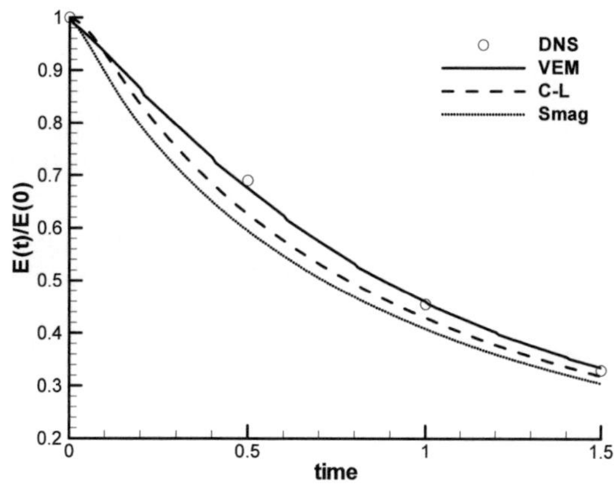

Fig. 3.4. The history of total energy decaying.

4. The choice of filters

The filter shape and filtering width are the two free parameters in LES. Each affects the LES results greatly. Designing suitable filter type and filtering width is important to get reasonable results. In dynamic Smagrinsky model and similarity model, the effect of the filtering width has been studied by Lund (Lund 1997), De Stefano and Vasilyev (De Stefano and Vasilyev 2002) etc. In order to separate these two effects from one another, the present study is focus on the importance of the filter shape.

Theoretically, the filtering operation should be repeated every time step because the nonlinear term continuously generates high frequency modes that need to be dissipated (Lund 1997). Depending on the type of filter, the SGS model should be adjusted in order to represent the dynamics of the unresolved scales correctly. Consequently the nature of the LES solution strongly depends on the filter shape. But for the traditional LES, especially for the eddy viscosity model, there is no explicit filtering process during the calculation in spite of the reasons mentioned above, i.e., the simulation result is independent of the filter. In the conventional practice, the filter has been only used as a concept (Fröhlich & Rodi 2001). The effect of the filter shape on LES is rarely discussed in the literature.

On the other hand, a suitable LES model is needed to test different filters. As just mentioned, most traditional eddy viscosity models do not have explicit filtering in the solution procedure. In the similarity models and the dynamical Smagorinsky model the filtering width of the test (second) filter plays a key role besides the filter shape. A more appropriate LES model, which can directly validate different filters, is therefore required. From section 3.2 we found that the filtering plays a key role in TNS. The dynamics of the large scales and the energy budget strongly depend on the filter shape. It is a very good model to study the filter effect.

There have been many filters proposed in the literatures that can be categorized into two groups: *smooth filters* and *discrete filters*. At the early stage of development, LES was mostly performed in spectral space in which the filters were defined as continuous in the whole domain. These filters are referred to as smooth filters. The most commonly used ones are the Tophat (box), the Gaussian, and the sharp spectral (Fourier cutoff) filters. Recently, the application of LES to solve real engineering problems in the complex flow has become realistic and, in fact, popular because of the urgent need from the industry. Finite difference scheme instead of pseudo-spectral method is now widely adopted in the numerical approach due to its flexibility in handling complex geometry and obtaining high order schemes (Lele 1992, Visbal & Gaitonde 2002). The finite difference discretization scheme, together with the limited grid resolution, can be seen as an implicit filtering as mentioned by many researchers (De Stefano and Vasilyev2002; Fröhlich & Rodi 2001; Lund 2003; Vasilyev 1998). However this kind of implicit filtering has some problems because of the interactions among the modified terms in the governing equations, the numerical error, and the order of the filter, etc.(Lund 2003; Vasilyev 1998). In order to avoid some of these problems, researchers tend to employ the explicit filtering to exert direct influence on the simulation result. These filters are usually defined on several adjacent points and, hence, denoted as discrete filters thereafter. There are several advantages using explicit filter: First it is easier to control the truncation and aliasing errors by removing the high wave number modes which is beyond the bandwidth allowed by the mesh. Second it can dump the oscillation at high frequency which comes from the numerical discretization scheme, boundary condition, etc. The amplitude of these oscillations usually is comparable to or even larger than that of the small scales after sufficiently long computation time, which tends to contaminate the final result of the simulation. By using the same explicit filter, it also makes the comparison with experiment or DNS data more direct.

4.1 Smooth filters

The smooth filters include the spectral filter, the Gaussian filter, the Tophat filter and those are defined continuously in the whole computation domain. The definitions for the first three can be easily found in some books (Pope 2000). Table 4.1 shows these filter functions in physical and spectral space respectively.

	Spectral space	Physical space
Spectral filter	$\hat{G}(k)=\begin{cases}1, & k\le k_c;\\ 0, & k>k_c\end{cases}$	$G(x)=\dfrac{\sin\left(\pi x/\bar{\Delta}\right)}{\pi x}$
Tophat filter	$\hat{G}(k)=\dfrac{\sin\left(0.5k\bar{\Delta}\right)}{0.5k\bar{\Delta}}$	$G(x)=\begin{cases}\dfrac{1}{\bar{\Delta}}, & \lvert x\rvert\le 0.5\bar{\Delta};\\ 0, & otherwise\end{cases}$
Gaussian filter	$\hat{G}(k)=\exp\left(-\dfrac{k^2\bar{\Delta}^2}{24}\right)$	$G(x)=\sqrt{\dfrac{6}{\pi\bar{\Delta}^2}}\exp\left(-\dfrac{6x^2}{\bar{\Delta}^2}\right)$

Table 4.1. Smooth filters in physical and spectral space $\bar{\Delta}=\pi/k_c$.

The main problem for the Tophat and Gaussian filters is that they remove too much energy of the large scales (Domaradzki et al 2002; Yang & Domaradzki 2004). The spectral filter is thought as the best among these three for LES because it keeps all the large scales while removes all the small scales. However filters defined in the physical space are much flexible because for most flows transformation to the spectral space is difficult. People are trying to find a filter that is defined in the physical space while has the property of the spectral filter or close to it at the same time.

Actually the filtering operation (2.1)(Leonard 1974) is a linear spatial averaging operation,

$$\bar{f}(x) = L_G(f(x)) = \int_D G(x,x';\bar{\Delta})f(x')dx' \tag{4.1}$$

A formal inverse of it in a power series expansion can be expressed as

$$L_G^{-1} = (I-(I-L_G))^{-1} = I + (I-L_G) + (I-L_G)^2 + \cdots \tag{4.2}$$

where I is the unity operator. The product of L_G and the first few terms of the above expansion (4.2) actually defines a suitable new filter (Domaradzki et al 2002) (the product of L_G and the full equation (4.2) is equal to I, of course). If only first few terms are selected, the new filter is close to the original filter L_G and the extra computation cost is small. When more terms are selected, the new filter is closer to unity. It has less effect on the large scales but needs much more computation time. Domaradzki *et. al.* (Domaradzki et al 2002) found that the combination of the first three terms in Eq. 4.2 is the best choice and denoted this filter as the physical filter

$$\bar{u} = 3\hat{u}_i - 3\hat{\hat{u}}_i + \hat{\hat{\hat{u}}}_i \tag{4.3}$$

where '^' is the original Tophat filter or Gaussian filter. One thing need to be pointed out is that the results of the Tophat, Gaussian and Physical filters strongly depend on the filter width $\bar{\Delta}$. However the objective of present work is to highlight the importance of the filter shape as mentioned above. In the following analysis, the filter width is fixed for these smooth filters, which is equal to 2 times of grid size Δ.

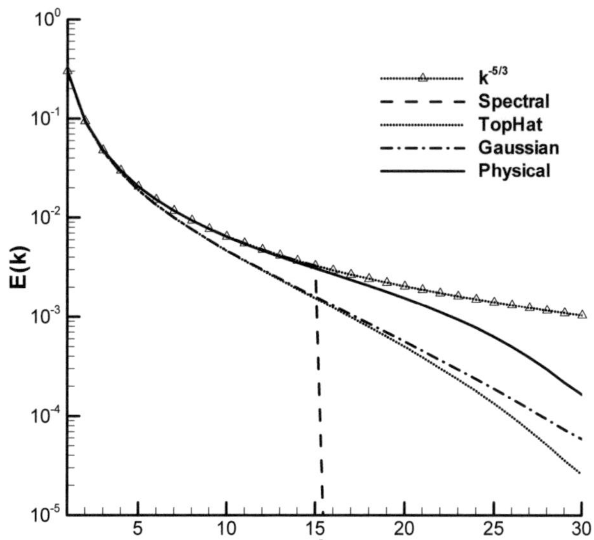

Fig. 4.1. Effect of the smooth filters on the $k^{-5/3}$ spectrum.

The effects of above filters on the $k^{-5/3}$ spectrum are shown in Fig.4.1. As can be seen, the Tophat and Gaussian filters remove too much energy of the low modes. The spectral filter only keeps the large scales. The physical filter strongly damps the small scales while affecting the large scales very little, which make it a good filter for LES.

Beside *a prior* test, the effects of these filters on a real three dimensional LES are also examined. Again the simplest homogeneous, isotropic decaying turbulence is utilized as the test case with two different initial conditions. The first has the initial condition of spectrum $E(k) = Ak^4 \exp\left(-2k^2 / k_p^2\right)$, where k_p is the peak mode and equals to 4. The grid resolution is 64^3 (In the following, the mesh size is 64^3 for all LES unless further specified). For comparison, the 256^3 DNS result is also included. The final energy spectrum is plotted in Fig. 4.2. It also shows that the Tophat filter removes too much energy (Since the Gaussian filter performs very similarly to the Tophat filter, we did not include it in the figure). The spectral and physical filters show very good agreement with the DNS data.

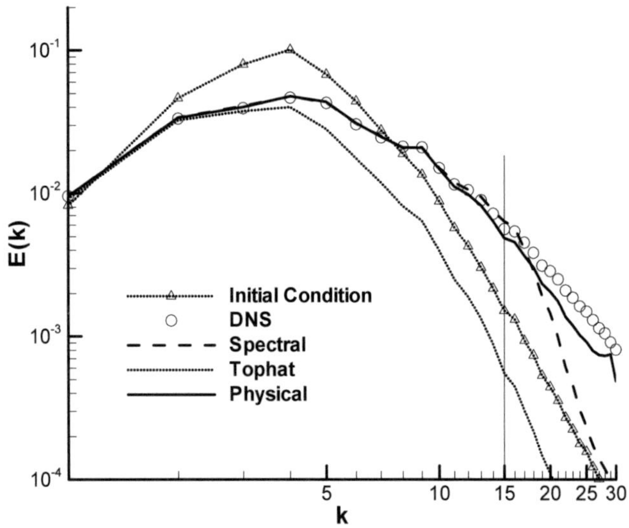

Fig. 4.2. Energy spectrum at final time for LES case 1.

The second case has a more critical initial condition as shown in Fig. 4.3. The initial condition is obtained from the 256^3 DNS data of Horiuti (Horiuti 1999) same as section 3. It is a challenging case for LES because the energy at cut-off mode k_c is not in the inertial range. The Tophat filter shows too much dissipation same as above. However the spectral filter delivers some undesirable behaviors this time. By removing all the small scales, it also shut down the energy transfer from the large to small scales completely. It will take some time for LES to rebuild the nonlinear interactions between the large and small scales, which leads to insufficient dissipation. Thus, the energy accumulates near the cutoff wavenumber as shown in Fig. 4.3. The physical filter provides the best result compared to the DNS data as also observed in paper ((Domaradzki et al 2002; Yang & Domaradzki 2004). The main reason is that the physical filter keeps a small part of the small scales which facilitates the energy transfer. Since this initial condition is a better case to test filters, we only run LES with case two in the following discussion.

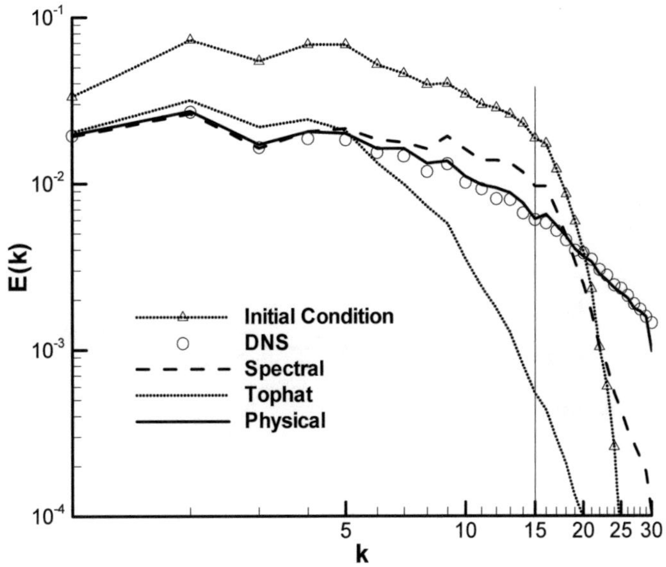

Fig. 4.3. Energy spectrum at final time for LES case 2.

The history of total kinetic energy decay for the smooth filters is plotted in Fig. 4.4. Corresponding to Fig. 4.3, the physical filter obtains better result compared to DNS. Since the spectral filter does not provide sufficient dissipation as shown in Fig. 4.3, its total energy is the biggest among all the results. The Tophat filter removes a part of large-scale energy each time when the filtering operation is applied. That is why the total energy jumps downwards periodically.

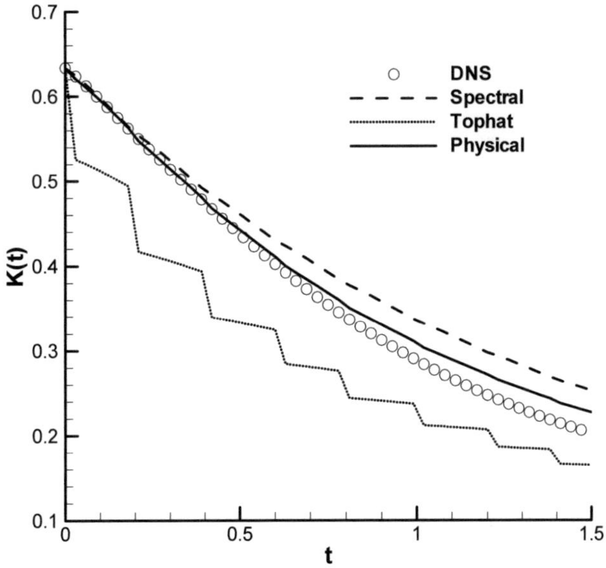

Fig. 4.4. The decay of the total kinetic energy for the smooth filters.

The effect of different grid resolutions is also investigated. The result of LES with grid 32^3 is shown in Fig4.5 and the result for 128^3 is plotted in Fig. 4.6. The behaviors of these smooth filters in coarse mesh (32^3) are almost the same as those in grid 64^3. Physical filter still gets the best results. For the fine mesh (128^3), all filters obtain good result except that the Tophat filter still dissipates a little more. The effect of the SGS model becomes small when the grid resolution increases, which is well known.

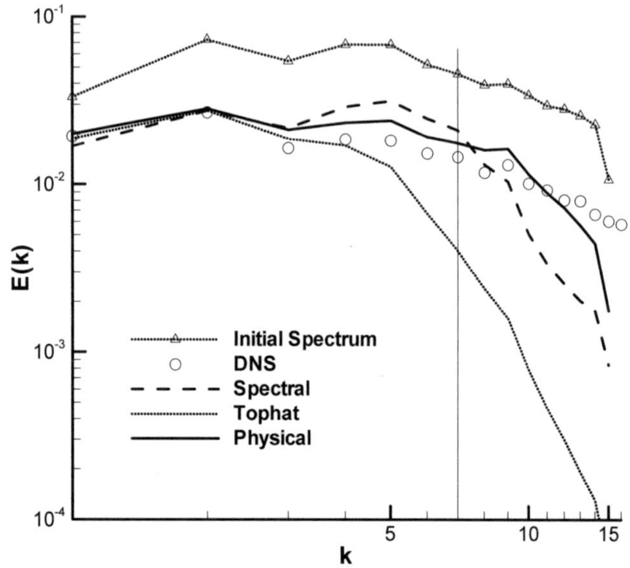

Fig. 4.5. Energy spectrum at final time for the smooth filters with grid 32^3.

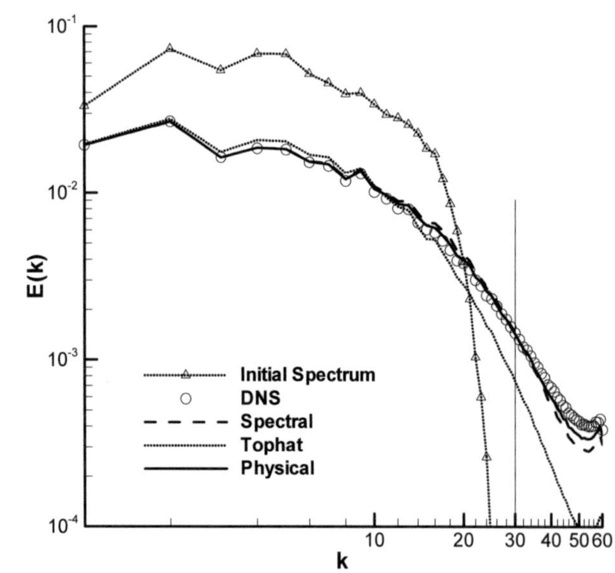

Fig. 4.6. Energy spectrum at final time for the smooth filters with grid 128^3.

4.2 Discrete filters

In order to handle complex geometry, finite difference scheme is widely used instead of the spectral method. The solution is available only on a set of discrete grid points. At most time, the filter for the whole domain does not exist due to the inhomogeneous and boundary condition. The discrete filters, including the discrete Tophat filter, the Padé filter (Visbal & Gaitonde 2002) and the filter series proposed by Vasilyev *et al.* (Vasilyev *et al.* 1998) are utilized rather than the spectral smooth filters

The main problem of the discrete filter is the commutation error between differentiation and filtering operation. Fortunately Vasilyev *et al.* (Vasilyev *et al.* 1998) gave out a solution which can control the commutation error to any specified order. Another problem is that if the order of the filter is too low, the error introduced by filtering may become larger than the magnitude of SGS term. Hence for traditional LES, the filter order is usually required to be higher than that of SGS term. But the filtering operation in TNS only acts as a dissipation source. The numerical error can be included into it as part of the dissipation. Low order filters can also obtain good results. It is similar to the strategy used by Mathew *et al.* (Mathew *et al.* 2003).

A one-dimensional filter given by Vasilyev *et al.* (Vasilyev *et al.* 1998) is defined as:

$$\bar{f}_j = \sum_{l=-K}^{L} w_l f_{j+l} \tag{4.4}$$

In order to control the commutation error to a specified order, the filter is required to have a different number of vanishing moments. Correspondingly, the weight factors w_i should satisfy a set of constrains. These filters are referred as V-filters in the following analysis.

Case	w_{-3}	w_{-2}	w_{-1}	w_0	w_1	w_2	w_3	w_4	w_5
1			1/4	1/2	1/4				
3			1/8	5/8	3/8	-1/8			
6		-1/16	1/4	5/8	1/4	-1/16			
7				31/32	5/32	-5/16	5/16	-5/32	1/32
9		-1/32	5/32	11/16	5/16	-5/32	1/32		
10	1/64	-3/32	15/64	11/16	15/64	-3/32	1/64		

Table 4.2. The weight parameters of the V-filters.

Several sets of weights for the V-filters are given in Table 4.2 which is similar to the Table 1 in Vasilyev *et al*'s paper (Vasilyev *et al.* 1998). The equation (4.4) defines a symmetric (center) scheme if K equals to L. The case 1, 6 and 10 are symmetric and have a commutation error of order 2, 4, 6 respectively. In order to handle boundary points, Vasilyev *et al* also proposed several asymmetric filters, i.e., K and L is different. For high asymmetric V-filters, such as the one side filter - case 7, it is found that too much unphysical energy is introduced to the high modes as also mentioned by Vasilyev *et al* (Vasilyev *et al.* 1998). This property is not desirable for TNS because it will lead to unphysical solution. Thus high asymmetric filters (case 2, 4 5, 7, 8) are not included in the following analysis. Only case 3 and 9 (whose order are 3 and 5 respectively) are tested as well as the symmetric ones.

Fig. 4.7 presents the filtering results of different V-filters applied to the $k^{-5/3}$ spectrum. For comparison, the result of the smooth physical filter is also included. Case 1 in fact is a discrete version of the Tophat filter using trapezoidal rule. Similar to the smooth one, it removes too much energy of the large scales. It is interesting that the asymmetric filters like case 3 and 9 keep more energy than the symmetric ones (case 6 and 10). Note case 3 and case 6 still remove a small part of the large-scale energy. While case 7 introduces too much energy at high wavenumber modes which will lead to an unphysical solution in a real LES run.

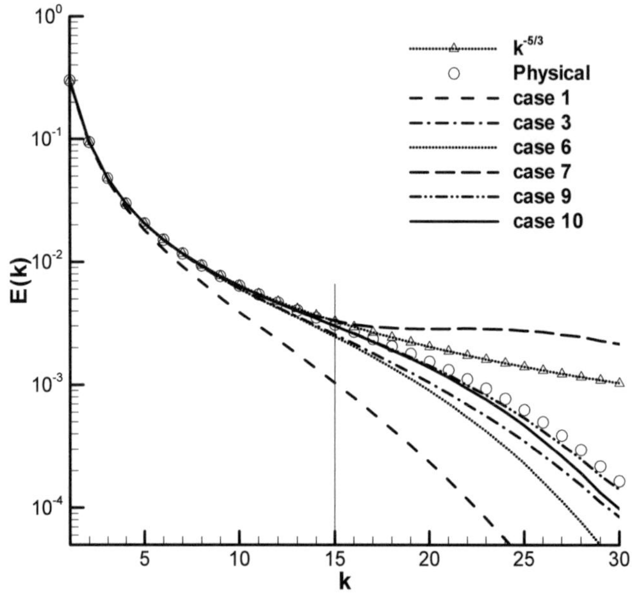

Fig. 4.7. Effect of the V-filters on the $k^{-5/3}$ spectrum.

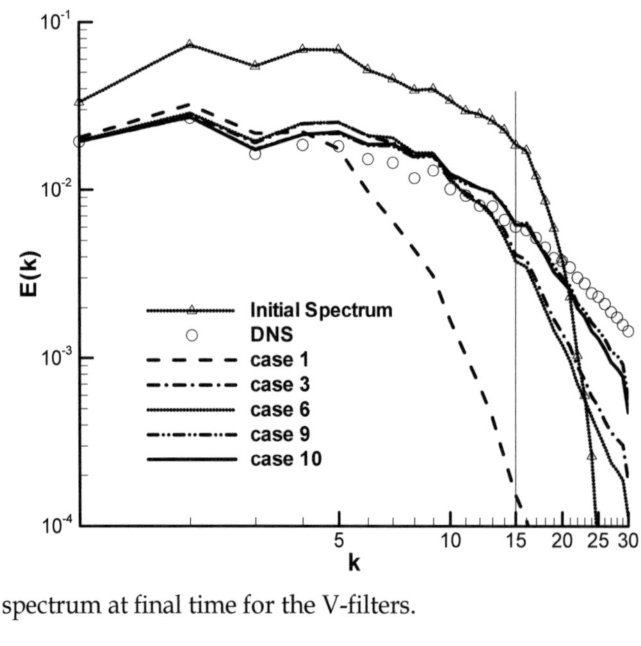

Fig. 4.8. Energy spectrum at final time for the V-filters.

Fig.4.8 shows the final energy spectrum of the V-filters in the same homogeneous run as Fig.4.3. As expected, case 1 dissipates too much energy. High order filters obtains better results. Corresponding to Fig.4.7, the result of the low order asymmetric filter case 3 (3rd order) is a little better than that of the high order symmetric filter case 6 (4th order). And the behaviors of case9 and case 10 are very similar. The reason is still attributed to the fact that a small amount of energy is introduced at high modes for the asymmetric filters. The decay of the total energy is plotted in Fig.4.9. Except case 1, all other cases show good agreement with the filtered DNS data. But there are small jumps for low order filters (case 3 and case 6) because of the undesirable effect to the large scales as shown in Fig.4.7. The effects of grid resolutions on V-filters are similar to the smooth ones, which are not included here.

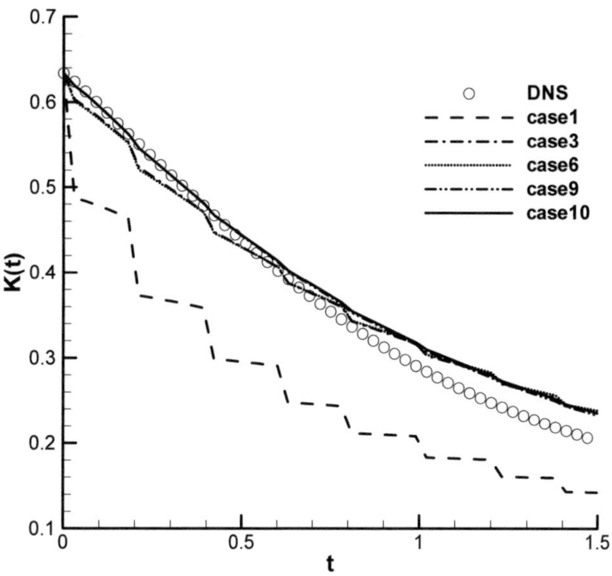

Fig. 4.9. The decay of the total kinetic energy for the V-filters.

Another series of discrete filters is the Padé filters. The Padé compact difference scheme can be regarded as an implicit filter (Visbal & Gaitonde 2002; Vasilyev et al 1998). Based on that, a set of Padé explicit filters is proposed by Visbal and Gaitonde (Visbal & Gaitonde 2002). For a variable *f*, the filtered value can be expressed as:

$$\alpha_f \bar{f}_{i-1} + \bar{f}_i + \alpha_f \bar{f}_{i+1} = \sum_{n=0}^{N} \frac{a_n}{2}\left(f_{i+n} + f_{i-n}\right) \tag{4.5}$$

where α_f is an adjustable parameters between (-0.5, 0.5) and high value of α_f means a less dissipative filter. N is the order of filter scheme, 2N+1 points give a 2N order filter. The coefficients a_n are listed in Table 4.3.

The filtering results of the $k^{-5/3}$ spectrum using different Padé filters are shown in Fig. 4.10. The smooth physical filter is also included as a benchmark. The 2nd order filter removes a small amount of the energy of the low modes, which may have undesirable effect on LES because of the unnecessary dissipation. The 4th order and above have little effect on the

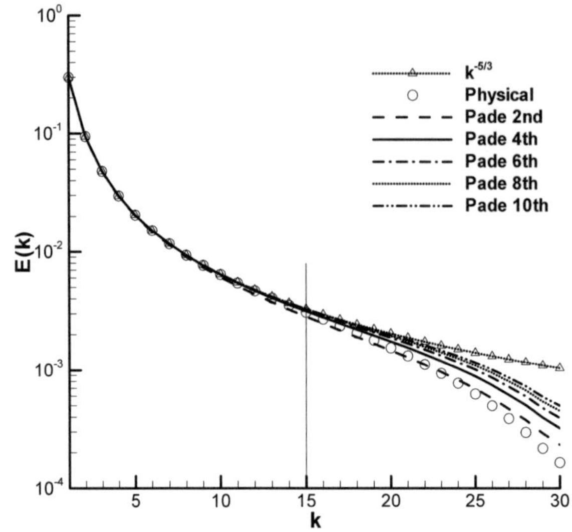

Fig. 4.10. Effect of the V-filters on the $k^{-5/3}$ spectrum.

Scheme	a_0	a_1	a_2	a_3	a_4	a_5
F2	$\frac{1}{2}+a_f$	$\frac{1}{2}+a_f$				
F4	$\frac{5}{8}+\frac{3}{4}a_f$	$\frac{1}{2}+a_f$	$-\frac{1}{8}+\frac{1}{4}a_f$			
F6	$\frac{11}{16}+\frac{5}{8}a_f$	$\frac{15}{32}+\frac{17}{16}a_f$	$-\frac{3}{16}+\frac{3}{8}a_f$	$\frac{1}{32}-\frac{a_f}{16}$		
F8	$\frac{93+70a_f}{128}$	$\frac{7+18a_f}{16}$	$\frac{-7+14a_f}{32}$	$\frac{1}{16}-\frac{a_f}{8}$	$\frac{-1}{128}+\frac{a_f}{64}$	
F10	$\frac{193+126a_f}{256}$	$\frac{105+302a_f}{256}$	$\frac{15(-1+2a_f)}{64}$	$\frac{45(1-2a_f)}{512}$	$\frac{5(-1+2a_f)}{256}$	$\frac{1-2a_f}{512}$

Table 4.3. The Coefficients of the Padé filters.

large scales. But higher the order is, the Padé filter tends to keep more small scales compared to the physical filter. In turn it may not provide enough dissipation for TNS.

The final energy spectra of the LES run with the Padé filters are plotted in Fig. 4.11 and the time evolutions of the total energy are shown in Fig. 4.12. Corresponding to Fig.4.10 the 2nd order filter overestimates the dissipation and subsequently provides the worst results among these runs. The 4th order and above show very good results as compared to the DNS data. However the 6th order and above filters keep more small-scale energy than DNS which may imply them do not provide enough dissipation.

From above results, it is found that the Padé filters show better results than the V-filters. It could be attributed to the fact that the Padé filters consider the effects of adjacent points. On the other hand, the calculation of the V-filters is much simple and straightforward. For the Padé filters we need to solve a tri-diagonal system. It is time consuming and may be infeasible for the inhomogeneous case. In the Section 4.1 the physical filter shows very good property but it is a smooth filter. So we modified it into a discrete version using the V-filters, i.e. in equation 4.3 we use the V-filters instead of the Tophat filter. Hereafter we denote it as PV-filter.

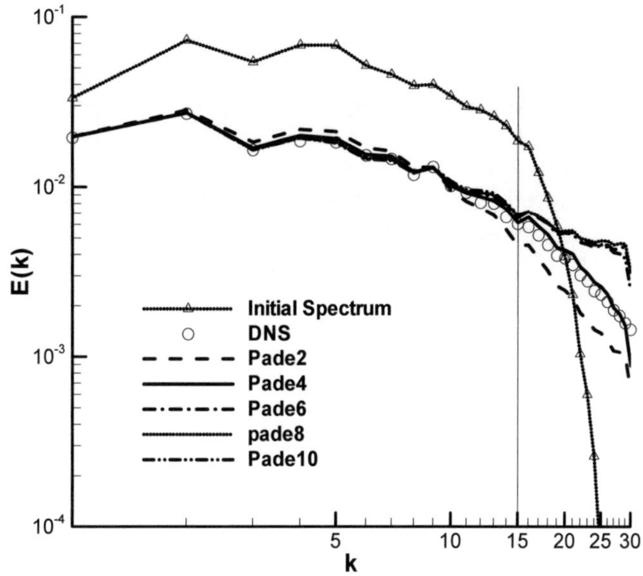

Fig. 4.11. Energy spectrum at final time for the Padé filters.

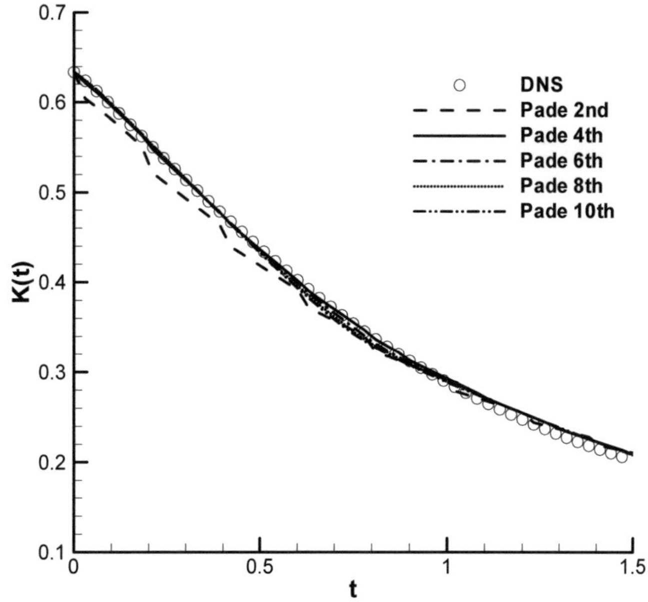

Fig. 4.12. The decay of the total kinetic energy for the Padé filters.

The results of a priori test and the LES run of the PV-filters are shown in Fig. 4.13, Fig. 4.14 and Fig. 4.15 respectively. For comparison, we also include the result of the original case 1 of the V-filter (V-case1) in Fig.4.13. It shows that the result of the 2nd order PV-case1 is improved significantly as compared to V-case1. As mentioned before V-case1 is actually a discrete version of the Tophat filter. Therefore the PV-case1 is a discrete version of the smooth physical filter. Since the result of smooth physical filter is much better than that of the Tophat filter as shown in Fig.4.1, it is no wonder that the PV-case1 is better than the V-case1. However, by comparing Fig.4.14 and Fig.4.3, it was found the results of this discrete version (PV-case1) are not as good as those of the smooth physical filter for a real LES run. Similar to Fig.4.7, the asymmetric filters (PV-case3 and PV-case9) show good behavior in Fig.4.13, keeping more energy than the symmetric ones (PV-case6 and PV-case10). But it was also found that small amount of nonphysical energy is introduced near the cutoff wavenumber. Correspondingly the behaviors of these asymmetric filters in a real LES run are not good as shown in Fig.4.14 and Fig.4.15 (PV-case3 is not shown in Fig.4.14 because the energy spectrum becomes so large that it is out of the scope range). The results of high order symmetric PV-filters are also improved compared to the original V-filters, but not too much.

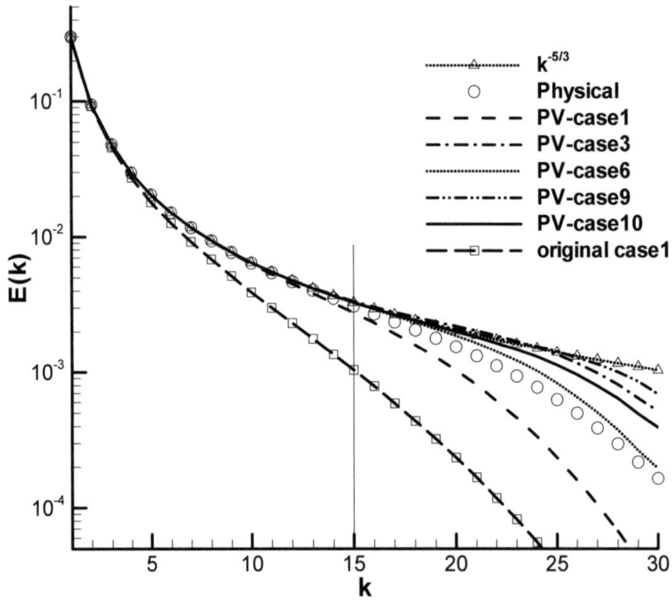

Fig. 4.13. Effect of the PV-filters on the $k^{-5/3}$ spectrum.

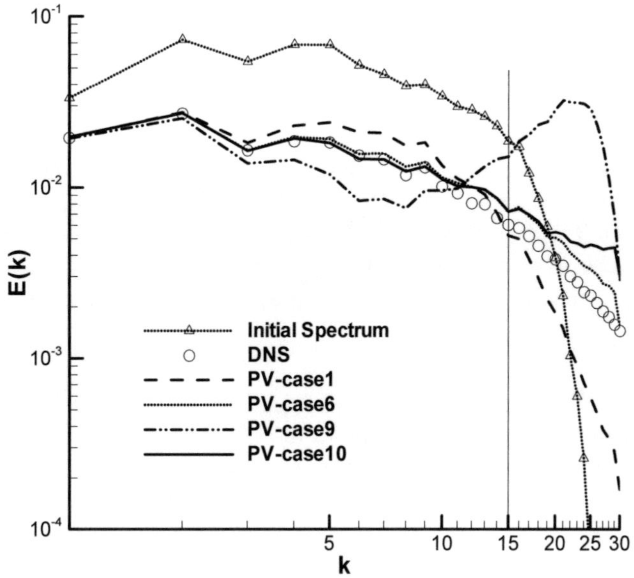

Fig. 4.14. Energy spectrum at final time for the PV-filters.

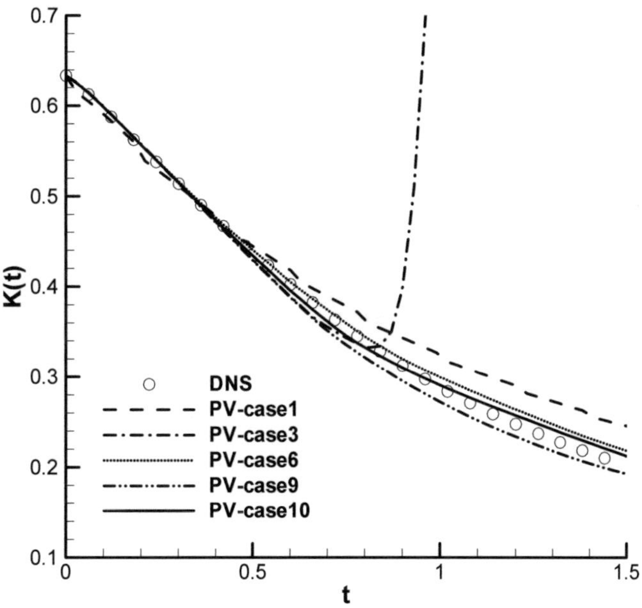

Fig. 4.15. The decay of the total kinetic energy for the PV-filters.

5. The effects of numerical errors on TNS

For DNS, the numerical errors mainly are aliasing and truncation errors (Chow 2003). As for LES, the small scales must be modelled because of the limited grid resolution which can not resolve all the scales. Therefore LES has an additional source of error comes from the SGS models. In general, it is required that all the source of errors can not overwhelm the contribution of SGS model in LES (Ghosal 1996; Chow 2003). In addition, unlike DNS the cut-off mode in LES is still energetic. As a result, LES is more sensitive to numerical errors. The numerical errors must be well controlled.

Note the numerical error in this section refers to aliasing and truncation errors introduced by spatial numerical scheme. Usually time discretization also introduces some computational errors (He et al 2004). Guo-Wei He etc studied the time correlation of several SGS model on LES (He et al 2004). Here we only focus on the spatial discretization error. In addition, the effect of the floating error of the computer is assumed to be small and ignored thereafter.

5.1 DNS results

We conduct DNS run at first in order to avoid the effect of SGS model. Also DNS data can provide benchmark for LES. The initial condition is the homogenous isotropic turbulence same as section 3 and 4. The grid resolution is 128×128×128 which is found fine enough to resolve the large scales for this simple flow. At Fig.1 the DNS results of 128^3 and 256^3 grid are compared. It is clear shows that they have a very good match for low wavenumber modes. In order to save computation time, only 128^3 runs are carried out thereafter.

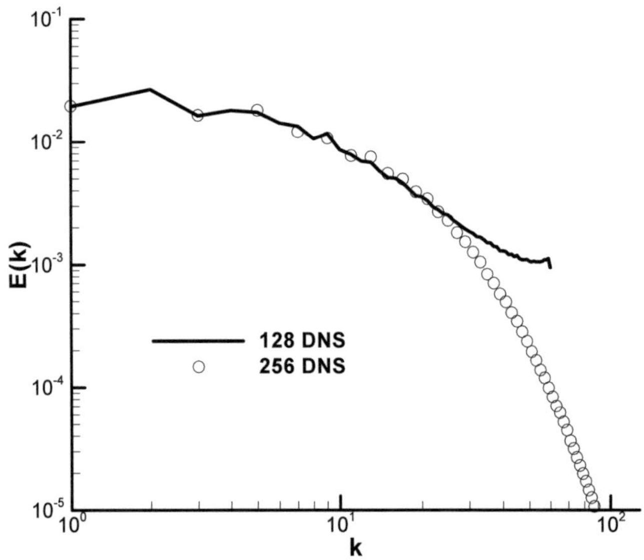

Fig. 5.1. The result of 128^3 DNS compared with 256^3.

As mentioned above, DNS only suffers from aliasing and discretization errors that depend on the numerical scheme used. When spectral method is used, the discretization errors is very small. So the numerical error is dominated by aliasing error. The main reason for aliasing error arising is that the gird resolution is limited. The modes beyond the grid cut-off wavenumber are incorrectly 'aliased' to wavenumbers that are resolved. Usually the contribution of aliasing errors is largest at the highest wavenumbers where any energy above the wavenumber cutoff incorrectly adds on the resolved spectrum. Without control, aliasing errors destroy the energy conservation and cause the solution to departure from physical solution. Usually a random shift technology is used to eliminate aliasing error. In order to identify the importance of aliasing error, we run two DNS: one uses anti-aliasing technology (the result marked as Dealiased) and the other one does not (the result denoted by Aliased). The simulation results are shown in Fig. 5.1. In Fig. 5.1a the energy spectrum at t=1 (the upper line) and t=3 (the lower line) are shown. And Fig. 5.1b gives the relative value of aliasing error, which is calculated as

$$\sigma(k) = \left(E(k)_{dealias} - E(k)_{alias}\right)/E(k)_{dealias} \tag{5.1}$$

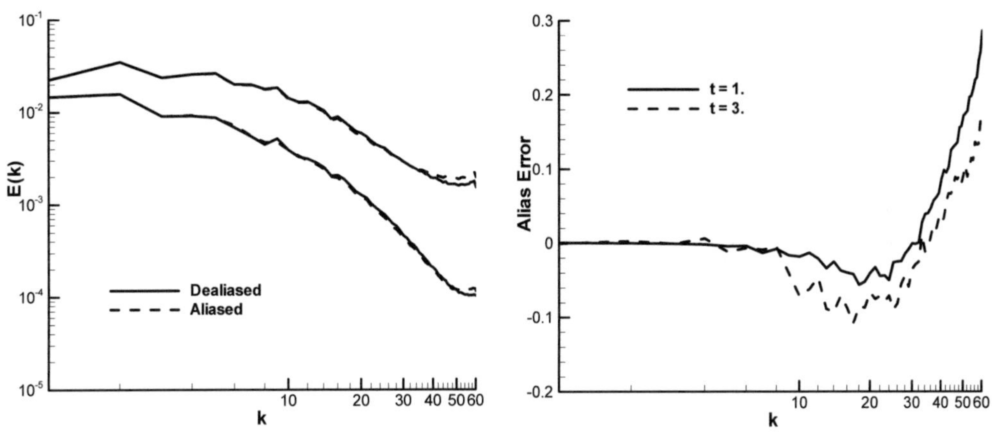

(a) (b)

Fig. 5.2. The aliasing errors for DNS using spectral method.

As we can see, the aliasing error is relatively small for DNS with spectral method. The largest error happens at high modes, which is consistent with the analysis of Park and Mahesh (Park & Mahesh 2007). The aliasing error can contaminate the low modes gradually with time evolution, as shown in Fig.5.1, but it is still very small.

For complex engineering problem, the spectral method is no longer suitable. Finite difference scheme or finite volume scheme is used instead. Same as section 4, the Padé compact scheme is used here. In order to examine the truncation error of different order of Padé scheme, one common used technology is to analysis the modified wavenumber in spectral space (Lele 1992). Similar to aliasing error, Padé scheme has little effect on low modes. The error is highest near the cut-off wavenumber. With higher order, the error is smaller and the result is more close to spectral method.

In order to isolate the discretization error, here we only apply the Padé scheme to the nonlinear term, which is similar to the way used by Kravchenko and Moin (Kravchenko & Moin 1997). The reason is that nonlinear term has important impact on SGS term. Also nonlinear term is a key factor which affects the stability of computation.

In Fig. 5.3 we compare the energy spectrum at different time for spectral method and different order Padé schemes. While the time evolution of total kinetic energy is shown in Fig. 5.4. As we can see, high order scheme, 6th order Padé scheme compares well with spectral method at all time. But for 4th order Padé scheme, at the initial stage (t=1), it compares well with spectral method at low modes, but shows some difference at high modes. The nonphysical energy introduced by discretization error accumulates at high modes and affects low modes gradually with time developing (t=3)

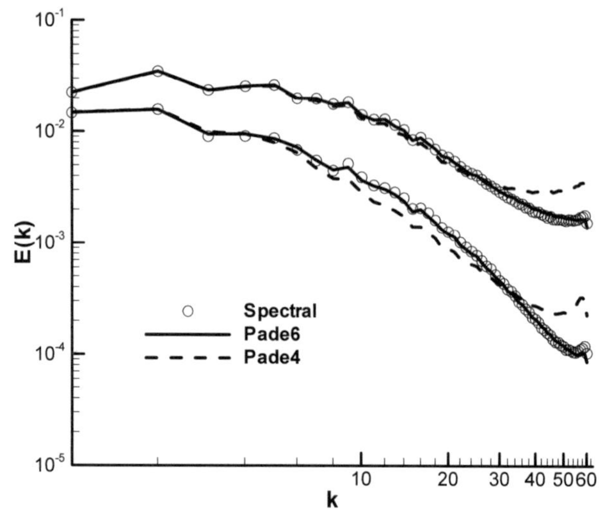

Fig. 5.3. The energy spectrum for DNS using different discretization schemes at t=1 and t=3 (from above to low).

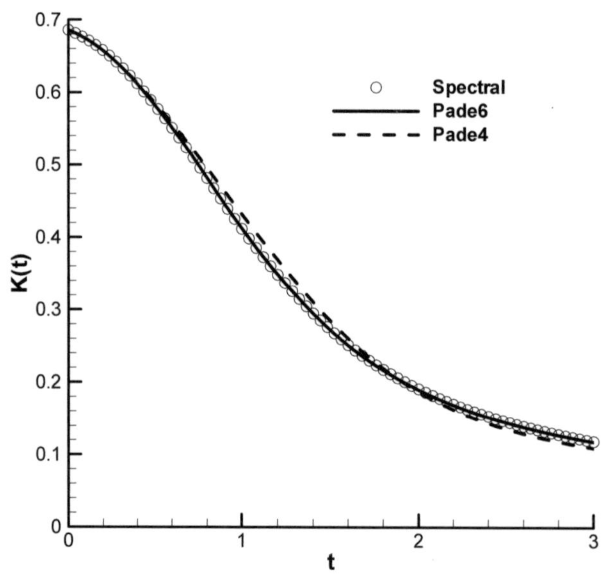

Fig. 5.4. The time evolution of total kinetic energy for DNS using different discretization schemes.

Note that 2nd order Padé scheme actually is the 2nd order center difference scheme. It is well known that it has the problem of even-odd oscillation which will leads to the computation diverging. We observe the same problem here. Usually an artificial viscosity is needed to dump the oscillation, which is beyond the research scope of this article. In Fig.5.5 the energy spectrum before computation fail is shown. It is clear seen that the nonphysical energy accumulates quickly at high modes which lead to the computation divergence. Park and Mahesh (Park & Mahesh 2007) gave a detail description about this problem. Interested reader should refer to their paper.

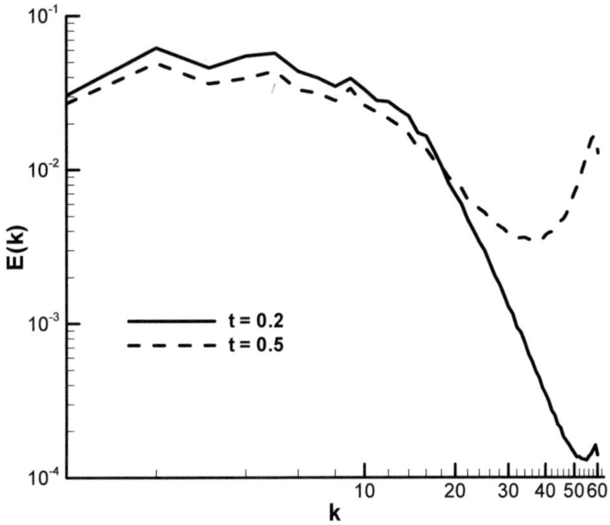

Fig. 5.5. The time evolution of energy spectrum for DNS using 2nd order Padé scheme.

The results for Padé schemes shown in Fig. 5.3 actually contain all the numerical errors, i.e. discretization and aliasing errors. Unlike spectral method, many researches thought that finite difference scheme can automatically decrease the aliasing error and therefore no anti-aliasing method is needed. Since the result of 6th order Padé scheme is the closest one to the spectral method, here we also apply the same anti-aliasing technology as used in spectral method to 6th order Padé scheme (denoted by Dealiased). The new result is then compared with the original one as shown in Fig. 5.6. Compared to spectral method, the magnitude of aliasing error does decrease. Note that actually it is very hard to isolate aliasing error from discretization error. The aliasing error shown above is not the actual aliasing error for 6th order Padé scheme. But anyway we can use that technology to determine the relative importance of aliasing error.

In general, the aliasing error in DNS can be well controlled. The main error is the truncation error of discretization scheme. Low order scheme is not suitable for simulation in some cases.

5.2 LES results

For the same simulations above, we also run the LES. The mesh size is 64×64×64. Spatial discretization adapts the same spectral and Padé compact schemes as in DNS. Note that LES has additional numerical error source which comes from the SGS model besides the aliasing error and discretization error for DNS. Again TNS approach is used to modelling the small scales. TNS model depends on periodic filtering to remove high modes energy. There are

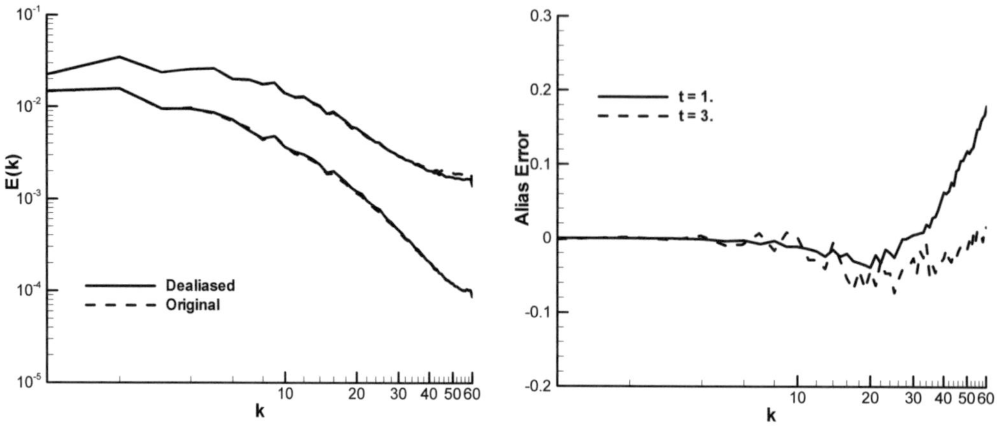

(a) (b)

Fig. 5.6. The aliasing error for DNS using 6th order Padé scheme.

many filters available as mentioned in section 4. Because we pay more attention to the possibility of applying LES to real engineering problem, only discrete filters are adapted here. Since Padé discrete filters show good results in section 4, we only focus on them to simply the research. Note that different order of Padé filter means the error introduced by SGS model is different.

In Fig. 5.7a, b, c, d it shows the final energy spectrum for spectral method and different Padé compact schemes (marked with 'd') combined with TNS model using different order Padé discrete filters (denoted as 'f'), i.e. 'd6f4' means 6th order Padé compact scheme and 4th order filter. As we can see, TNS model plays a key role in the simulations. Low order filter provides too much dissipation and performs poorly for all discretization schemes. High order filter (4th order and above) obtains good results compared with DNS. However higher the filter order is, it keeps more high modes energy and thus dissipates less. In return it decreases the performance of LES. TNS model with 4th order filter provides the best results. Compared to DNS, LES is not so sensitive to the order of the discretization scheme. Even 2nd order scheme can obtain reasonable results. The result is not as good as of high order scheme though, but much better than of DNS which diverges when using 2nd order scheme. The reason is that the discretization and aliasing errors cause the energy to accumulate at high modes; while TNS model removes high modes energy through filtering. The dissipation provided by SGS model dumps the unphysical energy increment. This result may help explain why low order scheme can obtain good results when applied to engineering problem.

In order to further comparing the effect of different discretization scheme on LES, here we run a series cases with the same TNS model (all using 6th order Padé filter) while the spatial discretization uses spectral method and different order of Padé schemes. The results are shown in Fig. 5.8 and Fig. 5.9. Similar to DNS, low order Padé discretization scheme leads energy to accumulate at high modes. Higher the order is, the result is more close to DNS. The spectral method is the best one. But different form DNS, low order (2nd order) scheme obtains reasonable result and does not cause divergence like DNS case in Fig. 5.5. It is because the TNS model removes the unphysical energy accumulated at high modes and thus dumps the discretization error.

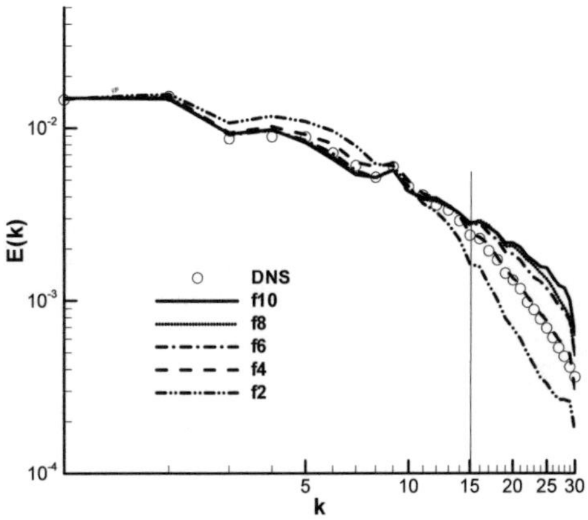

(a) spectral method

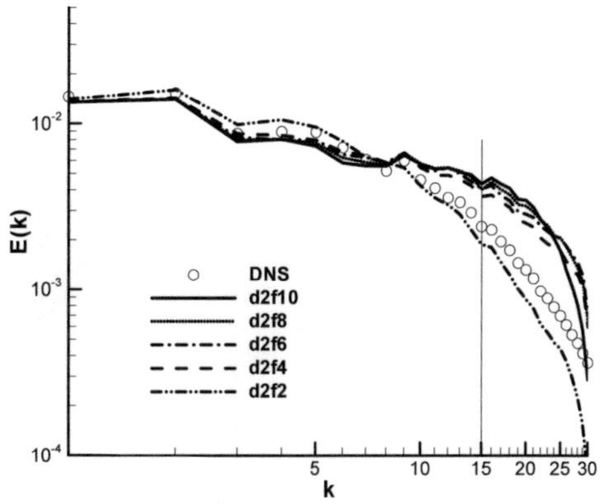

(b) 2nd order Padé scheme

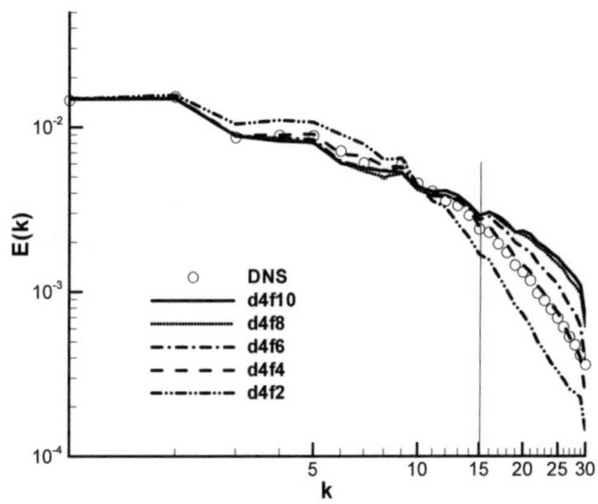

(c) 4th order Padé scheme

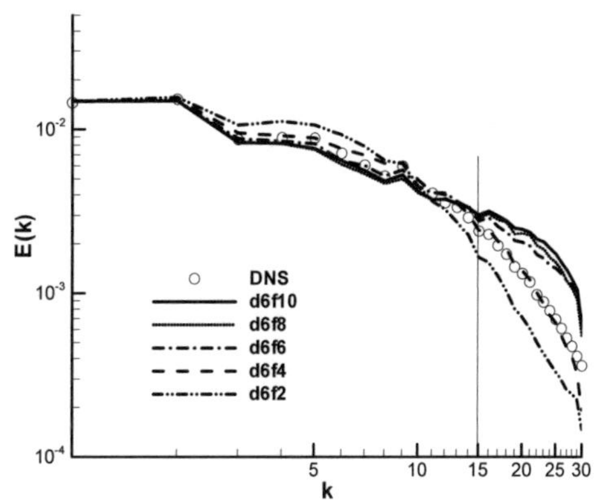

(d) 6th order Padé scheme

Fig. 5.7. The final energy spectrum for LES using spectral method, different order Padé schemes and TNS models.

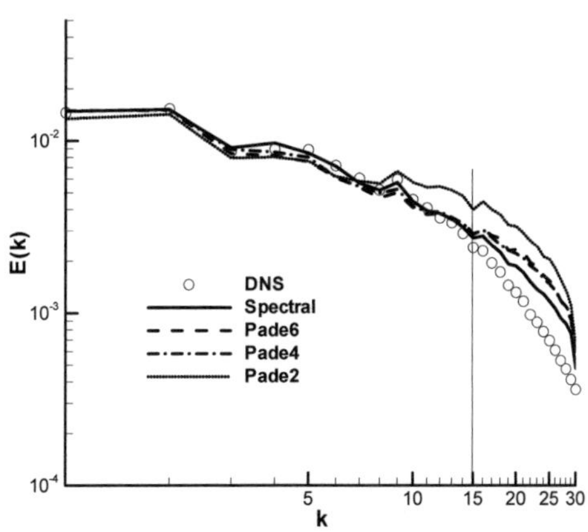

Fig. 5.8. The final energy spectrum for different discretization scheme with the same TNS model.

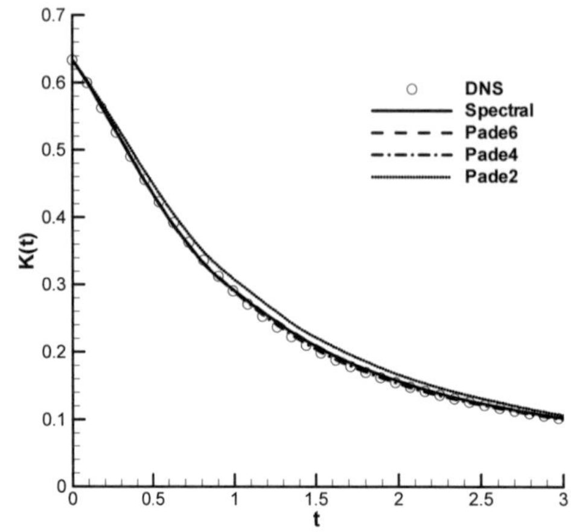

Fig. 5.9. The time evolution of total energy for different discretization scheme with the same TNS model.

Same to Fig. 5.6, we also try to investigate the effect of anti-aliasing method on the final results (only the case using 6th order Padé scheme, 6th TNS model is considered). The comparison is shown in Fig. 5.10. The aliasing error is still small. But for LES the energy at cut-off wavenumber is considerable large compared to DNS, the relative value of aliasing error increases.

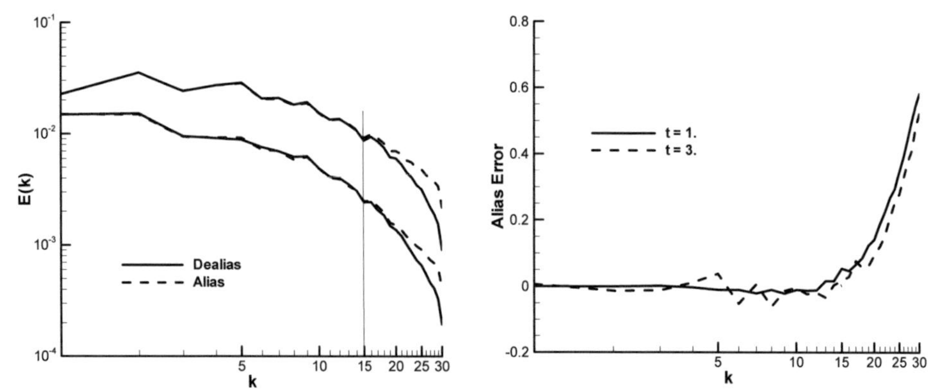

(a) (b)

Fig. 5.10. The aliasing error for LES using 6th Padé scheme and TNS model with 6th order filter.

6. Conclusion

In the past ten years significant progress has been made in the LES technology. LES has become one of the most promising and successful methodology available to solve the complex turbulent flows. However there are still some challenges before LES can be a mature tool to predict engineering problems, including reliable subgrid scale model, the choice of filter, near-wall treatment, numerical errors etc. And an accurate, fast and robust numerical algorithm for complex geometry is also needed. In this article, three key issues of

LES, namely the SGS models, the choice of filters and the effects of numerical errors, are investigated briefly.

The TNS approach is a simple and promising model. It actually is a DNS run with periodic processing of high modes. The basic assumption in TNS is that dynamics of small scales are strongly determined by the large eddies and the contribution of small scales to large scales are mostly contained within wavenumbers that are twice that of the cut-off wavenumber. By periodic removal of high mode energy using a filter, TNS provides necessary dissipation for small scales and thus avoids energy accumulation at high wavenumbers. It provides natural dissipation mechanism for low modes by nonlinear interactions between low modes and high modes at the cost of doubling the mesh. It can be expended to other flow easily because it does not have any empirical parameter.

The filtering operation plays a key role in TNS. It is responsible for removing the accumulated energy of the small scales at prescribed intervals. The filter type has direct effect on the final simulation results. Here a set of smooth filters and discrete filters are tested using TNS model. For the smooth filters, the physical filter is implemented in the physical space while it has similar property to the spectral filter at the same time. Also it keeps a part of the small-scale energy, which benefits the energy transfer. The Tophat and Gaussian filters are easy to implement but have serious undesirable effects on the large-scale energy. The discrete Padé filters exhibit advantages over the V-filters because the effect of adjacent points can be taken into account. The Padé filters can keep most of large-scale energy while maintaining sufficient amount of the small-scale energy at the same time. They show very good performance in all the runs, even better than the smooth physical filter. However the second order Padé filter still has effect on the large scales and the high order ones tend to keep too much small-scale energy, both of them may decrease the performance of TNS. The V-filters can be easily implemented to any specified order. However, high asymmetric filters should be avoided because they introduce too much nonphysical energy at high modes. The second order symmetric V-filter is actually a discrete version of the Tophat filter. It has the same problem as the smooth one, i.e., removing too much large-scale energy. When the smooth physical filter idea is applied to the V-filters, the results for the low order V-filters are improved significantly, but it is not necessary for high order V-filters. Note that the filter type should be adjusted according to the SGS model. So for LES with other SGS models, the effect of filters may be different.

The effects of numerical errors on LES are investigated briefly here, including discretization error, alias errors as well as SGS model error. As for DNS, no matter using spectral method or Padé compact scheme, the aliasing error can be well controlled. The final result is more affected by the truncation error of discretization scheme. High order scheme is preferred. Low order scheme is not suitable in some case. For example in our simulation, 2nd order discretization scheme leads energy to accumulate at high modes quickly and causes the solution unstable. As for LES, the interaction between numerical error and SGS model is complicated. Different model, such as TNS with different order filtering, can have different results. Low order filter brings in too much dissipation which is not a suitable property for LES; while the dissipation provided by high order filter is too small which also decreases the performance of TNS model. High order discretization schemes (4th order Padé scheme and above) plus middle order filters (4th or 6th order) can obtain good results compared with DNS. A more advantage is that TNS model not only avoids the small scales energy accumulating, but also dumps the side effect of discretization and alias errors to the high modes because TNS model removes the high modes energy periodically by filtering. This interaction between TNS model and numerical error benefits LES. So low order discretization scheme plus a more dissipative TNS model can get good enough result. In addition, the energy at cut-off wavenumber for LES is still relative large, so the effect of aliasing error increases. We have to admit that due to the time and our knowledge limitation, the study on the numerical error is not full enough. There are some excellent works by other researches available.

7. Acknowledgment

This research is supported by NSF China Grants No. 10502029, Hunan nature science found 10JJ3018 and the Science Fund of State Key Laboratory of Advanced Design and Manufacturing for Vehicle Body 31075013. I am greatly grateful to Dr. Domaradzki and Dr. Song Fu for many useful discussing and advising on this research.

8. References

Bertero, M and Boccacci P (1998). *Inverse Problems in Imaging*. Institute of Physics Publishing. ISBN 0750304359. Bristol, United Kingdom

Bouffanais, B. (2010). Advances and challenges of applied large-eddy simulation. *Computers & Fluids*, vol. 39, (December 2010), pp.735–738

Chollet, J. and Leiseur, M. (1981) Parameterization of small scales of three dimensional isotropic turbulence utilizing spectral closures. *J. Atmos. Sci.* Vol.38, (1981), pp.2747-2757

Chow, F. Moin P. (2003). A further study of numerical errors in large-eddy simulations[J]. *Journal of Computational Physics*, Vol.184, (2003), pp.366–380

Dahlstrom S and Davidson L. (2003). Large Eddy Simulation Applied to a High Reynolds Flow around an Airfoil close to stall. *AIAA paper 2003–0776*

De Stefano G. Vasilyev O. (2002). Sharp cutoff versus smooth filtering in large eddy simulation. *Physics of fluids*, Vol.14, No.1, (2002), pp.362-369

Domaradzki, J. Loh, K. Yee, P. (2002). Large eddy simulation using the subgrid-scale estimation model and truncated Navier-Stokes dynamics. *Theor. Comput. Fluid Dyn.*, Vol.15, No.6, (2002), pp.421-450

Domaradzki, J. Rogallo, R. (1990). Local energy transfer and nonlocal interactions in homogeneous, isotropic turbulence. *Phys. Fluids A*, Vol.2, (1990), pp.413.

Domaradzki, J. Saiki, E. (1997). A subgrid-scale model based on the estimation of unresolved scales of turbulence. *Phys. Fluids*, Vol.9, (1997), pp.2148

Fauconnier, D. Langhe, C. Dick E. (2009). A family of dynamic finite difference schemes for large-eddy simulation. *Journal of Computational Physics*, Vol.228, (2009), pp.1830–1861

Fröhlich J. Rodi W. (2001). Introduction to Large Eddy Simulation of Turbulent Flows, In: *Closure Strategies for Turbulent and Transitional Flows*, Launder and Sandham. pp.267-298, Cambridge University Press, ISBN 9780521792080, UK

Georgiadis, N. (2008). Large-eddy simulation - Current capabilities and areas of needed research. *Progress in Aerospace Sciences*, vol.44, (2008), pp.379–380

Germano, M. Piomelli, U. Moin, P. Cabot, W. (1991). A dynamic sub-grid-scale eddy viscosity model. *Phys. Fluids A*, Vol.3, No.7, (1991), pp.1760-765.

Ghosal, S. (1996). An analysis of numerical errors in large-eddy simulations of turbulence. *J. Comput. Phys.* Vol.125, (1996), pp.187–206

Hartel, C. Kleiser, L. Unger F. Friedrich, R. (1994). Subgrid-scale energy transfer in the near-wall region of turbulent flows. *Phys. Fluids*, Vol.6, (1994), pp.3130

He, G. Wang, M. Lele, S. (2004). On the computation of space-time correlations in decaying isotropic turbulence. *Physics of Fluids*, 2004, Vol.14, No.11, (2004), pp.3859-3867

Horiuti, K. (1999). Transformation properties of subgrid-scale models in a frame of reference undergoing rotation. *Submitted to the J. Fluid Mech.* (1999).

Kitoh, K. Oshima, N. Yamamoto, M. etc. (2009). A CFD Approach via Large Eddy Simulation to the Flow Field with Complex Geometrical Configurations: A Study Case of Vehicle Underbody Flows. *SAE 2009-01-0332*

Krajnovic, S. Davidson L. (2005). Flow Around a Simplified Car, Part 1: LES. *Journal of Fluids Engineering, Transactions of the ASME*, vol.127, (2005), pp.907 -918

Kravchenko, A. Moin, P. (1997). On the effect of numerical errors in large eddy simulations of turbulent flows. *Journal of Computational Physics*, Vol.131, No.2, (1997), pp.310–322

Lele, S. (1992). Compact finite difference schemes with spectral-like resolution. *Journal of Computational Physics*, Vol.103, (1992), No.1, (1992), pp.16-42

Leonard A. (1974). Energy cascade in large eddy simulations of turbulent fluid flows. *Adv. Geophys. A*, Vol.18, (1974), pp.237-248

Lesieur, M. (1990). *Turbulence in Fluids* (2nd Edition). Kluwer Academic Publishers. ISBN 978-1-4020-6434-0. Springer, The Netherlands.

Lilly, D. (1992). A proposed modification of the Germano subgrid-scale closure method. *Phys. Fluids A*, Vol.4, (1992), pp.633

Lilly, D. (1996). On the application of the eddy viscosity concept in the inertial subrange of turbulence. *NCAR manuscript 123*, (1996), NCAR, Boulder, CO.

Lund, T. (1997). On the use of discrete filters for large eddy simulation, *Center for Turbulence Research*, Annual Research Brief, (1997), pp.83

Lund, T. (2003). The Use of Explicit Filters in Large Eddy Simulation. *Computers and Mathematics with Applications*, Vol.46, (2003), pp.603-616

Mahesh, K. Constantinescu, G. Moin, P (2004). A numerical method for large-eddy simulation in complex geometries. *Journal of Computational Physics*, vol.197, (January 2004), pp.215–240

Mary I. and Sagaut P. (2001). Large Eddy Simulation of Flow Around an Airfoil. *AIAA paper 2001-2559*

Mathew, J. (2010). Large Eddy Simulation. *Defence Science Journal*, Vol.60, No.6, (November 2010), pp 598-605

Mathew, J. Lechner, R. Foysi, H. Sesterhenn, J. Friedrich, R. (2003) An explicit filtering method for large eddy simulation of compressible flows. *Physics of Fluids*, Vol.15, No.8, (2003), pp.2279-2289

McCallen, R. *et al.* (2006). DOE's Effort to Reduce Truck Aerodynamic Drag through Joint Experiments and Computations. (2006) DOE 21CTP-0003

Mellen, C. Fröhlich, J. Rodi, W. (2003). Lessons from LESFOIL project on large-eddy simulation of flow around an airforl. *AIAA Journal*, vol.41, No.4, (2003), pp.573-581

Minguez, M. Pasquetti R. Serre. E. (2008). High-order large-eddy simulation of flow over the 'Ahmed body' car model. *Physics of Fluids*, Vol.20, No.9, (2008), pp.95-101

Moin, P. (2002). Advances in large eddy simulation methodology for complex flows. *International Journal of Heat and Fluid Flow*, vol.23, (2002), pp.710–720

Park, N. Mahesh K. (2007). Analysis of numerical errors in large eddy simulation using statistical closure theory. *J. Comput. Phys.* Vol.222, (2007), pp.194–216.

Piomelli, U. (1999). Large-Eddy simulation: achievements and challenges. *Progress in Aerospace Science*. Vol.35, (1999), pp.335

Piomelli, U. Moin, P. Ferziger, J. (1988). Model consistency in large eddy simulation of turbulent channel flow. *Phys. Fluids*, Vol.31, (1988), pp.1884.

Pope, S. (2000). *Turbulent Flows*. Cambridge University Press. ISBN 0521591252. Cambridge, United Kingdom

Rodi, W. (2006). DNS and LES of some engineering flows. *Fluid Dynamics Research*, vol.38, (2006), pp.145-173

Rogallo, R. (1981). Numerical experiments in homogeneous turbulence. *NASA Tech. Memo.* 81835, 1981

Sagaut, P. (2006). *Large-eddy simulation for incompressible flows – an introduction* (3rd Edition). Springer. ISBN 978-3-540-26344-9. Berlin, German

Smagorinsky, J. (1963) General circulation experiments with the primitive equations I: The basic experiment. *Monthly Weather Review*. Vol.91, No.3, (1963), pp.99-165

Spalart, P. (2000). Strategies for turbulence modelling and simulations. *International Journal of Heat and Fluid Flow*. Vol.21, (2000), pp.252-263

Stolz, S. Adams, N. (1999). An approximate deconvolution procedure for large- eddy simulation. *Phys. Fluids*, Vol.11, (1999), pp.1699-701.

Tsubokura, M. Kobayashi, T. Nakashima, T. *et al.* (2009). Computational visualization of unsteady flow around vehicles using high performance computing. *Computers & Fluids*, Vol.38, (2009), pp.981–990

Vasilyev O. Lund, T. and Moin P. (1998). A general class of commutative filters for LES in complex geometries. *Journal of Computational Physics*, Vol.146, (1998), pp.82-104

Visbal M. Gaitonde D. (2002). On the use of higher-order finite-difference schemes on curvilinear and deforming meshes. *Journal of Computational Physics*, Vol.181, (2002), pp.155-185

Yang, X. Domaradzki J. (2004) Large eddy simulations of decaying rotating turbulence. *Physics of Fluids*, Vol.16, No.11, (2004), pp.4088-4104

Yang, X. Fu S. (2008). Study of numerical errors in direct numerical simulation and large eddy simulation. *Applied Mathematics and Mechanics*. Vol.29, No.7, (2008), pp.871-880

Zhou, Y. (1993). Interacting scales and energy transfer in isotropic turbulence. *Phys. Fluids A*, Vol.5, (1993), pp.2511

3

An Introduction of Central Difference Scheme Stability for High Reynolds Number

da Silva, A. R.; Silveira-Neto, A. and de Lima, A. M. G.
Federal University of Uberlândia/School of Mechanical Engineering
Brazil

1. Introduction

The quest for understanding the mechanisms responsible for the vortex shedding process comes from past decades, but it is still challenging. The turbulent wake downstream of bluff bodies induces alternating and dynamic loads in the bodies like (antennas, chimneys, suspended bridges, a set of risers and structures in general). These structures can produce disastrous results. Extrapolating the scale of the phenomena, one can refer to petroleum exploration, which starting from the platforms to the seabed, there are risers that are cylindrical tubes of great length. They are subjected to ocean currents and suffer fluid-dynamic effort. The consequence is that the phenomenon as fatigue and wear are accelerated, reducing the useful life of equipment and could lead them to collapse.

Thus, the study of problems involving immersed bodies is motivated by great technological challenges, both within the academic and industrial environment. Fluid-structure interaction is today one of the crucial problems in various areas of mechanical and civil engineering, because of the necessity of extensive structures subjected to fluid-dynamic random efforts. Therefore, it is important to appreciate the great importance of the study of flow around stationary circular cylinder in order to extrapolate to moving bodies or to set of moving bodies. This is a model, used to simulate, for example, a set of risers. We also emphasize the importance of such studies, including transition and turbulent flows, in order to better approximate the real conditions.

In the context of fluid mechanics, the study of fluid flows and how they interact with solid materials has been of great interest in various fields such as civil and mechanical engineering, meteorology and environment. In recent decades, great efforts have been made for the development of new numerical methods to analyze the wide range of problems in fluid mechanics, as well as improving existing ones. The Computational Fluid Dynamics has been considered an interesting tool to simulate various problems of practical interest in engineering. The literature shows different computational methods with several techniques to solve differential equations aiming to accuracy of results. Different numerical methods developed for the study of flow in the presence of immersed bodies are basically divided into techniques based on the immersed boundary method, and those based on meshes that are able to adapt to the immersed body inside the flow. However, there is no method that can be considered absolutely superior to others. The choice of the most appropriate method should be made case by case, taking into account the specific characteristics of the focused problem.

The Immersed Boundary Method (IBM), due to their capability to deal with problems of complex and mobile interfaces, becomes attractive, especially in cases involving large displacements. In the modeling process of physical problems, the equations that govern the physics of the problem appear naturally. These models can range from those involving only one differential equation to those involving a system of differential equations, which can be fully coupled. However, in most cases, exact solutions can not be obtained and numerical methods appear as a tool to solve these problems. The Immersed Boundary method is used here with the Virtual Physical Model in order to simulate two-dimensional incompressible flows over stationary, rotating and rotationally-oscillating circular cylinders. Different time discretization methods are used: first order Euler scheme and the second-order Adams-Bashforth and Runge-Kutta schemes. The sub-grid Smagorinsky model and a damping function are also used. Considering the existence of a mistaken view about the mentioned numerical methods, their stability analyses are made in the present work. The results are compared with numerical and experimental results obtained from the literature.

2. Mathematical modeling

The mathematical model that describes the flow consists of a set of coupled differential equations representing the physical phenomenon for which we want the solution. The literature has shown that only a fraction of practical problems can be resolved due to the complexity of the equations. Thanks to high-performance computers and numerical methods, the solution of several problems becomes possible. The formulations of the Immersed Boundary Method and Virtual Physical Model are briefly presented.

2.1 Immersed boundary method

The Immersed Boundary Method (Peskin, 1977) along with the Virtual Physical Model (Lima e Silva et al., 2007) are used to solve two-dimensional, incompressible, isothermal and transient flows. It is based on the motion equations plus a force term which model the interface. Thus, it becomes necessary to use two formulations: one for the fluid (Eulerian fixed mesh) and another for the immersed interface (Lagrangean mesh). These meshes are geometrically independent and coupled through the force term.

2.1.1 Mathematical formulation for the fluid

The Navier-Stokes equations, Eq. (1), and the continuity equation, Eq. (2), for a Newtonian fluid, are presented below using the tensor form:

$$\frac{\partial u_i}{\partial t}+\frac{\partial\left(u_i u_j\right)}{\partial x_j}=-\frac{1}{\rho}\frac{\partial p}{\partial x_i}+\frac{\partial}{\partial x_j}\left[\nu\left(\frac{\partial u_i}{\partial x_j}+\frac{\partial u_j}{\partial x_i}\right)\right]+f_i\,, \tag{1}$$

$$\frac{\partial u_i}{\partial x_i}=0\,, \tag{2}$$

where ρ [kg/m³] and ν [m²/s] are respectively the specific mass and the kinematic viscosity, properties that characterize the fluid. The variables of interest are represented by: the velocity components u_i [m/s], the pressure p [N/m²] and the components of the Eulerian force acting on the interface f_i [N/m³]. The force term only exists in Eulerian points coincident or close to the Lagrangean mesh, being zero for the remaining points of the calculation domain. This term is calculated by distributing the components of the Lagrangean interfacial force vector, using a distribution function (Peskin & McQueen, 1994):

$$f(x)=\sum_{k} D_{ij}(x-x_k)F(x_k)\Delta S^2(x_k) \tag{3}$$

where $f(x)$ [N] is the Eulerian force vector, x [m] and x_k [m] are respectively the position vectors of Eulerian and Lagrangean points, ΔS [m] is the arc length centered on each Lagrangean points, $F(x_k)$ [N] is the interfacial force calculated by the IBM and D_{ij} [m^{-2}] is a interpolation/distribution function, which properties are the same of the Gaussian function.

2.1.2 Mathematical formulation for the immersed interface – Virtual Physical Model (VPM)

The VPM allows the calculation of Lagrangean force based on physical interaction of the fluid and immersed solid surface in the flow. This model is based on applying the balance of momentum quantity over the fluid particles located at the Lagrangean points. The equation that determines this force is expressed as:

$$F(x_k,t)=\underbrace{\rho\frac{\partial V(x_k,t)}{\partial t}}_{F_a}+\underbrace{\rho\nabla\left(V(x_k,t)V(x_k,t)\right)}_{F_i}-\underbrace{\mu\nabla\left[\nabla V(x_k,t)+\nabla^T V(x_k,t)\right]}_{F_v}+\underbrace{\nabla p(x_k,t)}_{F_p} \tag{4}$$

where F_a [N] is the acceleration force, F_i [N] is the inertial force, F_v [N] is the viscous force and F_p [N] is the pressure force.

2.2 Turbulence model

Turbulence is one of the most challenging problems of modern physics and is among the most complex and beautiful phenomena in nature. Due to several practical implications for many sectors, the number of research related to understanding and controlling these flows has increased. The turbulence effects can be modeled and simulated since emprirical correlations and diagrams up to modern methodology of numerical simulation.

2.2.1 Turbulence equations

It is known that even for flows controled by moderate Reynolds numbers, it is not possible to solve directly all frequencies present in a turbulent flow. Reynolds (1894) proposed a decomposition process of the Navier-Stokes equations in a mean and floating part in order to solve the turbulent flow. The decomposition process of the scales yielded two groups of equations for the turbulence, the first being called Reynolds Averaged Navier-Stokes equations, and another called the filtered Navier-Stokes equations (Smagorinsky, 1963). After applying the filtering and the decomposition process and applying the definitions in Eqs. (1) and (2), we obtain the following equation:

$$\frac{\partial \overline{u}_i}{\partial t}+\frac{\partial\left(\overline{u}_i\overline{u}_j\right)}{\partial x_j}=-\frac{1}{\rho}\frac{\partial p^*}{\partial x_i}+\frac{\partial}{\partial x_j}\left[\nu_{ef}\left(\frac{\partial \overline{u}_i}{\partial x_j}+\frac{\partial \overline{u}_j}{\partial x_i}\right)\right]+f_i \tag{5}$$

$$p^* = \overline{p} + \frac{2}{3}\rho\, k \text{ and } \nu_{ef} = \nu + \nu_t \tag{6}$$

where ν_t is the turbulent viscosity.

2.2.2 Sub-grid modeling and large eddy simulation

The sub-grid models are suitable for the calculation of turbulent viscosity. The sub-grid Smagorinky model used here is based on the assumption that the production of sub-grid turbulent stress is equal to the dissipation. The turbulent viscosity is a function of strain rate and the length scale and is expressed as:

$$\nu_t = \left(C_S \ell\right)^2 \sqrt{2\overline{S}_{ij}\overline{S}_{ij}} \tag{7}$$

where ℓ is the characteristic length, S_{ij} is the strain rate, C_s is the Smagorinsky constant. Large eddy simulation allows us to obtain three-dimensional and transient results using the motion equations, as well as to simulate flows at high Reynolds numbers with the use of refined meshes. Like any methodology, the sub-grid model has some disadvantages, such as adjusting the constant in accordance with the problem, deficiency in modeling phenomena involving energy transfer from small scales to larger scales and disability in the calculation of viscosity near the walls, which may require the use of wall laws.

3. Numerical methodology

It is important to appreciate that numerical analysis of a two-dimensional flow is possible since that determine the values of the interest variables at discrete points. The result of a discretization process are finite difference equations, which are written for each point in the domain that we want to solve. After solving these equations, the approximated solution of the problem is found. As the number of grid points becomes large, the solution of discretized equations tends to the exact solution of the corresponding differential equation.

3.1 Fractional step method

The Fractional Step Method (Chorin, 1968) with displaced meshes for the coupling between the pressure and velocity fields is used here. This arrangement allows greater facility on discretization, without the need of mean calculus, because the velocity components are positioned on the face of control volume. Moreover, this arrangement provides more stability in the pressure-velocity coupling.

As the flow is incompressible, the pressure is no longer a function of specific mass, that is constant, ie, is not a function of the thermodynamic pressure of the fluid. The Fractional Step Method is a non-iterative method, where, from the force, velocity and pressure fields of the previous iteration, we estimate the velocity components fields. With these estimated fields, we calculate the pressure correction, through the solution of a linear system, by Modified Strongly Implicit Procedure (MSI) (Schneider & Zedan, 1981). The pressure acts as a Lagrange multiplier in minimization problems. The importance of the Poisson equation for pressure correction is that it makes the connection between the equations of motion and continuity. Provides values of p that allow that the values of velocities components, u^{n+1} v^{n+1}, obtained from the respective Navier-Stokes equations, satisfy the mass conservation at time $n+1$.

The spatial discretization is performed using the second order centered finite difference scheme and the time discretization with the first order Euler method, Adams-Bashforth and Runge-Kutta, both of second order.

3.2 Time discretization methods

It is presented, then, a brief description of the time discretization methods used here, already making an analogy with the motion equation.

3.2.1 Euler method

It is a first-order method for solving transient problems. With this method the time derivative $\frac{\partial u_i}{\partial t}$ can be approximated by:

$$\frac{\tilde{u}_i^{n+1} - u_i^n}{\Delta t} = f\left(u_i^n, u_j^n\right) - P_i^n + F_i^n \tag{8}$$

where f includes advective and diffusive terms of the motion equation. The index n, is related to time and Δt is the time step. This method is easy to implement, but requires the use of small time step to ensure the stability of the solution. The terms P_i^n and F_i^n are the pressure gradient and force field, respectively in the i direction. The term $\tilde{u}$ is an estimate of the velocity inherent of the coupling method used.

3.2.2 Second order Adams-Bashforth method

It is a multi-point method, where the velocity fields at the current time is obtained using information from two previous time instants. In other words, the advective and diffusive terms in n and $n-1$ are needed for the calculations in time $n+1$. Multipoint methods are easy to be implemented and require only an evaluation of the derivatives by time step, making them relatively inexpensive. The main disadvantage of these methods is that as they require information on previous points, they can not be started by themselves. For this purpose, we use the Euler method for initial calculus. For i component of the estimated velocity, this method can be represented by:

$$\frac{\tilde{u}_i^{n+1} - u_i^n}{\Delta t} = \frac{3}{2} f\left(u_i^n, u_j^n\right) - \frac{1}{2} f\left(u_i^{n-1}, u_j^{n-1}\right) - P_i^n + F_i^n \tag{9}$$

3.2.3 Second order Runge-Kutta method

It is a single stage method, ie, to determine $\tilde{u}_i^{n+1}$, one needs only the information available at the previous time u_i^n, u_j^n. In this method or in the superior orders the function in one or more additional points should be calculated. The first step until the middle of interval can be regarded as a predictor step, based on the explicit Euler method, which is accompanied by a correction to the end of the range. In summary, this method needs of information calculated only on the last time. Moreover, it requires the calculation of the function $f\left(u_i^n, u_j^n\right)$ twice and thus consumes more time. For the i component of the estimated velocity, this method can be represented by:

Predictor step:

$$\frac{\tilde{u}_i^{n+\frac{1}{2}} - u_i^n}{\frac{\Delta t}{2}} = f\left(u_i^n, u_j^n\right) - P_i^n + F_i^n \quad (10)$$

Corrector step:

$$\frac{\tilde{u}_i^{n+1} - u_i^n}{\Delta t} = f\left(\tilde{u}_i^{n+\frac{1}{2}}, \tilde{u}_j^{n+\frac{1}{2}}\right) - P_i^n + F_i^n \quad (11)$$

4. Problem description

Stability analysis of the second order spatial centered scheme with the time discretization schemes is performed by two-dimensional simulations of incompressible flows around a stationary circular cylinder. The rectangular domain is chosen to be $15d \times 30d$ with the cylinder located at 16.5 cylinder diameters from the inlet as illustrated in Fig. (1). The time step used in all simulations is 0.0001 s.

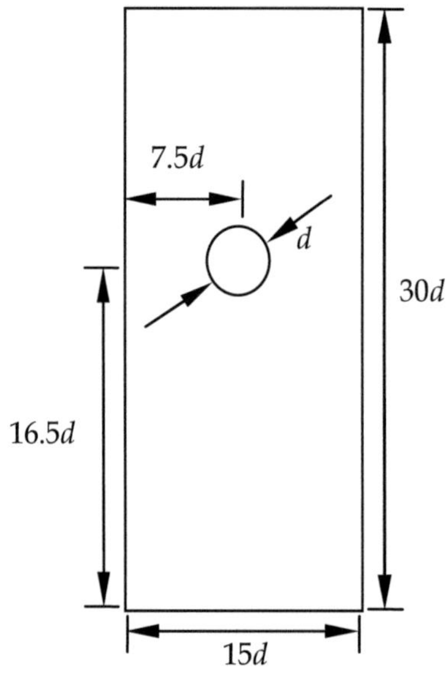

Fig. 1. Schematic illustration of the calculation domain.

The flow develops from the bottom to top and the boundary conditions for velocity are : in the inlet: $u = 0$ e $\upsilon = V$, in the outlet: $\frac{\partial u}{\partial y} = \frac{\partial \upsilon}{\partial y} = 0$ and in the lateral boundaries: $\frac{\partial u}{\partial x} = \frac{\partial \upsilon}{\partial x} = 0$. For the pressure, the boundary conditions used are: in the inlet: $\frac{\partial p}{\partial y} = 0$, in the outlet and in the lateral boundaries: $p = 0$.

4.1 Analyses of the grid refinement

For these simulations three grids are used, which are shown in the Tab. (1), along with the three time discretization schemes. It is observed through the mean values of drag coefficients (Table 2), the similarity of results when different time discretization methods were considered and the same grid refinement. Considering the various refinements, it is noted that with the coarser grid the destabilization of the flow occurs more slowly. With the grid refinement, which filters the instabilities of high frequency, the transition of the flow is faster. It is also observed that with the grid refinement from the grid 2 to grid 3, the mean values of drag coefficients are approximately the same, which leads to the independence of the results for finer mesh than 125x250. The Sthouhal number, obtained by Fast Fourier Transform (FFT) of the lift coefficient signal is also shown in Tab. (2) for Reynolds number 100.

Grid	Points number	Method
1	62x124	Euler Adams-Bashforth Runge-Kutta (R-K)
2	125x250	
3	250x500	

Table 1. Grids used for the three time discretization schemes, Re=100.

Re=100									
Grid	1			2			3		
Method	Adams	Euler	R-K	Adams	Euler	R-K	Adams	Euler	R-K
C_d	1.41	1.41	1.41	1.38	1.39	1.38	1.38	1.38	1.38
St	0.12	0.12	0.12	0.15	0.15	0.15	0.15	0.16	0.16

Table 2. Mean values of drag coefficients and Strouhal number for the three time discretization methods and different grids.

Note that the mean values of the drag coefficient decreases with grid refinement for the three methods. No significant difference is observed when passing from the intermediate to the most refined grid, as mentioned previously. These results are also visualized through the time evolution of the drag coefficient, Fig. (2), which presents the different grid refinement for each of the time discretization methods.

4.2 Stability of the time discretization schemes increasing the Reynolds number

For this analysis, simulations are carried out with the different time discretization methods mentioned and Reynolds numbers of 100, 300 and 1,000. For these simulations the grid is composed by 125x250 points, once, as analysed, the grid refinement did not alter significantly the inherent characteristics of the flow as the drag coefficient. Moreover, the cost of grid 3 is greater.

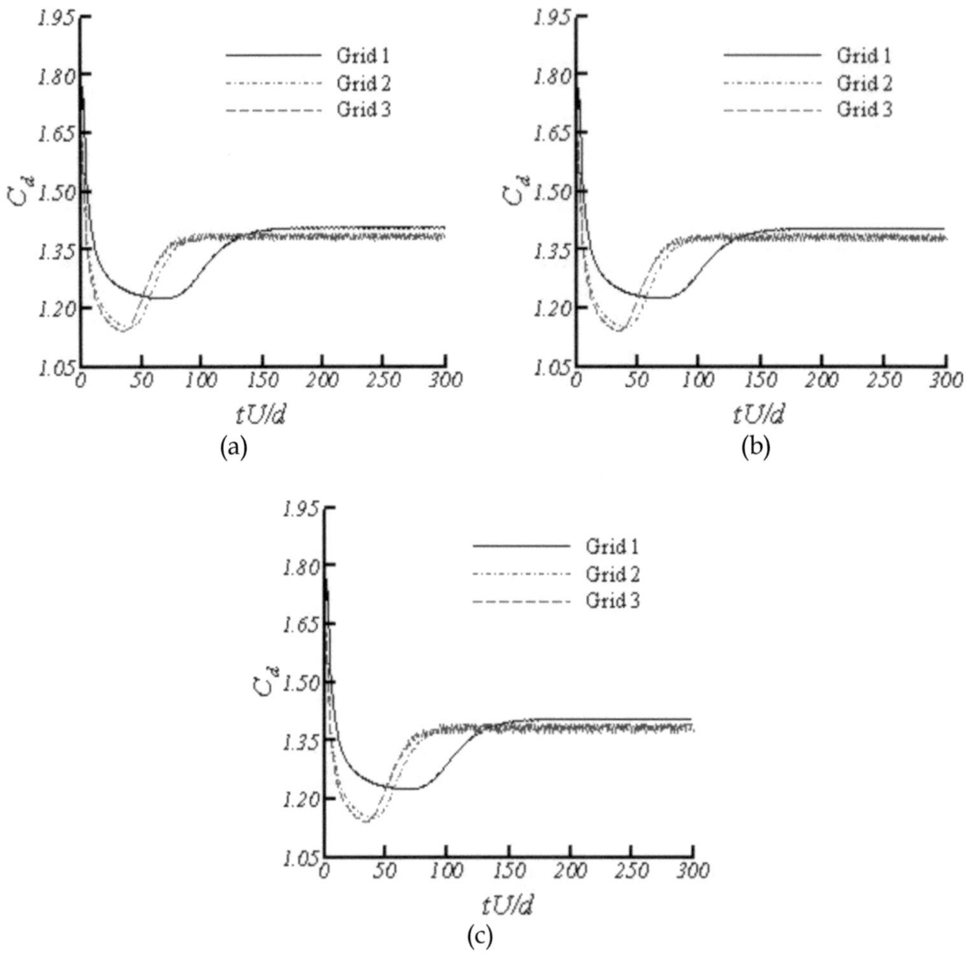

Fig. 2. Time evolution of the drag coefficient for the three grid refinement, at Re=100. Euler (a), Adams-Bashforth (b) and Runge-Kutta (c).

For Re=100, it is noted that the results are identical both qualitatively and quantitatively for the three time discretization methods (Fig. (2)). Again it is illustrated that the transient regime, with instabilities, appears later for the coarse grid (grid 1). For this grid, the start time of the instabilities formation is 150, while for the grids 2 and 3, this time is 75. Another interesting fact is that the drag coefficient oscillations is more pronounced for grids 2 and 3. This is due to the fact that the vortices are formed closer to the cylinder.

Increasing the Reynolds number from 100 to 300, it is found that the flow becomes more unstable, appearing instabilities and the drag coefficient decreases. Such instabilities can be related to the centered scheme of spatial discretization, where for this Reynolds number, the nonlinear effects become important. Figure 3 shows the time evolution of the drag and lift coefficients for the Euler, Adams-Bashforth and Runge-Kutta methods. There is a small difference in the results obtained with Euler's method when compared with the others two. When observe the lift coefficient in Fig. (3b) we see that the oscillations amplitude for Euler's method is larger than the amplitude of the signal for the others methods. This shows that the coupling of the spatial centered scheme with a second order temporal scheme makes the method more stable (Ferziger, 2002).

With further increase of Reynolds number for 1,000, there is an increase in the numerical instabilities in the three methods, being more pronounced in the Euler and Runge-Kutta methods. These instabilities were already expected once a turbulence model is not being used. Being the spatial discretization scheme, centered and without numerical diffusion, it is natural that the calculation becomes unstable, leading to divergence as seen through the time evolution of the dynamic coefficients in Fig. (4).

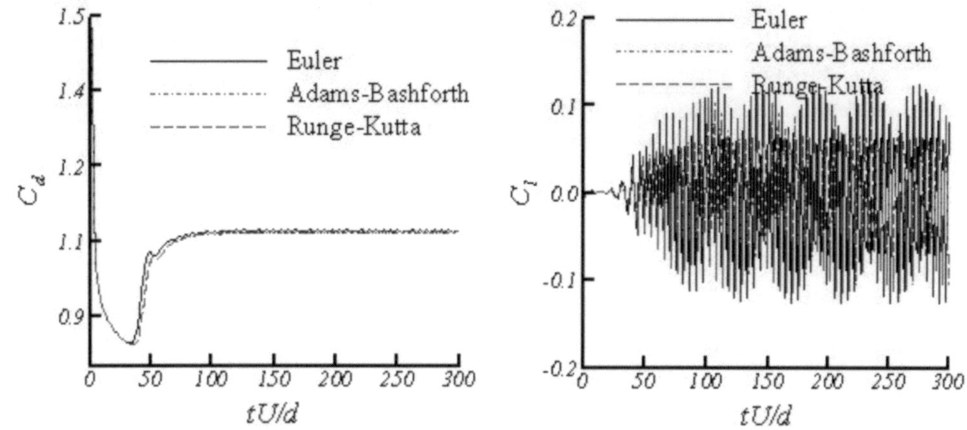

(a) (b)

Fig. 3. Time evolution of the drag (C_d) (a) and lift (C_l) (b) coefficients at Re=300, for the three time discretization methods.

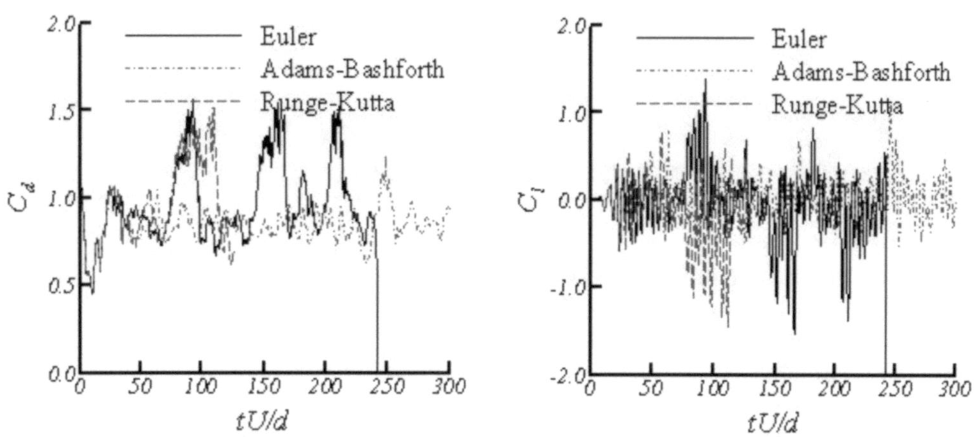

(a) (b)

Fig. 4. Time evolution of the drag (C_d) (a) and lift (C_l) (b) coefficients, at Re=1,000, for the three time discretization methods.

It is important to appreciate that for a high Reynolds number the turbulence model is needed to ensure that the kinetic energy of turbulence is carried by the wave number or cutoff frequency. The apparent convergence given by the Adams-Bashforth method can be misleading as will be seen in the item 4.3. It is noteworthy that the spatial centered schemes have no numerical viscosity, as in the case of upwind schemes, which are stable without turbulence model, even at high Reynolds numbers. The following are presented the simulations results with sub-grid Smagorinsky modeling, needed to ensure the stability of the methodology as previously commented.

4.3 Simulations with the sub-grid Smagorinsky modeling

The motion equations are sufficient to model flows in any regime and for any value of Reynolds number. However, as the Reynolds number increases the energy spectrum associated with the flow becomes wider, making it necessary the use of grid extremely fine, which implies high computational costs. Thus, with the use of coarse grids, the grid filtering process will eliminate all high frequencies providing only the low frequencies, hence the restriction on its use, without additional turbulence modeling. It is observed in Fig. (5) that even for the most stable method, Adams-Bashforth, for high Reynolds number (Re=10,000) the calculation diverges without turbulence modeling.

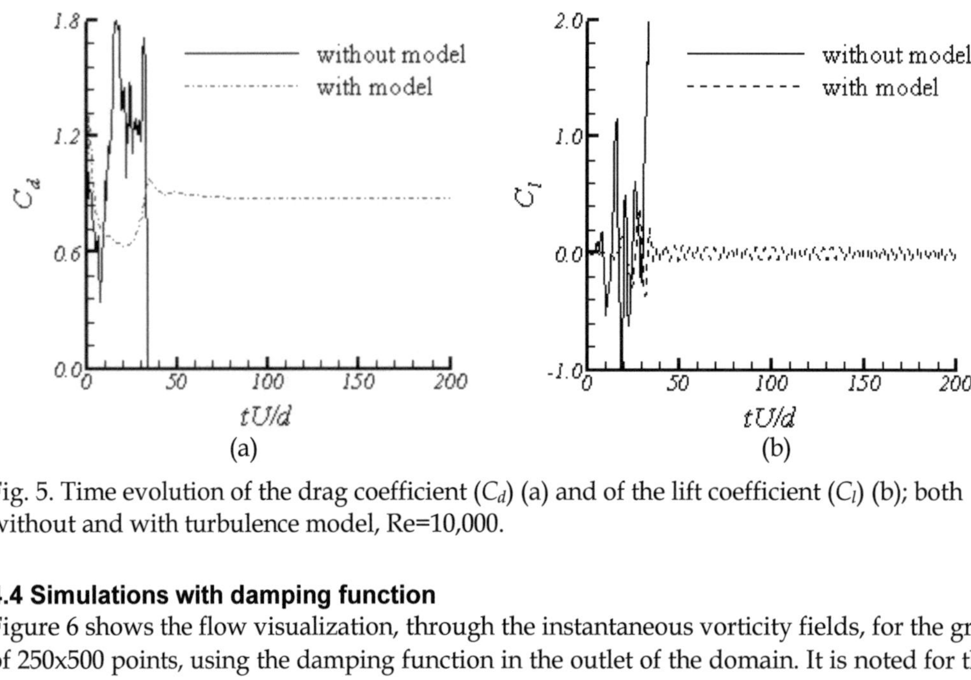

Fig. 5. Time evolution of the drag coefficient (C_d) (a) and of the lift coefficient (C_l) (b); both without and with turbulence model, Re=10,000.

4.4 Simulations with damping function

Figure 6 shows the flow visualization, through the instantaneous vorticity fields, for the grid of 250x500 points, using the damping function in the outlet of the domain. It is noted for the case without damping function, Fig. (6a) that the wake vortex presents an unusual behavior for two-dimensional flows, which can lead to divergence of the calculations. With the damping function, Fig. (6b), the calculation becomes more stable even at greater times of simulations. The damping function aims to remove the vortices in the outlet of the calculation domain, thus enabling the application of the boundary condition of the developed flow. This function eliminates the input of mass at the domain outlet that occur due to the vortices rotation. As verified in the presented results the second order spatial centered scheme with the second order time discretization scheme may be perfectly used for simulations at high Reynolds number since the turbulence modeling and the damping function is also applied to ensure the stability of the methodology.

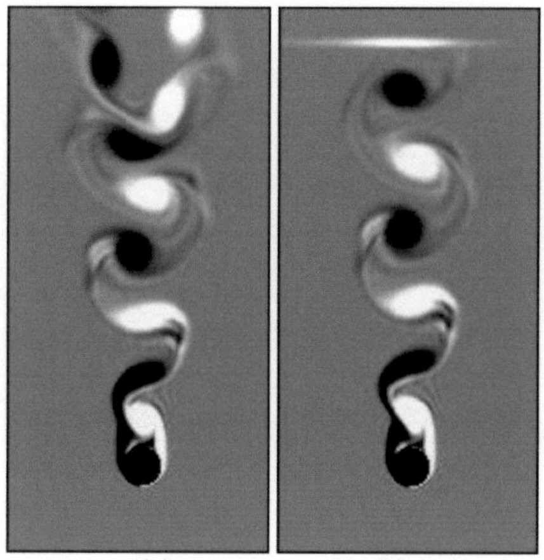

Fig. 6. Instantaneous vorticity fields for Re=10,000, Adams-Bashforth; without damping function (a), with damping function (b).

5. Applications of the immersed boundary methodology

Firstly, are presented, simulations'results of flow over a pair of cylinders of the same diameter, following by the results of rotating and rotationally-oscillating cylinder.

5.1 Flow around two circular cylinders in tandem configuration

One of the main applications of this type of study is to obtain a better understanding of the flow around a set of risers, which is subject to shear flows by ocean currents. The flow interference over bluff bodies is responsible for changes in characteristics of the fluid load that acts on immersed bodies. Consequently, the study of cylinders pair even in two-dimensional simulations has received considerable attention both from the standpoint of academic and industrial fields. In addition, flow over circular cylinders involve different fundamentals dynamic phenomena, such as boundary layer separation, shear layer development and vortex dynamic (Akbari & Price, 2005).

The configurations with a cylinders pair in tandem and side by side are the most extensively discussed in the literature (Sumner et al., 1999; Deng et al., 2006; Silva et al., 2009), although the form more general is the staggered configuration (Sumner et al., 2008; Sumner et al., 2005; Silva et al., 2009). According to the literature, there are various interference regimes, which were based on flow visualization in experiments. The wake behavior of two cylinders can be classified into groups according to the pitch ratio between the cylinders centers by diameter (*P/D*) (Sumner et al., 2005).

Here, the two cylinders have equal diameters d and the distance center to center of the cylinders, is called L. The cylinder A is located upstream and cylinder B is located downstream of the inlet. In all simulated cases, the two cylinders are disposed such that the minimum distance from the surface of each cylinder to the end of the uniform grid region is $1.25d$ in the x direction and $2d$ in the y direction as shown in Fig. (7). The non-uniform grid region is composed by 600x300 points, the Reynolds number equal to 39,500 and the pitch ratio equal to *L/D=2*.

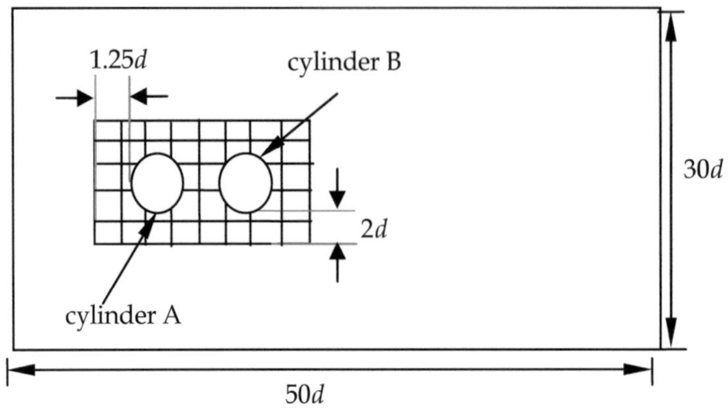

Fig. 7. Illustrative scheme of the distance from the cylinder surface to the uniform region boundaries.

5.1.1 Instantaneous vorticity fields

Figure 8 shows the flow visualization through the instantaneous vorticity field after the flow has reached steady state. It is noted that the shear layers originated from the surface of the upstream cylinder surrounding the downstream cylinder, forming a single wake behind the cylinder *B*. It is also noted, that the vortex wake oscillates around the symmetry line of the domain. The interaction between the two layers occurs only behind the downstream cylinder, which is within the wake of the upstream cylinder. For this case, the '2S' vortex shedding mode compose the wake. It is important to appreciate that for this pitch ratio and geometrical configuration, the two cylinders behave as a single body.

According to Naudascher & Rockwell (1994) no detectable vortex shedding behind the upstream cylinder occur, for *L/D<3.8*. Also according to these authors, as the spacing between the cylinders increases, vortex shedding occur in the upstream cylinder with a frequency that gradually approaches to the frequency for a stationary cylinder. Deng et al. (2006), in they work at low Reynolds number (Re=220), concluded that for two-dimensional simulations, each cylinder will produce a vortex wake only for $L/D \geq 4.0$, with no vortex shedding between the cylinders for $L/D \leq 3.5$. They also affirmed that even in three-dimensional flows, for this configuration and $L/D \leq 3.5$, the flow is equal to the two-dimensional.

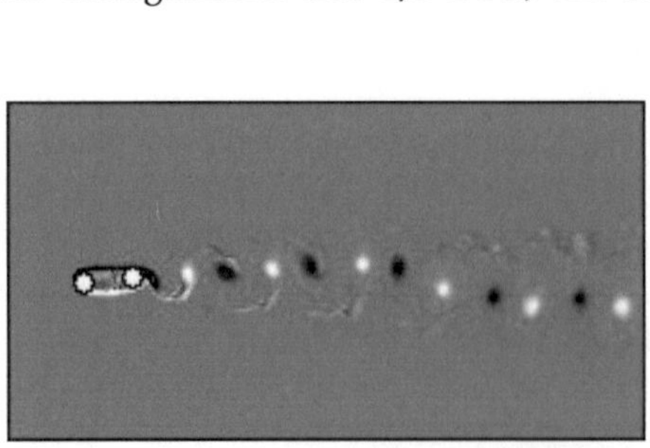

Fig. 8. Instantaneous vorticity field for *L/D*=2 and Re=39,500.

Figure (9a) shows the time evolution of the drag coefficient of the upstream (*A*) and downstream (B) cylinders and Fig. (9b) shows the time evolution of the lift coefficients. It is verified that the drag coefficient on the cylinder B is considerably smaller than the cylinder *A*, with mean close to zero. This can be understood by the fact that the cylinder B is inside of the upstream cylinder wake. The fluctuations of the lift coefficient of the two cylinders have zero mean, as shown in Fig. (9b). The amplitude obtained for the cylinder B is approximately seven times greater than the amplitude of cylinder *A*. The absence of vortices behind the upstream cylinder minimizes the lift fluctuations. Note also that the both fluctuations are in phase, Fig. (9b). This is consistent, once the vortices that are formed and transported induce forces on both cylinders simultaneously.

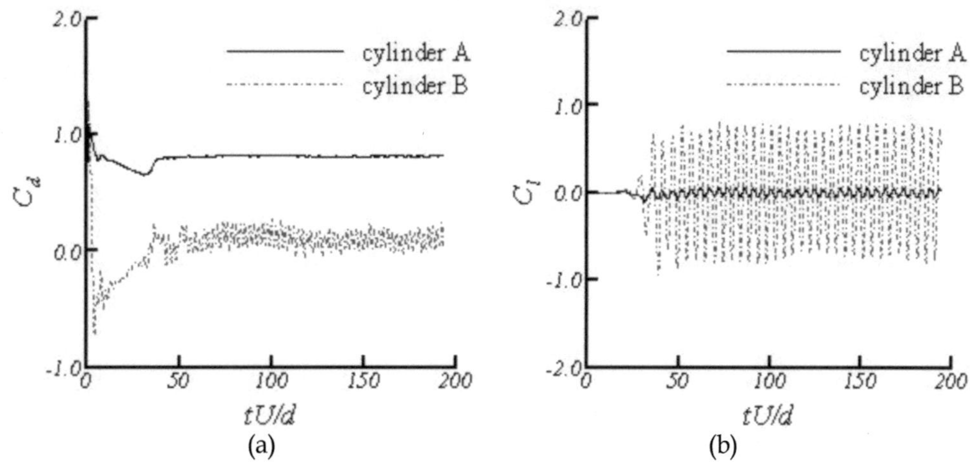

Fig. 9. Time evolution of the dynamic coefficients for Re=39,500 and *L/D*=2: a) drag coefficients and b) lift coefficients.

5.2 Flow around a rotating cylinder

The flow dynamics around a rotating cylinder is different from that observed for a stationary cylinder. The rotation of a cylinder in a uniform viscous flow modifies the vortices configuration and probably has an effect on flow-induced oscillations. As the cylinder rotates the flow is accelerated in one side and decelerated in the other side. This can be attributed to viscous effects injected by the cylinder on the flow. Therefore, the pressure on the accelerated side becomes smaller than the pressure at the decelerated side resulting on a lift force, transverse to the flow. In recent years more attention has been given to control the wake formed behind the cylinder, especially in order to suppress the vortices with the use of active or passive controls. The rotating motion of an immersed body can suppress partially or totally the vortex shedding process, so that the wake separation on one side of the body, be displaced from the axis of vertical symmetry.

5.2.1 Comparison of results

Aiming to compare the present results with the literature, simulations were carried out at low Reynolds numbers, which are 60, 100 and 200. For this simulations, the grid is composed by 200x125 points, refined over the cylinder (twenty grids per diameter) to ensure good accuracy in the results. The rotating moviment is imposed clockwise around its axis and is achieved by the imposition of the velocity components in each Lagrangean point. Figure 10 shows the amplitude of the drag and lift coefficients in function of the specific rotation α (the ratio of the tangential velocity and free-stream velocity) compared with the numerical results of Kang et al. (1999), for Re=60 and Re=100.

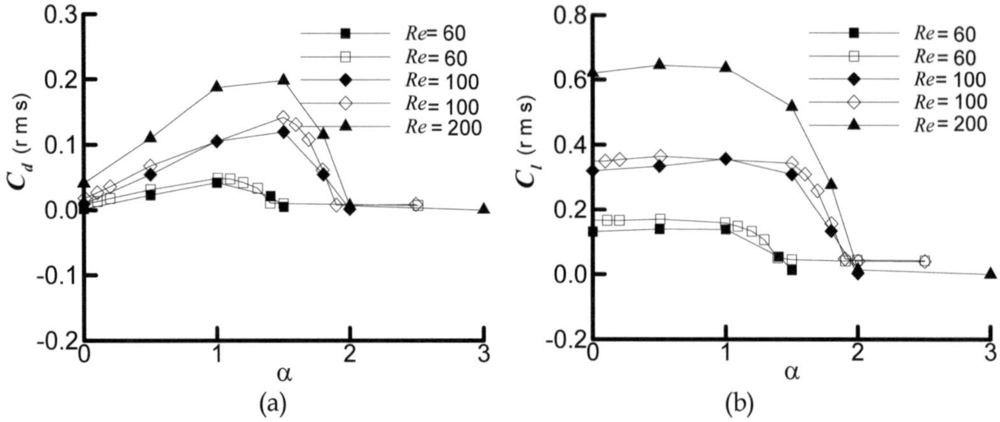

Fig. 10. Fluctuations amplitude of the dynamic coefficients: a) drag and b) lift. Full symbols: present work and empty symbols: Kang et al. (1999).

Note that the drag coefficient amplitude, Fig. (10a) increases until given α and then decreases, reaching a near-zero amplitude. Note also that the amplitudes increase with the Reynolds number and the rotation in which the amplitude decreases is different for each Reynolds number. For Re=60, the amplitude of the drag is reduced for α>1.0 and for Re=100 and Re=200, the reduction occur for α>1.5. On the other hand, the amplitude values of the lift coefficient, Fig. (10b), shows small variations for $\alpha \leq 1.0$, for all Reynolds numbers and then decreases, tending to zero. As observed, there was good agreement between the present results with those of Kang et al. (1999).

5.3 Flow over a rotationally-oscillating circular cylinder

For the stationary cylinder at low Reynolds numbers, it is known that the vortex wake is aligned and symmetrical about the central axis of the flow. The behavior is not verified when the cylinder is subjected to rotationally-oscillating moviment around its own axis. The mutual interaction between cylinder moviment and the adjacent fluid modifies the pattern wake of the flow through the acceleration and deceleration of the flow around the cylinder. Thus, there is a transition between different vortex shedding modes as the relationship between oscillation frequency and the vortex shedding frequency for the stationary cylinder varies for the same amplitude A. Commonly, some authors present two different flow regimes, being the no lock-in regime and the lock-in regime (Cheng et al. 2001a, 2001b). According to Löhner & Tuszynski (1998), the flow around a rotationally-oscillating cylinder is a forced oscillator form, or a nonlinear system, that in some cases, can become chaotic. Here, the rotationally-oscillating cylinder is started impulsively from rest and the tangential velocity on the cylinder is given by the expression:

$$V_{tg} = \omega R = A\sin(2\pi f_c t)R\,, \tag{12}$$

where ω is the angular velocity, A is the oscillation amplitude, R is the cylinder radius, f_c is the oscillation or imposed frequency and t is the physical time. The simulations were performed for Reynolds number equal to 1,000, the non-uniform grid is composed by 400x125 points and the turbulence model and damping function in the outlet of the domain were applied.

5.3.1 Different vortex shedding modes

In Fig. (11) the flow visualizations are presented, through the instantaneous vorticity fields for the dimensionless time equal to 200, at different amplitude values and frequency ratios. Figure (11a) corresponds to the stationary cylinder. Figures (11b) and (11c) correspond to A=1, for $f_c / f_o = 1.05$ and $f_c / f_o = 2.5$ respectively. Figures (11d) and (11e) correspond to A=2, for $f_c / f_o = 0.5$ and $f_c / f_o = 2.5$ respectively. Figures (11f), (11g) and (11h) correspond to A=3, for $f_c / f_o = 0.5$, $f_c / f_o = 2.5$ and $f_c / f_o = 6.0$ respectively. It is observed that there are different vortex shedding modes, when the same amplitude and different frequency ratios are considered.

In Fig. (11a), corresponding to the stationary cylinder, as already mentioned, there is the classical Von Kárman Street, represented by the classical '2S' vortex shedding mode. This mode indicates the generation of a positive vortex in one side of the cylinder and a negative vortex on the other side, at each oscillation cycle, forming a single vortex wake with displaced vortices around the symmetry line of the flow. In Fig. (11b), $f_c / f_o = 1.05$, the vortex wake is similar to pattern wake ('2S' mode), however, the vortices are presented more rounded and with smaller longitudinal and transversal spacing between them when compared with Fig. (11a). Increasing the frequency ratio to $f_c / f_o = 2.5$ and keeping the amplitude $A = 1$, Fig. (11c), there is a new vortex shedding mode called 'P+S'. This mode corresponds to a pair of vortices and single vortex composing the wake. Pairs of vortices having opposite signs are located at the inferior side of the central line of the flow, while the single vortices are released at the superior side of the cylinder.

For $f_c / f_o = 0.5$ and A=2 it is also observed a new vortex shedding mode called '2P ', which corresponds to pairs of vortices of opposite signs along the wake. Keeping the same oscillation amplitude and increasing the frequency ratio to $f_c / f_o = 2.5$, Fig. (11e), it is noted the same vortex shedding mode of the previous case, Fig (11d). Interesting to note, in this case, that the pairs are disposed symmetrically about the centerline of the flow forming a cone-shaped wake.

Increasing the amplitude to A=3, and taking $f_c / f_o = 0.5$ again, a new vortex shedding mode is obtained, called '2C ', as quoted in Williamson & Jauvtis (2004). It is noteworthy that the '2C' mode is not taken by other authors for the case of circular cylinder in rotationally-oscillating moviment. According to Williamson & Jauvtis (2004) this mode was obtained for pivoted cylinders. For $f_c / f_o = 2.5$, Fig. (11g), there is a new standard of vortex emission, in which the double vortex wake near the cylinder, composed by vortices of the same sign in each row, after a given distance away from the cylinder are coupled to form a single wake. The double wake length decreases with increasing the frequency ratio. In Fig. (11h), corresponding to $f_c / f_o = 6.0$ the instability caused by the cylinder oscillation is limited to a region near the cylinder, while far from the immersed body, the vortices reorient themselves to form the stable Von Kármán Street. Occurs, therefore, a vortex-vortex interaction of the same sign near the cylinder, resulting in large scale vortices, whose frequencies have values close to the vortex shedding frequency of the stationary cylinder (0.23). The return to the '2S' mode is observed for high f_c / f_o in all simulated amplitudes.

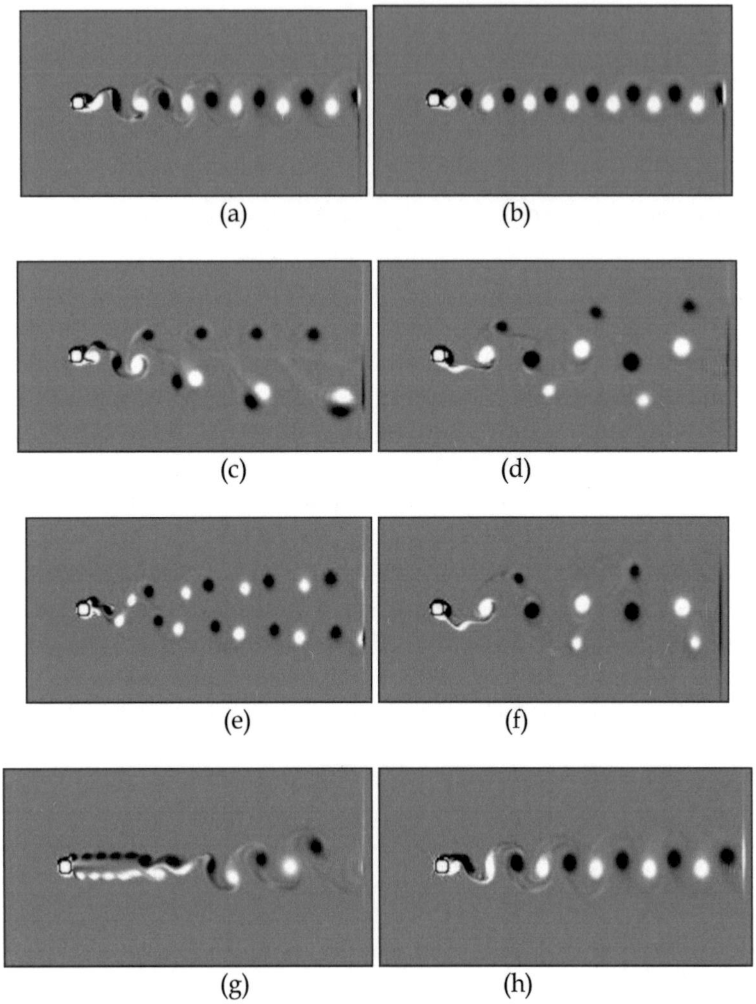

Fig. 11. Instantaneous vorticity fields for Re=1,000: a) stationary cylinder; b) and c) A=1 and $f_c / f_o = 1.05$ and $f_c / f_o = 2.5$ respectively; d) and e) A=2 and $f_c / f_o = 0.5$ and $f_c / f_o = 2.5$ respectively and f), g) and h) A=3 and $f_c / f_o = 0.5$, $f_c / f_o = 2.5$ and $f_c / f_o = 6.0$ respectively.

5.3.2 Vortex shedding frequency

Figure (12) shows the power spectra (E_{C_ℓ}) obtained by Fast Fourier Transform (FFT) of the lift coefficients signals. The frequency peak more energized are called by St_1 and St_2 where St_1 will be considered equal to the dimensionless frequency corresponding to the cylinder oscillation $St_c = f_c D / U$. When the power spectrum contains only one promiment peak it is

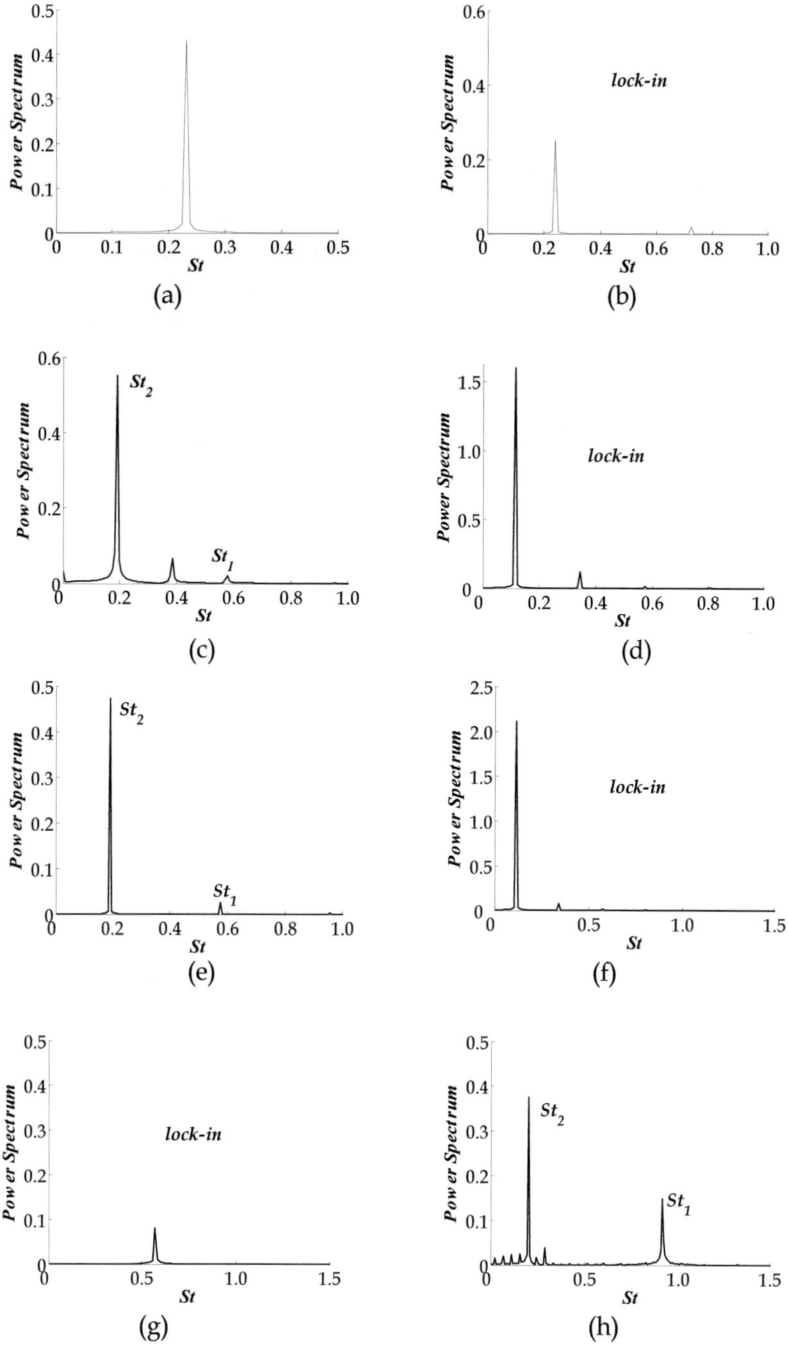

Fig. 12. Power Spectra for Re=1,000: a) stationary cylinder; b) and c) *A=1* and $f_c / f_o = 1.05$ and $f_c / f_o = 2.5$ respectively; d) and e) *A=2* and $f_c / f_o = 0.5$ and $f_c / f_o = 2.5$ respectively and f) g) and h) *A=3* and $f_c / f_o = 0.5$, $f_c / f_o = 2.5$ and $f_c / f_o = 4.0$ respectively.

called ressonance phenomenon or lock-in, ie, the cylinder is oscillating with a frequency equal to the vortex shedding frequency. It is worth remembering that the energy peaks corresponding to the harmonics are not considered here.

For the stationary cylinder case, Fig. (12a), the power spectrum shows a single energy peak, corresponding to the Strouhal number equal to 0.23. For *A=1* and $f_c / f_o = 1.05$ given in Fig. (12b), only one prominent peak is observed, corresponding to the lock-in regime. It is important to observe that the lower limit of the lock-in regime for this amplitude, starts for the studied cases, in $f_c / f_o = 0.6$. The ratio $f_c / f_o = 1.05$ correspond to the upper limit of this regime. Due to the large amount of data regarding all amplitudes and frequency ratios studied, only few results are reported here. With the increase of the frequency ratio and keeping the oscillation amplitude, Fig. (12c), there is more than one frequency peak in the spectrum, which indicates that the lock-in regime no longer exists. Interesting to note, for $f_c / f_o = 2.5$ ('P+S' mode, as Fig. (11c)), that for this vortex shedding mode, the frequency peak corresponding to St_1 has low energy level.

Increasing the amplitude for *A*=2 the lock-in regime range is greater, which is given by $0.5 \le f_c / f_o \le 1.05$. Figure (12d), $f_c / f_o = 0.5$, represents the lower limit of the lock-in regime for this amplitude. Note a considerable increase in energy level with the amplitude. For $f_c / f_o = 2.5$, Fig. (12e), out of lock-in regime, it is noted a great reduction in the energy level in comparison with Fig. (12d), inside the lock-in regime.

Considering *A*=3 and $f_c / f_o = 0.5$ in Fig. (12f), there is only one prominent peak, which indicates that this frequency ratio is within the lock-in regime. Comparing Figs. (12d) and (12f), corresponding to the same frequency ratio and different oscillation amplitude, there is an increase in energy level for a greater amplitude. It is noteworthy that the range of lock-in regime, for this amplitude is greater than for *A*=2, being $0.2 \le f_c / f_o \le 2.5$, as Fig. (12g) (upper limit of the regime). It is Interesting to note that, within the lock-in regime, the increase of the frequency ratio from $f_c / f_o = 0.5$ to $f_c / f_o = 2.5$ leads to a great reduction in energy level, as shown in Figs. (12f) and (12g). This reduction is associated with different vortex shedding modes, as shown in the Figs. (11f) and (11g). For $f_c / f_o = 4.0$ and *A*=3, Fig. (12h), one observes two frequency peaks, which indicates that, the lock-in regime no longer exists. It is verified for all considered amplitudes that as the frequency ratio is increased, the frequency called St_2 gradually recovers the frequency corresponding to the stationay cylinder, due to the fact that for high oscillation frequencies, there is no more synchronization between the oscillating cylinder and vortex shedding downstream of it. Thus, the vortices tend to reorient themselves to form a classical von Kárman Street and the frequencies match up again.

6. Conclusion

One of the goals that motivated the development of this work was to demonstrate through analysis of the important parameters such as dynamic coefficients, obtained through two-dimensional simulations of incompressible flows, that the second order centered spatial schemes can perfectly provide accurate results when used toghether the second order time discretization scheme. Another motivation was to continue the development of the Immersed Boundary method with the Virtual Physical model for further application in problems of interst both academic and industrial.

Firstly, simulations were performed with stationary cylinder, considering different Reynolds numbers and time discretization schemes. Results such as vorticity, time histories and fluctuations amplitude of dynamic coefficients and the Strouhal number are obtained. The concomitant use of second order temporal schemes with the spatial centered scheme is crucial for the stability of the methodology. The Adams-Bashforth temporal scheme presented more stable than the second order Runge-Kutta scheme. As the Reynolds number is increased the methodology showed to be unstable for all second-order temporal discretization schemes. This result is expected once the centered scheme has no numerical diffusion. Thus, it is concluded that for high Reynolds number, the use of turbulence modeling for the energy transfer process between the largest and smallest scales of turbulence is needed. It is important to appreciate that without the modeling and numerical diffusion the kinetic energy of the physical instabilities accumulates on the cutoff frequency and the simulation diverges. The cutoff frequency is determined by the mesh discretization.

It is known that the use of developed flow boundary condition at the outlet of the domain is common in the literature. However when there are physical instabilities, which must leave the domain, there may be problems of numerical stability, especially when using centered spatial schemes. This is due to the fact that the physical instabilities carry spurious information from the outside of the domain to inside. The result is also the divergence of the simulations. To solve this problem the use of a damping function is essential to ensure stability for higher values of Reynolds number.

Aiming to illustrate the applicability of the Immersed Boundary method used togheter the second order spatial centered scheme and second order temporal discretization scheme, simulations were carried out with a circular cylinder pairs, rotating cylinder and rotationally-oscillating cylinder. For the rotating cylinder case, the results showed good agreement with literature data. It was found that the rotation has greater influence on the amplitude of the drag coefficient than on the amplitude of the lift coefficient. It's worth noting that with increasing rotation the amplitude of the dynamic coefficients tends to null, as expected, once the vortex shedding process decreases.

For simulations with rotationally oscillating cylinder is analyzed the influence of amplitude and frequency ratio in the vortex shedding modes, as well as in the vortex shedding frequency. It is observed different vortex shedding modes when fixed the oscillation amplitude and varies the frequency ratios. It is important to appreciate the 2C mode obtained in this study once this mode is not found in the literature for rotatinally-oscillating cylinder and it is worth mentioning that, according to Williamson & Jauvtis (2004) the 2C mode is obtained for pivoted cylinder. It is also obtained for the amplitude and frequency ratios considered the lock-in regime, whose range increases as the oscillation amplitude increases.

7. Acknowledgments

The authors are deeply gratefully to the following organizations: Minas Gerais State Agency FAPEMIG for the continued support to their research work, especially through the post-doctorate scholarship granted to A.R. da Silva; Brazilian Research Council - CNPq for the financial support to their research activities; CAPES Foundation from the Brazilian Ministry of Education and the School of Mechanical Engineering College of the Federal University of Uberlândia, Brazil.

8. References

Akbari, M. H. & Price, S. J. (2005). Numerical investigation of flow patterns for staggered cylinder pairs in cross-flow, *Journal of Fluids and Structures,* Vol.20, pp. 533-554

Cheng, M.; Liu, G. R. & Lam, K. Y. (2001a). Numerical simulation of flow past a rotationally oscillating cylinder, *Computer & Fluids,* Vol.30, pp. 365-392

Cheng, M.; Chew, Y. T. & Luo, S. C. (2001b). Numerical investigation of a rotationally oscillating cylinder in mean flow, *Journal of Fluids and Structures,* Vol.15, pp. 981-1007

Chorin, A. (1968). Numerical solution of the Navier-Stokes equations, *Math. Comp.* , Vol.22, pp. 745-762

Deng, J.; Ren, A-L.; Zou, J-F. & Shao, X-M. (2006). Three-dimensional flow around two circular cylinders in tandem arrangement, *Fluid Dynamics Research,* Vol.38, pp. 386-404

Ferziger, J. H. & Peric, M. (2002). *Computational Methods for Fluid Dynamics, 3.* Ed. Berlin Springer-Verlag, pp. 423

Kang, S.; Choi, H. & Lee, S. (1999). Laminar Flow past a Rotating Circular Cylinder, *Physics of Fluid,* Vol.11, pp. 3312-3320

Lima e Silva, A. L. F.; Silva, A. R. & Silveira-Neto, A. (2007). Numerical Simulation of Two-Dimensional Complex Flows around Bluff Bodies using the Immersed Boundary Method, *J. of the Braz. Soc. Of Mech. Sci. & Eng.,* Vol.4, pp. 378-386

Naudascher, E. & Rockwell, D. (1994). *Flow-Induced Vibrations: An Engineering Guide,* Dover Publications, Inc. Mineola, New York, pp. 414

Peskin, C. S. (1977). Numerical Analysis of Blood Flow in the Heart, *Journal of Computational Physics,* Vol.25, pp. 220-252

Peskin, C. S. & McQueen, D. M. (1994). A General Method for the Computer Simulation of Biological Systems Interacting with Fluids, *SEB Symphosium on Biological Fluid Dynamics,* Leeds, England, (July 5-8)

Reynolds, O. (1894). On the dynamical theory of incompressible viscous fluids and the determination of the criterion, *Philosophical Transaction of the Royal Society of London,* Vol.186, Part I, pp. 122-164

Schneider, G. E. & Zedan, M. (1981). A Modified Strongly Implicit Procedure for the Numerical Solution of Field Problems, *Numerical Heat Transfer,* Vol.4, No.1

Silva, A. R.; Silveira-Neto, A.; Rade, D. A.; Francis, R. & Santos, E. A. (2009). Numerical Simulations of Flows over a Pair of Cylinders at Different Arrangements using the Immersed Boundary Method, *CMES: Computer Modeling in Engineering & Sciences,* Vol.50, No.3, pp. 285-303

Smagorinsky, J. (1963). General Circulation Experiments with Primitive Equations, *Mon. Weather Rev.,* Vol.91, pp. 99-164

Sumner, D.; Price, S. J. & Païdoussis, M. P. (1999). Tandem cylinders in impulsively started flow, *Journal of Fluids and Structures,* Vol.13, pp. 955-965

Sumner, D.; Richards, M. D. & Okasile, O. O. (2005). Two staggered circular cylinders of equal diameter in cross-flow, *J. of Fluids and Structures,* Vol. 20, pp. 255-276

Sumner, D.; Richards, M. D. & Okasile, O. O. (2008). Strouhal number data for two staggered circular cylinders, *Journal of Wind Engineering and Industrial Aerodynamics,* Vol. 96, pp. 859-871

Tuszynski, J. & Löhner, R. (1998). Control of a Kármán Vortex Flow by Rotational Oscillations of a Cylinder, *George Mason University, USA,* Vol.15, pp. 1-12

Williamson, C. H. K. & Jauvtis, N. (2004). A high-amplitude 2T mode of vortex-induced vibration for a light body in X-Y motion, *European Journal of Mechanics B/Fluids,* Vol.23, pp. 107-114

4

A Fourth-Order Compact Finite Difference Scheme for Solving Unsteady Convection-Diffusion Equations

Wenyuan Liao[1] and Jianping Zhu[2]
[1]*University of Calgary*
[2]*University of Texas at Arlington*
[1]*Canada*
[2]*USA*

1. Introduction

Convection-diffusion equations are widely used for modeling and simulations of various complex phenomena in science and engineering (Hundsdorfer & Verwer, 2003; Morton, 1996). Since for most application problems it is impossible to solve convection-diffusion equations analytically, efficient numerical algorithms are becoming increasingly important to numerical simulations involving convection-diffusion equations.

Recently a great deal of efforts have been devoted to developing high-order compact schemes, which utilize only the grid nodes directly adjacent to the central node. In (Noye & Tan, 1989), Noye and Tan derived a class of high-order implicit schemes for solving the one-dimensional unsteady convection-diffusion equations. This method is very stable and accurate (third-order in space and second-order in time). In (Gupta et al., 1984), a fourth-order finite difference scheme for a steady convection-diffusion equation with variable coefficients was proposed. The scheme is defined on a single square cell of size $2\Delta x$ over a nine-point stencil. In (Rigal, 1994), Rigal provided an extensive analysis of the properties of a class of two- and three-level second-order difference schemes which have been proposed in (Rigal, 1989; 1990). In (Spotz & Carey, 2001), the two-dimensional HOC (High Order Compact) scheme proposed in (Gupta et al., 1984) was extended to solve unsteady one-dimensional convection-diffusion equations with variable coefficients and two-dimensional diffusion equations. This method was further extended by Kalita et al. in (Kalita et al., 2002) to a class of HOC schemes with weighted time discretization, and successfully used to solve unsteady two-dimensional convection-diffusion equations. In (Karaa & Zhang, 2004), Karaa and Zhang proposed a novel high-order alternating direction implicit method, based on the technique in (Zhang et al., 2002), for solving unsteady two-dimensional convection-diffusion problems. This new method is second-order in time and fourth-order in space, and is computationally efficient. In (Tian & Dai, 2007), Tian and Dai proposed a class of high-order compact exponential finite difference methods for solving one- and two-dimensional steady-state convection-diffusion problems. This method is nonoscillatory, fourth-order in space, and easy to implement. Some more recent high-order ADI methods for unsteady convection-diffusion equations can be found in (Tian & Ge, 2007; You, 2006).

For simplicity, we will use the following one-dimensional equation to describe the new method developed in this chapter:

$$\begin{aligned} u_t &= au_{xx} + c(x)u_x + f(u), \\ 0 &< x < 1, 0 < t \le T, \\ u(0,t) &= g_1(t), u(1,t) = g_2(t), \\ u(x,0) &= h(x), \end{aligned} \tag{1}$$

where a is a constant. Extensions to more complicated equations in one-dimension(for example when a is not a constant) are straightforward; and extensions to higher-dimensional equations will be briefly discussed in Section 6.

The existence of the convection term in Eq. (1) creates several difficulties when the equation is solved numerically using the finite difference schemes. It is well-known (Hundsdorfer & Verwer, 2003; Morton, 1996) that the convection term needs to be discretized using proper upwind finite difference schemes to avoid oscillations in convection dominated problems. If the sign of $c(x)$ changes over the solution domain, the direction of the upwind scheme must also be changed accordingly. The order of accuracy of the upwind schemes is usually lower than the central difference schemes on the same finite difference stencil.

In addition, the convection term in Eq. (1) also makes it more difficult to use the fourth-order Padé approximations. For reaction-diffusion equations ($c(x) = 0$), the Padé approximation can be used to achieve fourth-order accuracy on a 3-point stencil typically used for the standard second-order algorithms(Gu et al., 2003):

$$\frac{u_i^{n+1} - u_i^n}{\Delta t} = a\frac{\delta^2 u_i^{n+1}}{\Delta x^2(1 + \frac{\delta^2}{12})} + f(u_i^{n+1}), \tag{2}$$

where $i = 0, 1, \cdots, M$, and $n = 0, 1, \cdots, N$ are indices for spatial and temporal grid points, respectively, u_i^n is the numerical approximation to the exact solution $u(x_i, t^n)$, and the central difference operator δ^2 is defined as $\delta^2 u_i^n = u_{i-1}^n - 2u_i^n + u_{i+1}^n$. Applying the operator $(1 + \frac{\delta^2}{12})$ to both sides of Eq. (2), we have

$$(1 + \frac{\delta^2}{12})\frac{u_i^{n+1} - u_i^n}{\Delta t} = a\frac{\delta^2 u_i^{n+1}}{\Delta x^2} + (1 + \frac{\delta^2}{12})f(u_i^{n+1}). \tag{3}$$

Eq. (3) is fourth-order accurate in space but contains only the second-order central difference operator δ^2 that requires only a 3-point stencil. This approach, however, does not work when the convection term is present in the equation. This is because the fourth-order Padé approximation for Eq. (1) leads to the following equation

$$\frac{u_i^{n+1} - u_i^n}{\Delta t} = a\frac{\delta^2 u_i^{n+1}}{\Delta x^2(1 + \frac{\delta^2}{12})} + c_i\frac{\delta u_i^{n+1}}{2\Delta x(1 + \frac{\delta^2}{6})} + f(u_i^{n+1}),$$

where the central difference operator δ is defined as $\delta u_i^n = u_{i+1}^n - u_{i-1}^n$. This equation cannot be simplified to an equation that is defined on a 3-point stencil in the same way as Eq. (2) is reduced to Eq. (3).

The new method discussed in this chapter eliminates the convection term u_x from Eq. (1) and solves $v = u_x$ directly along with u. This makes it possible to use central finite difference schemes and higher-order Padé approximations for accurate and efficient numerical solutions of convection-diffusion equations. It is unconditionally stable, and is particularly suitable for problems that require the solution of both u and u_x. For example, when solving the Black-Scholes option pricing model(Seydel, 2002)

$$\frac{\partial V}{\partial t} + \frac{1}{2}\sigma^2 S^2 \frac{\partial^2 V}{\partial S^2} + rS\frac{\partial V}{\partial S} - rV = 0, \tag{4}$$

both the solution V and its derivative V_S are desired. The solution V is the price of an option and its derivative V_S is called the hedge delta that represents the sensitivity of the option value to the change of the underlining stock price.

The rest of this chapter is organized as follows: The description of the new method is given in the next section. Proof of unconditional stability of the new method is given in Section 3. Computational complexity of this new method is analyzed and compared with upwind and standard central finite difference schemes in Section 4. Several numerical examples are presented in Section 5, followed by conclusions in Section 6.

2. The new method

In this section, we will first outline the new algorithm that eliminates the convection term in a convection-diffusion equation to facilitate the use of central finite difference schemes and then discuss how the initial and boundary conditions are handled using the new algorithm.

2.1 Description of the new method

Setting $v = u_x$ in Eq. (1), we have

$$u_t = au_{xx} + c(x)v + f(u) \tag{5}$$

Differentiating both sides of Eq. (1) with respect to x leads to

$$(u_x)_t = a(u_{xx})_x + c_x(x)u_x + c(x)(u_x)_x + f_u(u)u_x \tag{6}$$

which, considering $v = u_x$, can be written as

$$v_t = c(x)u_{xx} + av_{xx} + c_x(x)v + f_u(u)v \tag{7}$$

Eq. (5) and (7) now form a system of equations for u and v. They only involve diffusion term u_{xx} and v_{xx}, which can be discretized by the standard central finite difference schemes. If the 3-point second-order central difference scheme is used, the discretized equations will form a block tri-diagonal algebraic equation system with 2×2 blocks. For nonlinear $f(u)$, the Newton's method or its variations can be used to solve the nonlinear system of algebraic equations.

If the fourth-order Padé approximation is used for Eqs. (5) and (7), we have

$$\frac{u_i^{n+1} - u_i^n}{\Delta t} = a\frac{\delta^2 u_i^{n+1}}{\Delta x^2(1 + \frac{\delta^2}{12})} + c_i v_i + f(u_i^{n+1}), \tag{8}$$

$$\begin{aligned}\frac{v_i^{n+1} - v_i^n}{\Delta t} &= c_i\frac{\delta^2 u_i^{n+1}}{\Delta x^2(1 + \frac{\delta^2}{12})} + a\frac{\delta^2 v_i^{n+1}}{\Delta x^2(1 + \frac{\delta^2}{12})} \\ &+[(c_x)_i + f_u(u_i^{n+1})]v_i^{n+1}.\end{aligned} \tag{9}$$

Applying the operator $(1+\frac{\delta^2}{12})$ to both sides of these two equations, we obtain

$$(1+\frac{\delta^2}{12})\frac{u_i^{n+1}-u_i^n}{\Delta t} = a\frac{\delta^2 u_i^{n+1}}{\Delta x^2} + (1+\frac{\delta^2}{12})[c_i v_i + f(u_i^{n+1})], \tag{10}$$

$$\begin{aligned}(1+\frac{\delta^2}{12})\frac{v_i^{n+1}-v_i^n}{\Delta t} &= c_i\frac{\delta^2 u_i^{n+1}}{\Delta x^2} + a\frac{\delta^2 v_i^{n+1}}{\Delta x^2} \\ &+(1+\frac{\delta^2}{12})[(c_x)_i + f_u(u_i^{n+1})]v_i^{n+1}.\end{aligned} \tag{11}$$

Eqs. (10) and (11) are fourth-order accurate in space but only contains the second-order central difference operator δ^2 that is defined on a 3-point stencil. As a result, the discretized equations form a system of block tri-diagonal algebraic equations.

2.2 Initial and boundary conditions

The initial condition for v can be obtained by differentiating $h(x)$, the initial condition fro u given in Eq. (1) with respect to x, i.e.

$$v(x,0) = \frac{dh(x)}{dx}.$$

The boundary conditions for v, or for Eq. (7), are less straight forward. In the following, we discuss three different ways to generate boundary conditions for v at the spatial grid point $i=0$, assuming Dirichlet boundary conditions are given for u. The boundary conditions for v at the spatial grid point $i=M$ and other scenarios can be dealt with in similar ways.
Standard finite difference approximation: Since $v = u_x$, we have

$$v_0 = \frac{u_1 - u_0}{\Delta x}, \tag{12}$$

which provides an equation to complement the equation obtained by discretizing Eq. (7) at $i=1$. This approximation is first-order accurate in space. If necessary, higher-order one-sided finite difference schemes can be used to approximate $v = u_x$.
Padé approximation: We can use the fourth-order Padé approximation at $i=1$ for $v = u_x$

$$v_1 = \frac{\delta u_1}{2\Delta x(1+\frac{\delta^2}{6})} = \frac{u_2 - u_0}{2\Delta x(1+\frac{\delta^2}{6})}. \tag{13}$$

Applying $(1+\frac{\delta^2}{6})$ to both sides of Eq. (13), we have

$$(1+\frac{\delta^2}{6})v_1 = \frac{u_2-u_0}{2\Delta x}, \tag{14}$$

or

$$\frac{1}{6}v_0 + \frac{2}{3}v_1 + \frac{1}{6}v_2 = \frac{u_2-u_0}{2\Delta x}. \tag{15}$$

Solving v_0 from Eq. (15), we obtain the boundary condition

$$v_0 = \frac{3(u_2-u_0)}{\Delta x} - 4v_1 - v_2. \tag{16}$$

Direct integration of Eq. (1): This approach is particularly convenient for special cases of Eq. (1). For example, when dealing with steady state equation with a constant convection coefficient and constant $f(u)$, we have

$$au_{xx} + cu_x + d = 0, \tag{17}$$

where a, c and d are constants. Integrating this equation from x_0 to x_1, we have

$$au_x|_{x_0}^{x_1} + cu|_{x_0}^{x_1} + d(x_1 - x_0) = 0, \tag{18}$$

or

$$av_1 - av_0 + cu_1 - cu_0 + d\Delta x = 0. \tag{19}$$

Solving v_0 from Eq. (19), we obtain the boundary condition

$$v_0 = \frac{1}{a}(av_1 + cu_1 - cu_0 + d\Delta x). \tag{20}$$

This boundary condition has no truncation error since the integrations are carried out exactly. For more general cases when some of the terms in Eq. (1) cannot be integrated exactly, various numerical integration schemes, such as the second-order Trapezoidal scheme, can be used to generate boundary condition for v in a similar way.

3. Stability analysis

Stability is critical to numerical methods used to solve time-dependent systems. In this section, we conduct Von Neumann stability analysis for the new method combined with the standard second-order central difference scheme. The following one-dimensional linear convection-diffusion equation is used in the analysis

$$u_t = u_{xx} + cu_x \tag{21}$$

The new method combined with the second-order central difference for solving Eq. (21) is

$$\frac{u_i^{n+1} - u_i^n}{\Delta t} = \frac{1}{\Delta x^2}\delta^2 u_i^{n+1} + cv_i^{n+1}, \tag{22}$$

$$\frac{v_i^{n+1} - v_i^n}{\Delta t} = \frac{c}{\Delta x^2}\delta^2 u_i^{n+1} + \frac{\delta^2}{\Delta x^2}v_i^{n+1}. \tag{23}$$

Taking the discrete Fourier transform of the above equations, we have

$$M\begin{bmatrix}\hat{u}^{n+1}\\ \hat{v}^{n+1}\end{bmatrix} = R\begin{bmatrix}\hat{u}^{n}\\ \hat{v}^{n}\end{bmatrix}. \tag{24}$$

Thus

$$\begin{bmatrix}\hat{u}^{n+1}\\ \hat{v}^{n+1}\end{bmatrix} = M^{-1}R\begin{bmatrix}\hat{u}^{n}\\ \hat{v}^{n}\end{bmatrix}, \tag{25}$$

where

$$M = \begin{bmatrix}1 + 2\alpha\sin^2(\frac{\theta}{2}) & -\beta\\ 2\gamma\sin^2(\frac{\theta}{2}) & 1 + 2\alpha\sin^2(\frac{\theta}{2})\end{bmatrix},$$

and

$$R = \begin{bmatrix} 1 & 0 \\ 0 & 1 \end{bmatrix},$$

with $\alpha = \frac{\Delta t}{\Delta x^2}$, $\beta = c\Delta t$, and $\gamma = \frac{c\Delta t}{\Delta x^2}$.
Here $M^{-1}R$ is the amplification matrix at each time-step. In order for the numerical algorithm to be stable, the modulus of the eigenvalues of $M^{-1}R$ must be less than or equal to unity for all possible values of θ. For the 2×2 matrix, it is easy to see that it has two conjugate complex eigenvalues. If the modulus of the two eigenvalues is less than or equal to 1, then the method is unconditionally stable.
The eigenvalues of $M^{-1}R$ can be calculated as

$$\omega = \frac{1 + 2\alpha \sin^2(\frac{\theta}{2}) \pm i(c\sqrt{2\alpha\Delta t}\sin(\frac{\theta}{2}))}{1 + 4\alpha \sin^2(\frac{\theta}{2}) + 4\alpha^2 \sin^4(\frac{\theta}{2}) + 2c^2\Delta t \alpha \sin^2(\frac{\theta}{2})},$$

thus we have

$$|\omega|^2 = \frac{1}{1 + 4\alpha \sin^2(\frac{\theta}{2}) + 4\alpha^2 \sin^4(\frac{\theta}{2}) + 2c^2\Delta t \alpha \sin^2(\frac{\theta}{2})}.$$

Obviously, $|\omega|^2 \leq 1$ since $0 \leq \sin^2(\frac{\theta}{2}) \leq 1$ and $\alpha > 0$.

4. Computational complexity

In this section an estimation of computational cost of the new method is obtained, and computation times for three methods (upwind, standard central finite difference or standard cfd, and fourth-order new method) are compared using the following model equation

$$u_x - u_{xx} = 0, \quad u(0) = 0, \quad u(1) = 1, \tag{26}$$

with exact solution $u(x) = \frac{e^x - 1}{e - 1}$.
If the above model equation is discretized over n subintervals with equal size, and the numerical solution at the i-th grid point is denoted as u_i, the solutions can be obtained by solving the linear system $AU = b$. For both the upwind and standard central finite difference schemes, A is an $n \times n$ tridiagonal matrix and $U = (u_1, u_2, \cdots, u_n)$. For the fourth-order new method the matrix A is a $2n \times 2n$ banded matrix with a bandwidth of 7, and $U = (u_1, v_1, u_2, v_2, \cdots, u_n, v_n)$ contains the numerical solutions for both u and v, with $v = u_x$.
If an efficient algorithm is used to solve the tridiagonal linear system resulted from upwind and standard central finite difference schemes,a total of $2n - 1$ divisions, $3(n-1)$ multiplications, and $3(n-1)$ subtractions are needed. The computational complexity is $2(n-1) + 1 + 3(n-1) + 3(n-1) = 8n - 7 = 8n + \mathbf{O}(1)$ flops.
If the Gaussian elimination algorithm is used to solve the linear system resulted from the fourth-order new method, a total of $18n - 15$ divisions, $24n - 22$ multiplications, and $24n - 22$ subtractions are needed. The computational complexity is $66n - 59 = 66n + \mathbf{O}(1)$ flops.
Table 1 clearly shows that to achieve the same accuracy the fourth-order new method is much faster than both upwind and the standard second-order central finite difference schemes. For instance, to obtain an error less than 1.0E-05, the upwind scheme needs 68.054 seconds, and the standard second-order central finite difference scheme needs 0.0012 seconds, while the fourth-order new method needs only 0.0010 seconds to obtain an error of 7.4E-07. For the

Upwind		Stand-cfd		4th-order new	
Error	Time	Error	Time	Error	Time
9.7E-03	.0016	4.1E-04	.0011	7.4E-07	.0010
9.9E-04	.0098	9.8E-06	.0012	9.2E-09	.0012
1.0E-04	.5155	1.0E-06	.0016	1.8E-10	.0014
1.0E-05	68.05	1.0E-08	.0101	4.7E-12	.0016
1.0E-08	∞	1.0E-10	.4870	2.9E-13	.0022
1.0E-09	∞	1.5E-11	7.059	4.1E-14	.0035

Table 1. Computational cost vs accuracy for different algorithms

first-order upwind scheme, it is almost impossible to obtain an error less than $1.0E-08$ since a grid size of $h = 1.0E-08$ is needed.
Note that the symbol ∞ in Table 1 does not really represent infinity. It just represents an excessively large number. The computation time for each test case is the average of five runs. The unit for computation time is second.

5. Numerical results

Several numerical examples are presented here to compare the new method with the standard finite difference algorithms.
Example 1: In this example, we compare the accuracy of four different algorithms using the same 3-point finite difference stencil. The following steady state convection-diffusion equation is used in the example:

$$-au_{xx} + cu_x = 0, \quad u(0) = 0, u(1) = 1, \tag{27}$$

where a and c are constants. The exact solution is given as

$$u(x) = \frac{e^{\frac{c}{a}x} - 1}{e^{\frac{c}{a}} - 1}. \tag{28}$$

Δx	Upwind	2nd-stand	2nd-new	4th-new
1/10	1.32E-01	3.45E-02	1.41E-02	7.41E-04
1/20	7.64E-02	7.90E-03	3.70E-03	4.74E-05
1/40	4.17E-02	1.90E-03	9.52E-04	2.98E-06
1/80	2.18E-02	4.79E-04	2.39E-04	1.87E-07
1/160	1.12E-02	1.20E-04	5.98E-05	1.17E-08

Table 2. Errors between the exact solution and the numerical solution of Eq.(27) with $a = 0.1$ and $c = 1$.

Table 2. shows the error $\|u^e - u^c\|_\infty$ between the exact solution u^e and the numerical solution u^c calculated using the following four finite difference schemes with $a = 0.1$ and $c = 1$:

1. Upwind: First-order upwind difference for the convection term and second-order central finite difference for the diffusion term.
2. 2nd-stand: Second-order central difference for both the diffusion and convection terms.
3. 2nd-new: New method that uses second-order central difference for Eqs. (5) and (7).

4. 4th-new: New method that uses fourth-order Padé approximation for Eqs. (5) and (7).

All results are obtained using a 3-point stencil. It is clear from Table 2 that the accuracies of different schemes are as expected: when the grid size Δx is reduced by $\frac{1}{2}$, the errors are reduced by approximately $\frac{1}{2}$, $(\frac{1}{2})^2$ and $(\frac{1}{2})^4$ for the 1st-, 2nd- and 4th-order algorithms, respectively.

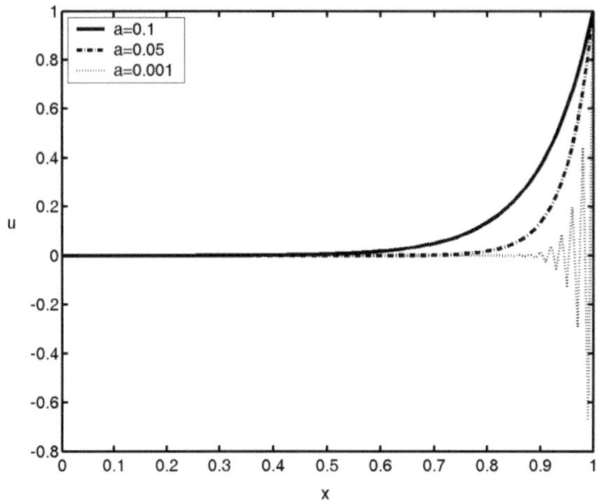

Fig. 1. Solution curves corresponding to $a = 0.1, 0.05, 0.001$ and $c = 1$ using the 2nd-stand algorithm with $\Delta x = 0.001$.

Although both the 2nd-stand and 2nd-new algorithms produced comparable results for the case of $a = 0.1$ and $c = 1$ shown in Table 2, the 2nd-new algorithm is much more robust when the boundary layer near $x = 1$ becomes steeper as a decreases. Fig. 1 and Fig. 2 show the solutions calculated using the 2nd-stand and 2nd-new central difference schemes, respectively. The three curves in each figure correspond to the diffusion coefficient $a = 0.1, 0.05$, and 0.001, respectively. It is clear from Fig. 1 that the solution calculated by the standard second-order central difference scheme becomes highly oscillatory when a reaches 0.001, while the solution calculated by the new second-order central difference scheme shown in Fig. 2 describes the steep boundary layer near $x = 1$ very well.

Example 2: In this example, we compare the robustness of three different algorithms. The governing equation for this example is

$$-au_{xx} + (x - \frac{1}{2})u_x = 0, \quad u(0) = 0, \quad u(1) = 1, \tag{29}$$

where a is a constant. The convection coefficient changes sign in the middle of the domain, which makes this turning point problem difficult (Morton, 1996).

Fig. 3 shows the solution curves obtained by the new method using the second-order central difference algorithm. The four solution curves in the figure correspond to diffusion coefficient $a = 1.0, 0.1, 0.01, 0.001$, respectively, all calculated with $\Delta x = 0.001$. It is clear that as a decreases, the boundary layers at $x = 0$ and $x = 1$ become steeper. Also note that all four solution curves pass the same point $x = 0.5$, where the convection coefficient is zero.

Fig. 4 shows the solution curves obtained by the standard finite difference schemes on the same grid with $\Delta x = 0.001$. The diffusion term is discretized by the second-order

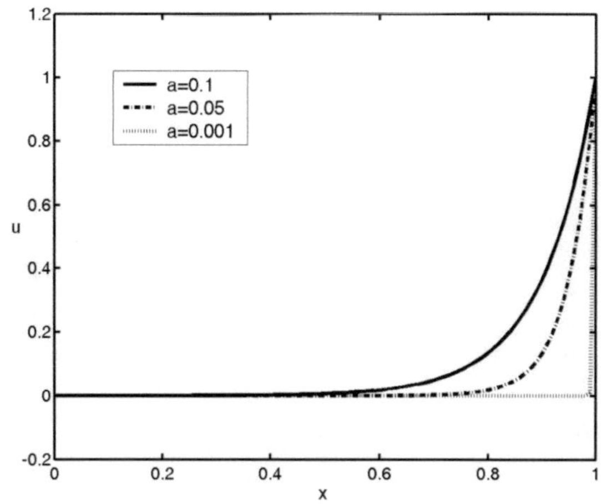

Fig. 2. Solution curves corresponding to $a = 0.1, 0.05, 0.001$ and $c = 1$ calculated using the 2nd−new algorithm with $\Delta x = 0.01$.

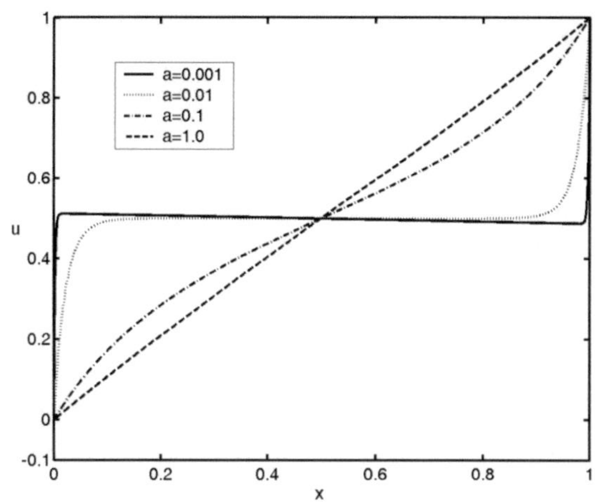

Fig. 3. Solution curves corresponding to $a = 1.0, 0.1, 0.01$ and 0.001 calculated by the new method using central difference scheme

central difference scheme and the convection term is discretized by the first-order upwind scheme assuming the convection coefficient is positive. The change of sign of the convection coefficient is not taken into consideration. The solution curves correspond to $a = 1.0$ and 0.1 look reasonable. But the solution curve correspond to $a = 0.01$ is not accurate. It does not cross the solution curves corresponding to $a = 1.0$ and 0.1 at $x = 0.5$. The solution curve corresponds to $a = 0.001$ does not resemble the correct solution at all. This is not surprising since the convection coefficient changes sign but the upwind scheme used in the calculation does not take this into consideration.

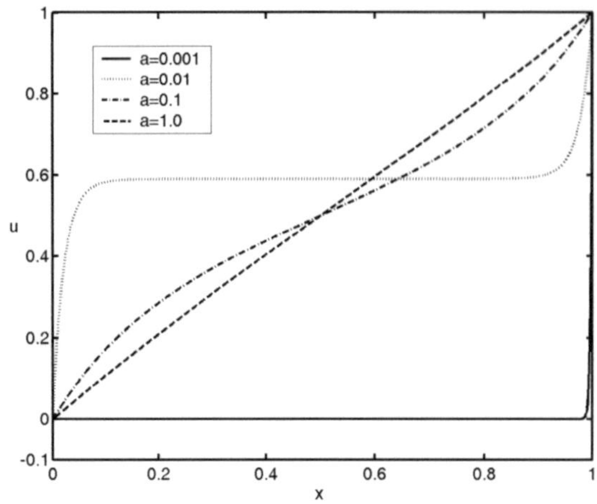

Fig. 4. Solution curves corresponding to $a = 1.0, 0.1, 0.01$ and 0.001 calculated by the upwind scheme without considering the change of sign of the convection coefficient.

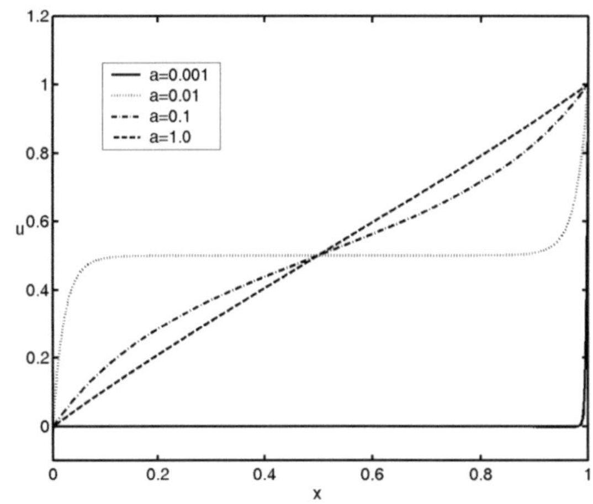

Fig. 5. Solution curves corresponding to $a = 1.0, 0.1, 0.01$ and 0.001 calculated by the upwind scheme taking into consideration the sign change of the convection coefficient.

Fig. 5 shows the solution curves obtained by the standard finite difference algorithm. The diffusion term is discretized by the second-order central difference scheme and the convection term is discretized by the first-order upwind scheme taking into consideration the sign change of the convection coefficient. We can see the solution curves correspond to $a = 1.0, 0.1$, and 0.01 are very similar to those in Fig. 3. All three solution curves cross each other at the same point $x = 0.5$. However, the solution curve corresponding to $a = 0.001$ does not resemble the true solution at all. This is somewhat surprising but probably can be attributed to the difficulty caused by the turning point at $x = 0.5$ where $c(x) = 0$. The situation does not improve even when the grid spacing Δx is further reduced.

Example 3: In this example we solve a nonlinear Black-Scholes equation, which is widely used to model option price when transaction cost is considered. It is well known that in the area of financial mathematics, the calculations of both the solution and its first derivative are required. The derivative is the so-called hedge delta, which actually represents the number of shares (of stock) that one should hold or sale, in order to maximize the profit. The nonlinear Black-Scholes equation solved in this chapter is given below. More details about this model can be found in (Barles & Soner, 1998).

$$u_t = (1 + \Phi[e^{(Kt+x)}a^2 E(u_{xx} + u_x)])(u_{xx} + u_x) - Ku_x,$$

with initial and boundary conditions

$$u(x,0) = max(1 - e^{-x}, 0), \quad u(-\infty, t) = 0, \quad u(\infty, t) = 1,$$

where a is transaction cost rate, E is the strike price, $K = \frac{2\rho}{\sigma_0^2}$, ρ is the risk-free interest rate, σ_0 is the volatility of the stock, and Φ is a function defined as the solution to the following ODE:

$$\Phi'(s) = \frac{\Phi(s) + 1}{2\sqrt{s\Phi(s)} - s}, \quad \Phi(0) = 0, \tag{30}$$

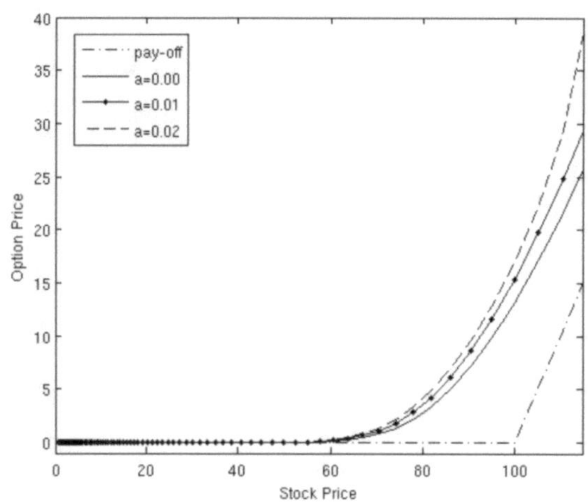

Fig. 6. Solution curves for option price corresponding to various transaction cost rates($a = 0.0, 0.01, 0.02$) and the pay-off curve.

In the numerical solution process, the infinite domain is approximated by a finite interval of sufficient length. In financial industry, one of the widely used methods for calculating hedge delta is to first solve the Black-Scholes equation to obtain numerical solution of u, and then apply finite difference schemes to the numerical solution to obtain approximations to u_x. With the new method discussed in this chapter, both the solution u and the hedge delta u_x are calculated simultaneously. Fig. 6 and Fig. 7 show the option price and the hedge delta for various transaction cost rates, respectively.

Example 4: In this example we solve a time dependent nonlinear equation, the Burgers' Equation:

$$u_t + uu_x = au_{xx}, \quad u(0,t) = 0, \quad u(1,t) = 1, \tag{31}$$

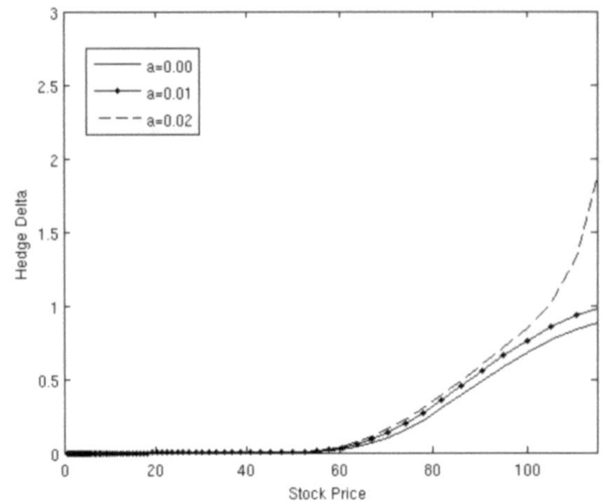

Fig. 7. Solution curves of the hedge delta $\frac{\partial V}{\partial S}$ corresponding to various transaction cost rate($a = 0.0, 0.01, 0.02$).

where a is a constant. We first solve the equation with the initial condition $u(x,0) = x(1-x)$, for which the analytic solution is not available. Figs. 8, 9, and 10 show the solution curves for various a values obtained by the standard central difference scheme (for both the convection and diffusion terms), the upwind (for convection)-central difference (for diffusion) scheme, and the new method using second-order central difference, respectively. It is clear that as a decreases, for instance, $a = 0.001$, the standard central difference scheme produces oscillations in Fig. 8.

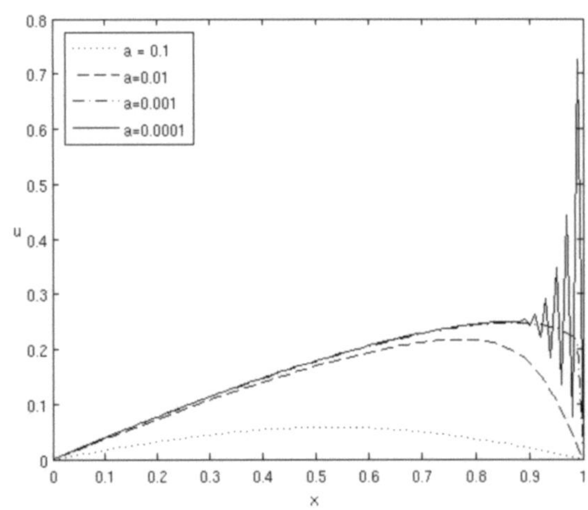

Fig. 8. Solution curves corresponding to $a = 0.1, 0.01, 0.001, 0.0001$ using the standard central difference scheme with $\Delta x = 0.01$.

The new method, on the other hand, produces solutions that are oscillation free as shown in Fig. 9. These solutions are similar to those produced by the upwind-central difference scheme shown in Fig. 10, and agree with the results reported in other works, such as (Hassanien et al., 2005).

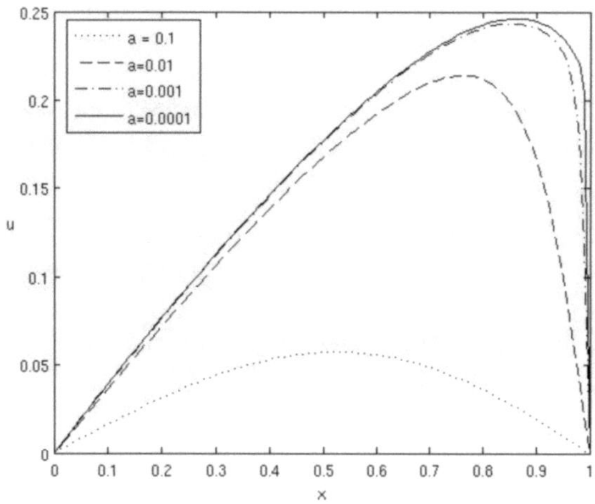

Fig. 9. Solution curves corresponding to $a = 0.1, 0.01, 0.001, 0.0001$ using the upwind scheme with $\Delta x = 0.01$.

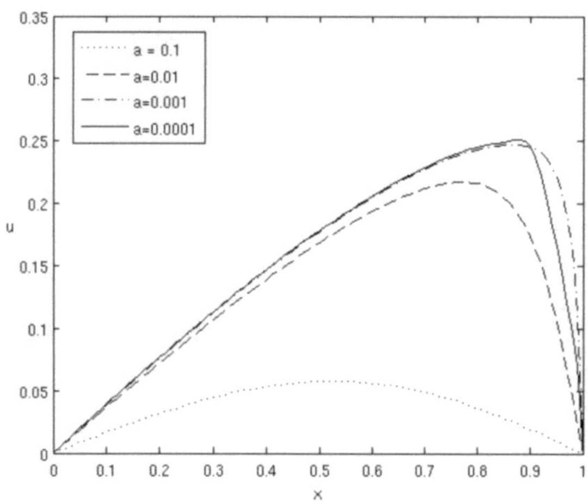

Fig. 10. Solution curves corresponding to $a = 0.1, 0.01, 0.001, 0.0001$ using the second-order new algorithm with $\Delta x = 0.01$.

Next we use the initial condition

$$u(x,0) = \frac{2a\pi \sin(\pi x)}{\kappa + \cos(\pi x)}, \tag{32}$$

with $\kappa > 1$, for which the exact solution to Eq. (31) is known as

$$u(x,t) = \frac{2a\pi e^{-\pi^2 at} \sin(\pi x)}{\kappa + e^{-\pi^2 at} \cos(\pi x)}. \tag{33}$$

We apply both the upwind-central scheme and the second-order new method to this example to compare the accuracy of the two algorithms. Table 3 shows the error $\|u^e - u^c\|_\infty$ between the exact solution u^e and the numerical solution u^c calculated using the two algorithms with $\kappa = 1.2$, for $a = 0.001$ and $a = 0.0001$. All results are obtained using a 3-point stencil. Since the main focus of the study is to compare spatial accuracy of the two algorithms, the first-order explicit time integration is used for simplicity with $\Delta t = 0.0001$ to ensure stability. It is clear from Table 3 that the accuracies of the two schemes are as expected: When the grid size Δx is reduced by $\frac{1}{2}$, the errors are reduced by approximately $\frac{1}{2}$ and $(\frac{1}{2})^2$ for the upwind-central and the 2nd−new schemes, respectively.

Δx	*upwind* $a = 0.001$	2nd-new $a = 0.001$	upwind $a = 0.0001$	2nd-new $a = 0.0001$
1/20	2.69E-04	1.48E-04	3.47E-06	2.31E-06
1/40	1.67E-04	3.87E-05	2.20E-06	6.11E-07
1/80	9.40E-05	9.79E-06	1.23E-06	1.67E-07
1/160	4.98E-05	2.45E-06	6.46E-07	4.13E-08

Table 3. Errors between the exact solution and the numerical solution of Eq. (31) with $a = 0.001$ and $a = 0.0001$.

The numerical examples presented in this chapter show that the standard central difference scheme is second-order accurate on a 3-point stencil but produces oscillatory solutions for convection dominated problems. The upwind scheme is more robust but is only first-order accurate on a 3-point stencil. The new method discussed in this chapter appears to combine the advantages of accuracy of the standard central difference algorithm with the robustness of the upwind scheme for convection dominated equations.

6. Conclusions

The method discussed in this chapter eliminates the convection term in Eq. (1) and makes it feasible to use central difference schemes to solve convection-diffusion equations accurately. The new method, combined with the central difference schemes, can achieve better accuracy than the upwind schemes on the same finite difference stencil, and is shown in the examples presented here to be as robust as the upwind schemes for convection dominated problems. It can also be easily combined with the Padé approximation to achieve fourth-order accuracy in space on a 3-point finite difference stencil.

The new method does incur a modest increase in computational complexity. Instead of just solving Eq. (1), the new method requires solving Eqs. (5) and (7). With a 3-point stencil, the standard upwind-central difference schemes will generate a system of tri-diagonal algebraic equations, while the new method discussed in this chapter will lead to a system of block tri-diagonal algebraic equations with 2×2 blocks. This increased complexity, however, can be compensated by the use of fewer grid points with the increased order of accuracy of the new method. Furthermore, for problems that require calculations of both the solutions and their derivatives, the new method eliminates the need to calculate the derivatives after solving Eq. (1).

The discussions of the new method in this chapter are based on one-dimensional problems. For higher-dimensional problems, a straightforward application of this method will lead to systems of four equations for two-dimensional problems and seven equations for three-dimensional problems. For better computational efficiency, operator splitting

(Gustafsson et al., 1995) should be used to first decompose the original equation into a series of one-dimensional problems. The new method discussed in this chapter can then be applied to these one-dimensional problems to calculate numerical solutions efficiently. Details will be presented in future papers.

7. References

Barles, G. & Soner, H. (1998). Option pricing with transaction costs and a nonlinear Black-Scholes equation, *Finance Stochast*, Vol. 2, 1998, pp. 369 - 397.

Gu, Y.; Liao, W. & Zhu, J. (2003). An efficient high order algorithm for solving systems of 3-D reaction-diffusion equations, *Journal of Computational and Applied Mathematics*, Vol. 155, 2003, pp. 1 - 17.

Gupta, M.; Manohar, R. & Stephenson, J. (1984). A single cell high-order scheme for the convection-diffusion equation with variable coefficients, *International Journal for Numerical Methods in Fluids*, Vol. 4, 1984, pp. 641 - 651.

Gustafsson, B.; Kreiss, H. & Oliger, J. (1995). *Time-Dependent problems and difference methods*, John Wiley & Sons, New York.

Hassanien, I; Salaman, A. & Hosham, H. (2005). Fourth-Order finite difference method for solving Burgers' equation, *Applied Mathematics and Computation*, Vol. 170, 2005, pp. 781 - 800.

Hundsdorfer, W. & Verwer, J. (2003). *Numerical solution of time-dependent advection-diffusion-reaction equations*, Springer, Berlin.

Kalita, J.; Dalal, D. & Dass, A. (2002). A class of higher order compact schemes for the unsteady two-dimensional convection-diffusion equation with variable convection coefficients, *International Journal for Numerical Methods in Fluids*, Vol. 38, 2002, pp. 1111 - 1131.

Karaa, S. & Zhang, J. (2004). High order method for solving unsteady convection-diffusion problems, *Journal of Computational Physics*, Vol. 198, no.1, 2004, pp. 1 - 9.

Morton, K. (1996). *Numerical solution of convection-diffusion problems*, Chapman & Hall, London.

Noye, B. & Tan, H. (1989). Finite difference methods for solving the two-dimensional advection-diffusion equation, *International Journal for Numerical Methods in Fluids*, Vol. 9, 1989, pp. 75 - 98.

Rigal, A. (1989). Numerical analysis of two-level finite difference schemes for unsteady diffusion-convection problems, *International Journal for Numerical Methods in Engineering*, Vol. 28, 1989, pp. 1001 - 1021.

Rigal, A. (1990). Numerical analysis of three-time-level finite difference schemes for unsteady diffusion-convection problems, *International Journal for Numerical Methods in Engineering*, Vol. 30, 1990, pp. 307 - 330.

Rigal, A. (1994). High order difference schemes for unsteady one-dimensional diffusion-convection problems, *Journal of Computational Physics*, Vol. 114, 1994, pp. 59 - 76.

Seydel, R. (2002). *Tools for computational finance*, Springer, Berlin.

Spotz, W. & Carey, G. (2001). Extension of high-order compact schemes to time-dependent problems, *Numerical Methods for Partial Differential Equations*, Vol. 17, 2001, pp. 657 - 672.

Tian, Z. & Dai, S. (2007). High-order compact exponential finite difference methods for convection-diffusion type problems, *Journal of Computational Physics*, Vol. 220, No.2, 2007, pp. 952 - 974.

Tian, Z. & Ge, Y. (2007). A fourth-order compact ADI method for solving two-dimensional unsteady convection-diffusion problems, *Journal of Computational and Applied Mathematics*, vol. 198, 2007, pp. 268-286.

Wood, W. (2006). An exact solution for Burgers' equation, *Communications in Numerical Methods in Engineering*, Vol. 22, 2006, pp. 797 - 798.

You, D. (2006). A high-order Padé ADI method for unsteady convection-diffusion equations, *Journal of Computational Physics*, Vol. 214, No. 1, 2006, pp. 1-11.

Zhang, J.; Sun, H. & Zhao, J. (2002). High order compact scheme with multigrid local mesh refinement procedure for convection diffusion problems, *Computer Methods in Applied Mechanics and Engineering*, Vol. 191, 2002, pp. 4661 - 4674.

5

Internal Waves Radiation by a Turbulent Jet Flow in a Stratified Fluid

Oleg Druzhinin
Institute of Applied Physics, Russian Academy of Sciences
Russia

1. Introduction

The radiation of internal gravity waves by stratified turbulent shear flows is encountered in many geophysical flows. Numerous applications include jet flows (Sutherland & Peltier 1994), grid-generated turbulence (Dohan & Sutherland 2003), boundary layers (Taylor & Sarkar 2007), collapse of mixed patches (Sutherland et al. 2007), wakes behind towed and self-propelled bodies (Lin & Pao 1979), and many others. The present paper deals with internal waves radiated by a jet flow that is created in the far wake of a sphere towed in a stratified fluid at large Froude and Reynolds numbers.

Experimental studies of internal gravity waves (IW) radiated by a towed sphere and its wake were performed both in a linearly stratified fluid by Bonneton, Chomaz & Hopfinger (1993) (further referred to as BCH) and in the presence of a thermocline by Robey (1996). The results show that internal waves radiated by the sphere (i.e. the lee waves) are stationary with respect to the sphere, and their amplitude is inversely proportional to the sphere Froude number, defined as $Fr = 2V / ND$ (where N is the buoyancy frequency, and V and D are the towing speed and the sphere diameter). On the other hand, internal waves, radiated by the turbulent wake are not stationary with respect to the sphere, and their amplitude grows as Fr increases. Experimental results obtained by BCH and Robey (1996) show that if the Froude number is sufficiently large ($Fr > 10$), non-stationary IW supercede the lee waves.

Experimental results obtained by BCH show that at early times ($Nt = O(10)$) internal waves are radiated due to the collapse of the vortex coherent structures developing in the near wake (Chomaz, Bonnet & Hopfinger (1993), further referred to as CBH). The wavelength of these waves (also called "random" waves) is of the order of the sphere diameter, and their dynamics is well described theoretically under an assumption that each collapsing coherent structure can be regarded as an impulsive source of IW. Visualization of the density distribution in a horizontal plane at a distance of three sphere radii below the towing axis at times $Nt < 40$ gives a rather complicated, irregular isophase pattern of these random internal waves.

The results of BCH show also that at later times ($Nt > 40$) random internal waves are superceded by waves whose initial spatial period is of the order of five sphere diameters. The isophase distribution of these waves, although being non-stationary with respect to the sphere, is reminiscent of the regular iso-phase pattern of the lee-waves. At sufficiently late times ($Nt > 50$), the random waves disappear, and there remain only coherent IW. BCH give no explanation of the observed dynamics of these coherent internal waves.

The experimental study of internal waves produced by a sphere towed under a thermocline at large Froude and Reynolds numbers was performed by Robey (1996). The results also show that the turbulent wake generates coherent internal waves which are non-stationary with respect to the sphere and whose amplitude grows linearly with *Fr*. In order to explain these experimental observations Robey (1996) considers a physical model of the IW radiation by the wake. According to this model, internal waves are emitted by vortices shed by the sphere, and each vortex can be regarded as a stationary source moving at a "resonance" speed, such that its effective Froude number is of order unity. Note however, that experimental results obtained by CBH do not support the assumption that such stationary vortices are present in the near wake.
Another theoretical model of IW radiation by the wake flow has been developed by Dupont & Voisin (1996). According to this model, internal waves are emitted by an oscillating source moving with the speed of a sphere. It is assumed that such a source adequately represents coherent vortex structures which are shed by the sphere at the frequency of a spiral instability mode of the near-wake flow (observed experimentally by CBH) and collapse under gravity. Dupont & Voisin (1996) performed numerical calculations based on the Green's function formalism developed by Voisin (1994). However, numerical results of Dupont & Voisin (1996) show that the IW phase pattern predicted by the model is rather complicated and does not reproduce the regular phase distribution related to the coherent internal waves observed experimentally by BCH.
Recently there have been successful attempts to perform DNS and LES of stratified wakes by Gourlay et al. (2001), Dommermuth et al. (2002) and Brucker & Sarkar (2010). Since the mean streamwise fluid velocity in the wake is much smaller than the sphere towing speed, the variation of the flow statistical properties along the streamwise (x) axis can be neglected in DNS in the considered flow region. Thus the flow in DNS/LES is initialized as a sum of a circular, mean streamwise velocity profile and an x-periodic, random velocity component accounting for the turbulent fluctuations. This turbulent component is prescribed as a sum of Fourier harmonics with independent random phases and given amplitude power spectrum. Numerical results of Gourlay et al. (2001) (such as the temporal development of the wake axis mean velocity, width and height and the instantaneous vorticity distribution) are in good qualitative agreement with the experimental data obtained by Spedding et al. (1996) and Spedding (2001). Dommermuth et al. (2002) performed the LES study of the stratified wake and used a relaxation procedure to bring to equilibrium the initially unrelated turbulent production and dissipation. Their results are similar to the results of Gourlay et al. (2001) and show that the relaxation procedure is essential for accurately simulating the near wake but is not important if only far wake is of interest. DNS of the turbulent wake flow at high Reynolds number (Re=50000) was performed recently by Brucker & Sarkar (2010) using the same flow initialization procedure. Both Gourlay et al. (2001) and Dommermuth et al. (2002) and Brucker & Sarkar (2010) conclude that startified wakes are capable of radiating internal waves, but do not examine in detail the physical mechanism of the IW radiation and the properties of waves kinematics and dynamics. The radiation of internal waves by a turbulent jet flow in a linearly stratified fluid was studied recently by performing DNS by Druzhinin (2009). The results show that IW radiation occurs at times $10 < Nt < 30$ and can be described as a result of an impulsive collapse of the vertical velocity fluctuation of the initially 3D turbulent flow.
The objective of the present paper is to study in more details the process of internal waves radiation by a temporally developing turbulent jet flow in a stratified fluid by direct numerical simulation. An initially circular, turbulent jet flow is considered with parameters

that match parameters of a far wake of a sphere towed in a stratified fluid at large Froude and Reynolds numbers (of order $O(10)$ and $O(10^4)$, respectively). The mathematical formulation and description of the numerical procedure are provided is Section 2. In Section 3 the properties of the jet flow and radiated internal waves obtained in DNS are described. In Section 4 a linear impulsive source theory is applied to explain the observed IW kinematics and dynamics, and final conclusions are found in Section 5.

2. Governing equations and numerical method

A circular jet flow with the initial (reference) Gaussian profile of the streamwise (x) velocity component is considered in the form:

$$U_{ref} = \exp\left(-4[y^2 + z^2]\right), \tag{2.1}$$

where y and z are the spanwise and vertical coordinates, respectively. Hereafter, all the variables are made dimensionless via normalizing by the velocity and length scales defined by the initial jet axis mean velocity and diameter, U_0 and L_0. For example, in the case of a wake created by a towed sphere, L_0 is close to the sphere diameter ($L_0 / D \approx 0.8$) and U_0 is defined by the towing speed V and the velocity deficit at the wake central axis at a given distance behind the sphere., e.g. $U_0 / V \approx 0.1$ at $x / D = 6$ (cf. Bevilaqua & Likoudis 1978). An initial linear, stable stratification of the fluid density is considered ($\rho_{ref} = -z$).
The Navier - Stokes equations for the fluid velocity are written under the Boussinesq approximation in the dimensionless form:

$$\begin{aligned} &\partial_t U_i + U_j \partial_j U_i + U_{ref} \partial_x U_i + \delta_{ix}\left(U_y \partial_y U_{ref} + U_z \partial_z U_{ref}\right) = \\ &-\partial_i P + \frac{1}{\mathrm{Re}} \partial^2 U_i + \frac{1}{\mathrm{Re}} \delta_{ix}\left(\partial^2_{yy} U_{ref} + \partial^2_{zz} U_{ref}\right) - \delta_{iz} Ri\, \rho, \end{aligned} \tag{2.2}$$

$$\partial_j U_j = 0. \tag{2.3}$$

The equation for the fluid density is written as:

$$\partial_t \rho + U_j \partial_j \rho + U_{ref} \partial_x \rho - U_z = \frac{1}{\mathrm{Re}\,\mathrm{Pr}} \partial^2 \rho . \tag{2.4}$$

In Eqs. (2.2) - (2.4), U_i $(i = x, y, z)$ and ρ are the instantaneous deviations of the fluid velocity and density from their respective reference profiles, and δ_{ij} is the Kroneker's symbol. The Reynolds number and the global Richardson number of the flow are defined as:

$$\mathrm{Re} = \frac{U_0 L_0}{\nu}, \tag{2.5}$$

and

$$Ri = \frac{g \Delta\rho_0}{\rho_0} \frac{L_0}{U_0^2}, \tag{2.6}$$

where ν is the fluid kinematic viscosity, g the acceleration due to gravity, and ($\Delta\rho_0 / \rho_0$) the absolute relative density variation in the vertical direction on scale L_0. (Note that since $U_0 / V \approx 0.1$, the Reynolds and Froude numbers of the sphere are about 10 times larger than Re and $Fr = Ri^{-1/2}$, respectively.) As follows from eqs. (2.2) - (2.6), the dimensionless buoyancy frequency equals $N = Ri^{1/2} = 1 / Fr$. The Prandtl number is set equal to unity. The results of DNS by Stadler et al. (2010) performed recently show that that Pr = 1 is a reasonable approximation for Pr = 7 which is the case of the thermal stratification in the ocean.

In order to perform numerical simulation in a region finite over the vertical coordinate and provide a sufficient resolution of the flow field, a mapping for the z-coordinate is employed in the form:

$$\xi = \tanh\frac{z}{9}, \tag{2.7}$$

so that

$$z = 4.5\ln\left(\frac{1+\xi}{1-\xi}\right), \tag{2.8}$$

and $-1 \le \xi \le 1$ for $-\infty < z < \infty$. The derivatives over z-coordinate in Eqs. (2.2)-(2.4) are rewritten as:

$$\frac{\partial}{\partial z} = \left(\frac{1-\xi^2}{9}\right)\frac{\partial}{\partial \xi}. \tag{2.9}$$

Equations (2.2) - (2.4) are discretized in a parallelepiped domain with sizes $0 \le x \le 36$, $-9 \le y \le 9$ and $-1 \le \xi \le 1$ by employing a finite difference method of the second-order accuracy on a uniform rectangular staggered grid consisting of 480 × 240 × 240 nodes in x, y, and $\xi(z)$ directions, respectively. The terms on the left hand side of equations (2.2) and (2.4), $U_{ref}\partial_x U_i$ and $U_{ref}\partial_x \rho$, that are responsible for the advection by the reference velocity $U_{ref}(y,z)$, are evaluated at each time step by Fourier interpolation which is a more accurate method to compute these terms as compared to a pure finite difference scheme (Gerz et al. (1989)). The integration is advanced in time using the Adams-Bashforth method with time step Δt = 0.0075. The shear-free (Neumann) boundary condition is prescribed in the spanwise and vertical directions (at y = ± 9 and ξ = ± 1), and x-periodic boundary condition is prescribed in the streamwise direction. The Poisson equation for the pressure is solved by fast Fourier transform over x-coordinate, cosine transform over y-coordinate, and Gauss elimination method over z-coordinate.

As it was observed by Gourlay et al. (2001) in their DNS study, internal waves radiated by the jet turbulence propagate away from the jet core toward the boundaries of the computational domain in the y and z directions. Thus one needs to avoid reflection of the waves from the boundaries and their coming back into the flow region. One way to do this is to prescribe the Sommerfeld radiation boundary condition (cf. e.g. Javam et al. 2000). In the present study we adopt a less computationally expensive approach analogous to that employed by Sutherland & Peltier (1994) in their numerical study of the instability development and IW radiation in a two-dimensional jet flow. In this approach, the absorption of internal waves radiated from the jet core is ensured by increasing the fluid kinematic viscosity in a layer near the boundaries of the computational domain. A similar viscous-sponge boundary condition was successfully employed recently by Taylor & Sarkar (2007) in their LES study of internal waves radiated by a turbulent boundary layer. Thus, in our DNS procedure the viscosity is increased by a factor of 20 in the region $\left|y^2+z^2\right|^{1/2}>7$, as compared to the viscosity in the rest of the computational domain (where it is constant and equals 1/Re). Our DNS results show that such artificial viscosity enhancement does not affect the jet flow dynamics and ensures complete absorption of internal waves radiated from the jet core region toward the boundaries.

In order to define the flow statistical characteristics at a given time moment (t), the x - averaged velocity and density fields are evaluated as:

$$<U_i>(y,z,t)=\frac{1}{L_x}\int_0^{L_x} U_i(x,y,z,t)dx+\delta_{ix}U_{ref}(y,z), \tag{2.10}$$

$$<\rho>(y,z,t)=\frac{1}{L_x}\int_0^{L_x} \rho(x,y,z,t)dx, \tag{2.11}$$

where $i=x,y,z$, and $L_x=36$. The jet maximum mean velocity (U_m) and its width and height ($L_{y,z}$) are further evaluated as:

$$U_m(t)=\max\{<U_x>(y,z,t)\}, \tag{2.12}$$

$$L_y(t)=\frac{1}{U_m}\int_{-\infty}^{\infty} <U_x>(y,z=0,t)dy, \tag{2.13}$$

$$L_z(t)=\frac{1}{U_m}\int_{-\infty}^{\infty} <U_x>(y=0,z,t)dz. \tag{2.14}$$

The instantaneous r.m.s. fluctuations of the velocity and density fields,

$$U'_i(y,z,t)=<U_i^2-<U_i>^2>^{1/2} \tag{2.15}$$

and

$$\rho'(y,z,t)=<\rho^2-<\rho>^2>^{1/2}, \tag{2.16}$$

and their amplitudes (the respective absolute maxima) are also evaluated.

The initial, random component of the fluid velocity is prescribed as a 3D homogeneous isotropic turbulence field consisting of a sum of Fourier harmonics with independent random phases and an isotropic amplitude power spectrum (Gourlay et al. 2001). We prescribe the initial turbulence spectrum to be uniform over the wavenumber range $0.5\le k\le 5$ and equal to zero for other k's (Fig. 1). Thus, the initial spectrum includes the most unstable (spiral) mode with k = 1.46 of an inviscid non-stratified circular jet flow (Batchelor and Gill 1962), as well as a higher-k axisymmetrical Kelvin-Helmholtz instability mode similar to that observed in the near wake flow (CBH 1993).

At present it is an open question whether the spiral shedding mode observed in the near wake (CBH 1993) is related to the spiral instability mode of the x-periodic circular jet, although the Strouhal numbers of the two modes are close (for the spiral mode St = $k/2\pi$ = 0.2 whereas for the shedding spiral mode St = 0.175, CBH 1993). It is possible that the two modes are related due to some correlation between the development of the instability of the near-wake flow and the location of the separation point of the boundary layer at the sphere and the development of the spiral shedding mode. It is important to note however that the development of the spiral instability mode is an intrinsic property of the circular jet/wake flow itself and not related to presence of the sphere.

Since at present there is no knowledge concerning the shape of the spectrum in the homogeneous near wake, we prescribe an initial uniform-amplitude spectrum. The initial amplitude of the random velocity component is prescribed to be about 40% of the mean velocity maximum. This value is close to the turbulence intensity measured by Bevilaqua and Lykoudis (1978) in a homogeneous turbulent wake at the distance $x/D = 6$ behind the sphere. The initial velocity field is further windowed with the reference profile $U_{ref}(y,z)$ (2.1) and made divergence-free , similarly to the initialization procedure employed by Gourlay et al. (2001).

The initial deviation of the density from the reference linear profile is prescribed to be zero. This is in agreement with the experimental observations of BCH showing that the effect of the turbulent mixing in the near wake of a towed sphere is weak and its contribution to the radiated IW field is negligible.

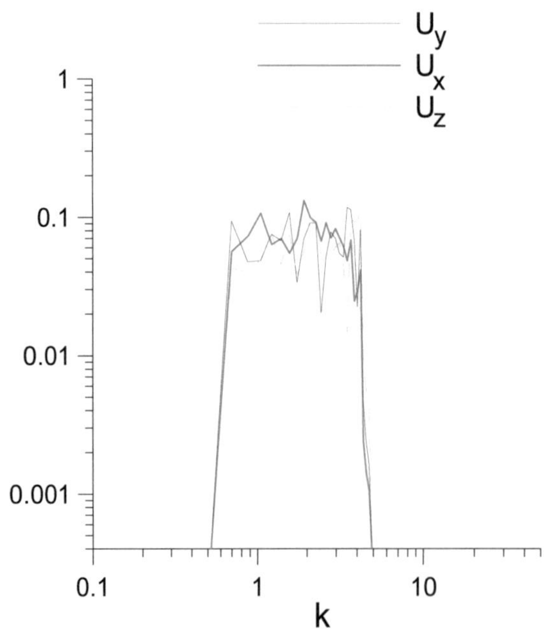

Fig. 1. The initial velocity spectrum.

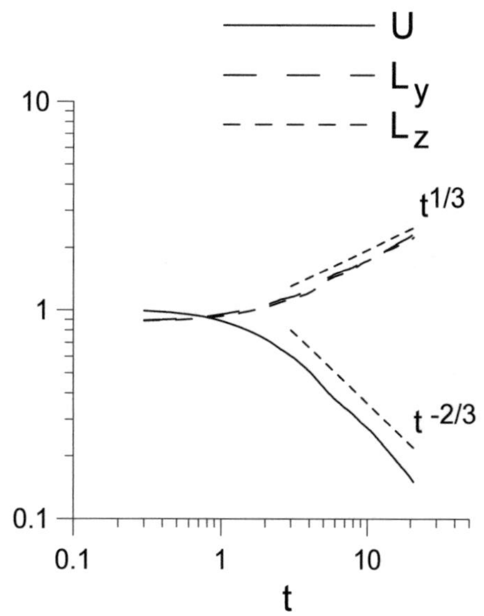

Fig. 2. Temporal development of the velocity and length scales of the non-stratified jet flow.

3. Numerical results

3.1 Jet flow properties

In order to verify the performance of our numerical procedure we performed DNS with Re = 700 of a homogeneous jet flow (where Ri = 0) and a stratified jet flow with two different Richardson numbers (Ri = 1 and Ri = 3) and compared our numerical results with well-known asymptotics of homogeneous and stratified far wakes.

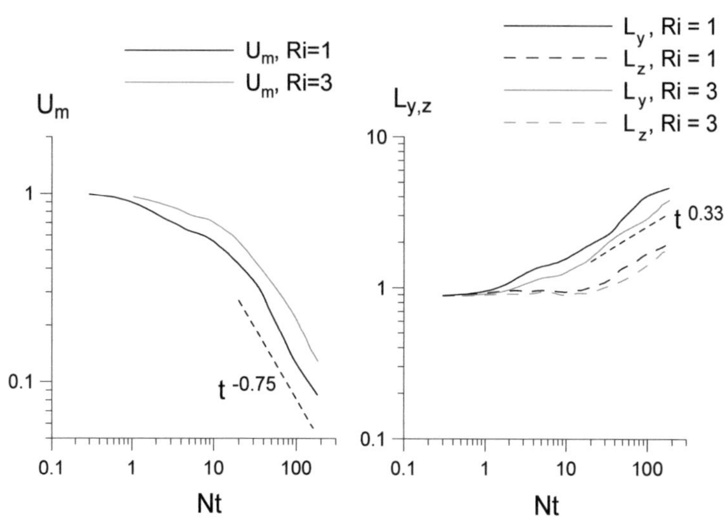

Fig. 3. Temporal development of the jet mean velocity maximum U_m (left) and its width L_y and height L_z (in dashed line) (right). Asymptotics $U_m \sim t^{-0.75}$ and $L_{y,z} \sim t^{0.33}$ are shown in dotted line.

Figures 2 and 3 compare the temporal development of the flow integral scales, such as the mean velocity maximum, and jet width and height obtained in our DNS, with the asymptotics $U_m \sim t^{-2/3}$ and $U_m \sim t^{-0.75}$ and $L_{y,z} \sim t^{0.33}$, observed in homogeneous and stratified wakes in laboratory experiments (Bevilaqua & Lykoudis 1978, Spedding 1997). In the case of a homogeneous wake, the agreement is very good for the considered times $t \leq 20$ (cf. Fig. 2). (It is important to note that since we normalize by the velocity deficit $U_0 / V \approx 0.1$, time moment t = 20 corresponds to the distance $x / D = tV / U_0 \approx 200$ behind the sphere.) In the stratified case, the agreement with the asymptotics $U_m \sim t^{-0.75}$ and $L_{y,z} \sim t^{0.33}$ is also quite satisfactory.

Figure 4 presents the temporal development of the velocity and density fluctuations amplitudes for Ri = 1 and 3. The figure shows that at early times ($Nt < 10$) the velocity fluctuations amplitudes are of the same order, i.e. the flow remains nearly isotropic. At later times, the vertical velocity decreases much faster as compared to the horizontal velocity components and at times $Nt > 30$ the amplitude U'_z becomes almost by two orders of magnitude smaller than the horizontal velocity amplitudes U'_x and U'_y. Thus, at that stage, the flow becomes quasi-two-dimensional.

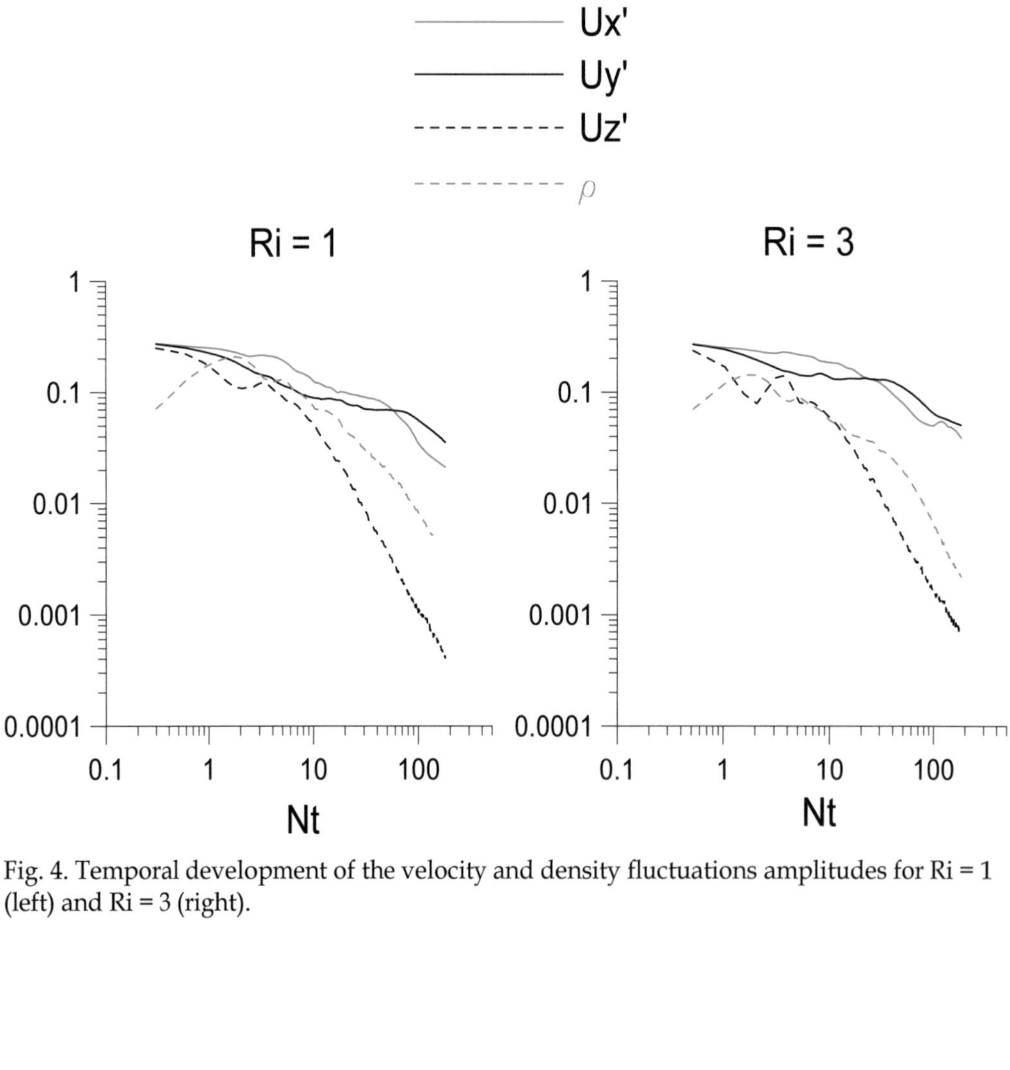

Fig. 4. Temporal development of the velocity and density fluctuations amplitudes for Ri = 1 (left) and Ri = 3 (right).

The density fluctuations amplitude ρ' increases and reaches its maximum at $Nt \approx 2$ due to the transfer of the initial turbulence kinetic energy into the potential energy of the displaced isopycnals. Then ρ' decreases, and this reduction is accompanied by the growth of the vertical velocity fluctuations until $Nt \approx 3.5$. At later times the anti-phase oscillations of ρ' and U'_z are smeared out due to their decay. Similar behavior was observed by Dommermuth et al. (2002) and interpreted as the radiation of internal waves by collapsing vertical velocity fluctuations in the wake.

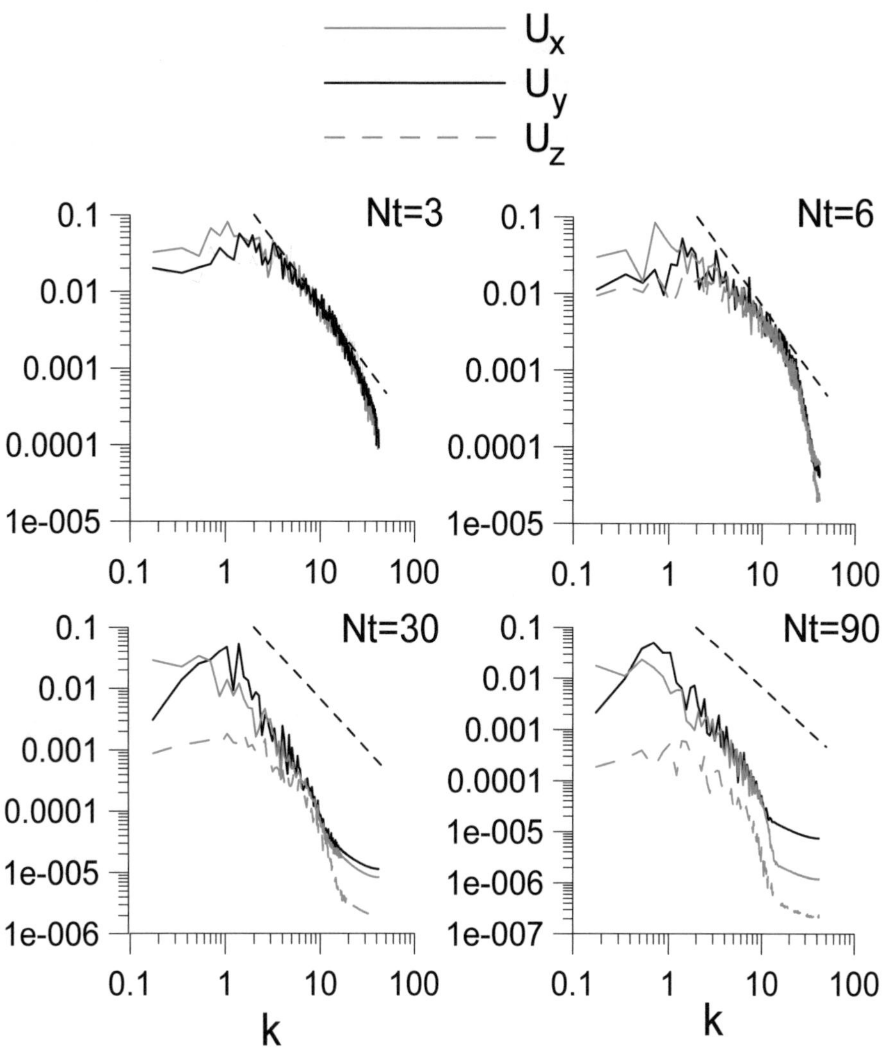

Fig. 5. Velocity fluctuations spatial spectra at different time moments. Asymptotics $k^{-5/3}$ is shown in dotted line. Here and below in Figs. 6, 7 Ri = 1.

Figure 5 shows the velocity wavenumber spectra $U_i(k)$ of the $i = x, y, z$ velocity components obtained in DNS for Ri = 1 at different time moments. Each spectrum is evaluated by a

Fourier transform of the velocity *i*-component $U_i(x,y,z)$ over the streamwise (x) coordinate and averaging over 9 x-realizations located in the jet core region $\left|y^2+z^2\right|<0.15$. The figure shows that at early time moments Nt = 3, 6 the spectra $U_i(k)$ are of the same magnitude, i.e. the velocity field remains isotropic. It is important to note that at these early times the spectra are characterized by distinctive peaks at $k \approx k_s$ (for y-component) and $k \approx 0.5k_s$ (for x-component) where $k_s = 1.46$ is the wavenumber of the spiral instability mode of the non-stratified jet flow (Batchelor & Gill 1962). At later times (Nt =30, 90) most of the energy becomes accumulated in the horizontal velocity components $U_x(k)$ and $U_y(k)$ with pronounced peaks at $k \approx 0.5k_s$.

The dynamics of the spectrum in Fig. 5 can be interpreted as follows. At early times (Nt < 10) there occurs a preferential growth of the most unstable mode which, in a certain sense, is analogous to the spiral instability mode of the non-stratified jet flow (Batchelor & Gill 1962). (This is in agreement with numerous experimental observations (cf. e.g. Spedding et al. (1996)) showing that at early times the stratified wake flow develops similarly to the homogeneous wake flow.) It is important to note that this instability mode is an *intrinsic* property of the jet flow itself and is not directly related to the shedding instability mode of the near-wake flow observed experimentally by CBH (1993). It is important to note also that, in our DNS, no selected modes are initially present (cf. Fig. 1). At later times (Nt > 30) the flow is governed by the non-linear interaction and competition between the most developed flow modes which leads to the preferential growth of a quasi-2D mode with wavenumber $0.5k_s$.

Figure 5 shows also that the fluid kinetic energy is negligible for wavenumbers larger than $k_{\max} = 20$ (the corresponding spatial scale is $l_{\min} = 2\pi / k_{\max} \approx 0.3$). Thus, for the considered spatial resolution (Δx = 0.075) the flow, including the smallest scales, is well-resolved in DNS.

Figure 6 presents the instantaneous distribution of the flow vorticity z-component, $\omega_z = \partial_x U_y - \partial_y (U_x + U_{ref})$ in the plane (x, y) at z = 0 obtained in DNS for Ri = 1 at time moments Nt = 6 and Nt = 90. The figure shows that at late times the vorticity distribution is characterized by the development of large-scale vortices of alternating polarity arranged in the horizontal plane (x, y) in the vicinity of the jet streamwise axis. Similar vortex structures (also called the "pancake" eddies) are known to be the common feature of stratified far wakes and observed both in laboratory experiments (cf. e.g. Spedding et al. (1996)) and in numerical simulations (Gourlay et al. (2001), Dommermuth et al. (2002)).

It is of interest to note that at times 30 < Nt < 90 the amplitude U'_y of the spanwise fluctuation velocity component remains almost constant whereas the streamwise velocity amplitude, U'_x, decreases with time, so that at sufficiently late times (Nt > 60) the spanwise velocity fluctuations prevail over the streamwise fluctuations (cf. Fig. 4). This behavior of U'_y and U'_x is more pronounced for a larger Richardson number (cf. cases Ri= 1 and Ri = 3 in Fig. 4). Figure 5 shows also that at that stage a distinct peak develops in the horizontal velocity spectra $U_{x,y}(k)$ at wavenumber $k \approx 0.5k_s$. This behavior of the spanwise velocity amplitude and the spectrum is in general agreement with the hypothesis put forward by Spedding (2001) who pointed out that an *intrinsic* mean flow sinuous instability may be responsible for the development of the large-scale coherent vortex structures in late stratified wakes.

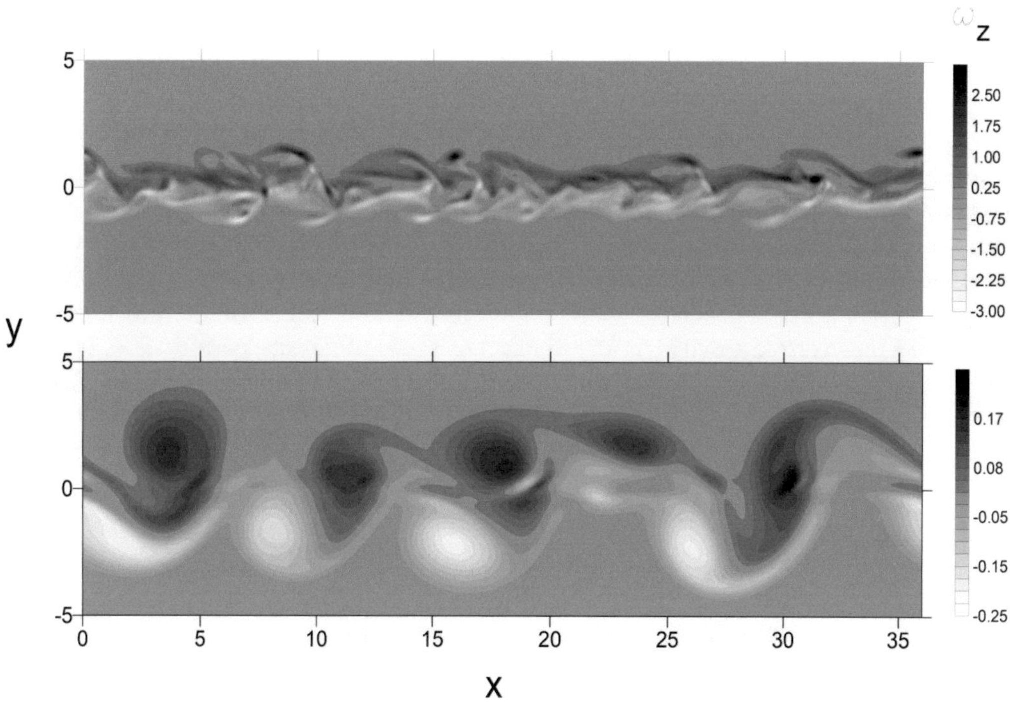

Fig. 6. Instantaneous contours of the vertical vorticity component ω_z in the horizontal central (x,y) plane at time moments Nt = 6 (top frame) and Nt = 90 (bottom frame). The mean flow is from left to right along the x-axis.

3.2 Internal waves radiation

Figure 7 shows the instantaneous distributions of the r.m.s. of the density and horizontal and vertical velocity fields, $\rho'(y,z)$, $U'_h(y,z)=\left(U'^2_x+U'^2_y\right)^{1/2}$ and $U'_z(y,z)$, evaluated from (2.15) and (2.16) at different time moments. The figure shows that at sufficiently late times ($Nt > 10$) the vertical velocity fluctuations, $U'_z(y,z)$, are mostly present in the region $|z|>1$ whereas the horizontal component, $U'_h(y,z)$, is most pronounced in a horizontal layer $|z|<1$ in the region $|y|<L_y$. At times Nt = 15, 30 the vertical velocity fluctuations are most pronounced in the elongated regions oriented at the angle θ with respect to the vertical axis in the range $40^0<\theta<60^0$. It is a well-known property of stratified turbulence that at sufficiently late times, after the initial collapse of 3D turbulence under the action of buoyancy force, the vertical velocity is associated mostly with propagating internal waves (IW) whereas the horizontal velocity is associated with quasi-2D fluid motions. Fig. 7 shows that at later times (Nt = 60, 90) amplitude U'_z decreases by the order of magnitude as compared to the time moment Nt = 15, and the regions of local maxima of $U'_z(y,z)$ are getting aligned with the vertical axis. This picture is similar to the one predicted by a linear theory for the IW radiated by an impulsive point source (Zavolski & Zaytsev 1984, Voisin 1991). According to this theory, amplitude of IW emitted impulsively by a point source has its maximum along the iso-phase line oriented at $\theta=\arctan\sqrt{2}\approx 55^0$ with respect to the vertical. At later times, at a given point, IW cancel out due to their mutual destructive interference and are superceded by small-amplitude, non-propagating buoyancy oscillations. (Below we discuss the application of the impulsive point theory in the considered case in more detail.)

Figure 7 shows also that the distribution of the density fluctuation in the vicinity of the jet core has a two-layer structure with local maxima of ρ' at $|z| \approx 0.5$, $y \approx \pm 2$. Now it is well known that the fluid density variations in a pancake vortex arise as a result of the cyclostrophic balance, where the centrifugal force inside the vortex is balanced by a vertical pressure gradient force that is provided by a perturbation of the local density (cf. Beckers et al. (2001)). This balance inside the individual vortex deflects isopycnals toward the vortex center and thus creates a two-layer distribution of the local density perturbation. Figure 6 shows that the centers of pancake vortices are located in the horizontal central plane at $y \approx \pm 2$. Thus it is plausible to assume that the local maxima of ρ' at $|z| \approx 0.5$, $y \approx \pm 2$ in the distribution of the density fluctuation (cf. Fig. 7, Nt = 60, 90) are due to the cyclostrophic balance inside the pancake eddies.

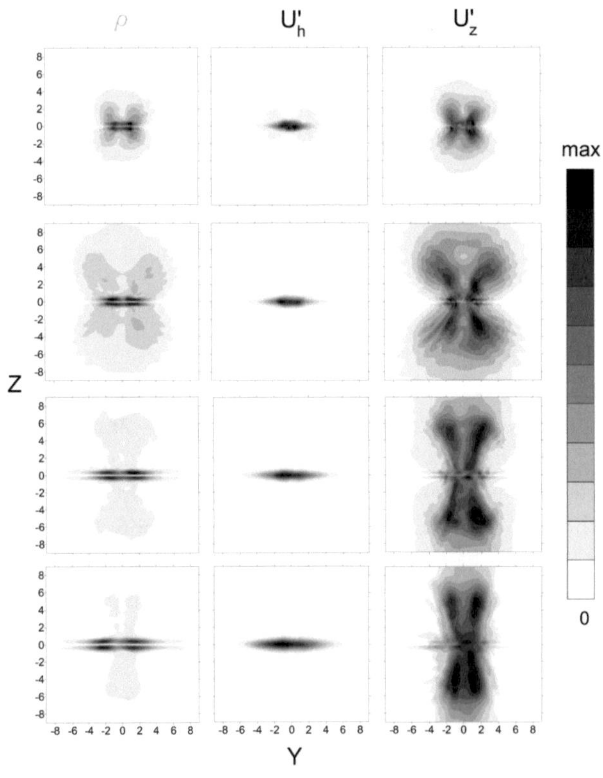

Fig. 7. Contours of the x-averaged density fluctuation ρ (left column), and horizontal (centre column) and vertical (right column) velocity fluctuations, U'_h and U'_z, obtained at time moments Nt = 15, 30, 60, 90 (from top to bottom). The respective maximum values are: 0.06, 0.12, 0.028 (Nt = 15); 0.03, 0.1, 0.0085 (Nt = 30); 0.016, 0.09, 0.0028 (Nt = 60); 0.0095, 0.07, 0.0012 (Nt = 90).

Figure 8 shows the instantaneous distribution of the vertical velocity component, U_z, in the vertical (x, z) planes at $y = 0$ and $y = 1.5$ obtained in DNS at time moments $Nt = 15$ and $Nt = 90$. The figure shows that at time moment $Nt = 15$, in the region sufficiently far away from the jet streamwise axis (for $|z| > 1$), IW isophase lines, which are associated with the regions of maxima and minima of U_z, are mostly in the direction of the mean flow and oriented at the angle of $\theta \approx 50^0$ with respect to the vertical. The velocity distribution has a nearly periodical spatial structure with a period of about 5 dimensionless units along the x-coordinate. The figure shows also that at time $Nt = 90$ the vertical velocity amplitude is diminished by the order of magnitude and its maxima and minima are arranged in columns with the same spatial periodicity. These maxima and minima can be associated with small-amplitude buoyancy oscillations which supercede impulsively radiated IW at that stage of the flow development (Voisin 1991).

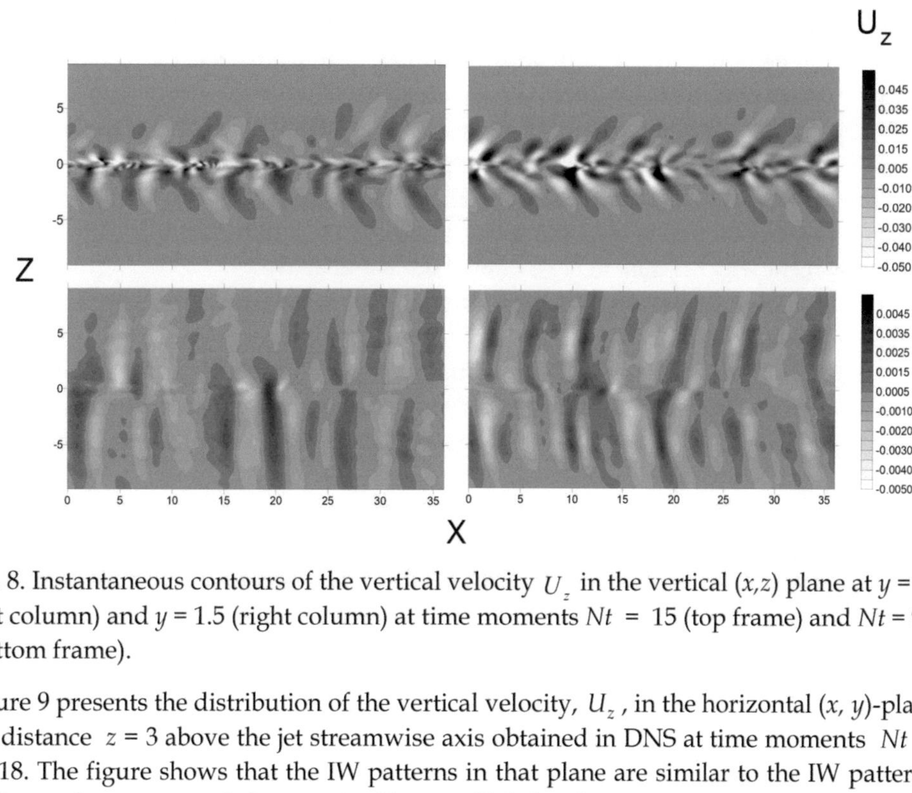

Fig. 8. Instantaneous contours of the vertical velocity U_z in the vertical (x,z) plane at $y = 0$ (left column) and $y = 1.5$ (right column) at time moments $Nt = 15$ (top frame) and $Nt = 90$ (bottom frame).

Figure 9 presents the distribution of the vertical velocity, U_z, in the horizontal (x, y)-plane at the distance $z = 3$ above the jet streamwise axis obtained in DNS at time moments $Nt = 12$, 15, 18. The figure shows that the IW patterns in that plane are similar to the IW patterns of stationary lee-waves and characterized by a well-defined streamwise spatial period of about 5 dimensionless units (or about 4-5 sphere diameters in the dimensional form). A similar isophase pattern was observed by BCH in the laboratory experiment in a horizontal plane at a distance of three sphere radii away from the towing axis. Note also that this spatial period is close to the wavelength of the spiral instability mode of the non-stratified jet flow $\lambda_s = 2\pi / k_s \approx 4.3$ for $k_s \approx 1.46$ (Batchelor and Gill 1962).
Figure 10 shows the temporal development of the vertical velocity and density, U_z and ρ, obtained in DNS at the point located at $x = 18$, with the angle with respect to the vertical $\theta =$

40^0 at the distance of $\left|y^2+z^2\right|=3$ from the jet streamwise axis for Richardson numbers Ri = 1 and Ri = 3. The figure shows that in both cases IW packet arrives at the observation point at time moment $Nt \approx 10$ which is independent of the Richardson number. At the given point, the IW paket amplitude grows at times $Nt < 20$ whereas the velocity U_z and density ρ oscillate with a phase shift $\pi/2$ typical of a monochromatic, linear internal wave (Phillips 1977). At times $Nt > 30$ the oscillations of U_z and ρ become incoherent and IW packet amplitude decreases. At sufficiently late times ($Nt > 60$) there remain only small-amplitude oscillations of the velocity and density with the buoyancy frequency N. These small-amplitude oscillations are similar to the buoyancy oscillations which supercede internal waves, which are mutually cancelled due to the destructive interference as their wavelengths become of the order of the source diameter (i.e. of order one in the considered case) (Voisin 1991).

Figure 11 presents spatially averaged frequency spectra of the vertical velocity obtained in DNS for Richardson numbers Ri = 1 and 3. Each spectrum was obtained by Fourier transform of time series $U_z(t)$ and averaged over 100 points located uniformly at a cylindrical surface with radius $\left|y^2+z^2\right|=3$ in the range $0^0 < \theta < 90^0$. The figure shows that the velocity spectra are characterized by a well pronounced peak at the frequency $\omega / N \approx 0.7$ which corresponds to the IW propagation angle $\arccos \omega / N \approx 45^0$. This value is close to the prediction of the linear theory stating that the amplitude of the waves radiated impulsively by a small-size source has a maximum at $\theta = \arctan\sqrt{2} \approx 55^0$. This is also in general agreement with the data in Figs. 7 and 8 discussed above.

Figure 12 presents the dependence of the internal waves amplitude (ρ_{iw}) vs. the inverse Richardson number (Ri^{-1}) obtained in DNS for two different values of the Reynolds number, Re = 400 and 700. The IW amplitude was evaluated in each DNS run as a maximum of the r.m.s. density fluctuation $\rho'(y,z,t)$ (2.16) at the distance $\left|y^2+z^2\right|=3$ from the jet streamwise axis. (Note that since we consider the linear reference density profile, $\rho'(y,z,t)$ is also equivalent to the average fluid particle vertical displacement amplitude i.e. the average IW amplitude.). The DNS results show that, for all considered Ri, the maximum of ρ' is observed at time moment $Nt \approx 15$ in the range $40^0 < \theta < 60^0$. Figure 12 shows that IW amplitude decreases with increasing Ri. The figure also shows an asymptotic estimate for the amplitude of the impulsively emitted internal waves (in dotted line).

Below in Section 4 the application of the impulsive source theory to explain the observed IW kinematics and dynamics is discussed.

4. Impulsive source model

Radiation of internal waves by the jet turbulence occurs due to the transfer of the kinetic energy of the vertical velocity fluctuations into the initial potential energy of isopycnal displacement and its further redistribution between the kinetic and potential energy of waves and turbulence. This transfer is most pronounced at the early stage of the jet flow evolution when the vertical velocity fluctuations are significant (i.e. for $Nt < 10$, cf. Fig. 4). The results in the previous section show that the properties of IW radiated by the jet flow turbulence are to some degree analogous to the properties of the internal waves radiated by an impulsive source. Let us consider this analogy in more detail.

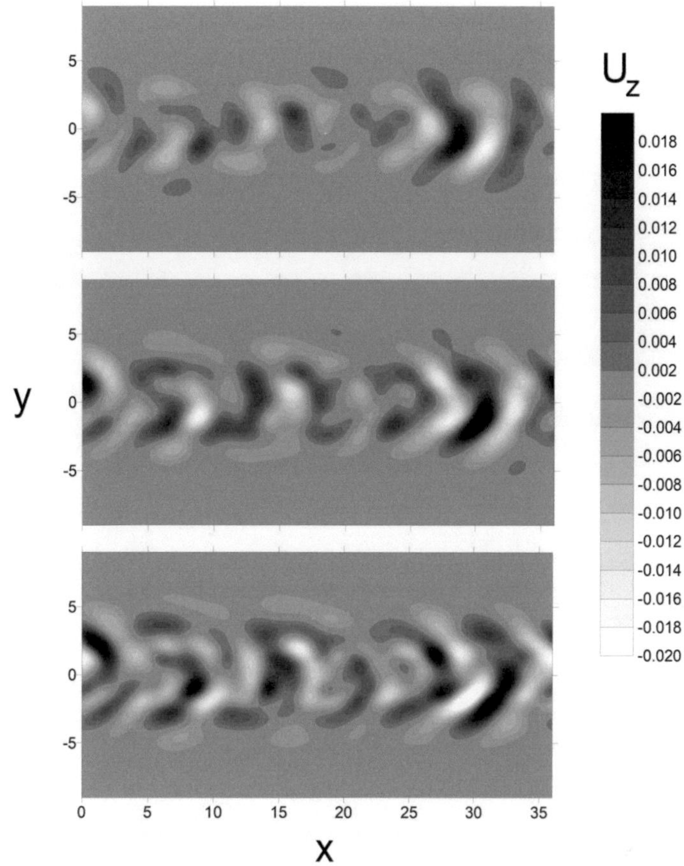

Fig. 9. Instantaneous contours of the vertical velocity U_z in the horizontal (x,y) plane above the jet streamwise axis at $z = 3$ at time moments $Nt =$ 12, 15, 18 (from top to bottom).

In the considered case, an IW radiation source function can be evaluated from the equation for the vertical velocity derived by Phillips (1977). In this equation, the non-linear terms are not discarded but can be regarded as an effective source of IW. This equation is derived in the inviscid case in the form:

$$\frac{\partial^2}{\partial t^2}\left(\nabla^2 U_z\right) + N^2 \nabla_h^2 U_z = Q(x,y,z,t) \tag{4.1}$$

where the IW source function is

$$Q(x,y,z,t) = \frac{\partial^3}{\partial x_\alpha \partial z \partial t}\left(U_j \frac{\partial U_\alpha}{\partial x_j}\right) - \nabla_h^2 \left\{ U_j \frac{\partial b}{\partial x_j} + \frac{\partial}{\partial t}\left(U_j \frac{\partial U_z}{\partial x_j}\right)\right\} \tag{4.2}$$

In (4.1) and (4.2) the notations are as follows: $\nabla^2 \equiv \frac{\partial^2}{\partial x^2} + \frac{\partial^2}{\partial y^2} + \frac{\partial^2}{\partial z^2}$, $\nabla_h^2 \equiv \frac{\partial^2}{\partial x^2} + \frac{\partial^2}{\partial y^2}$ are the full and horizontal Laplasian operators, respectively; summation over the repeated indexes

$\alpha = 1,2$ and j = 1, 2, 3 is performed; $(x_1, x_2, x_3) \equiv (x, y, z)$ are the Cartesian coordinates; $(U_1, U_2, U_3) \equiv (U_x, U_y, U_z)$ are the fluid velocity components; and $b = -Ri\rho$ is the buoyancy.

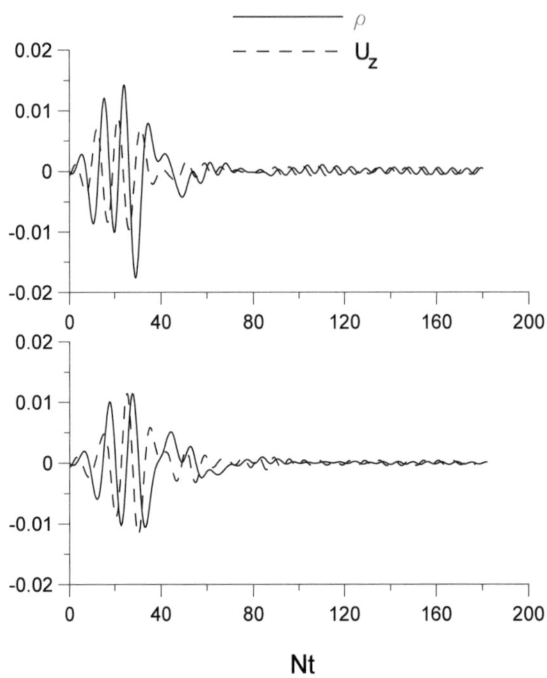

Fig. 10. Temporal development of the vertical velocity and density, U_z and ρ, obtained in DNS at x = 18 and θ = 40^0 (the angle with respect to the vertical) at the distance $\left|y^2 + z^2\right| = 3$ from the jet streamwise axis for Richardson numbers Ri =1 (top frame) and Ri = 3 (bottom frame).

Figure 13 shows an instantaneous distribution of the source function $Q(x, z, y = 0)$ evaluated in DNS in the central vertical plane at time moments Nt = 3 and 6. The figure shows that the distribution of Q is quite inhomogeneous and confined to the jet core region. Therefore, the effective source diameter is of the order of the initial jet flow diameter. The figure indicates also that the growth of the modes with wavenumbers $k \approx k_s$ and $k \approx 0.5k_s$ in the velocity spectra at time moments Nt < 10 (Fig. 5) leads to a modulation of the source function amplitude along the streamwise coordinate . (In Fig. 13 this modulation is more pronounced at time moment Nt = 6.)

Figure 14 presents the temporal development of the volume-averaged dispersion of the IW source function, $< Q(x, y, z, t)^2 >^{1/2}$, obtained in DNS for Ri = 1 and Ri = 3. The figure shows that, for all Ri, the dispersion increases by t = 2.5 by the order of magnitude. The figure shows also that at later times $< Q(x, y, z, t)^2 >^{1/2}$ decays, so that its amplitude is reduced by more than half by t = 5 and becomes negligible at Nt > 10. From the spectra in Fig. 11 the period of internal waves having the maximum amplitude can be evaluated as $NT_{IW} = 2\pi N / \omega \approx 8$ (cf. Fig. 11) and is almost twice as large as compared to the period of the IW source function half-decay.

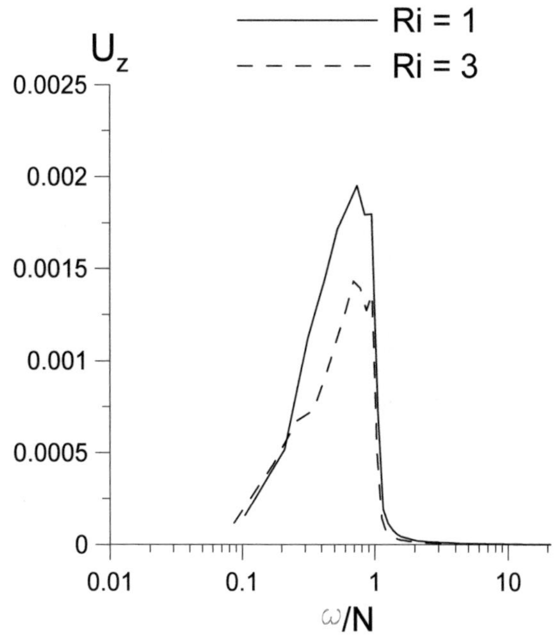

Fig. 11. Spatially averaged frequency spectra of the vertical velocity obtained in DNS for different Richardson numbers.

Thus Q in (4.1) can be regarded as an impulsive source function which brings about IW radiation by the jet flow turbulence. The temporal growth and maximum amplitude of this source function is controlled by the non-linear flow dynamics, not by buoyancy. Let us now make some estimates provided by the impulsive source theory (Zavolskii & Zaytsev 1984, Voisin 1991, BCH 1993) concerning the kinematics and dynamics of the radiated internal waves.

The time interval during which the IW packet, emitted impulsively by the source (S) at the angle θ with respect to the vertical (cf. Fig. 15), comes to the observation point (O) located at the distance $r = \left|y^2 + z^2\right|$, can be estimated with the use of the linear theory as follows. The group velocity (c_g) of internal waves with streamwise wavenumber k and the isophase line at the angle θ with respect to the vertical is evaluated as:

$$c_g = \frac{N}{2k}\sin 2\theta\,. \tag{4.3}$$

Thus the time interval, Nt_1, during which the IW wave packet comes from the source (S) to the observation point (O), is evaluated as:

$$Nt_1 = \frac{2kr}{\sin 2\theta}\,. \tag{4.4}$$

Eq. (4.4) shows that time interval Nt_1 does not depend on N in agreement with the DNS results in Fig. 10. Substitution of r = 3, $\theta = \arctan\sqrt{2}$, and $k = k_s \approx 1.3$ into (4.4) gives the estimate $Nt_1 \approx 8$, which is also in good agreement with the DNS results in Fig. 10.

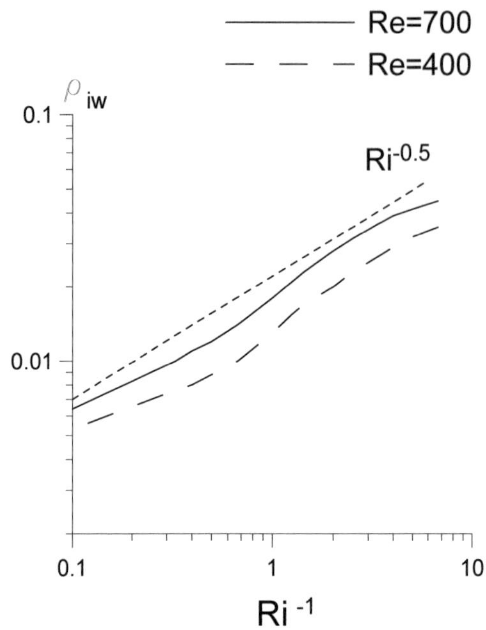

Fig. 12. The internal waves amplitude (ρ_{iw}) vs. inverse Richardson number obtained in DNS for different Reynolds numbers. The dotted line shows the asymptotic solution for the amplitude derived from the linear theory for an impulsive point source.

Figure 10 shows that at sufficiently late times (Nt > 40) the density oscillations at the considered distance from the jet streamwise axis (r = 3) are damped. The time moment (Nt_2) after which the IW amplitude decays at a given location can be estimated as follows. The wavelength λ of IW emitted impulsively by a source (S) at the angle θ with respect to the vertical at the distance r and coming to the observation point (O) at time t (cf. Fig. 15) can be evaluated as:

$$\lambda \approx \frac{2\pi r}{Nt\sin\theta}. \tag{4.5}$$

The theoretical analysis of the internal waves field generated by a sphere performed by Voisin (1994) shows that if λ becomes of the order of the sphere radius, the destructive interference of the waves emitted from different locations on the sphere leads to a decay of the wave amplitude. In the considered case, the cutoff wavelength is of the order of the jet initial diameter, i.e. $\lambda_c \approx 1$. Substitution of $\lambda = \lambda_c$ in (4.5) gives

$$Nt_2 \approx \frac{2\pi r}{\sin\theta}. \tag{4.6}$$

For $r = 3$ and $\theta = \arctan\sqrt{2}$ we obtain from (4.6) an estimate $Nt_2 \approx 30$, which is also in good agreement with the DNS results (Fig. 10). The linear theory also predicts that at times $Nt >> Nt_2$, the incoming waves are mutually cancelled, and there remain only buoyancy

oscillations of the density with the frequency N whose group velocity is identically zero. These buoyancy oscillations are present in Fig. 10 (for $Nt > 40$) and in the distributions of the vertical velocity in the form of columnar disturbances at time moment $Nt = 90$ in Figs. 7, 8.
The asymptotics for the IW amplitude in Fig. 12 is derived as follows. Using the same schematic in Fig. 15 the following estimate can be obtained for the amplitude of internal waves (ρ_{iw}) emitted impulsively by the source (S) and coming to the observation point (O) at time t (cf. e.g. BCH):

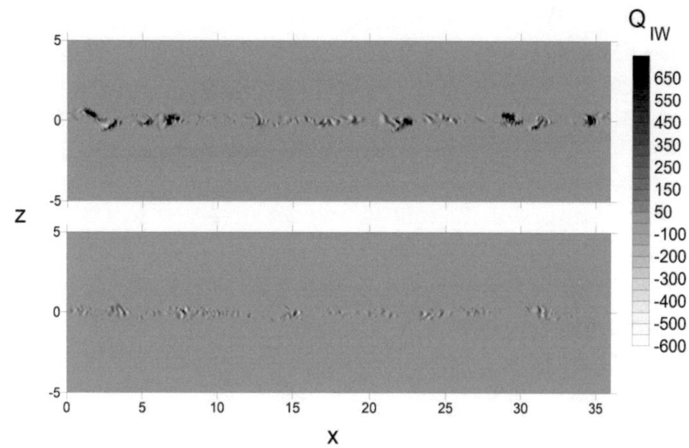

Fig. 13. Instantaneous contours of the IW source function Q_{IW} in the vertical central plane at time moments $Nt = 3$ (top frame) and $Nt = 6$ (bottom frame).

$$\rho_{iw} \sim \frac{\sin\theta\left[Nt\left|\cos\theta\right|\right]^{1/2}}{Nr}. \tag{4.7}$$

Eq. (4.7) shows that ρ_{iw} increases with time. As it was discussed above, the IW amplitude increases until time when the wavelength of incoming waves becomes of the order of the source size, i.e. for $Nt \le Nt_2$. Thus, the maximum amplitude ($\rho_{iw}^{\max}$) can be evaluated from (4.6) and (4.7) as:

$$\rho_{iw}^{\max} \sim \frac{\left[\pi\left|\sin 2\theta\right|\right]^{1/2}}{Nr^{1/2}}. \tag{4.8}$$

Eq. (4.8) shows that IW amplitude is inversely proportional to N, so that $\rho_{iw}^{\max} \sim Ri^{-0.5}$. (Note that the jet flow Froude number equals $Fr_j = 1/\sqrt{Ri}$, so that $\rho_{iw}^{\max} \sim Fr_j$.) This estimate is in good agreement with the results in Fig. 12 for sufficiently small amplitudes (for $\rho_{iw} < 0.03$). The growth of ρ_{iw} saturates for larger amplitudes, probably due to nonlinear effects, and increases for larger Reynolds number.

5. Conclusions and discussion

In the present paper, direct numerical simulation (DNS) has been performed in order to study the process of internal waves radiation by a stratified turbulent jet flow. An initially circular, turbulent jet flow with a Gaussian profile of the mean streamwise velocity component in a fluid with stable, linear density stratification is considered which models the flow created in the far wake of a sphere towed in a stratified fluid at large Froude and Reynolds numbers. The DNS results show that at early times ($Nt < 30$, where N is the buoyancy frequency) there occurs a collapse of the vertical velocity fluctuations which brings about the radiation of internal waves (IW). The characteristic spatial period of these waves is found to be close to the wavelength of the spiral instability mode of a non-stratified jet flow. The IW amplitude decreases with increasing the flow global Richardson number and is well described by the asymptotics $\rho_{iw} \sim Ri^{-0.5}$. At late times ($Nt > 60$) the jet flow becomes quasi-two-dimensional and is dominated by large-scale pancake vortices. At that stage, internal waves are superseded by non-propagating, columnar, small-amplitude buoyancy oscillations confined to a central vertical layer with a thickness of the order of the jet width. A linear model is proposed where the jet turbulence collapsing under the stabilizing effect of the buoyancy forces, is regarded as an impulsive source of IW radiation. The kinematics and dynamics of the internal waves observed in DNS are found to be in good agreement with the model prediction.

Note that a relatively narrow IW frequency range ($40^0 < \arccos\omega / N < 60^0$), similar to the one observed in our DNS, has been also observed in mixing-box experiments (Dohan & Sutherland 2003), in a flow over a vertical obstacle (Sutherland & Linden 1998), during the collapse of a mixed patch (Sutherland et al. 2007) and in LES of a density-stratified boundary layer (Taylor & Sarkar 2007). In these works, several models were proposed to explain the observed IW frequency range, and among them, perhaps, two pertain to the considered case of IW radiation by a temporally developing turbulent jet flow. Dohan and Sutherland (2003) employed stability criteria derived by Sutherland (2001) for low- and high-frequency waves which show that the largest critical IW amplitude corresponds to the waves propagating at $\theta = 45^0$.

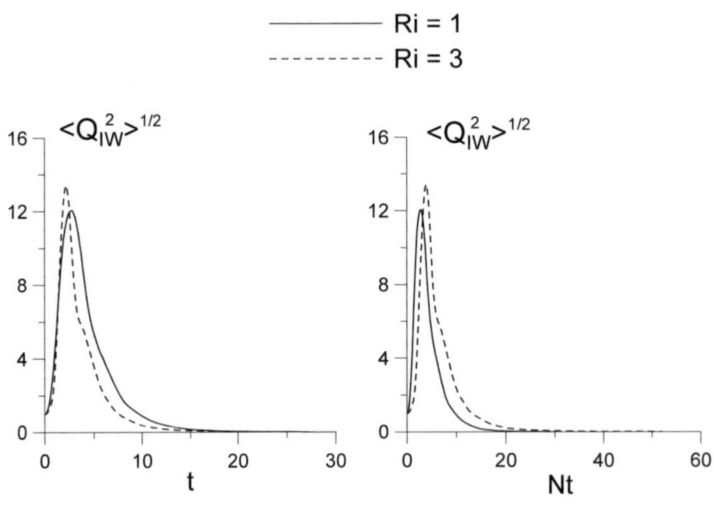

Fig. 14. Temporal development of the volume-averaged dispersion of the IW source function normalized by its initial value for different Richardson numbers. Note that the graph on the right is scaled with the buoyancy frequency.

Other waves become unstable at a lower amplitude and their breaking would explain the observed frequency selection. However, in our case the wave amplitude is much smaller than the critical value $A_{IW} / \lambda_x \approx 0.07$ (cf. Fig. 4 where $\rho_{\max}^{IW} \approx 0.05$ and $\rho_{\max}^{IW} / \lambda_x < 0.01$ for $\lambda_x \approx 5$) and this mechanism is not applicable. Taylor and Sarkar (2007) developed a linear viscous model to estimate the decay in wave amplitude. Waves with high and low frequencies have smaller vertical group velocities and dissipate more as compared to the waves with propagation angle in the vicinity of $\theta \approx 27^0$. Thus the viscous dissipation may cause the observed selected IW frequency range. However, our DNS results show that the selection of the IW propagation angle occurs in the close vicinity of the jet core region ($|z| > 1$) where viscous diffusion effects have not yet accumulated and are negligible as far as the frequency selection is concerned. Therefore, the impulsive source model considered in the present paper provides the most plausible explanation of the IW kinematics and dynamics observed in DNS.

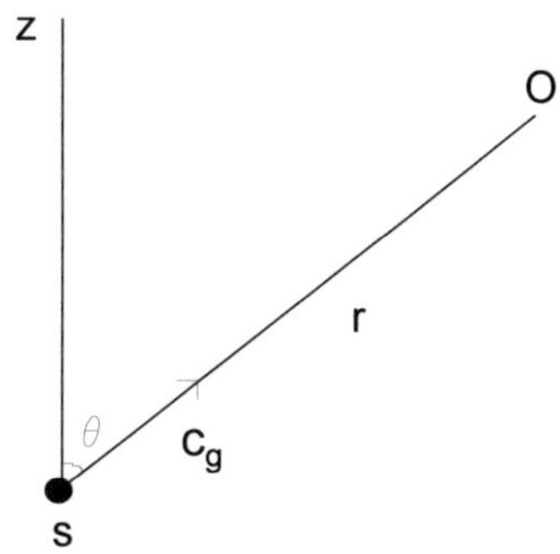

Fig. 15. Schematic of the radiation of the IW packet by an impulsive point source (S) with the group velocity c_g at the angle θ with respect to the vertical axis at the distance r from the observation point (O).

6. Acknowledgement

This work is supported by RFBR (10-05-00339, 10-05-91177, 09-05-00779, 11-05-00455, 10-01-00435).

7. References

Batchelor J.K. & Gill A.E. (1962). Analysis of the stability of axisymmetric jets. *J. Fluid Mech.* Vol. 14, pp. 559-551.

Beckers M., Verzicco R., Clercx H.J.H., & Van Heist G.J.F. (2001) Dynamics of pancake-like vortices in a stratified fluid: experiments, model and numerical simulations. *J. Fluid Mech.*Vol. 433, pp. 1-27.

Bevilaqua P.M. and Lykoudis P.S. (1978). Turbulence memory in self-preserving wakes. *J. Fluid Mech.* Vol. 89, pp. 589-606.

Bonneton P., Chomaz J.M., & Hopfinger E.J. (1993). Internal waves produced by the turbulent wake of a sphere moving horizontally in a stratified fluid. *J. Fluid Mech.* Vol. 254, pp. 23-40.

Brucker K.A. & Sarkar S. (2010a). A comparative study of self-propelled and towed wakes in a stratified fluid. *J. Fluid Mech.* Vol. 652, p. 373. Chomaz J.M., Bonneton P., & Hopfinger E.J. (1993). The structure of the near wake of a sphere moving horizontally in a stratified fluid. *J. Fluid Mech.* Vol. 254, pp. 1-21.

Dohan K. & Sutherland B.R. (2003). Internal waves generated from a turbulent mixed region. *Phys. Fluids* Vol. 15, pp. 488-498.

Dommermuth D.G., Rottman J.W., Innis G.E., & Novikov E.A. (2002). Numerical simulation of the wake of a towed sphere in a weakly stratified fluid. *J. Fluid. Mech.* Vol. 437, pp. 83-101.

Druzhinin O.A. (2009). Generation of Internal Waves by a Turbulent Jet in a Stratified Fluid. *Fluid Dynamics*, Vol. 44, No. 2, pp. 213-223.

Dupont P. & Voisin B. (1996). Internal waves generated by a translating and oscillating sphere. *Dyn. Atm. Oceans.* Vol. 23, pp. 289 - 298.

Gerz T., Shumann U., & Elghobashi S.E. (1989). Direct numerical simulation of stratified homogeneous turbulent shear flows. *J. Fluid Mech.* Vol 200, pp. 563-594.

Gourlay M.J., Arendt S.C., Fritts D.C., & Werne J. (2001). Numerical modeling of initially turbulent wakes with net momentum. *Phys. Fluids*. Vol. 13, pp. 3783-3802.

Javam A., Imberger J. & Armfield S.W. (2000). Numerical study of internal wave-wave interactions in a stratified fluid. *J. Fluid Mech.* Vol. 415, pp. 65-87.

Lin J.T. & Pao Y.H. (1979). Wakes in stratified fluid. *Annu. Rev. Fluid Mech.* Vol. 11, pp. 317-338.

Michalke A. & Hermann G. (1982) On the inviscid instability of a circular jet with external flow. *J. Fluid Mech.* Vol. 114, pp. 343-359 .

Phillips O.M. (1977). *Dynamics of the upper ocean.* 2nd ed. Cambridge Univ. Press.

Plaschko P. (1979). Helical instabilities of slowly divergent jets. *J. Fluid Mech.* Vol. 92, Part 2, pp. 209-215.

Spedding G.R. (1997). The evolution of initially turbulent bluff-body wakes at high internal Froude number. *J. Fluid Mech.* Vol. 337, pp. 283-301.

Spedding G.R. (2001). Anisotropy in turbulence profiles of stratified wakes. *Phys. Fluids*. Vol.13, pp. 2361-2372. Spedding G.R., Browand F.K., & Fincham A.M. (1996). Turbulence, similarity scaling and vortex geometry in the wake of a towed sphere in a stably stratified fluid. *J. Fluid Mech.* Vol. 314, pp. 53-103.

Stadler M.B., Sarkar S. & Brucker K.A. (2010). Effect of the Prandl number on a stratified turbulent wake. *Physics of Fluids*. Vol. 22, p. 095102.

Sutherland B.R. & Peltier W.R. (1994). Turbulence transition and internal wave generation in density stratified jets. *Phys.Fluids*. Vol.6, pp. 1267-1284.

Sutherland B.R. & Linden P.F. (1998). Internal waves excitation from stratified flow over a thin barrier. *J. Fluid Mech.* Vol. 377, pp. 223-252.

Sutherland B.R. (2001). Finite-amplitude internal wavepacket dispersion and breaking. *J. Fluid Mech.* Vol. 429, pp. 343-380.

Sutherland B.R., Chow A.N.F., & Pittman T.P. (2007). The collapse of a mixed patch in stratified fluid. *Phys. Fluids* Vol.19, pp. 116602-1-6.

Taylor J.R. & Sarkar S. (2007). Internal gravity waves generated by a turbulent bottom Ekman layer. *J. Fluid Mech.* Vol. 590, pp. 331-354.

Voisin B. (1991). Internal wave generation in uniformly stratified fluids. Part 1. Green's function and point sources. *J.Fluid Mech.* Vol. 231, pp. 439-480.

Zavolski N.A. & Zaitsev A.A. (1984). Development of internal waves generated by a concentrated pulse source in an infinite uniformly stratified fluid. *J. Appl. Mech. Tech. Phys.* Vol. 25, pp. 862-867.

6

Numerical Study on Flow Structures and Heat Transfer Characteristics of Turbulent Bubbly Upflow in a Vertical Channel

Mitsuru Tanaka
Kyoto Institute of Technology
Japan

1. Introduction

Turbulent bubbly flows have attracted a lot of attention because of their importance for many practical applications such as flows in chemical plants and nuclear power plants. Enhancement of heat transfer by bubble-induced turbulence also attracts a lot of attention from the view point of energy saving. Many studies have been conducted for the motion of bubbles and the characteristics of heat-transfer in turbulent bubbly flows. It is expected that the research on turbulent bubbly flows is accelerated by fully resolved simulations of bubble-turbulence interaction (Tryggvason et al., 2011).

The characteristics of bubbly upflow strongly depend on the motions of bubbles and resulting void fraction distribution in the flow. Serizawa et al. (1975) found that the local void fraction is high near the walls and is lower in the core region of upflow in a pipe. Liu (1993) also found in the experiments of turbulent bubbly upflow in a vertical channel that the void fraction has peaks near the walls for the bubbles smaller than 5-6mm, while it has a peak in the core of the channel for the bubbles larger than 5-6mm. Lu & Tryggvason (2008) also showed in their direct numerical simulations of turbulent bubbly upflow in a vertical channel that nearly spherical bubbles tend to concentrate on the near-wall regions, while strongly deformable bubbles tend to be expelled from the near-wall regions. They also showed that the turbulence structures are changed by the motions of bubbles. The detailed mechanism of turbulence modulation due to the bubbles, however, has not been fully clarified yet.

Some experimental studies have been conducted for heat-transfer enhancement by the injection of bubbles. Tamari & Nishikawa (1976) showed in their experiments of laminar natural convection heat transfer in water from a vertical plate that the heat transfer is enhanced by the injection of air bubbles. The enhancement of heat transfer by bubble injection was studied further in detail by Tokuhiro & Lykoudis (1994) and Kitagawa et al. (2008, 2010). However, the mechanism of the heat-transfer enhancement has not yet been fully clarified especially in turbulent flows.

In the present study, direct numerical simulations have been conducted for turbulent bubbly upflow between two parallel heating walls in order to clarify its heat transfer characteristics. The mechanism of the heat-transfer enhancement is examined by performing simulations with different values of control parameters. The performance of the heat-transfer enhancement is discussed based on the numerical results.

2. Direct numerical simulations of bubbly flows

2.1 Configuration

Figure 1 shows the spatial configuration considered in the present study. The x, y and z axes are assigned to the streamwise, wall-normal and spanwise directions, respectively. The gravitational force is assumed to point to the negative x direction. Here, we consider the system where the flow is heated with a uniform heat flux from both the walls and the mean temperature increases linearly in the streamwise (or vertical) direction. The wall heat flux, q_W, is determined so that the energy (enthalpy) of the system is conserved. In this situation, the wall heat flux is kept nearly constant for stationary turbulence.

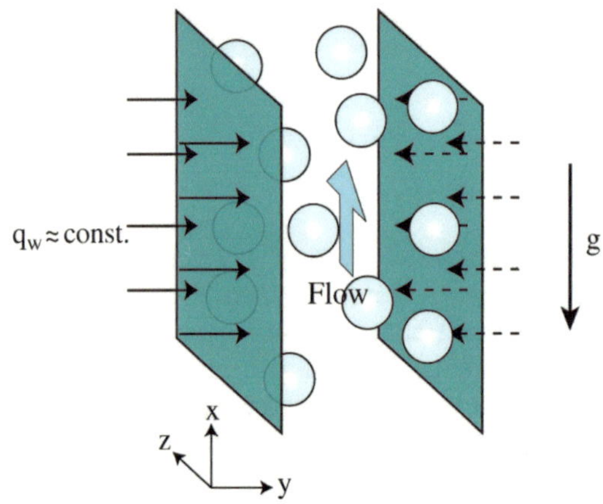

Fig. 1. Configuration.

It is assumed that the fluids are incompressible for both of the liquid (or continuous) and gas (or dispersed) phases in the present study. The buoyancy force originated from the non-uniform spatial distribution of temperature is assumed to be negligibly small. It is also assumed that the fluid properties do not depend on the temperature.

2.2 Basic equations

In this study, simulations of the bubbly flow are conducted by using VOF (Volume of Fluid) method. In the VOF mothod, the fraction of the bubble gas, F, occupying each computational grid cell is advected by using the equation

$$\frac{\partial F}{\partial t} = -u_i \frac{\partial F}{\partial x_i}, \tag{1}$$

where $x = (x_1,x_2,x_3) = (x,y,z)$ denotes the position, and $u = (u_1,u_2,u_3) = (u,v,w)$ represents the fluid velocity. In the present study, summation convention is applied to repeated subscripts if not otherwise specified.

The motions of incompressible fluid are governed by the Navier-Stokes (momentum) equations

$$\rho\left(\frac{\partial u_i}{\partial t} + u_k \frac{\partial u_i}{\partial x_k}\right) = -\frac{\partial (p-P)}{\partial x_i} + \frac{\partial \tau_{ij}}{\partial x_j} + f_{\sigma i} - \left(\rho - \langle\rho\rangle\right) g\delta_{i1} + \beta\delta_{i1}, \tag{2}$$

supplemented with the continuity equation

$$\frac{\partial u_k}{\partial x_k} = 0, \tag{3}$$

where

$$\tau_{ij} = \mu\left(\frac{\partial u_j}{\partial x_i} + \frac{\partial u_i}{\partial x_j}\right) \tag{4}$$

is the viscous stress. Here, ρ and μ denote the density and viscosity of the fluid. Their values for each grid cell are respectively given by the simple average,

$$\rho = F\rho_d + (1-F)\rho_c, \tag{5}$$

and the harmonic average,

$$\frac{1}{\mu} = F\frac{1}{\mu_d} + (1-F)\frac{1}{\mu_c}, \tag{6}$$

of the two fluids. The subscripts d and c denote the dispersed and continuous phases, respectively. p is the pressure and P denotes the mean pressure linearly decreasing in the vertical direction. $\mathbf{f}_\sigma$ represents the volume force associated with the interfacial surface tension of the bubbles, and g denotes the gravitational acceleration. $\langle \cdot \rangle$ represents the spatial average over the whole computational domain. The last term in Eq.(2) represents the total driving force exerted on the fluids flowing through the channel, and

$$\beta = -\frac{dP}{dx} - \langle \rho \rangle g. \tag{7}$$

For stationary turbulence, the temporal average of β equals to τ_W/δ, where τ_W represents the wall shear stress and δ denotes the channel half width.

Since the mean temperature increases linearly downstream, the temperature T is decomposed as $T = Gx - \Theta$, where G denotes the mean temperature gradient in the streamwise direction and Θ represents the temperature variance. The governing equation for Θ (or energy equation) is described by

$$(\rho C_P)\left(\frac{\partial \Theta}{\partial t} + u_k\frac{\partial \Theta}{\partial x_k} - Gu_1\right) = \frac{\partial}{\partial x_j}\left(k\frac{\partial \Theta}{\partial x_j}\right), \tag{8}$$

where

$$\rho C_P = F\rho_d C_{Pd} + (1-F)\rho_c C_{Pc} \tag{9}$$

and

$$\frac{1}{k} = F\frac{1}{k_d} + (1-F)\frac{1}{k_c} \tag{10}$$

represent the volume-averaged heat capacity (per unit volume) and heat conductivity, respectively. Here, C_P denotes specific heat.

2.3 Control parameters

The parameters which control the system considered in the present study are the channel Reynolds number Re_m, Eötvös number Eo, Morton number M, Archimedes number Ar, dispersed-phase Prandtl number $\mathrm{Pr}_d = \nu_d / a_d$, continuous-phase Prandtl number $\mathrm{Pr}_c = \nu_c / a_c$, the density ratio ρ_d / ρ_c, the viscosity ratio μ_d / μ_c, and the ratio of specific heat, C_{Pd} / C_{Pc}, where $a_d = k_d / (\rho_d C_{Pd})$ and $a_c = k_c / (\rho_c C_{Pc})$ are thermal diffusivities in the dispersed and continuous phases, respectively. First four parameters are defined as

$$\mathrm{Re}_m = \frac{2U_m \delta}{\nu_c}, Eo = \frac{\Delta \rho g d_0^2}{\sigma}, M = \frac{g \mu_c^4 \Delta \rho}{\rho_c^2 \sigma^3}, Ar = \frac{\rho_c \Delta \rho g d_0^3}{\mu_c^2}, \tag{11}$$

where $U_m = \langle u \rangle$, ν, d_0, and σ denote the mean velocity, kinematic viscosity, bubble diameter, and the surface tension coefficient, respectively. $\Delta \rho = \rho_c - \rho_d$ represents the density difference between the two phases.

The wall units are used to normalize the time, length, velocity and temperature. The friction velocity is defined by $u_\tau = \sqrt{\tau_W / \rho_c}$. The friction time and the friction length are defined by $t_\tau = \nu_c / u_\tau^2$ and $l_\tau = \nu_c / u_\tau$, respectively. The friction Reynolds number is defined as

$$\mathrm{Re}_\tau = \frac{u_\tau \delta}{\nu_c} = \frac{\delta}{l_\tau} = \frac{\mathrm{Re}_m}{2U_m^+}, \tag{12}$$

where the superscript '+' represents the values normalized by the wall units. The temperature is normalized by the friction temperature defined by

$$\Theta_\tau = \frac{q_W}{\rho_c C_{Pc} u_\tau}, \tag{13}$$

where q_W denotes the wall heat flux.

Eötvös number, Eo, represents the ratio of the buoyancy and surface-tension forces, while Archimedes number, Ar, represents the ratio of the buoyancy and viscous forces. Morton number, M, is not independent from Eötvös number Eo and Archimedes number Ar and is expressed as $M = Eo^2 / Ar^2$. The 'buoyancy parameter', which is defined by

$$Bu = \frac{\beta}{g \Delta \rho} = \left(\frac{\mathrm{Re}_\tau^2}{Ar} \right) \left(\frac{d_0}{\delta} \right)^3, \tag{14}$$

is also an important parameter. The buoyancy effect of bubbles may be large when this parameter is small.

The mean temperature

$$\Theta_m = \frac{\langle (\rho C_P) \Theta u \rangle}{\langle (\rho C_P) u \rangle}, \tag{15}$$

is used as the representative temperature of the fluid in the present study. The heat transfer coefficient can be defined as

$$h_t = \frac{q_W}{\Theta_m - \Theta_W}, \tag{16}$$

where Θ_W is the averaged temperature variance at the walls. The enhancement of heat transfer can be estimated by the Nusselt number which is defined by

$$Nu = \frac{2\delta h_t}{k_c} = \frac{2\mathrm{Re}_\tau \mathrm{Pr}_c}{\Theta_m^+ - \Theta_W^+}. \tag{17}$$

2.4 Numerical methods

2.4.1 PLIC-VOF algorithm

In the present study, we use a PLIC-VOF (Piecewise Linear Interface Calculation - Volume of Fluid) method to capture the interface of the bubble. The position of the interface is determined by the volume fraction F of the bubble. $F = 1$ represents a cell filled with the gas (dispersed-phase fluid) of the bubble, while $F = 0$ indicates that the cell is filled with the continuous-phase liquid. The cells of $0 < F < 1$ include the interface. The time evolution of F is estimated with a PLIC-VOF algorithm (Rudman; 1998, Scardovelli & Zaleski, 2003). In PLIC-VOF algorithm, we take account of the slope of the interface. Young and Parkar's method is used to estimate the normal vectors of the interface from the values of F in adjacent cells (Parker & Youngs, 1992). A mass-conserving scheme which also satisfies the consistency condition ($0 \le F \le 1$) is applied for the advection of the VOF function. The EI-LE (Eulerian implicit Lagrangian explicit) scheme (Scardovelli & Zaleski, 2003; Aulisa et al., 2003; Aulisa et al., 2007), which is an advection scheme originally designed for two-dimensional incompressible velocity field, is applied for the three-dimensional (3D) incompressible velocity field. The extension is conducted by decomposing the 3D velocity field into three two-component velocity fields by the use of Fourier transformation in the x and z directions.

2.4.2 Interfacial tension

In the continuum surface force (CSF) method, the interfacial tension force is calculated as

$$\mathbf{f}_\sigma = \sigma \kappa \mathbf{n} \delta_S, \tag{18}$$

where σ is the coefficient of the interfacial tension, κ is the curvature, $\mathbf{n}$ is the normal to the interface, and δ_S is a delta function concentrated on the interface. The interfacial tension force in Eq.(2) is calculated by using Eq.(18) and the relation $\mathbf{n}\delta_S = -\nabla F$, which holds in the continuum limit. The curvature, κ, is calculated with a high degree of accuracy by using height functions (Lorstad & Fuchs, 2004), which effectively eliminates spurious currents for a static drop (Francois et al., 2006).

2.4.3 Collision between bubbles

In a general VOF method, two interfaces inside the same grid cell cannot be distinguished. Thus, coalescence occurs when two bubbles are very close to each other. To avoid this type of coalescence, separate VOF functions are assigned to the bubbles. A repulsive force is applied when two bubbles come very close to each other to avoid the overlap of the bubbles. Suppose Bubble 1 and Bubble 2 approach each other and their VOF functions are given by F_1 and F_2. We make use of their smoothed functions $\tilde{F}_1$ and $\tilde{F}_2$ which are obtained by the convolution using the kernel:

$$K(r,\gamma)=\begin{cases}1-6(r/\gamma)^2+6(r/\gamma)^3 & (r/\gamma<1/2)\\ 2(r/\gamma)^3 & (1/2\le r/\gamma<1)\\ 0 & (1\le r/\gamma)\end{cases} \quad . \tag{19}$$

The repulsive force

$$\mathbf{f}_{R1}=-CF_1\nabla\tilde{F}_2, \tag{20}$$

is exerted on Bubble 1, where C is a positive constant. Similarly, the force

$$\mathbf{f}_{R2}=-CF_2\nabla\tilde{F}_1, \tag{21}$$

is exerted on Bubble 2. The integral of $\mathbf{f}_{R1}+\mathbf{f}_{R2}$ over the whole computational domain is exactly zero. Therefore, this repulsive force does not affect the total momentum in the system. In the present study, we set $\gamma=3\Delta x$ – $4\Delta x$, where Δx is the grid spacing. Smoothed VOF functions are also utilized for the estimation of the fluid and thermal properties in Eqs.(5), (6), (9) and (10) with $\gamma=2\Delta x$ (Lorstad & Fuchs, 2004).

2.4.4 Time integration and spatial discretization

The momentum and energy equations are solved on a collocated grid by using the finite difference schemes. All of the velocity components and the pressure are defined at the center of the grid cell. The time-integration is based on a fractional-step method where a pseudo-pressure is used to correct the velocity field so that the continuity equation is satisfied. A balanced force algorithm developed by Francois et al. (2006) is used to suppress unphysical flows (or spurious currents) resulting from the unbalance between the interfacial tension and the pressure difference across the interface. Poisson's equation for the pseudo-pressure is solved by using a multigrid method.

The QUICK method (Leonard, 1979) is applied in the finite differencing of the convection terms of momentum and energy equations. The second-order central difference scheme is applied for the finite differencing of the viscous terms of the momentum equations and the diffusion term of the energy equation. The 2nd-order improved Euler method is used for the time-integration of the convective and viscous (or diffusion) terms (Rudman, 1998). The velocity field at $t^n+\Delta t/2$ is used to advect the VOF function.

2.5 Validation of numerical scheme

We compared the rise velocity of a bubble in otherwise quiescent fluid with that in Bunner & Tryggvason (2002). The bubble rise velocity can be described by the bubble Reynolds number, $\mathrm{Re}_d=u_b d_0/\nu_c$, where u_b and d_0 denote the rise velocity and the bubble diameter, respectively. Numerical parameters were the same as that in Bunner & Tryggvason (2002). The computational conditions are summarized in Table 1. There cases with different grid resolutions were examined with $32\times32\times32$, $64\times64\times64$, and $128\times128\times128$ grid points. For the three cases, the bubble diameter equals to $15.5\Delta x$, $31.1\Delta x$, and $62.2\Delta x$, respectively. Here, Δx denotes the grid spacing. Periodic boundary conditions were imposed in all directions. Domain size was set to be $2\pi\times2\pi\times2\pi$.

Eötvös number	1.0
Archimedes number	900
Density ratio	0.02
Viscosity ratio	0.02
Void fraction	0.06

Table 1. Computational conditions for a rising bubble.

Fig. 2 shows the time evolution of the bubble rise velocity for the three cases. The horizontal straight line of $\mathrm{Re}_d = 31.74$ represents the terminal velocity in the case of $d_0 = 38.9\Delta x$ in Bunner & Tryggvason (2002). The tendency of convergence is clearly seen as the grid resolution is increased. This indicates the validity of our numerical scheme.

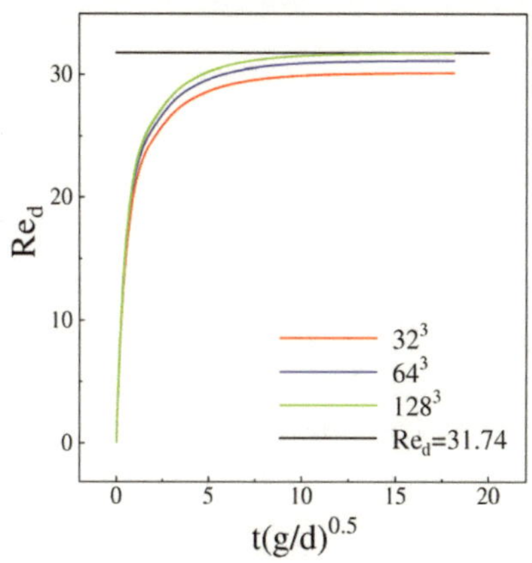

Fig. 2. Time evolution of rise velocities for a single bubble.

It was found by an oscillation test that more than 24 grid points per bubble diameter are needed to simulate oscillation motions of bubbles. A static drop test was also conducted under the same condition as in Francois et al. (2006) to find that the magnitude of the spurious current is as small as theirs.

2.6 Computational conditions

Since many grid points are needed to resolve the fluid motions around and inside the bubbles, simulations are limited to low Reynolds numbers with small computational domains. We utilize so-called 'minimal turbulent channel' in the present study. The simulations are performed on the domain of $\pi\delta \times 2\delta \times (\pi/2)\delta$ as in Lu & Tryggvason (2008). In the simulation of Lu & Tryggvason (2008), the constant pressure gradient to drive the flow was set so that the friction Reynolds number Re_τ was 127.2. Therefore, the size of the computational domain was $400 \times 254.4 \times 200$ in wall units, and the domain was sufficiently large to sustain turbulence, as was shown in Jimenez & Moin (1991). The resulting channel Reynolds number was 3786 in their simulation of the single-phase turbulent flow. In their flow laden with nearly spherical bubbles, the channel Reynolds number was reduced to less than 2000, which may be too low to examine turbulence statistics of a bubbly flow. In the present study, the channel Reynolds number is set at 3786, and the volume flow rate is kept constant. Notice that the friction velocity (and the friction Reynolds number) is generally changed by the effects of the bubbles.

Non-slip boundary conditions are imposed in the wall-normal direction for the velocity components. Periodic boundary conditions are imposed in the x and z directions for the velocity, the pressure variance, $p-P$, and the temperature variance, Θ. As mentioned above, we assume a constant temperature gradient in the vertical (streamwise) direction. We impose a uniform heat flux from both walls. In the present study, the energy (enthalpy) of the system is kept constant, so that the instantaneous wall heat flux q_W is given by

$$q_W = \frac{1}{2} G \int_0^{2\delta} \overline{\rho C_P u}(y) dy. \tag{22}$$

Here, $\overline{\cdot}$ represents the spatial average in the x and z directions.

2.6.1 Bubbly flow

The simulations are performed with $256 \times 256 \times 128$ rectangular grid cells. We set the fluid density inside the bubbles (density of the dispersed-phase fluid) to be one-tenth of that of the liquid (continuous-phase fluid) $(\rho_d/\rho_c = 0.1)$, and we set the viscosities to be equal $(\mu_d/\mu_c = 1.0)$ to reduce the computational cost as in Lu & Tryggvason (2008). Air bubbles with a diameter of 1-2mm in water are considered in the present study. Eötvös number, Morton number, and Archimedes number of the bubbles are 0.36, 2.91×10^{-10}, and 12700, respectively. These parameters correspond to a 1.64mm air bubble in the fluid whose viscosity is 1.84 times higher than that of the water at room temperature. Twelve bubbles with a diameter of 0.4δ are introduced randomly into the turbulent single-phase flow in the channel. Computational conditions are summarized in Table 2.

Although most of the parameters employed here are quite close to those in Lu & Tryggvason (2008), the buoyancy parameter, Bu, is considerably higher than their value of 0.018. This indicates that the buoyancy effects are less important in our simulation. In order to assess the importance of the buoyancy effects, we conduct a simulation for neutrally buoyant droplets, where Bu is infinite , as will be explained in 2.6.2.

The thermal properties employed in the present simulation are summarized in Table. 3. The Prandtl number for the liquid (continuous-phase fluid) is set at a low value of 2.0 ($\mathrm{Pr}_c = 2.0$) to maintain high numerical accuracy. The Prandtl number for the gas (dispersed-phase fluid) is also set at 2.0 ($\mathrm{Pr}_d = 2.0$). In this case, the ratio of heat capacities per unit volume, $\rho_d C_{Pd}/\rho_c C_{Pc}$, is 0.1 and the ratio of thermal conductivity, k_d/k_c , is 1.0, respectively. Hereafter, we call this run Case B1. For comparison, three cases (Cases B2-B4) with different thermal porperties are simulated. In Case B2, we change the Prandtl number of the continuous-phase fluid to 1.0 to examine Prandtl number dependence of the heat transfer characteristics of the turbulent bubbly flow. In Cases B3 and B4, we change the thermal properties inside the bubbles. In Case B3, the thermal conductivity inside the bubbles is set at $1/10$ of that in the surrounding liquid in order to examine the heat insulating effect due to the bubbles. In Case B4, the specific heat of the gas inside the bubble is set to be 10 times larger ($\rho_d C_{Pd}/\rho_c C_{Pc} = 1.0$) to clarify the effect of lower heat capacity inside the bubbles.

In order to check the accuracy of the simulation, we have conducted a simulation under the same physical conditions with a lower grid resolution. The parameters for this simulation are summarized in Table 4.

Channel Reynolds number	3786
Domain size	$\pi\delta \times 2\delta \times (\pi / 2)\delta$
Number of grid points	$256 \times 256 \times 128$
Time increment	$\Delta t^+ = 4.54 \times 10^{-3}$ $\Delta t/T_\sigma = 0.063$
Grid resolution	$\Delta x^+ = \Delta z^+ = 2.00$ $\Delta y^+ = 0.38 - 2.17$
Density ratio	0.1
Viscosity ratio	1.0
Diameter of bubbles	$0.4\delta(\approx 32.6\Delta x)$
Number of bubbles	12
Eötvös number	0.36
Morton number	2.91×10^{-10}
Archimedes number	1.27×10^4
Void fraction	0.04
Buoyancy parameter *Bu*	8.17×10^{-2}

Table 2. Computational conditions for the bubbly flow. T_σ represents the timescale of the smallest resolved capillary wave, and is described by $T_\sigma = \left[(\rho_c + \rho_d)(\Delta x)^3/\pi\sigma\right]^{1/2}$.

Case	B1	B2	B3	B4
Prandtl number (liquid)	2.0	1.0	2.0	2.0
Prandtl number (bubble)	2.0	1.0	20.0	20.0
Ratio of specific heat	1.0	1.0	1.0	10.0
Ratio of thermal conductivity	1.0	1.0	0.1	1.0

Table 3. Thermal properties for the bubbly flow.

Number of grid points	$192 \times 192 \times 96$
Time increment	$\Delta t^+ = 7.89 \times 10^{-3}$ $\Delta t/T_\sigma = 0.073$
Grid resolution	$\Delta x^+ = \Delta z^+ = 2.64$ $\Delta y^+ = 0.51 - 2.79$
Diameter of bubbles	$0.4\delta(\approx 24.4\Delta x)$

Table 4. Computational conditions for the simulation with lower grid resolution.

2.6.2 Droplet flow

As mentioned above, we conduct a simulation for neutrally buoyant droplets in order to assess the importance of the buoyancy effects. The density ratio of the dispersed-phase fluid is changed to 1.0 from 0.1 in the bubbly flow. Computational conditions are summarized in

Table 5. Two cases with different Prandtl numbers are examined. Since the fluid density is uniform throughout the computation domain, the pressure Poisson equation is directly solved by the use of fast Fourier transform. The time increment and grid spacings are $\Delta t^+ = 7.56\times10^{-3}$, $\Delta x^+ = \Delta z^+ = 2.34$, $\Delta y^+ = 0.35-1.93$.

Case	D1	D2
Density ratio	1.0	1.0
Viscosity ratio	1.0	1.0
Prandtl number (continuous)	2.0	1.0
Prandtl number (dispersed)	2.0	1.0
Ratio of specific heat	1.0	1.0
Ratio of thermal conductivity	1.0	1.0

Table 5. Computational conditions for the droplet flow.

2.6.3 Single-phase flow

For comparison, a long simulation without bubbles was also conducted at the same channel Reynolds number of 3786 and Prandtl numbers of $\mathrm{Pr}_c = 1, 2$. The computational conditions are summarized in Table 6. Statistical quantities were obtained by taking averages over the period of about 30,000 in wall units. The time-averaged friction Reynolds number was 127.2 as in Lu and Tryggvason (2008).

Number of grid points	$96\times192\times96$
Grid type	Collocated grid
Convection term	QUICK
Time increment	$\Delta t^+ = 4.66\times10^{-2}$
Grid spacing	$\Delta x^+ = 4.16, \Delta z^+ = 2.08$ $\Delta y^+ = 0.30-2.42$

Table 6. Computational conditions for the single-phase flow

Number of grid points	$48\times128\times48$
Grid type	Staggered grid
Convection term	2nd central (consistent scheme)
Time increment	$\Delta t^+ = 4.66\times10^{-2}$
Grid spacing	$\Delta x^+ = 8.33, \Delta z^+ = 4.16$ $\Delta y^+ = 0.30-4.12$

Table 7. Computational conditions for the centered 2nd-order scheme.

In order to estimate the effects of the numerical diffusion caused by the QUICK scheme, a simulation was conducted by using the centered 2nd-order scheme (consistent scheme) for the convection terms in a staggered grid system (Kawamura et al., 1998). It is found that the amplitude of the streamwise component of vorticity is slightly (about 1.5%) lower in the case with the QUICK scheme than that with the centered 2nd-order scheme. The Nusselt number for higher Prandtl number of $\mathrm{Pr}_c = 2$ is also slightly (about 1%) lower. It can be concluded that the effects of the numerical diffusion due to the QUICK scheme are small.

3. Results and discussion

The turbulent bubbly (or droplet) flow and the temperature field reached a fully developed state about $t^+ = 1000$ after the injection of the bubbles (or the droplets). After the turbulence reached the fully developed state, the simulation has further been conducted for the period of $700\,t_\tau$ (or $1400\,t_\tau$) for the bubbly (or droplet) turbulent flow to obtain statistical quantities. The longer simulation for $2900\,t_\tau$ has been performed for the bubbly flow with the lower grid resolution.

Since the simulations are performed under the condition of constant volume flow rate, the wall friction and therefore wall units are generally changed by the injection of the bubbles. Hereafter, the normalization of physical quantities is performed by the use of either the wall units, $u_\tau, t_\tau, l_\tau, \Theta_\tau$, in each flow or those, $u_{\tau 0}, t_{\tau 0}, l_{\tau 0}, \Theta_{\tau 0}$, in the single-phase flow, depending on the situation. The quantities normalized by the wall units in the single-phase flow are denoted by the superscript '+0'.

3.1 Flow structures of turbulent bubbly flow

3.1.1 Wall shear stress and friction Reynolds number

In table 8, the relative magnitude of the wall shear stress τ_W/τ_{W0} and the friction Reynolds number $\mathrm{Re}_\tau/\mathrm{Re}_{\tau 0}$ are shown for the bubbly and droplet flows. Note that these two quantities are related with the wall units as

$$\frac{\mathrm{Re}_\tau}{\mathrm{Re}_{\tau 0}} = \frac{l_{\tau 0}}{l_\tau} = \frac{u_\tau}{u_{\tau 0}}, \quad \frac{\tau_W}{\tau_{W0}} = \frac{t_{\tau 0}}{t_\tau} = \left(\frac{\mathrm{Re}_\tau}{\mathrm{Re}_{\tau 0}}\right)^2 \tag{23}$$

when δ and ν_c are fixed. The wall shear stress is increased by the factor of 1.65 (or 1.37) for the bubbly (or droplet) flow.

	τ_W/τ_{W0}	$\mathrm{Re}_\tau/\mathrm{Re}_{\tau 0}$
Bubbly flow	1.65 (1.61)	1.28 (1.27)
Droplet flow	1.37	1.17

Table 8. Wall shear stress and friction Reynolds number. The values in the parentheses represent those for the bubbly flow with the lower grid resolution.

3.1.2 Bubble motions and vortices

Fig. 3(a) shows a typical snapshot of the bubbles and the vortical structures visualized by the second invariant of velocity gradient tensor, $Q^+ = 0.0125$. It is clearly seen that the bubbles tend to collect on the near-wall regions of the channel. The bubbles are slightly deformed form the spherical shape. As is shown in Fig. 3(b), the droplets are distributed rather uniformly throughout the channel though some droplets are located close to the walls as in the case of the bubbly flow.

It is seen in the case of the bubbly flow that the vortices are locally activated by the bubbles in the near-wall regions. In the case of the droplet flow, strong vortices are observed even in the central region of the channel. Notice that the normalized values of Q are used for visualization in Figs. 3 and that the vortices are considerably strengthened due to the injection of the bubbles.

Figs. 4(a) and 4(b) show the time evolution of the locations of the bubbles and the droplets, respectively. The bubbles rise along the walls almost all the time. As is shown in Fig. 4(c), the void fraction has sharp peaks near the walls as a result of bubble accumulation toward the walls. Horizontal motions are much more noticeable for the droplets. Some droplets rise along the walls as the bubbles, however. This is also confirmed by the profile of the volume fraction of the droplet in Fig. 4(c).

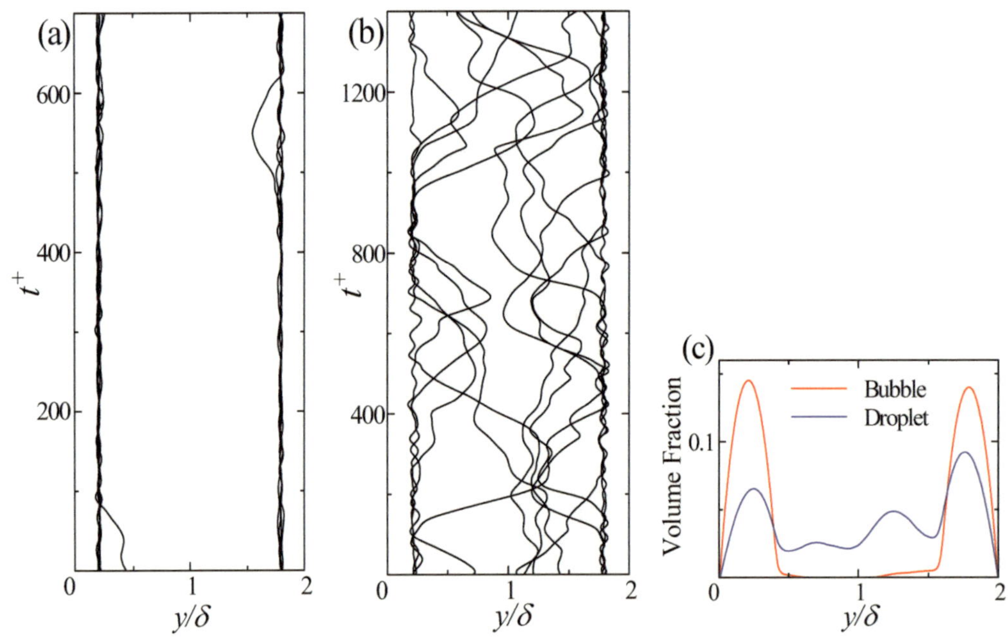

Fig. 4. The path of (a) bubbles and (b) droplets. (c) Profiles of volume fraction.

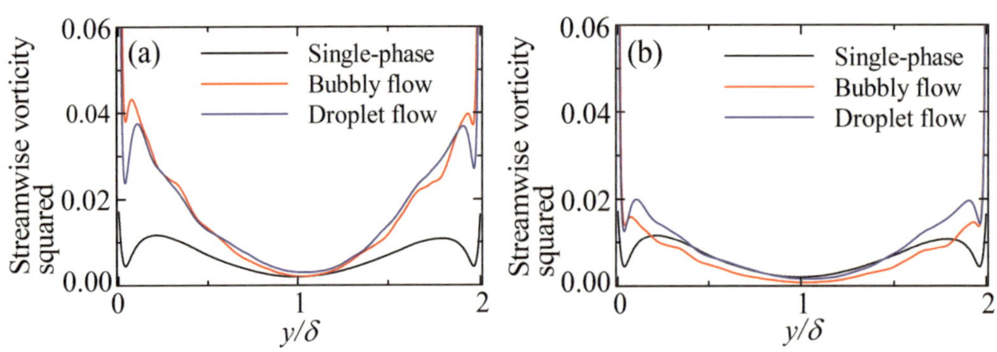

Fig. 5. Profiles of streamwise vorticity squared that is normalized by (a) $t_{\tau 0}^{-2}$ and (b) t_{τ}^{-2}.

Fig. 5(a) shows the profiles of the streamwise vorticity squared which is normalized by the friction time for the single-phase flow, $\left\langle(\omega_x^{+0})^2\right\rangle$. The vorticities in the bubbly and droplet flows have high values compared with the single-phase flow, indicating that the generation of the streamwise vortices is enhanced by the injection of the bubbles or droplets. There are peaks at $y/\delta = 0.07$ and 1.93 near the walls in the profile of the bubbly flow. The corresponding peaks for the droplet flow are more distantly positioned from the walls, and the peaks in the single-phase flow are further away from the walls. In general, these peaks approach the walls as the friction Reynolds number is increased. We have conducted a simulation of the single-phase turbulent flow at a higher $\mathrm{Re}_\tau (\approx 160)$, which is comparable with that of the turbulent bubbly flow, to find that the peaks in the vorticity profile are located at $y/\delta = 0.19$ and 1.81. This indicates that the bubbles (or droplets) rising along the walls enhance the generation of quasi-streamwise vortices in the regions very close to the walls. This is verified by the visualization of the vortical structures around the bubbles (see Figs. 3).

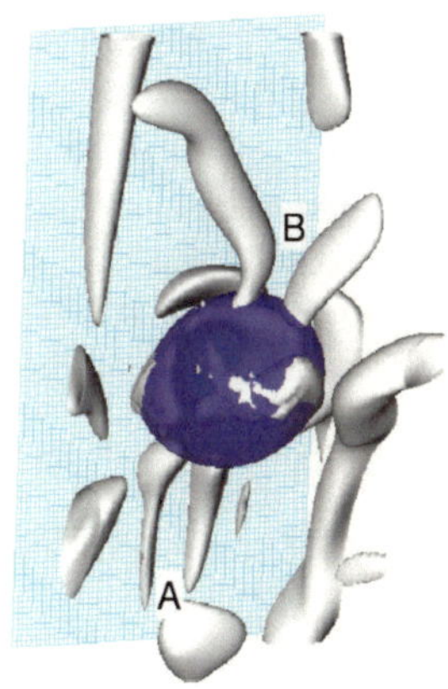

Fig. 6. A bubble and vortices. Light blue represents a wall.

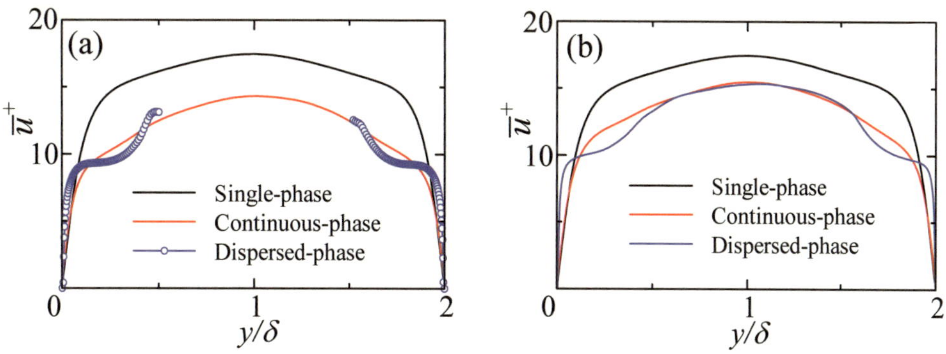

Fig. 7. The mean velocity profile for (a) bubbly flow and (b) droplet flow.

In the profile for the bubbly flow, there are small bumps at $y/\delta \approx 0.3$ and 1.7 in addition to the two peaks near the walls. As is shown in Fig. 6, these peaks and bumps correspond to the trailing vortices around the bubbles. Relatively small trailing vortices are seen on the wall side of the bubble (e.g. a vortex pair marked by A), while relatively large vortices are also seen on the side of the channel center (e.g. vortices marked by B).

In Fig. 5(b), the profiles of the streamwise vorticity squared which is normalized by the friction time for each flow, $\langle(\omega_x^+)^2\rangle$, are shown. The vortices is relatively weak in the central region of the channel in the bubbly flow.

3.1.3 Mean velocity profiles

Fig. 7(a) shows the mean velocity profiles for the bubbly flow. The black line represents the liquid velocity in the single-phase flow, and the red line and blue circles represent the liquid and gas velocities in the bubbly flow, respectively. Note that the gas velocity is not the rise velocity of the bubble centroids, but just the velocity of the gas inside the bubbles. Note also that the bubble diameter is 0.4δ. Since the wall shear stress is increased with the flow rate fixed, the mean velocity normalized by the friction velocity is reduced compared with that for the single-phase flow.

The gas velocity is higher than the liquid velocity near the walls, while it is lower in the regions around $y/\delta = 0.25$ and 1.75. The bubbles are exposed to high shear near the walls. The balance between this shear stress and the interfacial surface tension leads to the higher gas velocity near the walls and the lower gas velocity on the central side of the channel. In fact, the streamwise velocity is homogenized by the circulating flow inside the bubble.

Fig. 7(b) shows the mean velocity profiles for the droplet flow. The velocity for the dispersed-phase fluid is remarkably lower than that for the continuous-phase fluid in the regions around $y/\delta = 0.25$ and 1.75, indicating that the droplets are moving more slowly than the surrounding fluid.

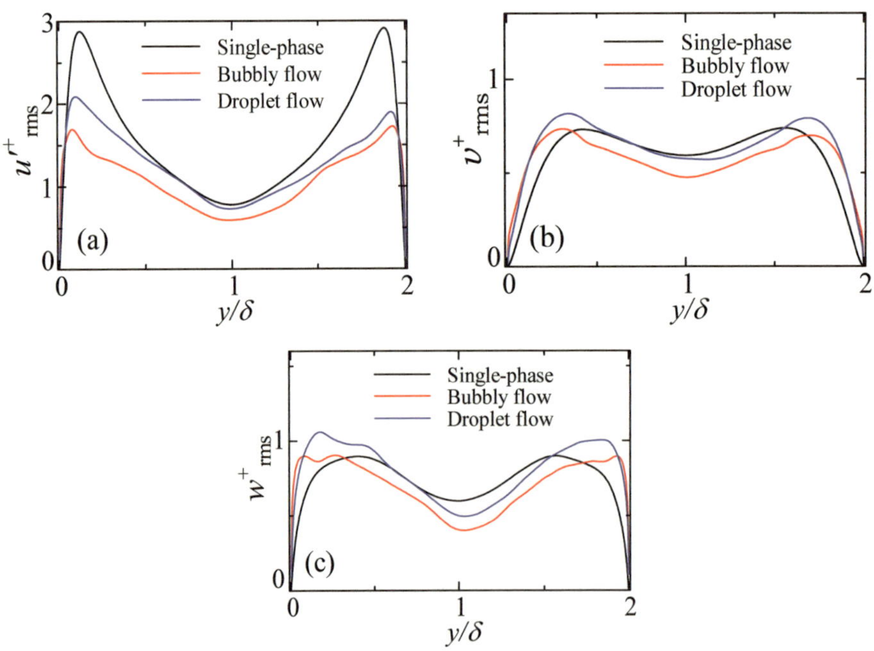

Fig. 8. The rms velocity fluctuation profiles.

3.1.4 Turbulence intensities

Figs. 8 show the profiles of velocity fluctuations of the liquid (continuous-phase fluid) for the single-phase, bubbly and droplet flows. In the case of the droplet flow, the streamwise component of the turbulence intensities decreases near the walls due to the droplets. The wall-normal and spanwise components, on the other hand, increase due to the presence of the droplets in the near-wall regions. The fluid motions normal to the interfaces of droplets are directly suppressed or induced by the presence of droplets. The droplets, on the other hand, indirectly affect the fluid motions. The turbulence is augmented by the droplets, and the redistribution mechanism of Reynolds stresses is enhanced. This may be one of the reasons for the decrease in the streamwise component and the increase in the wall-normal and spanwise components near the walls.

The profiles of turbulence intensities in the bubbly flow resemble those in the droplet flow when they all are normalized by the friction velocity of the single-phase flow (figures not shown). When normalized by each value of the friction velocity, all components are considerably low in the turbulent bubbly flow compared with those in the droplet flow as is shown in Figs. 8. This is because the increase in the wall shear stress (and the friction velocity) is brought about by the factors other than turbulence augmentation, as is discussed in 3.1.5.

3.1.5 Shear-stress profiles

The wall-friction drag is increased due to the injection of the bubbles (Note that the volume flow rate is kept constant in the computation). Now, we examine the mechanism for the increase of the drag by considering the balance of forces in the channel. Taking the average of Eq.(2) over time and the x and z directions and integrating the averaged equation with respect to y, we obtain the relation

$$-\overline{\rho u \mathrm{v}}(y)+\tau(y)+\int_0^y \overline{f_{\sigma x}}(y')dy'-g\int_0^y \overline{(\rho-\langle\rho\rangle)}(y')dy'=\tau_W\left(1-\frac{y}{\delta}\right). \quad (24)$$

Here, $\tau=\overline{\mu du/dy}$ denotes the viscous shear stress and $\tau_W=\tau(0)=\tau(2\delta)$. The first, second, third, and fourth terms on the right-hand side of Eq.(24) represent the Reynolds shear stress, the viscous shear stress, the surface-tension term, and the buoyancy term, respectively.

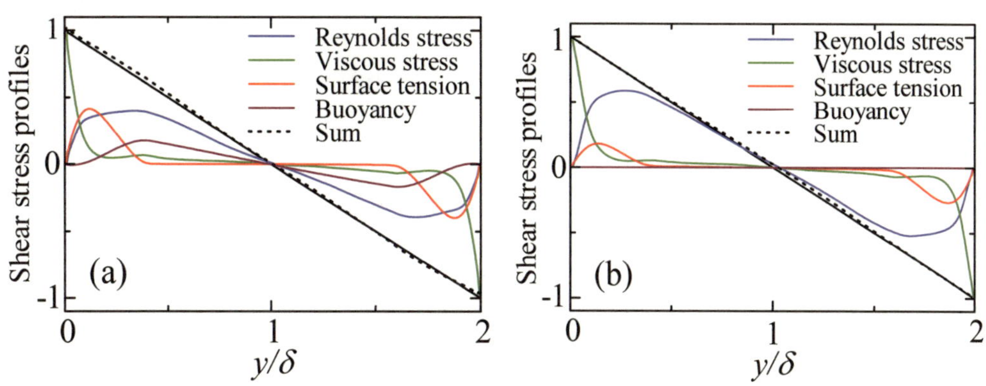

Fig. 9. Budget for shear stress.

The profiles of these four terms are drawn in Fig. 9. They are normalized by the wall shear stress. The sum of the four terms and the straight line of $(1-y/\delta)$ are also plotted in the figure. They agree well with each other, which indicates that the overall balance of forces is satisfied. The viscous shear stress is dominant in the near-wall regions as in the case of single-phase flows. The surface-tension term has large values in the regions of high void fractions (see Fig. 4). The bubbles are deformed by the mean shear in the near-wall regions and a restoring force due to the interfacial tension is acting to the liquid fluid. Since this term has large values near the walls, it makes a major contribution to the increase in the friction drag. The buoyancy term has relatively large values in the core region of the channel, which reduces the relative magnitude of the Reynolds shear stress there.
For the droplet flow, the buoyancy term is obviously zero. The surface-tension term has relatively large values near the walls since some droplets are located there. Its magnitude is smaller than that in the bubbly flow, however. Instead, the relative magnitude of the Reynolds shear stress is large in the droplet flow.

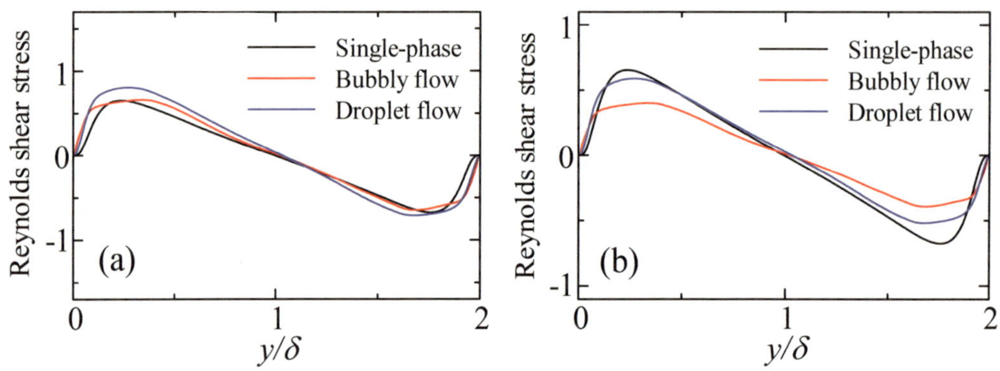

Fig. 10. Profiles of Reynolds shear stress normalized by (a) τ_{W0} and (b) τ_W .

Figs. 10 show the profiles of the Reynolds shear stress. They are normalized by the wall shear stress, τ_{W0}, for the single-phase flow in Fig. 10(a). It is clearly seen that the magnitude of Reynolds shear stress is increased in the near-wall regions due to the presence of the bubbles (or droplets). This is because the momentum exchange is enhanced by the vortices generated around the bubbles (or droplets) near the walls. This increase of the Reynolds shear stress near the walls contributes to the increase in the wall friction. When normalized by τ_W, the amplitude of the Reynolds stress is substantially reduced in the bubbly flow except in the close vicinity of the walls. This indicates that the relative role of the turbulence in the shear stress becomes diminished in the bubbly flow.

3.2 Heat transfer characteristics of turbulent bubbly flow

3.2.1 Friction temperature and Nusselt number

The friction temperature is also altered by the injection of the bubbles or droplets. The relative magnitude of the friction temperature is shown in Table 9. The time-averaged values of the Nusselt number in the single-phase flow are 15.8 and 20.6 for $\mathrm{Pr}_c = 1$ and $\mathrm{Pr}_c = 2$, respectively (see Table 10). In the bubbly flow, the time-averaged Nusselt number for $\mathrm{Pr}_c = 1$ (Case B2) and $\mathrm{Pr}_c = 2$ (Case B1) are 19.5 and 27.3, which are 1.23 and 1.33 times higher than the corresponding values in the single-phase flow, respectively. In the droplet flow, the Nusselt numbers for $\mathrm{Pr}_c = 1$ (Case D2) and $\mathrm{Pr}_c = 2$ (Case D1) are respectively 19.8 and 27.1, which are very close to the corresponding ones in the bubbly flow in spite of the difference in the wall shear stress. By comparing Case B1 and Case B3, it is found that the reduction in the Nusselt number due to the insulating effect of the bubbles is very small. By comparing Case B1 and Case B4, we notice that the low heat capacity of the gas inside the bubbles leads to some amount of reduction in the Nusselt number.

Case	B1, B2, B3	B4	D1, D2
$\Theta_\tau/\Theta_{\tau 0}$	0.76 (0.76)	0.78(0.79)	0.85

Table 9. The values of $\Theta_\tau/\Theta_{\tau 0}$.

Case	Single Phase		B1	B2	B3	B4	D1	D2
	Pr=2	Pr=1						
Nu	20.6	15.8	27.3 (27.6)	19.5 (19.6)	27.1 (27.4)	29.5 (29.3)	27.1	19.8

Table 10. Time-averaged Nusselt numbers. The values in the parentheses represent those for the bubbly flow with the lower grid resolution.

3.2.2 Mean temperature profiles

The profiles of the mean temperature variance, $\overline{\Theta^+ - \Theta_W^+}$, are drawn in Figs. 11. The temperature variance is decreased in the whole region of the channel for the droplet flow. In the case of the bubbly flow, the temperature difference is decreased except in the core region of the channel. This increase in the core region indicates that the enhancement of fluid mixing due to the bubbles is rather confined to the near wall regions. The difference between the mean fluid temperature and the wall temperature is smaller in the multiphase flows than in the single-phase flow, which means that the increase of the Nusselt number exceeds that of the friction Reynolds number (see Eq.(17)).

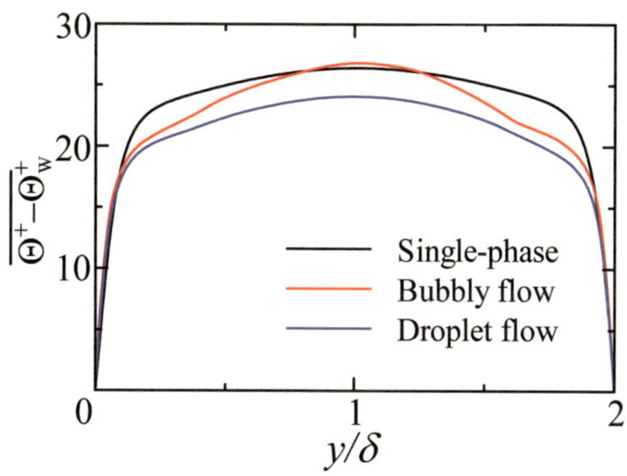

Fig. 11. The mean temperature profiles for the single-phase flow, Case B1 and Case D1.

3.2.3 Heat flux profiles

Now, we examine the mechanism for the enhancement of heat transfer by considering the energy balance in the channel. The averaging of the energy equation, Eq.(8), over time and the x and z directions, and the integration of the averaged equation with respect to y yield

$$q_W - G\int_0^y \overline{\rho C_P u}(y')dy' = k\overline{\frac{\partial \Theta}{\partial y}}(y) - \overline{\rho C_P \Theta \mathrm{v}}(y). \tag{25}$$

The left-hand side of Eq.(25) represents the total heat flux in the wall-normal direction, and the first and the second terms on the right-hand side represent the molecular heat flux and the turbulent heat flux, respectively. In the figures below, each term is normalized by the wall heat flux of each case.

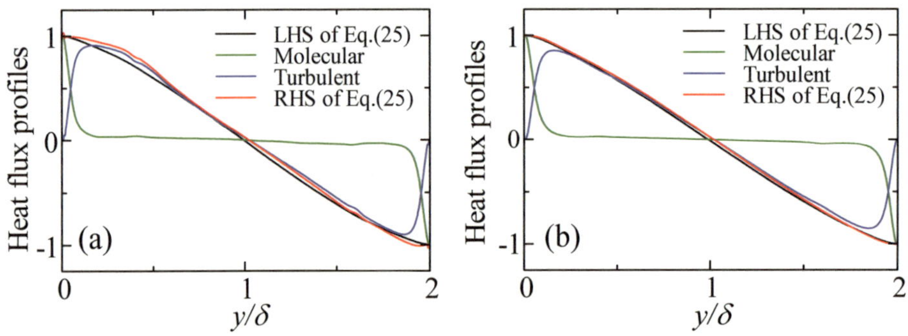

Fig. 12. Heat flux profiles for (a) Case B1 and (b) Case D1.

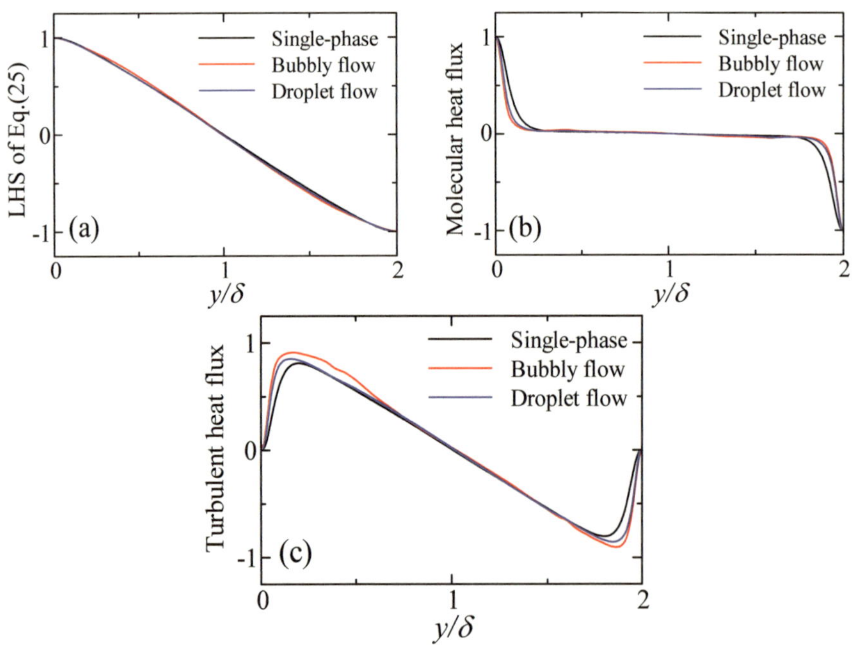

Fig. 13. The profiles of (a) the left-hand side of Eq.(25), (b) the molecular heat flux and (c) turbulent heat flux.

The profiles of these three terms are drawn in Figs. 12 for Case B1 and Case D1. The sum of the molecular and turbulent fluxes is also plotted in the figures. In both cases, the sum agrees well with the left-hand side of Eq.(25), which indicates that the overall balance of heat transfer is satisfied.

Fig. 13(a) shows the profiles of the left-hand side of Eq.(25) for the single-phase flow, Case B1 and Case B2. Clear differences are not seen among three cases, indicating that the change in the profile of heat-capacity flow rate due to the bubbles or droplets has an insignificant effect on the enhancement of heat transfer. The profiles of the molecular heat flux are shown in Fig.13(b). The molecular heat flux in the bubbly (or droplet) flow is reduced near the walls compared with the case of the single-phase flow. This indicates that the effective heat conductivity is increased due to the bubbles (or droplets).

Fig. 13(c) shows the profiles of turbulent heat flux. The turbulent heat flux is increased by the effects of bubbles (or droplets) in the regions near the walls. As is shown below, this is caused by the vortices whose generation is activated by the bubbles (or droplets). This increase in the turbulent heat flux in the near-wall regions is responsible for the increase in the effective heat conductivity of the fluid near the wall, which enhances the heat transfer. In summary, the enhancement of heat transfer in the bubbly or droplet flow is caused by the increase of the turbulent heat flux near the walls.

3.2.4 Effects of thermal properties of gas inside bubbles

Figs. 14 show the distribution of the temperature variance, $\Theta_W^+ - \Theta^+$, in the x-y plane for the three cases (Case B1, B3, B4) with different thermal properties for the gas inside the bubbles. Red and blue represent the regions of $\Theta_W^+ - \Theta^+ \geq 0$ and $\Theta_W^+ - \Theta^+ \leq -30$, respectively. Contour lines represent the cross-sections of the bubbles. The temperature is high near the walls and low in the center of the channel. The flow is going upward. It is found in Figs. 14 that the temperature field is almost uniform inside the droplet. This is due to the circulating flow inside the bubble (figures not shown). The change of the temperature distribution is small if the thermal conductivity of the gas is reduced. This is because the effect of convection dominates that of conduction inside the bubbles.

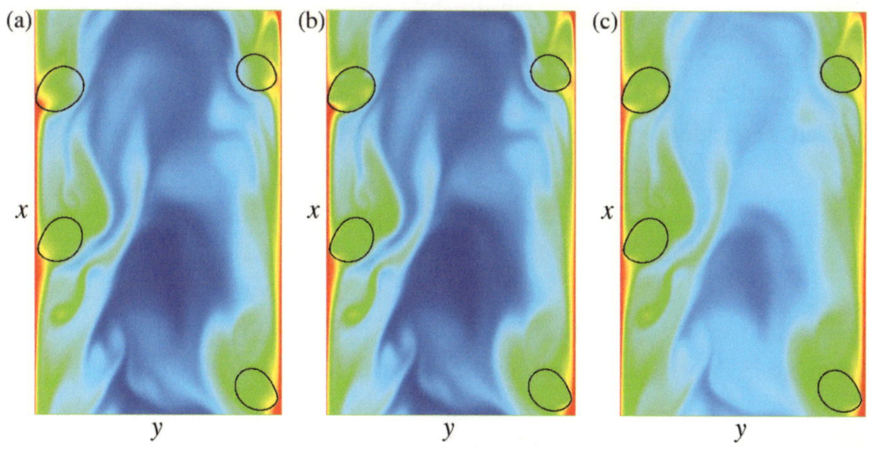

Fig. 14. Temperature distribution in an x-y plane for the bubbly flow. (a) Case B1, (b) Case B3, (c) Case B4.

3.2.5 Heat transfer enhancement and vortices

In Figs. 15(a) and 15(b) the instantaneous temperature field, $\Theta_W^+ - \Theta^+$, and the cross-sections of vortices are shown in a horizontal (*y*-*z*) plane for the bubbly flow (Case B1) and the droplet flow (Case D1). Those for the single-phase flow are also drawn in Fig. 15(c) for comparison. Notice that the temperature field is normalized by the friction temperature of each case. Red and blue represent the regions of $\Theta_W^+ - \Theta^+ \geq 0$ and $\Theta_W^+ - \Theta^+ \leq -30$, respectively. The cross-sections of vortices are represented by the contour lines of the second invariant of velocity gradient tensor of $Q^+ = 0.0125$.

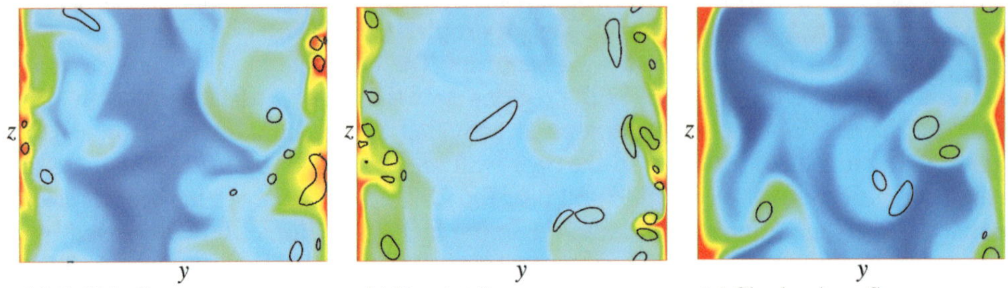

(a) Bubbly flow (b) Droplet flow (c) Single-phase flow

Fig. 15. Temperature distribution in *y*-*z* planes for (a) the bubbly flow (Case B1), (b) the droplet flow (Case D1) and (c) single-phase flow.

In the single-phase turbulent flow, the vortices are located only in the low-temperature regions away from the walls. In the bubbly and droplet turbulent flows, on the other hand, they are also located in the near-wall regions where the temperature gradient is relatively high. It is obvious that the vortices near the walls play a major role in the heat-transfer enhancement.

It is interesting to know how the heat-transfer enhancement depends on the continuous-phase Prandtl number. As is shown in Table 11, the heat-transfer enhancement is more noticeable at higher Prandtl numbers. Since the thermal boundary layer is thinner at a higher Prandtl number, the vortices near the walls, which are generated by the bubbles or droplets, more effectively enhance the heat transfer. The ratio $Nu(\mathrm{Pr}=2)/Nu(\mathrm{Pr}=1)$ is weakly dependent on the friction Reynolds number in single-phase turbulent flows. We performed a simulation for the single-phase turbulence at $\mathrm{Re}_\tau \approx 160$ and obtained the value of 1.33, which is considerably lower than 1.40 in the bubbly flow at $\mathrm{Re}_\tau \approx 160$.

Case	Single Phase	Bubble	Droplet
$\frac{Nu(\mathrm{Pr}=2)}{Nu(\mathrm{Pr}=1)}$	1.31	1.40	1.37

Table 11. The ratio of the Nusselt number at $\mathrm{Pr}_c = 2$ to that at $\mathrm{Pr}_c = 1$. The ratio of the Nusselt number in Case B1 to that in Case B2 is shown for the bubbly flow.

3.3 Performance of heat transfer enhancement

As was shown above, the Nusselt number is increased by the injection of the bubbles or droplets in the present simulations. This heat transfer enhancement is accompanied by the increase of the wall-friction, however. Reynolds analogy provides a useful concept for the evaluating the performance of heat transfer enhancement. Colburn (1933) stated that Reynolds analogy is described by the relation

$$St\,\mathrm{Pr}_c^{2/3} \equiv j = c_f/2, \tag{26}$$

where

$$St = \frac{q_W}{\rho_c C_{Pc} U_m(\Theta_m - \Theta_W)} = \frac{Nu}{\mathrm{Re}_m \mathrm{Pr}_c}, \tag{27}$$

is the Stanton number, j denotes the j-factor, and

$$c_f = \frac{\tau_W}{\frac{1}{2}\rho_c U_m^2} \tag{28}$$

is the fricition coefficient. Eq.(26) holds for laminar and turbulent flow over flat plates and turbulent flow in smooth ducts. The equation $2j/c_f = 0.25 Nu\,\mathrm{Pr}_c^{-1/3}\mathrm{Re}_m \mathrm{Re}_\tau^{-2} = 1$ gives a relation between friction due to surface shear and heat transfer.

As is shown in Table 12, the injection of the bubbles or droplets leads to the reduction of $2j/c_f$. The forces resulting from the interfacial surface tension (and the buoyancy) significantly contribute to the increase of the wall shear stress in addition to the convection in turbulence. Heat transfer enhancement, on the other hand, is mainly caused by the increase in turbulent heat flux. Since the effects of the surface tension are more significant in the bubbly flow, the reduction is more noticeable in the bubbly flow than in the droplet flow.

The value of $2j/c_f$ is larger for higher Prandtl numbers for all cases. The reduction of $2j/c_f$ due to the injection of the bubbles or droplets is less significant for higher Prandtl numbers where the convection term plays more important roles.

The above results indicate that the performance of heat transfer is not so good in the bubbly and droplet turbulent flows. In the case of bubbly flows, however, the buoyancy force exerted on bubbles, $g\Delta\rho\alpha$, may be used as a driving force for the upflow through the channel, where α is the mean void fraction. When all of this buoyancy force can be used to reduce the extra driving force, the extra wall shear stress, which balances the extra driving force, is given by $\tau'_W = \tau_W - (g\Delta\rho\alpha)h = \tau_W(1-\alpha/Bu)$. The values in the rightmost column of Table 12 are obtained by replacing τ_W in Eq.(28) by τ'_W. These values exceed 1, suggesting that the performance of heat transfer enhancement may be improved in the bubbly flow.

	Bubble	Droplet	Single-phase	Bubble
$\mathrm{Pr}_c = 1$	0.69	0.84	0.92	1.38
$\mathrm{Pr}_c = 2$	0.77	0.92	0.96	1.54

Table 12. The value of $2j/c_f$ .The rightmost column corresponds to the case in which the buoyant effect of bubbles is considered.

3.4 Future research

We still have many issues to resolve in order to clarify the heat transfer characteristics of turbulent bubby upflows. Firstly, the size of the computational domain is possibly too small to obtain the correct statistics of the turbulent bubbly flow since we utilized a minimal channel. In addition, statistical errors may be large since the number of bubbles is small and the computational time is relatively short to obtain the turbulence statistics. Larger and longer simulations are required to resolve these problems. Secondly, we set the density ratio at 0.1 and the viscosity ratio at 1.0, which are much higher than the corresponding values in an air-water system. The bubble motions and the generation of vortices due to the bubbles should be examined by changing the values of these two ratios. The continuous-phase Prandtl number of 2.0 employed in the present study is low compared with that of about 7 at room temperature. Simulations at higher Prandtl numbers are desirable. Thirdly, only two flow patterns (the bubbly and the droplet flows) have been simulated in the present study. As was shown in Lu & Tryggvason (2008), the bubble distribution consists of a core where the flow is essentially homogeneous, and a wall layer with a larger number of bubbles sliding along the wall in the case where the buoyancy effect is dominant. This interesting situation should be examined in the future study. The heat transfer characteristics of bubbly drag-reducing flows is also an interesting topic to explore.

4. Conclusion

Direct numerical simulations have been conducted for turbulent bubbly upflow between two parallel heating walls at a constant volume flow rate in order to clarify its heat transfer characteristics. For comparison, simulations for neutrally buoyant droplets have also been performed. We have obtained the following results.

- The bubbles accumulate in the vicinity of the wall and slide along the wall in the turbulent channel upflow.
- The droplets are distributed rather uniformly throughout the channel though some tendency of accumulation in the vicinity of the walls is observed.
- The turbulence production is enhanced by the bubbles or the droplets in the near-wall regions.
- The wall friction is increased by the injection of bubbles. This is mainly caused by the interfacial surface tension resulting from the deformation of the bubbles due to high shear near the walls.
- The heat transfer is enhanced by the injection of bubbles (or droplets). This is because the turbulent heat flux is augmented by the generation of the vortices due to the bubbles (or droplets).
- The reduction in the Nusselt number due to the insulating effect of the bubbles is very small, while the low heat capacity of the gas inside the bubbles causes some amount of reduction.
- The heat-transfer enhancement is more noticeable at higher Prandtl numbers.
- The performance of heat transfer enhancement is not good in the bubbly and droplet turbulent flows. However, the performance is improved in the bubbly flow if the buoyancy force exerted on bubbles is available as a driving force of the upflow.

5. References

Aulisa, E.; Manservisi, S.; Scardovelli, R. & Zaleski, S. (2003) A geometrical area-preserving Volume-of-Fluid advection method. *Journal of Computational Physics*, Vol.192, p.355-364

Aulisa, E.; Manservisi, S.; Scardovelli, R. & Zaleski S. (2007) Interface reconstruction with least-squares fit and split advection in three-dimensional Cartesian geometry. *Journal of Computational Physics*, Vol.225, pp.2301-2319

Bunner, B. & Tryggvason, G. (2002). Dynamics of homogeneous bubbly flows Part.1 Rise velocity and microstructure of the bubbles. *Journal of Computational Physics*, Vol.466, pp.17-52

Colburn, A. P. (1933). A method of correlating forced convection heat transfer data and a comparison with fluid friction. *Transactions of the AIChE*, Vol.29, pp.174-210.

Francois M.M.; Cumminsa, S. J.; Dendya, E. D.; Kothea, D. B.; Siciliana, J. M. & Williams, M. W. (2006). A balanced-force algorithm for continuous and sharp interfacial surface tension models within a volume tracking framework. *Journal of Computational Physics*, Vol. 213, pp.141-173

Kawamura, H.; Ohsak, K.; Abe, H. & Yamamoto, K. (1998). DNS of turbulent heat transfer in channel flow with low to medium-high Prandtl number fluid. *International Journal of Heat and Fluid Flow*, Vol.19, pp.482-491

Kitagawa, A.; Kosuge, K.; Uchida, K. & Hagiwara, Y. (2008). Heat transfer enhancement for laminar natural convection along a vertical plate due to sub-millimeter-bubble injection. *Experiments in Fluids*, Vol.45, pp.473-484

Kitagawa, A.; Kitada, K. & Hagiwara, Y. (2010). Experimental study on turbulent natural convection heat transfer in water with sub-millimeter-bubble injection. *Experiments in Fluids*, Vol.49, pp.613-622

Leonard, B. P. (1979). A stable and accurate modelling procedure based on quadratic upstream interpolation. *Computer Methods in Applied Mechanics and Engineering*, Vol.19, pp.59-98

Liu, T. J. (1993). Bubble size and entrance length effects on void development in a vertical channel. *International Journal of Multiphase Flow*, Vol.19, No.1, pp.99-113

Lorstad, D. & Fuchs, L. (2004). High-order surface tension VOF-model for 3D bubble flows with high density ratio. *Journal of Computational Physics*, Vol.200, pp.153-176

Lu, J. & Tryggvason, G. (2008). Effect of bubble deformability in turbulent bubbly upflow in a vertical channel. *Physics.of Fluids*, Vol.20, 040701, pp.1-6

Parker, B. J. & Youngs, D. L. (1992). Two and three dimensional Eulerian simulations of fluid flow with material interface, Technical Report, 01/92, Atomic Weapons Establishment, Aldermaston, Berkshire, February, 1992.

Rudman, M. (1998) A volume-tracking method for incompressible multifluid flows with large density variations, *International Journal for Numerical Methods in Fluids*, Vol.28, pp.357-378

Scardovelli, R. & Zaleski, S. (2003). Interface reconstruction with least-square fit and split Eulerian-Lagrangian advection. *International Journal for Numerical Methods in Fluids*, Vol.41, pp.251-274

Serizawa, A.; Kataoka, I. & Michiyoshi, I. (1975). Turbulence Structure of Air-Water Bubbly Flow- II. Local Properties. *International Journal of Multiphase Flow*, Vol.2, pp. 235-246

Tamari, M. & Nishikawa, K. (1976). The Stirring Effect of Bubbles upon the Heat Transfer to Liquids. *Heat Transfer -- Japanese Reserch*, Vol.5, No.2, pp.31-44

Tokuhiro, A. T. & Lykoudis, P. S. (1994). Natural Convection Heat Transfer from A Vertical Plate-I. Enhancement with Gas Injection. *International Journal of Heat and Mass Transfer*, Vol.37, No.6, pp.997-1003

Tryggvason, G.; Scardovelli, R. & Zaleski, S. (2011). *Direct Numerical Simulations of Gas-Liquid Multiphase Flows*, Cambridge University Press, ISBN 978-0-521-78240-1, Cambridge, UK

7

Mathematical Modelling of the Motion of Dust-Laden Gases in the Freeboard of CFB Using the Two-Fluid Approach

Alexander Kartushinsky[1] and Andres Siirde[2]
[1]*Tallinn University of Technology, Faculty of Science, Laboratory of Multiphase Media Physics, Tallinn,*
[2]*Tallinn University of Technology, Faculty of Mechanical Engineering, Department of Thermal Engineering, Tallinn, Estonia*

1. Introduction

Fluidized beds are the units designed to provide fluid-solid contacting by the fluid flow through a bed of particles (Andrews and Arthur 2007). A number of thermal processes in technology take advantage of the importance of gas-solid interaction in fluidized beds to carry out gas-solid reactions, heterogeneous catalysis and particle drying. The gas-solid fluidization process in circulating fluidized beds is widely applied in many industrial branches. Characterization of the gas-solid particle flow in a circulating fluidized bed (CFB) riser is important for the process optimization. The particle size distribution has significant influence on the dynamics of gas-solid flow (He et al., 2008) along with another important property of the giving system, such as difference in the physical densities of the used materials. The gas-fluidized beds consist of fine granular materials that are subject to the gas flow from below giving the transport velocity that is large enough to overcome the gravity by the viscous drag force and thus the particles can suspend and be fluidized. When in the fluidized state, the moving particles work effectively as a mixer resulting in a uniform temperature distribution and high mass transfer rate, which are beneficial for the efficiency of many physical and chemical processes (Wang et al., 2005). For this reason the gas-fluidized beds are widely applied in different industries: thermal, energy, chemical, petrochemical, metallurgical, and environmental industries in large-scale operations involving adhesion optimized coating, granulation, drying, and synthesis of fuels and base chemicals (Kunii & Levenspiel, 1991). In general, the lack of understanding of fundamentals of the dense gas–particle flows has led to severe difficulties in design and scale-up of these industrially important gas-solid contactors (van Swaaij, 1985). In most cases, the design and scale-up of fluidized bed reactors is a fully empirical process based on preliminary tests on pilot-scale model reactors, which is a very time consuming and thus expensive activity. Clearly, computer simulations can be a very useful tool to aid this design and scale-up process.

In the CFB furnaces the ash solids and inert materials like sand particles are mainly used as a solid heat carrier – separated in a hot cyclone and cooled after that in a heat exchanger while the ash particles come back into the furnace. The temperature level in the furnace can be held in the given range by circulating the ash/sand masses. While the heat capacity of ash is quite low, the circulating ash mass must be huge. One way of optimization is to keep up higher heat capacity by adding inertial sand particles. The high ash concentration in furnace gases can be attained with i) high velocity of gas in bed when the fuel particles carried out of bed are burned and their ash fills the whole volume of furnace and ii) ash circulation. The CFB combustion technology enables to bind the sulphur components with the carbonate components added to the fuel or existing within the mineral part of the fuel. A disadvantage of CFB is that some fuel ash particles become too fine during the circulation and therefore the size of ash particles contained in the fuel gas exiting the hot cyclone is too small. As a result of disintegration, the mass of fine ash particles, which are not separated from flue gases or captured in the connective flue ducts and multicyclone increases. The high concentration of particles in the fire gases of CFB furnace chamber contributes to the formation of particle clusters with the solid phase concentration within 0.1 - 0.2 m^3/m^3. At the exit of CFB boiler furnace the density of solid phase is within 5 - 20 kg/m^3.

The given paper is an advanced research of two previous references: "Numerical simulation of uprising gas-solid particle flow in circulating fluidized bed" (Kartushinsky et al., 2009) and "Numerical simulation of uprising turbulent flow by 2D RANS for fluidized bed conditions" (Krupenski et al., 2010) where the mathematical modelling of CFB has been performed. The first one is related to the numerical simulations of CFB where the two-phase turbulent boundary layer approach (TBL) was included. The latter concerns modelling of CFB processes by the RANS approach, which has been developed for both, the gaseous and solid phases, implementing the Euler/Euler approximations or a two-fluid model. Both papers have their advantages and disadvantages. For instance, in the TBL approach the diffusive source terms were retained only in one direction, namely, in the transverse direction, and the magnitude of average transverse velocity components in the gas- and dispersed phases were much less than that of longitudinal components of the corresponding velocities in the gas- and dispersed phases. Such an approach is fully valid and used in the pipe channel flows as well as in the turbulent round jets and flows past the rigid shapes (Hussainov et al., 1995, 1996, Frishman et al., 1997). Nevertheless, a more rigorous and accurate solution was obtained with the help of RANS approach where there are no artificial predictions attached to the TBL approach. However, in both papers only one component of solid admixture, namely, the ash particles are used to simulate the motion of particulate solid phase as a whole.

The current mathematical performance assesses the effect of the presence of two coexisting solid substances, such as ash (light) and sand (heavy) particles with the particle size distribution for each component of solids. This system represents one step further for the mathematical approach to capture real physical processes in CFB. Besides, by making calculations in the real CFB conditions (high temperature of the process) we take into account the amount of heat that must be separated from the combustor by the sensible heat of ash and solid sand particles. The approach enables to optimize particle mass concentration of ash and sand solid particles in fire gases.

The problem is solved by using elaborated mathematical modelling with the help of 2D RANS approach that applies to two coexisting phases. The numerical simulations are performed in the vertical freeboard CFB flow conditions when the temperature of carrier gas-phase fluid is 1123K. Therefore the corresponding magnitudes of parameters of the gaseous phase such as kinematic viscosity coefficient and density of the gaseous phase must

be increased by the factor ten and decrease by factor three, respectively, versus their magnitudes obtained for the normal flow conditions at the temperature 293K.
The following practical initial data were used in calculations:

Generic name		*Dimension*	*Minimal*	*Average*	*Maximal*
Pipe data	**Diameter**	m	0.0305	0.0305	0.0305
	Height	m	1.525	1.525	1.525
Ash concentration		kg/nm³	10	20	20
Ash density		kg/m³	2000	2000	2000
Ash particle size		m	0.005	0.0075	0.01
Sand density		kg/m³	2600	2600	2600
Sand particle size		m	0.005	0.0075	0.01

Table 1. The initial data for calculations.

For these media we have chosen the initial data very close to the medium in the Estonian oil-shale CFB furnace. The problems of two-phase flows in the CFB risers have been analyzed in certain publications (Hussain et al., 2005, Moscow Energija, 1973), but these studies do not consider dependence of the amount of sensible heat carried by solid particles on the mass flow loading magnitude. The numerical parametric study deals with the influence of the parameters of various riser exits on the hydrodynamics of gas-solid two-phase flow in the CFB riser (Hussain et al., 2005, Moscow Energija, 1973).
The freeboard CFB used in the given research represents a cylindrical symmetric pipe flow domain occupied by the giving mixture of gas and two types of solid particles. Since the two-fluid model or Euler/Euler approach is applied for the description of the behaviour of solid particles as continuous co-existing phases, the numerical performance is carried out with the finite (control) volume method (Perić & Scheuerer, 1989 and Fertziger & Perić, 1996) written in numerical codes. Another mathematical modelling method, which also operates with the Euler/Euler (or coexisting) approximation deals with the high density or packed particulate flows and solution is obtained with applying the theory of granular flows, for example, that by book of Multiphase Flow and Fluidization: *Continuum and Kinetic Theory Descriptions* (Gidaspov, 1994). In such particulate flows, the particle-turbulence interaction phenomenon is less significant in comparison with the particle-particle collision phenomenon. On the contrary to the Euler/Euler approach, another well-known approximation, which is frequently applied for modelling, the dispersed phase is the Lagrangian Particle Tracking method. The Lagrangian method deals usually with huge numbers of tracking particles (up to several millions of tracking particles depending on the mass flow loading) to obtain a converged solution and also to take into account the particles feedback in the primary fluid (gas-phase). One mathematical technique that can be used for the calculation of flow parameters, including the coupling effect, is given by the particle-cell source method (Crowe et al., 1977). Helland et al., (2000) using the Lagrangian Particle-Tracking approach to calculate the two-dimensional gas-solid particles flow in a CFB riser with the 3% total volume concentration of solids. To take into account the effect of the inter-particle collisions within the Lagrangian approach, (Sommerfeld, 2001) developed a stochastic inter-particle collision model with the introduction of a fictitious particle with which the traced particles might collide.

To sum up with introduction one can underline an importance of sought problem, that is the key study of given process is taken place in freeboard of furnace of CFB steam-generator and which is under numerical investigation.

2. Theoretical terms of the model

2.1 Governing equations for the two dimensional RANS model

In the area of multiphase flows there has been developed a lot of models for particulate flows in several papers e.g.(Pfeffer et al., 1966, Michaelides, 1984). A "two-fluid model" is being used in the modelling of dispersed two-phase systems where the gas and particles are considered as two coexisting phases that reach the entire flow domain. To describe the flow of the particulate phase, one of the possibilities is using the Reynolds-Averaged Navier-Stokes (RANS) method. The general equations of this method were examined by plenty of experiments, which showed that with using this method it is possible to discover, for example, the boundary conditions using the wall-functions approach and it is quite easy to implement it numerically. In this work the RANS method is used for both coexisting phases, namely the gas- and solid phases with the closure equations. Two basic predictions were used for closure of the governing equations of gaseous and dispersed phases:
i) the four-way coupling model (Crowe, 2000) by that captures one capture the particle-turbulence interaction phenomena and ii) the inter-particle collision closure model (Kartushinsky & Michaelides 2004) to assess an the particles interaction. The both models are used for receiving an output of necessary data which are the axial and radial velocities, turbulent energy and the particle mass concentration. The information on these parameters will be much useful for evaluation of the relevant processes occurred in particulate flows like CFB processes.
This model is based on the complete averaged Navier-Stokes equations applied for the axisymmetrical upward gas-solid particle turbulent flow in the freeboard CFB processes. The governing equations present the carrier fluid (gas-phase) and solid (polydispersed) phase which is considered a co-existing flow and consists of a continuity equation for the gas-phase and mass conservation equation in the dispersed phase together with the momentum equations for both phases in the longitudinal and radial directions. In addition, the moment of momentum equation is included for the solid phase because of Magnus lift force and plausible particle rotation stemmed from the wall interaction. The solid phase is considered a polydispersed phase, which consists of two particle fractions - light (ash) particles and heavy (sand) particles. The present governing equations along with the corresponding boundary conditions are given by Kartushinsky and Michaelides (2004, 2006, 2009) and are the following:

1. Continuity for the gaseous phase:

$$\frac{\partial u}{\partial x}+\frac{\partial (rv)}{r\partial r}=0 \tag{1}$$

2. Linear momentum equation in the longitudinal direction for the gaseous phase:

$$\frac{\partial}{\partial x}\left(u^2-\nu_t\frac{\partial u}{\partial x}\right)+\frac{\partial}{r\partial r}r\left(uv-\nu_t\frac{\partial u}{\partial r}\right)=-\frac{\partial p}{\rho\partial x}+\frac{\partial}{\partial x}\nu_t\frac{\partial u}{\partial x}+\frac{\partial}{r\partial r}r\nu_t\frac{\partial v}{\partial x}$$

$$-\sum_{i=1,3}\alpha_i\left(\frac{u_{ri}}{\tau_i'}+C_{Mi}\Omega_i v_{ri}\right) \tag{2}$$

3. Linear momentum equation in the radial direction for the gaseous phase:

$$\frac{\partial}{\partial x}\left(uv-\nu_t\frac{\partial v}{\partial x}\right)+\frac{\partial}{r\partial r}r\left(v^2-\nu_t\frac{\partial v}{\partial r}\right)=-\frac{\partial p}{\rho\partial r}+\frac{\partial}{\partial x}\nu_t\frac{\partial u}{\partial r}+\frac{\partial}{r\partial r}r\nu_t\frac{\partial v}{\partial r}$$

$$-\frac{2\nu_t v}{r^2}-\sum_{i=1,3}\alpha_i\left(\frac{v_{ri}}{\tau_i'}-(C_{Mi}\Omega_i+F_{si})u_{ri}\right) \tag{3}$$

4. Turbulence kinetic energy equation for the gaseous phase:

$$\frac{\partial}{\partial x}\left(uk-\nu_t\frac{\partial k}{\partial x}\right)+\frac{\partial}{r\partial r}\left(vk-\nu_t\frac{\partial k}{\partial r}\right)=$$

$$\nu_t\left\{2\left[\left(\frac{\partial u}{\partial x}\right)^2+\left(\frac{\partial v}{\partial r}\right)^2+\left(\frac{v}{r}\right)^2\right]+\left(\frac{\partial u}{\partial r}+\frac{\partial v}{\partial x}\right)^2\right\}$$

$$-\varepsilon_h+\sum_{i=1,3}\frac{\alpha_i}{\tau_i}\left(u_{ri}^2+v_{ri}^2+0.5(\overline{u_{si}'^2}+\overline{v_{si}'^2})\right) \tag{4}$$

5. Mass conservation equation for the solid phase:

$$\frac{\partial}{\partial x}(\alpha_i u_{si})+\frac{\partial}{r\partial r}(r\alpha_i v_{si})=-\frac{\partial}{\partial x}\left(D_{si}\frac{\partial\alpha_i}{\partial x}\right)-\frac{\partial}{r\partial r}\left(rD_{si}\frac{\partial\alpha_i}{\partial r}\right) \tag{5}$$

6. Momentum equation in the longitudinal direction for the solid phase:

$$\frac{\partial}{\partial x}(\alpha_i u_{si}u_{si})+\frac{\partial}{r\partial r}(r\alpha_i u_{si}v_{si})=$$

$$-\frac{\partial}{\partial x}\left(\alpha_i\overline{u_{si}'^2}\right)-\frac{\partial}{r\partial r}\left(r\alpha_i\overline{u_{si}'v_{si}'}\right)+\alpha_i\left[\frac{u_{ri}}{\tau_i'}+C_{Mi}\Omega_i v_{ri}-g\left(1-\frac{\rho}{\rho_p}\right)\right] \tag{6}$$

7. Momentum equation in the radial/transverse direction for the solid phases:

$$\frac{\partial}{\partial x}(\alpha_i v_{si}u_{si})+\frac{\partial}{r\partial r}\left(r\alpha_i v^2{}_{si}\right)=$$

$$-\frac{\partial}{\partial x}\left(\alpha_i\overline{u_{si}'v_{si}'}\right)-\frac{\partial}{r\partial r}\left(r\alpha_i\overline{v_{si}'^2}\right)+\alpha_i\left[\frac{v_{ri}}{\tau_i'}-(C_{Mi}\Omega_i+F_{si})u_{ri}\right] \tag{7}$$

8. Angular momentum equation for the solid phases:

$$\frac{\partial}{\partial x}\left(\alpha_i \omega_{si} u_{si}\right) + \frac{\partial}{r\partial r}\left(r\alpha_i \omega_{si} v_{si}\right) =$$

$$-\frac{\partial}{\partial x}\left(\alpha_i \overline{u'_{si}\omega'_{si}}\right) - \frac{\partial}{r\partial r}\left(r\alpha_i \overline{v'_{si}\omega'_{si}}\right) - \alpha_i C_{\omega i}\frac{\Omega_i}{\tau_i} \tag{8}$$

Here p is the pressure, u, u_s, v_s, ω_s are the longitudinal, radial, angular velocity components of gas- and solid phases (subscript s), respectively, and α the particle mass concentration. The subscript "i" corresponds to the number of particle fraction and varies in the range ($1 \le i \le 3$), which composes the polydispersed phase. The particle void fraction is linked with the particle mass concentration as $\alpha = \beta\rho / \rho_p$ (β is solids void fraction). The closure equations of gas-phase are performed by using $k - L_h$ four-way coupling model of Crowe (2000) where k is the turbulent energy of carrier fluid and L_h is the hybrid length scale. This parameter is computed as a harmonic average of the integral turbulence length scale of single phase pipe flow, L_0 ($L_0 = k_0^{3/2} / \varepsilon_0$) and inter-particle spacing, λ, defined as $\lambda = \delta\sqrt[3]{\left(\rho_p / \alpha\rho\right) - 1}$. Thus, the hybrid length scale or scale of dissipation rate of turbulent energy in particulate flows is determined as $L_h = 2L_0\lambda / \left(L_0 + \lambda\right)$ [Crowe 2000]. The values, ρ_p and ρ are the densities of the particle materials and gas-phase, δ is the particle size. The coefficient of turbulent viscosity is calculated as $\nu = \sqrt{k}L_0$, by the turbulent energy of particulate flow and turbulence length scale related to the single phase flow. Thus, the parameters of the single phase flow (subscript 0), the average velocity components, turbulent energy, k_0, its dissipation rate, ε_0, together with L_0 (while $T_0 = k_0 / \varepsilon_0$ is integral turbulence time scale) have to be calculated in advance (in preliminary calculations) for completion modelling in the pipe gas-solid turbulent flow system. An advantage of the four-way coupling model of (Crowe, 2000) (with the inclusion of particle collision) is that it includes the turbulence enhancement by the presence of particles, expressed via the term $\frac{\left(u_r^2 + v_r^2\right)}{\tau}$ ($u_r = u - u_s$ and $v_r = v - v_s$ is the slip velocity between the gas- and solid phases along the streamwise and radial directions) and turbulence attenuation via the increase of its dissipation rate by particles, $\varepsilon_h = k^{3/2} / L_h$ (in the right-hand side terms of Eq. 4). $\tau = \frac{\rho_p\delta^2}{18\rho\nu}$ is the particle response time for the Stokes regime (ν is the kinematic viscosity coefficient) and $\tau' = \tau / C'_D$ for the non-Stokes regime expressed via the particle Reynolds number, $\mathrm{Re}_s = \delta\sqrt{u_r^2 + v_r^2} / \nu$ and $C'_D = 1 + 0.15\mathrm{Re}_s^{0.687}$. By determining of the coefficients of C_{Mi} and F_{si} one can correct the values of the lift Magnus and Saffman forces and $C_{\omega i}$ for the particles rotation are taken from (Crowe et al., 1998) for relevant range of change of the particle Reynolds number, Re_s. $\Omega = rot\vec{V} - \omega_s$ is the angular velocity slip of particles while the differential mathematical operator "rot" over the gas velocity vector $\vec{V}$ is defined for the 2D motion, as $rot\vec{V} = \frac{1}{2}\left(\frac{\partial v}{\partial x} - \frac{\partial u}{\partial r}\right)$. The average values, $\overline{\alpha' u'_s}$, $\overline{\alpha' v'_s}$, $\overline{u'^2_s}$, $\overline{v'^2_{si}}$, $\overline{u'_s v'_s}$, $\overline{u'_s \omega'_s}$, and $\overline{v'_s \omega'_s}$ are the particles stress tensors originated from their turbulent fluctuation along with their inter-collisions calculated from (Kartushinsky & Michaelides, 2004). Due to the particle turbulent diffusion and particle collision the diffusion coefficient has two components: $D_s = D_{sturb} + D_{col}$. The first term in expression for the particle diffusion coefficient is calculated as $D_{sturb} = \frac{2}{3}k(\tau + T_0)\left[1 - \exp\left(-\frac{T_0}{\tau}\right)\right]$ from the PDF model of Zaichik & Alipchenkov (2005) and the second term is taken from the particle's collision model of Kartushinsky & Michaelides (2004).

3. Results and discussions

The numerical method: In the given RANS computations the *control volume* (cv) method was used. The governing equations (1-9) were solved using a strong implicit procedure with the lower and upper matrix decomposition and up-wind scheme for convective fluxes (Perić & Scheuerer, 1989 and Fertziger & Perić, 1996). For the considered computations, 145,000 uniformly distributed control volumes were utilized for running the numerical codes. The wall functions were incorporated at a dimensionless distance from the wall as follows, $y^+ = \frac{\Delta y \cdot v_*}{\nu} = \frac{\Delta y \cdot c_\mu \sqrt{k}}{\nu} = 10$, where Δy and c_μ are the control volume size and the empirical constant that equals to $c_\mu = 0.09$ and k is the turbulent energy, respectively.

All computations were extended from the pipe entrance to a short distance up to *x/D=50* (D is the pipe diameter) similar to the height of the freeboard of CFB. For the particulate phase, when the size of particles is often larger than the size of the viscous boundary sub-layer, the volume domain occupied by the dispersed phase has slightly shrunk, which gives always positive values for the solids' velocities in the wall vicinity. This method follows the numerical approach by Hussainov et al., (1996) has been employed here.

All results are presented in the dimensionless way: the velocities of both phases are related to the gas-phase velocity at the centre of the flow (r=0), the turbulent energy is normalized to a square of the gas-phase velocity, and particle mass concentration is normalized to its value at (r=0).

The numerical results. The effect of inter-particle collisions is very important for the particulate flows when the ratio of $\tau_c / \tau < 1$ (where τ_c is the time of inter-particle collision and τ is the particle response time). In the considered freeboard CFB, for the particulate flows with a high mass flow ratio about or above 10kg dust/kg air the given ratio of τ_c / τ is less unit resulted in accounting of the collision process in CFB by utilizing "collision terms" in equations (5-8). These terms are responsible for inter-particle collisions. These are terms for the production of longitudinal and radial components of linear velocity correlations and deriving linear and angular velocity correlations of the solid phase, such as $\overline{u'^2_s}$, $\overline{v'^2_{si}}$, $\overline{u'_s v'_s}$, $\overline{u'_s \omega'_s}$, $\overline{v'_s \omega'_s}$. These velocity correlations are due to the particle collision between various fractions and they are computed from the difference in average velocities

of various sizes of particles and from that in particle material densities (light and heavy particles). An analytical expression for given velocity correlations of the dispersed phase along with the closure approach of the governing equations of polydispersed phase, Eqs. (5-8), are given in model of (Kartushinsky & Michaelides, 2004).
The results of numerical simulation are shown in the following Figures 1-7. The axial velocity distribution of dispersed phase is calculated as an average velocity of the mixture of ash particles of different sizes or as a mixture of ash and sand particles with applying the formulae, $\overline{u_s} = \sum_i \alpha_i u_{si} / \sum_i \alpha_i$ where u_{si}, and α_i are the axial linear velocity and particle mass concentration of ash or ash and sand particles, respectively. The Fig.1 shows longitudinal distribution of the gas- and solid phases for three examined cases: mixture1 is the ash ($\rho_p = 2000\mathrm{kg/m^3}$) and sand particles ($\rho_p = 2600\mathrm{kg/m^3}$) of the same size, 500μm with the total mass flow loading of 10kg/kg equally distributed between the ash and sand particle fractions; mixture2 is the composition of ash particles of two sizes, 500 and 1000μm and sand particles of 500μm with the total mass flow loading of 10kg/kg, which are equally distributed between these three particle fractions, and finally, mixture3 consists of ash and sand particles of the same size 500μm with the higher total mass flow ratio of 20kg/kg where the mass fractions are equally distributed between the ash and sand particles. The calculations were performed for the conditions of CFB, namely, when the density of the gaseous carrier fluid was ρ=0.3kg/m³ and kinematic viscosity of the carrier fluid $\nu = 1.5 \cdot 10^{-4}$ m²/s. This corresponds to the flow parameters of hot gases at the temperature of T=1123K.

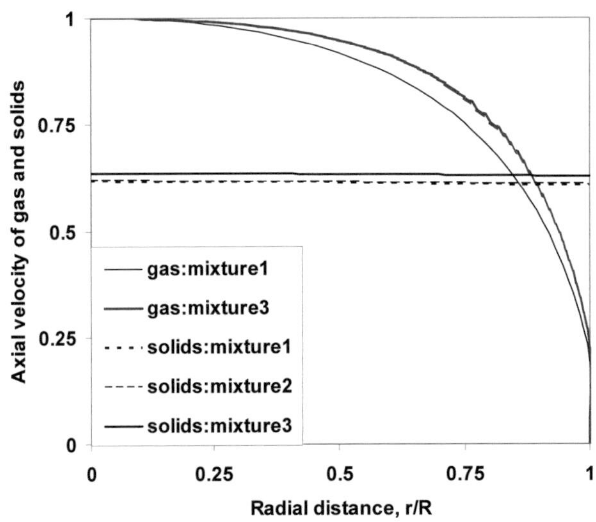

Fig. 1. Axial velocity distribution of gas- and dispersed phases for their average axial velocity by different flow conditions for mixtures 1, 2 and 3.

As one can notice, the gas velocity profile is similar to the typical turbulent velocity profile, however in a dense flow with high mass loading, e.g., 20kg/kg loaded by coarse particles, the velocity profile of the carrier gas-phase becomes flatter (diffusive line in Fig.1). It comes from the effect of turbulence enhancement by the motions of coarse particles, which modify

the velocity profile to its shape of "fully" turbulent regime. At the same time the average magnitude of the longitudinal velocity component of solids slightly increases with the growth of the mass flow ratio (cf. straight dashed and bold solid lines in Fig. 1). Such tendency in the two-phase turbulent jet has been experimentally observed by Laats & Mulgi (1979). Fig. 1 gives also the distribution of longitudinal velocity components of different solid particles. As the modelling shows, the velocity distribution of solid phase is less sensible to the variation of particle sizes than to the change of mass flow loading (cf. longitudinal velocity profiles for mixture1 and mixture3, straight lines in Fig. 1).
The following Figs. 2 and 3 show the detailed distribution of longitudinal velocity components for each particle fraction of solids presented separately. The cases of mixture1 and mixture3 show similar particle sizes of 500µm, but different material densities (light and heavy particles) and also different mass flow ratios: 10 and 20kg/kg (Fig. 2). The other cases are the mixture1 and the mixture2 with the particle sizes and material densities distributions obtaining for the same total mass flow loading 10kg/kg (Fig. 3). As one can notice, the ash particles have higher velocity than heavy sand particles (cf. dashed and solid dashed lines, Fig.2) that could be observed for both mass flow loadings: 10kg/kg (mixture1) and 20kg/kg (mixture3). Mixture2 is a more complicated case of particle composition. Considering the above, we can see that the larger ash particles have a lower velocity value than the smaller ones (cf. light and dark diffused lines for 500 and 1000µm particles, Fig.3). However, at the same time the heavier sand particles of 500µm have larger velocity magnitude than the lighter ash particles of 500 and 1000µm, which show smaller velocity magnitude (Fig.3). This trend is probably caused by the higher rate of particle collision between the light ash particles of different sizes than that between the light and heavy particles of the same size. It is difficult to predict such a tendency, but, it can be observed in numerical simulations.

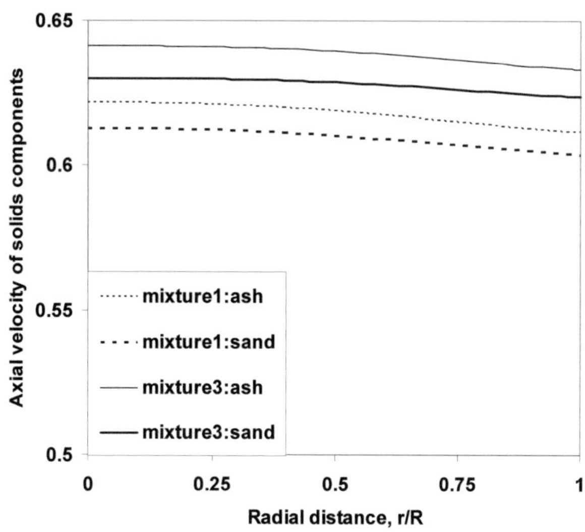

Fig. 2. Axial velocity profiles of ash and sand particles for various flow conditions: mixture1: ash and sand particles of 0.5mm for 10kg/kg and mixture3: ash and sand 0.5mm for 20kg/kg.

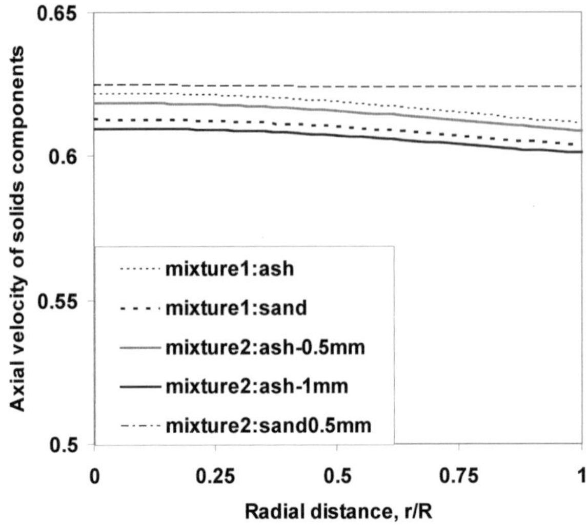

Fig. 3. Axial velocity profiles of ash and sand particles for various flow conditions: mixture1: ash and sand particles of 0.5mm and mixture2: ash 0.5 and 1mm and sand 0.5mm for 10kg/kg.

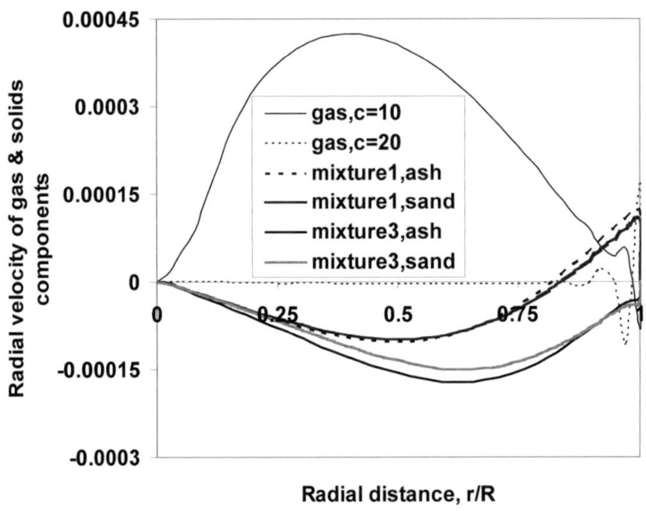

Fig. 4. Radial velocity profiles of gas phase and two components of solids for various flow conditions: mixture1 and mixture3 for ash and sand solid phases with different mass loadings, 10 and 20 kg/kg, respectively.

Fig. 4 shows the distribution of radial velocity components of gas- and dispersed phases. The profiles of radial velocities of ash and sand particles have been plotted separately for different mass loadings: 10 (mixture1) and 20kg/kg (mixture3). As one can notice, increase of mass flow loading results in change of shape and magnitude of the radial gas velocity profile (cf. dashed and solid lines, Fig. 4). Different behaviour in the distribution of radial velocity components of solid and gas-phase can also be observed. Namely, the profiles of solid phase have concave shape while the profile of gas-phase is convex. This means that the increase of mass flow loading results in the increase of radial velocity component of both fractions whatever particles are considered - the ash or sand particles (cf. solid and diffused lines for mixture3 versus the dashed bold and diffused bold lines for mixture1, Fig. 4). This comes from the effect of attenuation of the gas-phase by a larger amount of solid particles in the flow.

The effect of lift forces is given in Fig. 5 in terms of the distribution of angular velocity of particles. Fig. 5 shows the distribution of angular velocity of ash and sand particles separately and also their average angular velocity calculated analogously to the above-mentioned calculation of average linear velocity of solids in the given form: $\overline{\omega_s} = \sum_i \alpha_i \omega_{si} / \sum_i \alpha_i$ where ω_{si} is the angular velocity of composed particle fractions. As the figure shows, the angular velocity of particles is gradually increasing towards the wall and light ash particles have higher rotation in the vicinity of the wall than heavy sand particles. The increase of particle rotation is obviously stemmed from effect of diminishing of the particles inertia. The particle rotation results indirectly from the intensification of the mixing process, because of the growth of Magnus lift force that causes the particle migration across the flow.

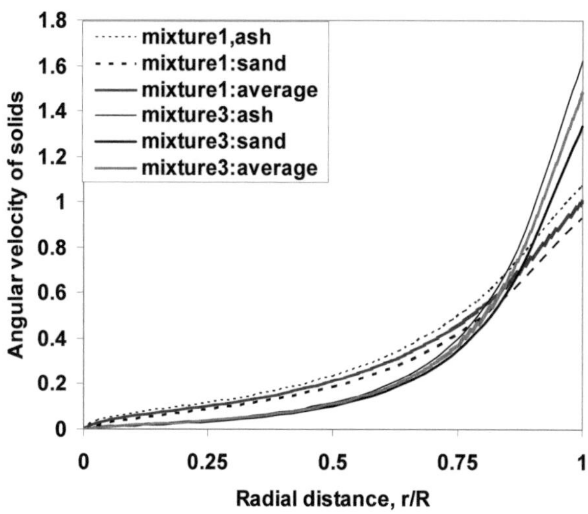

Fig. 5. Angular velocity profiles of ash and sand particles and average profile of the mixture of particles $\overline{\omega_s}$ for the same flow conditions in Fig. 4 for mixtures 1 and 3.

Fig. 6 shows the distribution of particle mass concentration across the two regimes of the flow, which depends on the mass flow ratio: mixture1 with 10kg/kg and mixture3 with 20kg/kg. As the figure shows the lower mass flow ratio results in the slower decrease of mass concentration towards the wall versus the increase of mass concentration of particles for higher mass loading of the flow. As numerical results show, the profile of particle mass concentration is close to the flat shape, which can be observed in the flow loaded by coarse particles. In fact, the numerically obtained profiles of particle mass concentration are highly appreciated because of the efficient operation of CFB units. On the contrary, in the flow domain the gradient profiles of mass concentration can cause retard of enhancement of the combustion process. Thus, an additional sand mass fraction brought to the flow domain may contribute to the improvement of the combustion process in CFB cycles.

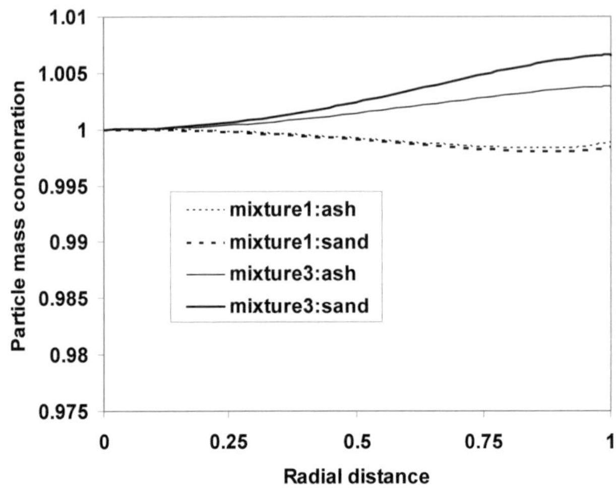

Fig. 6. Distribution of particle mass concentration for ash and sand solid phases in different flow conditions shown in previous Figs. 4 and 5: for mixtures 1 and 3.

Finally, the Fig. 7 shows distribution of turbulent the energy across the flow. All considered results for given three different regimes: mixture1, mixture2 and mixture3 are matched between each other and versus also turbulent energy of single phase flow. As a whole, the trend shows that the particles in all the observed regimes generate the turbulence, which stems from the vortex shedding phenomenon behind the particles which is input to the level of turbulence generated by the flow itself. This effect of turbulence modulation, namely, the turbulence enhancement due to the presence of coarse particles is explained and computed using the four-way coupling model by Crowe (2000). This amount of an additional turbulent energy is proportional to the square of velocity slip between the gaseous and the solid phases following the model by Crowe (2000) and it is substantial because of large velocity slip between the phases owing to high inertia of large particle size. Following to the model of Crowe (2000), this generation term is balanced by the introduced dissipation rate of turbulent energy and calculated via the hybrid turbulence length scale (last term in the right-hand side of Eq. 5). The given four-way coupling model by Crowe (2000) is based on the criteria of turbulence modulation by particles considering the ratio of particle size to the integral turbulence length scale. In accordance with this criterion for the considered cases of two-phase turbulent flow loaded by 500 and 1000μm particles, this scale ratio is far above 0.1 and therefore the particles enhanced the turbulence of the carrier gas-phase flow. In addition, the effect of increase of polydispersity grade, i.e. particle size variation from 500 up to 1000μm occurred for the mixture2 (only with ash particles) is less pronounced than that with increase of mass flow ratio up to 20kg/kg occurred in the case of the mixture3 (cf. bold dashed line in Fig. 7), on forming the shape and magnitude level of turbulent energy.

Feeding of particles into the flow field may create some reason for additional turbulence generation and it is much appreciated because the intensification of mixing process in CFB can be substantially improved, and as a result, higher efficiency of the combustion process in CFB units can be obtained.

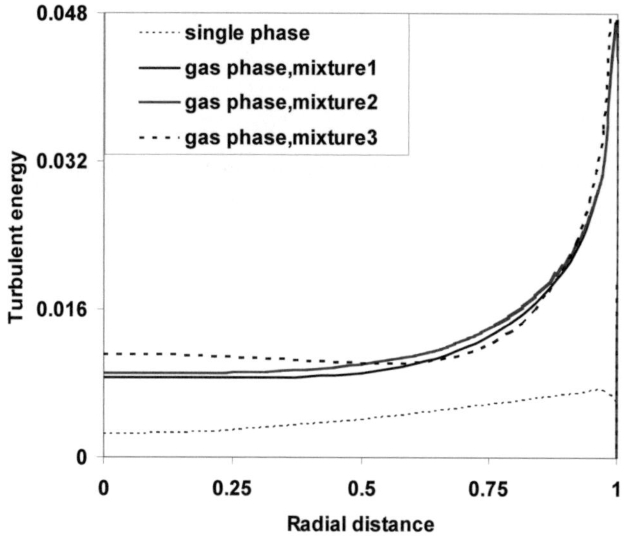

Fig. 7. Turbulent energy profiles of single and gas phases for mixtures 1, 2 and 3 with different particle sizes of ash: 0.5 and 1 mm and sand 0.5 mm and for the mass loadings (10 and 20 kg/kg).

4. Comparison of the results

Comparing the results with our previous research (Kartushinsky et al., 2009 and Krupenski et al., 2010) in which the theoretical initial data were used we can notice the following perceptible fact:
Inclusion of second (heavier) particle fraction modifies the turbulence of carrier fluid resulting in the intensification of mixing process in the freeboard area of CFB.

5. Conclusions

The numerical study of particulate turbulent flow modelled by 2D RANS (Euler/Euler) approach showed importance of addition of second solid fraction, characterized by heavy (sand) particles along with existence of first solid fraction of lighter (ash) particles in the mixing process taken place in freeboard CFB process. The main contribution to the flow formation stems from the inclusion of inter-particle collisions and four-way coupling turbulence modulation due to the presence of polydispersed solid particles with various physical properties. Other forces exerted on the motion of solids are: the gravitation, viscous drag and lift forces. On the basis of the performed calculations one can conclude:

a. variation of solids material properties results in the enhancement of flow turbulence in comparison with the turbulence level of the flow loaded by one particle fraction;

b. increase of mass loading of the flow is more pronounced for turbulence enhancement than the increase of particle size;
c. increase of mass flow ratio intensifies the mixing process resulting in uniform distribution of mass concentration of solids;

The obtained results can be implemented for updating/refurbishing of the industrial scale CFB risers using the real sizes distribution of solid particles of ash and sand for the combustion of Estonian oil-shale particles.

6. Acknowledgements

The work was support from target financing of the Project SF0140070s08 (Estonia). The authors are grateful for the technical support of cluster computers from the Universities of Texas at Austin and San Antonio (USA).

7. References

Andrews, A.T. (2007). IV Filtered Models for Gas-Particle Flow Hydrodynamics. *PhD Thesis*, 235 pages.

Crowe, C.T.; Stock, D.E. & Sharma, M.P. (1977). The Particle-Source-In Cell "PSI-CELL" Model for Gas-Droplet Flows. *ASME Transactions, Series I - Journal of Fluids Engineering*, Vol.99, 325-332.

Crowe, C.; Sommerfeld, M. & Tsuji, M. (1998). *Multiphase Flows with Droplets and Particles*. CRC Press LLC, Boca Raton, Florida. ISBN 0-8493-9469-4.

Crowe, C.T. (2000). On Models for Turbulence Modulation in Fluid-Particle Flows. *International Journal of Multiphase Flow*, Vol.26, No.5, pp. 719-727.

He, Y.; Deen, N.G.; van Sint Annaland, M. & Kuipers, J.A.M. (2008). Gas-Solid Turbulent Flow in a Circulating Fluidized Bed Riser; Numerical Study of Binary Particles Mixtures, *9th International Conference on Circulating Fluidized Beds*, Germany.

Fertziger, J.H. & Perić, M. (1996). *Computational Method for Fluid Dynamics*. Springer-Verlag Berlin Heidelberg. ISBN 3540594345.

Frishman, F.; Hussainov, M.; Kartushinsky A. & Mulgi A. (1997). Numerical Simulation of a Two-Phase Turbulent Pipe-Jet Flow Loaded with Polyfractional Solid Admixture. *International Journal of Multiphase Flow*, Vol.23, No.4, pp. 765-796.

Gidaspov, D. (1994). *Multiphase Flow and Fluidization: Continuum and Kinetic Theory Description*. Boston: Academic Press. ISBN 10: 0-12-282470-9.

Helland, E.; Occelli, R. & Tradist, L. (2000). Numerical study of cluster formation in a gas-particle circulating fluidized bed. Power Technology, Vol.110, No.3, pp. 210-221.

Hussainov, M.; Kartushinsky, A.; Mulgi, A.; Rudi Ü. & Tisler, S. (1995). Experimental and Theoretical Study of the Distribution of Mass Concentration of Solid Particles in the Two-Phase Laminar Boundary Layer on a Flat Plate. *International Journal of Multiphase Flow*, Vol.21, No.6, pp. 1141-1161. ISSN 0301-9322.

Hussain, A.; Ani, F. N.; Darus, A. N.; Mustafa, A. & Salema, A. A. (2005). *Proceedings of the 18th International Conference on Fluidized Bed Combustion*, ASME Publication, pp. 1-7.

Hussainov, M.; Kartushinsky, A.; Mulgi, A. & Rudi, Ü. (1996). Gas-solid flow with the slip velocity of particles in a horizontal channel. *Journal of Aerosol Science*. Vol.27, No.1, pp. 41-59.

Kartushinsky, A. & Michaelides, E.E. (2004). An Analytical Approach for the Closure Equations of Gas-Solid Flows with Inter-Particle Collisions. *International Journal of Multiphase Flow*, Vol.30, No.2, pp. 159-180.

Kartushinsky A. & Michaelides, E.E. (2006). Particle-laden gas flow in horizontal channels with collision effects. *Powder Technology*, Vol.168, pp. 89-103.

Kartushinsky, A.; Michaelides, E.E. & Zaichik, L.I. (2009). Comparison of the RANS and PDF Methods for Air-Particle Flows. *International Journal of Multiphase Flow*, Vol.35, pp. 914-923.

Kartushinsky, A.; Martins, A.; Rudi, Ü.; Shcheglov, I.; Tisler, S.; Krupenski, I. & Siirde, A. (2009). Numerical Simulation of Uprising Gas-Solid Particle Flow in Circulating Fluidized Bed. *Oil-Shale*, Vol.26, No.2, pp. 125-138.

Krupenski, I.; Kartushinsky, A.; Siirde, A. & Rudi, Ü. (2010). Numerical Simulation of Uprising Turbulent Flow by 2D RANS for Fluidized Bed Conditions. *Oil-Shale*, Vol.27, No.2, pp. 147-163.

Kunii, D. & Levenspiel, O. (1991). *Fluidization Engineering*. Butterworth Heinemann E.U.A. (Ed), London, UK.

Laats, M.K. & Mulgi, A.S. (1979). Experimental Investigation of Kinematic Picture of Solid Particles in Pipe Flow. *Proceedings of Estonian Academy of Sciences*, Tallinn, pp. 32-46 (in Russian).

Michaelides, E.E. (1984). A Model for the Flow of Solid Particles in Gases. *International Journal of Multiphase Flow*, Vol.10, pp. 61–75.

Peric, M. & Scheuerer, G. (1989). CAST - A Finite Volume Method for Predicting Two-Dimensional Flow and Heat Transfer Phenomena, *GRS – Technische Notiz*, SRR-89-01.

Pfeffer, R.; Rosetti, S. & Licklein, S. (1966). Analysis and Correlation of Heat Transfer Coefficient and Heat Transfer Data for Dilute Gas–Solid Suspensions. *NASA rep. TND-3603*.

van Swaaij, W.P.M. (1985). *Chemical reactors*. Fluidization 2nd Edition, Academic Press, London, UK. (Davidson, J. F., Clift, R. and Harrison, D. Ed.), pp. 595-630.

Sommerfeld, M. (2001). Validation of a stochastic Lagrangian Modelling Approach for Inter-Particle Collisions in Homogeneous Isotropic Turbulence. *International Journal Multiphase Flow*, Vol.27, pp. 1829–1858.

Wang, S.; Liu, H.; Lu, H.; Liu, W.; Jiamin, D. & Li, W. (2005). Flow Behaviour of Clusters in a Riser Simulated by Direct Simulation Monte Carlo Method. *Chemical Engineering Journal*, Vol.106, pp. 197-211.

Zaichik, L. I. & Alipchenkov, V. M. (2005). Statistical Models for Predicting Particle Dispersion and Preferential Concentration in Turbulent Flows. *International Journal of Heat and Fluid Flow*, Vol.26, pp. 416-430.

Thermal Calculation of Power Generators (Standard Method). Moscow, Energija, 1973, 295 pages [in Russian].

8

Computation of Non-Isothermal Reversed Stagnation-Point Flow over a Flat Plate

Vai Kuong Sin and Chon Kit Chio
University of Macau
Taipa, Macao SAR, China

1. Introduction

The full Navier-Stokes equations are difficult or impossible to obtain an exact solution in almost every real situation because of the analytic difficulties associated with the nonlinearity due to convective acceleration. The existence of exact solutions are fundamental not only in their own right as solutions of particular flows, but also are agreeable in accuracy checks for numerical solutions.

In some simplified cases, such as two-dimensional stagnation point flows, by introducing coordinate variable transformation, the number of independent variables is reduced by one or more. The governing equations can be simplified to the non-linear ordinary differential equations and are analytic solvable. The classic problems of two-dimensional stagnation-point flows can be analyzed exactly by Hiemenz Hiemenz (1911), one of Prandtl's first students. These are exact solutions for flow directed perpendicular to an infinite flat plate. Howarth Howarth (1951) and Davey Davey (1961) extended the two-dimensional and axisymmetric flows to three dimensions, which is based on boundary layer approximation in the direction normal to the plane.

The similarity solutions for the temperature field were studied by Eckert Eckert (1942). Case corresponding a step change in wall temperature or in wall heat flux in laminar steady flows at a stagnation point has been also investigated by several authors (see Chao et al. Chao & Jeng (1965), Sano Sano (1981) and Gorla Gorla (1988)). Further, Lok et al. Lok et al. (2006) investigated the mixed convection near non-orthogonal stagnation point flow on a vertical plate with uniform surface heat flux, where the results published are very good with present value of $\theta(0)$ for the constant wall temperature boundary condition. On the contrary, reversed stagnation-point flow over an infinite flat wall does not have analytic solution in two-dimensional steady state case.

The aim of this study is to investigate the unsteady viscous reversed non-isothermal stagnation-point flow, which is started impulsively in motion with a constant velocity away from near the stagnation point. A similarity solution of full Navier-Stokes equations and energy equation are solved by applying numerical method. Studies of the reversed stagnation-point flow have been considered during the last few years, as this flow can be applied in different important applications that occur in oil recovery industry, as shown in Fig. (1).

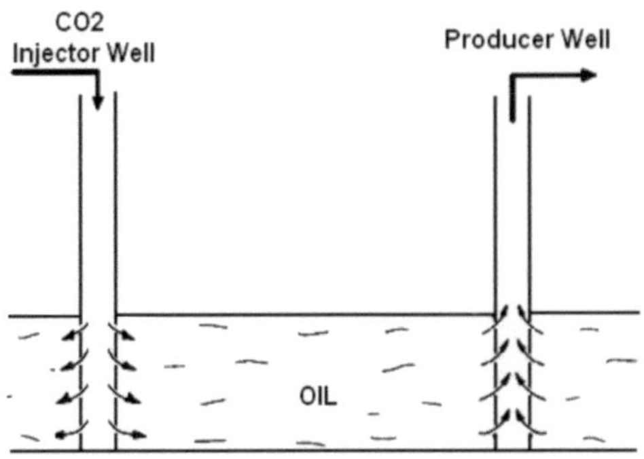

Fig. 1. Oil recovery industry

2. Governing equation

2.1 Momentum equation

The viscous fluid flows in a rectangular Cartesian coordinates (x, y, z), Fig. 2, which illustrates the motion of external flow directly moves perpendicular out of an infinite flat plane wall. The origin is the so-called stagnation point and z is the normal to the plane.

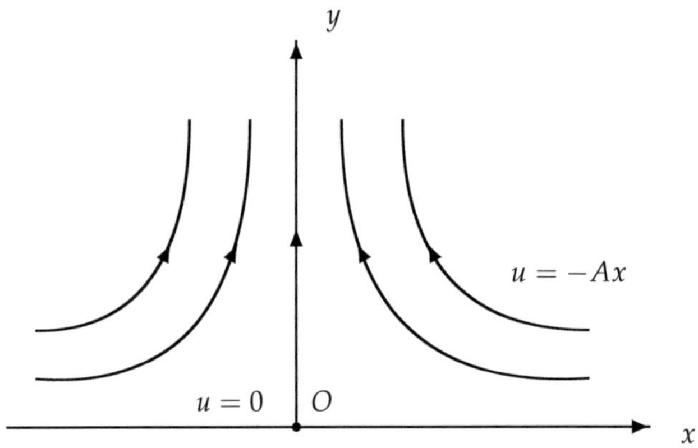

Fig. 2. Cooridnate system of reversed stagnation-point flow

By conservation of mass principle with constant physical properties , the equation of continuity is:

$$\frac{\partial u}{\partial x} + \frac{\partial v}{\partial y} = 0 \tag{1}$$

We consider the two-dimensional reversed stagnation-point flow in unsteady state and the flow is bounded by an infinite plane $y = 0$, the fluid remains at rest when time $t < 0$. At $t = 0$, it starts impulsively in motion which is determined by the stream function

$$\psi = -\alpha xy \tag{2}$$

For a viscid fluid the stream function, since the flow motion is determined by only two factors, the kinematic viscosity ν and α, we consider the following modified stream function

$$\psi = -\sqrt{A\nu}xf(\eta,\tau) \tag{3a}$$

$$\eta = \sqrt{\frac{A}{\nu}}y \tag{3b}$$

$$\tau = At \tag{3c}$$

where η is the non-dimensional distance from wall and τ is the non-dimensional time. Noting that the stream function automatically satisfies equation of continuity 1 . The Navier-Stokes equations White (2003) governing the unsteady flow with constant physical properties are

$$\frac{\partial u}{\partial t} + u\frac{\partial u}{\partial x} + v\frac{\partial u}{\partial y} = -\frac{1}{\rho}\frac{\partial p}{\partial x} + \nu(\frac{\partial^2 u}{\partial x^2} + \frac{\partial^2 u}{\partial y^2}) \tag{4a}$$

$$\frac{\partial v}{\partial t} + u\frac{\partial v}{\partial x} + v\frac{\partial v}{\partial y} = -\frac{1}{\rho}\frac{\partial p}{\partial y} + \nu(\frac{\partial^2 v}{\partial x^2} + \frac{\partial^2 v}{\partial y^2}) \tag{4b}$$

where u and v are the velocity components along x and y axes, and ρ is the density.
From the definiton of stream function, we have

$$u = \frac{\partial \psi}{\partial y} = -Axf_\eta \tag{5a}$$

$$v = -\frac{\partial \psi}{\partial x} = \sqrt{A\nu}f \tag{5b}$$

Substituting u and v into the governing equations results a simplified partial differential equation

$$f_{\eta\tau} - (f_\eta)^2 + ff_{\eta\eta} - f_{\eta\eta\eta} + 1 = 0, \tag{6}$$

with the boundary conditions

$$f(0,\tau) = f_\eta(0,\tau) = 0 \tag{7a}$$

$$f_\eta(\infty,\tau) = 1. \tag{7b}$$

Equation (6) is the similarity equation of the full Navier-Stokes equations at two-dimension reversed stagnation point. The coordinates x and y are vanished, leaving only a dimensionless variable η.
When the flow is in steady state such that $f_{\eta\tau} = 0$, it can be proved that the differential equation does not have solution under the boundary conditions Davey (1961). Thus we concentrate on the transient behavior in other section.

2.2 Energy equation

In this section, we shall focus on the non-isothermal flow which is at a temperature T different from that of the wall T_w. By solving the energy equation, we are able to determine the temperature distribution in the reversed stagnation-point flow.

For constant-property fluid such as results, the transient energy equation Burmeister (1993) is given as follow

$$\rho c_p \left(\frac{\partial T}{\partial t} + u\frac{\partial T}{\partial x} + v\frac{\partial T}{\partial y} \right) = k \left(\frac{\partial^2 T}{\partial x^2} + \frac{\partial^2 T}{\partial y^2} \right) + \mu \Phi \tag{8}$$

where k is the thermal conductivity and c_p is the heat capacity.
Note that u and v are the velocity components. These give

$$u = -Axf_\eta \tag{9a}$$

$$v = \sqrt{A\nu} f \tag{9b}$$

and Φ is defined as

$$\Phi = 2\left[\left(\frac{\partial u}{\partial x} \right)^2 + \left(\frac{\partial v}{\partial y} \right)^2 \right] + \left(\frac{\partial u}{\partial y} + \frac{\partial v}{\partial x} \right)^2 - \frac{2}{3}\left(\frac{\partial u}{\partial x} + \frac{\partial v}{\partial y} \right)^2 \tag{10}$$

and is called the viscous dissipation since it represents the irreversible conservation of mechanical forms of energy to a thermal form.
To transform equation (8) into a nondimensional form, a dimensionless temperature θ is defined as

$$\theta = \frac{T - T_w}{T_\infty - T_w}. \tag{11}$$

where T_∞ is the ambient temperature. Noting that both T_w and T_∞ are constant,

$$T(0,t) = T_w, \;\; T(\infty,t) = T_\infty, \tag{12}$$

the temperature distribution T can be considered as a function of y and t only.
Under the assumption that the viscous dissipation is negligible compared to conduction at the wall, the energy equation may be written as

$$\theta_{\eta\eta} - \frac{\rho c_p \nu}{k} f\theta_\eta = \frac{\rho c_p \nu}{k}\theta_\tau \tag{13}$$

subject to the boundary conditions

$$\theta(0,\tau) = 0 \qquad \theta(\infty,\tau) = 1 \tag{14}$$

Equation (13) is a second-order partial differential equation with variable coefficients $f(\eta,\tau)$ and the Prandtl number $Pr = \rho c_p \nu / k$ is assumed to be constant. Consider the fluid of which $Pr = 1$, the thermal boundary layer and the velocity boundary layer collapse, and thus, substituting $\theta = f'$, equation (6) and (13) represent the same equation.

3. Asymptotic solution

3.1 Velocity distribution

When τ is relatively small, Proudman and Johnson Proudman & Johnson (1962) first considered the early stages of the diffusion of the initial vortex sheet at $y = 0$. They suggested that, when the flow is near the plane region, the viscous forces are dominant, and the viscous term in the governing Navier-Stokes equations is important only near the

boundary. On the contrary, the viscous forces were neglected away from the wall. The convection terms dominate the motion of external flow in considering the inviscid equation in the fluid. According to their solution, the general features of the predicted streamline are sketched in Fig. (3).
We therefore consider the similarity of the inviscid equation

$$f_{\eta\tau} - (f_\eta)^2 + f f_{\eta\eta} + 1 = 0. \tag{15}$$

Proudman and Johnson obtained a similarity solution of (15) is in the form

$$f(\eta, \tau) = e^{\tau} F(\gamma) \tag{16}$$

and the further integration provides an exact solution

$$F(\gamma) = \gamma - \frac{2}{c}(1 - e^{-c\gamma}) \tag{17}$$

where c is a constant of integration; the improved numerical evaluations of Robins and Howarth Robins & Howarth (1972) estimate the value of c to be approximately 3.51. This solution describes the flow in the outer region. When $\tau \to \infty$ and η/e^{τ} is relatively small, the solution (17) yields

$$F \sim -\gamma = -\eta e^{-\tau}$$

and

$$f = -\eta, \quad f' = -1 \tag{18}$$

Substituting in equation (6) becomes

$$f''' - f f'' + (f')^2 - 1 = 0 \tag{19}$$

with the boundary conditions

$$f(0) = f'(0) = 0 \tag{20a}$$
$$f'(\infty) = -1 \tag{20b}$$

This is exactly the classic stagnation-point problem Hiemenz (1911)) by changing the sign in f. It is a third-order nonlinear ordinary differential equation and does not have an analytic solution, and thus it is necessary to solve it numerically and the result is show in Fig. 4 .

3.2 Temperature distribution

Wen $\tau \to \infty$, we have an exact solution of the momentum equation in outer region, and thus, we still apply the same procedure to solve the temperature profiles in outer region. Consider the following transformation:

$$\theta(\eta, \tau) = \Theta(\gamma) \tag{21}$$

where

$$\gamma = \eta e^{-\tau}$$

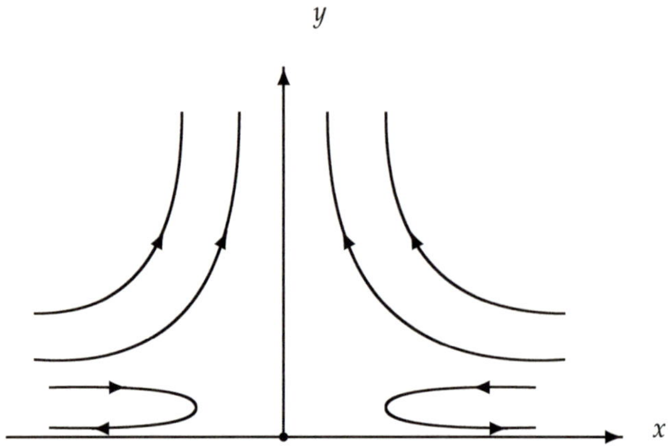

Fig. 3. Streamlines of reversed stagnation-point flow

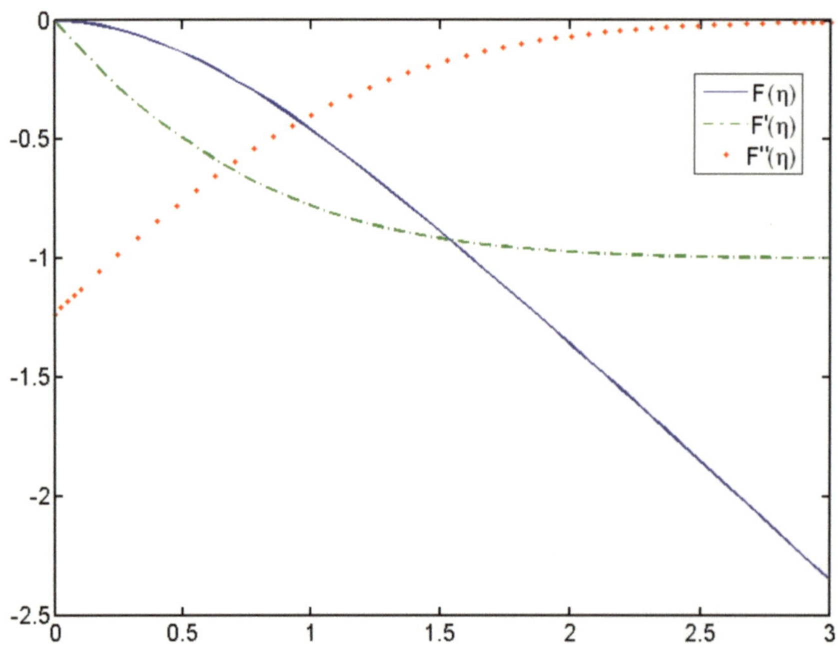

Fig. 4. Numerical solutions of stagnation-point flow

if we consider a finite value of τ, equation (13) becomes an ordinary differential equation

$$\Theta'' + \frac{2Pr\, e^{2\tau}}{c}(1 - e^{-c\Upsilon})\Theta' = 0 \tag{22}$$

subject to the boundary

$$\Theta(0) = 0, \;\; \Theta(\infty) = 1 \tag{23}$$

where

$$c = 3.51.$$

The following pages (Figs. (5) to (6)) show the asymptotic solution of temperature distributions with Pr in outer region.

4. Finite-difference formulations

4.1 Governing equations

According to the previous work, the governing equations in reversed stagnation-point flow are

$$f_{\eta\tau} - (f_\eta)^2 + f f_{\eta\eta} - f_{\eta\eta\eta} + 1 = 0. \tag{6}$$

$$\theta_{\eta\eta} - Pr\, f\theta_\eta = Pr\, \theta_\tau \tag{13}$$

The above equations (6) and (13) subject to the boundary conditions are are nonlinear third-order partial differential equations. They do not admit similarity solution and numerical or perturbation methods are needed to solve the equation.
We shall, however, use here a numerical method. It is an implicit finite-difference method with second-order accuracy. The partial differential equations can be expressed as approximate expressions, so that it is easy to program the solution of large numbers of coupled equation.

We start with rewriting the partial differential equations in the form:

$$f_{\eta\tau} = f_{\eta\eta\eta} + (f_\eta)^2 - 1 + f f_{\eta\eta} \tag{24a}$$

$$\theta_\tau = \frac{1}{Pr}\theta_{\eta\eta} - f\theta_\eta \tag{24b}$$

and introducing the new dependent variables

$$h = 1 - f_\eta \tag{25a}$$

$$g = \theta \tag{25b}$$

The equations can be rewritten as

$$h_\tau = h_{\eta\eta} + 2h - h^2 + h_\eta \int (1 - h)\, d\eta \tag{26a}$$

$$g_\tau = \frac{1}{Pr} g_{\eta\eta} - g_\eta \int (1 - h)\, d\eta \tag{26b}$$

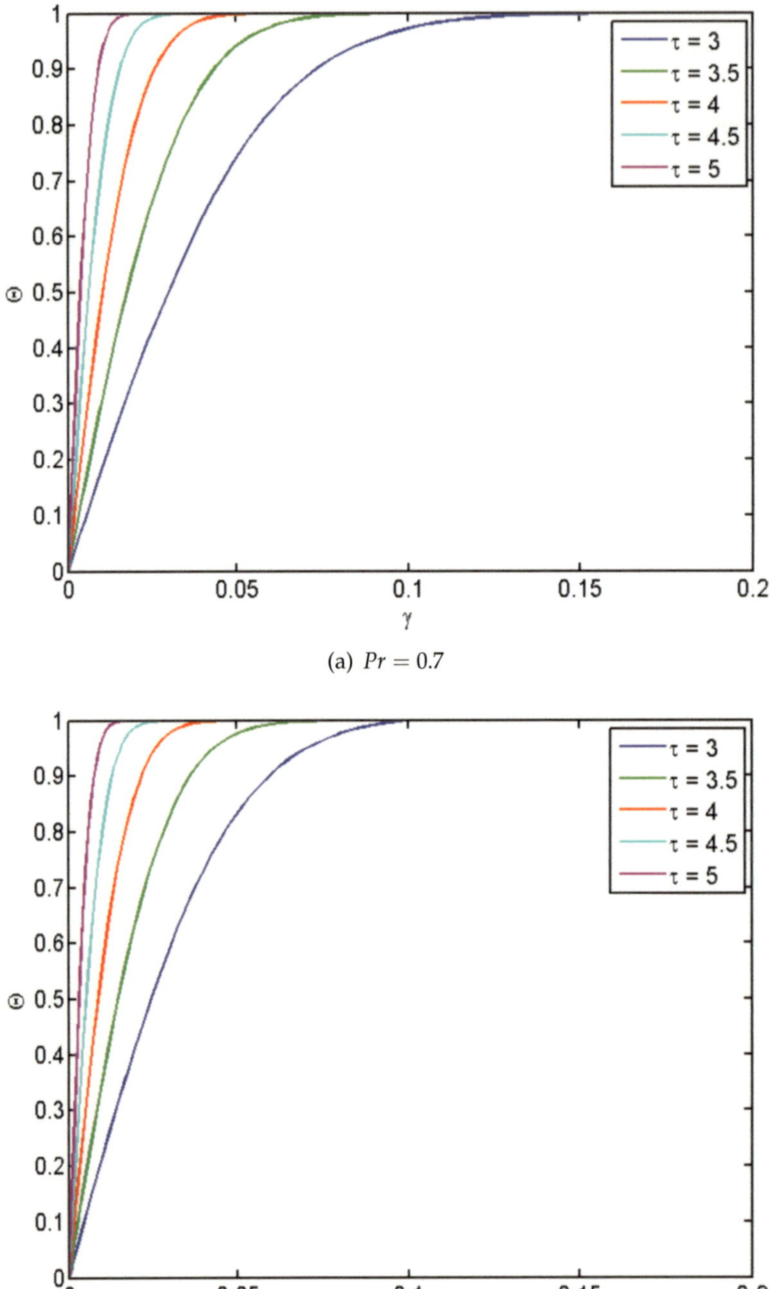

(a) $Pr = 0.7$

(b) $Pr = 1$

Fig. 5. Asymptotic temperature solution Θ for various value of γ

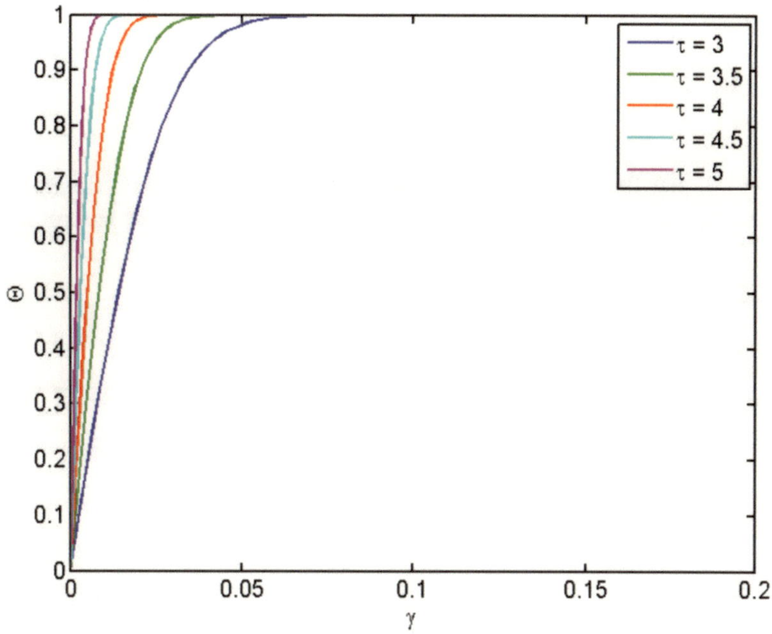

(a) $Pr = 3$

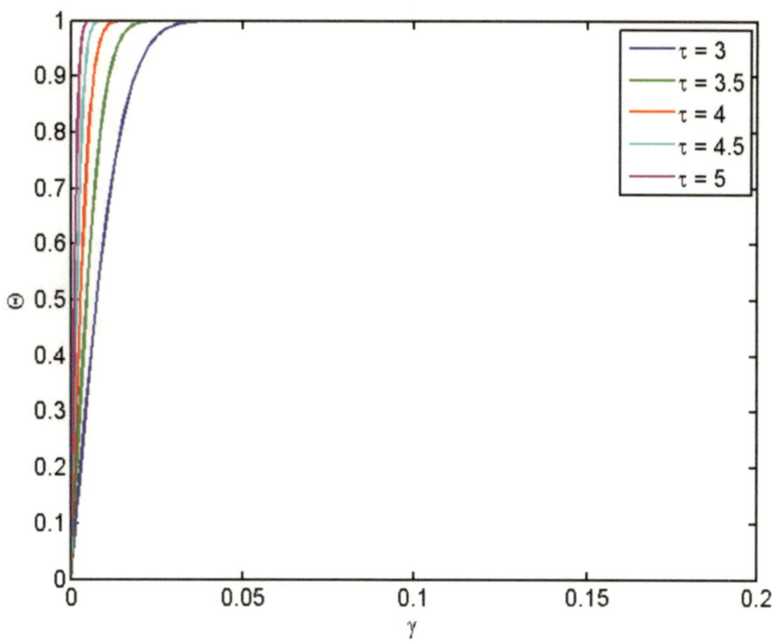

(b) $Pr = 10$

Fig. 6. Asymptotic temperature solution Θ for various value of γ

We now consider the net rectangle in the $\tau - \eta$ plane shown in Fig. (7) and the net points defined as below:

$$\eta^0 = 0, \quad \eta_j = \eta_{j-1} + \Delta\eta, \ \ j = 1, 2, ...J, \ \eta_J = \eta_\infty$$

$$\tau^0 = 0, \quad \tau^n = \tau^{n-1} + +\Delta\tau, \ \ n = 1, 2, ...J,$$

Here n and j are just the sequence of numbers that indicate the coordinate location, not tensor indices or exponents. The partial differential equations are easily discretized by central

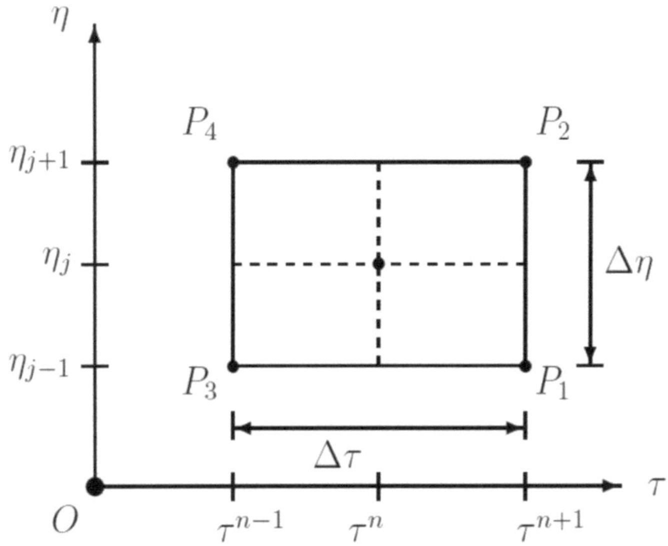

Fig. 7. Net rectangle for finite-difference method

difference representations with second-order accuracy, for example the finite-difference forms for any points are

$$h_\eta = \frac{h^n_{i+1} - h^n_{i-1}}{2\Delta\eta} \tag{27}$$

and

$$h_{\eta\eta} = \frac{h^n_{i+1} - 2h^n_i + h^n_{i-1}}{\Delta\eta} \tag{28}$$

When $i = 0$, since the value of h^n_{i-1} is not logical, the derivative is replaced by the forward difference with second-order accuracy

$$h_\eta = \frac{-h^n_{i+2} + 4h^n_{i+1} - 3h^n_i}{2\Delta\eta} \tag{29}$$

The finite-difference form of the ODE is written for the midpoint $(\tau^n,\ \eta_j)$, the discretized equation takes the form.

$$\frac{h_i^{n+1}-h_i^n}{\Delta\tau} = \frac{h_{i+1}^{n+1}-2h_i^{n+1}+h_{i-1}^{n+1}}{(\Delta\eta)^2} + 2h_i^n - (h_i^n)^2 - \frac{h_{i+1}^n - h_{i-1}^n}{2\Delta\eta}\int_0^{i\Delta\eta}(1-h)\,d\eta \tag{30a}$$

$$\frac{g_i^{n+1}-g_i^n}{\Delta\tau} = \frac{g_{i+1}^{n+1}-2g_i^{n+1}+g_{i-1}^{n+1}}{Pr(\Delta\eta)^2} - \frac{g_{i+1}^n - g_{i-1}^n}{2\Delta\eta}\int_0^{i\Delta\eta}(1-h)\,d\eta \tag{30b}$$

This procedure yields the following linear tridiagonal system:

$$-\beta h_{i+1}^{n+1} + (1+2\beta)h_i^{n+1} - \beta h_{i-1}^{n+1} = h_i^n + \Delta\tau\left[2h_i^n - (h_i^n)^2 - \frac{h_{i+1}^n - h_{i-1}^n}{2}\sum_0^i(1-h_i^n)\right] \tag{31a}$$

$$-\frac{\beta}{Pr}g_{i+1}^{n+1} + (1+\frac{2\beta}{Pr})g_i^{n+1} - \frac{\beta}{Pr}g_{i-1}^{n+1} = g_i^n - \Delta\tau\,\frac{g_{i+1}^n - g_{i-1}^n}{2}\sum_0^i(1-h_i^n) \tag{31b}$$

where $\beta = \Delta\tau/(\Delta\eta)^2$.

4.2 Initial flow

The initial condition is the solution of the following linear partial differential equations

$$h_\tau = h_{\eta\eta} \tag{32a}$$

$$g_\tau = \frac{1}{Pr}g_{\eta\eta} \tag{32b}$$

an the required solutions are

$$h = 1 - erf\left(\frac{\eta}{2\sqrt{\tau}}\right) \tag{33a}$$

$$g = erf\left(\frac{\eta}{2\sqrt{\tau/Pr}}\right) \tag{33b}$$

where the error function $erf(z)$ is defined as

$$erf(z) = \frac{2}{\sqrt{\pi}}\int_0^z exp(-\xi^2)\,d\xi \tag{34}$$

When $\tau \to 0$, the boundary conditions are convenient to write in the form

$$h_0^n = g_0^n = 0,$$

$$h_i^0 = erf\left(\frac{\eta_i}{2\sqrt{\tau}}\right),$$

$$g_i^0 = erf\left(\frac{\eta_i}{2\sqrt{\tau/Pr}}\right) \tag{35}$$

Equations (31) are defined as being implicit, as more than one unknown appears in the left hand side. They are unconditionally stable, however, set of linear algebraic equations is required to be solved by the tridiagonal matrix algorithm (TDMA), also know as the Thomas algorithm, which is a simplified form of Gaussian elimination that is applied to evaluate tridiagonal systems of equations.
The procedure is straightforward, except for the algebra. The resulting algorithm of the finite-difference method is written in MATLAB, a numerical computing environment allowing matrix manipulations and plotting of functions and data.

5. Numerical result

The following figure (Figs. (8)) shows the velocity distribution f. From the solution 17, we have

$$log(1 - f_\eta) = -c\eta + log\,2 \tag{36}$$

and if the similarity solution holds, then the graph of $log(1 - f_\eta)$ against $\eta e^{-\tau}$ should provide a straight line of gradient $-c$, except for small values of η, In Figs. (8), the values of $log(1 - f_\eta)$ are plotted against $\eta e^{-\tau - 3.5}$ at different value of τ. The value of c is 3.51 which is consistent with the previous discussion.
Next, we show the numerical solution of temperature distributions with Pr in Figs. (9) through (10)) . It is noticed that the dimensionless wall temperature gradient $\Theta'(0)$ raises with increase of Prandtl number, but the thermal boundary layer thickness decrease with increase of Prandtl number. The thermal boundary layer thickness is the distance from the body at which the temperature is 99% of the temperature obtained from an inviscid solution. The decrease of thickness can be explained by the definition of Prandtl number that Prandtl number is inversely proportional to the molecular thermal diffusivity α. If the Prandtl number is greater than 1, the thermal boundary layer is thinner than the velocity boundary layer. If the Prandtl number is less than 1, which is the case for air at standard conditions, the thermal boundary layer is thicker than the velocity boundary layer.
In comparison to the asymptotic solution, we note that increase in non-dimensional time τ leads to an increase in temperature profiles in both cases. Near the wall region where γ is small, the dimensionless wall temperature gradient of the numerical solution is lower than that of the asymptotic solution. It is because the asymptotic solution is only valid for the outer region. At our level of discretization, however, we are only able to resolve in small time range.

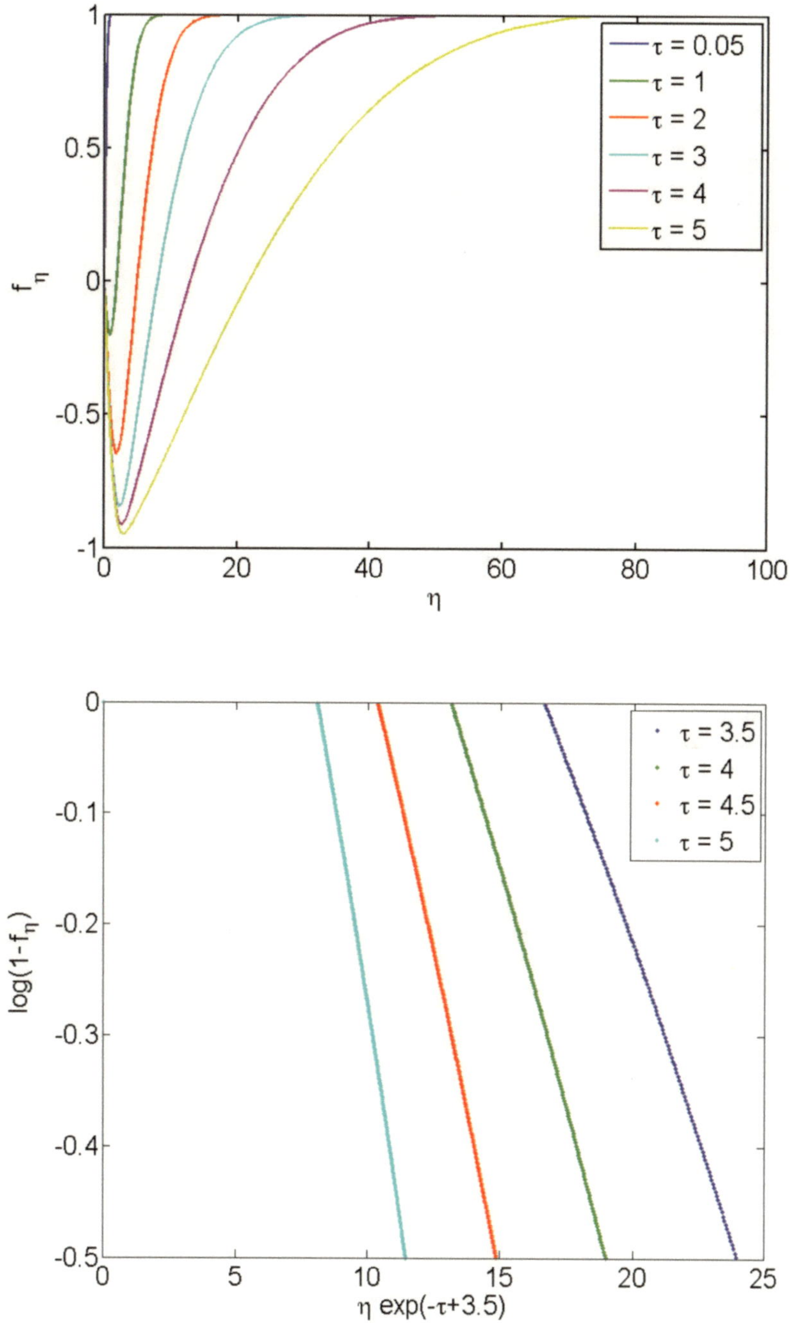

Fig. 8. Numerical solution of Eq. (17) against (a) τ, (b) $\eta e^{-\tau}$

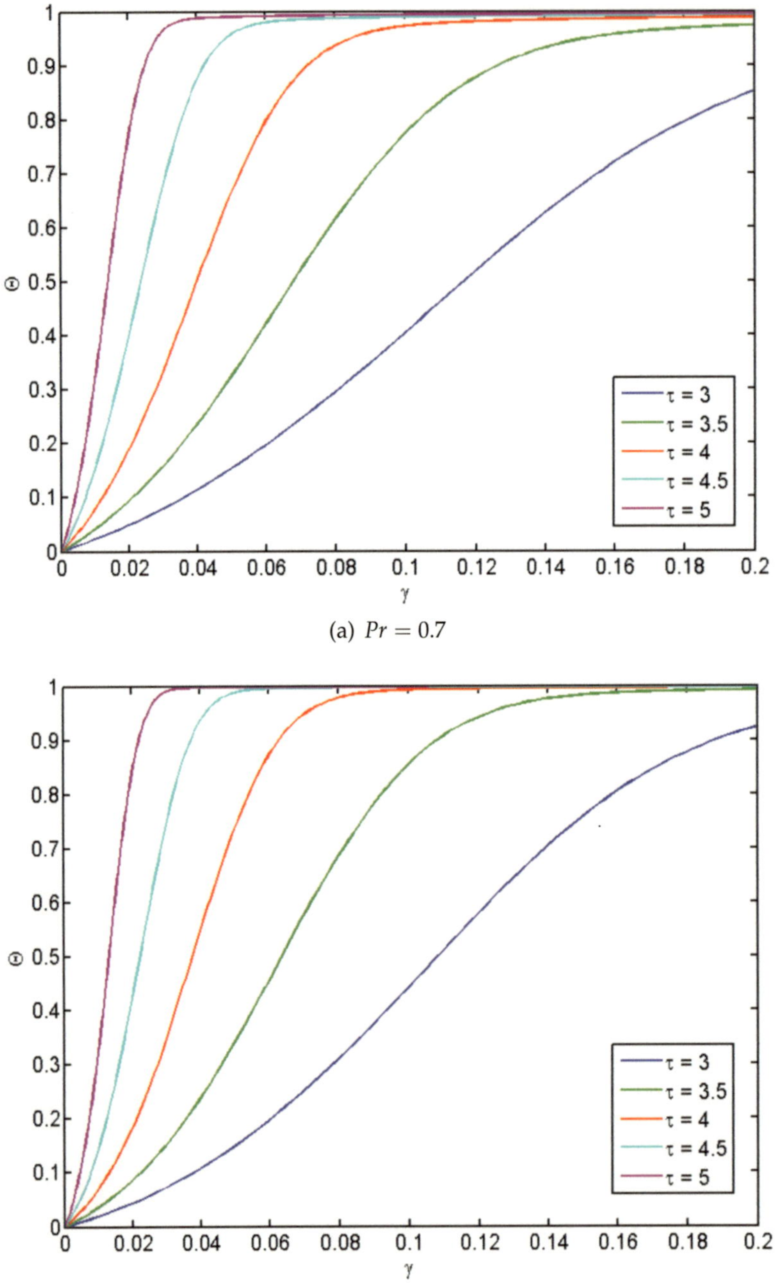

(a) $Pr = 0.7$

(b) $Pr = 1$

Fig. 9. Numerical temperature solution Θ for various value of γ

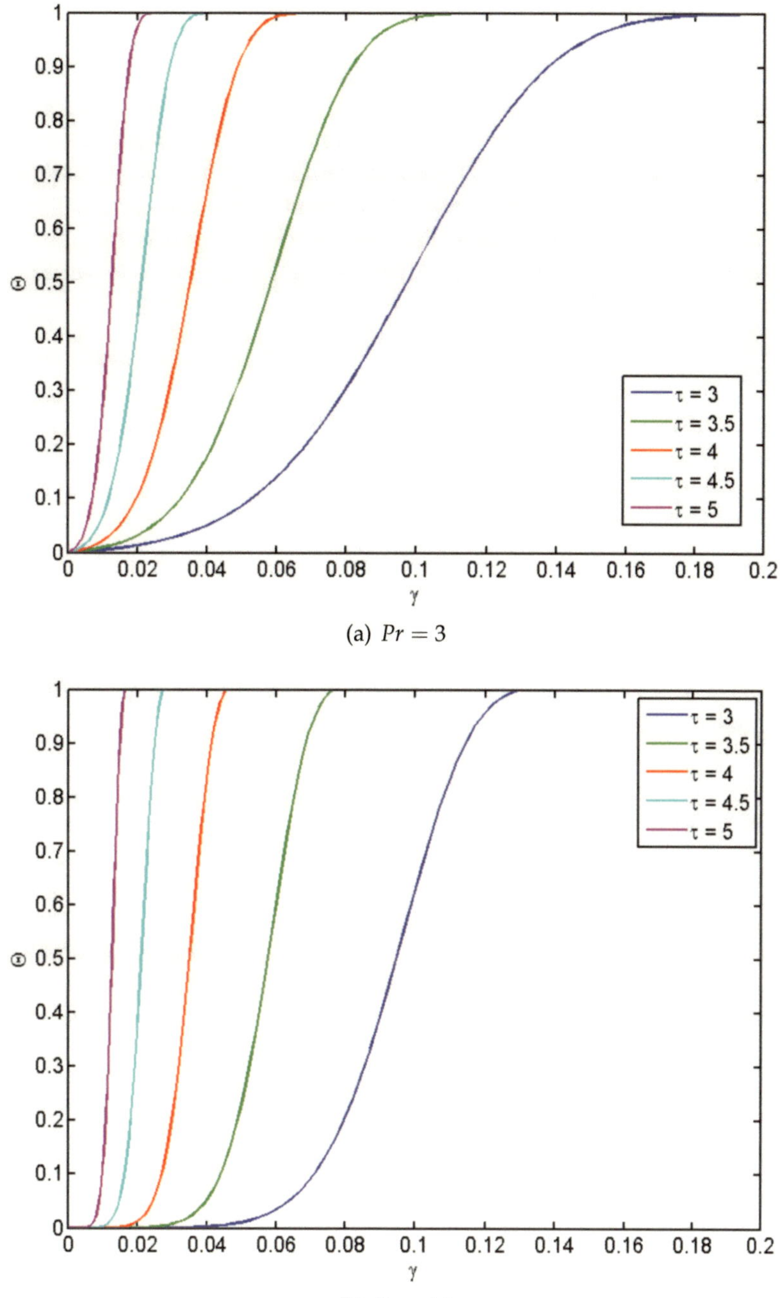

(a) $Pr = 3$

(b) $Pr = 10$

Fig. 10. Numerical temperature solution Θ for various value of γ

6. Conclusion

This study provides velocity and temperature distributions at different locations along the wall of a reversed stagnation-point flow by solving the numerical solution of full Navier-Stokes equations with finite difference method. Numerical findings show that velocity profiles obtained from similarity solution and numerical simulation are in tremendously good agreement and in region close to the stagnation point. Discrepancy of results in velocity profiles increases in region which is away from the reversed stagnation-point flow.
With the establishment of this frame work, the more important practical properties in engineering and technology application, like the velocity of wall is function of time, the temperature of wall is function of time and distance from wall, can be investigated and they would be the next phase of this study.

7. References

Burmeister, L. C. (1993). *Convective heat transfer*, A Wiley-Interscience publication, Wiley.

Chao, B. & Jeng, D. (1965). Unsteady stagnation point heat transfer, *J. Heat Transfer* 87: 221–230.

Davey, A. (1961). Boundary-layer flow at a saddle point of attachment, *Journal of Fluid Mechanics* 10: 593–610.

Eckert, E. (1942). *Die Berechnung des Wärmeübergangs in der laminaren Grenzschicht umströmter Körper*, VDI-Forschunhsheft.

Gorla, R. (1988). The final approach to steady state in a nonsteady axisymmetric stagnation point heat transfer, *Heat and Mass Transfer* 22(1): 37–44.

Hiemenz, K. (1911). Die Grenzschicht an einem in den gleichförmigen Flüssigkeitsstrom eingetauchten geraden Kreiszylinder, Dingl. Polytech, *J* 326: 321–410.

Howarth, L. (1951). CXLIV. The boundary layer in three dimensional flow.-Part II. The flow near a stagnation point, *Philosophical Magazine (Series 7)* 42(335): 1433–1440.

Lok, Y., Amin, N. & Pop, I. (2006). Mixed convection near a non-orthogonal stagnation point flow on a vertical plate with uniform surface heat flux, *Acta Mechanica* 186(1): 99–112.

Proudman, I. & Johnson, K. (1962). Boundary-layer growth near a rear stagnation point, *Journal of Fluid Mechanics* 12(02): 161–168.

Robins, A. & Howarth, J. (1972). Boundary-layer development at a two-dimensional rear stagnation point, *Journal of Fluid Mechanics* 56(01): 161–171.

Sano, T. (1981). Unsteady stagnation point heat transfer with blowing or suction, *Journal of Heat Transfer* 103: 448.

White, F. (2003). Fluid Mechanics. 5th edt.

Part 2

Applications Involving Computational Fluid Dynamics

9

Numerical Modelling and Optimization of the Mixture Formation Process by Multi-Hole Injectors in a GDI Engine

Michela Costa and Luigi Allocca
CNR – Istituto Motori
Italy

1. Introduction

The problem of the environmental impact of energy conversion systems is particularly felt in the automotive field as a consequence of the wide diffusion of internal combustion engines within the transportation systems, and of the very high concentration of vehicles in the urban areas. Several actions, therefore, are today being taken by car manufacturers and researchers towards the development of more and more efficient propulsion systems, characterised by lower and lower pollutants emissions. In fact, despite the recent efforts aimed at developing alternative technologies, it is likely that the internal combustion engine will remain dominant for the next 30 years and beyond. This implies that the study and the optimisation of the thermo-fluid-dynamic processes characterising its operation will undoubtedly continue to play a determining role in the forthcoming scenario.

The major difficulties today encountered in the experimental characterization of combustion and pollutants formation in both spark ignition (SI) and compression ignition (CI) engines rely in the low spatial and temporal resolution achievable from measurements, as well as in the possible influence of instruments on the same phenomena to be investigated. The diagnostics capability surely benefits of the development of non-intrusive optical techniques, although constructive and economic problems still hinder their broad use. On the other hand, the introduction of increasingly accurate physical and chemical models and the simultaneous growth of the processors speed have led to a diffuse use of computational fluid dynamics (CFD) techniques, especially in the phase of engine design. A wide variety of geometrical configurations or sets of engine parameters, indeed, are today suitable of being analysed into detail through models of various complexities at relatively low costs, or optimised according to predefined objectives.

As regards SI engines, in particular, the most pursued solution for the improvement of fuel economy relies on engine downsizing, coupled with turbo-charging and direct injection (DI): the engine displacement is reduced, whereas an increase of the low end torque is realised by air boosting, compression ratio rising and gasoline injection directly in the combustion chamber. These measures allow overwhelming the main shortcoming of engines mounting port fuel injection (PFI) systems, with mixture formation occurring within the intake ducts, namely the significant engine pumping losses at part-load operation (where the engine works during most of an urban driving cycle), caused by the throttle load control. The more precise gasoline dosage determines mixture formation processes the more effective for the development and stability of combustion. Knock arising benefits of the charge cooling effect offered by directly injecting the fuel into the cylinder. The engine can even be operated with overall lean mixtures through the so-called stratification of the charge, namely by creating a zone with stoichiometric air-to-fuel ratio around the spark plug and leaner conditions close to the cylinder walls. This reduces the wall heat losses, the unburned hydrocarbons (HC) and the carbon monoxide (CO) formation, and, at the same time, strongly increases the engine volumetric efficiency.

A lean engine operation, to the sake of truth, is generally feasible only at low loads and speeds, while at the higher loads, and at all loads and high speeds, the engine better works as homogeneous/stoichiometric. In fact, the in-cylinder turbulence intensity increases with the engine speed, hindering stable stratifications to be achieved at the higher regimes; on the other hand, increasing loads while attempting to maintain a stratified charge leads to mixtures locally excessively rich, that may cause an undesired increase of soot formation.

The realization of these different mixture conditions, namely of what is commonly called "mixed mode" direct injection boosting, encounters several difficulties in the practice. These range between the need of having at disposal increasingly efficient after-treatment systems for lean operation and the will to gain further insight into the in-cylinder mixture formation and combustion processes [Küsell *et al.*, 1999; Çelik and Özdalyan, 2010; Alkidas, 2007]. At present, technical solutions aimed at realising mixture conditions optimal for stable combustion, with low emissions and gasoline consumption over the whole engine working map, mainly rely on the employment of new generation high pressure GDI injectors (especially in the multi-hole configuration), as well as on the possibility to resort to split injections in the low speed regimes.

By controlling the spray orientation and fragmentation, a flexible charge stratification can be achieved, that, case by case, as the engine load and speed are changed, is able to give rise to an optimal combustion processes development.

Present work is focused on two activities performed by authors within the CFD approach to the study of in-cylinder processes in SI engines: the development of a three-dimensional (3D) numerical model for the GDI spray dynamics [Costa *et al.*, 2010], whose prediction capability is improved through a Simplex optimization algorithm, and the assessment of a procedure for the fuel consumption reduction based on the optimal synchronization of injection within the engine working cycle [Costa *et al.*, 2011]. The work is organised as following.

A certain insight into the behaviour of new generation GDI multi-hole injectors is first given, by experimentally characterizing three different devices both at the mass flow rate test bench and in an optically accessible vessel. Single and double injection strategies are considered.

The experimental activity is finalised to the creation of a database to be used for the assessment of a 3D numerical model for the GDI spray dynamics. The model is developed within the AVL Fire™ code [www.avl.com] and exploits a log-normal distribution for the initial droplets diameter, whose expected value and variance are properly defined.

Hints for a GDI engine design are then given. One of the three injector is considered as mounted on a single-cylinder engine, four-valve, four-stroke, 638 cc displacement, suitable for motorbike applications. A 3D model able to reproduce the in-cylinder energy conversion process, namely the whole pressure cycle, is build within the same commercial software environment. Two typical engine operating conditions are taken under examination, a high-

load and a moderate-load. In this last case, a globally lean stratified operation is studied. The influence of important parameters, as the injector orientation, the start of injection (SOI), the time of spark ignition (SI) and the injection pressure on the mixture formation and combustion processes are discussed.
Results of a study of split injection under lean-mixture, moderate-speed, moderate-load working conditions are finally presented. Major aim is the application of an optimization technique for the individuation of the mixture formation process realising a combustion the most effective for the maximization of the engine work. The software modeFRONTIER™ is chosen to automatically run the 3D numerical engine model. The Simplex algorithm is adopted to draw the choice of the input parameters in the design of experiments (DOE) space.

2. Experimental characterisation of the GDI spray dynamics from multi-hole injectors

Either the desired charge stratification around the spark plug in lean-mixture operation, or the greatest homogeneity under stoichiometric conditions, is achievable in GDI engines through different modes of gasoline-air mixture formation. In the so-called *wall-guided* mode the gasoline spray is directed towards the piston, which exhibits a properly shaped "nose" deflecting the mixture cloud in the vicinity of the spark plug. In the *air-guided* mode the mixture richer region is brought towards the ignition location by the tumble motion of the air entering from the intake ducts. Finally, in the *jet-guided* or *spray-guided* mode typically the spacing between the injector and the spark is smaller, with the fuel spray injected close to the ignition location [Stan, 2000].
Several kinds of injectors for GDI applications are today available. The earliest solution to reduce the rapidly changing fuel concentration gradients as the fuel passes the spark location during the injection period, hence to increase the combustion robustness, relies on the adoption of air-assisted injection systems, such as the one developed by Orbital Engine [Cathcart and Railton, 2001]. This technology is today still applied, because it offers an additional degree of freedom constituted by the direct injection of air, that allows a more effective control of local oxygen concentration, temperature and charge motion through the cycle [Shim *et al.*, 2008]. Alternative solutions, better meeting the requirements for the development of more efficient GDI engines, are the high pressure injectors: the swirl type injector generates an hollow-cone fuel spray by providing a swirl rotational motion to the fuel, that widely disperses and well-atomizes the spray at moderate injection pressures [Brewster *et al.*, 2008]; the multi-hole configuration, on the other hand, exhibits flexible spray patterns that reduce the fuel impingement on the cylinder walls and improve the spray stability (cone shape) with respect to the existing backpressure.
Three commercial multi-hole injectors suitable to be mounted on high-performances SI engines are tested within the present work. As mentioned in the Introduction, the major aim is the assessment of a complete database for the development of a 3D numerical model for the spray dynamics. Table 1 reports the holes number and diameter, as well as the exact flow rates of the considered injectors. The axes of the single jets coming from the nozzles are configured to depict different spray footprint structures. Two injectors are manufactured by Bosch, type HDEV 5.1, differing for the holes number, six for Injector #1, seven for Injector # 2, distributed regularly on a circumference to form an ellipsoidal-like hollow-cone geometry. The third injector is a six-hole Continental device, with five holes distributed over

a circumference and the sixth one in central position. Fig. 1 represents three sketches, each drawing the position of the holes on the relevant injector and the footprint of the spray axes on a plane placed at a distance of 30 mm from the holes themselves.

Injector Type	holes number	Hole diameter (mm)	Static Flow at 10 MPa (g/s)
Injector #1 BOSCH HDEV 5.1	6	0.193	13.7
Injector # 2 BOSCH HDEV 5.1	7	0.179	13.7
Injector # 3 CONTINENTAL	6	0.190	13.1

Table 1. Geometrical and flow rate characteristics of the three tested injectors.

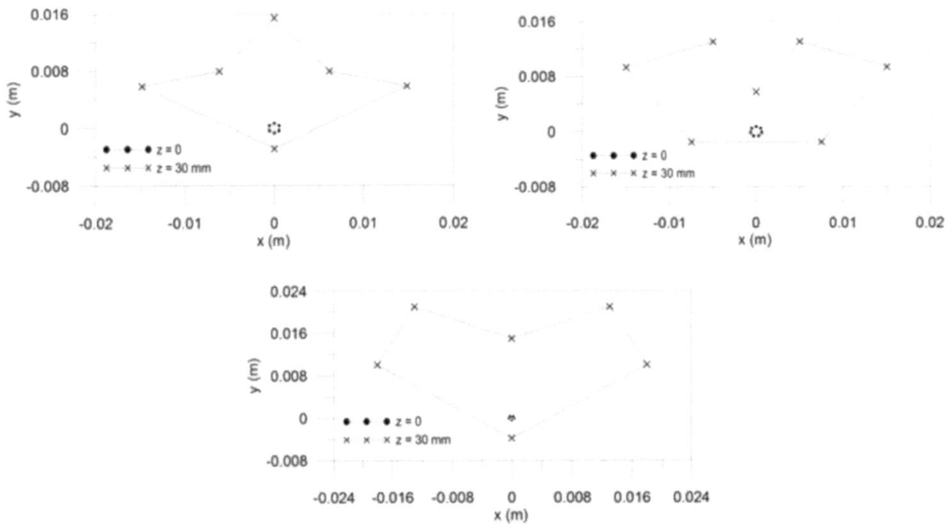

Fig. 1. Holes distribution and spray footprint on a plane placed at 30 mm from the injector tip. Injector #1 (top left), Injector #2 (top right) and Injector #3 (bottom).

The maximum operating pressure for all the three injectors is forced up to 25 MPa for Injector #1 and #2, up to 20 MPa for Injector #3. Commercial gasoline is used (ρ=740 kg/m^3) delivered by a hydro-pneumatic injection system without rotating organs. The system is managed by a programmable electronic control unit (PECU) enabling to define the strategy typology in terms of number of injection events, durations and dwell times.
Two types of analysis are conducted: instantaneous mass flow rates of gasoline are measured by means of an AVL meter operating on the Bosch principle [Bosch, 1966; Wallace, 2002] under both single and double injection strategies; image processing techniques are applied to derive the single jet penetration length and cone angle over time in the single injection case. The measured instantaneous mass flow rate profile is integrated over the injection interval of time to gain the total injected mass, and to verify that the value of this last quantity is in accordance with that measured by means of a precision balance. The study of the fuel dispersion, instead, is realized in an optically-accessible high-pressure

quiescent vessel containing air at atmospheric backpressure and ambient temperature. The jets are enlightened by powerful flashes at different instants from SOI. Images are captured through a high resolution CCD camera, 0.5 μs shutter time, 12 bit, at different times from SOI. The optical axis of the CCD is oriented either in a parallel or in an orthogonal way with respect to the spray propagation. Alignments of the jet directions with respect to the camera axis are actuated by a wet seal spherical holder enabling to tilt the injector in the angular range +/- 15°. The tip penetration of the considered jet, as well as the cone angle, is collected as a function of time. The images processing is based on background subtraction, filtering and edges determination. All the measurements are made on five-image averaged pictures for a statistical analysis of the cycle-to-cycle dispersion. A plateau value of the cone angle is achieved when the spray is completely developed (t ~ 500 μs).
The injection strategies in the experimental campaign cover the entire injection pressure range for the three injectors. The pulse durations are calibrated to deliver 10, 20 and 50 mg of gasoline at different injection pressures. Some single injection tests are reported in Table 2. Fig.2 reports a typical energizing current signal to the solenoid for injecting 20 mg of fuel at the pressure of 10 MPa, and the correspondent fuel injection rate signals, as collected for the three injectors. The signals are averaged over one hundred shots. A shift of 0.35 ms is registered between the start of energizing current and the exiting of fuel from the nozzle, indicating a postponed answer of the mechanical parts. This delay remains practically unchanged for all the three devices. Differently, the fuel injection rate signals show different rise times: for both the Bosch injectors it is of about 70 μs, while for the Continental one it is of about 170 μs. Furthermore, the closure time for Injector #3 is longer than for the others, namely it is of about 70 μs. The precise overlapping between signals relevant to Injectors #1 and #2 is indicative of an analogue behaviour of the moving equipment, while the Injector #3 has a slight larger inertia, hence greater opening and closing delays. This implies a different promptness availability of the fuel with the same command signals.

P_{inj} (MPa)	3	6	10	10	15	20	23
t_{inj} (μs)	1000	1900	1450	3600	2900	2600	2500
m_f (mg)	10	20	20	50	50	50	50

Table 2. Time durations of the pulses for the desired fuel amounts at the indicated injection pressures.

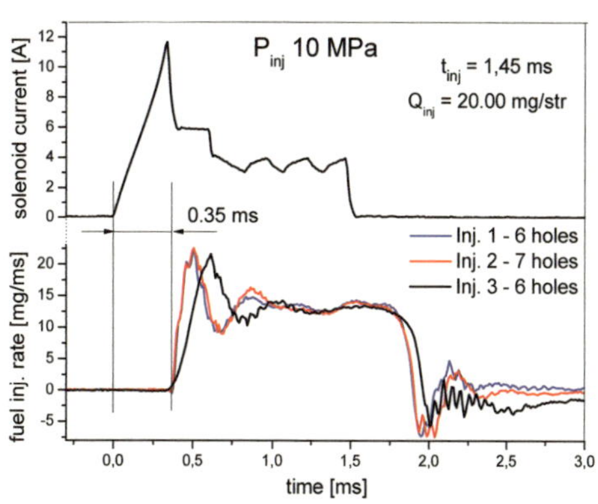

Fig. 2. Energizing solenoid current (top) and fuel injection rates (bottom) for the three considered injectors at P_{inj}=10 MPa, m_f = 20 mg.

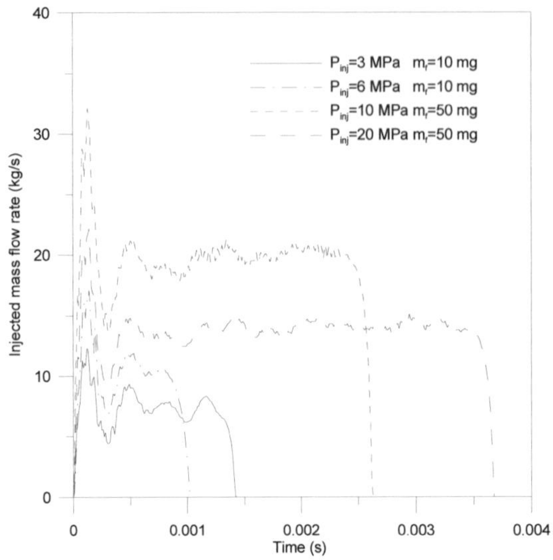

Fig. 3. Measured mass flow rates for four injection pressures and two values of the total injected mass for Injector #1.

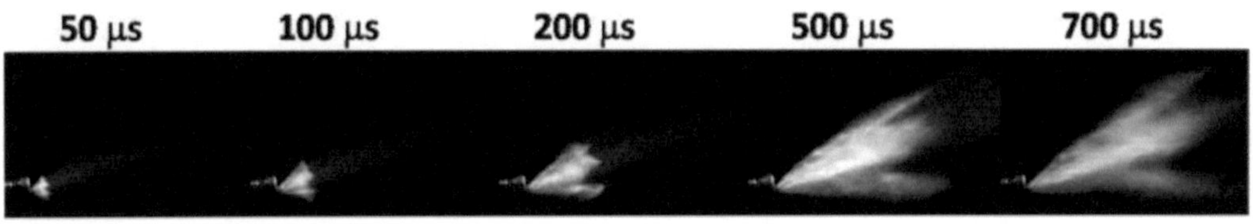

Fig. 4. Sequence of sprays from Injector #1 taken at different time from the SOI at $P_{inj} = 10$ MPa, $m_f = 50$mg.

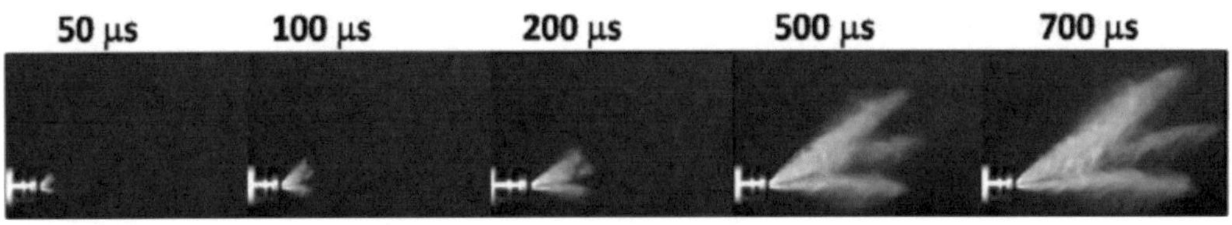

Fig. 5. Sequence of sprays from Injector #2 taken at different time from the SOI at $P_{inj} = 10$ MPa, $m_f = 50$mg.

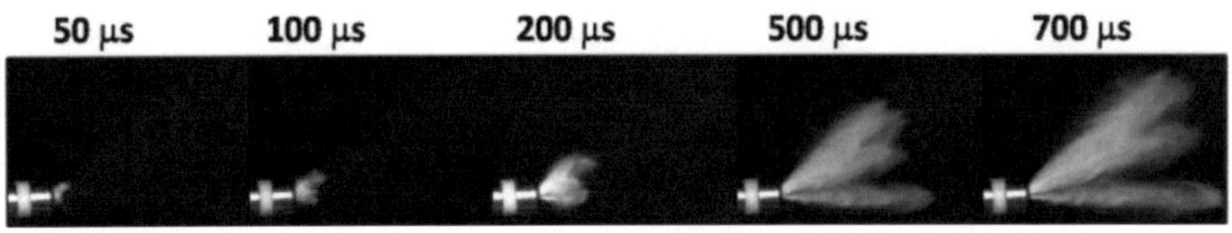

Fig. 6. Sequence of sprays from Injector #3 taken at different time from the SOI at $P_{inj} = 10$ MPa, $m_f = 50$mg.

Fig.3 is drawn to give an idea of the operation of one of the considered injectors, namely Injector #1, under different injection pressures and with current signals set to deliver two injected quantities, m_f=10 mg and m_f=50 mg. The injection pressure is equal to 3 and 6 MPa for m_f=10 mg, and 10 and 20 MPa for m_f=50 mg. The figure highlights the great flexibility of the injector in its capability to range from what are low to high load engine conditions.
Images of the jets evolving in the optically accessible vessel at different instants from SOI are reported in Figs. 4-6. Fig. 4 is a sequence of the propagating jets produced by the Injector #1 at 50, 100, 200, 500 and 700 μs from the SOI at the injection pressure of 10 MPa and 50 mg delivered gasoline. The lateral view of the spray allows distinguishing the origin of the single jets close to the nozzle exit. Four single well-confined arrows appear in the CCD view plane, while the last two are in the back side. The chosen orientation of the injector enables a complete view of the jet placed in the bottom part of the figure (horizontal), and permits a precise determination of its length, under the main hypothesis that all the jets behave in a similar way. In Figs. 5 and 6 the propagating sprays for the Injector #2 and Injector #3 are reported, respectively, under the same injection conditions of Fig. 4. Differences in the structure of the global spray appear due to the different number of holes and directions, although the overall behaviour appears almost unchanged. Injectors #1 and #2 assume analogues total angle while Injector #3 has a larger one. Detectable differences should appear from the punctual measurements of the penetrations and cone-angles.
The spray images highlight a complex structure of the evolving jets with inner bunches or fuel pockets picked out by the highest intensities of the scattered light. This aspect is indicative of a non homogeneous distribution of the fuel and is peculiar of the injection process. Fig. 7 reports an example of the front-view images of the sprays from the three injectors taken at 700 μs from the SOI, 10 MPa injection pressure and 50 mg injected fuel. The number of jets, their directions and the difference in the footprint figures for the diverse devices are evident. The six jets of Injector #1 are gathered together with respect to the other two. Injector #2 has a wider rose of the jets, with the seven sprays well distinguishable.

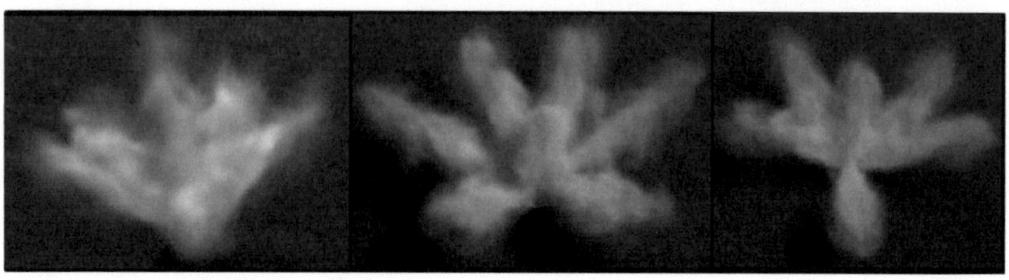

Fig. 7. Frontal-view images for the sprays issuing from the three considered injectors at 700 μs from the SOI, P_{inj} = 10MPa, m_f = 50 mg.

An idea of the behaviour of Injectors #1 and #2 under double strategies is given in Figs. 8 and 9. Fig. 8 reports the fuel injection rate signal collected for a double-pulse strategy at the injection pressure of 6 MPa for Injector #1, together with the timing of the solenoid driving current. Each pulse is equal to 0.9 ms in duration, hence the gasoline injected mass is split in percentages equal to 50% plus 50% of the total amount. Stability and repetitiveness of the injection events is studied by varying the value of the dwell time, dw, from the minimum value up to 1.5 ms. The minimum value of this variable, below which the opening of the second injection event interferes with the closing of the previous one, due to the electro-hydraulic inertia of the internal mobile equipment, is equal to 320 μs. Fig. 9 represents four different strategies of Injector #2, all delivering a total mass equal to 20 mg at the injection pressure of 10 MPa. It is to be remarked that also for this injector the minimum dwell time allowing distinguishable events is equal to 320 μs. The top of Fig. 9 shows the single pulse strategy. The setting for a 50% fuel injected during the first pulse and the remaining 50% delivered during the second one is then plotted. The successive strategy exhibits a 30+70% splitting, while at the bottom of the figure the 70+30% case is represented. This last could serve to realize, in the engine working cycle, a homogeneous combustion followed by a post-injection aimed at improving the exhaust conditions for a more effective catalytic conversion. Note that these percentages are just indicative and can be varied at will by modulating the energizing currents duration. Since no memory of the first pulse is induced in the second one above the minimum dwell time, the regulation of the percentages is a mere question of current settings.

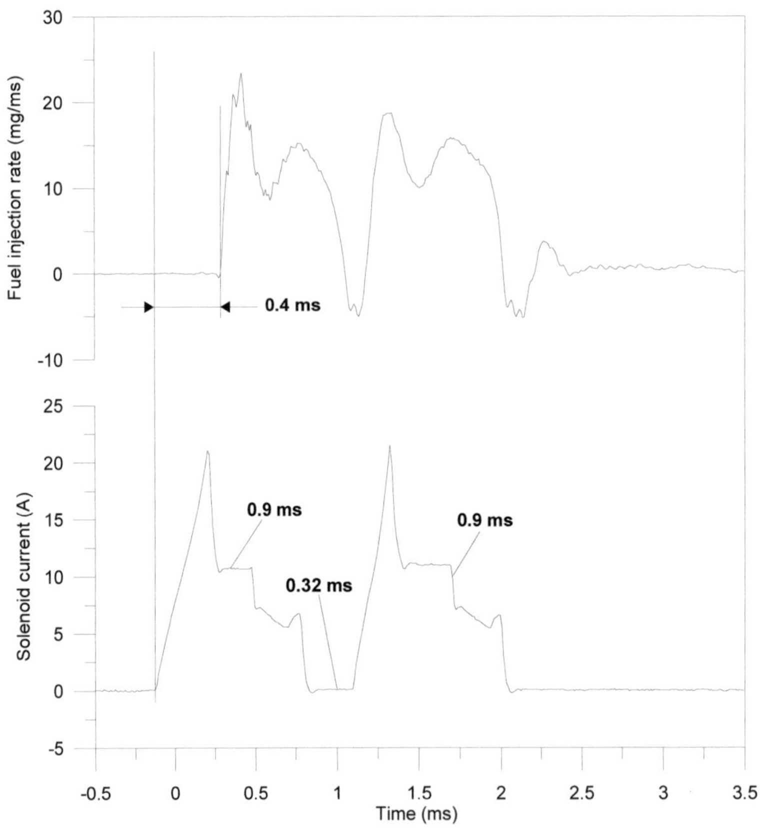

Fig. 8. Fuel injection rate for a double injection strategy at the minimum dw (top) with the corresponding exciting solenoid currents (bottom) for Injector #1. P_{inj}= 6 MPa.

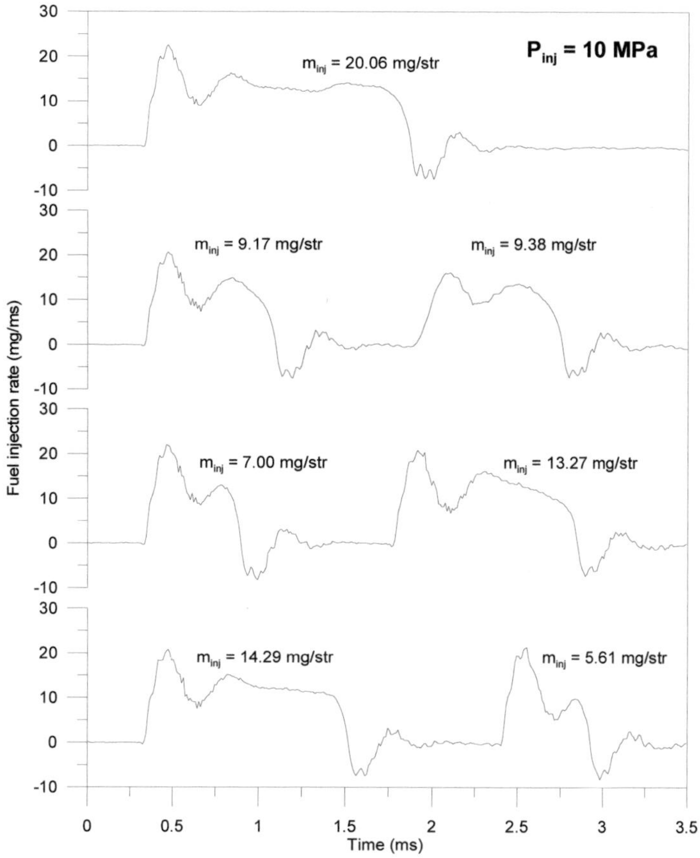

Fig. 9. Fuel injection rates for a single injection and for double injection strategies split at 50+50%, 30+70% and 70+30% for Injector #2.

3. Numerical simulation of the GDI spray dynamics

Reducing development time, improving performances and reliability of numerical models is of crucial importance for the design of new engine components. The use of optimization methods coupled with modern CFD tools is today very effective to accomplish these tasks, especially where uncertainty exists about a number of involved constants. Numerical procedures, in fact, may be used to generate a series of progressively improved solutions to the optimization problem, starting from an initial one. The process is terminated when some convergence criterion is satisfied.

In the present section the assessment of a simulation tool reproducing the spatio-temporal dynamics of sprays issuing from new generation high pressure injectors under various operating conditions is presented. The model, developed within the AVL Fire™ code environment, is conceived to exploit the previously described experimental data in part as input parameters, in part as terms of comparison for the numerical results.

In order to numerically simulate the effected tests, the spray is hypotesised to enter the top surface of a properly dimensioned computational domain of cylindrical shape, where the injector is supposed to be placed in central position. According to the discrete droplet method (DDM), the spray is considered as a train of droplets of given size, suffering various concurring effects as they travel within the computational domain. Turbulent dispersion, coalescence and break-up affect the droplets diameter within a Lagrangian approach coupled with the Eulerian description of the surrounding air motion. Break-up is simulated according to the model of Huh-Gosman [Huh and Gosman, 1991], whose constant C_1 (regulating the break-up time) is properly adjusted in the model tuning procedure. Initial droplets size at the nozzle exit section, is considered as not constant, but variable according to a probabilistic log-normal distribution, whose expected value is given by the following theoretical diameter:

$$D_{th} = C_d \left(\frac{2\pi\tau_f}{\rho_g u_{rel}^2} \right) \lambda^* \tag{1}$$

being τ_f the gasoline surface tension, ρ_g the surrounding gas density, u_{rel} the relative velocity between the fuel and the gas, C_d a constant of the order of the unity (indeed taken equal to the unity), and the parameter λ^* deriving from the hydrodynamic stability analysis and indicating the dimensionless wavelength of the more unstable perturbation to the liquid-gas interface at the injector exit section. The variance of the distribution, σ, is another parameter of the model to be properly tuned.
It is worth noticing that the definition of a probabilistic distribution of initial droplets size at the nozzle exit section corresponds to specify the occurrence probability for each particle diameter entry in the particle size distribution. The sum of all elements is used to normalize the distribution. The number of particles per parcel is determined by the particle probability distribution, the number of introduced parcels per time step and the assigned mass flow rate. The number of introduced parcels per time step is fixed a priori, and the injection velocity is evaluated in such a way to fulfil the continuity equation. The single jet cone angle is set as an input parameter, according to the effected measurements.

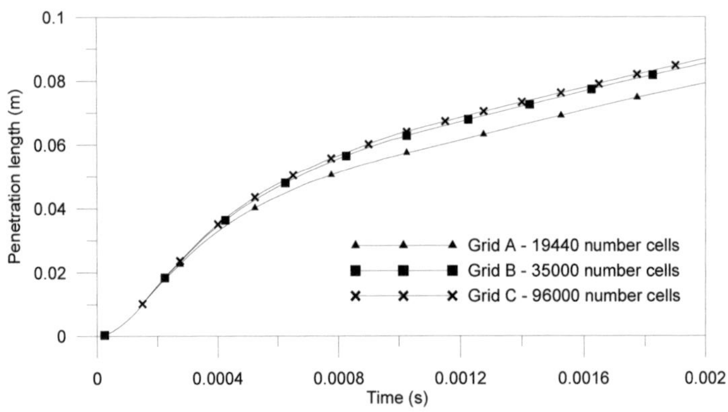

Fig. 10. Results dependency on the grid size.

In order to assess the numerical results dependency on the grid cell size, preliminary tests are made. As shown in Fig. 10, the penetration length in a certain test case, as averaged on the six jets issuing from the Injector #1, is practically unchanged as computed over a grid made of 35000 cells and over a grid made of 96000 cells. The former, therefore, is found being sufficient to perform the computations with a reasonable accuracy and low computational effort. In the following, however, results relevant to a grid made of about 60000 cells are presented.

Tuning of the Huh-Gosman model constant and of the distribution variance is here discussed as made by means of an optimization algorithm, instead than through a trial and error procedure. At each injection pressure, the error between the numerically computed penetration length, as averaged over the six jets, and the experimentally measured one is minimised by varying the value of both C_1 and σ in a properly defined DOE space. A sketch of the tuning procedure, as developed within the modeFRONTIER software, is represented in Fig. 11. The Simplex algorithm is used. The results of the automatic model tuning are reported in Fig.12. The top of the figure represents the value of the C_1 constant minimizing the error between numerical and experimental data as a function of the injection pressure for the three injectors. The bottom of the figure reports the value of the variance of the corresponding distribution of initial droplets size.

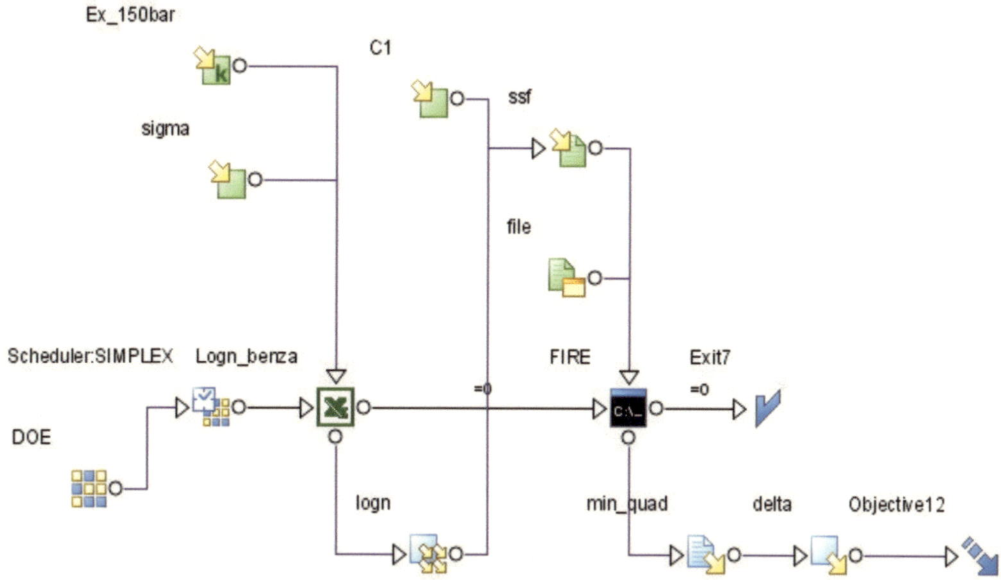

Fig. 11. Sketch of the numerical model constants tuning procedure.

A similitude of behaviour between Injector #1 and #2 is evident, since the values of C_1 are found comparable. The values relevant to Injector #3 are slightly higher, probably due to the differences in the injector geometrical characteristics, hence in the way internal perturbations affect the issuing flow. A slight increase of the variance with injection pressure may be assumed, according to a former authors' idea, physically consistent with the reduction of droplets initial diameter consequent the increase of injection pressure. A similar conjecture may apply to the trend of the Huh-Gosman constant, which slightly increases to account for the greater injection velocity. The low dispersion of the optimal values of the model constants confirms the good prediction capability of the model. The combined use of the Huh-Gosman break-up model and of a properly defined log-normal distribution for the initial droplets size allows overwhelming the problems generally encountered in the simulation of GDI sprays from new generation injectors.

The dependence of the break-up process upon injection pressure, indeed, is a challenging issue, since it is well known that increasing injection pressure has a twofold effect on the

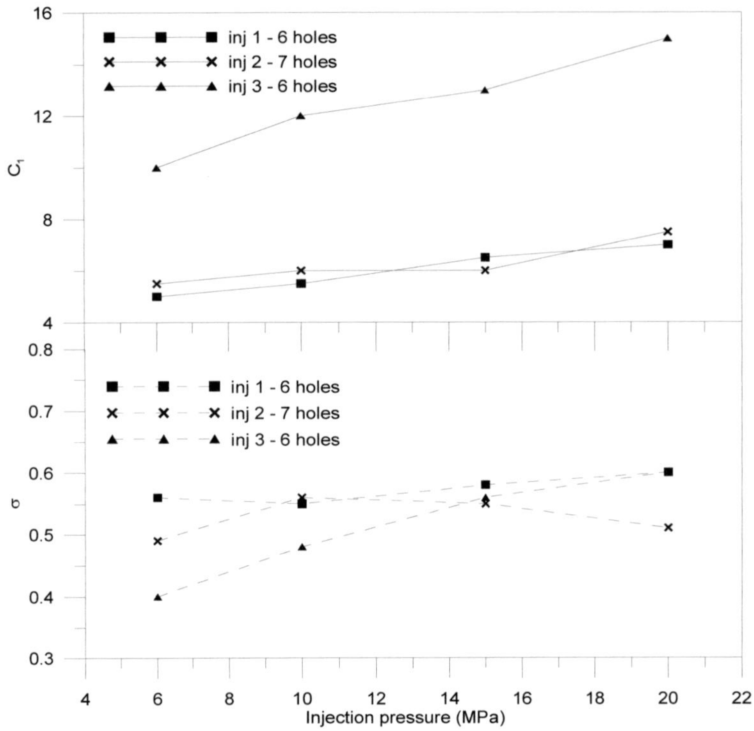

Fig. 12. Results of the tuning procedure of the two model constants.

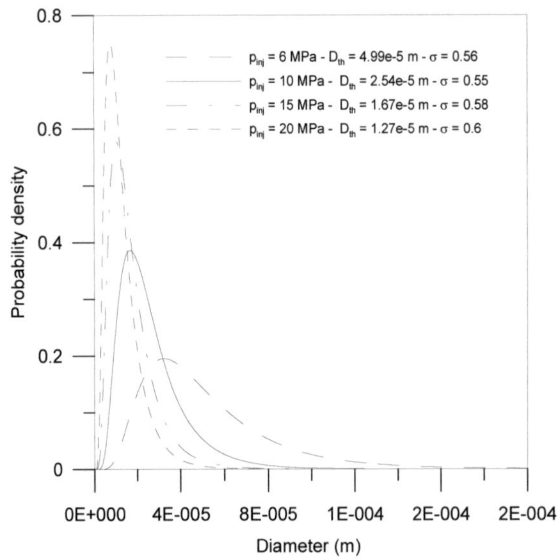

Fig. 13. Log-normal distribution of the initial droplets size for Injector #1 as a function of the injection pressure.

spray behavior. From one hand, the spray fragmentation is enhanced and the droplets diameter reduced, from the other, injection velocity is increased. The two effects have opposite consequences on the overall spray length, that should be reduced by the presence of smaller droplets, but should be increased by the greater velocities. The last effect is indeed dominant, as confirmed by the experiments, but may be overestimated in the phase of spray modeling. Malaguti *et al.* [Malaguti *et al.*, 2010], say, faced the problem by resorting to what authors call an "artificial" introduction of atomized droplets made at a given distance from the injector tip: a Rosin-Ramler distribution whose average diameter was computed to match the experimentally measured penetration length and droplets size was used. Present idea is believed to better follow the actual physics of the phenomenon, since the expected value of the initial droplets distribution, inserted at the nozzle exit section, is a theoretical diameter linked to the injection pressure through the value of the relative velocity between the liquid and the air, that moves towards lower values as injection pressure is raised. The distribution variance may be maintained almost constant or slightly increasing with injection pressure, as confirmed by the here presented optimization procedure. Fig. 13, as an example, reports the distributions used for the four considered injection pressure for Injector #1. Analogous shapes are relevant to the other two injectors. All the distributions are cut at the value corresponding to the nozzle hole diameter.

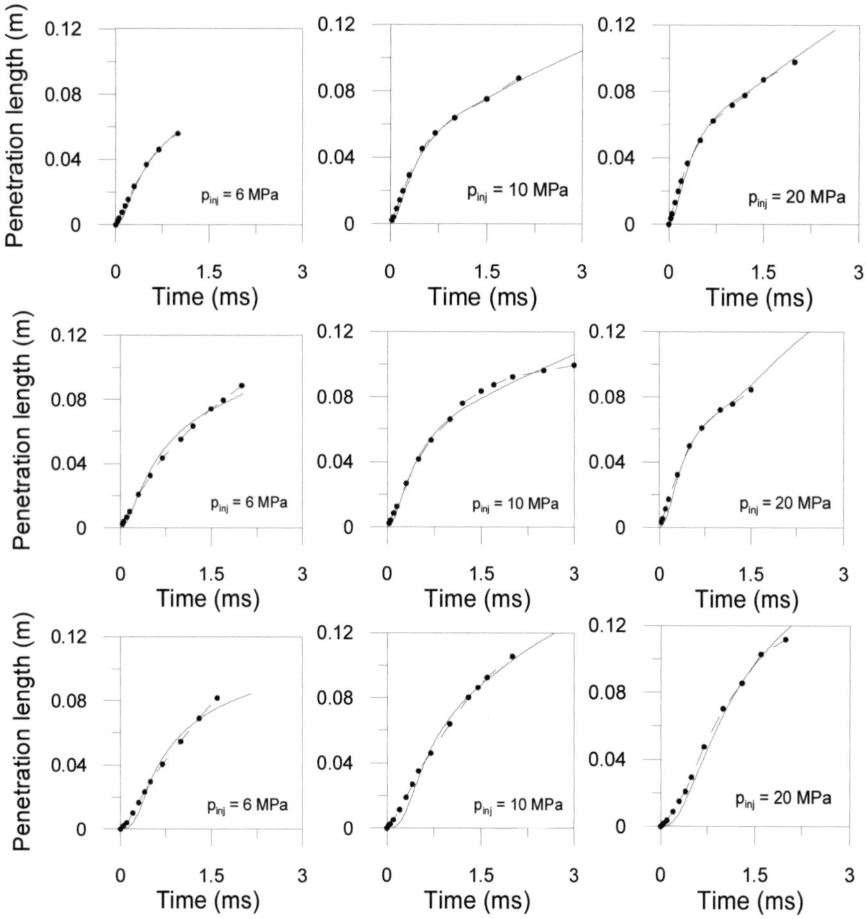

Fig. 14. Numerical (continuous line) and experimental (dashed line with dots) penetration lengths for Injector #1 (top), #2 (centre), #3 (bottom).

The prediction capability of the model is demonstrated in Fig. 14, where a comparison between the computed and the measured penetration lengths relevant to the three injectors are reported. The agreement is satisfactory under all the injection pressures considered.

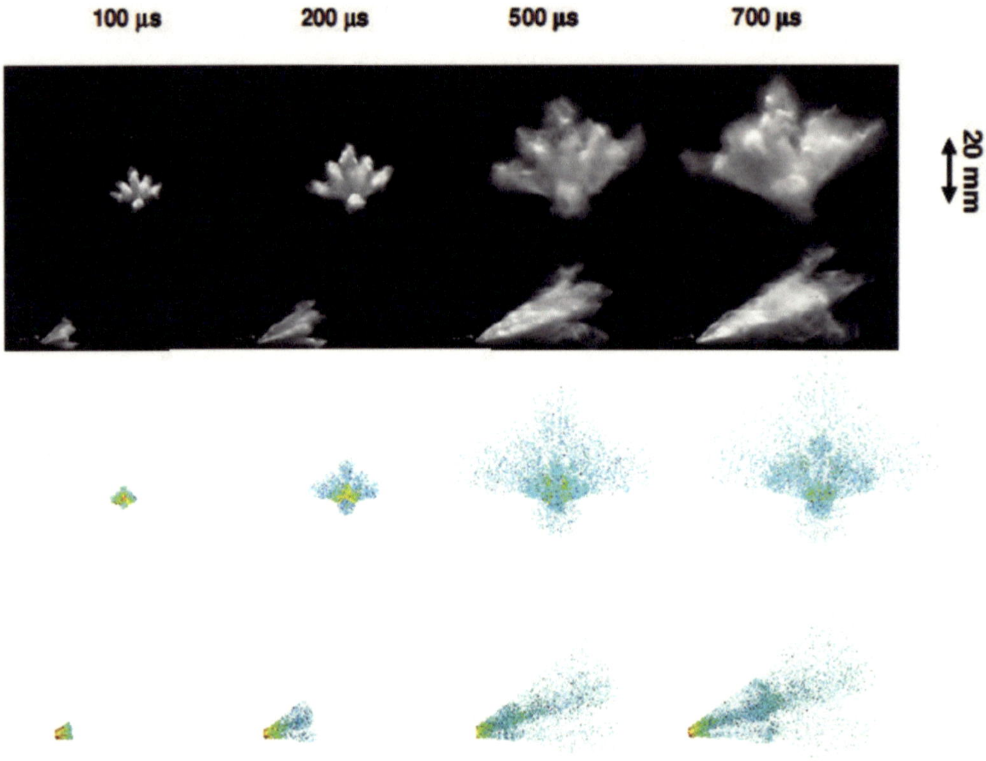

Fig. 15. Experimentally collected images (top) and numerically computed sprays (bottom) for Injector #1 under injection pressures of 20 MPa. Frontal and lateral views.

The spray structure is represented in Figs. 15 and 16. Fig. 15 is a sequence of images of the evolution of the spray issuing from Injector #1, in two different views, as experimentally collected and as numerically simulated for an injection pressure P_{inj}=20 MPa and an injected total mass m_f=50 mg. The frontal view of the sprays allows appreciating the jet propagation. The regularity appears destroyed for the 500 and 700 µs images, where the interference between the single jets is evident and the single jet evolution cannot be longer followed. The fuel has to be considered as a single, large and composite spray. Fig. 16 shows experimental images and numerically computed sprays from Injector #2 at various instants of time from the SOI at the injection pressure of 10 and 15 MPa. The greater penetration length at the higher pressure is evident. Slight differences appear in the spray tip, that is sharper in the experiments. This discrepancy can be reduced by further adjusting the far field break-up characteristic time of droplets, although it is to be considered that, at the distance from the nozzle where the differences become appreciable, the effect of evaporation should be also taken into account under real engine working conditions.

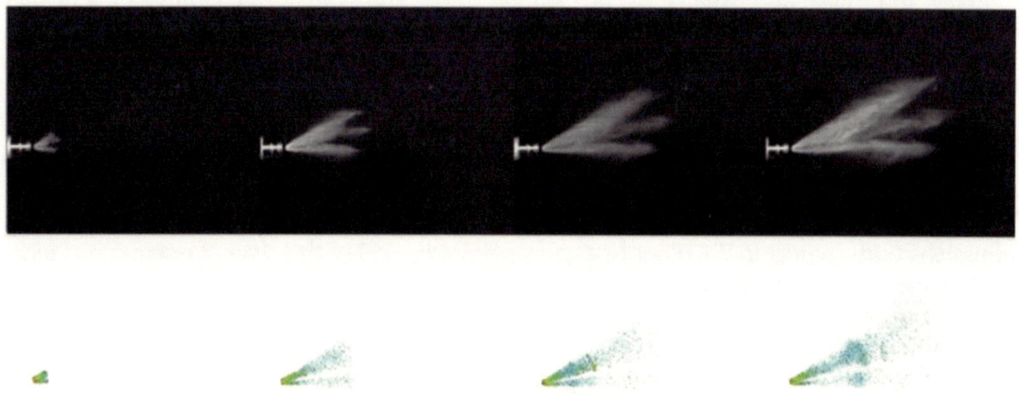

100 μs 300 μs 500 μs 700 μs

P_{inj}= 10 MPa

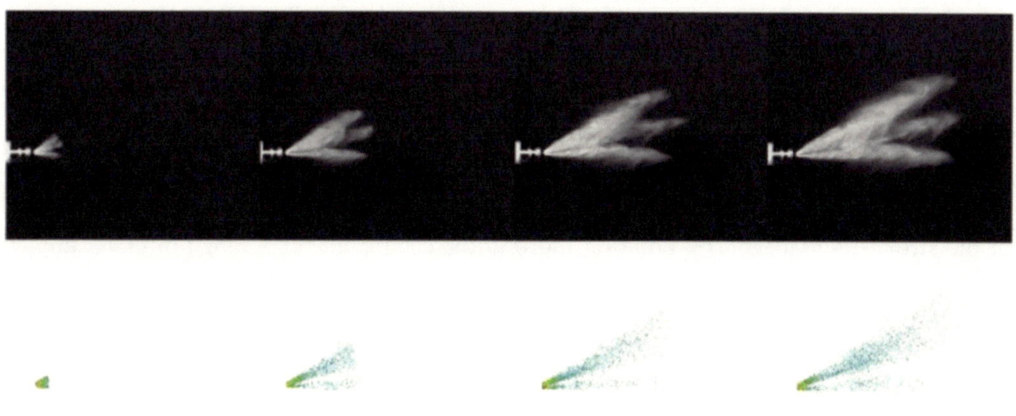

100 μs 300 μs 500 μs 700 μs

P_{inj}= 15 MPa

Fig. 16. Numerically computed (top) and experimentally collected (bottom) images of the spray issuing from the Injector #2 under injection pressures equal to 10 and 15 MPa.

4. Development of the 3D GDI engine model and its application in the design phase

The effects of the injection strategy on the combustion process of a GDI engine are discussed in this section. In particular, a single cylinder engine, four-valve, four-stroke, 638 cc displacement, suitable for motorbike applications is analysed. A 3D numerical model of the cylinder and intake and exhaust ducts, using as initial and boundary conditions the results of a 1D simulation of the entire propulsion systems, is presented, as developed by authors within the AVL Fire™ environment. Gasoline injection is simulated according to the previously discussed model, under both single and double strategies, as issuing form Injector #1. In positioning the injector within the combustion chamber, the *spray guided* mixture formation mode is preferred, since it offers the greatest possibilities of extending the limits of lean engine operation. In fact, low combustion efficiency losses and combustion phasing losses, resulting in a significant further improvement in fuel economy and noxious emissions with respect to the other two concepts are typical of this way of operation [Piock, 2003, Landenfeld *et al.*, 2004]. The considered engine is at a design stage, therefore major choices improving the engine operation are discussed, as firstly derived on the ground of parametric analyses.

4.1 Moving mesh generation

The discretisation of the moving boundary computational domain is realized by means of the pre-processing software included in the same Fire™ Graphical User Interface (GUI), called Fame Engine Plus (FEP). This allows performing a semi-automatic moving mesh generation, where the user can control the cell size by thickening nodes where particular geometric conformations of the outer surfaces are present, or where intense gradients of the thermo-fluid variables are expected. This is made through the choice of appropriate selections on the surfaces, or the surfaces edges, in the vicinity of which the spacing of the grid is determined ad hoc, depending on the particular crank angle position and differently from the rest of the domain.

The mesh relevant to the simulation of the four-stroke engine cycle is made by accounting for both the sequence of steps in which the cycle itself may be decomposed (intake, compression, expansion and exhaust stroke) and the subdivision of the domain in three main parts, namely the cylinder, the intake ducts and the exhaust ducts. The time sequence of the strokes is managed by building more grids, each used for a range of crank angles defined *a priori*, that avoids an excessive cell distortion. The transition from one grid to the next is carried out by re-mapping the thermo-fluidynamic variables on the nodes, according to a procedure called *rezone* in the Fire™ environment. In order to maintain the computational time within reasonable limits, the grids are considered active only in physical domains of interest: when intake and exhaust valves are closed the grid is built only in the cylinder; the intake and exhaust ducts are added geometrically, and numerically solved, only at those crank angles for which these zones are actually put into contact with the cylinder by the valves opening. The error resulting from not having simulated the flow in the pipes when valves are closed, is controlled by setting appropriate conditions of pressure and temperature at the crank angles where these domains are connected with the cylinder.

Fig. 17 shows a view from the top of the surface of the complete computational domain, with the four pipes. The spark plug is assumed as mounted in central position, while the injector is positioned between the two intake pipes at a distance of 39.6 mm from the

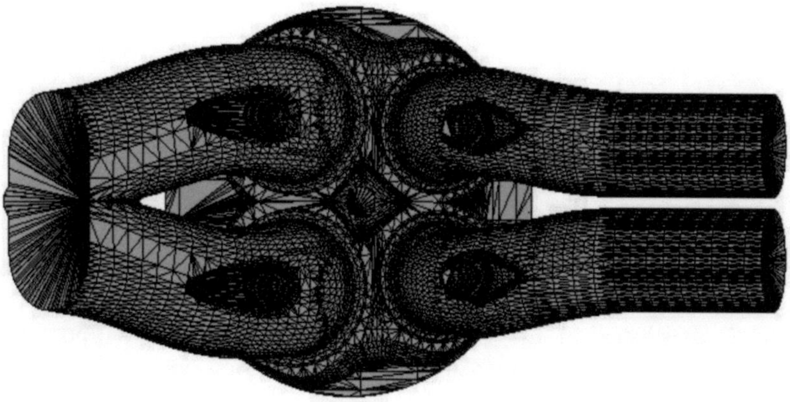

Fig. 17. Top view of the complete engine surface.

cylinder axis. Fig. 18 represents one of the grids used for the range of valves overlap, particularly at 380°, together with a table reporting its geometrical characteristics. Note the thick part on the right of the exhaust ducts, which is a part added properly to avoid numerical errors due to reflections from the outlet surface.

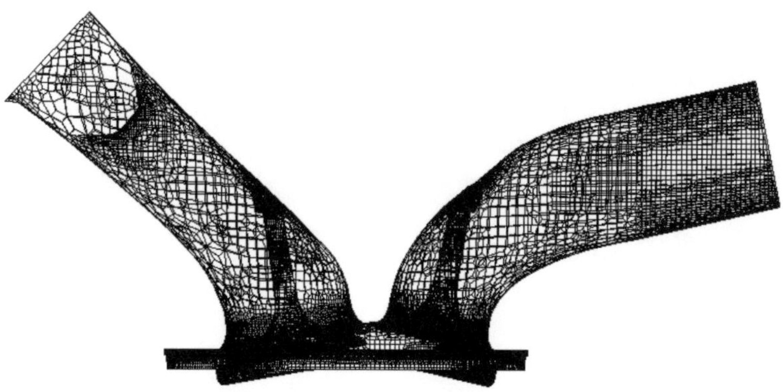

Number of tetrahedrical cells	7698
Number of Hexahedrical cells	613785
Number of piramidal cells	67811
Number of prismatic cells	133259
Total number of cells	822553

Fig. 18. Computational grid (cells on surface) corresponding to a crank angle of 380° and characteristic data.

For the sake of clarity, Table 3 reports the instants of intake and exhaust valves opening (intake valves opening, IVO, exhaust valves opening, EVO) and closing (intake valves closing, IVC, exhaust valves closing, EVC), and the position of the top dead centre (TDC).

IVO	IVC	EVO	EVC	TDC (valves overlap)	TDC (combustion)
330°	608°	120°	390°	360°	720°

Table 3. Relevant crank angle positions.

4.2 Simulation of the in-cylinder processes

Boundary and initial conditions for the 3D simulation are derived from a 1D model of the whole propulsion system, including all the elements from the intake mouth to the exhaust. The model is developed at the University of Naples - DIME, within the 1Dime code environment, by accurately schematising all the engine components [Bozza *et al.*, 2001]. The 1Dime code is a well assessed gas-dynamic tool, using the two-zone fractal combustion model and validated under various engine configurations by Bozza *et al.* [Bozza and Torella, 2004; Bozza *et al.*, 2008].
To give an example of the boundary conditions set at the intake pipes inlet and at the exhaust pipes outlet of the 3D model, Figs 19 and 20 are drawn. These show, respectively, the static pressure set at the exhaust and the total pressure and static temperature set at the intake at the engine speed of 7500 rpm, motored conditions. Note that the engine under investigation is characterized by the presence of intense pressure wave propagation in the intake system, strongly affecting the cylinder volumetric efficiency. Imposing a transient boundary condition at the intake ducts inlet is required to get a good prediction of the overall trapped mass. On the other hand, no problem derives from this assumption, as no unphysical/spurious oscillations arise, between the imposed 1D total pressure and the static pressure resulting from the 3D computations.
The comparison between the in-cylinder motored pressure cycle calculated by means of the 1D and the 3D models at 7500 rpm is reported in Fig. 21. The agreement is good, both as regards the charge substitution phase, and the compression and expansion strokes.

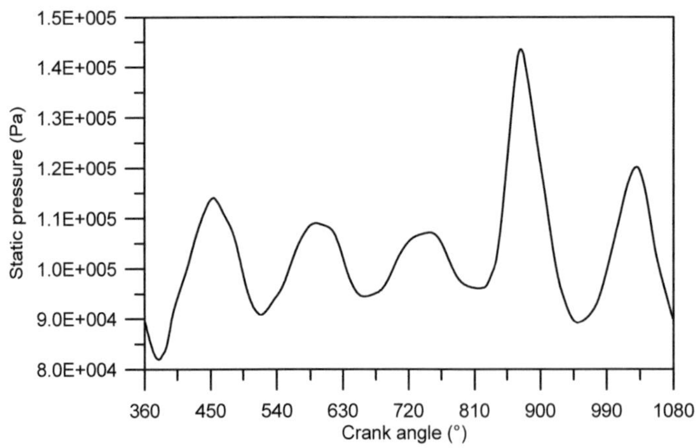

Fig. 19. Outlet boundary condition. Static pressure.

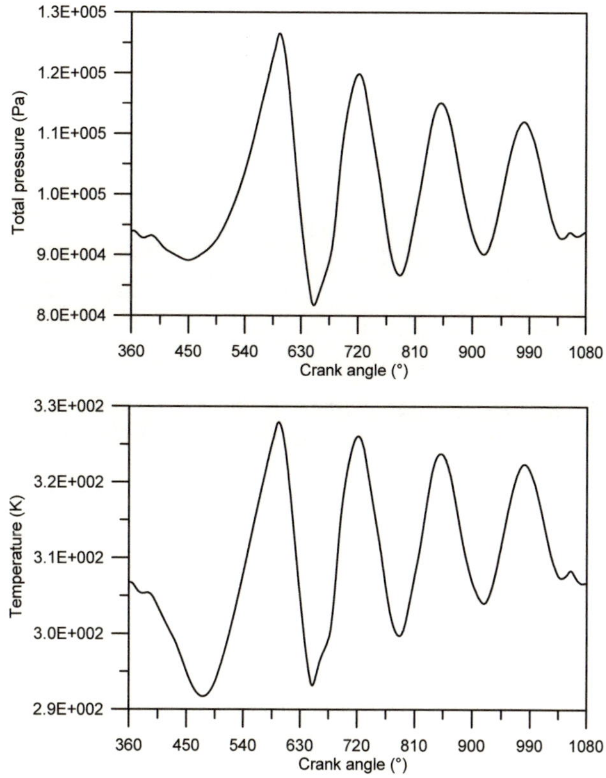

Fig. 20. Inlet boundary conditions. Total pressure (top) and static temperature (bottom).

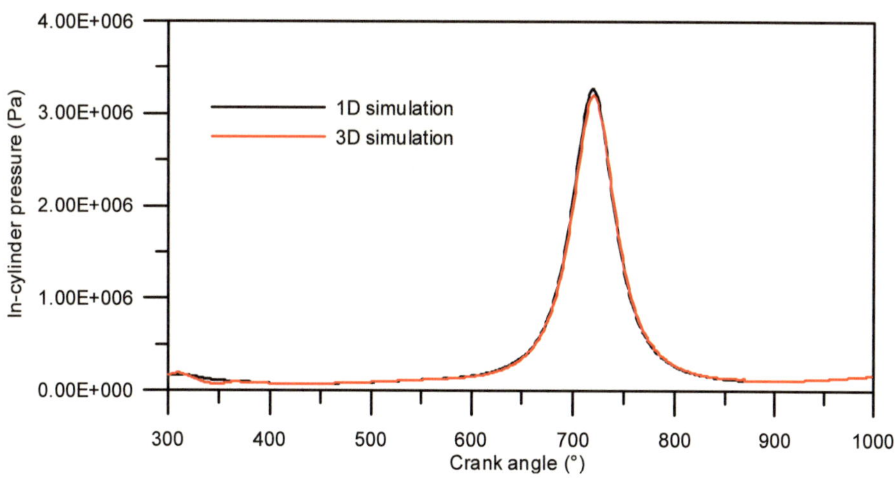

Fig. 21. 1D and 3D in-cylinder pressure cycles. Motored conditions.

When simulating typical engine working cycles, spray dynamics is simulated by following the previously described approach, combustion according to the Extended Coherent Flame Model (ECFM) model [Colin *et al.*, 2003].

Results relevant to different engine representative working conditions, including mixture formation and combustion processes, are discussed hereafter. Table 4 summarises data relevant to a full-load case and a moderate-load case: speed, air-to-fuel ratio A/F, injected gasoline mass and injection pressure and injection duration are reported.

	Speed (rpm)	BMEP (MPa)	A/F	P_{inj} (MPa)	m_f (mg)	Injection duration (ms)	Injection duration (°)
Full-load	7500	1.28	13	10	50	3.44	155
Moderate-load	5000	0.3	17	6	19.4	2.07	62°

Table 4. Numerical tests cases.

The first considered operating condition refers to an engine speed equal to 7500 rpm and full load, namely brake mean effective pressure BMEP=1.28 MPa and A/F=13, according to data derived from the 1D simulation. After the definition of the best inclination of the injector with respect to the cylinder axis, different crank angles of start of injection (SOI) at the injection pressure P_{inj}=10 MPa are discussed, for fixed instants of time of spark ignition (SI). In a second step, the injection pressure is changed with fixed SOI and fixed SI. As P_{inj} raises from 10 MPa to 20 MPa, the injection duration is reduced from 3.44 ms to 2.63 ms, hence from 155° to 118°.

Another considered representative operating condition is of moderate-load, for an engine speed equal to 5000 rpm, namely BMEP=0.3 MPa, with A/F=17. Injection pressure is assumed at 6 MPa, injected mass is m_f= 19.4 mg, SI is varied to reach the maximum brake torque (MBT). This case is examined with the scope of highlighting advantages deriving from adopting overall lean stratified mixtures.

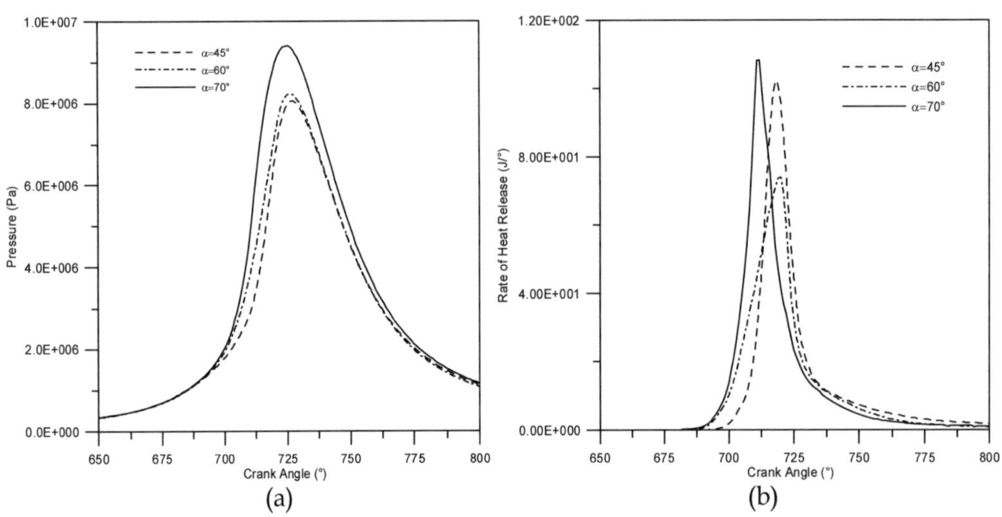

Fig. 22. In-cylinder pressure (a) and rate of heat release (b) for three different inclinations of the injector w.r.t. the cylinder axis.

The analysis leading to the choice of the Injector #1 inclination angle is first discussed. The injection strategy shown in Fig. 3, characterised by an injected mass equal to 50mg at a pressure of 10 MPa, is chosen to effect the study. The injector is assumed mounted on the cylinder head in such a way that its axis and the cylinder axis form angles of 45°, 60° and 70°. SOI is set at 470°, angle of maximum intake valves lift, SI is fixed at 675°. Valves and spark plug wetting are avoided by choosing the best injector orientation with respect to its own axis, namely by directing the previously mentioned insulated jet, of the six composing the spray, towards the engine head. The dramatic effect of the injector inclination on the pressure cycle and the rate of heat release is shown in Fig. 22. An angle of 70° is demonstrated to increase the pressure cycle area by increasing the release of heat within the combustion chamber.

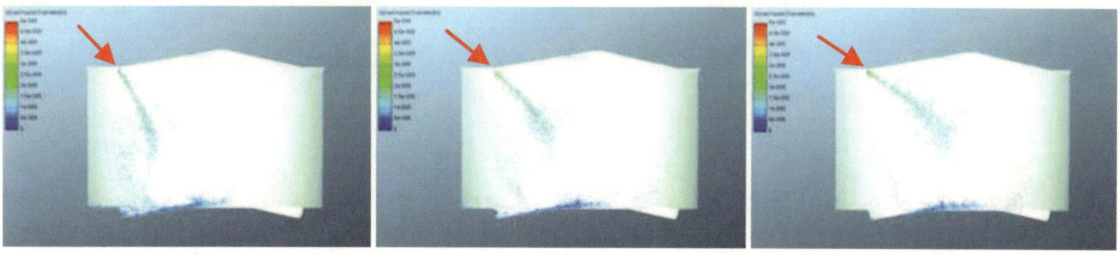

(a) (b) (c)

Fig. 23. Spray droplets visualization at the crank angle corresponding to the end of the intake stroke. The injector axis is inclined at 45° (a), 60° (b) and 70° (c) w.r.t. the cylinder axis. A red arrow indicates injector position.

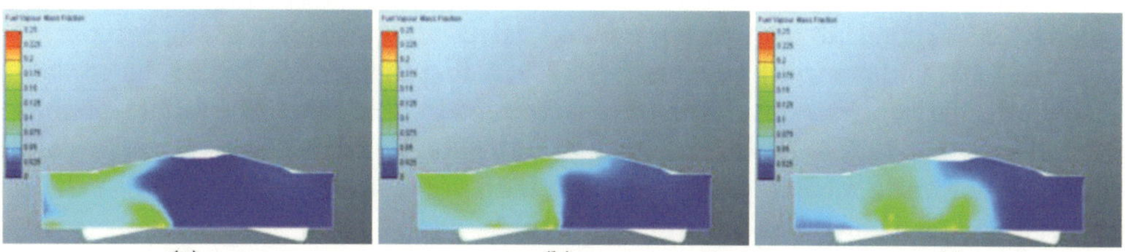

(a) (b) (c)

Fig. 24. Gasoline vapour distribution on a plane passing through the spark plug at 675°. The injector axis is inclined at 45° (a), 60° (b) and 70° (c) w.r.t. the cylinder axis. A red arrow indicates injector position.

This consideration is justified by the better quality of the mixture formation process relevant to the higher inclination angle, as demonstrated by Figs. 23 and 24. Fig. 23 reports the spray visualization in the cylinder at the crank angle of 600°. At this instant, which is 130° after the SOI, and only 25° before its end, only a small part of the fuel injected is evaporated, due to the low temperature existing in the cylinder during the intake stroke and at the initial stage of compression. As expected, the air motion significantly affects the droplets trajectory by deviation towards the spark plug, and reduces the penetration as a consequence of an increased dispersion. A large number of droplets impacts on the piston surface, particularly with the injector angles of 45° and 60°. A greater inclination indeed realises a more effective vapour distribution of gasoline. Fig. 24 demonstrates that the greater concentration of fuel vapour around the spark plug, on a plane passing through the spark axis, at the crank angle of 675° is reached for the inclination angle of 70°.

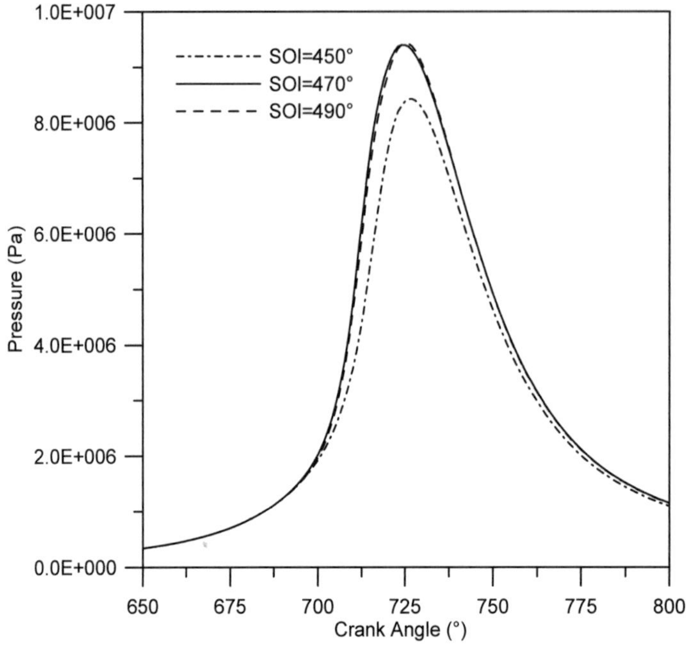

Fig. 25. In-cylinder pressure for three vales of SOI at full load.

The effect of changes in SOI on the engine pressure cycle at full-load is shown in Fig. 25. Three values of SOI ranging between 450° and 490° are considered. As already noticed, the angle 470° corresponds to the maximum intake valves lift. Spark ignition, SI, is set at 676°. No appreciable variations are observed by anticipating SOI during the intake stroke. In other words, the numerical results highlights the need to fully exploit the turbulent motion of the entering air, and to initiate the mixture formation process before the starting of the intake valves reverse motion, due to the quite long duration of injection (155°) under full load conditions at the injection pressure P_{inj}= 10 MPa.

The comparison between simulations effected at high load under different injection pressures, P_{inj}= 10 MPa and P_{inj}= 20 MPa, is made in Figs. from 26 to 28. SI is assumed at 691°. Injection always starts at the crank angle of 470°. Fig. 26 represents the spray visualisation within the cylinder at the crank angle of valves closure. The stronger atomisation pertinent to P_{inj}= 20 MPa is well evident. The increased quality of the mixture formation process determines a better vapour distribution within the combustion chamber, whose effect is well evident on the resulting in-cylinder pressure cycle (Fig. 27.a). The faster release of heat in the case of higher injection pressure determines, on the other hand, far worst conditions for the in-cylinder NO formation, as highlighted in Fig. 27.b, that represents the mean NO mass fraction as a function of the crank angle. Hence, the choice of the injection pressure must consider different aspects, including the coupling with the exhaust after-treatment system. Fig. 28, indeed, reports the injected and the evaporated gasoline mass within the cylinder, as a function of the crank angle for the two injection pressures. It is evident that injection starts at 470° and has different durations, evaporation is faster for the case P_{inj}=20 MPa, but, anyway, it is practically complete at the time of spark ignition for both the cases.

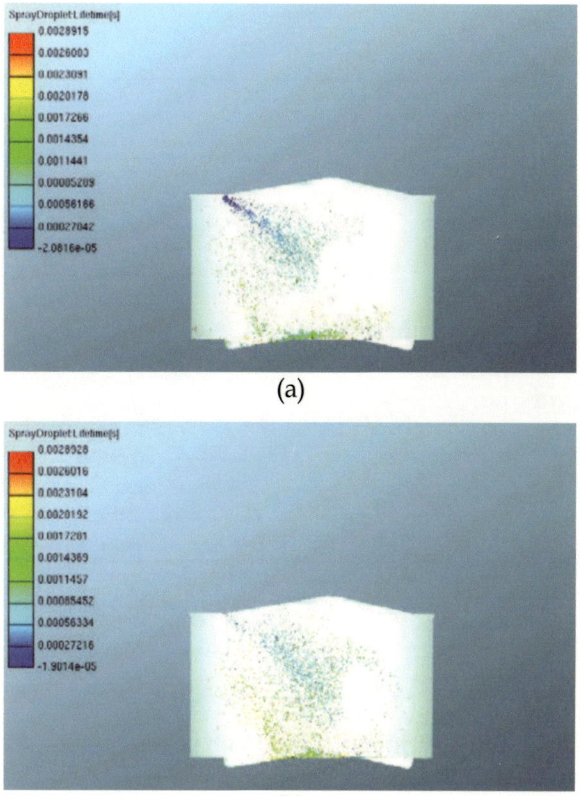

(a) (b)

Fig. 26. Spray droplets visualization at IVC for P_{inj}=10 MPa (a) and P_{inj} =20 MPa (b), full load.

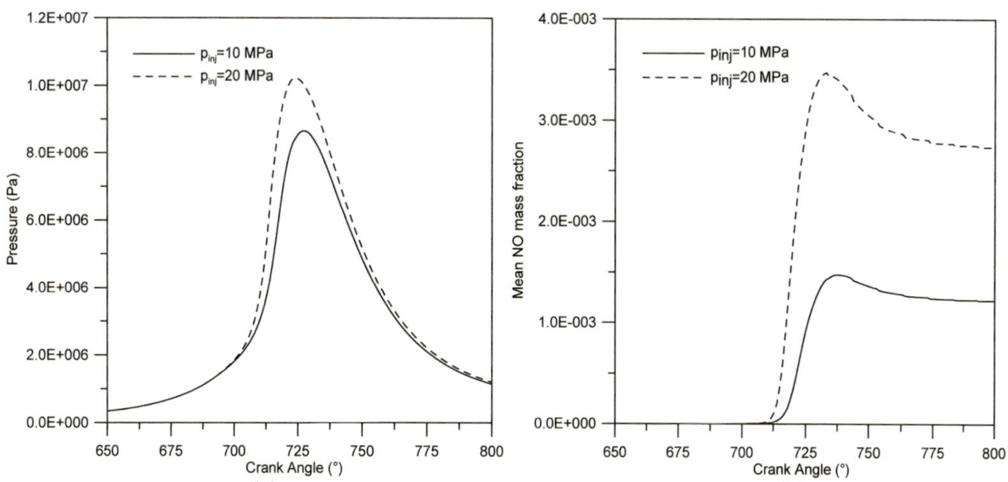

(a) (b)

Fig. 27. In-cylinder pressure (a) and mean NO mass fraction (b) for P_{inj}=10 MPa and P_{inj}=20 MPa (a), full load.

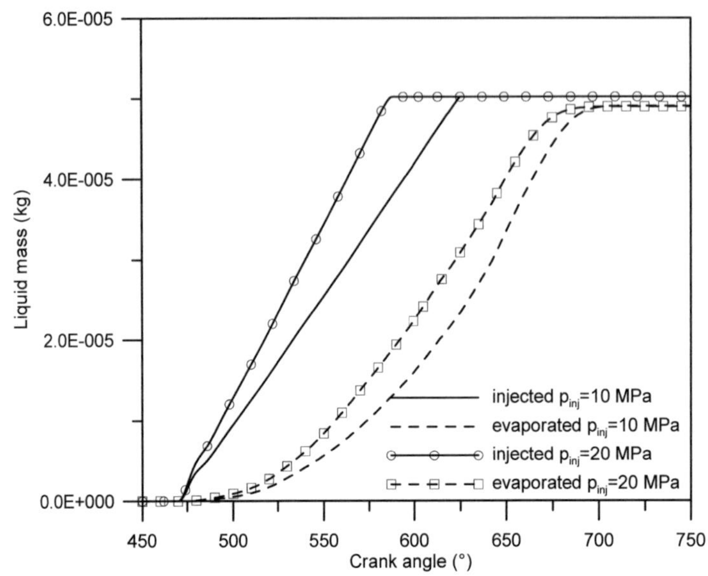

Fig. 28. Injected and evaporated gasoline mass for P_{inj}=10 MPa and P_{inj}=20 MPa.

Results relevant to the 3D simulation of the moderate-load overall lean condition (A/F=17) at 5000 rpm are summarised in Fig. 29.

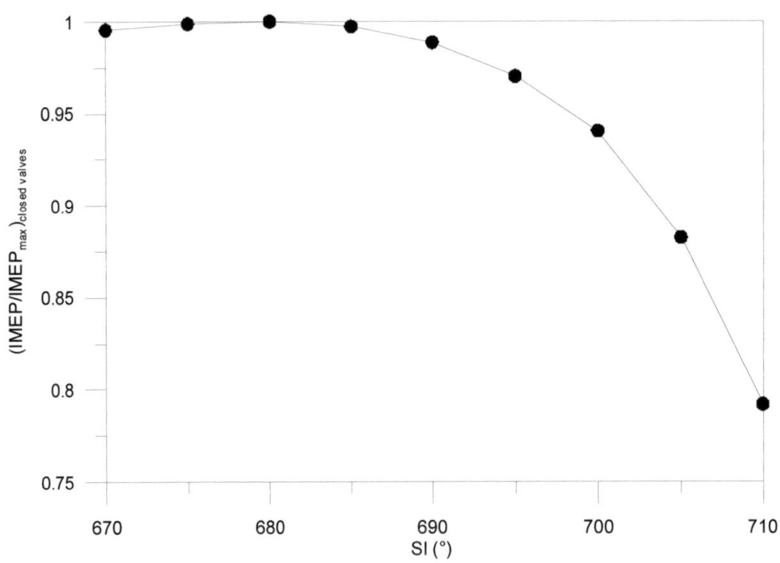

Fig. 29. Normalized mean indicated pressure in the closed valve period under moderate-load as a function of SI.

Injection is realized in a single event, as characterized by an injection pressure equal to 6 MPa, hence by a duration, at the considered engine speed, of about 60°. SOI is fixed at 450° and SI is varied between 670° and 710°, step 5°. The value of SOI is assumed on the ground of the physical consideration that the injection has to fully exploit the motion of the air entering the cylinder, hence by accounting for the fact that the maximum intake valves lift occurs at 470°. The indicated mean pressure, relevant to the closed valves period and normalized with respect to its maximum value, is reported in Fig. 8 as a function of SI. The maximum value of the curve, hence the maximum brake torque (MBT), is attained in correspondence of SI at 680°, namely 40° before the top dead centre (BTDC). This situation is hereafter considered as a reference case to be used as a term of comparison for the following analysis (starting point).

5. The optimization problem

Reducing costs, improving performances and system reliability and shortening the time to market is of crucial importance in the design of technical systems and components. The use of rigorous methods of decision-making, such as optimization methods, coupled with modern tools of numerical simulation, is today very effective to accomplish these tasks, especially in complex systems. Numerical procedures, in fact, may be used to generate a series of progressively improved solutions to the optimization problem, starting from an initial one. The process is terminated when some convergence criterion is satisfied.

The optimization problem here discussed is intended to the reduction of the fuel consumption of the considered single cylinder engine, through the more proper choice of the injection strategy under moderate load, moderate speed, lean mixture condition. The underlying design variables are identified in the time of spark ignition (SI) and in the start of the single injection event. More into detail, since both single and double injection strategies are considered, the variable is just the hereafter called SOI in the case of single injection, or the start of the first injection event, SOI_1, and the dwell time between two successive pulses, dw, in the case injection is split in two parts. The choice of the range of variation of the samples, as well as of the step between successive samples, is a subjective matter, strongly affecting the efficiency and speed of the optimization procedure. Physical considerations are made in the assessment of the DOE space, as avoiding injection in the valves overlap period, or considering the existence of a MBT value corresponding to a given SI, which helps in limiting the interval of variation of this last quantity.

The objective function is chosen as the cycle area in the pressure-volume plane, relevant to the closed valves period. This function is to be maximised. As an example, Fig. 30 shows the flow-chart of the optimization problem, in the case of split injection.

The algorithm chosen for the maximisation of the objective function, the Simplex, by Nelder & Mead, is an optimization algorithm seeking the vector of parameters corresponding to the global extreme (maximum or minimum) of any N-dimensional function $F(x_1, x_2,..,x_N)$ in the parameter space. This algorithm for non-linear optimization problems does not require derivates evaluations, so it is more robust than algorithms based on local gradients.

Two successive analyses are effected in the single injection case: the first consists in fixing the time of SI just at the found value of 680° and varying SOI in a pre-defined range, the second in assuming both SOI and SI as input variables for the optimization procedure. In both the situations the Simplex algorithm is used to search for the inputs maximizing the mean indicated pressure in the closed valves period.

The optimization of the time of SOI alone is effected in order to understand how the injection event has to be synchronized with the intake or the compression phase. The interval of explored crank angles starts at 445° and ends at 615°, thus covering situations where the injection is fully realized at open intake valves or completely during compression with closed valves. As previously said, the maximum intake valves lift is at 470°, whereas their closing angle occurs at 608°. The results of the optimization analysis lead to state that the maximum work, hence the minimum fuel consumption, is realized starting the injection at 475°. This can be deduced from Fig. 31, where the optimized variable is reported as a function of the SOI. The starting point is indicated, whereas the maximum increase in the optimised variable is evident at 475°.

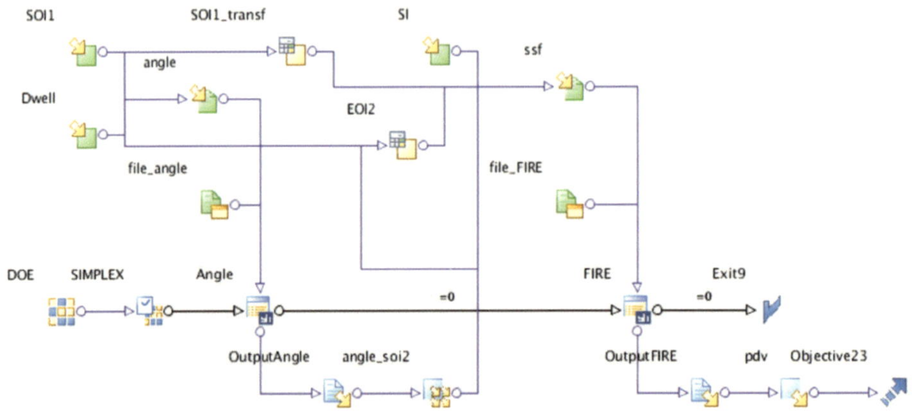

Fig. 30. Flow chart of the optimization problem in the case mixture formation is realized through split injection.

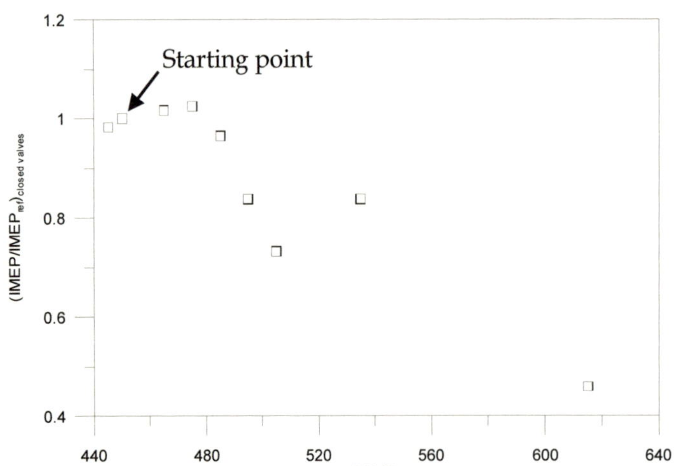

Fig. 31. Normalized mean indicated pressure in the closed valve period for the first optimization problem as a function of SOI.

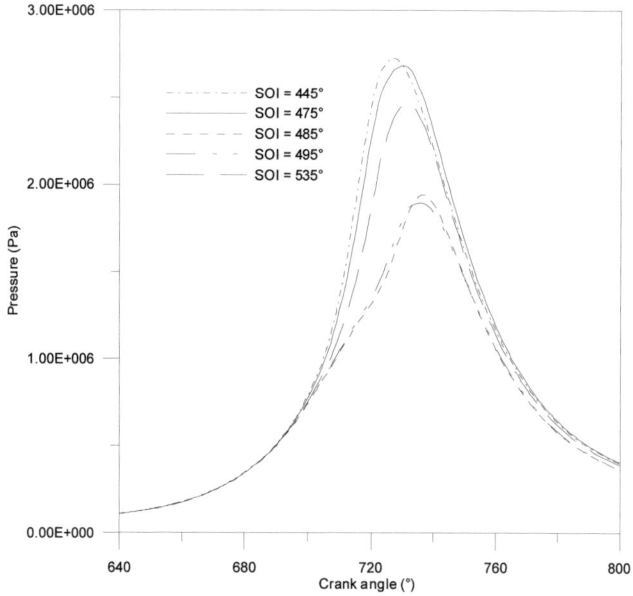

Fig. 32. Pressure cycles relevant to five different values of SOI.

The dramatic effect of a change in SOI on the in-cylinder pressure at moderate-load is visualized in Fig. 32, where five different cycles are plotted, chosen between those computed during the optimization procedure. All of them have the SI at the same crank angle, 680°. It is evident that injection has to be not so much delayed, and has to really exploit the motion of the air entering the cylinder, before the valves lift decreases too much. The optimal choice of the start of the injection event allows an increase of the 5.3% of the pressure cycle area with respect to the assumed starting point.

Results of the second optimization analysis relevant to the single injection case are reported in Figs. 33. It is evident that the couple of values of SOI and SI maximizing the engine performances is SOI at 475° and SI at 680°. The value of SOI coincides with the one found in the first optimization analysis, where the value of SI is considered as fixed. This last, on the other hand, is found equal to the value previously set on the ground of the parametric analysis. The gain in the pressure cycle area with respect to the starting point is clearly visible.

Effects of splitting the injection in two successive events characterized by a same injected mass (50%+50%), is discussed by varying SI and the starts of both the first and the second injection event. More precisely, as previously said input variables are assumed as SI, SOI_1, SOI of the first injection, and the dwell time between the two injection events. Fig. 34 represents the modeFRONTIER results, which show the optimal values being SOI_1 at 450° and a dwell time equal to about 80°. The optimal spark advance remains at 680°, although the relevant graph is here not reported. Splitting injection in two events allows an increase of the work greater than the 8% with respect to the case assumed as starting point, with injection realized in one shot.

The comparison between the in-cylinder pressure cycles found as optimal in the single injection case and in the double injection case is made in Fig. 35. The total injected mass is the same, namely 20 mg/str. The increase in the cycle area is well visible. It corresponds to a decrease equal to 2.6 % in the fuel consumption.

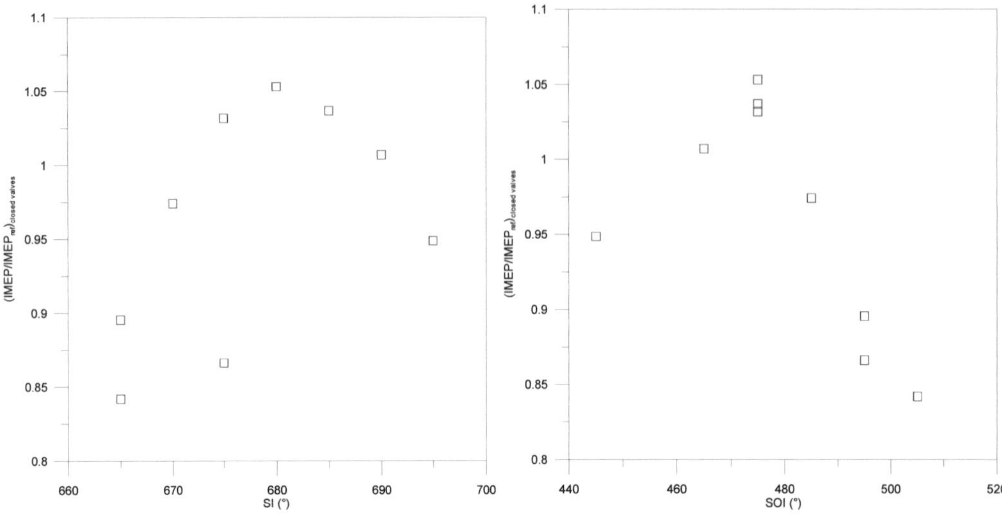

(a) (b)

Fig. 33. Results of the second optimization as a function of SOI (a) and SI (b).

The explanation of the better performances relevant to the double injection case is simply drawn on the ground of the work of Li *et al.* [Li *et al.*, 2007], and by looking at Fig. 36, where the equivalence ratio distribution on a plane passing through the spark plug, at the crank angle of SI, is visualized in the two cases of single and double injection. The spark is in central position on the engine head. The occurrence of a quite well stratified charge is evident, although a rich zone still appears close to the piston wall opposite to the injector location. This is represented as a red arrow in the figure.

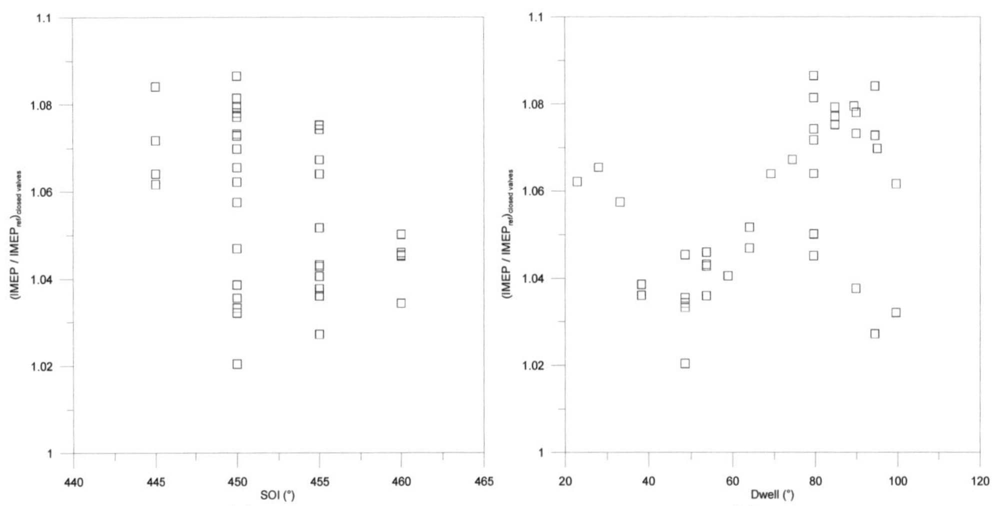

(a) (b)

Fig. 34. Optimal synchronization of two injection events w.r.t. SOI (a) and dwell time (b).

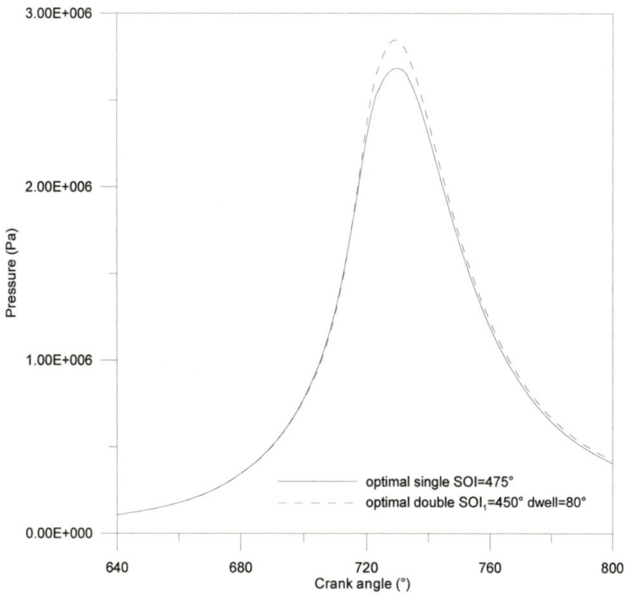

Fig. 35. Optimal pressure cycles relevant to single injection and double injection.

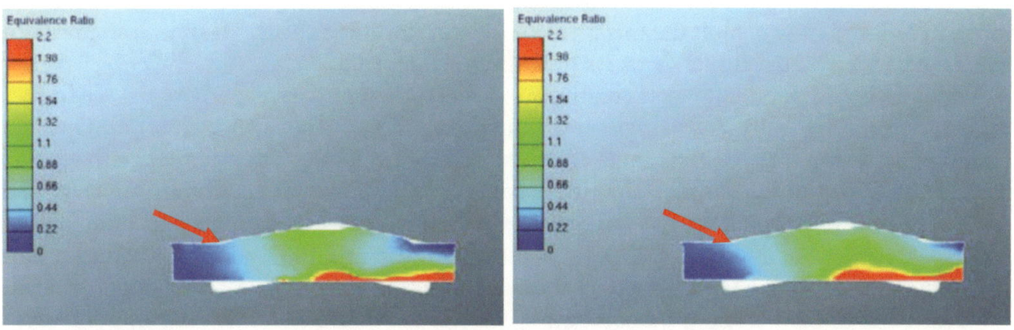

Fig. 36. Equivalence ratio distribution on a plane passing through the spark location in the optimal single injection case (left) and in the optimal double injection case (right) at the crank angle of SI.

The double injection event, with the second pulse entirely realized during the compression stroke, gives rise to a more effective charge stratification around the spark plug. This implies a faster propagation of the flame front within the combustion chamber. The problem of the presence of a rich zone closest to the cylinder walls and opposite to the injector position is not avoided, but can be solved by possibly reducing the injection pressure.

6. Conclusion

The application of CFD techniques to the study and optimisation of the combustion process in a GDI engine is presented.
A first part of the work is devoted to the numerical multidimensional modelling of the dynamics of sprays issuing from new-generation multi-hole injectors for GDI applications.

Three injectors are preliminary experimentally investigated with the aim of building a comprehensive database for the assessment of a proper spray model. The injectors are all characterised, under various injection strategies, in terms of both measurement of the instantaneous mass flow rate and visualization of the fuel dispersion in an optically accessible vessel. The developed spray model exploits a log-normal distribution of the initial droplets size of given expected value and variance. The expected value is theoretically determined as a function of the experimental injection velocity and backpressure, whereas the variance is properly tuned, together with a constant regulating the adopted droplets break-up model. Tuning of the constants is realised by assessing an automatic novel procedure within an optimisation software. The model portability with respect to the injection pressure and the kind of injector is demonstrated.

A 3D CFD model able to define the main guidelines for the management of the mixture formation process in a high performance GDI engine is then assessed. Simulation of the whole four-stroke engine cycle is effected by considering gasoline adduction during intake through one of the tested injectors. Boundary and initial conditions for the 3D model are defined, as a function of time, on the ground of a 1D simulation of the whole propulsion system.

The mixture formation process under high-speed high-load working conditions is shown to be strongly affected by the choice of the angle of inclination of the injector axis w.r.t. the cylinder axis. For lower angles, the gasoline droplets remains confined in the vicinity of the walls or quickly reach the surface of the piston, where they remain for a long time, especially during compression due to the motion of the piston itself. The choice of the SOI is made in order to fully exploit the turbulent motion of the entering air. The injection pressure must not be increased so much in order to limit the NO formation.

A moderate speed, moderate load condition is also studied into detail, where the air-to-fuel ratio is maintained lean. Both single and double injection events are considered. Optimal choice of both the start of the single injection strategy and the time of spark advance is realized by means of the Simplex algorithm, in order to minimize the fuel consumption. The same criterion is adopted in the numerical study of mixture formation and combustion consequent a double injection. The start of the first pulse and the dwell time between two successive pulses, both characterized by the same gasoline mass, are searched, together with the best time of SI. The optimal solution is shown to reduce the fuel consumption with respect to the case injection is realized in one shot, thus confirming the possibility to resort to split injections to improve the quality of the charge stratification under lean operation.

The assessed procedure, where a properly developed 3D engine model is coupled with an optimization tool, is proven to be a valuable tool in the phase of engine design.

7. Acknowledgment

Authors wish to thank Mr. Alessandro Montanaro, Mr. Ugo Sorge and Mr. Salvatore Alfuso for the long day assistance in the development of the work here presented. A special thank goes to Prof. Fabio Bozza for the important support given in the 1D engine modelling.

8. References

Küsell, M.; Moser, W.; Philipp, M. (1999). Motronic MED7 for gasoline direct injection engines: engine management system and calibration procedures, SAE Paper 1999-01-1284

Çelik, M. B.; Özdalyan, B. (2010). Gasoline direct injection, In: *Fuel Injection*, D. Siano, (Ed.), Sciyo, ISBN: 978-953-307-116-9, available from: http://www.intechopen.com/articles/show/title/gasoline-direct-injection

Alkidas, A. C. (2007). Combustion advancements in gasoline engines, *Energy Conversion and Management*, Vol. 48, pp. 2751-2761

Costa, M.; Sorge, U.; Allocca, L. (2010). Numerical study of the mixture formation process in a four strokes GDI engine for two-wheels applications, *Simulation Modelling Practice and Theory J.*, Vol. 19 (4), pp. 1212-1226

Costa, M.; Sorge, U.; Allocca, L. (2011). Optimization of the mixture formation process by split injection in a GDI engine for two-wheel applications, submitted to *Advences in Engineering Software*

AVL Fire v2010 Users Guide - ICE Physics & Chemistry, available from: www.avl.com

Stan, C. (2000). *Direct Injection Systems for Spark-Ignition and Compression-Ignition Engines*, SAE Publication

Cathcart, G.; Railton D. (2001). Improving robustness of spray guided DI combustion systems: the air-assisted approach, JSAE 2001 Spring Convention, Paper 20015 360

Shim, Y. S.; Choi, G. M.; Kim, D. J. (2008). Numerical modelling of hollow-cone fuel atomisation, vaporisation and wall impingement processes, *International Journal of Automotive Technology*, Vol. 9(3)

Brewster, S.; Cathcart G., Zavier C. (2008). The potential of enhanced HCCI/CAI control through the application of spray guided direct injection, SAE Paper 2008-01-0035

Bosch, W. (1966). The fuel rate indicator: a new measuring instrument for display of the characteristics of individual injection", SAE Paper 6607496

Wallace, I. (2002). *Injection Rate Gauge: Pass Off Information and User Instructions.* Fuel & Engine Management Systems, Graz

Piock, W. (2003). Spark-Ignition Internal Combustion Engine with Direct Injection", US Patent 6578547 B2

Landenfeld, T.; Kufferath, A.; Gerhard, J. (2004). Gasoline Direct Injection - SULEV Emission Concept, SAE Paper 2004-01-0041

Huh, K. Y.; Gosman, A. D. (1991). A phenomenological model of diesel spray atomization, Int. Conf. on Multiphase Flows; Tsukuba, Japan

Malaguti, S.; Fontanesi, S.; Cantore, G. (2010). Numerical characteriztion of a new high-pressure multi-hole GDI injector, ILASS Europe, Brno (CZ)

Bozza, F.; Gimelli. A.; Senatore, A.; Caraceni A. (2001). A theoretical comparison of various VVA systems for performance and emission improvements of SI-engines, SAE Paper 2001-01-0671

Bozza, F.; Torella, E. (2004). The employment of a 1D simulation model for the A/F ratio control in a VVT engine, *SAE Transactions, Journal of Engines, vol.* 3, p. 112

Bozza, F.; Gimelli, A.; Andreassi, L.; Rocco, V.; Scarcelli R. (2008). 1D-3D analysis of the scavenging and combustion process in a gasoline and natural-gas fuelled two-stroke engine, SAE Paper 2008-01-1087

Colin, O.; Benkenida, A.; Angelberger, C. (2003). 3D modeling of mixing, ignition and combustion phenomena in highly stratified gasoline engines, *Oil & Gas Science and Technology - Rev. IFP Energies Nouvelles*, Vol. 58(1), pp. 47-62

Li, T.; Nishida, K.; Zhang, Y.; Hiroyasu, H. (2007). Effect of split injection on stratified charge formation of direct injection spark ignition engines, *International Journal of Engine Research*, Vol. 8, pp. 205-218

10

Turbulent Combustion Simulation by Large Eddy Simulation and Direct Numerical Simulation

Fang Wang
Beihang University
China

1. Introduction

Combustion is a natural phenomenon. It happens in forest, automotive engine and gas cooker. In Computational Fluid Dynamics (CFD), the combustion phenomenon complies with a set of partial differential equations. According to the resolution scale, from big to small, the simulation methods in combustion are Reynolds Averaged Navior Stokes method (RANS), Large Eddy Simulation (LES), and Direct Numerical Simulation (DNS). Combustion model research in RANS and LES was, is and will still be a hot topic.

In this chapter, an Algebraic Sub-grid Scale turbulent Combustion Model (ASSCM) for LES is brought forward. Then this model is applied to a partly diffusion jet flame and a pre-mixed flame, after that, the database of the LES simulation results is used to test a RANS turbulent combustion model closure idea. Finally, a DNS by spectral method (Xu et al, 1996) in channel flow is carried on with consideration of buoyancy effects, and the database of the DNS simulation results is used to study RANS and LES turbulent combustion models.

2. Turbulent combustion models in LES

The Sub-Grid Scale (SGS) turbulent combustion model is a key point in LES study. There are two methods in modelling: one is to build the turbulent combustion model for all turbulence scale, the other is to build the models for big scale and small scale separately. Generally, there are probability density function models, laminar flame-let models, eddy break up model, and ASSCM sub-grid scale model, etc.

As for probability density function models, there are filtered density function method (FDF), probability density function method (PDF), and filtered mass density function method (FMDF), which are similar methods and all rooted in the probability function. They solve the PDF transport equation by the Lagrangian Monte Carlo scheme without using the assumed PDF functions. Also the detail chemical reaction kinetics can be applied directly without models, while the mixing term and the convection term need to be closed. The value of the filtered scaler, such as the averaged temperature, can be calculated by the integration over the composition space. When the FMDF or FDF method extended into turbulent combustion SGS model, the joint probability density function of the sub-grid-scale (SGS) scalar quantities are obtained by solution of its modelled transport equation. In the work of Colucci et al 1998 and James et al 2000, the FMDF combined with detail reaction gave good prediction in temperature and species profiles. The SGS PDF method still use Monte Carlo method to solve the transport equation of the SGS PDF function (Gao et al 1993). Renfo et al 2004 used this method and Smagorinsky model to predict the [OH] time series in H_2/N_2 jet turbulent flame. The predicted power spectral densities and the [OH] time scale are close to the measurements.

The SGS laminar flame-let model is a quick reaction model, that means it assumes that the chemical time scales are shorter than the turbulent time scales. It uses a conservation scalar, such as the mixture fraction, to define the flow variables, such as the species concentration. Assumed PDF functions, as the double-delta function, the clipped Gaussian function and the Beta-pdf function are commonly used. The filtered mixture fraction and its variance can be calculated by transport equations. The relational expression also can be defined by experimental data. DesJardin et al 1999, using the experiential expressions, simulated the ethyne-air jet flame, the temperature prediction is higher than the experimental data in some regions. Jones 2002 applied this method in jet flame and combustion chamber in gas turbine engine, with Smagorinsky turbulent model. The averaged velocity and mixture fraction are close to the experimental data. In the simulation of the gas turbine chamber, the temperature predictions are close to the experimental data in the down stream regions. The instantaneous vortex structures showed detail flow information in the combustion chamber.

The Eddy Break Up (EBU), Eddy Dissipation Concept (EDC) and other similar concept SGS model are rooted from the same type RANS model. The turbulent time scale is rescaled by the Kolmogorov turbulent time scale, and the concentrations were calculated by the filtered values. Yaga 2002 applied this model in a swirl combustion chamber with Smagorinsky turbulent model and three steps reaction kinetics. The prediction results of the temperature and the methane concentration are in good agreement with the experimental data while the CO concentration is not very well.

An ASSCM sub-grid scale model is proposed by author and colleagues. In the filtered species equation, there are two reaction terms:

$$\frac{\partial \rho \tilde{Y}_s}{\partial t} + \frac{\partial}{\partial x_j}(\rho \tilde{u}_j \tilde{Y}_s) = \frac{\partial}{\partial x_j}\left(\frac{\mu}{Sc_s}\frac{\partial \tilde{Y}_s}{\partial x_j}\right) - \tilde{w}_{L,s} - w_{S,s} - \frac{\partial g_{Sj,s}}{\partial x_j} \tag{1}$$

The instantaneous reaction expression for s species is in the Arrhenius form:

$$w_s = B\rho^2 Y_{fu} Y_{ox} \exp(-E/RT) = \rho^2 K Y_{fu} Y_{ox} \tag{2}$$

B is the pre-exponential factor, E is the activation energy and R is the universal gas constant. If the fluctuation of density can be neglected, in order to shorten the expression, the exponential term and the pre-exponential factor can be merged into one parameter K. The filtered 'big' scale reaction rate is defined as:

$$\tilde{w}_{L,s} = \rho^2 \tilde{K} \tilde{Y}_{fu} \tilde{Y}_{ox} \tag{3}$$

The filtered SGS reaction rate is:

$$w_{S,s} = \rho^2 (\widetilde{K Y_{fu} Y_{ox}} - \tilde{K} \tilde{Y}_{fu} \tilde{Y}_{ox}) \tag{4}$$

The exact expression of the SGS reaction rate is very complex. Anyway it presents the influence from the turbulent fluctuation under the grid scale. Conceptually, comparison with the Reynolds decomposition and the correlation of the turbulent fluctuation, the expression is rewritten as:

$$w_{S,s} = \rho^2 \left[\tilde{K}(\widetilde{Y_{fu} Y_{ox}} - \tilde{Y}_{fu}\tilde{Y}_{ox}) + \tilde{Y}_{ox}(\widetilde{KY_{fu}} - \tilde{K}\tilde{Y}_{fu}) + \tilde{Y}_{fu}(\widetilde{KY_{ox}} - \tilde{K}\tilde{Y}_{ox}) \right] \tag{5}$$

$\tilde{K}$ is the integral value in the control volume. The separate subtract terms in the SGS reaction rate denote the contribution from the 'small' scale turbulence fluctuation, and they can be closed by the products of the gradient of the filtered values:

$$(\widetilde{KY_{OX}} - \tilde{K}\tilde{Y}_{OX}) = C_{K,Y_{OX}} L_S^2 \frac{\partial \tilde{K}}{\partial x_j} \frac{\partial \tilde{Y}_{ox}}{\partial x_j} \tag{6}$$

The $C_{K,Yox}$ is the constant, between 0.05 to 0.005 and L_s is the SGS mixing length.

3. Jet flame simulation and premixed flame simulation using LES

The ASSCM sub-grid scale turbulent combustion model is applied to a partly diffusion jet flame and a premixed flame after a bluff body. The SGS turbulent combustion model is verified by the experimental data and the LES database is used to verified the RANS turbulent combustion model. The instantaneous turbulent and flame structures are studied too. The implicit box filter function and the Smagorinsky-Lilly's eddy viscosity turbulent model are used. The Smagorinsky constant is 0.1 in this chapter. The SGS mass flux and heat flux are in gradient models. Second order upwind scheme in space, second order central difference scheme for momentum equation, second order in temporal, and PISO algorithm are used. A random velocity component, satisfying Gaussian distribution is superposed at the inlet boundary. The grid size near inlet is 0.5mm around, and under 2mm in the simulation domain. The time step is 0.1ms. Each time step, it iterated 25 steps. As a comparison, the RANS model is applied for the jet flame too.

The methane-air jet flame, the 'Flame D', is measured by the Sandia Laboratory. The sketch map of this flame is shown in the figure 1. The central flow consists of 25% methane and 75% dry air, the inlet velocity is 29.7m/s, and the inlet temperature is 294K. The annular flow velocity is 6.8m/s and its temperature is 1880K. The surrounding flow velocity is 0.9m/s, and its temperature is 291K. The exit is located at a distance of 1m from the jet exit. The methane air reaction kinetics is taken from Westbrook as:

$$w_{fu} = 2.119 \times 10^{11} Y_{ox}^{1.3} Y_{fu}^{0.2} \exp(-2.027 \times 10^8 / RT) \tag{7}$$

The specific heat for all the species are using subsection polynomial expression, such as the specific heat value of methane when the temperature is between 300K to 1000K:

$$C_p = 403.58 + 9.0575T - 0.014425T^2 + 1.5805 \times 10^{-5} T^3 - 6.3431 \times 10^{-9} T^4 \tag{8}$$

Figure 2 is the averaged temperature comparison between the RANS unified second order moment (USM) transportation turbulent combustion model prediction results and the LES ASSCM turbulent combustion model prediction results with the experimental results. In most regions the, the prediction value of the ASSCM model are very close to the experimental data. The RANS model can give the same trend of the temperature profiles.

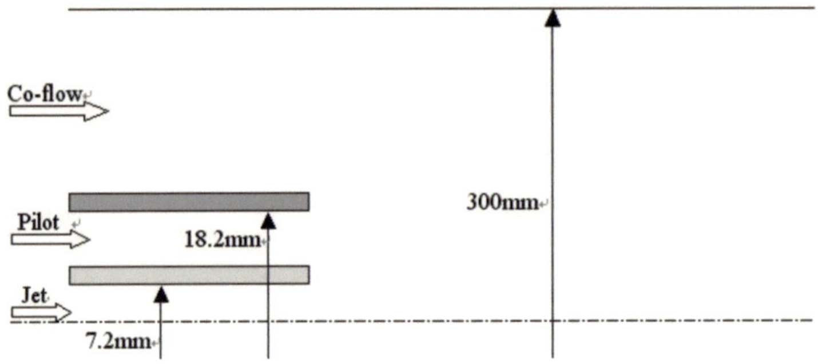

Fig. 1. The sketch map of the jet flame and its dimension.

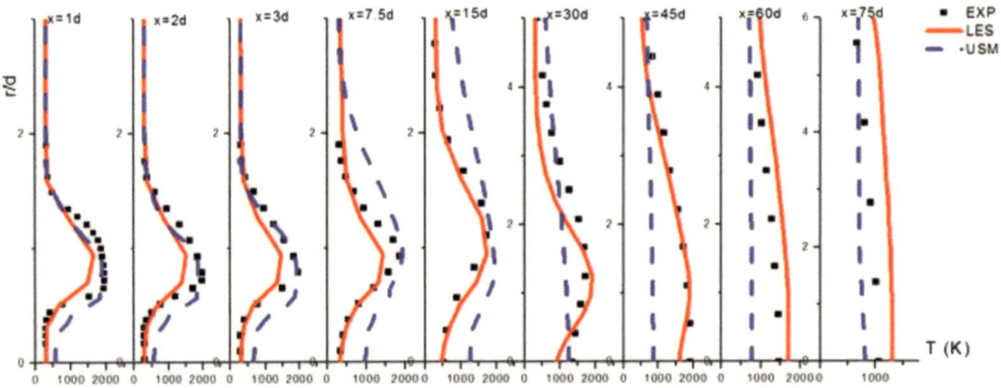

Fig. 2. The average temperature profiles.

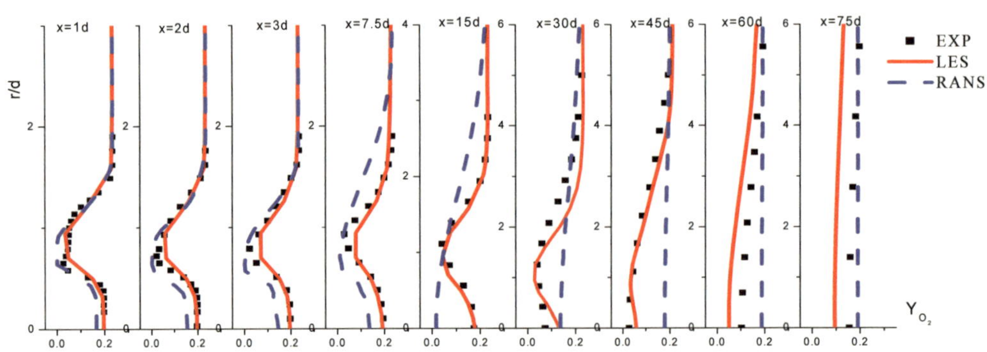

Fig. 3. The average oxygen concentration profiles.

Figure 3 shows the averaged oxygen concentration profiles comparison amongst the LES, RANS and the experimental data. In most regions, the LES ASSCM model gives good results. While the RANS predictions also are close to the experimental data in most regions. Considering RANS 1/500 computing time, it is still useful and popular in industry field. The big difference between the RANS prediction results and the experimental data is mainly from the shear layer gradient assumption and one global step reaction kinetics.

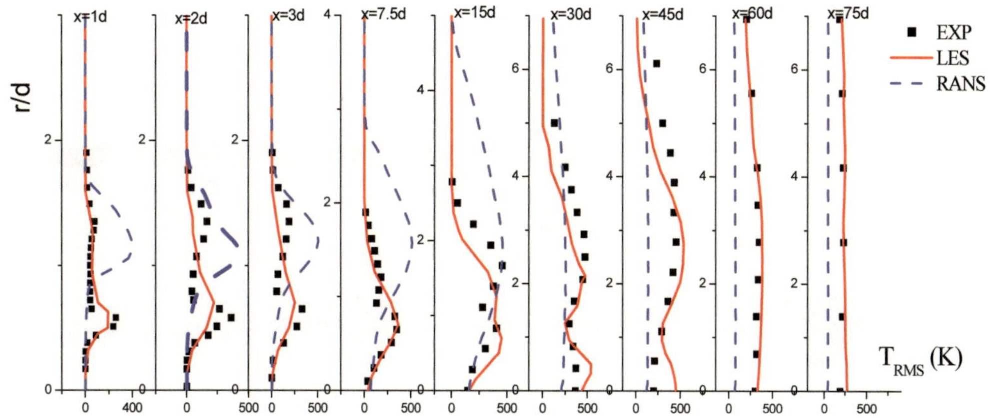

Fig. 4. The root mean square (RMS) value of the temperature.

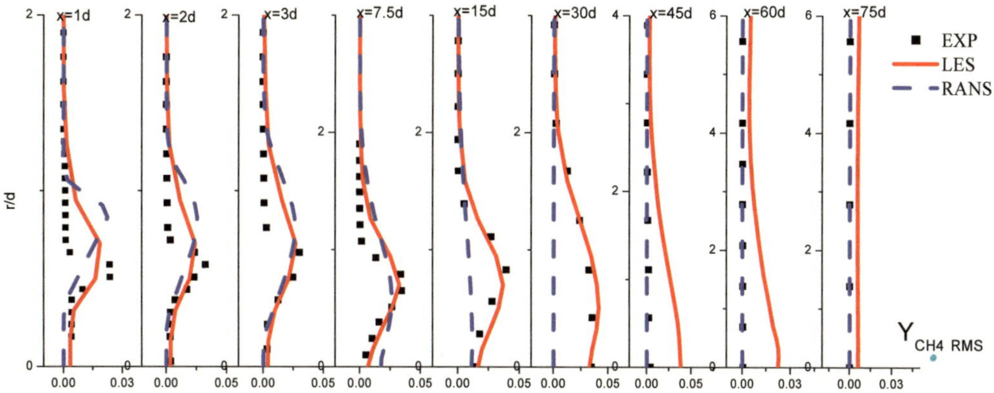

Fig. 5. The RMS value of the methane concentration.

The RMS value of the LES ASSCM model and the RANS model prediction results are shown in the figure 4 and 5, as well as the comparison with the experimental data. Generally, the LES RMS predictions are worse than the LES average value predictions, especially in the regions near the methane jet area: x=1d, x=2d, and x=3d sections. These regions have great gradient value of temperature and concentration, and there are more active turbulence fluctuations. As for the prediction of the turbulent character, the LES is much better than the RANS method.

Figure 6 is the instantaneous stain rate contour at the central axis section. The high velocity jet flow mixed with the low velocity co-flow air, then the mixing layer induced vortex and higher stain rate regions.

Figure 7 and figure 8 are instantaneous temperature contour in different time step. From these two pictures, the temperature in the central jet flow remains low for quite long distance from the inlet. The pilot flow ignite the jet flow and the flame spread downstream.

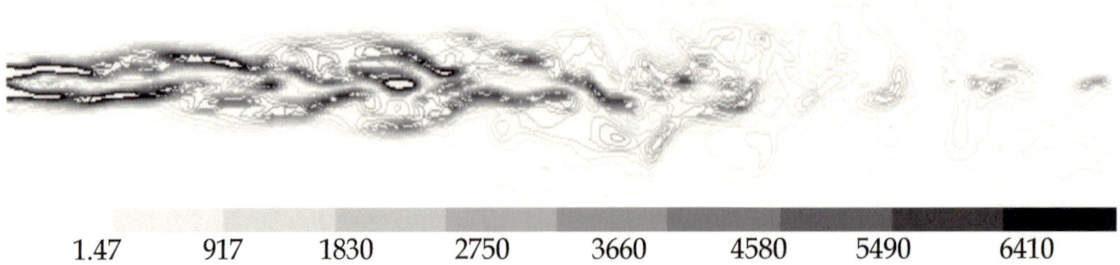

Fig. 6. The instantaneous stain rate contour (1/s).

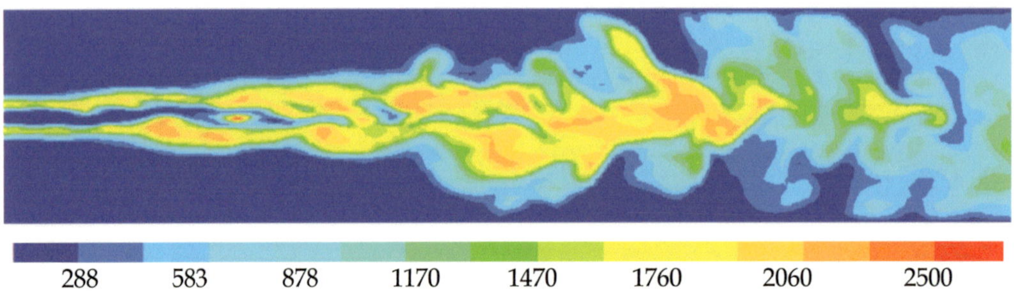

Fig. 7. The instantaneous temperature contour (K, t=0.8990s).

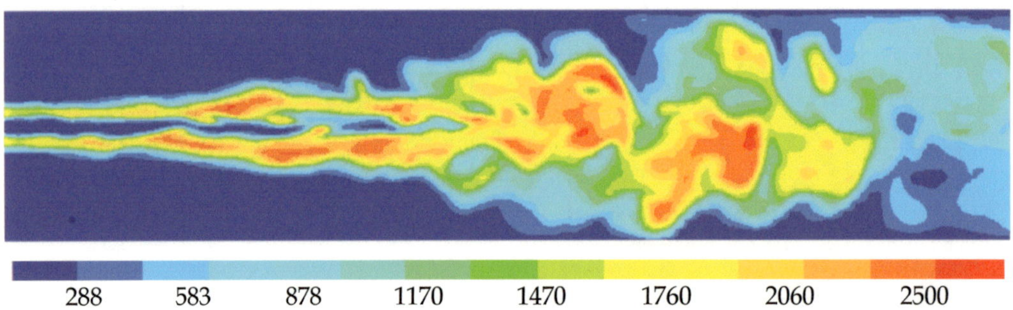

Fig. 8. The instantaneous temperature contour (K, t=1.1094s).

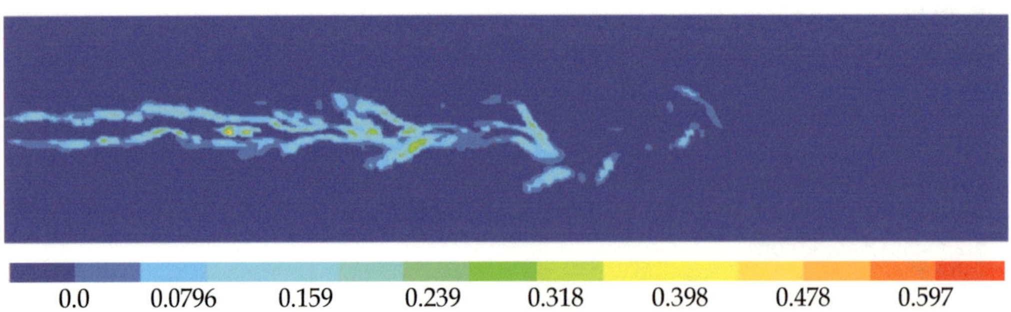

Fig. 9. The instantaneous reaction rate contour (kmol/m^{3}s).

The co-flow air was entraining to the combustion flames. The high temperature areas changed temporally. The unsteady flame is similar to the candle flickers. It also can be seen the wrinkle flame structures. Figure 9 is the instantaneous reaction rate contour. The high reaction rate area is the low concentration area. Reaction also happens in some isolated 'islands'.

Then, a propane air premixed flame is studied. The combustion chamber is shown in the figure 10 (Giacomazzi 2004). The inlet velocity is 17m/s, temperature is 288K, and the equivalence ratio is 0.65. The final mesh section is shown in figure 11, the maximum grid size is 0.5mm. Time step is 0.1ms, and 35 iterations during each time step.

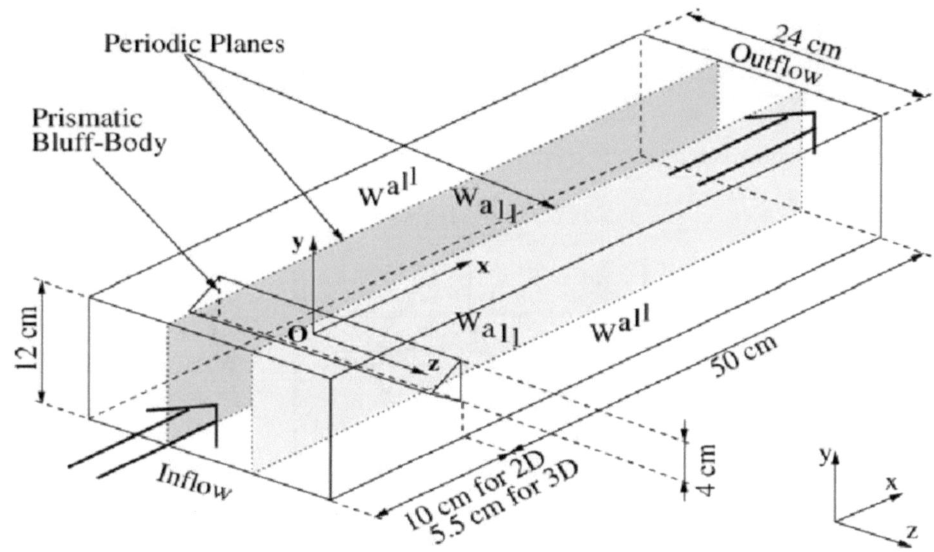

Fig. 10. The premixed chamber with bluff body (Giacomazzi 2004).

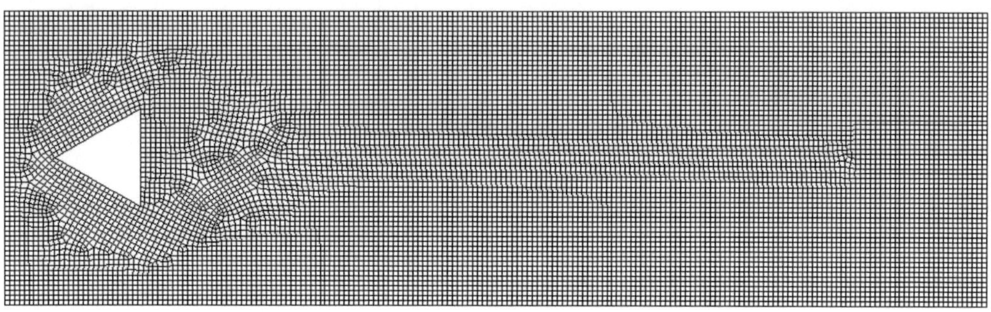

Fig. 11. The final mesh at z=0 section.

The laminar reaction rate is:

$$w_{fu} = 4.836 \times 10^9 Y_{ox}^{1.65} Y_{fu}^{0.1} \exp(-1.51 \times 10^4 / T) \tag{9}$$

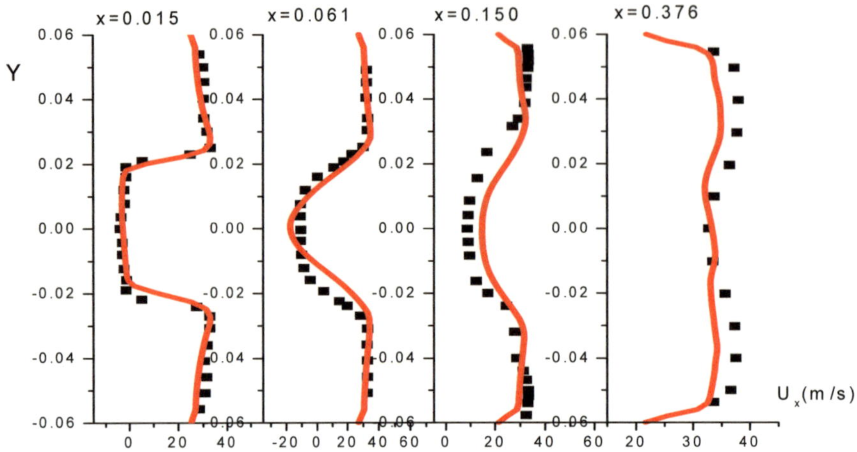

Fig. 12. The averaged x velocity with combustion.

3

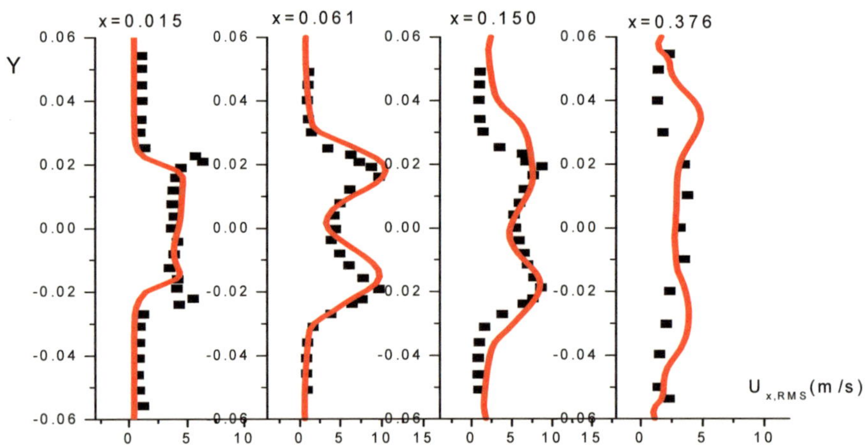

Fig. 13. The RMS value of the x velocity with combustion.

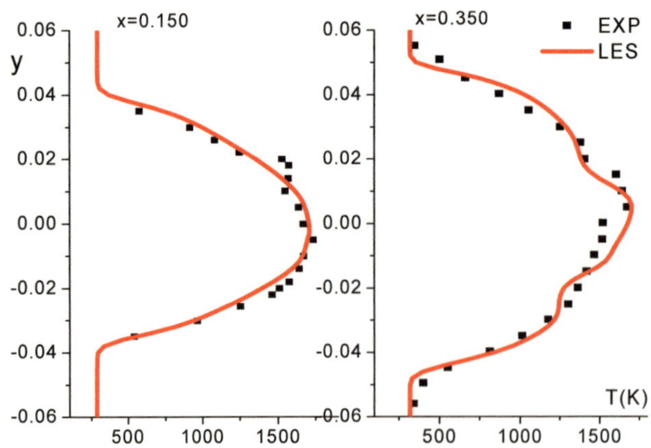

Fig. 14. The averaged temperature profiles with combustion.

In figure 15 and 13, the x velocity and its RMS value are compared with the experimental data generally. The predictions are close to the experimental data. Figure 14 is the averaged temperature profiles. The LES predictions are in good agreement with the experimental data. So the LES ASSCM model with the Smagorinsky-Lilly model can properly predict the combustion flow in this premixed case.

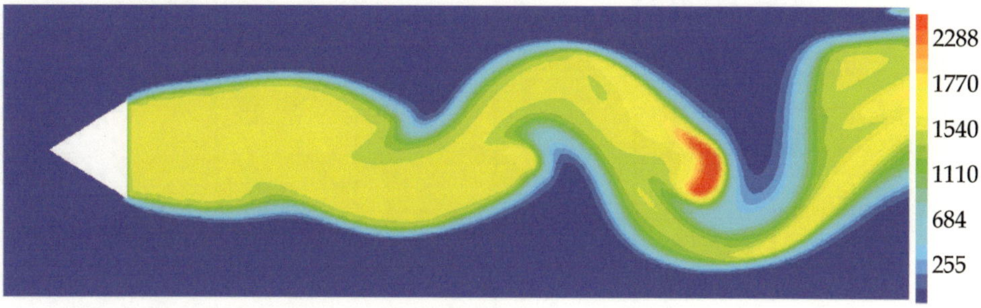

Fig. 15. The instantaneous temperature contour (K).

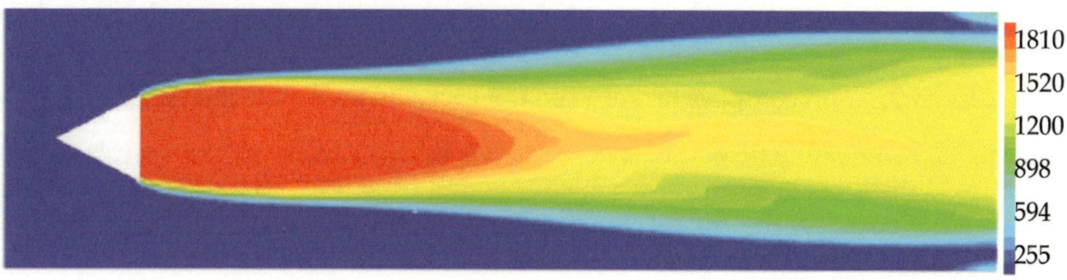

Fig. 16. The averaged temperature contour (K).

The section results are shown in figure 15 and 16: the instantaneous temperature contour and the averaged temperature contour. The bluff body in the combustion chamber works as a flame stabilizer: the premixed flame attached behind the bluff body. The high temperature regions changed a lot in pace with the time steps. The instantaneous high temperature regions are different from the averaged high temperature regions. There are wrinkled flame structures. There are vortex 'source' in the after side of the bluff body. The vortex is generated, stretched and mixed along the combustion chamber.

Because LES method can give much better predictions on turbulent fluctuations, the LES database can be used as a preliminary test source for the RANS combustion model. In RANS USM model, the correlations are solved by transportation equations, such as the transport equation of the correlation of the reaction rate factor K and a species concentration:

$$\frac{\partial}{\partial t}\left(\rho\overline{K'Y'}\right)+\frac{\partial}{\partial x_j}\left(\rho\overline{u_j}\overline{K'Y'}\right)=\frac{\partial}{\partial x_j}\left(\frac{\mu_e}{\sigma_g}\frac{\partial\overline{K'Y'}}{\partial x_j}\right)+ \\ c_{g1}\mu_T\frac{\partial\overline{K}}{\partial x_j}\frac{\partial\overline{Y}}{\partial x_j}-c_{g2}\rho\left(\frac{a}{\tau_A}+\frac{b}{\tau_T}\right)\overline{K'Y'} \tag{10}$$

As for the ASOM model, the expression of the the correlation of the reaction rate factor K and concentration is:

$$\overline{K'Y_1'} = C_{KY_1} \frac{k^3}{\varepsilon^2} \frac{\partial \overline{K}}{\partial x_j} \frac{\partial \overline{Y_1}}{\partial x_j} \tag{11}$$

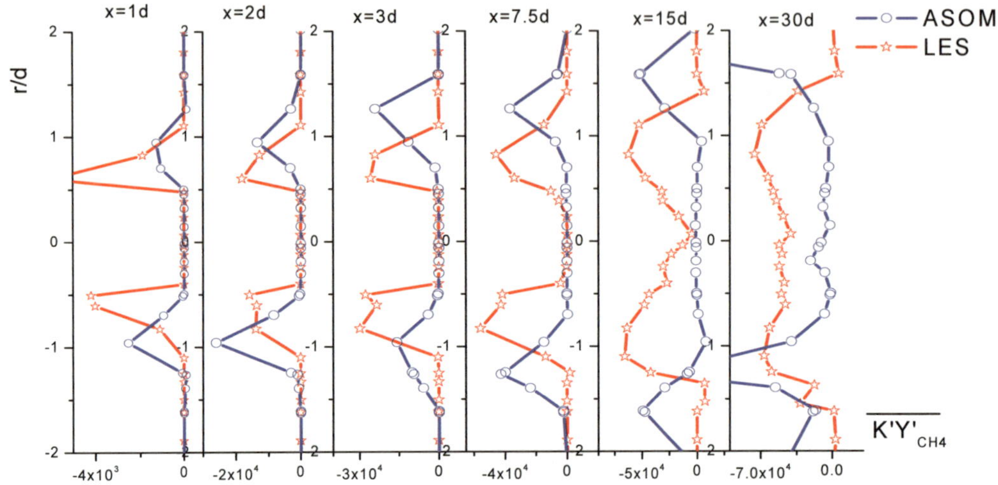

Fig. 17. The correlation comparison between the LES statistic value and ASOM model value.

From the jet flame simulation database here, the RANS ASOM model correlation value is close to the statistic correlation value which is gotten from the LES database, which is shown in figure 17. Generally, the model value is in the same trend with the statistic value and consistent with positive and negative symbols.

The concentration correlation comparison between the model value and the statistic value is shown in figure 18. In most regions, the model values are close to the statistic values. Generally, the model value is of the same magnitude order with the statistic value. The similar statistic calculation is applied in the premixed case too, and the comparison result is shown in figure 19. The model value is close to the statistic value in all the sections.

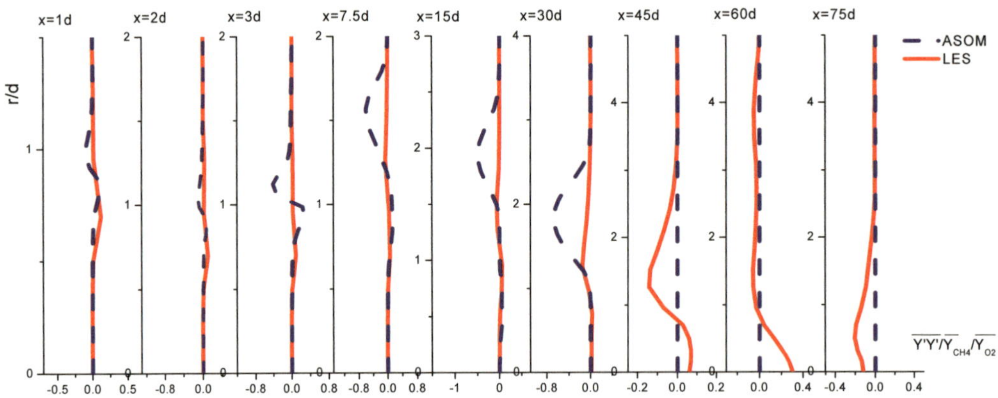

Fig. 18. The relative correlation comparison between the LES statistic and ASOM model value.

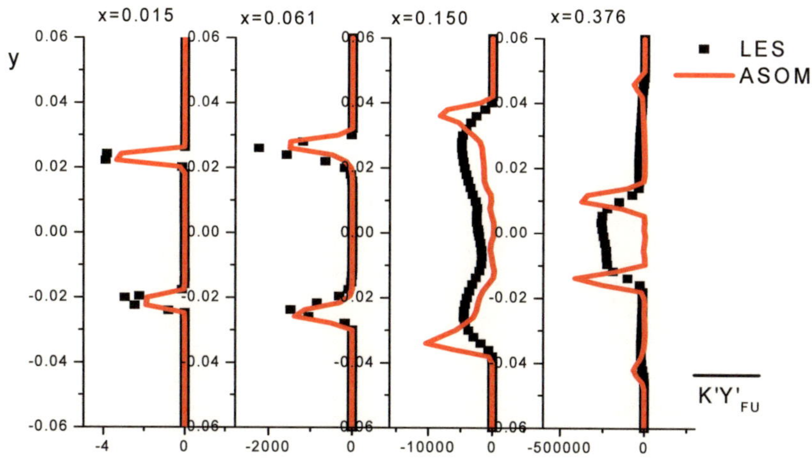

Fig. 19. The correlation comparison between the LES statistic and ASOM model value.

4. Direct numerical simulation for reacting flows

Along with the development of computational technology, direct numerical simulation becomes more and more popular in combustion simulation studies. It is a powerful tool for fundamental study and test sources for RANS and LES models.

In this chapter, a DNS of turbulent reacting channel flows with the consideration of the interaction between the velocity and scalars by buoyancy effect is performed using a spectral method. The instantaneous reaction rate is in Arrhenius form. The computational domain and coordinate system are shown in figure 20. x, y, z are the flow direction, normal direction, and span-wise direction separately. The height of the channel is 2H, the length in the stream-wise is 12.6H and the width in the span-wise direction is 6.28H. The flow is fully developed and the reactants mixed sufficiently.

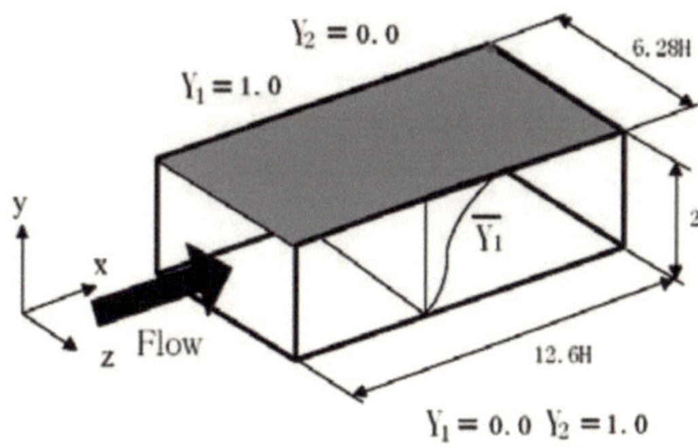

Fig. 20. The computation domain for DNS.

The instantaneous continuity, momentum, species concentration and energy equations of incompressible turbulent reacting flows, with consideration of the buoyancy effect using Boussinesq approximation and taking the Arrhenius expression of one-step kinetics.

$$\frac{\partial u_i}{\partial x_i} = 0 \tag{12}$$

$$\frac{\partial u_i}{\partial t} + u_j \frac{\partial u_i}{\partial x_j} = -\frac{\partial p}{\partial x_i} + \frac{\partial}{\partial x_j}[\nu(\frac{\partial u_i}{\partial x_j} + \frac{\partial u_j}{\partial x_i})] - F_i \tag{13}$$

$$\frac{\partial}{\partial t}(Y_1) + \frac{\partial}{\partial x_j}(u_j Y_1) = \frac{\partial}{\partial x_j}(D\frac{\partial Y_1}{\partial x_j}) - w_1 / \rho \tag{14}$$

$$\frac{\partial}{\partial t}(Y_2) + \frac{\partial}{\partial x_j}(u_j Y_2) = \frac{\partial}{\partial x_j}(D\frac{\partial Y_2}{\partial x_j}) - w_2 / \rho \tag{15}$$

$$\frac{\partial}{\partial t}(T) + \frac{\partial}{\partial x_j}(u_j T) = \frac{\partial}{\partial x_j}(\frac{\lambda}{c_p \rho}\frac{\partial T}{\partial x_j}) + w_1 Q_1 / (c_p \rho) \tag{16}$$

The F_i term in momentum equation stands for the effect from buoyancy force which caused by the difference of the temperature, also it induces the scalar and velocity interaction. The Reynolds number Re_m defined by the channel half width H and average velocity U_m is 3000. The parameters in DNS cases are given in Table 1.

For all cases, the mass fraction of species 1 (fuel) is given as 1.0 at the top wall and 0.0 at the bottom wall, whereas the mass fraction of species 2 (oxidizer) is given as 0.0 at the top wall and 1.0 at the bottom wall. The wall temperature is given as 900K. Periodic boundary conditions are used in the longitudinal and spanwise directions and solid-wall boundary conditions are used on the top and bottom boundaries.

Case	B	E/R (K)	Q (kJ/kg)	F_y (m/s^2)
1	0	0	0	0
2	0.1	0	0	0
3	1.0	0	0	0
4	10^8	15000	100	0
5	10^8	20000	100	0
6	10^{10}	20000	100	0
7	10^8	20000	100	-0.5
8	10^8	15000	100	F_y
9	10^8	20000	100	F_y

Table 1. Parameters for DNS Cases.

For numerical simulations, the Galerkin-Tau spectral expansion method is adopted. The Fourier transform is used in x and z directions and the Chebyshev transform is used in the y direction. Uniform grid distribution is in x and z directions and the Gauss-Lobatto nonuniform grid distribution is used in the y direction. The number of grid nodes in x and z directions is 128, and in the y direction is 129. This results a total of 2.11 million nodes. The time step used is 0.01H/Um. A third-order scheme is used for time marching.

The statistical RMS value of velocities and a correlation were compared with the literature data (Kawamura 2000), which are shown in figure 21 and 22. The predictions from this chapter are labelled by SM DNS, and the predictions from literature are labelled by FD DNS.

In the SM DNS simulation results, U_τ=0.063845247, Re_τ=191.54. The two DNS results are very close to each other.

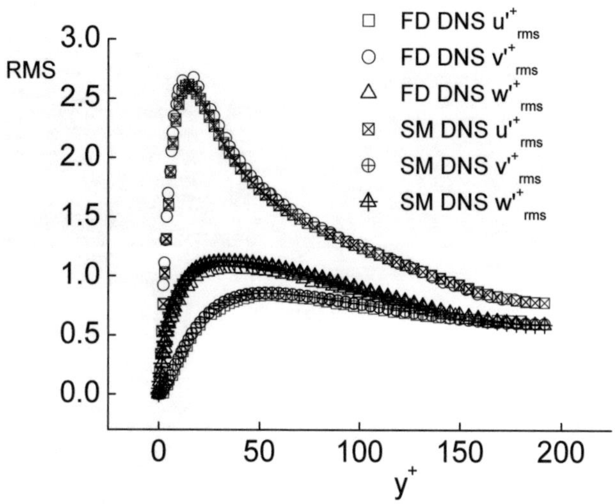

Fig. 21. The RMS value of velocities.

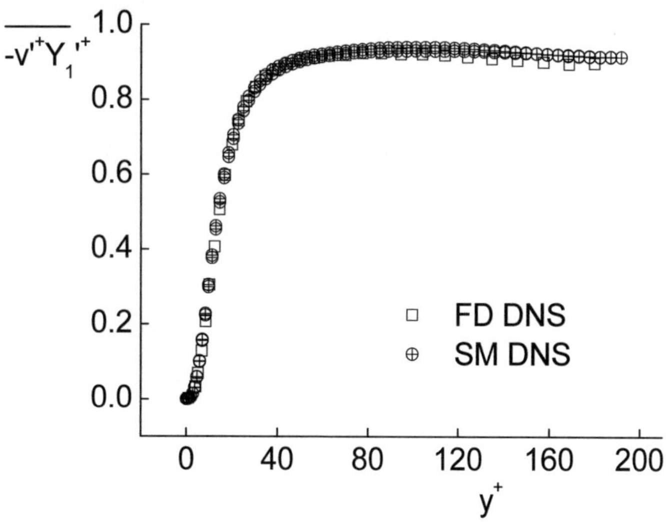

Fig. 22. The averaged value of the correlation of concentration and v velocity

The instantaneous contour of temperature and species are shown in figure 23 and 24. The plenty turbulent structures and near-wall stripe structures can be seen. The statistical averaged reaction factor K profiles is shown in figure 25.

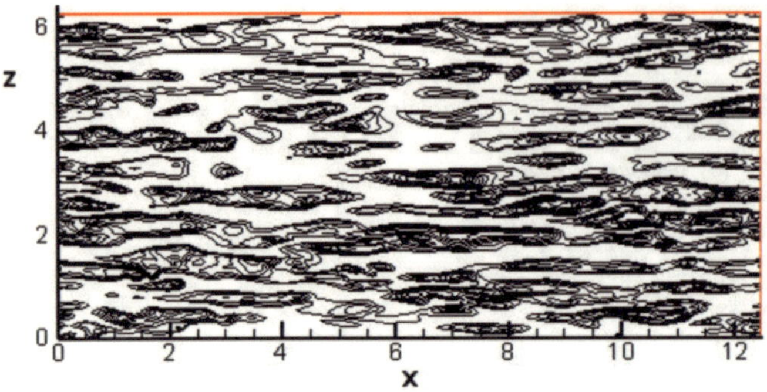

(a)

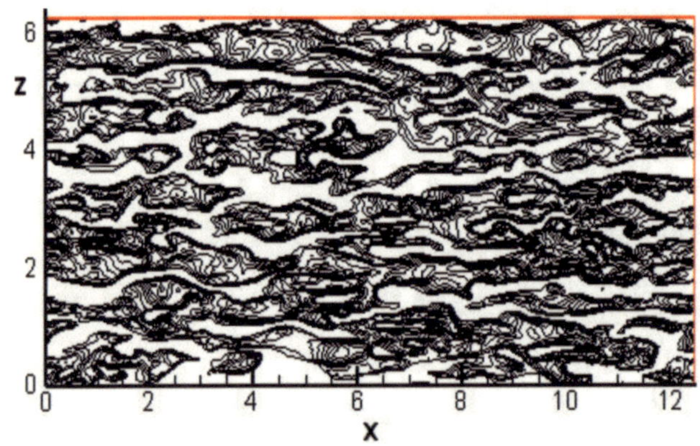

(b)

Fig. 23. The instantaneous contour of temperature fluctuations in case 5 (a-y^+=8.2, b-y^+=24.9)

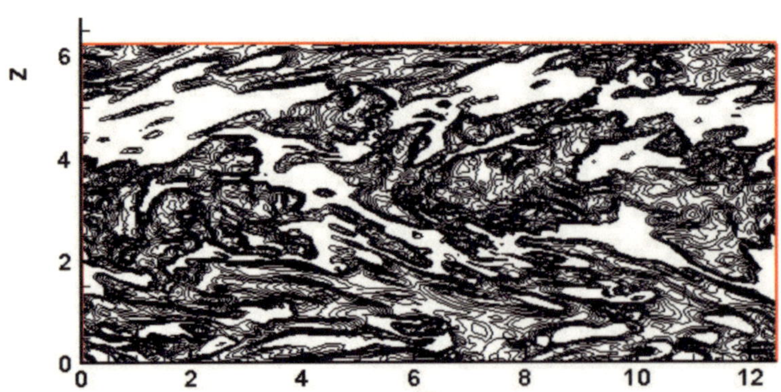

Fig. 24. The instantaneous contour of concentration fluctuation (case 8, y^+=8.2)

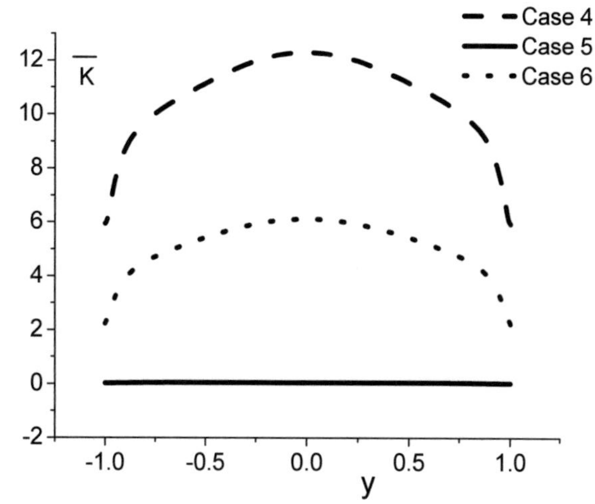

Fig. 25. The averaged reaction factor K profiles.

5. Turbulent combustion model study by DNS

The DNS database is used for the scalar fluctuation correlations transportation equations' budget. The exact values are compared with the model values, and then the improvement is given in the turbulent combustion model.

Firstly, a RANS transport equation combustion model is studied. In turbulent combustion model, the correlations are important terms. As for incompressible flow, c_p is constant, $D = \frac{\lambda}{\rho c_p}$, and put $w_1 = w_2 = B\rho^2 Y_1 Y_2 \exp(-\frac{E}{RT}) = \rho^2 Y_1 Y_2 K$ reaction term into the equations, then the exact transportation equation for $\overline{T'Y_1'}$, $\overline{K'Y_1'}$ and $\overline{Y_1'Y_2'}$ are:

$$\frac{\partial \overline{Y_1'T'}}{\partial t} + \overline{u}_j \frac{\partial \overline{Y_1'T'}}{\partial x_j} = -\overline{T'u_j'}\frac{\partial \overline{Y_1}}{\partial x_j} - \overline{Y_1'u_j'}\frac{\partial \overline{T}}{\partial x_j} - \frac{\partial \overline{u_j'Y_1'T'}}{\partial x_j} + D\frac{\partial}{\partial x_j}\left(\frac{\partial \overline{Y_1'T'}}{\partial x_j}\right) - 2D\overline{\frac{\partial T'}{\partial x_j}\frac{\partial Y_1'}{\partial x_j}} + \frac{\rho Q_1}{c_p}\overline{Y_1'Y_1Y_2K} - \rho\overline{T'Y_1Y_2K} \tag{17}$$

$$\frac{\partial \overline{K'Y_1'}}{\partial t} + \overline{u}_j \frac{\partial \overline{K'Y_1'}}{\partial x_j} = -\overline{u_j'K'}\frac{\partial \overline{Y_1}}{\partial x_j} - \overline{u_j'Y_1'}\frac{\partial \overline{K}}{\partial x_j} - \frac{\partial \overline{u_j'K'Y_1'}}{\partial x_j} + D\frac{\partial}{\partial x_j}\left(\frac{\partial \overline{K'Y_1'}}{\partial x_j}\right) - 2D\overline{\frac{\partial Y_1'}{\partial x_j}\frac{\partial K'}{\partial x_j}} - \frac{\lambda}{\rho c_p}\frac{E}{R}\overline{\frac{Y_1'}{T^2}\frac{\partial K}{\partial x_j}\frac{\partial T}{\partial x_j}} - \frac{2\lambda}{\rho c_p}\overline{\frac{Y_1'}{T}\frac{\partial K}{\partial x_j}\frac{\partial T}{\partial x_j}} - \rho\overline{K'Y_1Y_2K} + \frac{E\rho Q_1}{Rc_p}\overline{\frac{Y_1'KY_1Y_2K}{T^2}} \tag{18}$$

$$\frac{\partial \overline{Y_1^{'}Y_2^{'}}}{\partial t}+\overline{u_j}\frac{\partial \overline{Y_1^{'}Y_2^{'}}}{\partial x_j}=-\overline{u_j^{'}Y_2^{'}}\frac{\partial \overline{Y_1}}{\partial x_j}-\overline{u_j^{'}Y_1^{'}}\frac{\partial \overline{Y_2}}{\partial x_j}-\frac{\partial \overline{u_j^{'}Y_1^{'}Y_2^{'}}}{\partial x_j}+$$
$$D\frac{\partial}{\partial x_j}(\frac{\partial \overline{Y_1^{'}Y_2^{'}}}{\partial x_j})-2D\overline{\frac{\partial Y_1^{'}}{\partial x_j}\frac{\partial Y_2^{'}}{\partial x_j}}-\rho\overline{Y_1^{'}Y_1Y_2K}-\rho\overline{Y_2^{'}Y_1Y_2K} \tag{19}$$

The statistical correlation values are shown in figure 26 to 29. The temperature fluctuation is very important in reaction correlations. Then the budgets are studied and shown in figure 30 to 32. In these results, $\overline{K'Y_1'}$ value changes greatly and $\overline{T'Y_1'}$ are more important than $\overline{Y_1^{'}Y_2^{'}}$ according to the average value.

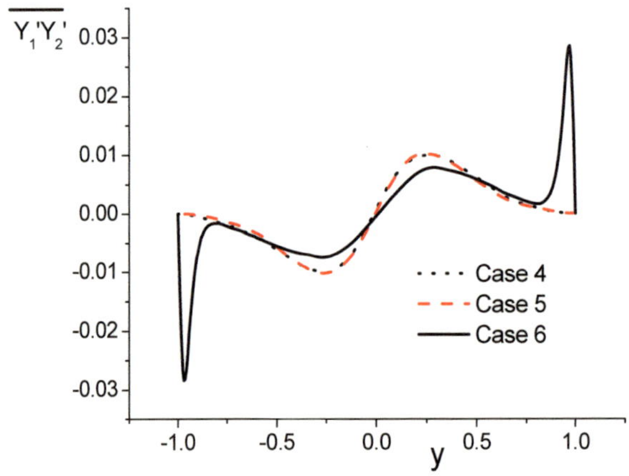

Fig. 26. The profiles of the $\overline{Y_1^{'}Y_2^{'}}$.

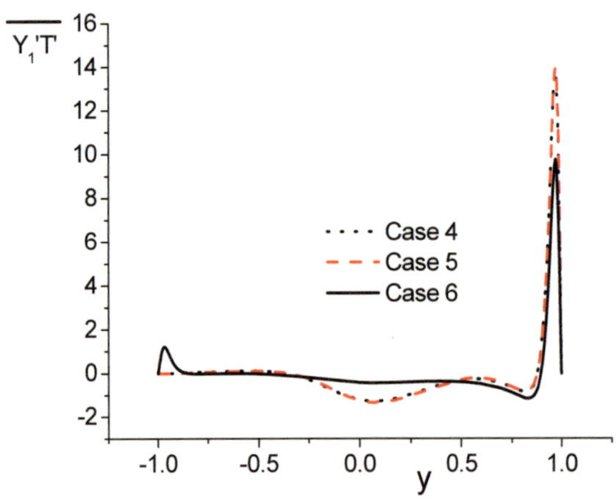

Fig. 27. The profiles of the $\overline{T'Y_1'}$.

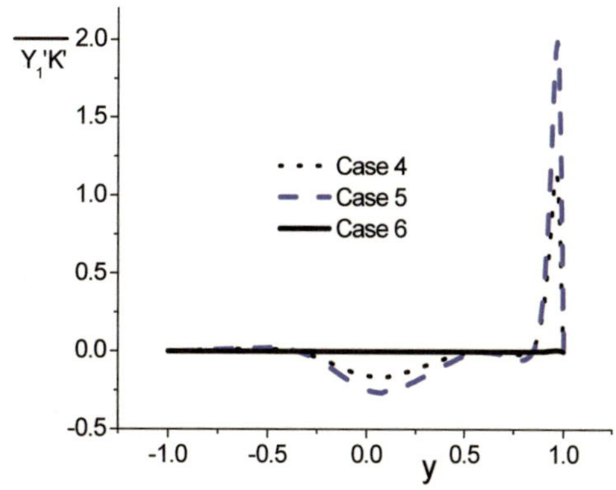

Fig. 28. The profiles of the $\overline{K'Y_1'}$.

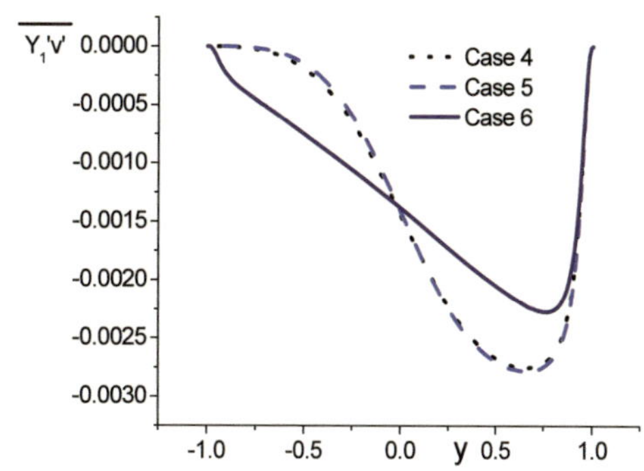

Fig. 29. The profiles of the $\overline{v'Y_1'}$.

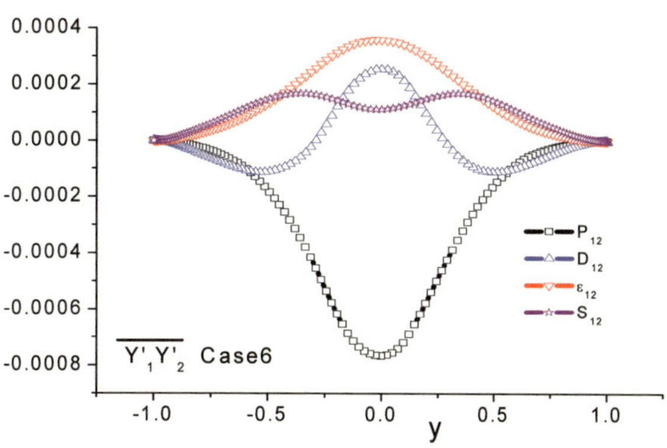

Fig. 30. The budget of the $\overline{Y_1'Y_2'}$ equation.

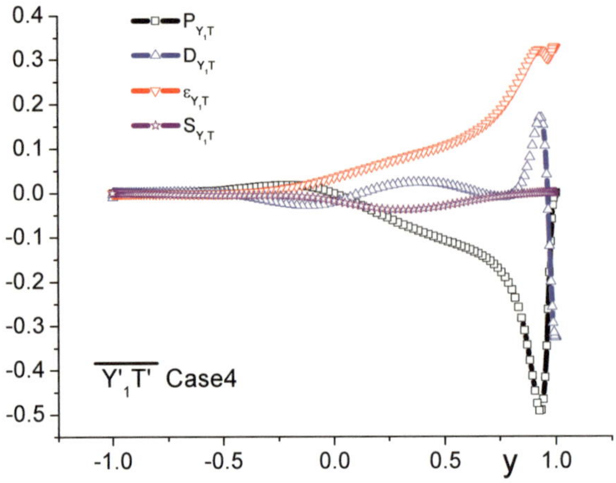

Fig. 31. The budget of the $\overline{T'Y_1'}$ equation.

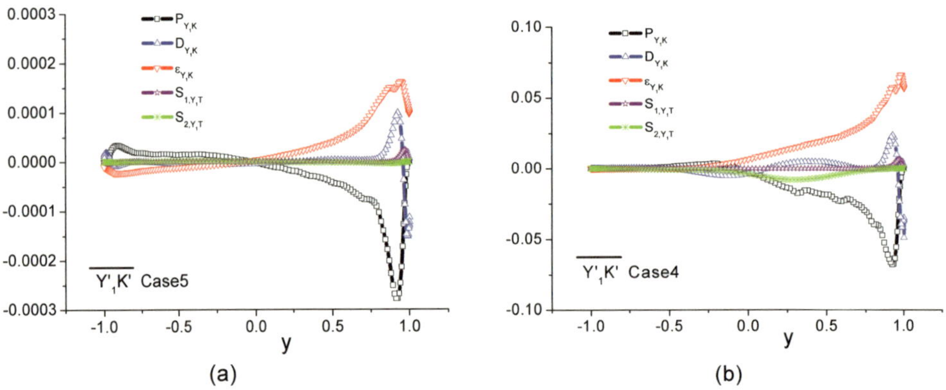

Fig. 32. The budget of the $\overline{K'Y_1'}$ equation.

From the magnitude and distribution, the chemistry affects a lot in correlations and their budget. In RANS model, the correlation transportation equations need to be closed with the production term, turbulent diffusion term and the dissipation term. As for the production term, the isotropic turbulent model is applied with σ_Y = 0.7. It is assumed that the dissipation of the correlation is direct proportion to itself. And gradient model is used in the diffusion term.

$$\frac{\partial \overline{K'Y_1'}}{\partial t}+\overline{u}_j\frac{\partial \overline{K'Y_1'}}{\partial x_j}=\frac{C_1\mu_t}{\rho\sigma_{KY}}\frac{\partial \overline{Y_1}}{\partial x_j}\frac{\partial \overline{K}}{\partial x_j}+\frac{\mu_e}{\sigma_{KY}}\frac{\partial}{\partial x_j}\left(\frac{\partial \overline{K'Y_1'}}{\partial x_j}\right)$$
$$-C_2\frac{\varepsilon}{k}\overline{K'Y_1'}-C_3[B\rho(\overline{Y_1}+\beta\overline{Y_2})\exp(-\frac{E}{R\overline{T}})]\overline{K'Y_1'} \qquad (20)$$

$$\frac{\partial \overline{Y_1'Y_2'}}{\partial t}+\overline{u}_j\frac{\partial \overline{Y_1'Y_2'}}{\partial x_j}=\frac{C_1\mu_t}{\rho\sigma_{YY}}\frac{\partial \overline{Y}_1}{\partial x_j}\frac{\partial \overline{Y}_2}{\partial x_j}+\frac{\mu_e}{\sigma_{YY}}\frac{\partial}{\partial x_j}\left(\frac{\partial \overline{Y_1'Y_2'}}{\partial x_j}\right)$$
$$-C_2\frac{\varepsilon}{k}\overline{Y_1'Y_2'}-C_3[B\rho(\overline{Y}_1+\beta\overline{Y}_2)\exp(-\frac{E}{R\overline{T}})]\overline{Y_1'Y_2'} \tag{21}$$

In which, $C_1=11.5$, $\sigma_{KY}=\sigma_{YY}=0.7$, $C_2=0.005$, $C_3=0.012$, $\beta=1.0$.

The comparison of the DNS exact values and the RANS model values are shown in figure 33 and 34. Generally, the model values of the production term (a), diffusion term (b) and the total dissipation term (c) are close to the exact values from DNS database. The difference between the exact values and the model values is rooted from the model assumption.

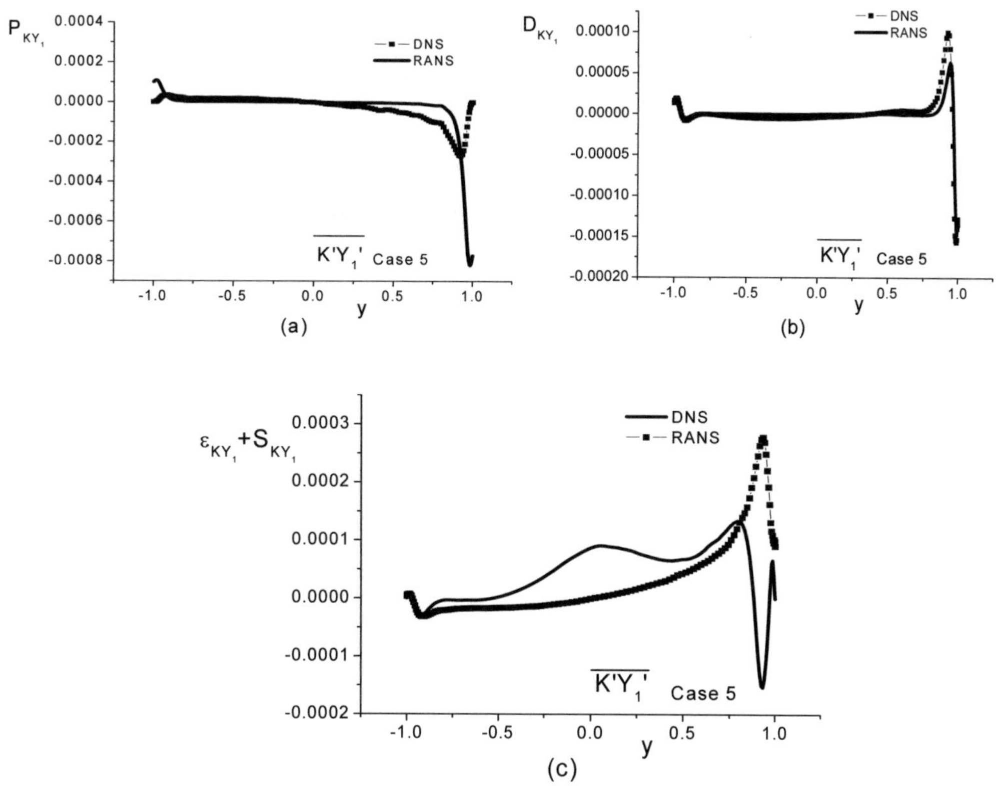

Fig. 33. The DNS statistical value and RANS model value of terms in $\overline{K'Y_1'}$ correlation equation in case 5.

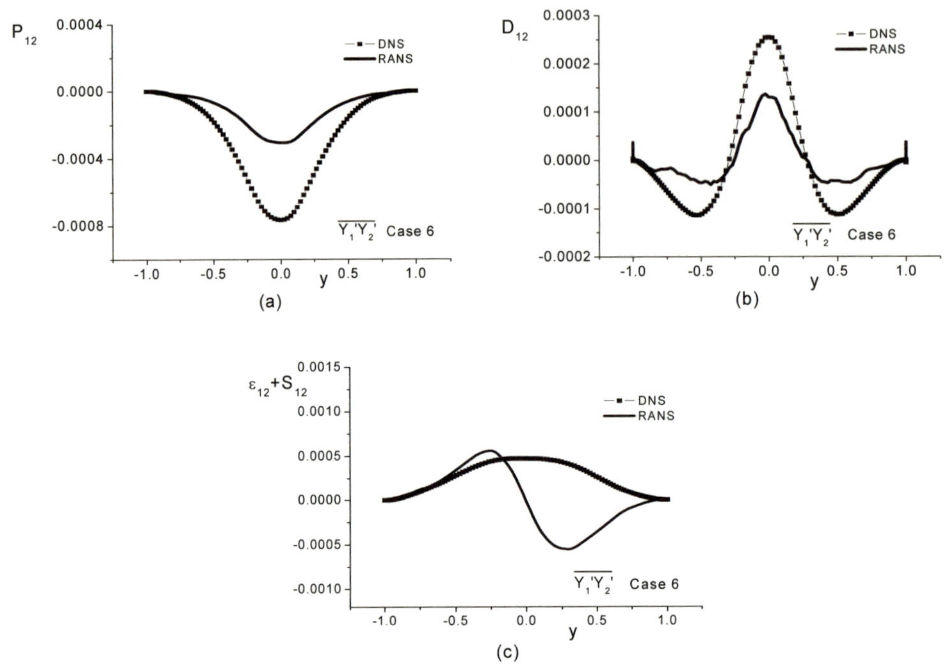

Fig. 34. The DNS statistical value and RANS model value of terms in $\overline{Y_1^{'}Y_2^{'}}$ correlation equation in case 6.

The algebraic second order moment (ASOM) RANS turbulent combustion model is quite simple but have been applied in jet flame successfully. The model expression is:

$$\overline{Y_1^{'}Y_2^{'}} = C_{YY}\frac{k^3}{\varepsilon^2}\frac{\partial \overline{Y_1}}{\partial x_j}\frac{\partial \overline{Y_2}}{\partial x_j} \tag{22}$$

$$\overline{K^{'}Y_1^{'}} = C_{KY_1}\frac{k^3}{\varepsilon^2}\frac{\partial \overline{K}}{\partial x_j}\frac{\partial \overline{Y_1}}{\partial x_j} \tag{23}$$

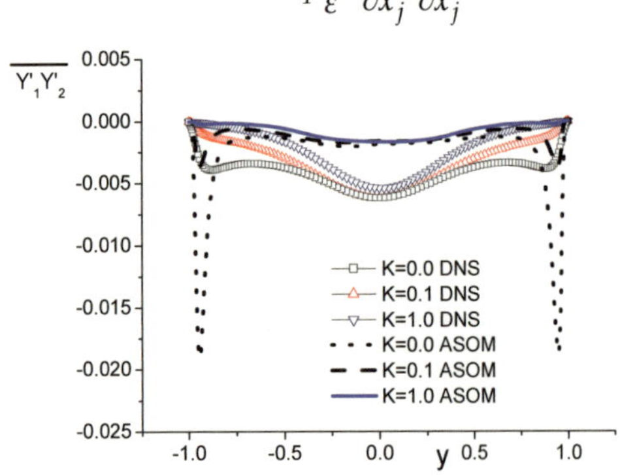

Fig. 35. The DNS statistical value and RANS model value of correlation $\overline{Y_1^{'}Y_2^{'}}$

The comparison between DNS exact values and the algebraic model values are shown in figure 35 and 36. The model values are in same trend with the exact values while in some regions, the model values are rather of distortion. The overestimated value in the near wall regions and the underestimations in the main flow regions resulted from the gradient simplification. The model constant in ASOM model is 0.005. These results show the reasonableness of ASOM model.

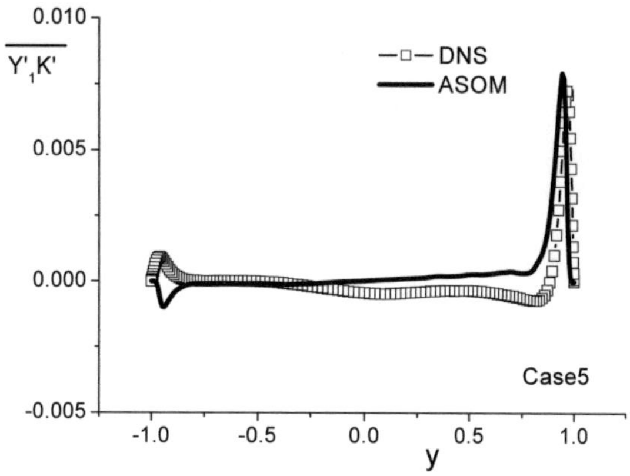

Fig. 36. The DNS statistical value and RANS model value of correlation $\overline{K'Y_1'}$.

As for the ASSCM SGS model in LES, the small scale reaction is calculated by:

$$\widetilde{Y_1Y_2K} - \tilde{Y}_1\tilde{Y}_2\tilde{K} = \tilde{K}(\widetilde{Y_{OX}Y_{Fu}} - \tilde{Y}_{OX}\tilde{Y}_{Fu}) + \tilde{Y}_{OX}(\widetilde{KY_{Fu}} - \tilde{K}\tilde{Y}_{Fu}) + \tilde{Y}_{Fu}(\widetilde{KY_{OX}} - \tilde{K}\tilde{Y}_{OX}) \quad (24)$$

The three quasi-correlation parts in the right hand side, shortened as $R_{Y_1Y_2}$, R_{Y_1K} and R_{Y_1T}, are

$$R_{\Phi\Psi} = \widetilde{\Phi\Psi} - \tilde{\Phi}\tilde{\Psi} = C_{\Phi,\Psi}L_S^2\frac{\partial\tilde{\Phi}}{\partial x_j}\frac{\partial\tilde{\Psi}}{\partial x_j} \quad (25)$$

Initially, the turbulent model is Smagorinsky-Lilly SGS model with $L_S = C_S\Delta$. While this model get bigger dissipation in flow regions especially in the near wall region, then a damping correction is used [zhang 2005]:

$$L_S = C_S\Delta[1-\exp(-y^+ / A^+)] \text{ , } C_S = 0.2, \ A^+ = 26 \quad (26)$$

In the spectral method, each variable in flow can be expended as Fourier function, in this chapter, the DNS wave number is 128, then assumed that the cut-off wave number in LES is 64, thus the DNS results can be divided into two parts: the low-pass value represents the resolvable value in LES and the rest high order value represents the sub-grid scale value. Using the filtering function, the statistic value of SGS correlation R_{Y_1K} and R_{Y_1T} from DNS database and SGS model value are shown in figure 37 to 42. R_{Y_1T} and R_{Y_1K} have same trend, and they have similar distribution in all domain.

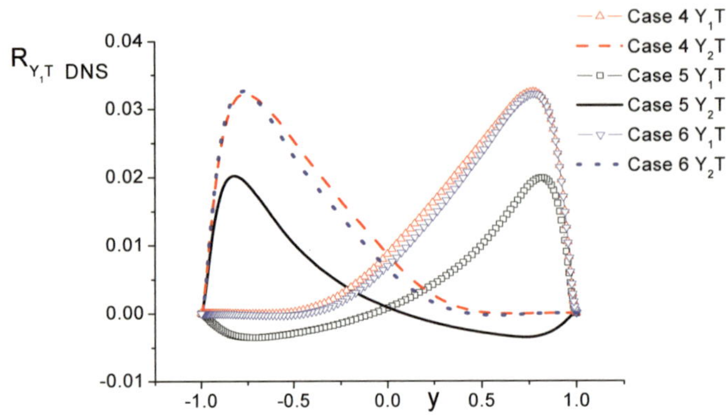

Fig. 37. The DNS value of SGS R_{Y_1T} .

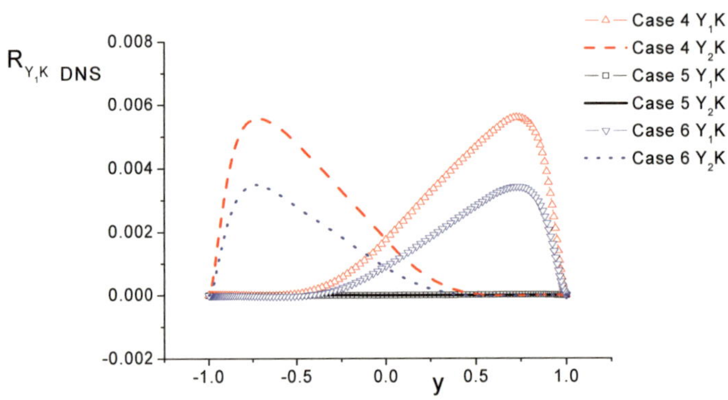

Fig. 38. The DNS value of SGS R_{Y_1K} .

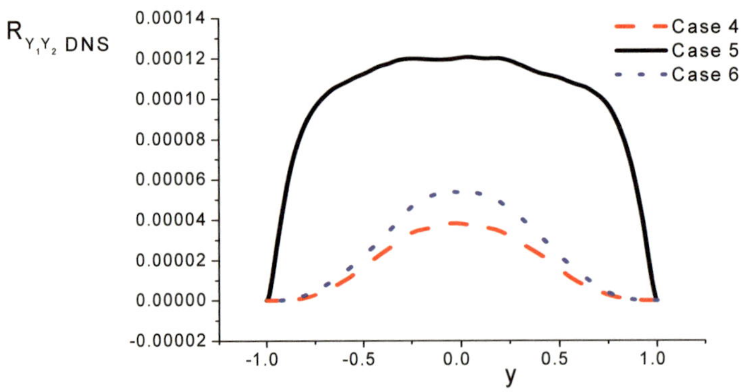

Fig. 39. The DNS value of SGS $R_{Y_1Y_2}$.

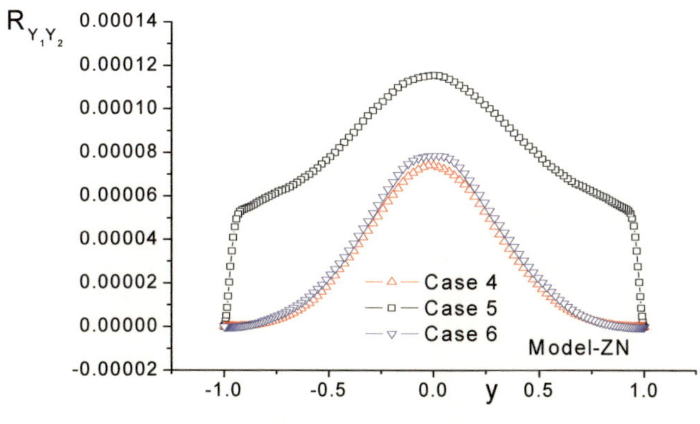

Fig. 40. The DNS value of SGS $R_{Y_1Y_2}$ with wall correction.

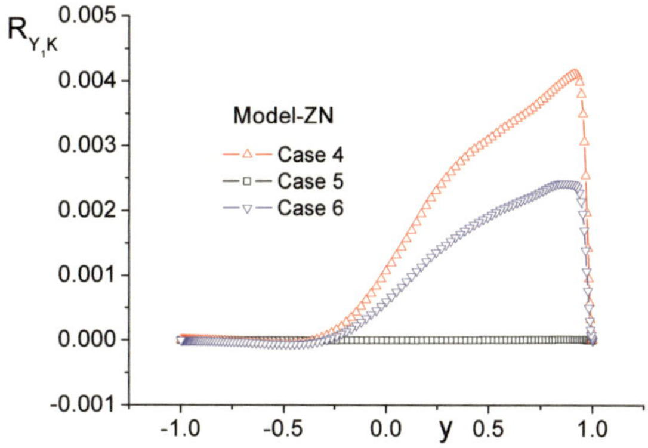

Fig. 41. The DNS value of SGS R_{Y_1K} with wall correction.

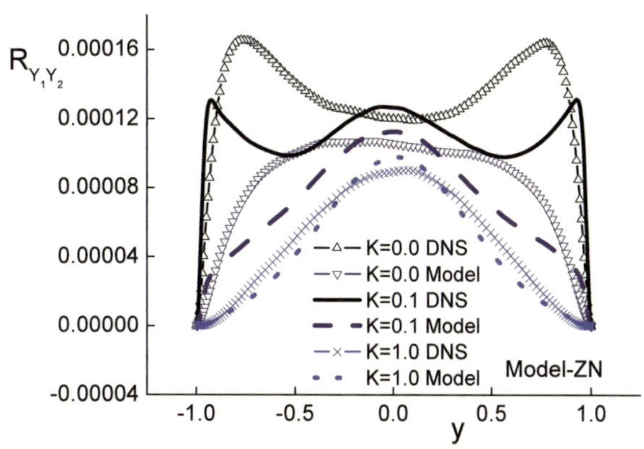

Fig. 42. The DNS value of SGS $R_{Y_1Y_2}$ with wall correction

In ASSCM turbulent SGS combustion model, the model factor is constant, while the exact value for model factor is shown in figure 43. It can be treat as a constant in most regions, but changes a lot in the near wall regions and varies according to different cases.

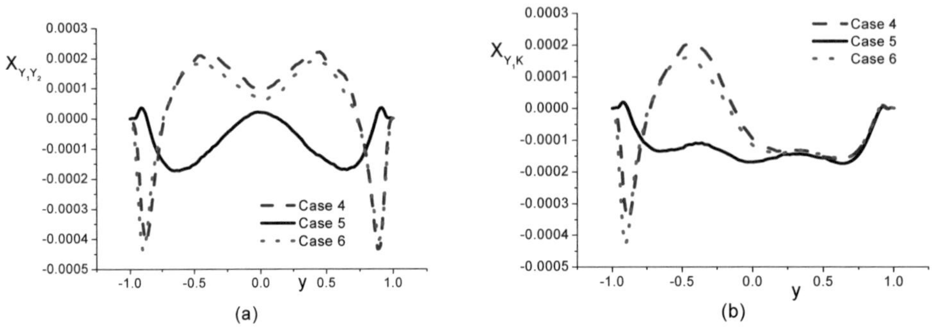

Fig. 43. The SGS model factor from DNS statistic.

While the model factor value with the near wall damping modification is shown in figure 44.

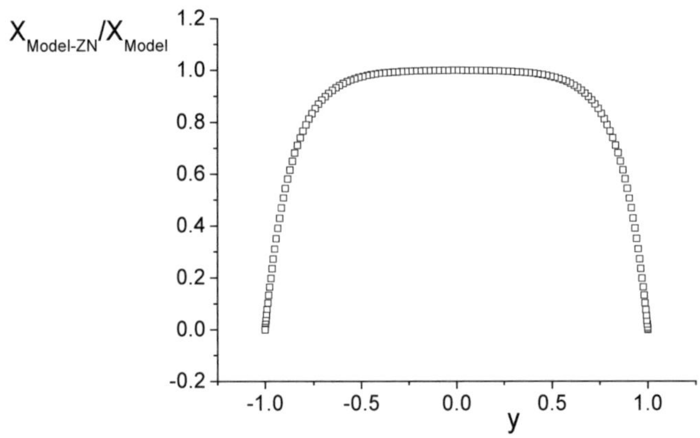

Fig. 44. The modified SGS model factor ($X_{Model-ZN}$) divided by constant model value (X_{Model})

According to the figures above, it is clearly that the modified model ($X_{Model-ZN}$) is better than the constant value model (X_{Model}) in the near wall regions because its value is closer to the exact DNS statistic value, so the damping model can give more reasonable prediction results.

The SGS scalar flux model is using gradient model with damping modification:

$$g_{u_jY_1} = C_{u_jY_1}\frac{\gamma_T}{\sigma}\frac{\partial \tilde{Y}_1}{\partial x_j} \tag{27}$$

Sum up the main points in this part, briefly, there are typical strip structures in the velocity and scalar field. The chemical reaction enhanced the turbulence especially in high shear regions. In the transportation equations of correlations, the production term and the dissipation term are more important. Comparison with the exact value from DNS, the RANS second order moment turbulent combustion model and the RANS algebraic second order moment turbulent model can give reasonable predictions in most regions. The damping modification model can give better prediction results than the constant value model because it is closer to the exact model factor value.

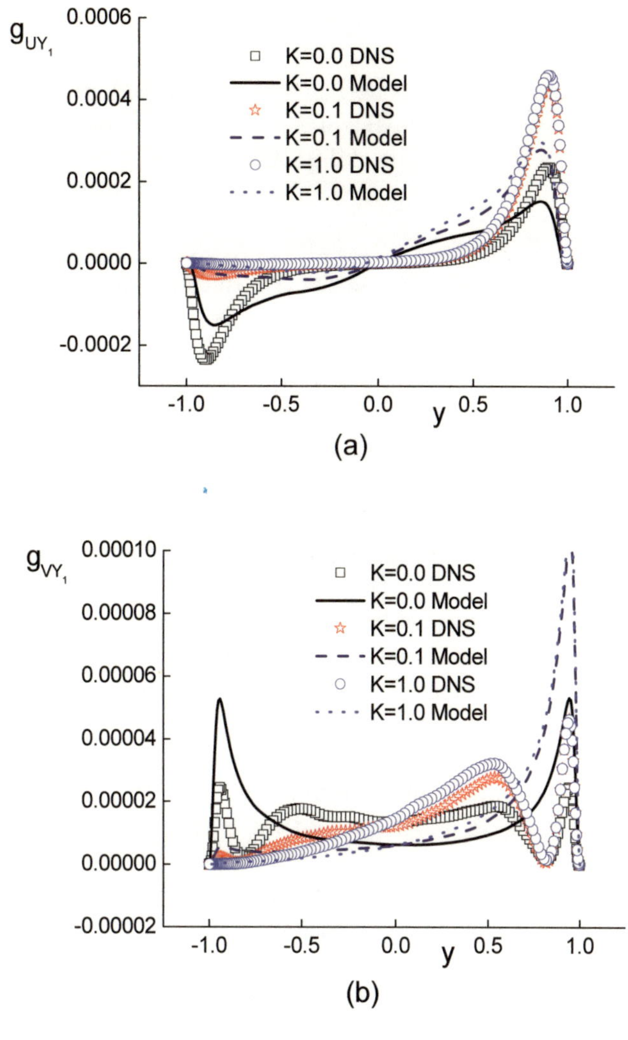

Fig. 45. The SGS flux model tested with damping model.

6. Conclusion

The LES and DNS methods are more and more important recently. There are many SGS turbulent combustion models for LES. The algebraic sub-grid scale turbulent combustion is quite simple in expression, while it is successfully applied in partly diffusion jet flame and premixed after bluff body flame. The predicted temperature, species, velocity and RMS values are all close to the experimental data in the most regions.

A spectral method DNS is carried in a channel reaction flow. The results are used for turbulent model research. It is shown that the ASSCM SGS model value is close to the exact value mainly, so ASSOM model is reasonable again.

The ASOM RANS turbulent combustion model is tested by LES and DNS results. Though this model is simple, its value has same trend with the exact value and quite close to the exact value sometimes. It can give quick and roughly prediction for average parameters but not RMS value.

The correlations in turbulent combustion model are studied in DNS, the temperature fluctuation is very important. The RANS equations were modelled. The near wall damping modification can improve the prediction ability of SGS model.

7. References

Colucci P J, Jaberi F A, Givi P. Filtered density function for large eddy simulation of turbulent reacting flows. Physics of Fluids, 1998, 10(2):499~515

DesJardin P E, Frankel S H. Two-dimensional large eddy simulation of soot formation in the near-field of strongly radiating nonpremixed acetylene-air turbulent jet flame. Combustion and Flame, 1999, 119:121~123

Gao F, Obrien E E. A large-eddy simulation scheme for turbulent reacting flows. Phys Fluids A, 1993, 5(6):1282~1284

Giacomazzi E, Battaglia V, Bruno C. The coupling of turbulence and chemistry in a premixed bluff-body flame as studied by LES. Combustion and Flame, 2004, 138:320~335

James S, Jaberi F A. Large scale simulations of two-demensional nonpremixed methane jet flames. Combustion and Flame, 2000, 123:465~487

Jones W P. Large eddy simulation of turbulent combustion processes. Computer Physics Communications, 2002, 147:533~537

Kawamura H, Abe H, Shingai K. DNS of turbulence and heat transport in a channel flow with different Reynolds and Prandtl numbers and boundary conditions. In: Nagano Y, Hanjalic K, Tsuji, eds. 3rd Int. Symp. on Turbulence, Heat and Mass Transfer. Tokyo, 2000. 15~32

Renfro M W, Chaturvedy A, King G B. Comparison of OH time-series measurements and large-eddy simulations in hydrogen jet flames. Combustion and Flame, 2004, 139:142~151

Westbrook C K, Dryer F L. Simplified Reaction Mechanisms for the Oxidation of Hydrocarbon Fuels in Flames, Combust. Sci. Tech. 1981, 27(1-2): 31-43

Xu C, Toonder J M J, Nieuwstadt F T M, et al. Origin of high kurtosis levels in the viscous sublayer. Direct numerical simulation and experiments. Physics of Fluids, 1996, 8(7):1938~1944

Yaga M, Endo H, Yamamoto T, et al. Modeling of eddy characteristic time in LES for calculating turbulent diffusion flame. International Journal of Heat and Mass Transfer, 2002, 45:2343~2349

Zhang Z S, Cui G X, Xu C X, Theory and modelling of turbulence, Beijing, Qsinghua University Press, 2005

11

Numerical Simulation of Dense Gas-Solid Multiphase Flows Using Eulerian-Eulerian Two-Fluid Model

Teklay Weldeabzgi Asegehegn,
Matthias Schreiber and Hans Joachim Krautz
Brandenburg University of Technology Cottbus
Germany

1. Introduction

Gas-solid fluidized beds are widely applied in chemical processes such as drying, combustion, synthesis of fuels, granulation, polymerization etc. They have several advantageous properties including; excellent heat and mass transfer, nearly isothermal conditions due to intense gas-solid mixing, large gas-solid surface area, smooth transport of solids, uniform solid product in batch processes, and possibility of continuous and large-scale operations. On the other hand, these reactors have several drawbacks that provide a strong motivation for further studies and developments. These include; difficulty in scaling-up and design, erosion of vessel and internals, formation of agglomerates, non-uniform products due to non-uniform solids residence time during continuous operation, and high particle entrainment. These drawbacks are bottlenecks for practitioners to reliably design and scale-up commercial fluidized bed reactors. The main reason for this is that the gas-solid multiphase flow dynamics coupled with heat and mass transfer and chemical reactions that occur in these systems are very complex and not yet fully understood.

In bubbling gas-solid fluidized beds, bubble characteristics such as size, shape, velocity, distribution have a vital influence on the hydrodynamics of bed and hence on its performance as a chemical reactor and/or a heat exchange unit. The extent of gas-solid mixing and segregation, heat and mass transfer as well as reaction conversion are governed by the number, size and motion of bubbles passing through the bed (Kunii & Levenspiel, 1991). Therefore, fundamental understanding of the hydrodynamics of fluidized beds thereafter their heat and mass transfer as well as chemical conversion come only after a sound understanding of bubbling behaviour is achieved. However, prediction of bubble characteristics is extremely complex as bubbles can grow, coalesce, split or even disappear as they move from the distributor where they are formed to the top of the bed where they finally erupt. Moreover, bubble characteristics vary with geometric construction of the bed and operating conditions. In many applications, heat exchanger tubes are inserted to enhance the rate of heat and mass transfer and chemical conversion, control the operating temperature, promote good mixing and reduce gulf circulation of solids. In these systems, the bubbling behaviour is also strongly influenced by the geometry and arrangement of the internals (Yates et al., 1990; Hull et al., 1999; Asegehegn et al., 2011a). Therefore, fundamental understating of the bubble hydrodynamics is necessary for better understanding of the complex gas-solid flow dynamics. This will lead to better optimize and improve the design, scale-up and operation procedure of the systems as well as to extend their use to novel applications.

Several experimental techniques have been developed for the past several decades in an attempt to measure and understand the bubble characteristics in laboratory-scale fluidized beds. Unfortunately, these laboratory-scale data do not necessarily scale-up accurately. To better understand the hydrodynamics in a commercial-scale fluidized bed reactor, it is necessary to study a vessel of that size. However, such experiments are not only prohibitive due to their capital and operational cost but also provide little information on the bubbling properties of the bed. In case of parametric studies, it is not practical or even impossible to vary the geometry and operating conditions of commercial-scale fluidized beds during experimentation. Moreover, due to the harsh environment and opaque nature of gas-solid flow structure of fluidized beds, it is difficult to observe the flow structure of the bed using many of the experimental techniques developed so far. Thus, together with the development of dedicated experimental techniques the development of fundamental hydrodynamic models is of utmost importance to achieve a better understanding of fluidization. Eventually this will lead to the improvement of existing processes, improved scale-up and the design of more efficient future processes. In recent years, together with rapid development of high performance computers and numerical algorithms, the rapid growth of interest in understanding the physical mechanisms responsible for the complex behaviour of gas-solid systems has helped to spark the development of fundamental approaches based on Computational Fluid Dynamics (CFD). Though empirical correlations are still largely used for designing gas-solid fluidized beds, these CFD models have been seen as fundamental tools in the study of the hydrodynamics and to aid in the design process of these systems. Numerical models are more flexible and less expensive specially when performing parametric studies for different bed geometries and operating conditions. Moreover, they provide extensive data for bubble characteristics for the entire cross section of the bed regardless of the complexity of bed geometry and operating conditions. However, further model development and validation of the models are still needed. It is believed that such validated CFD models can contribute to the successful understanding of bubble characteristics hence the design and optimization of these industrially relevant reactors.

Broadly speaking, there are two types of CFD models for gas-solid multiphase flow simulations that are widely applied today; namely, the Discrete Particle Model (DPM) and the Two-Fluid Model (TFM). In the DPM approach, which is based on the Eulerian-Lagrangian approach (Tsuji et al., 1993; Hoomans et al., 1996), the gas phase is treated as a continuous phase described by locally averaged Navier-Stokes equations on a computational cell scale, whereas the motion of particles is modelled as a discrete phase, described by Newton's laws of motion on an individual particle scale. A comprehensive review of the state of the Eulerian-Lagrangian model with a detailed description and governing equations as well as their application in the study of fluidized beds can be found elsewhere in the literature (e.g. Deen et al., 2007). In the TFM, which is based on the Eulerian-Eulerian approach (Anderson & Jackson, 1967), both the gas and solid phases are treated as fully interpenetrating continua. They are described by separate conservation equations for mass and momentum with appropriate interaction term between the phases included as a source terms in the conservation equations to couple the two phases.

Practically the motion of gas-particle flow systems present in fluidized beds should be expressed at least by the Eulerian-Lagrangian approach with the Newtonian equations of motion for the suspended particles. However, when the system comprises a large number of closely spaced particles, as in the case of fluidized bed, the problem is far too difficult to allow direct solution by tracking individual particles. Despite the rapid growth in computer capacity, it is only possible to track less than 10^6 particles (much less than the practical number of particles found in industrial scale fluidized beds) using the DPM. Since both CPU time and the required memory scales linear with the number of particles, it is obvious that DPM simulations of engineering size fluidized beds are beyond the capability of commercially available computer facilities within the foreseeable future. Therefore, DPM is not a natural choice for hydrodynamic modelling of gas-solid systems. For practical purposes, it is necessary to seek some way of simplifying it so that it can be described by a relatively small number of partial differential equations. One way of simplifying this problem is to replace the point mechanical and fluid mechanical variables by an appropriate locally average value of the corresponding variables to formulate the integral balances for mass, momentum and energy for a fixed control volume containing both phases. Hence describing the motion of the fluid and particles as though they were interpenetrating continua (Anderson and Jackson, 1967). In such continuum model, the equations are a generalization of the Navier-Stokes equations for interacting continua. This means that instead of knowing the positions and velocities of each particle, only the volume fraction of each phase and the average volume flow pattern are known. Though the local instantaneous value of variables vary rapidly on a scale comparable with the particle spacing the averaged variables are smoothed by averaging over regions large compared with the particle spacing but small compared with the size of complete system. The main advantage of this model is that the averaging techniques allow us to use relatively coarser grids and longer time steps so that the computational effort is significantly reduced, hence larger scale simulations can be performed, using less computation time.

In fact, the continuum model suffers from some limitations in modelling of the gas-solid flow. It does not provide information about the hydrodynamics of individual particles and thus has limitations in predicting certain discrete flow characteristics such as particle size and density effect. Nevertheless, it remains the only feasible approach for performing parametric investigation and scale-up and design studies of industrial scale systems and dense gas-solid beds (van Wachem et al., 2001; van der Hoef et al., 2008). Detail comparisons of the DPM and the TFM can be found elsewhere in the literature (e.g., Gera et al., 1998; Chiesa et al., 2005; van der Hoef et al., 2008)

2. The Eulerian two-fluid model

Most literatures give tribute to the paper by Davidson (1961) as the first to apply the concept of hydrodynamic model in fluidized beds in his analysis of a single isolated bubble rising in an unbounded fluidized bed. However, Anderson & Jackson (1967) were the first to formulate the complete CFD TFM for gas-solid multiphase flows in the mid 60's. Since then many have made significant efforts to develop detailed microbalance models to study the complex hydrodynamics of gas-fluidized beds (e.g., Gidaspow, 1994; Enwald et al., 1996; Kuipers & van Swaaij, 1998).

Owing to the continuum description of the particulate suspension, the TFM requires additional closure laws for the solid rheology. Two of the most important transport variables that appear in the momentum equation of the solid are the solids stress tensor and solids pressure. These variables depend strongly on the collisional behaviour of the individual particles, hence difficult to express. So far, there are two types of approaches to treat these variables. The first one is commonly known as the Constant Viscosity Model (CVM) and was applied by many of the early TFM computer simulations (e.g. Gidaspow & Ettehadieh, 1983; Tsuo & Gidaspow, 1990; Kuipers et al., 1992, 1993; Enwald et al., 1996). This approach assumes a constant value for the solids viscosity obtained from some experimental and empirical correlations. The solids phase pressure, which prevents particles from reaching impossibly low values of void fraction, was assumed to depend on the solid volume fraction and it is determined from experiments. The advantage of this model is its simplicity and thus easy to implement in a computer codes. However, it is difficult to take into account the underlying characteristics of the solid phase rheology due to mutual particle collisions. The second approach makes use of the Kinetic Theory of Granular Flow (KTGF) and develops some relations as a function of the particle velocity and position (Ding & Gidaspow, 1990). One of the advantages of the KTGF is that it can give a more fundamental insight of the particle-particle interactions. Detail explanation of this model is presented in section 3.3 below.

Over the past 20 years, a large number of researchers have devoted significant effort to apply and validate the TFM based on the KTGF for different flow regimes and particle classes. For example, Boemer et al. (1997, 1998), van Wachem et al. (1998, 1999, 2001), Hulme et al. (2005), Patil et al. (2005), Lindborg et al. (2007) have been devoted to validate the model for bubble behaviour in gas-solid fluidized beds. The majority of these and other validation works are only relevant for beds without immersed tubes and to date little has been done to validate the TFM for fluidized beds with immersed obstacles. Those who performed numerical simulation using the TFM for beds with immersed tubes are mainly limited to beds with single or few tubes. Moreover, their validations involved mainly qualitative comparisons such as voidage distribution and solid circulation near the tube surface in an attempt to investigate the heat transfer coefficient or erosion characteristics of the tubes (Bouillard et al., 1989; Gamwo et al., 1999; Gustavson & Almstedt, 2000; Yurong et al., 2004; Schmidt & Renz, 2005; Gao et al., 2007). There are also attempts in validating the TFM using time-averaged bubble properties (Das Sharma & Mohan, 2003; Asegehegn et al., 2011a). Nevertheless, these are limited to only few immersed horizontal tubes.

In this chapter of the book, numerical simulations of gas-solid fluidized beds were performed using the granular TFM for beds without and with dense immersed tubes. The results of bubble properties were thoroughly analyzed and validated with experimental results obtained from pseudo-2D bed. Moreover, comparisons between 2D and 3D simulations were performed.

3. Numerical modelling using the Granular two-fluid model

3.1 Governing equations

The conservation of mass for both the gas and the solids phase can be written as:

$$\frac{\partial(\varepsilon_g \rho_g)}{\partial t} + \nabla \cdot \left(\varepsilon_g \rho_g \boldsymbol{u}_g\right) = 0 \tag{1}$$

$$\frac{\partial(\varepsilon_s \rho_s)}{\partial t} + \nabla \cdot \left(\varepsilon_s \rho_s \boldsymbol{u}_s\right) = 0 \tag{2}$$

The volume fractions are related as:

$$\varepsilon_s + \varepsilon_g = 1 \tag{3}$$

The conservation of momentum for the gas and the solids phase are described by:

$$\frac{\partial(\varepsilon_g \rho_g \boldsymbol{u}_g)}{\partial t} + \nabla \cdot \left(\varepsilon_g \rho_g \boldsymbol{u}_g \boldsymbol{u}_g\right) = \nabla \cdot \left(\boldsymbol{\tau}_g\right) - \varepsilon_g \nabla P - \beta\left(\boldsymbol{u}_g - \boldsymbol{u}_s\right) + \varepsilon_g \rho_g \boldsymbol{g} \tag{4}$$

$$\frac{\partial(\varepsilon_s \rho_s \boldsymbol{u}_s)}{\partial t} + \nabla \cdot \left(\varepsilon_s \rho_s \boldsymbol{u}_s \boldsymbol{u}_s\right) = \nabla \cdot \left(\boldsymbol{\tau}_s\right) - \varepsilon_s \nabla P - \nabla P_s + \beta\left(\boldsymbol{u}_g - \boldsymbol{u}_s\right) + \varepsilon_s \rho_s \boldsymbol{g} \tag{5}$$

3.2 Interphase momentum transfer

In the TFM the two phase are coupled through the interphase momentum transfer, hence it is one of the most important and dominant force in modelling gas-solid systems. The drag force acting on a particle in fluid–solid systems is generally represented by the product of a momentum transfer coefficient and the slip velocity ($u_g - u_s$) between the two phases. Numerous empirical correlations for calculating the momentum transfer coefficient, β, of gas-solid systems have been reported in the literature. These have been compared and validated by different researchers before, e.g. van Wachem et al. (2001), Taghipour et al. (2005), and Vejahati et al. (2009). All these researchers reported that the different drag models available gave quantitatively similar predictions of the macroscopic bed characteristic and bubble properties. As a result, the most commonly used drag model of Gidaspow (1994) was used in this work.

$$\beta = 150 \frac{\left(1-\varepsilon_g\right)^2}{\varepsilon_g} \frac{\mu_g}{\left(d_p\right)^2} + 1.75\left(1-\varepsilon_g\right) \frac{\rho_g}{d_p} \left|u_g - u_s\right|, \quad if \quad \varepsilon_g \leq 0.8 \tag{6}$$

$$\beta = \frac{3}{4} C_d \frac{\varepsilon_g\left(1-\varepsilon_g\right)}{d_p} \rho_g \left|u_g - u_s\right| \varepsilon_g^{-2.65}, \qquad if \quad \varepsilon_g > 0.8 \tag{7}$$

Where,

$$C_d = \begin{cases} \frac{24}{Re_p}\left[1 + 0.15\left(Re_p\right)^{0.687}\right] & , Re_p \leq 1000 \\ 0.44 & , Re_p > 1000 \end{cases} \tag{8}$$

The particle Reynolds number is given by:

$$Re_p = \frac{\varepsilon_g \rho_g \left|u_g - u_s\right| d_p}{\mu_g} \tag{9}$$

3.3 Kinetic theory of granular flow

Almost all recent TFM of gas-solid systems used the Kinetic Theory of Granular Flow (KTGF) principle to derive the constitutive equations to describe the rheology of the particulate phase, i.e., the particulate phase viscosity and the particulate phase pressure gradient. The KTGF is basically an extension of the classical kinetic theories of non-uniform gases as described by Chapman & Cowling (1970). It was first applied to granular flows by Jenkins & Savage (1983) and Lun et al. (1984). Later Sinclair & Jackson (1989) applied this theory to model gas-solid flow in a pipe. The model was further developed and applied to dense gas-solid fluidized beds by Ding & Gidaspow (1990) and Gidaspow (1994). The extensions were made to include the dissipation of kinetic fluctuation energy in the granular medium during mutual non-ideal particle-particle collisions due to inelastic deformation and friction of particles with the surrounding fluid.

In gas-solid flow, the interaction of the particles and the gas is restricted to a mutual drag force. Since the gas does not slip freely at the wall of the vessel, there is a gas velocity profile in fully developed flow, with the maximum velocity on the axis of the pipe, and the drag forces exerted by the gas on the particles induce a corresponding profile of particle velocity. As a result of this shearing motion the particles collide with each other, resulting in a random granular motion of particle. Thus, the instantaneous particle velocity can be decomposed into a local mean velocity and random fluctuation velocity. The random velocity fluctuations then generate an effective pressure in the particle phase, together with an effective viscosity that resists shearing of the particle assembly. Similar to the usual thermodynamic temperature in gases, a pseudo-temperature, known as the granular temperature Θ is defined as one third of the mean square of the random velocity component of the velocity, u', (Jenkins & Savage, 1983) as:

$$\Theta = \frac{1}{3}u'^2 \tag{10}$$

This granular temperature is the measure of the particle velocity fluctuation mainly due to the particle-particle collision and varies with time and position in the fluidized bed. Therefore, both the effective pressure and the effective viscosity are functions of the granular temperature. As a result, an additional conservation equation representing a balance for this kinetic energy of the random motion of the particles is required to determine the pseudo (granular) temperature distribution. This pseudo-thermal energy is generated by the working of the effective shear stresses in the particle phase, dissipated by the inelasticity of collisions between particles and conducted from place to place as a result of gradients in the particle temperature. The additional conservation equation of the particle velocity fluctuations is described by a separate conservation, the so-called granular temperature equation:

$$\frac{3}{2}\left(\frac{\partial(\varepsilon_s\rho_s\Theta)}{\partial t} + \nabla\cdot(\varepsilon_s\rho_s u_s\Theta)\right) = (-P_s I + \tau_s):\nabla u_s - \nabla\cdot q - \gamma_s - J_s \tag{11}$$

The left hand side of this equation is the net change in fluctuating energy. The first term on the right hand side is the generation of fluctuating energy due to local acceleration of the particles, which includes solid pressure and shear tensor. The second term is the diffusion of fluctuating energy. The third term on the right hand side is the dissipation of fluctuating energy due to inelastic particle-particle collision and the last term is the exchange of fluctuation energy between gas and solid phases, which accounts for the loss of granular energy due to friction with the gas.

Instead of solving the complete granular temperature equation Syamlal et al. (1993) proposed an algebraic form of the equation. They assumed a local equilibrium between generation and dissipation of the granular energy as these terms are the most dominant terms in dense regions. Thus, the convection and diffusion terms can be neglected. Boemer et al. (1997) and van Wachem et al. (2001) showed that using the algebraic form instead of the full partial differential equation hardly affects simulation results while significant computational time can be saved. By neglecting the convection and diffusion terms and retaining only the generation and the dissipation terms, Eq. 11 is reduced to:

$$0 = (-P_s I + \tau_s) : \nabla u_s - \gamma_s \tag{12}$$

For detail discussions and derivation of the kinetic theory, interested readers are referred to the book by Gidapow (1994) and papers by Jenkins & Savage (1983), Lun et al. (1984), Ding & Gidaspow (1990).

3.3.1 Gas phase stress tensor

Gases are usually assumed Newtonian fluids thus the stress tensor is modelled using the Newtonian stress-strain relation as:

$$\boldsymbol{\tau}_g = -\varepsilon_g \left[\left(\xi_g - \frac{2}{3}\mu_g \right) (\nabla \cdot \boldsymbol{u}_g) \boldsymbol{I} + \mu_g \left((\nabla \boldsymbol{u}_g) + (\nabla \boldsymbol{u}_g)^T \right) \right] \tag{13}$$

For the gas phase, the bulk viscosity ξ_g is usually set to zero while the shear viscosity μ_g is assumed to be constant.

3.3.2 Solids phase shear stress tensor

The solids phase is also assumed Newtonian and the stress tensor is given by:

$$\boldsymbol{\tau}_s = -\varepsilon_s \left[\left(\xi_s - \frac{2}{3}\mu_s \right) (\nabla \cdot \boldsymbol{u}_s) \boldsymbol{I} + \mu_s \left((\nabla \boldsymbol{u}_s) + (\nabla \boldsymbol{u}_s)^T \right) \right] \tag{14}$$

In fluidized beds the bulk and shear viscosities of the particulate phase are of the same order and thus bulk viscosity is not neglected.

Solids bulk viscosity

Solids bulk viscosity describes the resistance of particle suspension against compression. In general the model proposed by Lun et al. (1984) used and is given by:

$$\xi_s = \frac{4}{3} \varepsilon_s \rho_s d_p g_o (1+e) \sqrt{\Theta/\pi} \tag{15}$$

Solids shear viscosity

Shear viscosity represents the tangential forces due to translational and collisional interaction of particles. In general it is written as the sum of a collisional and a kinetic part:

$$\mu_{s,KTGF} = \mu_{s,col} + \mu_{s,kin} \tag{16}$$

There are several models for the shear viscosity expression in the literature. Basically all use similar expression for the collision contribution however their expression for the kinetic contribution of the solids shear viscosity differs. van Wachem et al. (2001) compared the performance of the most commonly used models and they reported that the models differ mainly in the dilute region ($\varepsilon_s < 0.3$), which is of minor importance in bubbling fluidized beds. In dense solid systems, there is no difference in the predicted solids viscosity of the models. Therefore, the model proposed by Gidaspow (1994) was used in this work.

$$\mu_{s,col} = \frac{4}{5} \varepsilon_s \rho_s d_p g_o (1+e) \sqrt{\Theta/\pi} \tag{17}$$

$$\mu_{s,kin} = \frac{1}{15} \sqrt{\Theta\pi} \rho_s d_p g_0 \varepsilon_s^2 (1+e) + \frac{1}{16} \sqrt{\Theta\pi} \rho_s d_p \varepsilon_s + \frac{10}{96} \sqrt{\Theta\pi} \frac{\rho_s d_p}{g_0(1+e)} \tag{18}$$

3.3.3 Dissipation of granular energy

The dissipation term in the fluctuating granular energy equation (Eq. 11 and 12) represents the dissipation of granular energy due to inelastic particle-particle collisions and is usually expressed by the model of Lun et al. (1984) as:

$$\gamma_s = 12(1 - e^2)\frac{\varepsilon_s^2 \rho_s g_0}{d_p\sqrt{\pi}}\Theta^{3/2} \tag{19}$$

3.3.4 Radial distribution function

The radial distribution function can be interpreted as the probability of a single particle touching another particle (probability of particle collision) in the solids phase. The value of the radial distribution function varies from one at zero solids volume fractions and tends to infinity when the solids volume fraction reaches the maximum packing limit, due to constant contact of the particles. The function allows a tight control of the solids volume fraction, so that maximum packing is not exceeded and more accurate flow characteristics can be achieved. There are several empirical models for the radial distribution function and have been compared by van Wachem et al. (2001). In this work the model proposed by Ma & Ahmadi (1986) was used.

$$g_0 = 1 + 4\varepsilon_s \left\{ \frac{1+2.5\varepsilon_s+4.5904\varepsilon_s^2+4.515439\varepsilon_s^3}{\left[1-\left({\varepsilon_s}/{\varepsilon_{s,max}}\right)^3\right]^{0.67802}} \right\} \tag{20}$$

3.3.5 Solids pressure

The solids pressure represents the normal forces due to particle-particle interactions and it prevents the solids phase from reaching unrealistic high solids volume fractions. It also helps to make the system numerically stable by converting imaginary characteristics into real ones (Kuipers et al., 1992). It is written as the sum of the kinetic and collisional term as given by Lun et al. (1984):

$$P_{s,KTGF} = \varepsilon_s \rho_s \Theta + 2 g_o \varepsilon_s^2 \rho_s \Theta (1 + e) \tag{21}$$

3.3.6 Frictional stresses

When particles are closely packed, as in the case of dense fluidized beds, the behaviour of the granular flow is not adequately described by kinetic theory, which assumes collisions to be binary and quasi-instantaneous. In regions with high particle volume fractions multi-particle contacts (frictional stresses) dominate the stress generation mechanism. Hence, it is necessary to include these stresses in the model. Similar to shear stress, frictional stress is composed of the frictional shear viscosity and frictional solids pressure, which includes tangential and normal frictional forces. The frictional stresses are simply added to the solid stresses from KTGF when the solids volume fraction exceeds a certain value $\varepsilon_{s,min}$, which is set to 0.6 in this work.

$$\mu_s = \mu_{s,KTGF} + \mu_{s,f} \tag{22}$$

$$P_s = P_{s,KTGF} + P_{s,f} \tag{23}$$

Here the Schaeffer (1987) model for frictional shear viscosity and the Johnson et al. (1990) model for frictional pressure were used:

$$\mu_{s,f} = \frac{P_s \sin\phi}{2\sqrt{I_{2D}}} \tag{24}$$

$$P_{s,f} = Fr\frac{\left(\varepsilon_s - \varepsilon_{s,min}\right)^n}{\left(\varepsilon_{s,max} - \varepsilon_s\right)^p} \tag{25}$$

3.4 Initial and boundary conditions

The initial conditions for all simulation cases were set to the minimum fluidization condition with a bed voidage of 0.38 and bed height at minimum fluidization of 0.5 m. At the inlet the velocity inlet boundary condition with uniform superficial velocity of the gas phase was set. At the outlet the pressure outlet boundary condition was set for the mixture phase and the height of the free board was made long enough so that fully developed flow was achieved for the gas phase. At the side and tube walls the gas phase was assumed to have a no-slip boundary condition. For the particulate the partial-slip boundary condition of Johnson & Jackson (1987) was used.

$$\tau_w = \frac{\pi}{6}\sqrt{3}\phi'\frac{\varepsilon_s}{\varepsilon_{s,max}}\rho_s g_0\sqrt{\Theta}u_{slip} \tag{26}$$

3.5 Simulation parameters and procedure

The two different bed geometries shown in Fig. 1 were used for the numerical simulations. All the dimensions of the beds were similar to the experimental setup except for the 2D simulation. For the solution the commercial CFD code ANSYS FLUENT 12.1 (ANSYS, 2009) was used. A uniform quadratic mesh with a size of 5 mm was applied with slight refinement of up to 2 mm near the tube surfaces to capture the higher velocity gradients there. The QUICK and second order upwind scheme were employed for spatial discretization of the continuity and momentum equations respectively and time was discretized using second order implicit. The Phase-Coupled SIMPLE algorithm was used for the pressure-velocity coupling. A fixed time step of 2.5×10^{-5} s was used. Table 1 shows additional simulation parameters that were used.

Parameter	Value
Gas density, kg/m^3	1.2
Gas viscosity, Pa·s	$1.79 \cdot 10^{-5}$
Particle density, kg/m^3	2500
Particle diameter, μm	246, 347
Minimum fluidization velocity, U_{mf}, m/s	0.0876, 0.144
Minimum fluidization solid volume fraction	0.62
Bed height at minimum fluidization, m	0.5
Restitution coefficient	0.95
Superficial velocity, m/s	$2U_{mf}$, $3U_{mf}$, $4U_{mf}$
Maximum particle packing limit	0.65
Specularity coefficient	0.50
Angle of internal friction, °	28.5
Time step size, s	$2.5 \cdot 10^{-5}$

Table 1. Additional simulation parameters.

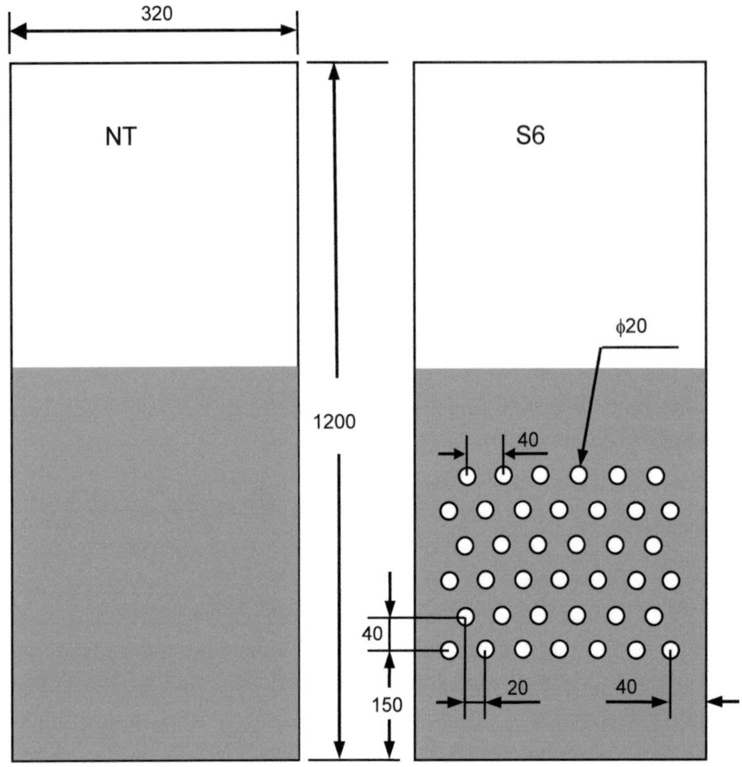

Fig. 1. Bed geometries: left - without immersed tubes (NT) and right with staggered tube arrangement (S6). All dimensions are in mm.

4. Experimental procedure

The experimental studies were performed using a specifically designed and constructed pseudo-2D fluidized bed. The bed was 0.32 m wide, 1.2 m high and 0.02 m thick and almost 2D thus allowing visual observations of bubble dynamics within the bed. The front and back sides were made of polycarbonate plastic in order to allow easy drilling of holes for assembly of the simulated tubes and allow full transparency of light. Bubble properties were calculated with the help of a Digital Image Analysis Technique (DIAT). DIAT was seen as a powerful method especially for the analysis of bubble properties as it provides rigorous and detailed information about the flow structure of the whole bed without interfering the flow dynamics. With the help of MATLAB Image Processing Toolbox, an in-house software was developed to fully automate the image acquisition and data processing procedure for the analysis of bubble properties for fluidized bed with and without immersed tubes. Detail description of the procedure was presented in our previous publication and interested readers are referred to it (Asegehegn et al., 2011b). The in-house software was developed to handle simulation results as well.

Once the bubbles are delineated and identified their projected areas A_B, horizontal and vertical coordinates of their centroids and horizontal and vertical extremes are measured. Then the bubble properties (bubble aspect ratio, diameter, rise velocity and location of the rise velocity) are calculated using equations 27 to 30 respectively.

The bubble aspect ratio, AR, is defined as:

$$AR = d_y/d_x \tag{27}$$

Where d_y and d_x are the vertical and horizontal extremes shown in Fig. 2.

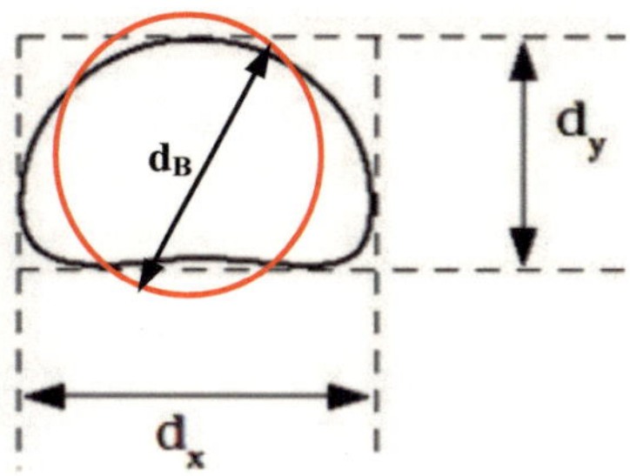

Fig. 2. Bubble dimensions.

The bubble diameter was calculated from the area equivalent A_B as:

$$d_B = \sqrt{4A_B/\pi} \tag{28}$$

The rise velocity was calculated from the difference in the vertical-coordinate of the centriod between consecutive time frames and dividing by the time interval between the frames.

$$u_B = \left(y_g(t+\Delta t) - y_g(t)\right)/\Delta t \tag{29}$$

Where y_g is the vertical component of the centre of gravity of the bubble, t is the time and Δt is the time delay between consecutive frames of the images, 1/50 s in this case. The velocity is attributed to the mean vertical height according to:

$$h = \left(y_g(t+\Delta t) + y_g(t)\right)/2 \tag{30}$$

Once the instantaneous bubble properties at each section of the bed are calculated, a number averaging was used to calculate the time-averaged bubble properties with bed height.

$$\theta = \sum_{i=1}^{n}(\theta_i)/N \tag{31}$$

Where θ is any of the bubble property such as aspect ratio, diameter, rise velocity, and N is total number of bubble properties recorded during the total averaging time considered.

5. Results and discussions

All simulations were performed for 20 s of real flow time and the first 5 s were neglected to reduce the start-up effect. Thus, the results reported were averaged over the last 15 s of real flow time. Bubble properties were calculated from the volume fraction contours produced by the CFD software, Fig. 3.

These volume fraction contours were then analysed by the in-house code. The first step in analysing bubble properties is to discriminate the bubble from the rest of the bed. This was done by setting a solid volume fraction cut-off point to produce discriminated volume fraction contours from the CFD code (ANSYS FLUENT 12.1) used. In the results reported in this book, a bubble was assumed to be the area with solid volume fraction of less than or equal to 0.2. There is no uniform definition of bubble boundary in literature with threshold values ranging from 0.15 to 0.30 for the solid volume fraction with 0.2 mostly used. Some sensitivity analyses performed showed that there is no significant difference in rise velocity and bubble shape with the different bubble boundaries used while the mean bubble diameter slightly varied with the threshold values (Asegehegn et al., 2011a). In this work, 50 frames per seconds were sampled to be consistent with the experimental analysis. Therefore, for the total 15 seconds of real flow time 750 frames are analysed for the statistical analysis of bubble properties. Though this was much less than the number of frames in the experimental results, considering the computational effort needed it was found to be sufficient for the statistical analysis of bubble properties.

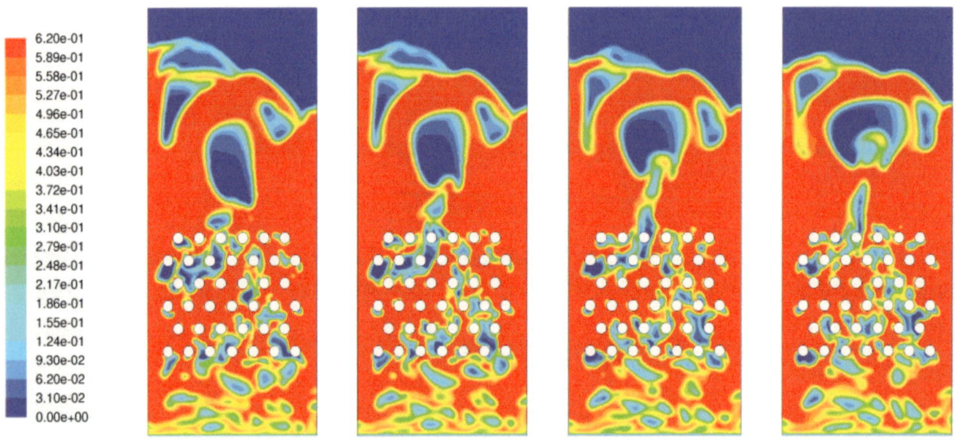

Fig. 3. Instantaneous volume fraction contour plots.

5.1 Influence of grid size

It is common practice to perform grid sensitivity analyses in order to ensure grid independent solution during numerical simulations. However, it is usually difficult to achieve grid independent solution using the granular kinetic theory as the granular theory closure equations do not give grid independent solutions with reasonable grid sizes. However, in this work a grid sensitivity analysis was performed at least to ensure the mean bubble properties are not significantly affected by the grid size used. For this purpose simulations were performed for both beds with grid sizes ranging from 2 mm to 10 mm. The results are plotted in Fig. 4 and 5 for the mean bubble diameter and mean bubble rise velocity respectively. With the exceptions of a grid size of 10 mm other sizes (5 mm, 4 mm, 2 mm) provided comparable results hence the grid size of 5 mm was selected taking into account the accuracy and computational time required.

In Table 2 the different computational times needed per one second of real flow time is presented for the different grid sizes as well as 2D and 3D simulations. All simulations were performed on a Quad-Core Intel Xeon processor (3 GHz each) workstation and a time step of 2.5×10^{-5} s was used. It can be clearly seen that the simulation time significantly increased as the grid size reduced. The difference between the NT and S6 can be attributed to the increase in number of cells in S6 as a result of the refinement near the tube surfaces.

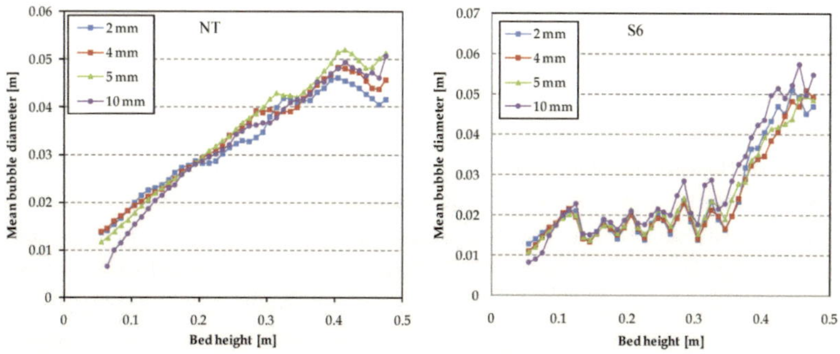

Fig. 4. Comparison of mean bubble diameter for different grid sizes.

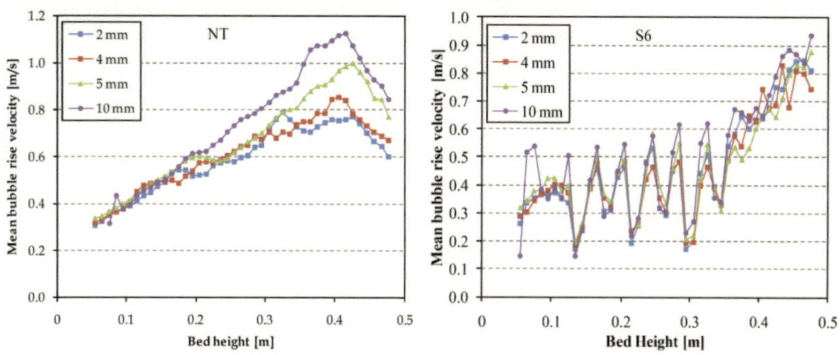

Fig. 5. Comparison of mean bubble rise velocity for different grid sizes.

Domain	Geometry	Grid size [mm]	Number of cells	Simulation time per second of real flow time [h]
2D	NT	2	96000	70
		4	24000	18
		5	15300	12
		10	3840	5
	S6	2	101838	75
		4	27694	27
		5	18469	16
		10	5190	11
3D	NT	4	120000	159
		5	61440	75
	S6	4	145705	219
		5	72924	105

Table 2. Computational time requirements for different solution domains, bed geometries and grid sizes.

5.2 Two-dimensional versus three-dimensional simulation

Generally, all practical gas-solid flows are three-dimensional (3D) in nature and numerical simulations in 3D domain should be performed to validate and study these 3D flows.

However, even with improved computational facilities, 3D simulations are still computationally prohibitive even for engineering-scale fluidized beds. Therefore, the majority of simulation studies encountered in the literature are limited to two-dimensional (2D) coordinate system to simulate 3D fluidized beds. However, there are no studies proving that 2D computations are sufficient for validation and parametric study of fluidized beds. 2D simulations are most likely to be successful in cases where the flow is presumed to be 2D, that is in cases where the variations in space and time in a given direction of the physical space are negligible compared to the variations encountered in the other directions. This is typically in the case of pseudo-2D beds, which have small depth compared to the height and width. In such cases, the particle motion can be effectively suppressed in the depth direction thus resembling 2D motion of the particles in the axial and radial directions only. Many researchers have applied 2D Cartesian simulations to model such rectangular pseudo-2D beds and found reasonable agreement between model prediction and experimental results. However, such comparisons leave an important difference between the pseudo-2D experimental beds and 2D numerical models. The front and back walls, which are neglected in the numerical model, could have considerable influence on the hydrodynamics of the fluidized beds. So far, only Li et al. (2010) have performed both 2D and 3D simulations of a pseudo-2D and compared the results with experimental measurements. They found considerable difference in the bubble rise velocity predicted by the 2D and 3D simulations while the bubble diameter predicted by both domains is generally comparable. Cammarata et al. (2003) performed simulations using 2D and 3D domains of a rectangular bed and the results of bubble diameter were compared with correlation from the literature. These authors found considerable difference of the bubble diameter predicted by the simulations. On the other hand, Peirano et al. (2001) analysed and compared simulation results of the power spectra of pressure fluctuations, bed height, and probability density function of particle volume fraction with experimental measurements. They observed a significant difference between 2D and 3D simulations and concluded that 2D simulations should be used with caution and only for sensitivity analysis. Though all the above authors concluded that 3D simulations should be preferably performed except maybe in cases where the flow is by nature 2D, they also indicate that 2D simulations could be used to conduct sensitivity analyses.

In this work, simulations were performed for two different particle sizes and two bed geometries with and without immersed horizontal tubes using 2D and 3D domains and the results were compared to experimental data obtained from pseudo-2D bed. The mean bubble diameter and rise velocity are shown in Fig. 6 and 7 respectively for the particle with mean diameter of 347 μm. Similar results were obtained for the other particle size as well but the results are not presented here to reduce redundancy. As shown in Fig. 6 the mean bubble diameter predicted by both 2D and 3D simulations are generally in very good agreement with the experimental though the 2D simulations predicted slightly smaller bubbles than the 3D. This was consistent with the results of Li et al. (2010) while Cammarata et al. (2003) reported otherwise. The results obtained from 2D simulations showed greater divergence from the experimental data with increasing bed height. Though not shown here, this was more pronounced with increasing superficial velocity. A significant difference between 2D and 3D simulations was observed in mean bubble rise velocity, Fig. 7. 2D simulations predicted much higher rise velocity than 3D simulations and significantly deviate from the experiment measurements. This was largely attributed to the wall effect. It was believed that neglecting the front and back walls in the 2D simulations resulted in higher bubble rise velocities. In the experiment as well as 3D simulations, as a result of small bed thickness, the down flowing particles along the front and back walls increased the drag experienced by the bubbles, thus slowed the bubbles. On the other hand these walls were neglected in the 2D simulations and bubbles could move freely in the bed without experiencing the drag of down flowing particles as well as the friction of walls. Others also reported similar results, e.g. Krishna et al. (2000) and Li et al. (2010). Krishna et al. (2000) studied the influence of walls on bubble rise velocity for both gas-liquid and gas-solid systems and they reported that the rise velocity of single gas bubbles was significantly reduced as the ratio of bubble to bed width increased. Though 2D simulations have certain limitations and are physically different form the 3D flow exit in practical applications, they can provide quiet satisfactory results compared to experimental observations. It is clear that 3D simulations are more realistic and should be preferred, but with current, even in the near future, computer capacity these are far from reaching. Comparing the computational time needed for 2D and 3D simulations as shown in Table 2 above, it was found that 3D simulations are 5 to 9 times more expensive than their 2D equivalents. As an example in order to simulate 20 s of real flow time in the 2D grid with a mesh size of 5 mm using the no tube geometry 240 h (approx. 10 days) of simulation time were necessary while this was increased to 1500 h (approx. 62 days) in the case of 3D simulations. Therefore, as also deduced by Xie et al. (2008) and Cammarata et al. (2003), especially for conducting extensive parametric studies, 2D simulations remain indispensable.

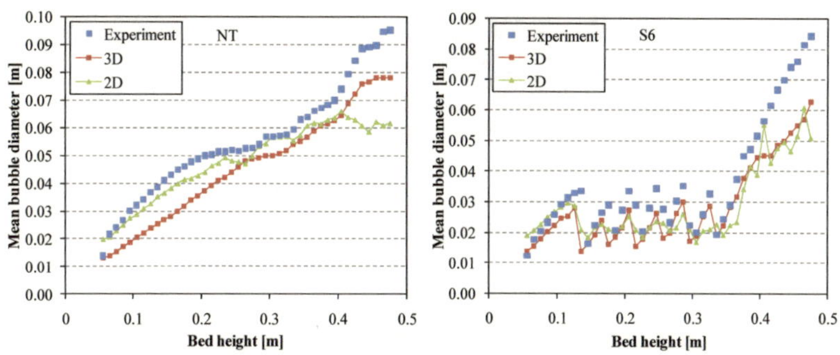

Fig. 6. Comparison of mean bubble diameter between 2D and 3D simulations, d_p = 347 μm, u=2.0U_{mf}.

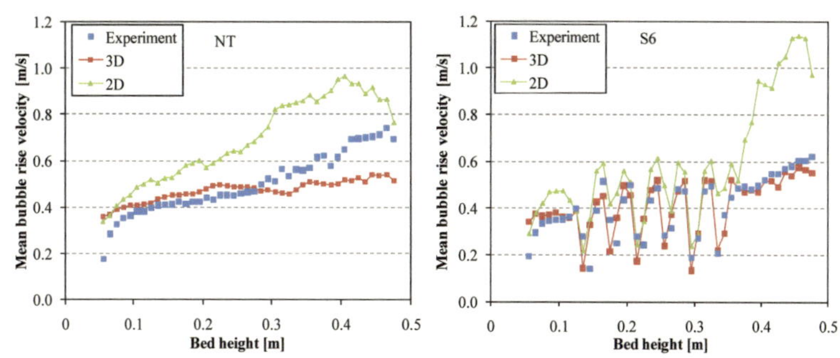

Fig. 7. Comparison of mean bubble rise velocity between 2D and 3D simulations, d_p = 347 μm, u=2.0U_{mf}.

5.3 Influence of immersed horizontal tubes

5.3.1 Bubble aspect ratio

Aspect ratio is an important characteristics of a bubble since it strongly influence the bubble's hydrodynamics. Fig. 8 shows the mean bubble aspect ratio for the two bed geometries (NT and S6) and different superficial velocities. Similar results were obtained for the second particle size and the graphs are not shown here to reduce redundancy. In general, the simulation showed good agreement with the experimental data for all geometries. For the bed without internal tubes both the simulation and experimental results predicted an increase in aspect ratio with bed height. This indicated the flattening and vertical stretching of bubbles with increasing bubble size. Generally, for beds without internal obstacles, the bubble shape was found to be nearly circular when the bubble was smaller and flattened, distorted and elongated when the bubble was bigger. Similar results were reported by Hatano et al. (1986) from experimental observations.

In the case of beds with internal horizontal tubes bubble aspect ratio was found to depend more strongly on tube geometry rather than bubble size or bed height. Bubbles were seen to elongate vertically when they moved between the tubes in a row and retained their original shape and became nearly circular when they were away from the tube rows. This resulted in oscillation of the aspect ratio in the tube bank region as shown in Fig. 8. The elongation of bubbles in the vertical direction was mainly seen as a result of the reduction in flow area and bubbles squeezed and deformed to fit the space between the tubes. As a bubble squeezed it stretched and elongated vertically as the area/volume of the bubble should at least remain the same provided that no splitting has occurred during the process. Qualitatively the simulation predicted a similar trend for fluctuations in the aspect ratio in the tube bank region, however, it predicted bubbles that were relatively circular as opposed to the corresponding experimental data. This could be associated with the no-slip boundary condition imposed on the walls for the gas phase.

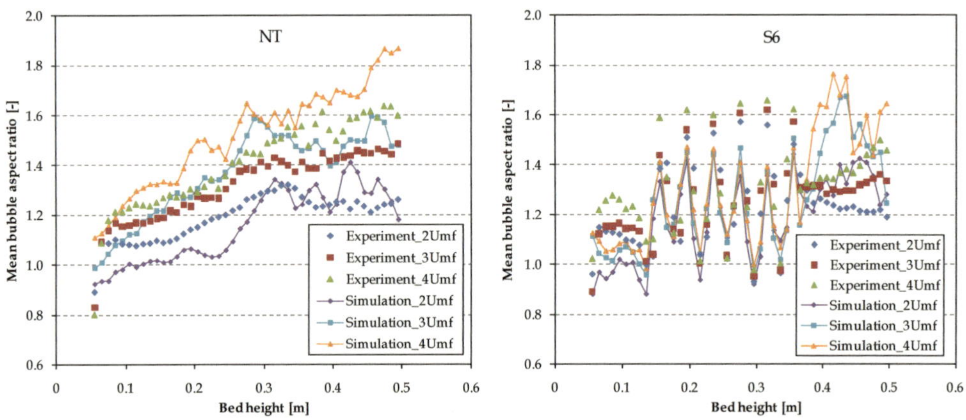

Fig. 8. Comparison of mean bubble aspect ratio between simulation results and experimental data for beds with and without immersed tubes and different superficial velocities, d_p= 246 mm and U_{mf}=0.0876 m/s.

5.3.2 Bubble size

Fig. 9 and 10 present the simulation results and comparisons with experimental data of mean bubble diameter for the two bed geometries (NT and S6) and two different particle sizes. For beds without immersed tubes the simulation and experimental results were in very good agreement until a certain height near the eruption zone. After this height the simulation predicted no growth of bubbles while a continuous growth of bubbles was observed from the experiment.

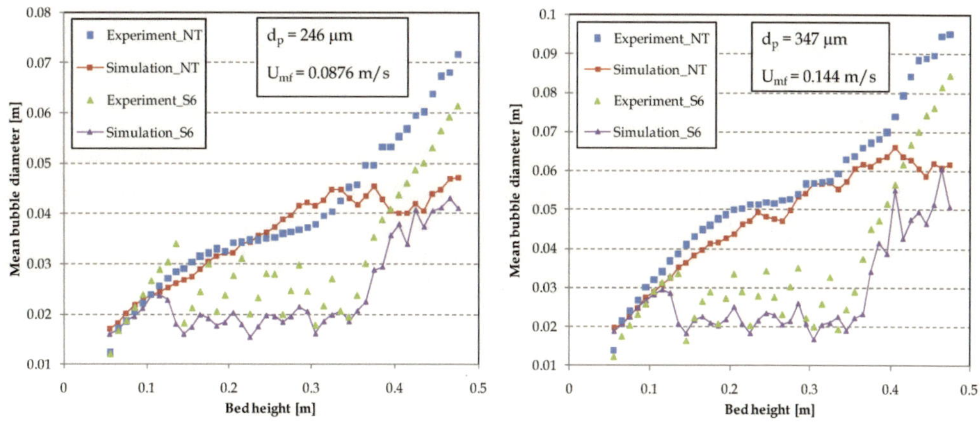

Fig. 9. Comparison of mean bubble diameter between simulation results and experimental data for beds with and without immersed tubes and two different particle sizes, $u=2U_{mf}$.

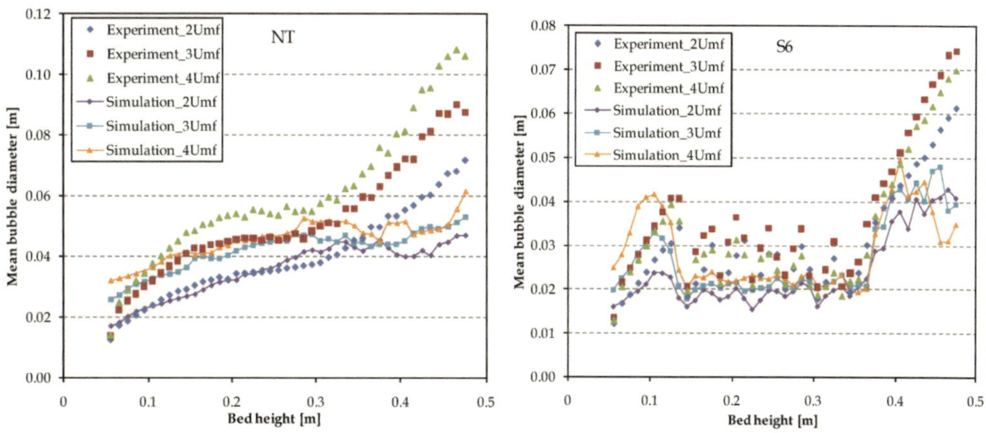

Fig. 10. Comparison of mean bubble diameter between simulation results and experimental data for beds with and without immersed tubes and different superficial velocities, d_p= 246 mm and U_{mf} = 0.0876 m/s.

In the case of beds with horizontal tubes good qualitative agreement was achieved between the simulation and experimental results for both particle sizes. However, the simulation slightly underpredicted bubble diameter in the tube bank region. This was partially attributed to the wall effect that was neglected in the numerical simulation while the experiments were performed using pseudo-2D beds. From both simulation and experiment it can be concluded that the presence of tubes resulted in higher bubble splitting and coalescence which eventually reduced the mean bubble size. Small bubbles formed at the distributor rose and grew by coalescence until they reached the first row of tubes. Upon reaching the first row of tubes they split then grew by coalescence until they reached the second row of tubes. This continued until the last row of tubes after which bubbles rapidly grew without restriction until they finally reached the top of the bed and erupted. As shown in Fig. 10 both the simulation and experiment showed that the growth of bubbles in the tube bank region was mainly dictated by tube bank geometry rather than superficial velocity or bed height. In the tube free region, below and above the tube bank, bubble growth resembled a similar trend as in the case of the bed without immersed tubes.

5.3.3 Bubble rise velocity

Fig. 11 and 12 illustrate comparisons between simulation and experimental results for bubble rise velocities for the two bed geometries and particle sizes. For beds both with and without immersed tubes the simulation overpredicted rise velocity as compared to the experimental results and it was more pronounced at the upper part of the beds. This was largely associated with the wall effect as discussed above.

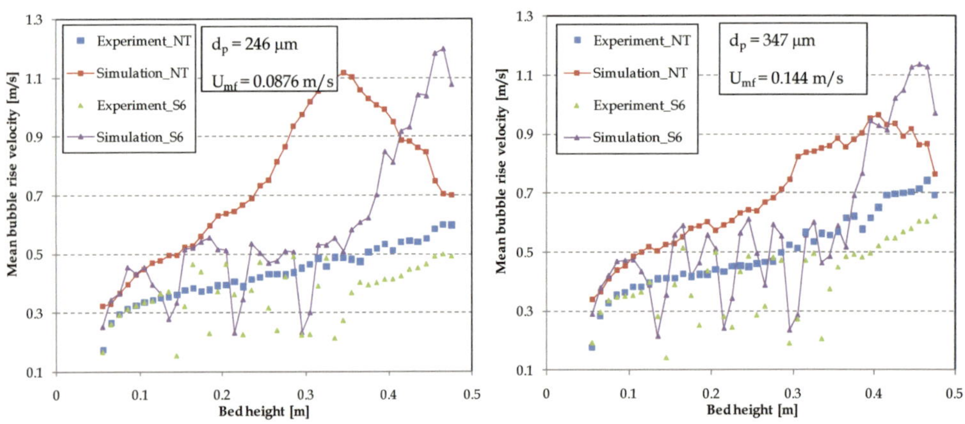

Fig. 11. Comparison of mean bubble rise velocity between simulation results and experimental data for beds with and without immersed tubes and two different particle sizes, $u=2U_{mf}$.

In the tube bank region the rise velocity was highly influenced by the presence of tubes. The reduction in bubble size due to frequent splitting in the tube bank region caused a decrease in bubble rise velocity compared to beds without internal obstacles. Both the experiment and the simulation showed higher rise velocity at the upper part of the tubes and lower rise velocity at the lower part of the tubes. The higher rise velocity seen at the upper part of the tube rows can be explained mainly due to the elongation of bubbles. As a result of elongation of a bubble and stretching the centroid of the bubble moved further in distance than it would if it were circular. This caused the centroid of the bubbles to move further in the vertical direction than they usually do. It was observed that bubbles with higher aspect ratios had higher rise velocities than those with lower aspect ratios. Hatano et al. (1986) also reported similar results for beds without internal obstacles. The reason for the lower mean rise velocity at the bottom of the tubes was due to the semi-stagnant bubbles that occurred at this location as a result of small bubble formation and splitting of bubbles into large and small daughters (Asegehegn et al. 2011a).

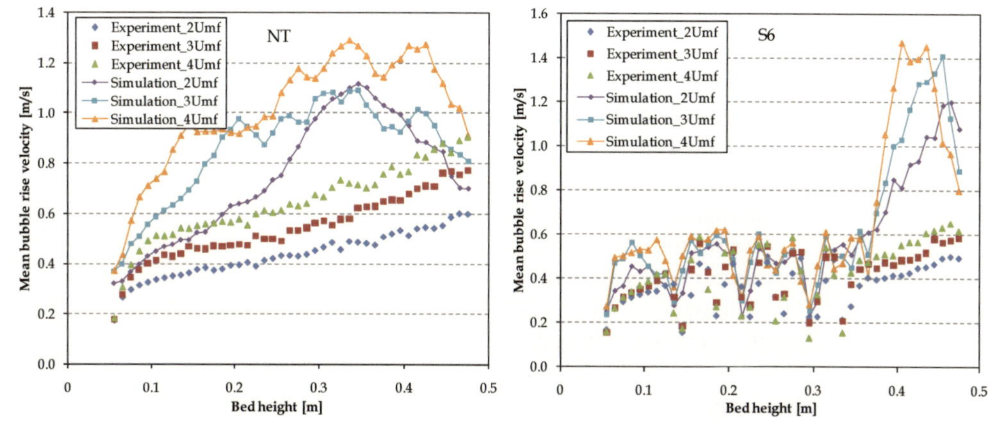

Fig. 12. Comparison of mean bubble rise between simulation results and experimental data for beds with and without immersed tubes and different superficial velocities, d_p= 246 mm and U_{mf} = 0.0876 m/s.

6. Conclusion

Numerical simulations using the Eulerian-Eulerian TFM were performed for pseudo-2D gas-solid fluidized beds with and without immersed horizontal tubes. The simulation results of bubble characteristics were compared and validated with experimental data obtained by a digital image analysis technique. From the results of this work the following conclusions can be drawn:

The two-fluid model is capable of predicting the main bubble characteristics such as bubble aspect ratio, diameter and rise velocity with and without immersed tubes. The calculated bubble properties were in general in good agreement with the experimental data.

3D simulations gave better results than 2D simulations compared with experiments. However, they are computationally expensive and 2D simulations can be successfully used for parametric study of gas-solid fluidized beds of engineering scale without losing much of the information.

The major difference between 2D and 3D simulations was observed in predicting the bubble rise velocity where 2D simulations overpredicted the bubble rise velocity compared to the corresponding 3D simulations and experimental data.

As a result of higher bubble splitting and coalescence as well as additional drag, the bubble diameter and rise velocity were lower for beds with horizontal tubes than beds without tubes. Moreover, bubble diameter and rise velocity were found to strongly depend on the tube bank geometry rather than the superficial velocity in the case of beds with dense immersed tubes while these bubble properties strongly vary with superficial velocity in the case of beds without immersed tubes.

7. Acknowledgment

The authors gratefully acknowledge the funding of this research project by the "Entrepreneurial Regions"-Initiative established by the German Federal Ministry of Education and Research and Research and COORETEC-Initiative from the Federal Ministry of Economics and Technology.

8. Nomenclature

Symbols:

A_B	Project area of a bubble, m^2
C_d	Drag coefficient
d	Diameter, m
d_x	Horizontal extreme of a bubble, m
d_y	Vertical extreme of a bubble, m
e	Coefficient of restitution
Fr	Constant in Johnson et al. (1990) friction model, N/m^2
g	Gravitational acceleration, m/s^2
g_0	Radial distribution function
I	Unit tensor
I_{2D}	Second invariant of the deviatoric stress tensor, s^{-2}
J	Granular energy transfer, $kg/m/s^3$
N	Number of bubbles, Eq. 31
n	Constant in Johnson et al. (1990) friction model
p	Constant in Johnson et al. (1990) friction model
P	Pressure, Pa
q	Diffusion of fluctuating energy, kg/s^3
Re	Reynolds number
t	Time, s
u	Velocity, m/s
u′	Fluctuating velocity, m/s

Greek Letters:

β	Interphase drag coefficient, $kg/m^3/s$
γ	Dissipation of fluctuating energy, $kg/m/s^3$
ε	Volume fraction
Θ	Granular temperature, m^2/s^2
θ	Bubble property, Eq. 31
μ	Shear viscosity, Pa·s
ξ	Bulk viscosity, Pa·s
ρ	Density, kg/m^3
τ	Shear stress tensor, N/m^2
ϕ	Angle of internal friction, °
ϕ'	Specularity coefficient

Subscripts:

B	Bubble
col	Collisional
f	Frictional
g	Gas phase
kin	Kinetic
KTGF	Kinetic Theory of Granular Flow
max	Maximum
mf	Minimum fluidization

min Minimum
p Particle
s Solids phase
sl Slip

9. References

Anderson, T.B. & Jackson, R. (1967). A Fluid Mechanical Description of Fluidized Beds Equations of Motion. *Industrial & Engineering Chemistry Fundamentals*, Vol.6, No.4, (November 1967), pp. 527-539, ISSN 0196-4313

ANSYS Inc. (2009). Eulerian Model Theory. Ansys Fluent 12.0 Theory Guide, Chapter 16.5, Lebanon.

Asegehegn, T.W.; Schreiber, M. & Krautz, H.J. (2011a). Numerical study of bubble gas-solid fluidized bed hydrodynamics: Influence of immersed horizontal tubes and data analysis. *International Journal of Chemical Reactor Engineering*, Vol. 9, A16, ISSN 1542-6580

Asegehegn, T.W.; Schreiber, M. & Krautz, H.J. (2011b). Investigation of bubble behaviour in fluidized beds with and without immersed horizontal tubes using a digital image analysis technique. *Powder Technology*, Vol. 210, No 3, (July 2011), pp. 248-260, ISSN 0032-5910

Boemer, A.; Qi, H. & Renz, U. (1997). Eulerian simulation of bubble formation at a jet in a two-dimensional fluidized bed. *International Journal of Multiphase Flow*, Vol.23, No.5, (September 1997), pp. 927-944, ISSN 0301-9322

Boemer, A.; Qi, H. & Renz, U. (1998). Verification of Eulerian Simulation of Spontaneous Bubble Formation in a Fluidized Bed. *Chemical Engineering Science*, Vol.53, No.10, (May 1998), pp. 1835-1846, ISSN 0009-2509

Bouillard, J.X.; Lyczkowski, R.W. & Gidaspow D. (1989). Porosity distributions in a fluidized bed with an immersed obstacle. *AIChE Journal*, Vol.35, No.6, (June 1989), pp. 908-922, ISSN 0001-1541

Cammarata, L.; Lettieri, P.; Micale, G.D.M.; & Colman, D. 2D and 3D CFD simulations of bubbling fluidized beds using Eulerian-Eulerian models. *International Journal of Chemical Reactor Engineering*, Vol. 1, A48., ISSN 1542-6580

Chapman, S. & Cowling, T.G. (1970). *The mathematical theory of non-uniform gases*, Cambridge University Press, ISBN 978-052-1408-44-8, Cambridge, UK

Chiesa, M., Mathiesen, V., Melheim, & Halvorsen, B. (2005). Numerical simulation of particulate flow by the Eulerian-Lagrangian and Eulerian-Eulerian approach with application to a fluidized bed. *Computer & Chemical Engineering*, Vol. 29, No. 2, (January 2005), pp. 291-304, ISSN 0098-1354

Das Sharma, S.K. & Mohan, R. (2003). Numerical study of the influence of horizontal tube banks on the hydrodynamics of a dense gas-solid bubbling fluidized bed. *International Journal of Chemical Reactor Engineering*, Vol.1, A26, ISSN 1542-6580

Davidson, J.F. (1961). Symposium on fluidization-discussion. *Transactions of the Institution of Chemical Engineers*, Vol. 39, pp. 230-232 ISSN 0371-7496

Deen, N.G.; van Sint Annaland, M.; van der Hoef, M.A. & Kuipers, J.A.M. (2007). Review of discrete particle modeling of fluidized beds. *Chemical Engineering Science*, Vol.62, No.1-2, (January 2007), pp. 28-44, ISSN 0009-2509

Ding, J. & Gidaspow, D. (1990). A bubbling fluidization model using kinetic theory of granular flow. *AIChE Journal*, Vol.36, No.4, (June 1990), pp. 523-538, ISSN 0001-1541

Enwald, H.; Peirano, E. & Almstedt, A.E. (1996). Eulerian two-phase flow theory applied to fluidization. *International Journal of Multiphase Flow*, Vol.22, Suppl.1, (December 1996), pp. 21-66, ISSN 0301-9322

Gamwo, I.K.; Soong, Y. & Lyczkowski, R.W. (1999). Numerical simulation and experimental validation of solids flows in a bubbling fluidized bed. *Powder Technology*, Vol.103, No.2, (Juli 1999), pp. 117-129, ISSN 0032-5910

Gao, W.M.; Kong, L.X. & Hodgson, P.D. (2007). Computational simulation of gas flow and heat transfer near an immersed object in fluidized beds. *Advances in Engineering Software*, Vol.38,No.11-12, (November-December 2007), pp. 826-834, ISSN 0965-9978

Gera, D., Gautam, M., Tsuji, Y., Kawaguchi, T. & Tanaka, T. (1998). Computer simulation of bubbles in large-particle fluidized beds. *Powder Technology*, Vol. 98, No. 1 , (July 1998), pp. 38-47, ISSN 0032-5910

Gidaspow, D. (1994). *Multiphase flow and fluidization: Continuum and kinetic theory descriptions*, Academic Press, ISBN 978-012-2824-70-8, Boston, USA

Gidaspow, D. & Ettehadieh, B. (1983), Fluidization in two-dimensional beds with a jet. 2. hydrodynamic modeling. *Industrial & Engineering Chemistry Fundamentals*, Vol.22, No.2, (May 1983), pp. 193-201, ISSN 0196-4313

Gustavsson, M. & Almstedt, A.E. (2000). Numerical simulation of fluid dynamics in fluidized beds with horizontal heat exchanger tubes. *Chemical Engineering Science*, Vol.55, No.4, (February 2000), pp. 857-866, ISSN 0009-2509

Hatano, H.; Khattab, I.A.H.; Nakamura, K. & Ishida, M. (1986). Spatiotemporal measurement of bubble properties in free-bubbling fluidized beds. *Journal of Chemical Engineering of Japan*, Vol.19, No.5, (September 1986), pp. 425-430, ISSN 0021-9592

Hoomans, B.P.B.; Kuipers, J.A.M.; Briels, W.J. & van Swaaij, W.P.M. (1996). Discrete particle simulation of bubble and slug formation in a two-dimensional gas-fluidized bed: A hard-sphere approach. *Chemical Engineering Science*, Vol.51, No.1, (January 1996), pp. 99-118, ISSN 0009-2509

Hull, A.S.; Chen, Z.; Fritz, J.W. & Agarwal, P.K. (1999). Influence of horizontal tube banks on the behavior of bubbling fluidized beds: 1. bubble hydrodynamics. *Powder Technology*, Vol.103, No.3, (July 1999), pp. 230-242, ISSN 0032-5910

Hulme. I.; Clavelle, E.; van der Lee, L. & Kantzas, A. (2005). CFD modeling and validation of bubble properties for a bubbling fluidized bed. *Industrial & Engineering Chemistry Research*, Vol.44, No.12, (May 2005), pp. 4254-4266, ISSN 0888-5885

Jenkins, J.T. & Savage, S.B. (1983). A Theory for the rapid flow of identical, smooth, nearly elastic, spherical particles. *Journal of Fluid Mechanics*, Vol.130, pp. 187-202, ISSN 0022-1120

Johnson, P.C.; Nott, P. & Jackson, R. (1990). Frictional-collisional equations of motion for particulate flows and their application to chutes. *Journal of Fluid Mechanics*, Vol.210, pp. 501-535, ISSN 0022-1120

Johnson, P.C. & Jackson, R. (1987). Frictional-collisional constitutive relations for granular materials, with application to plane shearing. *Journal of Fluid Mechanics*, Vol.176, pp. 67-93, ISSN 0022-1120

Krishna, R.; van Baten J.M.; Urseanu, M.I. & Ellenberger, J. (2000). Rise velocity of single circular-cap bubbles in two-dimensional beds of powders and liquids. *Chemical Engineering and Processing*, Vol.39, No.5, (September 2000), pp. 433-440, ISSN 0255-2701

Kuipers, J.A.M. & van Swaaij W.P.M. (1998). Computational fluid dynamics applied to chemical reaction engineering. *Advances in Chemical Engineering*, Vol.24, pp. 227-328

Kuipers, J.A.M.; van Duin K.J.; van Beckum, F.P.H. & van Swaaij, W.P.M. (1992). A numerical model of gas-fluidized beds. *Chemical Engineering Science*, Vol.47, No.8, (June 1992), pp. 1913-1924, ISSN 0009-2509

Kuipers, J.A.M.; van Duin K.J.; van Beckum, F.P.H. & van Swaaij, W.P.M. (1993). Computer simulation of the hydrodynamics of a two-dimensional gas-fluidized bed. *Computers & Chemical Engineering*, Vol.17, No.8, (August 1993), pp. 839-858, ISSN 0098-1354

Kunii, D. & Levenspiel, O. (1991). *Fluidization Engineering, 2nd ed.*, Butterworth-Heineman, ISBN 978-040-9902-33-4, Boston, USA

Li, T.; Grace, J.R. & Bi, X. (2010). Study of wall boundary condition in numerical simulations of bubbling fluidized beds. *Powder Technology*, Vol.203, No.3, (November 2010), pp. 447-457, ISSN 0032-5910

Lindborg, H.; Lysberg, M. & Jakobsen, H.A. (2007). Practical validation of the two-fluid model applied to dense gas-solid flows in fluidized beds. *Chemical Engineering Science*, Vol.62, No.21, (Nove,ber 2007), pp. 5854-5869, ISSN 0009-2509

Lun, C.K.K.; Savage, S.B.; Jeffrey, D.J. & Chepurniy, N. (1984). Kinetic theories for granular flow: Inelastic particles in couette flow and slightly inelastic particles in a general flow field. *Journal of Fluid Mechanics*, Vol.140, pp. 223-256, ISSN 0022-1120

Ma, D. & Ahmadi, G. (1986). An equation of state for dense rigid sphere gases. *Journal of Chemical Physics*, Vol.84, No.6, pp. 3449-3450, ISSN 0021-9606

Patil, D.J.; van Sint Annaland, M. & Kuipers, J.A.M. (2005). Critical comparison of hydrodynamic models for gas-solid fluidized beds - Part II: Freely bubbling gas-solid fluidized beds. *Chemical Engineering Science*, Vol.60, No.1, (January 2005), pp. 73-84, ISSN 0009-2509

Peirano, E.; Delloume, V. & Leckner B. (2001).Two- or three- dimensional simulations of turbulent gas-solid flows applied to fluidization. *Chemical Engineering Science*, Vol. 56, No. 16, (August 2001), pp. 4787-4799, ISSN 0009-2509

Schaeffer, D.G. (1987). Instability in the evolution equations describing incompressible granular flow. *Journal of Differential Equations*, Vol.66, No.1, (January 1987), pp. 19-50, ISSN 0022-0396

Schmidt, A. & Renz, U. (2005). Numerical prediction of heat transfer between a bubbling fluidized bed and an immersed tube bundle. *Heat Mass Transfer*, Vol.41, No.3, pp. 257-270, ISSN 0947-7411

Sinclair, J.L. & Jackson, R. (1989). Gas-particle flow in a vertical pipe with particle-particle interactions. *AIChE Journal*, Vol.35, No.9, September (1989),pp. 1473-1486, ISSN 0001-1541

Syamlal, M.; Rogers, W. & O'Brien, T.J. (1993). *MFIX Documentation: Theory guide*. National Technical Information Service, DOE/METC-94/1004, Springfield, USA

Taghipour, F.; Ellis, N. & Wong, C. (2005). Experimental and computational study of gas-solid fluidized bed hydrodynamics. *Chemical Engineering Science*, Vol.60, No.24, (December 2005), pp. 6857-6867, ISSN 0009-2509

Tsuji, Y.; Kawaguchi, T. & Tanaka, T. (1993). Discrete particle simulation of two-dimensional fluidized bed. *Powder Technology*, Vol.77, No.1, (October 1993), pp. 79-87, ISSN 0032-5910

Tsuo, Y. & Gidaspow, D. (1990). Computation of flow patterns in circulating fluidized beds. *AIChE Journal*, Vol.36, No.6, (June 1990), pp. 885-896, ISSN 0001-1541

van der Hoef, M.A.; van Sint Annaland, M.; Deen, N.G. & Kuipers, J.A.M. (2008). Numerical simulation of dense gas-solid fluidized beds: A multiscale modeling strategy. *Annual Review of Fluid Mechanics*, Vol.40, pp. 47-70, ISSN 0066-4189

van Wachem, B.G.M.; Schouten, J.C.; Krishna, R. & van den Bleek, C.M. (1998). Eulerian simulation of bubbling behaviour in gas-solid fluidized beds. *Computers and Chemical Engineering*, Vol.22, Suppl.1, (March 1998), pp. S299-S306, ISSN 0098-1354

van Wachem, B.G.M.; Schouten, J.C.; Krishna, R. & van den Bleek, C.M. (1999). Validation of the Eulerian simulated dynamic behaviour of gas-solid fluidized beds. *Chemical Engineering Science*, Vol.54, No.13-14, (July 1999), pp. 2141-2149, ISSN 0009-2509

van Wachem, B.G.M.; Schouten, J.C.; van den Bleek, C.M.; Krishna, R. & Sinclair, J.L. (2001). Comparative analysis of CFD models of dense gas-solid systems. *AIChE Journal* Vol.47, No.5, (May 2001), pp. 1035-1051, ISSN 0001-1541

Vejahati, F.; Mahinpey, N.; Ellis, N. & Nikoo, M.B. (2009). CFD simulation of gas-solid bubbling fluidized bed: A new method for adjusting drag law. *The Canadian Journal of Chemical Engineering*, Vol.87, No.1, (February 2009), pp. 19-30, ISSN 1939-019X

Xie, N.; Battaglia, F. & Pannala, S. (2008). Effects of using two- versus three-dimensional computational modeling of fluidized beds: Part 1, Hydrodynamics. *Powder Technology*, Vol.182, No.1, (February 2008), pp. 1-13, ISSN 0032-5910

Yates, J.G.; Ruiz-Martinez, R.S. & Cheesman, D.J. (1990). Prediction of size in a fluidized bed containing horizontal tubes. *Chemical Engineering Science*, Vol.45, No.4, pp. 1105-1111, ISSN 0009-2509

Yurong, H.; Huilin, L.; Qiaoqun, S.; Lidan, Y.; Yunhua, Z.; Gidaspow, D. & Bouillard, J. (2004). Hydrodynamics of gas-solid flow around immersed tubes in bubbling fluidized beds. *Powder Technology*, Vol.145, No.2, (July 2004), pp. 88-105, ISSN 0032-5910

12

Numerical Simulation Techniques for the Prediction of Fluid-Dynamics, Combustion and Performance in IC Engines Fuelled by CNG

Mirko Baratta and Ezio Spessa
IC Engines Advanced Laboratory – Politecnico di Torino, Torino
Italy

1. Introduction

The design of modern internal combustion (IC) engines requires the understanding and quantification of many physical phenomena, including their impact on engine performance and emissions. In fact, the investigation of thermo-fluid-dynamic processes, combustion, performance and emissions is essential to fulfil the emission regulations, that are becoming more and more severe. Although the experimental analysis of such processes is mandatory to obtain fully quantitative results, the application of numerical simulation techniques is continuously increasing in popularity amongst the research community. This is due, on one hand, to the increased accuracy of specific sub-models, which are dedicated to several physical aspects in IC engines, and, on the other hand, to the availability of computational resources of increasing power. Nowadays, simulation tools can range from zero-dimensional analysis tools of the combustion process in the engine chamber, to complete three-dimensional simulation models of turbulent flows and combustion.
This chapter is intended as an overview of the state-of-the-art of 1-D computational fluid-dynamics (CFD) and thermo-dynamic tools applied to IC engines, with specific reference to compressed natural gas (CNG) fuelling. Moreover, the specific modelling approaches of the authors are presented, within the 0-D and 1-D frameworks.

2. 1-D engine simulation

1-D simulation tools are based on the solution of the inviscid form of the conservation laws of mass, momentum and energy (Euler equations). The equations are actually written in a 'generalized' form, in which ad-hoc terms are added, in order to properly simulate the friction and heat-exchange effects at the pipe walls. Furthermore, they are written in a quasi 1-D approach, as the variations of any dependent variable in a direction orthogonal to the flow direction are neglected, and at the same time the changes in the flow cross-section along the pipe axis are accounted for.
In the last two decades, several commercial 1-D CFD tools have specifically been developed for engine flow simulation: among others, GT-Power (Gamma Technologies), Wave (Ricardo), Boost (AVL), and AMESim (LSM). Among the different classes of computational models, such tools are often a good compromise between accuracy, the required CPU time, and completeness of the engine system that can be analyzed.

1-D codes are designed to simulate the unsteady flow throughout the whole engine system, as well as throughout the whole engine cycle. The essential processes of the complete engine system are described by means of mathematical equations in such a way that the physical states, such as pressures, temperatures and mass flows, can be calculated in all the computational volumes and at all the instants. These codes allow the calculation of any engine-relevant cycle-averaged parameter which is useful for the assessment of the engine performance: torque, power, indicated work, volumetric efficiency, fuel consumption, and so on. Engine-oriented 1-D codes have increasingly been used in order to support the engine design phase (Winterbone & Pearson, 1990; Blair, 1999). Their application usually starts from the calibration of an engine model in a 'baseline' configuration, on the basis of experimental data. Then, the predictive model is used to estimate the impact of a different engine configuration on the performance, the efficiency and the emission levels: among others, the inlet and exhaust pipes length and diameter, the turbocharger characteristics, the valve actuation and timing, and the combustion-management strategies, can be modified (Badami et al., 2002; Baratta et al., 2010; Galindo et al., 2004; Vitek et al., 2006). 1-D codes are often used to provide time-dependent boundary conditions for three-dimensional in-cylinder turbulent-flow simulations.

The quasi 1-D approach is adopted in the engine intake and exhaust systems, which can be considered as assemblies of pipe elements. Other engine components are modelled by means of the zero-dimensional approach, usually combined with ad-hoc lumped parameter models or performance maps. Cylinders, injectors, valves, compressors and turbines are simulated in this way, and their behaviour is properly coupled to that of the 1-D computational domain.

A brief overview of the main engine-components modelling approaches is provided hereafter. Then, the main issues concerning the model tuning procedure are discussed.

2.1 Cylinders

For the mathematical description of the physical processes that occur within cylinders, it is worth distinguishing between the gas exchange and the high-pressure phase. Only during the gas exchange, do mass flows occur between the cylinder and the connected pipes and manifolds through the valves. Cylinders are usually zero-dimensional parts in which a uniform pressure is assumed. The temperature is considered uniform in the gas exchange phase and in the high-pressure cycle prior to the start of combustion, whereas a two-zone (burned-unburned) methodology is followed after the start of combustion and prior to the opening of the exhaust valve (see, for example, Gamma Technologies, 2009). Sometimes a multizone approach is followed, in order to accurately describe the burned-gas temperature distribution and the pollutant formation mechanisms (Baratta et al., 2006, 2008; Onorati et al., 2003).

When one or more valves are open, the cylinder-content evolution is governed by the continuity equation and the First Law of Thermodynamics:

$$dm_{cyl} = \left(\dot{m}_{in} - \dot{m}_{out}\right)dt \tag{1}$$

$$-dQ + pdV_{cyl} = d\left(m_{cyl}U_{cyl}\right) + \left(\dot{m}_{out}i_{cyl} - \dot{m}_{in}i_{in}\right)dt \tag{2}$$

in which the symbols U and i denote the internal energy and the enthalpy, respectively, Q is the heat transfer to the walls, and V_{cyl} is the instantaneous chamber volume. During the high-pressure phase, flow leakages from the combustion chamber are usually neglected, which means that the trapped-air mass m_{cyl} is considered constant. The charge thermodynamic state can be calculated, prior to the start of combustion, by solving the First Law of Thermodynamics, under the assumption of a constant mass and considering a uniform temperature distribution inside the chamber (single-zone approach):

$$-dQ + pdV_{cyl} = m_{cyl}dU_{cyl} \tag{3}$$

It should be noted that a suitable correlation for the heat transfer between the charge and the cylinder walls is needed (Catania et al., 2001; Heywood, 1988): this point will be discussed in the following subsection.

After the onset of combustion, four variables are required, whenever the two-zone approach is followed, to define the charge state, at each time step: pressure (p), unburned and burned-gas temperature (T_u and T_b, respectively), and burned-mass fraction ($x_b = \frac{m_b}{m_{tot}} = \frac{m_b}{m_b + m_u}$).

Although the exact set of equations which is actually implemented can be different from one distributed code to another, a general framework exists. The required variables are calculated by implementing a suitable form of the energy conservation equation for the unburned zone and for the whole cylinder content, of the conservation of the instantaneous cylinder volume, and of a so-called 'combustion model'.

The formulation of the energy conservation law is common to both simulation and diagnostic models, and can be written in the following form (Catania et al., 2003):

Unburned-gas region:

$$-dQ_u + V_u dp = (1 - x_b) m_{cyl}\, di_u \tag{4}$$

Cylinder content:

$$-(dQ_u + dQ_b) + V_{cyl}dp = (i_b - i_u) m_{cyl}\, dx_b + (1 - x_b) m_{cyl}\, di_u + m_{cyl}\, x_b\, di_b \tag{5}$$

The conservation of the chamber volume can be used to derive an equation that links the pressure at a given crank angle to T_u, T_b, and x_b (Baratta et al., 2006):

$$\mathrm{p} = \frac{m_{cyl}}{V_{cyl}}\left[(1 - x_b) R_u T_u + x_b R_b T_b\right] \tag{6}$$

The enthalpy of the burned and unburned gases is determined in Eqs. (4-5) for each chemical species, by means of polynomial functions of the gas temperature. JANAF tables can be used for this purpose (Baratta et al., 2006; Catania et al., 2003, 2004). The unburned-gas enthalpy includes the contribution of the fuel chemical energy which is released during combustion. The equation set is closed by introducing a 'combustion model', that allows x_b in Eqs. (4-6) to be defined. Combustion modelling is a fundamental feature of engine simulation codes. Its primary objective is to predict, or to specify, the rate of heat release (that is, the rate at which the chemical energy of a fuel is converted into thermal energy of burned gases) and hence the in-cylinder pressure evolution. Basically, the combustion model can be non-predictive or predictive.

A non-predictive combustion model simply imposes a burn rate as a function of the crank angle. The prescribed burn rate will be followed, regardless of the conditions inside the

cylinder. With reference to SI engines, the Wiebe function allows the almost S-shape of experimentally observed burn rates to be reproduced (Heywood, 1988). The Wiebe function is completely straightforward to apply, but on the other hand, it does not contain any description of the various physical phenomena, such as the in-cylinder turbulence level or flame-turbulence interaction. Hence, such an approach should only be followed when the purpose of the engine simulation model is to investigate the effect of a variable that virtually does not influence the burn rate. The accuracy of the Wiebe-function approach can be enhanced by including ad-hoc lookup tables in the model for the Wiebe parameters. This procedure has successfully been followed by many researchers (see, for example, Baratta et al., 2010; Lefebvre & Guilain, 2005). In (Baratta et al., 2010), a large number of experiments were carried out on an engine test rig under steady-state operating conditions at different engine speed (N) and brake mean effective pressure (bmep) values. A heat-release analysis was then carried out with the specific tools embedded in GT-Power, and the obtained parameters were organized in lookup tables as functions of N and bmep.
An alternative approach, which was pioneered in (Blizzard & Keck, 1974), is to use predictive combustion models. These models consist of phenomenological correlations for the turbulent burning speed, and are based on physical principles, so that they can account for any changes in the in-cylinder flow, combustion chamber geometry, mixture properties and thermodynamic state, spark timing, and so on. The topic of predictive combustion models will be dealth with in a dedicated section of this chapter.

2.2 In-cylinder heat transfer

In a zero-dimensional first-law analysis of the indicated cycle in an IC engine (Eqs. 1-6), the heat transfer term has to be estimated. This is usually done on an instantaneous, spatially average basis, using Newton's law:

$$\frac{dQ}{dt} = h \cdot A \cdot (T - T_w) \tag{7}$$

where h is the convective heat-transfer coefficient, A is the gas-wall contact area, T is the gas temperature, T_w is the wall temperature. The Woschni correlation (Sihling & Woschni, 1979; Woschni, 1967) is by far the most frequently applied relation for this purpose. The Woschni correlation defines a spatially-averaged convective coefficient:

$$h\left[\frac{W}{m^2K}\right] = c_0 \cdot D[m]^{-0.2} p[bar]^{0.8} T[K]^{-0.55} w\left[\frac{m}{s}\right]^{0.8} \tag{8}$$

where, in the original Woschni's paper, c_0=130, and w is an average gas velocity, which was assumed to be made up of a term proportional to the mean piston speed, and another proportional to the difference between the instantaneous pressure and the instantaneous motored pressure (at the same crank angle).
As far as the c_0 coefficient is concerned, there is evidence in the literature that a fine tuning is needed if accurate results are desired (Baratta et al., 2005; Catania et al., 2003; Guezennec & Hamada, 1999). Tuning can be performed when the Woschni correlation is applied to estimate the heat transfer in a diagnostic tool, in which the experimental in-cylinder pressure trace is analyzed and the heat-release law is calculated. For example, a method for calibrating the heat transfer coefficient was proposed and assessed in (Catania et al., 2003), based on the measurement of the exhaust emissions, with specific reference to HC, CO, and

H_2, and on an energy balance of the whole cylinder charge, from the start to the end of combustion. When the correlation is employed for predictive indicated-cycle calculations, the heat transfer coefficient can be set on the basis of experience previously acquired on similar engines, or can be calibrated at a few engine working points with the support of experimental tests, combined with diagnostic analysis. Lookup tables for c_0 can then be included in the engine model.

A different approach can be followed if a predictive combustion model is applied, as will be detailed in the 'Predictive 0-D combustion models' section of this chapter. Since such a combustion model needs the support of a zero-dimensional in-cylinder fluid flow and turbulence submodels, the same flow model is sometimes used to estimate an equivalent fluid velocity and, hence, the convective heat transfer coefficient (see, for example, Gamma Technologies, 2009; Hountalas & Pariotis, 2001; Morel & Keribar, 1985).

Although most of engine 1-D simulation codes determine the instantaneous heat flux through Eq. (7), many research works (Alkidas, 1980; Catania et al., 2001; Enomoto & Furuhama, 1989) have pointed out a phase lag and an attenuation of the heat flux calculated using the conventional convection law, with respect to the measured heat-flux distributions vs. crank angle. For this reason, in order to take the unsteadiness of the gas-wall temperature difference into account, the following unsteady formulation for Newton's convection law was proposed in (Catania et al., 2001):

$$Q = h \cdot A \cdot \left[T - T_w + K \frac{B}{S_p} \frac{d(T - T_w)}{dt} \right] \qquad (9)$$

where: B is the bore diameter, S_p the mean piston speed, and K a dimensionless coefficient that has to be calibrated.

2.3 Turbochargers

The turbocharger sub-model is a critical part of the overall model of a turbocharged engine. The approach followed in most 1-D simulation tools is to include turbocharger performance data in the form of lookup tables (Gamma Technologies, 2009), which are processed by the software in order to obtain the final interpolated maps. The interpolation procedure can be either fully automatic or partially controlled by the user. However, the final map quality is dependent to a great extent on the amount and quality of the available experimental data, which are usually measured in a flow rig under steady-state conditions.

The detailed turbocharger modelling technique which is followed by the GT-Power code is described hereafter. The approach is similar to those followed by the other codes that are available in the market.

GT-Power handles measured compressor and turbine performance tables in SAE format, in which the data are organized as several "speed lines" according to standards J922 and J1826. The data for each speed line consist of mass flow rate, pressure ratio and thermodynamic efficiency triplets. As an example, Fig. 1 shows the raw turbine map data for a turbocharger which is installed on a 7.8 litre CNG engine (Baratta et al., 2010), in terms of reduced mass flow (graph on the left) and efficiency (graph on the right) versus pressure ratio for different speed lines. Quantities on abscissa and vertical axis have been normalized to their maximum value. Each coloured line refers to a different reduced speed n_{red}. In GT-Power, the performance tables are pre-processed so as to create internal maps that define the performance of the turbine and compressor over a wide range of operating conditions. The topic of turbine table pre-processing is described hereafter, as it is generally accepted that turbine data quality is the most critical point in turbocharged engine simulation (Baratta et al., 2010; Westin & Ångström, 2003; Westin et al., 2004; Winkler & Ångström, 2007). Turbine data pre-processing uses the well-known characteristics of turbines regarding efficiency, reduced mass flow rates and blade speed ratio (BSR). Namely, for a fixed-geometry turbine, the efficiency and reduced mass flow rate should lie on specific trend lines when plotted against $BSR = U/C_S$, provided each quantity is normalized to its value at the maximum efficiency point on the actual speed line. U is the rotor blade tip speed and C_S is the gas velocity that would be achieved by an isentropic expansion across the turbine stage. The application of the GT-Power approach to the turbocharger data in Fig. 1 is shown in Fig. 2a,b. The agreement between the experimental data and the fit curves in Fig. 2a,b highlights the accuracy of the procedure for a wide range of BSR values. Figures 2c,d show the complete extent of the mass flow and efficiency maps, which are obtained on the basis of the fit curves, including the extrapolated ranges of n_{red} and PR. These plots are a graphical representation of the maps used internally by the code for the turbocharger simulation.

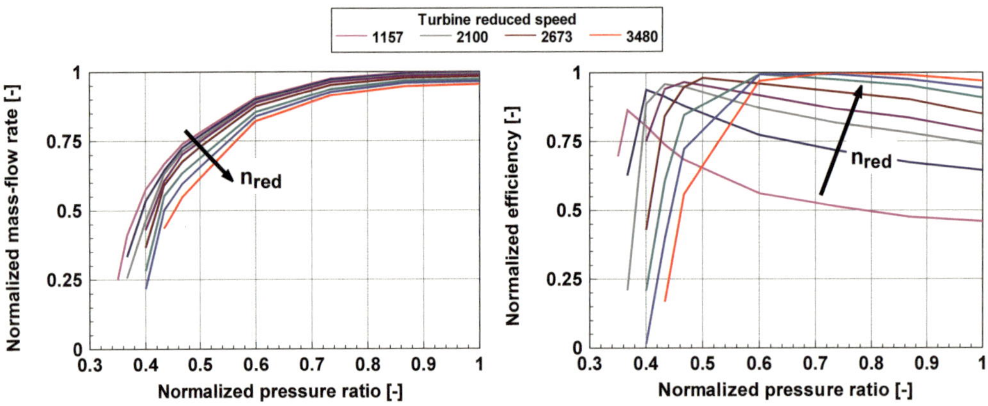

Fig. 1. Raw turbine performance maps. Each quantity is normalized to a specific value (Baratta et al., 2010).

The turbocharger maps are lumped-parameter models which are fluid-dynamically coupled to the surrounding 1-D pipe elements. For a given pressure ratio (imposed by the pipes at the compressor and turbine boundaries), and for a given shaft speed, which is the same for both the compressor and the turbine, the maps provide a value of the mass-flow rate and the efficiency. Such values can be adjusted by means of a mass-flow and an efficiency multiplier (MFM and EM, respectively), and are then used in the calculations. The mass-flow rate is imposed as a boundary condition in the adjacent pipes, and the PR and the efficiency are used to compute the instantaneous turbine and compressor power. The unbalance between these powers determines the change in the shaft speed in the actual time step, according to the following equation:

$$\frac{1}{\omega_{shaft}}\left(\dot{m}_{exh}\eta_{trb}c_p{}'T^0_{in,trb}\cdot\left(1-PR^{\frac{1-\gamma'}{\gamma'}}\right)-\dot{m}_{air}\frac{1}{\eta_{cmp}}c_pT^0_{in,cmp}\left(PR_{cmp}^{\frac{\gamma-1}{\gamma}}-1\right)\right)=I_{TC}\frac{d\omega_{shaft}}{dt} \quad (10)$$

where $\dot{m}_{air}$ is the mass flow rate through the compressor, $\dot{m}_{exh}$ is the mass flow rate of the exhaust gases through the turbine, c_p is the specific heat at a constant pressure of the air, γ is the ratio of the specific heats of the air, γ' is the ratio of the specific heats of the exhaust gases, $T^0_{in,cmp}$ is the total gas temperature at the compressor inlet, PR_{cmp} is the pressure ratio across the compressor, and η_{cmp} and η_{trb} are the efficiencies of the compressor and the turbine, respectively. Finally, ω_{shaft} is the shaft rotational speed, and I_{TC} denotes the whole turbocharger (compressor, turbine and shaft) inertia.

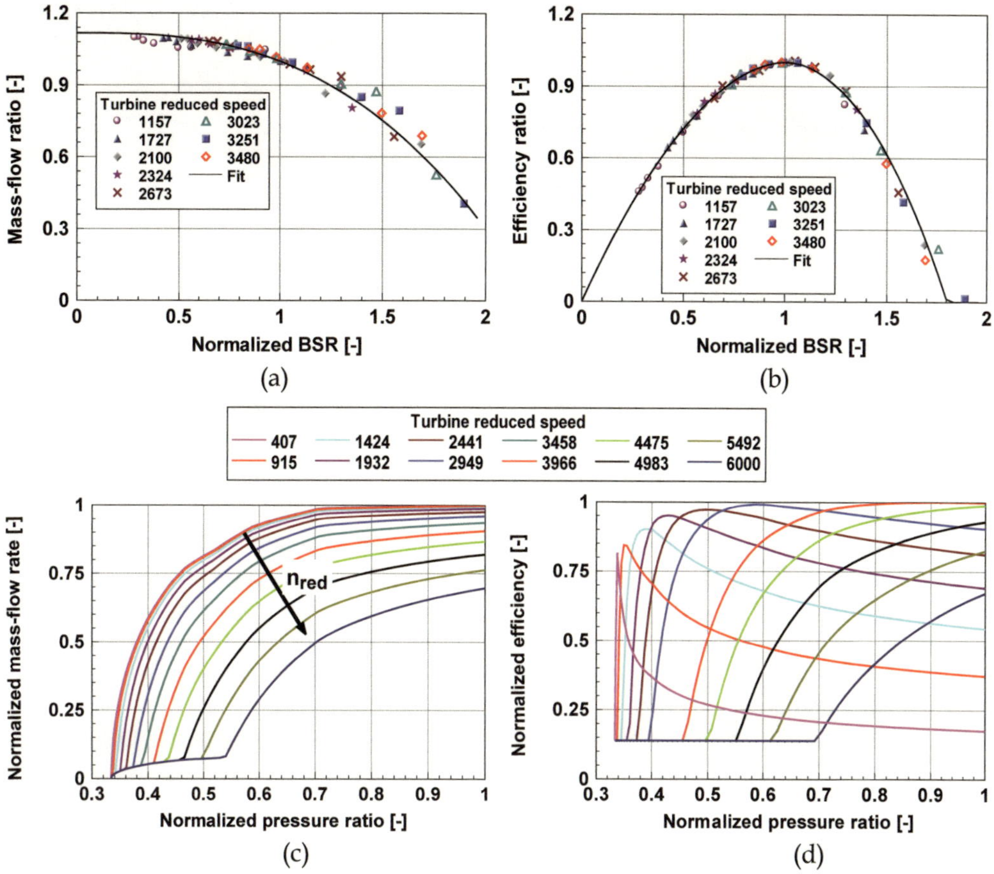

Fig. 2. Turbine performance maps. (a), (b) mass flow and efficiency fit versus data as functions of BSR; (c), (d) final turbine mass flow and efficiency maps, including the extrapolated range of reduced speed and PR (Baratta et al., 2010).

2.4 Performance of compressors and turbines

The potential need to adjust the mass-flow or the efficiency multipliers has long been known (Baratta et al., 2010; Gamma Technologies, 2009; Westin & Ångström, 2003; Westin et al., 2004).

As far as the compressor is concerned, differences in installation may influence the compressor surge-line shape, as surge depends on the compressor inlet and delivery arrangements (Baines, 2005). The position of the surge line will therefore vary from the gas stand to the engine, and from one engine installation to another. Fortunately, these variations are quite small in many cases. Due to the limited extent of the pulsating flow, which is usually observed at the compressor side, it has been found that the compressor averaging point can be predicted with good accuracy without having to adjust the compressor map. Both the compressor speed and pressure ratio usually fit well the measured values (Westin & Ångström, 2003).

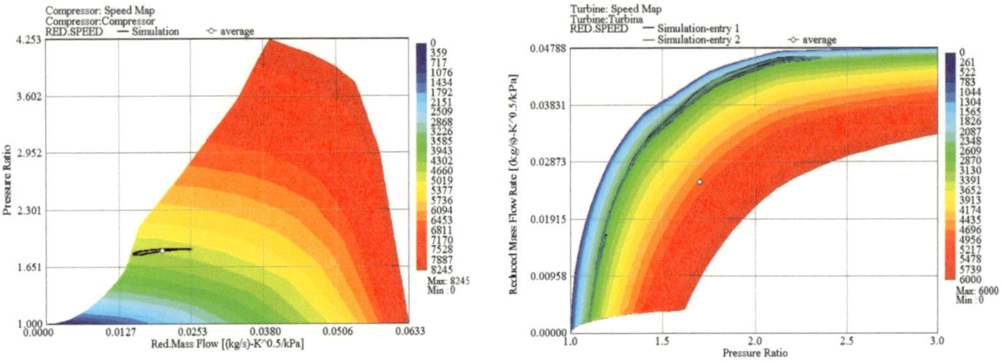

Fig. 3. Simulated compressor and turbine operating points for the maximum torque operation point of a TC 7.8 litre CNG engine. Steady-state engine operating conditions, $N = 0.55\ N_{max}$.

Conversely, the power from the turbine often has to be adjusted for each single operating conditions for many reasons (Westin et al., 2004):

- The flow entering the turbine in the engine installation is heavily pulsating, whereas the turbine performance maps are usually measured under steady-state conditions;
- During each engine cycle, the pulsating flow covers a large operating range, and this means that a large portion of the map is covered for each cycle. Often, the map is not measured with a large enough range, thus the software needs to extrapolate it, and this extrapolation may be a source of error;
- In most cases, the maps are not measured for the low-speed range of the turbocharger. Consequently, for low engine speeds, the calculation depends on a map portion which is usually extrapolated;
- The engine exhaust temperatures can be substantially higher than the gas temperatures used when measuring the maps.

Figure 3 shows the simulated compressor and turbine operating points for the maximum torque operation point of a TC 7.8 litre CNG engine (Baratta et al., 2010), under steady-state engine operating conditions. The black lines show the excursion of the compressor and turbine working point on the map during the engine cycle (two lines are plotted for the turbine, which is of the twin-entry type). The empty circles denote 'average' points, which are given by the time-average of the mass-flow rate and pressure ratio. The different extent of the pulsating flow at the compressor and at the turbine side is apparent.

As regards the turbine, the EM factor actually accounts for two processes (Baines, 2005): the fraction of the exhaust-gas energy that is available at the turbine inlet, which depends on the engine exhaust-pipes arrangements, and the efficiency with which the turbine converts this energy into shaft work. The correction does not, therefore, necessarily mean higher or lower turbine efficiency under pulse-flow conditions, but rather that the overall efficiency of the whole exhaust system is different. This has recently been referred to as 'apparent pulse turbine efficiency' (Baines, 2005; Watson & Janota, 1982).

The necessity of adjusting the turbine efficiency for each operation point would mean that is practically impossible to build a fully predictive 1-D model for a turbocharged engine. However, the problem can be overcome by organizing the turbine efficiency multipliers, obtained in the calibrated points, in a suitable form. For example, in (Baratta et al., 2010), the calibration of the turbine efficiency was carried out over a wide range of engine speeds and loads, with reference to a Heavy-Duty turbocharged CNG engine, and the obtained efficiency multiplier resulted to have a well defined trend when plotted against the turbine expansion ratio, as shown in Fig. 4. Such a trend is in agreement with the findings of (Watson & Janota, 1982), as well as with those of (Westin & Ångström, 2003), who calculated a multiplier value of 1.42 at partial load (i.e., low turbine expansion ratio) and of 0.69 at full load, for a 4-cylinder 2 litre gasoline-fuelled SI engine. $\eta_{trb,apparent}$ in Fig. 4 corresponds to η_{trb} in Eq. (10).

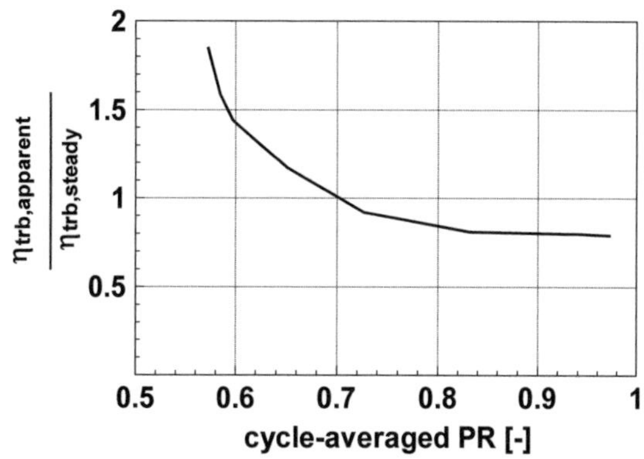

Fig. 4. Ratio of apparent turbine efficiency under pulsating flow conditions to steady-state flow efficiency. Cycle-averaged PR is normalized to a specific value (Baratta et al., 2010).

The turbine efficiency multiplier data, organized as in Fig. 4, can be very useful to allow the model to make reliable predictions of the turbine behaviour outside the calibration points. Furthermore, they are even more important if a transient simulation has to be performed. For example, (Baratta et al., 2010) considered the simulation of engine load transients at fixed speed, and almost the whole curve reported in Fig. 4 was used by the software during the calculations.

Finally, it is worth stressing that heat losses from the turbine are usually neglected in the simulations. (Westin et al., 2004) proposed an approach, based on experimental heat-transfer measurements, to account for the heat transferred from the turbine to the surroundings. In this way, the magnitude of the correction needed for the turbine efficiency decreased.

2.5 Engine-model tuning procedure

It is generally accepted that 1D models need a careful calibration procedure in order to obtain accurate results (Baratta et al., 2010; Gamma Technologies, 2009; Westin & Ångström, 2003), especially for turbocharged engine applications. In fact, due to their combined one-dimensional and zero-dimensional nature, these models are characterized by a simplified description of many physical phenomena, such as: wall friction and heat transfer, concentrated losses, flow through the valves, fuel injection, and so on. Thus, they are generally not able to describe the engine fluid-dynamics accurately, unless semi-empirical input data are provided by means of the model calibration, which is usually carried out by adjusting specific model coefficients so as to accurately reproduce the experimental measurements taken at selected steady-state operating conditions.

In order to calibrate the flow losses in the intake and exhaust pipelines of a SI engine, points at wide-open throttle are more significant, due to the very high mass-flow rate. However, part-load data should also be acquired, in view of using the model for predictive purposes over a wide range of operating conditions. In general, a 1-D model will unlikely be fully predictive (i.e., quantitative) outside the calibration region, though its results may still be significant as trends. If an engine is in the early stages of design, the experimental database may be incomplete, but measurements from other engines with common or similar components may still be useful.

2.5.1 Combustion and in-cylinder heat-transfer model calibration

The accurate prediction of the in-cylinder pressure trace is mandatory for a good estimation of the engine indicated power, which in turn is fundamental to achieve the correct value of the brake power and torque. For this reason, the in-cylinder pressure is almost always acquired, on a crank angle basis, on engine test rigs. Experimental in-cylinder pressure is the main reference data for the calibration of combustion and in-cylinder heat transfer models. The x_b profile versus crank angle can be extracted by means of a diagnostic analysis (also known as heat-release analysis), (Catania et al., 2003; Guezennec & Hamada, 1999; Heywood, 1988). Then, the 'experimental' x_b profile can constitute the basis for the calibration of a predictive combustion model, can be used to set up specific lookup tables for the Wiebe parameters ('semi-predictive' approach), or it can be directly imposed in the model.

Some commercial codes, such as GT-Power, embed tools that are specifically developed for this purpose (Gamma Technologies, 2009). Using these embedded tools, most of the needed inputs for the burn rate calculation (such as trapped air-mass and residual fraction) can be worked out directly by running the simulation of the engine model. In addition, diagnostics is carried out with the same thermodynamics and chemistry as that used for the predictions. Sometimes, heat-release (HR) profiles from external diagnostic tools may be available. However, it should be pointed out that the different thermodynamic models between the diagnostic and the simulation codes can introduce additional uncertainties into the calculation of the gas thermodynamic properties as functions of temperature. For this reason, the tools provided by the adopted 1-D code for HR analysis should be used whenever possible.

As far as the calibration of the heat transfer within the cylinder is concerned, two alternatives are possible.

a. If the HR is worked out internally, the procedure allows the calibration of the heat transfer at the same time (Gamma Technologies, 2009). For example, the diagnostic tool embedded in GT-Power ('EngBurnRate' template) provides a few parameters that allow the heat-transfer calibration to be assessed. In particular, the heat transfer multiplier can be calibrated to minimize both the deviations of the so-called fuel 'lower heating value multiplier' (LHVM) from unity and the 'cumulative compression heat release'. The code determines LHVM on the basis of an energy balance, that is similar to the one proposed in (Baratta et al., 2005; Catania et al., 2003).

b. If the heat release has been determined previously and is directly imposed, the heat transfer can only be calibrated on the basis of the match between the experimental and numerical in-cylinder pressure. However, in this case, such a calibration is also affected by an additional uncertainty, due to the calculation of the gas thermodynamic properties with different sub-models. In some applications, it may be acceptable to keep the standard C_0 coefficient, and to match the cylinder pressure by slightly shifting the HR profile. However, the alternative a) is preferable.

Once the heat transfer model has been calibrated at all the engine working points which have been investigated experimentally, the related heat-transfer multiplier values can be organized in lookup tables and then included in the engine model.

2.5.2 Turbocharged engines

The calibration procedure is more complex in the case of turbocharged engines, in which the compressor, the engine and the turbine are fluid-dynamically coupled. For turbocharged engine applications, it is not advisable to tune the entire model, consisting of the engine and the turbocharger, from the beginning. In fact, slight inaccuracies that are usually present before model tuning can make the compressor operation point (and, hence, the boost level) deviate to a great extent from the real one. In this case, it is very difficult to isolate the root cause of a performance problem (Baratta et al., 2010; Gamma Technologies, 2009; Westin & Ångström, 2003). For this reason, an engine model without the turbocharger should be built first. The intercooler outlet and the turbine inlet should be replaced by two environments in which pressure, temperature and fluid composition are properly set on the basis of measured data, and the model should be calibrated, as in the case of a naturally-aspirated engine.

2.6 Steady-state engine-model tuning example

The procedure outlined above allows the 1-D model of a turbocharged engine to obtain a rather high degree of predictability, not only in a qualitative sense, but also from a quantitative point of view. It was followed almost exactly in this way in (Baratta et al, 2010), from which Fig. 5 is taken. The engine features are reported in Table 1.

As can be seen, the engine model is generally well calibrated in all the tested cases. With reference to the whole intake system, and the portion of the exhaust ports within the cylinder head, the wall temperatures at the fluid side were set to specific values, which were selected on the basis of the outcomes of the experimental tests. The wall temperature was evaluated taking account of the gas-wall heat transfer for the pipes downstream from the exhaust ports and the external temperature was set equal to the value in the cell cabinet. The intake and exhaust ports were modelled as straight pipes, and heat-transfer multipliers were thus introduced to account for the bends, roughness, the additional surface area and turbulence caused by the valves and stems (Gamma Technologies, 2009). There was no need to set heat-transfer multipliers elsewhere in the intake system or to add friction multipliers to the model because the pressures and temperatures in the engine manifolds and ports were well reproduced (Fig. 5a,c,d). The agreement between the simulated and experimental values of PFP (peak firing pressure, Fig. 5e) and engine brake torque (Fig. 5f) demonstrate the accuracy of the combustion and engine friction sub-models, respectively. The above

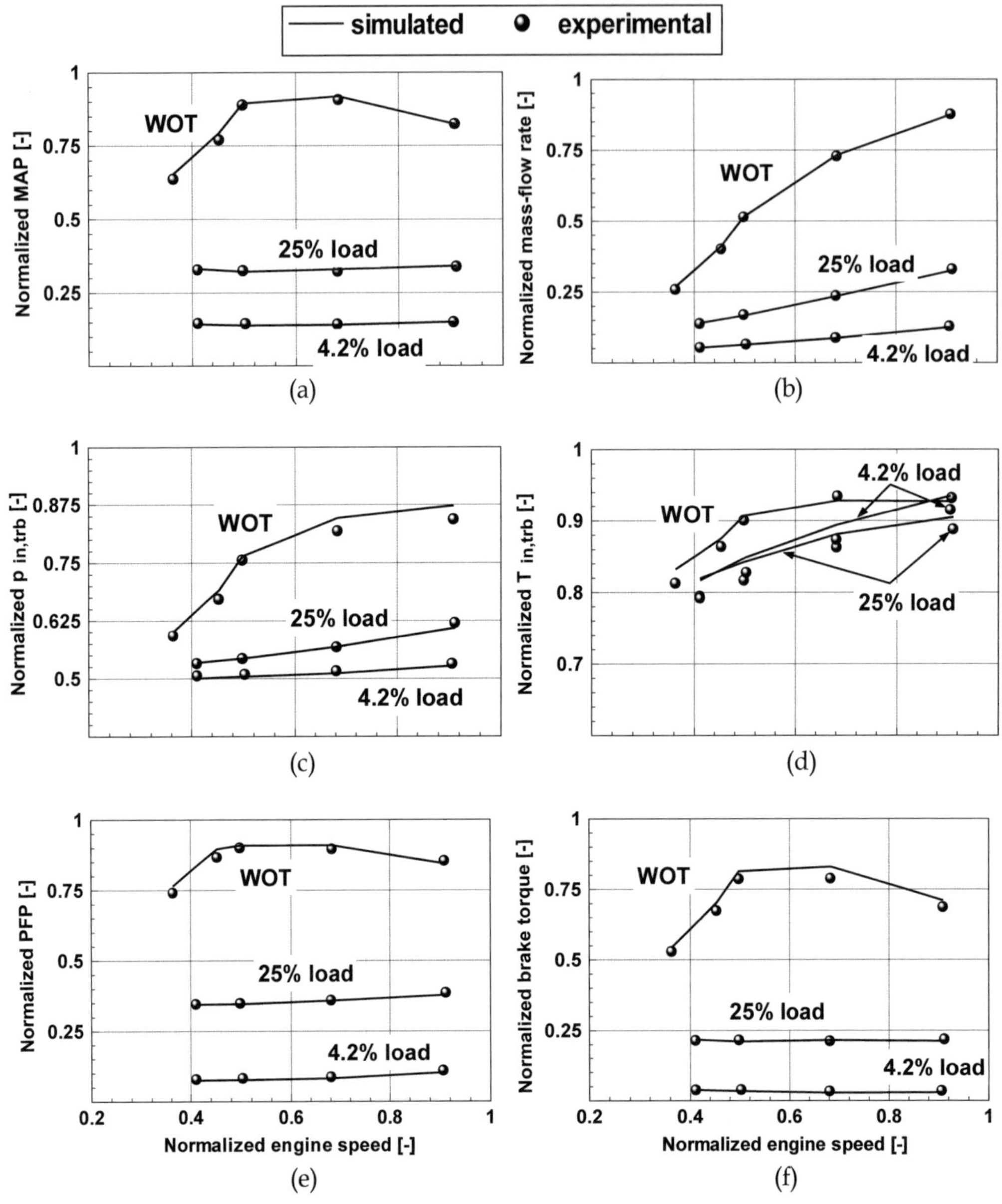

Fig. 5. Model results under steady-state working conditions, as functions of the engine speed. (a): Manifold Absolute Pressure; (b): air mass-flow rate; (c): Pressure at the turbine inlet (cylinder 1 side); (d): Temperature at the turbine inlet; (e): Peak Firing Pressure (cylinder 1); (f): Engine brake torque. Each quantity is normalized to a specific value (Baratta et al., 2010).

calibration was made with reference to the engine model without the turbocharger. Subsequently, turbocharger and intercooler (IC) were added and the pressure at the turbine outlet was tuned first, acting on the friction multipliers of the pipes located downstream from the turbine. Then, the turbine MFM and EM were adjusted so as to match both the experimental pressure at the turbine inlet and the experimental shaft speed, and to balance the turbine and compressor cycle-averaged power:

$$\int_0^{T_{cycle}}\left[\dot{m}_{air}\cdot\frac{1}{\eta_{cmp}}\cdot c_p T^0_{in,cmp}\cdot\left(PR_{cmp}^{\gamma-1/\gamma}-1\right)\right]dt=\int_0^{T_{cycle}}\left[\dot{m}_{exh}\cdot\eta_{trb}\cdot c_p{}'T^0_{in,trb}\cdot\left(1-PR^{1-\gamma'/\gamma'}\right)\right]dt \quad (11)$$

Number of cylinders	6 (in line)	Displacement	7.78 dm^3
Number of valves	4 (per cylinder)	Compression ratio	11:1
Bore	115 mm	Turbocharged	Yes
Stroke	125 mm	Intercooler	Yes

Table 1. Characteristics of a 7.8 litre turbocharged CNG engine (Baratta et al., 2010).

In particular, it is worth referring to the WOT conditions in Fig. 5, in which the first three points (engine speeds between 0.35 and 0.5 on the normalized scale) were characterized by a closed waste-gate (WG) valve, whereas the WG was partially open for the remaining two points. In those cases, the EM was selected on the basis of both the shaft speed and the pressure at the turbine inlet. MFM was selected so as to match the experimental $p_{in,trb}$ in the closed-WG points, and was then kept constant in the open-WG ones. The combined effect of MFM, EM, and WG position resulted in a slight overestimation of the turbine backpressure compared to the experiments for the open-WG points (Fig. 5c), although the differences are consistent with the uncertainty of the pressure measurements.

2.7 Transient engine simulation

The simulation of the transient behaviour of an engine by means of a 1-D simulation code is more challenging than a steady-state modelling approach. In fact, in a steady-state simulation, only the 'converged' results are significant, and the code is run until the differences in the engine variables are negligible in two consecutive simulated cycles. In a transient simulation, in which the engine speed and/or load versus time change, the model should accurately reproduce not only the engine variable at the end of the transient, but also their evolution versus time.

Engine models that have to be used for transient simulation need a more careful calibration. In particular, it is not sufficient to set the model parameters with reference to the steady-state full-load conditions. This holds for all submodels, and was demonstrated in (Lefebvre & Guilain, 2006) for the combustion model. In fact, by simulating load transients using constant full-load combustion parameters, the model results presented unacceptable deviations from the experimental ones, and did not allow transient behaviour to be predicted correctly, or different engine configurations to be compared. The model inaccuracy decreased when the combustion process was modelled as a function of the engine load and speed, and the maps were included in GT-Power, and it was further reduced when the same procedure was followed for the in-cylinder heat-transfer coefficient (c_0 in Eq. (8)). A similar procedure was followed in (Baratta et al., 2010). The following aspects should also be taken into account:

- The engine transient simulation should start from an already converged solution or, in other words, the 'actual' transient should be properly distinguished from the 'numerical' one. This can be achieved by running the model for a few seconds before the start of the 'actual' transient phase.

- The friction, filling, and heat-exchange phenomena in the intake and the exhaust manifolds should be accurately simulated. This is mandatory for turbocharged engines, in order to reproduce the experimental pressure and temperature time-history at the turbine inlet. The thermal inertia of the pipes should be taken into account in the 'actual' transient, whereas it should be neglected during the 'numerical' one, in order to shorten the thermal transient phase of the model. (Galindo et al, 2006) pointed out the great importance of the heat-transfer model in the transient calculations of a 1-D engine model. They presented a heat transfer model that is suitable to predict the transient operation of HSDI turbocharged engines when implemented in a 1-D gas-dynamic model. The model includes some selected correlations for the heat transfer coefficient for the different ducts and the engine cylinder. An important contribution of the work is the calculation of the wall temperatures by means of a three-node finite-differences scheme that accounts for thermal inertia.
- The turbine EM should be quite accurate for turbocharged engines, during the whole simulation, as it influences the slope of the boost curve versus time. Besides, it could be useful to reduce the turbocharger inertia during the 'numerical' transient. Acceptable results were obtained in (Westin & Ångström, 2003) by calibrating the turbine efficiency in the initial and in the final points of a load transient, under steady-state conditions, and by operating a linear EM interpolation during the transient evolution. In (Baratta et al., 2010), the EM was organized in a lookup table as a function of PR (see Fig. 4), and then included in the model. This led to a good model accuracy in different load-transient simulations.

Figure 6 (Baratta et al., 2010) shows the model calibration results for a tip-in event of the engine under study. The throttle was opened abruptly and the torque was varied from about 4.2% load to the steady-state values at WOT. Before applying the model to the transient simulations, the following changes were made:

- The temperature time-history for the pipes between the compressor and the intercooler was accurately simulated, taking the gas-wall heat transfer into account;
- the catalyst friction multiplier was organized in a lookup table as a function of the mass flow and was included in the model.

The model resulted to be well calibrated. In fact, not only were the asymptotic values well reproduced but also the simulated slopes that occurred during the transient were comparable to the experimental ones. However, some discrepancies were observed in the time-histories of the temperature at the turbine inlet (Fig. 6d) and the brake torque (Fig. 6f). The main differences between simulated and experimental $T_{in,trb}$ time-histories are that:

- The simulated asymptotic value at the end of the transient is higher than the experimental one. This can be ascribed to an underestimation of the measured gas temperature, which is due to the heat transferred from the thermocouple to the pipe walls by both radiation and conduction, through the thermocouple stem (Baratta et al., 2010; Westin & Ångström, 2003; Westin, 2005).
- Due to thermocouple thermal inertia, the slopes of the simulated and measured temperature rise are different. Fast temperature oscillations, such as those calculated during the first transient phase, cannot be measured by the thermocouple (Westin & Ångström, 2003).

- The computed gas temperature, before the tip-in event, is lower than that measured during the experiment. Under such a partial load, the turbocharger group produces virtually no boost, which in turn has no practical influence on the transient simulation. Therefore, the calibration of the exhaust-pipe heat-transfer multiplier and wall temperature were not performed at this operating condition, and this likely contributed to the observed difference in gas temperatures.

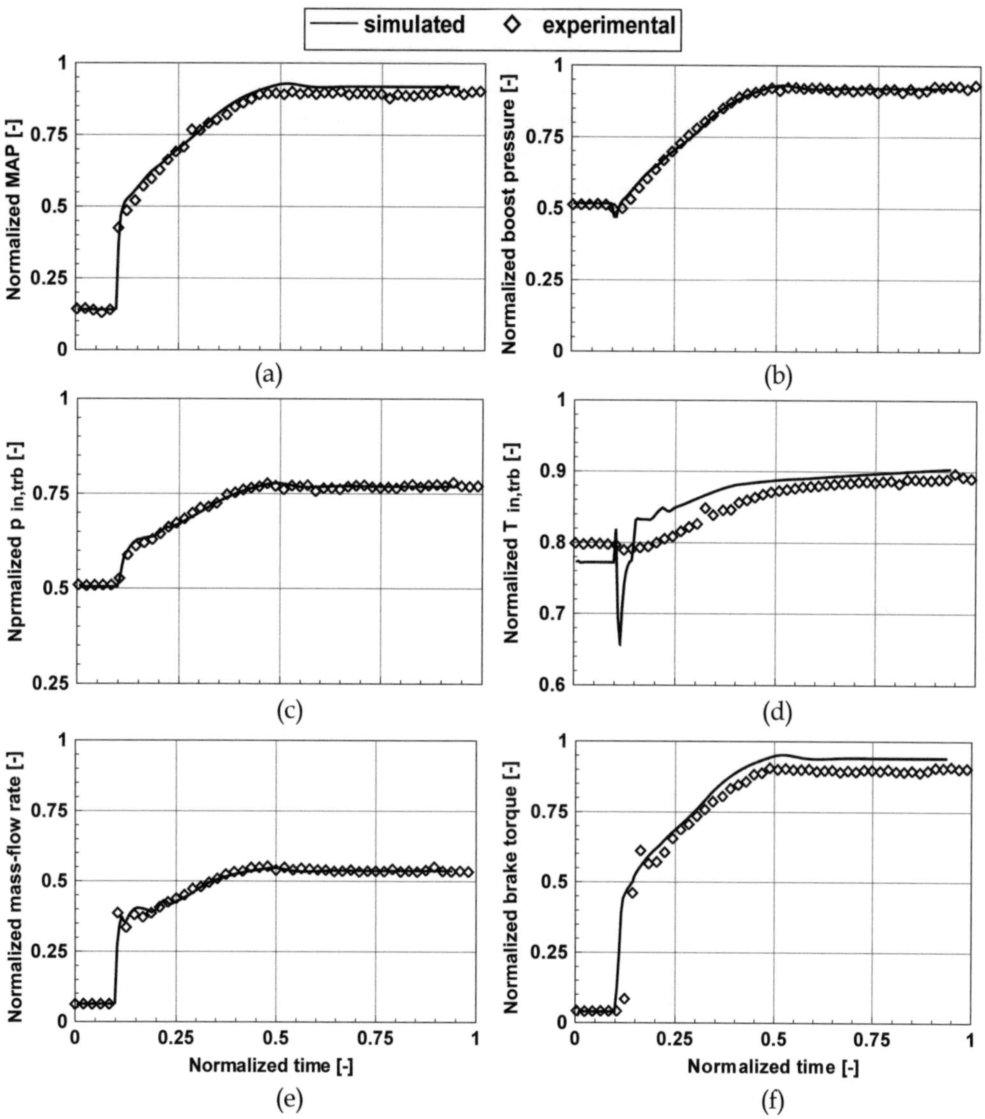

Fig. 6. Model results under transient working conditions (load step at constant engine speed, N = 0.55 N_{max}). (a) manifold absolute pressure, (b) boost pressure, (c) pressure at the turbine inlet (cylinder 1 side), (d) temperature at the turbine inlet (cylinder 1 side), (e) air mass-flow rate, (f) engine brake torque. Each quantity is normalized to a specific value (Baratta et al., 2010).

The slight difference between the calculated and the measured brake torque at the transient end (Fig. 6f) can primarily be ascribed to an underestimation of the gas pressure contribution to the friction mean effective pressure under full-load operations.
(Baratta & Spessa, 2009) modified the previous model with reference to the engine installation on a commercial vehicle for urban transportation. The model was extensively revised by modifying the pertinent pipe, bend and 'flowsplit' objects. In addition, the following differences were considered with respect to the dyno test-bed configuration:

- The bus IC was of the air-to-air type, and displayed different volumes and temperatures than the water-to-air IC installed on the dyno test rig. This influenced the engine volumetric efficiency, the charge temperature and the wave propagation phenomena within the intake system. Therefore, it was necessary to revise the IC calibration, with specific reference to flow losses and heat transfer effects (surface roughness and material, and the related multipliers).
- In the bus layout, the auxiliary components are driven by the engine, while most of them have an independent energy source or are even absent on the dyno test rig. For this reason, the engine friction-model was re-tuned in order to achieve a reliable estimation of the engine brake torque.

The new model was tuned on the basis of a specific test, in which the hydraulic torque converter of the considered urban bus was kept under stall conditions by means of the vehicle brakes, while a quick opening of the throttle valve was actuated. Throughout this transient process, the engine torque demand was thus proportional to N^2. As an example, Fig. 7 compares the experimental (black solid line) and simulated (red dotted line) time-histories of the boost pressure, mass flow rate and engine speed for a load step from $N / N_{max} = 0.3$ to 0.8. The same EM profile versus PR was used as in (Baratta et al., 2010).

3. Predictive 0-D combustion models

The reliability of the 1-D approach can be improved if predictive 0-D combustion models are used to predict the heat-release rate within the engine combustion chamber. The turbulent combustion process is a complex phenomenon that involves many chemical, thermo-dynamic and fluid-dynamic aspects, which should be studied by adopting a three-dimensional approach. However, as discussed in great detail by (Lipatnikov & Chomiak, 2002), even in this case, the development of a fundamentally substantiated model, that is, a model which is based only on the application of 'first principles', is very difficult. A possible, practical solution is that of shifting from the first principles to phenomenology, i.e., in the use of well established experimental facts and approximate descriptions of selected combustion-process characteristics which are assumed to be the main controlling factors. Similarly, predictive 0-D combustion models, which are the topic of this section, are based on a phenomenological description of the turbulent combustion process of a premixed fuel-air mixture. Although they generally need a preliminary tuning procedure, they can potentially predict the dependence of the heat-release rate on, among other factors, in-cylinder flow, combustion chamber geometry, mixture composition, thermodynamic state, and spark timing. Since the pioneering work of (Blizzard & Keck, 1974), a large number of papers have been published, which have focused on the development and/or the application of predictive combustion models to SI engines. A rather good review of the main aspects that have to be faced in a thermodynamic combustion model formulation can be found in (Velherst & Sheppard, 2009).

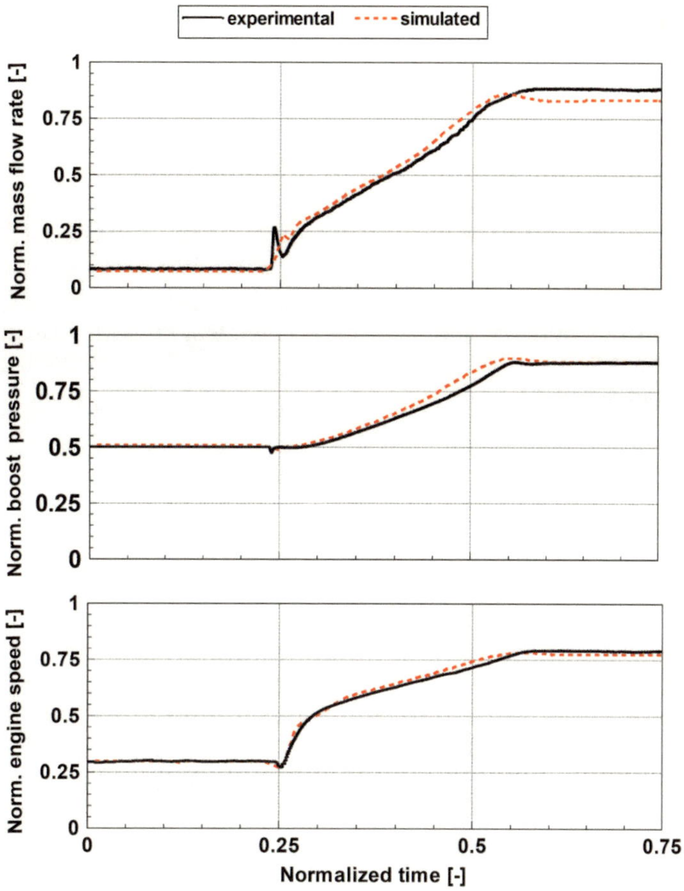

Fig. 7. Load step for an engine coupled to a stalled torque converter (Baratta & Spessa, 2009): experimental (solid black line) and simulated (red dotted line) time histories. Each quantity is normalized to a specific value.

3.1 Introduction and overview

The goal of a predictive combustion model is to predict the rate at which the unburned mixture is converted into burned gases. This allows the computation of the in-cylinder pressure through Eqs. (4-6). The different models are based on the definition of a 'turbulent burning velocity', S_b, and of a flame burning-front area A_{bf}, whereas the flame-brush thickness is generally neglected. The flame area is often modelled assuming a spherical shape of the flame front, which gradually intersects the combustion chamber surfaces as it grows (see, among others, Baratta et al., 2008; Bozza et al., 2005; Wahiduzzaman et al., 1993). This assumption has been confirmed by experiments, at least for combustion chambers with sufficiently low swirl and tumble ratios. In a thermo-dynamic modelling approach, this is also the most reasonable a priori choice. In fact, a sub-model for the flame deformation by the in-cylinder flow would need detailed information on the flow motion characteristics, which is not compatible with the thermo-dynamic nature of the overall model.
The evolution equation for the burned-gas mass fraction x_b can be derived adopting two different approaches (Baratta et al ., 2006).

a. the 'prompt burning' approach: the mixture that is entrained through the flame front burns promptly. Thus, it follows that the increment in x_b for each computational step of the combustion phase is:

$$dx_b = \frac{1}{m_{cyl}} \rho_u A_{bf} S_b \frac{d\theta}{\omega} \tag{12}$$

Examples of models based on such an approach can be found in the literature (Baratta et al., 2008; Bozza et al., 2005; D'Errico et al., 2002; Wu et al., 1993; Yoshiyama et al., 2001).

b. the 'entrainment + burning' approach: the entrainment process is followed by a laminar burnout process in the region behind the flame front. The process is described by the following equations:

$$dx_e = \frac{1}{m_{cyl}} \rho_u A_{bf} S_b \frac{d\theta}{\omega} \tag{13}$$

$$dx_b = \frac{x_e - x_b}{\tau} \tag{14}$$

x_e being the entrained mass fraction (Brown et al., 1996; Grill et al., 2006; Hattrel et al., 2006; Poulos & Heywood, 1983; Wahiduzzaman et al., 1993). The rate of laminar burnout in eq. (14) is assumed to be proportional to the unburned mass behind the flame front. Since the burnout is postulated to take place at the laminar flame speed and over a typical length scale of the turbulence microscale, the time constant τ in eq. (14) is given by the ratio of the Taylor turbulence microscale, λ, and of the laminar flame speed S_L (Wahiduzzaman et al., 1993):

$$\tau = \frac{\lambda}{S_L} \tag{15}$$

The calculation of the turbulent flame speed S_b, to be used in Eqs. (12) or (13), involves the evaluation of the laminar burning speed, S_L, of the in-cylinder turbulence generation, as well as of the turbulence-flame interaction (Baratta et al., 2006). As will be shown later on, each of these aspects can exert a remarkable influence on the indicated cycle prediction. For this reason, the assessment of the accuracy of each of the adopted sub-models is often very difficult. A comparison between simulated and experimental or diagnosed combustion-related quantities generally allows one to assess the overall simulation-model accuracy, which depends on how the different sub-model results are combined. A critical discussion of the main sub-models which are required is provided hereafter.

3.2 In-cylinder turbulence sub-model

In-cylinder turbulence modelling is required in a predictive combustion model, in order to quantify the increase in burning velocity, due to the turbulence, with respect to the case of laminar combustion. In the framework of thermo-dynamic models, a zero-dimensional model is usually applied, which provides a uniform value of the mean-flow velocity and of the root mean square (rms) turbulent fluctuation. The turbulence model results can also be used by the in-cylinder heat-transfer sub-model, in order to derive a value for the convective heat-transfer coefficient.

A rather simple, but quite widely applied model is the K-k one (Poulos & Heywood, 1983), which is based on a zero-dimensional energy cascade from the mean flow to the viscous eddy dissipation. According to such a model, the rates of change in the mean flow kinetic energy ($K = 1/2\, m_{cyl} U^2$) and in the turbulent kinetic energy ($k = 3/2\, m_{cyl} u'^2$) are, respectively:

$$\frac{dK}{dt} = \frac{1}{2}\dot{m}_i v_i^2 - P - K\frac{\dot{m}_o}{m_{cyl}} \tag{16}$$

$$\frac{dk}{dt} = P - m_{cyl}\varepsilon - k\frac{\dot{m}_o}{m_{cyl}} \tag{17}$$

where: U is the average mean-flow velocity, u' is the rms turbulent velocity, $\varepsilon \cong \frac{u'^3}{L_i}$ is the rate of turbulent kinetic energy dissipation per unit mass, L_i is the characteristic size of the large-scale eddies, m is the mass in the cylinder, $\dot{m}_i$ is the mass flow rate into the cylinder, $\dot{m}_o$ is the mass flow rate out of the cylinder, v_i is the jet velocity entering the chamber and P is the rate of turbulent kinetic energy production. Since the turbulence model does not spatially resolve the flow parameters, the production term P is empirically estimated from mean flow quantities:

$$P = 0.3307\, c_\beta \frac{K}{L_i}\left(\frac{k}{m}\right)^{1/2} \tag{18}$$

where the turbulent dissipation constant c_β is adjusted to give the expected profiles of u' and U throughout the whole cycle. It is worth pointing out that the accuracy of a turbulent burning-speed model depends to a great extent on the unburned-gas turbulence evolution during combustion, which is normally thought to present a maximum near firing TDC (Baratta et al., 2008, Bozza et al, 2005, Heywood, 1988; Poulos & Heywood, 1983; Yoshiyama et al., 2001). Although the magnitude of such a maximum depends, among other factors, on the configuration of the combustion chamber and, to a lesser extent, on the intake system, its presence is generally modelled by means of heuristic approaches that add turbulence during compression and combustion. As an example, it can be seen that, in (Baratta et al., 2006, 2008; Poulos & Heywood, 1983), as soon as the combustion starts, Eq. (17) is no longer integrated, and the evolution of the turbulence intensity and of the spatial macro scale is calculated by assuming conservation of angular momentum for large scale eddies, which gives rise to an increase in the unburned-gas turbulence. Eqs. (16) and (17) have recently been modified by adding ad-hoc compression-related terms that account for the density variation in the cylinder during the compression and expansion strokes. If such terms are introduced into the K-k model equations, these also have to be integrated through the combustion phase (Bozza et al., 2005).

The main advantage of the K-k model is that of its simplicity. However, since the energy cascade is governed by the dissipation constant c_β, such a constant has to be set by the user, taking the combustion chamber geometry into account. In (Baratta et al., 2006), a sensitivity analysis of the computed mean velocity and turbulence intensity was carried out in a range of c_β values of between 0.75 and 3.0. The experimental turbulence data close to TDC, taken in a similar motored engine to that under study, were in good agreement with the calculated levels when the value c_β=3.0 was employed.

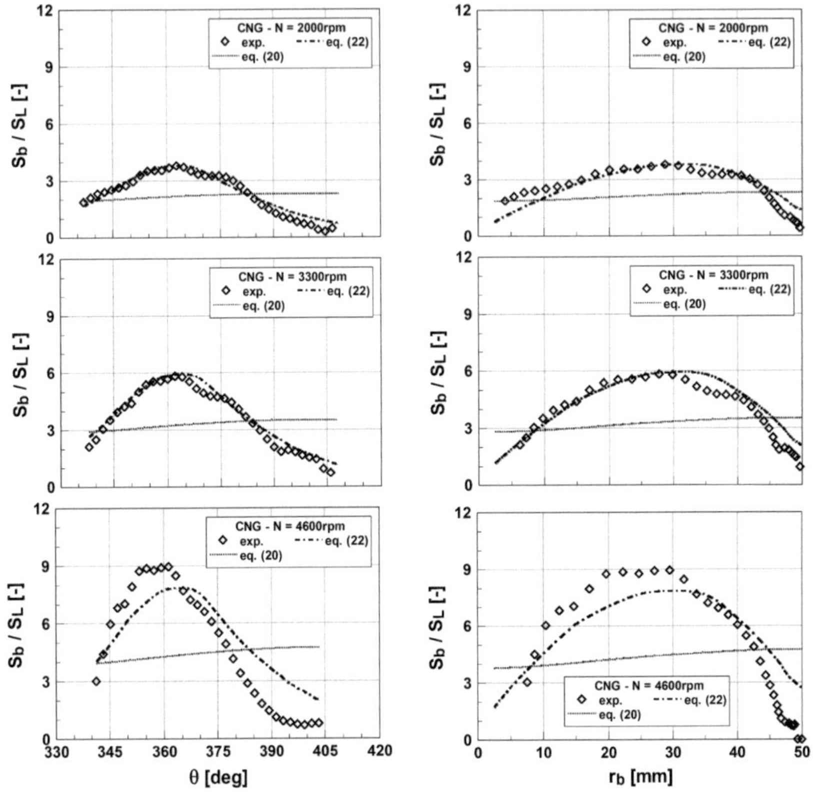

Fig. 8. Distributions of diagnosed and computed Sb/SL, versus θ (column on the left) and rb (column on the right), for different engine speeds – 2000cc 16v NA engine, CNG fuelling, bmep = 440 kPa, RAFR = 1.0, MBT timing (Baratta et al., 2006).

(Morel & Keribar, 1985) tried to develop a rather innovative flow model, with an expanded physical basis, in order to reduce the necessity of adjustments to account for engine-to-engine differences. The model was initially developed with reference to convective heat-transfer estimation in Diesel engines, and was then extended to SI engines and to the prediction of the turbulence level, for S_b prediction purposes (Morel et al., 1988). The cylinder volume is divided into multiple regions: the central core region, the squish region, the head recess region, and the piston cup region. Some axial and radial velocities are calculated, at each time step in each region, from mass conservation and piston kinematics, whereas the other radial and axial velocities, which are essentially three-dimensional, are included in the turbulence. A swirl equation, based on the conservation of angular momentum under the hypothesis of solid-body rotation, is solved for each region. The turbulent kinetic energy and the dissipation rate evolution are predicted by means of the k-ε model equations (Wilcox, 1994), which were rewritten to account for a discretization into a few regions, rather than into a multitude of computational nodes. Thus, the turbulent kinetic energy actually includes a wide range of scales, which are partially superimposed onto the mean-flow spectrum. A turbulence production term, due to the unburned-gas compression, is also included (Morel et al., 1988). As far as the prediction of the convective heat-transfer coefficient is concerned, Morel & Keribar's model is expected to require fewer adjustments when it is applied to a new engine, due to its expanded physical basis compared to the previous models. However, when the accurate prediction of in-cylinder turbulence is required, as is the case of a predictive combustion model implementation, the proposed discretization of the k-ε model equations does not seem to be much more accurate than the very simple production term formulation given by Eq. (18). In particular, since a portion of the kinetic energy associated with the mean-flow scales is included in the turbulence terms, the simulated u′ velocity may be different from the turbulent velocity which is presumed to affect the combustion velocity.

3.3 Turbulent flame-speed model

Turbulent burning-velocity models start from laminar burning speed (S_L) data for the burning mixture, and are based on the evaluation of both the turbulence level and the turbulence-flame interaction. The latter can be modelled through either a non-fractal or a fractal approach, taking the turbulence level into account. In the first approach, the entrainment velocity S_b is the sum of a convective component and a diffusive one (Wahiduzzaman et al., 1993):

$$S_b = S_L + C_s u' \left(1 - \frac{1}{1 + C_k r_b^2 / L_i^2}\right) \tag{19}$$

r_b being the burned-gas radius, L_i the turbulence macroscale and C_s and C_k two fitting parameters. The term in brackets modulates the contribution of u′, in order to avoid an overprediction of the flame speed at the initial stage of combustion, when the size of the flame kernel is comparable with that of the turbulence eddies.

The second approach is based on the fractal and laminar flamelet concepts (Baratta et al., 2006; Gouldin & Miles, 1995), in order to represent the turbulent premixed flames. The laminar flamelet concept assumes that the combustion within a turbulent flame is confined to asymptotically thin moving laminar flamelets that are embedded in the turbulent flow. Since these thin layers behave like laminar flames, the turbulent burning velocity can be evaluated as the product of the surface area of the flamelets and the laminar burning speed, which is corrected to take stretch and flame curvature effects into account. The characterization and evaluation of the flamelet surface area, in relation to the turbulence properties, have been the subjects of many studies (Gülder and Smallwood, 1995; Gülder et al., 2000; North & Santavicca, 1990). According to the fractal theory, the general expression of the correlation that links the turbulent flame surface area and speed to the laminar ones is:

$$A_T / A_L = S_b / S_L = \left(\varepsilon_o / \varepsilon_i\right)^{D-2} \tag{20}$$

where A_T and A_L are the wrinkled and mean flame front surface areas, S_b and S_L represent the turbulent burning speed and the laminar flame velocity, ε_o and ε_i are the so-called outer and inner turbulence cutoff length scales, and D is the fractal dimension of the flame front surface. The success and the applicability of these models depend to a great extent on the availability of reliable values for the inner and outer cutoff length scales and for the fractal dimension. Correlations to evaluate the cutoff length scales have been proposed, namely in (Gülder and Smallwood, 1995).

The inner cutoff length scale ε_i is taken equal to the turbulence micro scale η:

$$\varepsilon_i = \eta = L_i \left({u' L_i}/{\nu} \right)^{-3/4} \tag{21}$$

The outer cutoff length scale has been taken equal to the integral turbulence scale, L_i, in many studies (D'Errico et al., 2002; Wu et al., 1993). However, although this choice could be acceptable for stationary flames issuing from burners (Gülder et al., 2000), in SI engine combustion, in which the mean flame front is assumed to be spherical, the wrinkling effect of turbulence on the flame front should be a function of the ratio between the characteristic flame-front and eddy dimensions, because the initially regular flame front surface progressively becomes more and more wrinkled as its dimension increases with respect to turbulent eddies. Therefore, (Baratta et al., 2006, 2008) replaced the integral length scale in Eq. (20) with a characteristic linear dimension of the flame front, i.e., the square root of its surface area. Furthermore, (Gülder et al., 2000) pointed out that, if the fractal geometry approach yields a true measure of the wrinkled surface area of the flame front, then Eq. (20) may not be a reasonable assumption for the turbulent premixed flames in the flamelet regime. In fact, small-scale turbulence can enhance the transfer of heat and species across the flame front. For this reason, (Baratta et al., 2006, 2008) introduced a pre-multiplying factor in Eq. (20), and argued that such a factor should be proportional to the average charge density, as an increased density means higher concentrations of reactive species near the flame front. Thus, the proposed formula for the turbulent burning speed was:

$$\frac{S_b}{S_L} = \left(\frac{\rho}{\rho_0} \right)^n \left(\frac{C_L \sqrt{A_{bf}}}{\eta} \right)^{D-2} = \left(\frac{\rho}{\rho_0} \right)^n \left(\frac{C_L \sqrt{A_{bf}}}{C_L \left(h_{\min} + S_p \right) \left(\frac{u' C_L \left(h_{\min} + S_p \right)}{\nu} \right)^{-3/4}} \right)^{D-2} \tag{22}$$

where h_{min} is the clearance height, S_p the instantaneous piston displacement from TDC, A_{bf} the unwrinkled flame-front area, and C_L a closure coefficient that depends on the engine fuelling and speed. n was found to be 1.25 for two different engines and ρ_0 is the average density evaluated at a reference crank angle, which depends on the specific engine (Baratta et al., 2008).

Although predictive combustion models have been developed as phenomenological models, they can simply be considered as mathematical descriptions that agree with the S-shaped mass-fraction burned observations. It is reasonable to use either Eq. (19) or the fractal approach (Eqs. (20) or (22)), coupled to the 'prompt burning' or the 'entrainment + burning' approaches, provided appropriate choices are made for A_{bf}, τ and the specific model's constants. However, though it is not a general rule, virtually all the fractal models used in the literature are coupled to the 'prompt burning' approach, whereas the non fractal ones are implemented with the 'entrainment + burning' formulation.

The results of the application of the Baratta et al. model are reported in Fig. 8, in terms of predicted S_b/S_L profiles versus crank angle and versus burned-gas radius. In the figure, 'exp.' denotes the results of the multizone diagnostic model application (Catania et al., 2004). Two calculation results are plotted: one is obtained through Eq. (22) and the other with the original Eq. (20) in which L_i is used as the outer cutoff scale. The general good agreement between the predicted and experimental results in Fig. 8 clearly shows the capability of the model to describe the flame-turbulence interaction in the overall flame propagation interval, from the development to the extinction of the flame. Furthermore, as can be inferred from this figure, Eq. (22) can extrapolate a value of S_b/S_L that is almost equal to 1 as r_b approaches zero, in agreement with the flame propagation theory (Baratta et al., 2006; Velherst & Sheppard, 2009). This supports the correctness of the introduction of the term $\sqrt{A_{bf}}$ into the definition of ε_o, as well as of the term $(\rho/\rho_0)^n$ to account for the reduced species and heat transfer across the flame front at low in-cylinder densities. If Eq. (20) is applied with $\varepsilon_o=L_i$, the modulation of S_b/S_L is insufficient, and the model generally needs special measures for a correct end-of-combustion simulation (Bozza et al., 2005; D'Errico et al., 2002; Wu et al., 1993).

The model developed in (Baratta et al., 2008) resulted to be in quite good agreement with the experimental or diagnosed combustion-related parameters. The main attractiveness of this model is given by its 'intrinsic' capability to reproduce, with good accuracy, the S_b/S_L modulation through combustion, as well as its straightforward calibration. In fact, the crank angle at which the ρ_0 term is evaluated in Eq. (22) is the only parameter that should be set for a specific engine, and it is virtually independent of fuelling and operating conditions. An example of model validation is given in the column on the left of Fig. 9: with the exception of a couple of points, the agreement of the maximum in-cylinder pressure p_{max} and the maximum heat-release rate HRR_{max} is within a few percent. Obviously, the model accuracy could be improved if an ad-hoc model tuning is carried out for each operating point, but even with a fixed calibration set for a given engine and fuelling, the degree of accuracy is acceptable, and the model can be used for predictive purposes.

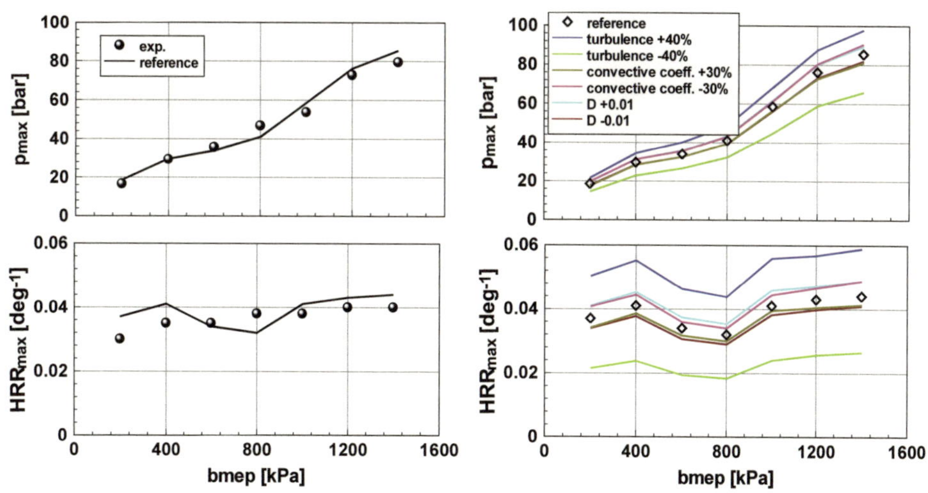

Fig. 9. Comparison between experimental/diagnosed and simulated quantities (left) and model sensitivity analysis (right) - 1200cc 8v TC engine, Methane fuelling, N = 3000 rpm, RAFR = 1.0, MBT timing.

The column on the right in Fig. 9 provides an example of the influence of the main sub-models on the results of the overall model. In-cylinder turbulence and heat-transfer sub-models are considered, and in addition, the influence of a slight change in the fractal dimension, D, is assessed. The 'reference' series is the same as in the first column, and represents the calibration in (Baratta et al., 2008). The deviation from the 'reference' calibration for each sub-model has been set on the basis of the uncertainty that can be expected in the adopted modelling framework. In particular, a deviation of 40% was considered for the turbulence level at the spark discharge, due to the significant approximations in the K-k model. An error of 30% is reasonable for the heat-transfer, especially if a diagnostic tool is not available for its calibration. Finally, the uncertainty on the fractal dimension D can be even higher than 0.01, since at present there is no agreement on its value (Baratta et al., 2006). As can be seen, for the considered deviation values, an increase in the heat-transfer coefficient has almost the same effect as a decrease in the fractal dimension. Both parameters can influence the model performance to a certain extent. As can be expected, the turbulence level exerts a remarkable influence on the overall model output. In particular, the bell-like shape of the u' profile versus crank angle, although obtained through empirical formulas, is very important to obtain an acceptable S_b/S_L profile.
The above discussion confirms that the overall model accuracy depends on each specific sub-model formulation, as well as on the related calibration. A precise model prediction can be obtained by adopting very accurate sub-models, but also when the sub-models error cancel each other. A good predictive combustion model should be formulated and calibrated so as to be able to reproduce the engine indicated cycle with a reasonable accuracy over a wide range of operating conditions, and to capture the engine performance trends when a design or operation variable is modified.

4. Conclusions

In the present chapter, the problem of the 1-D simulation the fluid-dynamics, combustion and performance of SI engines has been analyzed in detail. Among the different aspects that have to be faced when approaching this problem, the discussion has been focused on the in-cylinder pressure evolution versus crank angle, paying specific attention to the closed-valve phase, and on the turbocharger modelling. An accurate model tuning procedure has been outlined for both topics, and indications have been given on how the model could be made predictive, even in the presence of variable coefficients (such as, for example, the in-cylinder heat-transfer coefficient and the turbine efficiency multiplier).
Although quite good results can be obtained adopting of the Wiebe approach for the simulation of combustion, provided lookup tables can be built from combustion experimental data for its coefficients, the reliability of the 1-D approach can be improved to a great extent if a predictive combustion model is used for the heat-release calculations. In this case, the researcher has different options, within the fractal or non-fractal frameworks. Attention has mainly been focused on the authors' combustion model, but acceptable results can also be obtained with any model from the literature. In general, the accuracy of the overall simulation model depends on how the various sub-model results are combined.

5. References

Alkidas, A.C., "Heat Transfer Characteristics of a Spark-Ignition Engine," ASME Trans., Journal of Heat Transfer, Vol. 102, pp.189-193, 1980.

Badami, M., Millo, F., and Giaffreda, G., "Experimental and Computational Analysis of a High Performance Four-Stroke Motorcycle Engine Equipped with a Variable Geometry Exhaust System", SAE Paper 2002-01-001, 2002.

Baines, N.C., "Fundamentals of Turbocharging", Concepts NREC, White River Junction, Vermont, USA, 2005.

Baratta, M., d'Ambrosio, S., Spessa, E., and Vassallo, A., "Analysis of Cyclic Variability in a Bi-Fuel Engine By Means of a 'Cycle-Resolved' Diagnostic Technique", ASME Paper ICEF2005-1214, 2005 Fall Technical Conference of the ASME ICED, Ottawa, ON, Canada, September 11-14, 2005.

Baratta, M., Catania, A.E., Spessa, E., and Vassallo, A., "Development and Assessment of a Multizone Combustion Simulation Code for SI Engines Based on a Novel Fractal Model", SAE Paper No. 2006-01-0048, SAE 2006 World Congress, Detroit, MI, USA, April 3-6, 2006.

Baratta, M., Catania, A.E., d'Ambrosio, S., and Spessa, E., "Prediction of Combustion Parameters, Performance and Emissions in CNG and Gasoline SI Engines", ASME Transactions, Journal of Engineering for Gas Turbines and Power, Vol. 130, pp. 062805-1/11, 2008.

Baratta, M., and Spessa, E., "Turbocharged CNG Engines for Urban Transportation: Evaluation of Turbolag Reduction Strategies by means of Computational Analyses", ASME Paper No. ICES2009-76067, 2009 Spring Technical Conference of the ASME ICED, Milwaukee, Wisconsin, USA, May 3-6, 2009.

Baratta, M., Spessa, E., and Mairone, P., "Numerical Investigation of Turbolag Reduction In HD CNG Engines By Means Of Exhaust Valve Variable Actuation and Spark Timing Control", KSAE International Journal of Automotive Technology, Vol. 11 (3), pp. 289–306, 2010.

Blair, G.P., "Design and Simulation of Four Stroke Engines", SAE R-186 ISBN 0-7680-0440-3, 1999.

Blizzard, N.C., and Keck, J.C., "Experimental and Theoretical Investigation of Turbulent Burning Model for Internal Combustion Engines," SAE Paper No. 740191, 1974.

Bozza, F., Gimelli, A., Merola, S. S., and Vaglieco, B. M., "Validation of a Fractal Combustion Model Through Flame Imaging," SAE Paper No. 2005- 01-1120, 2005.

Brown, A.G., Stone, C.R., and Beckwith, P. "Cycle-by-Cycle Variations in Spark Ignition Engine Combustion - Part I: Flame Speed and Combustion Measurement and a Simplified Turbulent Combustion Model", SAE Paper No. 960612, 1996.

Catania, A.E., Misul, D., Mittica, A., and Spessa, E., "Unsteady Convection Model for Heat Release Analysis of IC Engine Pressure Data," SAE Transactions, Journal of Engines, Vol.109, pp.1610-1620, 2001.

Catania, A.E., Misul, D., Mittica, A., and Spessa, E., "A Refined Two-Zone Heat Release Model for Combustion Analysis in SI Engines," JSME International Journal, 2003, Series B, Vol. 46, No.1, pp. 75-85.

Catania, A. E., Misul, D., Spessa, E., and Vassallo, A., 2004, "A New Quasi-Dimensional Multizone Combustion Diagnostic Model for the Analysis of Heat Release, Flame

Propagation Parameters and Nitric Oxide Formation in SI Engines," Comodia '04, Yokohama, Japan, Aug. 2–5, JSME Paper No. 04-202.

D'Errico, G., Ferrari, G., Onorati, A., and Cerri, T., "Modeling the Pollutant Emissions from a S.I. Engine," SAE Paper No. 2002-01-0006, 2002.

Enomoto Y., and Furuhama, S., "A Study of the Local Heat Transfer Coefficient on the Combustion Chamber Walls of a Four-Stroke Gasoline Engine," JSME International Journal, Series II, Vol. 32, No. 1, pp.107-114, 1989.

Galindo, J., Luján, J.M., Serrano, J.R., Dolz, V., and Guilain, S., "Description of a Heat Transfer Model Suitable to Calculate Transient Processes of Turbocharged Diesel Engines With One-Dimensional Gas-Dynamic Codes", Applied Thermal Engineering, Vol.26, pp. 66–76, 2006.

Galindo, J., Luján, J.M., Serrano, J.R., Dolz, V., and Guilain, S., "Design of an Exhaust Manifold To Improve Transient Performance of a High-Speed Turbocharged Diesel Engine", Experimental Thermal and Fluid Science, Vol. 28, pp.863–875, 2004.

Gamma Technologies Inc., "GT-SUITE Engine Performance Application Manual", 2009.

Gülder, Ö.L., and Smallwood, G.J., "Inner Cutoff Scale of Flame Surface Wrinkling in Turbulent Premixed Flames," Combustion and Flame, Vol. 103, pp. 107-114, 1995.

Gülder, Ö.L., et. al., "Flame Front Surface Characteristics in Turbulent Premixed Propane/Air Combustion," Combustion and Flame, Vol. 120, pp. 407-416, 2000.

Gouldin, F.C., and Miles, P.C., "Chemical Closure and Burning Rates in Premixed Turbulent Flames", Combustion and Flame, Vol. 100, pp. 202-210, 1995.

Grill, M., Billinger, T., and Bargende, M., "Quasi-Dimensional Modeling of Spark Ignition Engine Combustion with Variable Valve Train" SAE Paper No. 2006-01-1107, SAE 2006 World Congress, Detroit, MI, USA, April 3-6, 2006.

Guezennec, Y.G., and Hamada, W., "Two-Zone Heat Release Analysis of Combustion Data and Calibration of Heat Transfer Correlation in an I.C. Engine," SAE Paper No. 1999-01-0218, 1999.

Hattrlel, T., Sheppard, C.G.W., Burluka, A.A., Neumeister, J., and Cairns, "Burn Rate Implications of Alternative Knock Reduction Strategies for Turbocharged SI Engines", SAE Paper No. 2006-01-1110, 2006.

Heywood, J.B., "Internal Combustion Engine Fundamentals," McGraw-Hill International Editions, 1988.

Hountalas, D.T., and Pariotis, E.G. "A Simplified Model for the Spatial Distribution of Temperature in a Motored DI Diesel Engine", SAE Paper no. 2001-01-1235; 2001.

Lefebvre, A., and Guilain, S., "Modelling and Measurement of the Transient Response of a Turbocharged SI Engine", SAE Paper 2005-01-0691, 2005. DOI 10.4271/2005-01-0691.

Lipatnikov, A.N., and Chomiak, J., "Turbulent Flame Speed and Thickness: Phenomenology, Evaluation, and Application in Multi-Dimensional Simulations", Progress in Energy and Combustion Science, Vol. 28, pp. 1-74, 2002.

Morel, T., and Keribar, R., "A Model for Predicting Spatially and Time Resolved Convective Heat Transfer in Bowl-in-Piston Combustion Chambers," SAE Paper 850204, 1985.

Morel, T., Rackmil, C., Keribar, R., and Jennings, M.J., "Model for Heat Transfer and Combustion in Spark Ignited Engines and its Comparison with Experiments", SAE Paper No. 880198; 1988.

North, G.L., and Santavicca, D.A., "The Fractal Nature of Premixed Turbulent Flames," Combustion Science and Technology, Vol. 72, pp. 215-232, 1990.

Onorati, A., Ferrari, G., D'Errico, G., and Montenegro, G., "The Prediction of 1D Unsteady Flows in the Exhaust System of a S.I. Engine Including Chemical Reactions in the Gas and Solid Phase", SAE Transactions, J. Engines, SAE paper 2002-01-0003; 2003.

Poulos, S.G., and Heywood, J.B., "The Effect of Chamber Geometry on Spark-Ignition Engine Combustion," SAE Paper No. 830334, 1983.

Sihling , K., and Woschni, G.: "Experimental Investigation of the Instantaneous Heat Transfer in the Cylinder of a High Speed Diesel Engine," SAE paper 790833, 1979.

Velherst, S., and Sheppard, C.G.W., "Multi-Zone Thermodynamic Modelling of Spark-Ignition Engine Combustion - An Overview", Energy Conversion and Management, Vol. 50, pp. 1326-1335, 2009.

Vítek, O., Macek, J., and Polàšek, M., "New Approach to Turbocharger Optimization using 1-D simulation tools", SAE Paper 2006-01-0438, 2006.

Wahiduzzaman, S., Morel, T., and Sheard, S., "Comparison of Measured and Predicted Combustion Characteristics of a Four-Valve SI Engine," SAE Paper No. 930613, 1993.

Watson, N., and Janota, M.S., "Turbocharging the Internal Combustion Engine", MacMillian, 1982.

Westin, F., and Ångström, H.E., "Simulation of a Turbocharged SI-Engine with Two Software and Comparison with Measured Data", SAE Paper No. 2003-01-3124, 2003.

Westin, F., Rosenqvist, J., and Ångström, H.E., "Heat Losses from the Turbine of a Turbocharged SI Engine - Measurements and Simulation", SAE Paper No. 2004-01-0996, 2004.

Westin, F., "Simulation of Turbocharged SI Engines–With Focus on the Turbine", Ph. D. Dissertation, The Royal Institute of Technology, Sweden, 2005.

Wilcox, D.C., "Turbulence Modeling for CFD", DCW Industries Inc., La Canada, California (USA), 1994.

Winkler, N., and Ångström, H.E., "Study of Measured and Model Based Generated Turbine Performance Maps within a 1D Model of a Heavy-Duty Diesel Engine Operated During Transient Conditions", SAE Paper No. 2007-01-0491, 2007.

Winterbone, D.E., and Pearson, R.J., "Design Techniques for Engine Manifolds", Professional Engineering Publishing, London, 1990.

Woschni, G., "A Universally Applicable Equation for the Instantaneous Heat Transfer Coefficient in the Internal Combustion Engine," SAE Trans., Vol. 76, pp.3065-3083, 1967.

Wu, C.M, Roberts, C.E., Matthews, R.D., and Hall, M.J., "Effects of Engine Speed on Combustion in SI Engines: Comparisons of Predictions of a Fractal Burning Model with Experimental Data", SAE Paper No. 932714, 1993.

Yoshiyama, S., Tomita, E., Zhang, Z., and Hamamoto, Y., "Measurement and Simulation of Turbulent Flame Propagation in a Spark Ignition Engine by Using Fractal Burning Model," SAE Paper No. 2001-01-3603, 2001.

13

Development of Two-Phase Flow Correlation for Fluid Mixing Phenomena in Boiling Water Reactor

Hiroyuki Yoshida and Kazuyuki Takase
Japan Atomic Energy Agency
Japan

1. Introduction

The two-phase fluid mixing phenomena in fuel bundles of BWR plays an important role in the thermal-hydraulic performance of the fuel rod bundle, because it has strong effects on spatial distributions of the void fraction, quality and mass flow rate within it. The subchannel analysis method has been used for the prediction of the macroscopic thermal-hydraulic characteristics, such as critical power and pressure loss, of a wide variety of fuel rod bundle designs. This method evaluates the fluid mixing effects using a unique model, known as a "cross flow model". The first successful cross flow model for gas-liquid two-phase flow was devised by Lahey and Moody (1993). In their model, cross flow phenomena were decomposed into three components, namely flow diversions caused by transverse pressure gradients, turbulent mixing caused by stochastic pressure and flow fluctuations and a void drift that is unique to gas-liquid two-phase flow.

Recently, there were studies of cross flow model improvements. Kawahara et al. (1999) presented an improved turbulent mixing model based on RMS (Root Mean Square) values of subchannel-to-subchannel differential pressure fluctuations. One of the advantages of this model was its ability to consider channel gap geometries and scales. Sumida et al.(1995) and Takemoto et al.(1997) supposed that the turbulent mixing and void drift phenomena were only transient components of the diversion cross flow caused by differential pressure fluctuations between the subchannels, and formulated the model known as the "fluctuating pressure model". Although both models appear promising for predicting the fluid mixing phenomena however, their applicability under actual plant operation conditions is presently unclear because it is impossible to simulate differential pressure fluctuations under steam-water high-pressure conditions without relying on experimental data. Although the cross flow model remains the most popular approach today, the mechanics of the third component, the void drift, are still unclear and there is no widely accepted understanding of it yet.

In the cross flow model and subchannel analysis, two-phase flow correlations are used to evaluate effects of flow conditions on two-phase flow characteristic easily. To create, modify or confirm these correlations, "actual scale tests" those simulate flow conditions and flow channel of actual fuel bundles are required. In actual BWR, pressure and temperature equals to about 7.2MPa and 560K respectively. Then the actual scale tests take a long time and

entail great cost, development of a method that enables the thermal-hydraulic design of BWRs without these actual size tests is desired.
It is expected that large scale numerical simulations (numerical simulations by large scale computer) would replace certain large-scale tests and thermal-hydraulic information, some of which is currently difficult or impossible to measure experimentally, would be obtained. And new design method will be developed based on these numerical simulations.
For this reason we developed an advanced thermal-hydraulic design method for BWRs using innovative two-phase flow simulation technology. For this, the following are required: (1) an advanced simulation method with high accuracy prediction, (2) verification of simulation method; and, (3) analytical method to confirm or modify the correlations by detailed numerical simulation data. In this study, we are developing the method to create or modify the two-phase flow correlations for the fluid mixing phenomena in BWR based on advanced numerical simulation technic.

2. Numerical simulation method

The fluid mixing phenomena dominates water and steam distribution in the fuel bundles and is one of the most important phenomena that affect boiling transition (BT) of BWRs. Surface tension at gas-liquid interface (interface), shapes of interfaces and pressure difference fluctuation between subchannels play important roles in these phenomena. Then an advanced simulation method developed in this study must evaluate surface tension, interface shape and pressure fluctuation accurately. To satisfy these requirements, we developed an advanced simulation code: TPFIT and an advanced interface tracking method. Detail of the TPFIT and the advanced interface tracking method are explained in this section.

2.1 Governing equation and numerical simulation

To calculate surface tension and interface shapes by realistic computational resources, the TPFIT adopt interface tracking method. In two-phase flow in rod bundles, compressibility of steam has important influence for pressure difference fluctuation between subchannels. In TPFIT, considering the time-dependent Navier-Stokes equation for two phase compressible flow, conservative equations of mass of liquid, mass of gas, momentum and energy are described as follows:
Mass of liquid:

$$\frac{\partial(\rho f)_l}{\partial t} + \frac{\partial u_k(\rho f)_l}{\partial x_k} = 0 \tag{1}$$

Mass of gas:

$$\frac{\partial(\rho f)_g}{\partial t} + \frac{\partial u_k(\rho f)_g}{\partial x_k} = 0 \tag{2}$$

Momentum:

$$\frac{\partial u_i}{\partial t} + u_k \frac{\partial u_i}{\partial x_k} = -\frac{\partial p}{\partial x_i} + \frac{1}{\rho}\frac{\partial \tau_{ik}}{\partial x_k} + g_i + \sigma_i \tag{3}$$

Energy:

$$\frac{\partial e}{\partial t}+u_k\frac{\partial e}{\partial x_k}=-\frac{p}{\rho}\frac{\partial u_k}{\partial x_k}+\frac{1}{\rho}\frac{\partial}{\partial x_k}\left(\lambda\frac{\partial T}{\partial x_k}\right)+q \tag{4}$$

where u, p, e, T are velocity, static pressure, internal energy and temperature, and g and σ in the momentum equation are gravity and surface tension force, respectively. In above equations, subscripts g and l are used to represent gas and liquid phases. The mass of liquid and gas phases in two phase flow are defined as following equation.

$$\begin{aligned}(\rho f)_l &= \rho_l f_l \\ (\rho f)_g &= \rho_g f_g\end{aligned} \tag{5}$$

In Eq. (5), f is volume fraction of fluid, and Volume fraction of gas phase is evaluated by use of volume fraction of liquid.

$$f_g = 1 - f_l \tag{6}$$

Two-phase fluid density ρ is calculated as sum of mass of both phases:

$$\rho = (\rho f)_l + (\rho f)_g \tag{7}$$

Eqs. (1) and (2) are solved in the advanced interface tracking method described in sec.2.2. The momentum equation (Eq. (3)) is solved by the CIP (Cubic Interpolated Pseudo-particle) method (Yabe and Aoki, 1991). The energy equation (Eq. (4)) is used to obtain the Poison equation for static pressure. Temperature is estimated by means of a fluid property routine based on the static pressure and local density of both phases. The ILUCGS method is used to solve the Poison equation for static pressure. In the TPFIT code, a Cartesian coordinate system and staggered grid are used. The surface tension force in the momentum equation is estimated using the CSF model (Blackbill et al., 1992). In the CSF model, volume fraction of liquid f_l is required and evaluated in the advanced interface tracking method, too. The local viscosities and thermal conductivities of liquid and gas were evaluated using solved static pressure and temperature fields based on the fluid property routine.

2.2 Outline of advanced interface tracking method

The fundamental concept of the advanced interface tracking method is quite simple. That is, a transported volume of liquid and gas between neighboring calculation control volumes during each time step is calculated through the movement of approximated gas-liquid interfaces, as estimated in the Lagrangian system. Schematic drawings of the major three operational steps within each time step in the two-dimensional case are shown in Figure 1.

In the first step (reconstruction step), as shown in Figure 1 (a), a gas-liquid interface in each control area for calculations is reconstructed, taking account of the liquid fraction represented by it and its surroundings. In the reconstruction step, the gas-liquid interface is approximated by a linear function: $F(\mathbf{x})$ as same as PLIC (Gueyffier, et al., 1999) method (see Fig.2 for 3-dimensional case). The function $F(\mathbf{x})$ is expressed as follows:

$$F(\mathbf{x}) = \sum_{i=1}^{n_m} a_i x_i + b,\ \mathbf{x} = (x_1, x_2, x_3) \tag{8}$$

In the equation, n_m represents dimension of simulation, and is 2 or 3. x_i is the coordinate position of the definition point of scalar quantities. A unit normal vector to the interface $\mathbf{a}=(a_1,a_2,a_3)$ and segment b in Eq.(8) must be estimated.
To evaluate the function $f(\mathbf{x})$, we assumed that the interface exists in the position where volume fraction of liquid f_l equals to 0.5. By least-squares method (choose eight nearest neighbors for 2-dimensional case, 26 nearest neighbors for 3-dimensional case), linear function is obtained.

$$F(\mathbf{x}) = f_l - 0.5 = \sum_{i=1}^{n_m} a_i x_i + b_0 \tag{9}$$

In the equation, b_0 is segment of linear function evaluated by least square method. Control volume is divided into two polyhedrons by the linear functions. If gray polyhedron in Fig.2 corresponds to liquid region in control volume, volume of this polyhedron: V_l must be equals to proper volume of liquid. Thus,

$$V_l = f_l \Delta V \tag{10}$$

where ΔV is a volume of computational cell given by following equation for 3-dimensional cases.

$$\Delta V = \Delta x_1 \cdot \Delta x_2 \cdot \Delta x_3 \tag{11}$$

To satisfy Eq. (10), the segment b is adjusted as fraction $V_l/\Delta V$ agrees with volumetric fraction of fluid. Between the volume of fluid V_l and segment b, there is the relation that is expressed as the following equation for three dimensional cases.

$$V_m = \frac{1}{6a_1a_2a_3}\left\{ b^3 - \sum_{i=1}^{3}\left[\max\left(b - a_i\Delta x_i, 0\right)\right]^3 - \sum_{i=1}^{3}\left[\max\left(b - b_m + a_i\Delta x_i, 0\right)\right]^3 \right\} \tag{12}$$

In this equation, b_m is the maximum value that b can take:

$$b_m = \sum_{i=1}^{3} a_i \Delta x_i \ . \tag{13}$$

In this study, the Newton's method is used to estimate the segment b that satisfies Eq. (12).
In the next step (transportation step), polyhedrons within each control volume are transported along a surrounding velocity field (Fig.1 (b)). Some parts of the volume of this polyhedron are transported to surrounding control volume. For example, in Fig.1(b), δV is transferred from control volume 1 to control volume 2. Each transferred volume of liquid is calculated in this step. And each transferred volume of gas is also calculated by a procedure same as the volume of liquid.

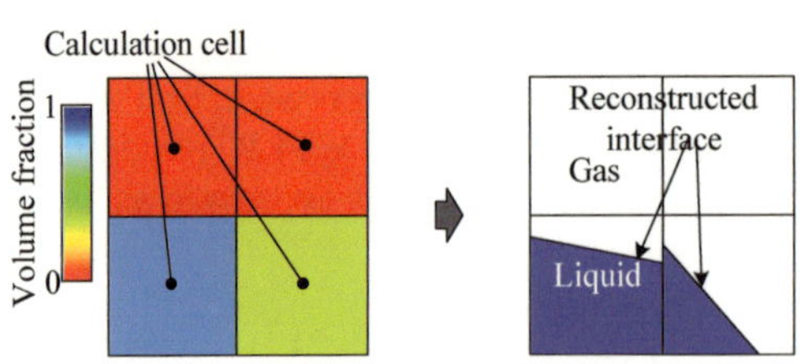

Fig. 1. (a) Reconstruction step

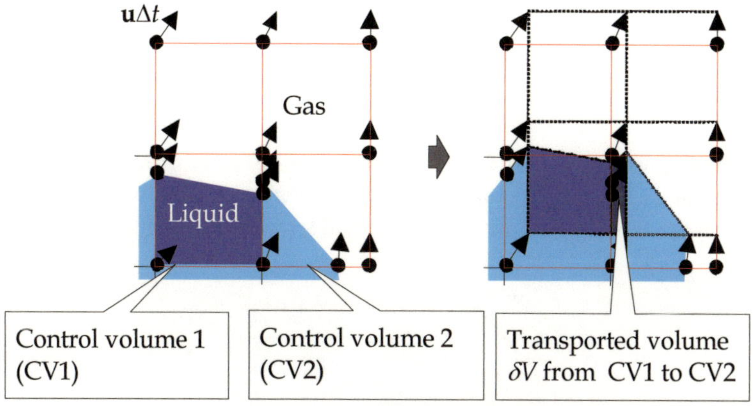

(b) Transportation step

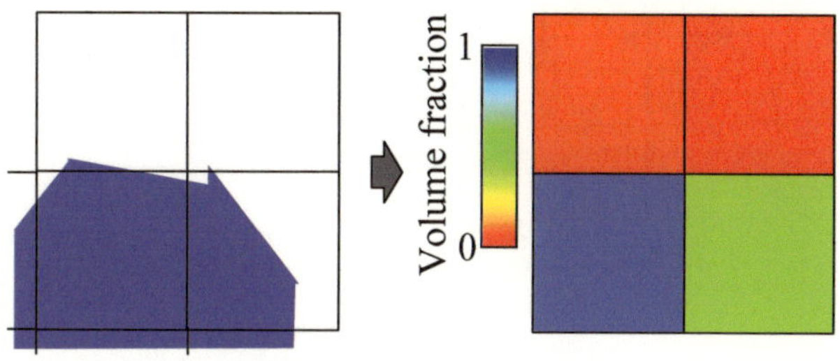

(c) Redistribution step

Fig. 1. Schematic drawings of volume fraction transport calculation using the advanced interface tracking method (2-dimensional case).

In transportation step, transfer volume of both phases is calculated. In the last step (redistribution step), as shown in Fig.1(c), transferred mass of both phases can be evaluated by multiplying density by transferred volume. Mass at new time step can be calculated by summing these transferred mass.

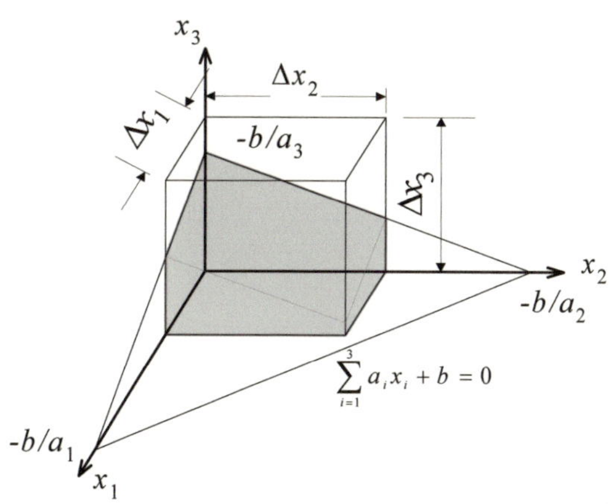

Fig. 2. Approximated fluid segment in control volume (3-dimensional case).

3. Validation of TPFIT for fluid mixing phenomena

We try to validate the TPFIT with the advanced interface tracking method developed in this study for fluid mixing phenomena.

3.1 Verification and validation of TPFIT for simple flow configuration

Before validate the TPFIT for fluid mixing phenomena, we check basic performance of the TPFIT for two-phase flow by performing numerical simulation in simple flow configuration

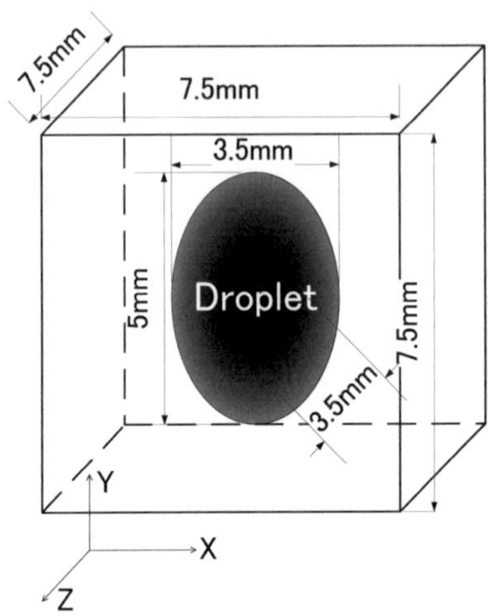

Fig. 3. Initial arrangement of droplet.

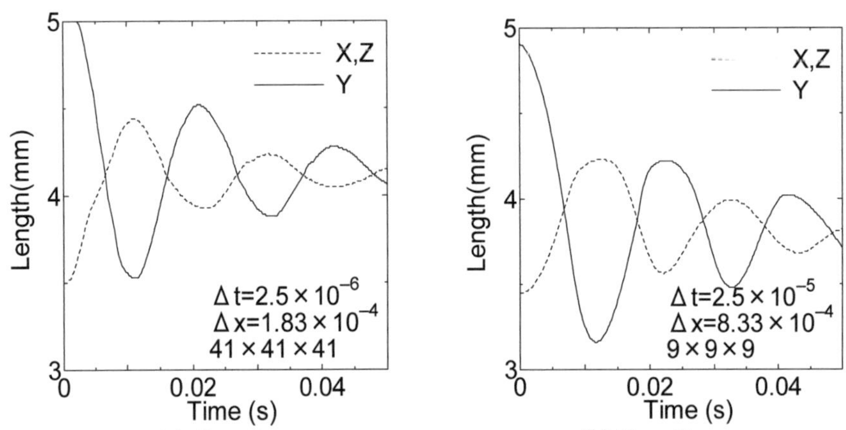

(a) Case A (b) Case B

Fig. 4. Time change of diameters of droplet.

3.1.1 Vibrating droplet under the zero gravity

In order to verify the potential of the advanced interface tracking method, 3-dimensional analyses of the vibration of a liquid drop under zero gravity were carried out. Initial arrangement of the droplet is shown in Fig.3. In the simulations, two computational grids were used, one is a fine grid (41×41×41, case A) and another is a course grid (9×9×9, case B). Time changes of diameters of the droplet are shown in Fig.4. The vibration cycle is about 0.022 seconds and agrees with the theoretical value that expressed as following equation (Rayleigh, 1879).

$$\tau = \pi\sqrt{\frac{\rho_l r^3}{2\sigma}} \tag{14}$$

The results of the case A and those of the case B are almost the same, and the effect of the different grid number is small. The diffusion at the gas-liquid interface was not observed. Then we confirmed the effectiveness of the advanced interface tracking method.

3.1.2 Liquid film falling down on inclined flat plate

In the fluid mixing phenomena, bubble, bubble/slug, slug and slug/churn flow are important. However, in slug flow, liquid film is observed between slug bubble and wall. Then verification of the TPFIT must be performed for film flow.

The TPFIT code was applied to numerical simulation of liquid film falling down on inclined flat plate. Simulations were performed with the same conditions as the experiment by Moran et al. (2003) (see Fig.5). Physical properties of the liquid were as follows: kinematic viscosity, ν_l=2×10^{-5} m^2/s, density, ρ_l=960 kg/m^3, and surface tension, σ=2.06×10^{-2} N/m. And air properties at 300K and atmospheric pressure were used as gas properties. On all walls, non-slip boundary condition was assigned, and inlet pressure was fixed at atmospheric pressure.

The flow conditions were summarized in Table 1. The analysis conditions were set up to compare the probability density function (PDF) of local film thickness with the experimental results. In the table 1, δ_N represents Nusselt's mean film thickness (Nusselt, 1916), and is evaluated by the following equation:

$$\delta_N = \left(\frac{3\nu_l J}{g_z}\right)^{1/3} \tag{15}$$

In this equation, g_z is flow direction acceleration by gravity force, and J is mass flow rate of the liquid.

Case	Inlet flow rate J (l/min)	Film Reynolds number	δ_{ave_exp}	δ_{ave_cal}	δ_N
1	0.333	13	0.91	0.85	0.84
2	2.55	106	1.73	1.67	1.66
3	5.45	220	2.31	2.15	2.14

Table 1. Numerical conditions.

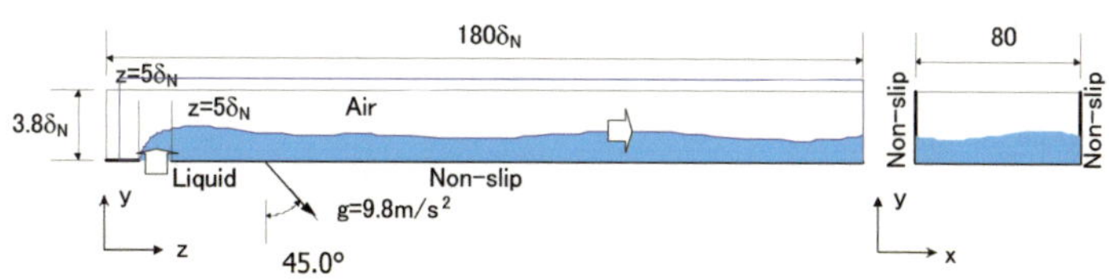

Fig. 5. Analytical geometry of a liquid film.

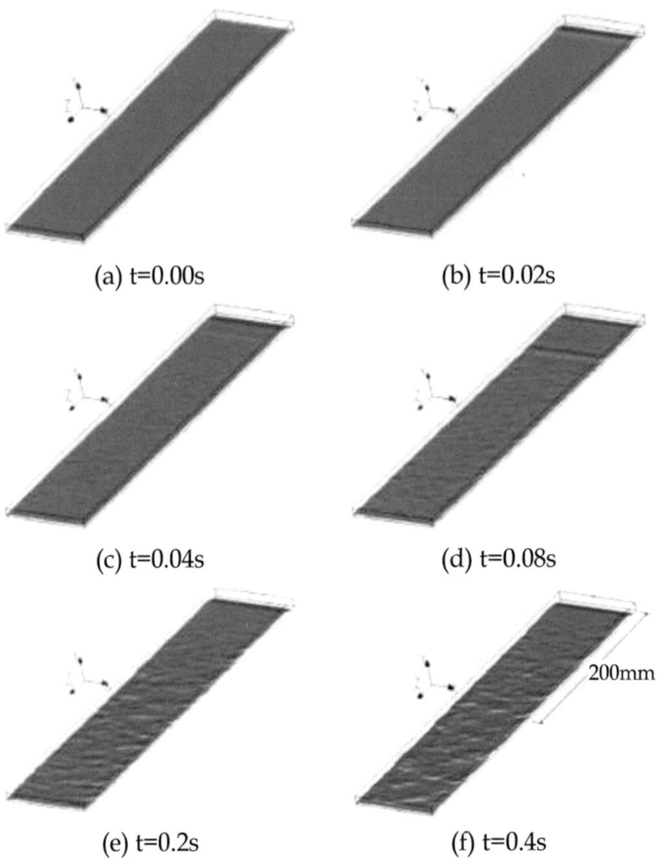

Fig. 6. Observed liquid film shapes.

Figure 6 shows snapshot of the numerical results of the Case 3. In this study, the calculated gas-liquid interfaces were defined as isosurface at a volume fraction of liquid of 0.5. In 0.02s, two-dimensional wave was observed near liquid inlet section, and this wave moves to the downstream section. From 0.04 seconds later, small three-dimensional waves occurred on the surface of the liquid film. After that, these small waves gradually becomes big until t=0.2s. At t=0.4s, the liquid film exhibited a smooth, flat gas-liquid interface upon immediate entrance to the test section, but after a short distance small, small ripples were observed at the interface. At approximately 200mm (about z=100 δ_N) from the inlet, the small ripples developed into a three-dimensional structure characterized by large waves, and wave structures were almost developed at this point. In general, the degree of waviness increased with increasing film Reynolds number. The average local film thicknesses in the numerical result (δ_{ave_cal}) at x=20mm and z=175 δ_N are shown in Table 1 and almost agreed with Nusselt's mean film thickness. However, δ_{ave_cal} were slightly smaller than the average film thickness in the experimental results (δ_{ave_exp}).

The probability density functions (PDF) of liquid film thickness at x=20mm and z=175 δ_N were evaluated to compare numerical results with the experimental results quantitatively. Figure 7 shows the PDF of film thickness. At low Reynolds numbers (Re_f=13), the PDF distributions showed a sharp peak (first peak) at about average film thickness, but remained close to zero for greater thickness values, indicating existence of few waves. At low film Reynolds number, the position and height of the first peak agreed well in the analysis and experiment.

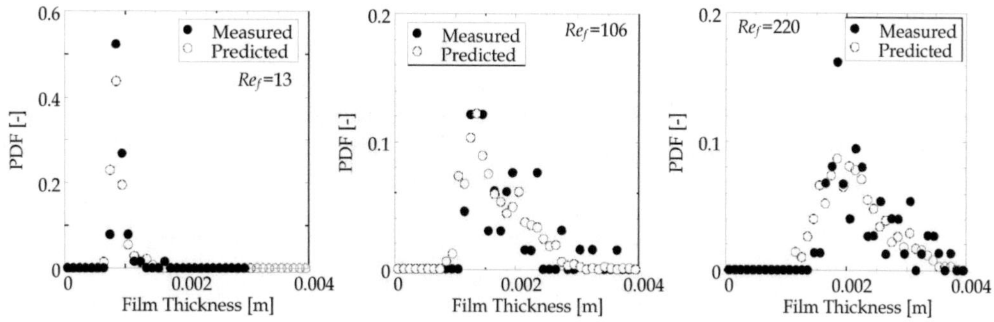

(a) Case 1 (b) Case 2 (c) Case 3

Fig. 7. Probability density function of liquid film thickness.

In the experimental results, at relatively high Reynolds number (Re_f=106 and 220), additional smaller peaks (second peaks) appeared to the right of the main peaks. Because the sampling numbers (n_s) used in the processing of the experimental data (n_s = 60) were smaller than those in the numerical results (n_s =1200), scattered results were observed in the experimental PDF distributions. As shown in Fig.8, the numerical result agreed well with the experimental result including existence of second peaks and these positions. The predicted values of minimum liquid film thickness by the numerical simulations were slightly smaller than those measured by the experiments without relying on the mass flow rate of the liquid. It is thought that because the predicted minimum liquid film thicknesses were thin, the average liquid film thicknesses became smaller in comparison with the experimental results.

3.1.3 Bubbly and slug flow in square duct

By two-phase correlations for fluid mixing phenomena, volume or mass cross flow rate or mixing coefficients are evaluated. Then volume and mass conservation of two-phase flow is important function. As mentioned above, volume conservation equations for both phases are not solved, and the TPFIT has no special treatment to keep volume conservation. Then we must check volume conservation of the TPFIT. In two-phase flow fluid mixing phenomena, the maximum value of mixing gas flow rate is around 10% of gas flow rate in flow channel. An error of the volume conservation must be done below 1% if we want to predict mixing coefficient with accuracy of less than 10%.

Case	Fluid	Inlet	Inlet void fraction: α_{in}	Inlet velocity: w_{in}
1	Air-water at 0.1MPa and 300K	A	0.307	0.5 m/s
2		B	0.111	
3	Steam-water at 7.2MPa and 560K	A	0.307	
4		B	0.111	

Table 2. Numerical condition for bubbly flow in square duct.

To check volume conservation, the TPFIT was applied to bubbly and slug flow in square duct. Numerical domain is shown in Fig.8 (a), and numerical conditions are shown in table 2. In the simulations, air-water and steam-water two-phase flow were used. Air-water two-phase flow at atmospheric pressure is used as working fluid in many experimental researches, and the TPFIT was applied to these experiments for validation. Then we used in this simulation. Steam-water two-phase flow at 7.2MPa and 560K (saturation temperature at 7.2MPa) is appeared in real (actual) reactor conditions. Two-phase flow correlations will be checked or examined at this conditions, we also used in this simulation. On all walls, non-slip boundary condition was assigned, and inlet velocity and volume fraction of liquid were fixed. Outlet pressure was also fixed at atmospheric pressure or 7.2MPa.

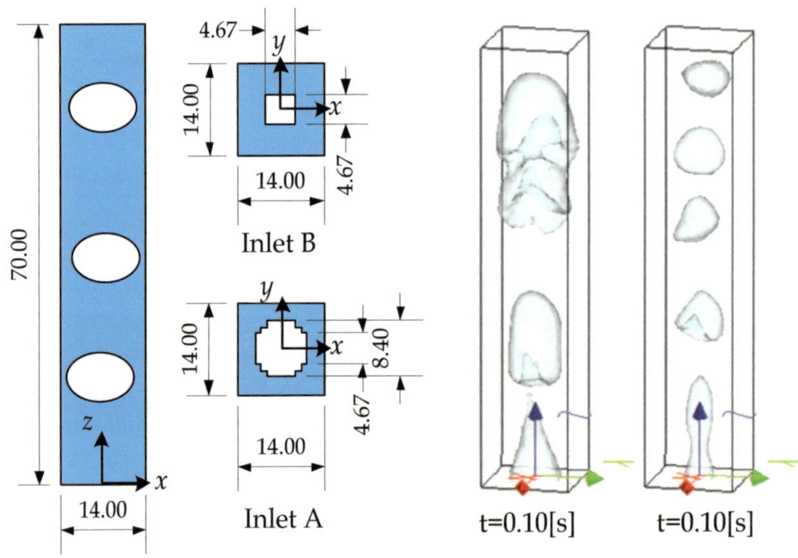

(a) Numerical Domain (b) Example of Interface shape

Fig. 8. Numerical domain and example of interface shape.

Figure.8 (b) shows example of interface shapes. Different two-phase flows were formed in a square duct by the difference in inlet volume fraction. And complicated interface shapes were observed in higher volume fraction case (Case 1). Figure 9 shows evaluated volume conservation error. In this figure, E_{vol} was volume conservation error and defined as following equation.

$$E_{vol} = \frac{Vol_g}{Vol_{g,in}} - 1, \tag{16}$$

where Vol_g is calculated total gas volume in a square duct by use of simulated results. And $Vol_{g,in}$ is total gas volume calculated by use of inlet condition of simulations:

$$Vol_{g,in} = \alpha_{in} \cdot w_{in} \cdot A \cdot t, \tag{17}$$

where, A is area of square duct (=14×14=196mm^2), t is time. In Case 1 and 2, differences between gas density and liquid density was relatively large, and effects of compressibility of gas was also large. Then, large fluctuation of E_{vol} in Case 1 and 2 was observed. However, except these fluctuations, the maximum value of volume conservation error: E_{vol} were less than 0.2%. Therefore, it was confirmed that the TPFIT has enough performance of volume conservation to simulate two-phase flow fluid mixing phenomena.

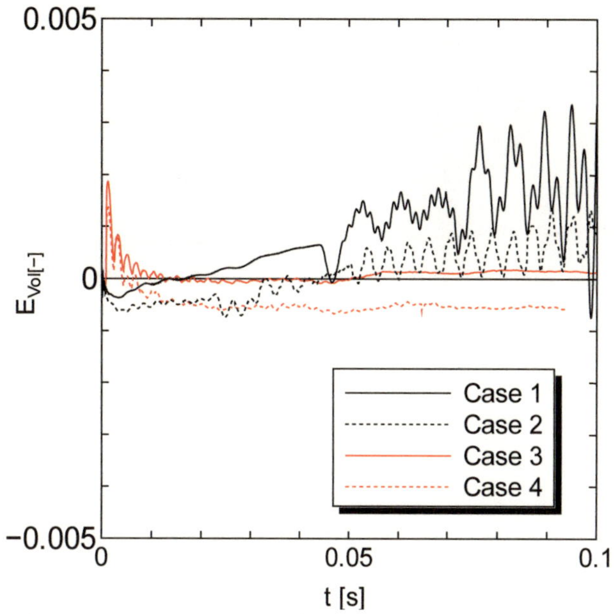

Fig. 9. Evaluated volume conservation error for two-phase flow in square duct.

3.2 Verification for fluid mixing phenomena by experimental data

In the next step, we must validate TPFIT for fluid mixing phenomena. To evaluate TPFIT performance for two-phase flow fluid mixing phenomena between the subchannels, numerical simulations for two-phase flow fluid mixing tests were performed.

3.2.1 Air-water fluid mixing test

TPFIT code was applied to 2-channel air-water mixing tests (Yoshida, 2007). The dimension of calculated test channel is shown in Fig.10 (a). The test channel, which consists of two parallel subchannels with an 8×8 mm square cross section and the interconnection, is 220 mm long and air and water flow upwards in it. The interconnection's gap clearance, horizontal and vertical length are 1.0 mm, 5.0 mm and 20 mm respectively. An irregular mesh division in the Cartesian system was adopted and two subchannels and the interconnection were formed by using obstacles as shown in Fig.11. The total number of effective control volumes was 428,680 respectively. The fluid mixing was observed at interconnection in the experiments. A non-slip wall, constant exit pressure and constant inlet velocity were selected as boundary conditions for each subchannel. The time step was controlled with a typical safety factor of 0.2 to keep it lower than the limitation value given by the Courant condition and stability condition of the CSF model. Calculation conditions are shown in Table 3.

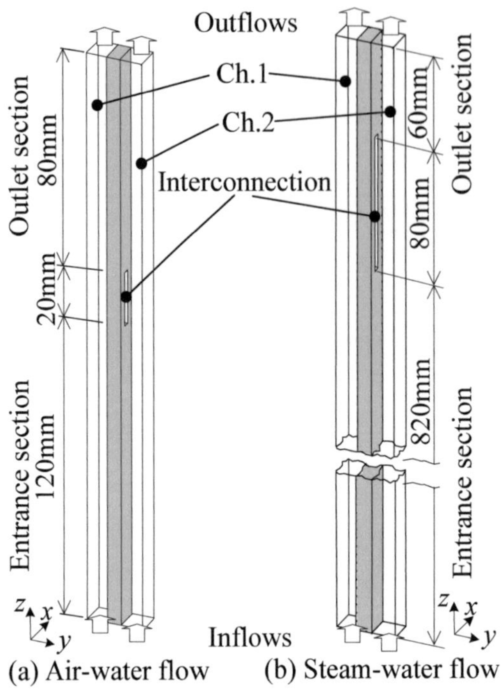

Fig. 10. Calculated test channel.

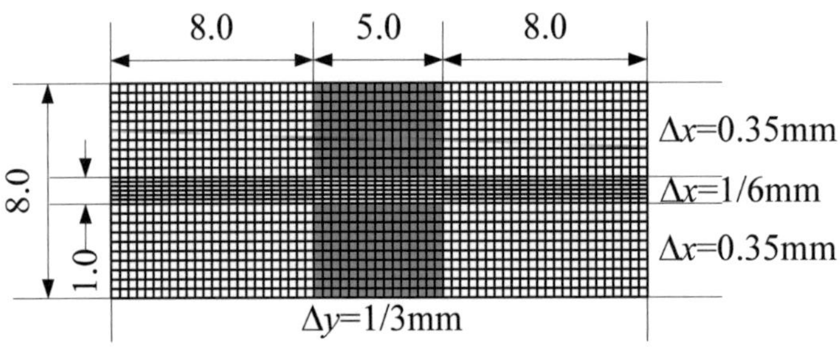

Fig. 11. Calculation meshes in channel cross section for air-water fluid mixing test.

Water inlet velocity (m/s)		Injected air volume (cc)	
Ch.1	Ch.2	Ch.1	Ch.2
0.26	0.26	1.27	1.50

Table 3. Air-water flow calculation condition.

The slug behavior observed around the interconnection is shown in Fig.12 (a). Once the top of an ascending air slug in Ch.1 reaches the center height of the interconnection, part of it starts to be drawn toward Ch. 2. Then the tip of stretched part of the air slug flows into Ch.2 through the interconnection and is separated to form a single bubble. The calculated air slug behavior is shown in Fig.12 (b). As shown in Fig.12 (b), any intrusion of air into the interconnection as well as any separation of the air slug can be effectively calculated. The moved bubble volumes from Ch.1 to Ch.2 were estimated to be 0.087cc in the observation and 0.094cc in the calculation.

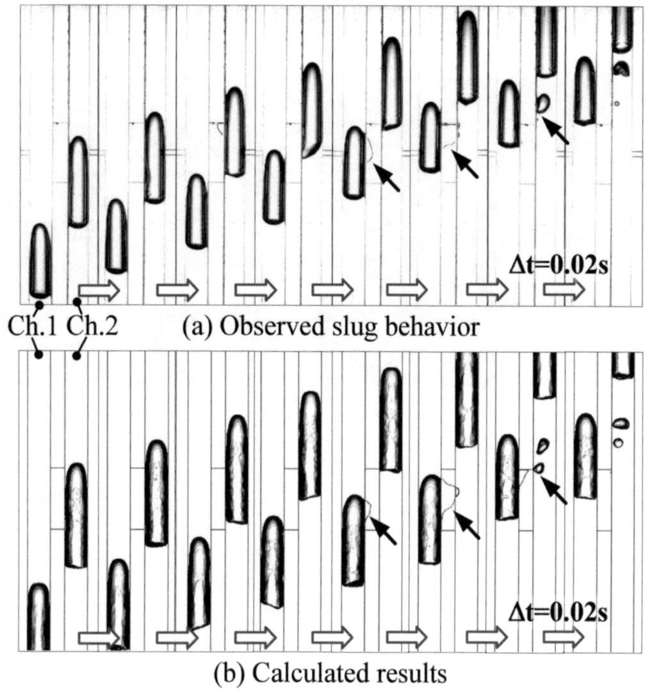

Fig. 12. Observed and calculated slug behavior of air-water fluid mixing test around the interconnection.

3.2.2 Steam-water fluid mixing under high pressure

The TPFIT was applied to steam water fluid mixing test (Yoshida, 2007). Calculated test channels used in these simulations are shown in Fig.10 (b). The calculation conditions are shown in Table 4. An irregular mesh division in the Cartesian system was adopted and two subchannels and the interconnection were formed by using obstacles as shown in Fig.13. The total number of effective control volumes was 2,647,400 respectively. A non-slip wall, constant exit pressure, and constant inlet velocity were selected as boundary conditions for each subchannel.

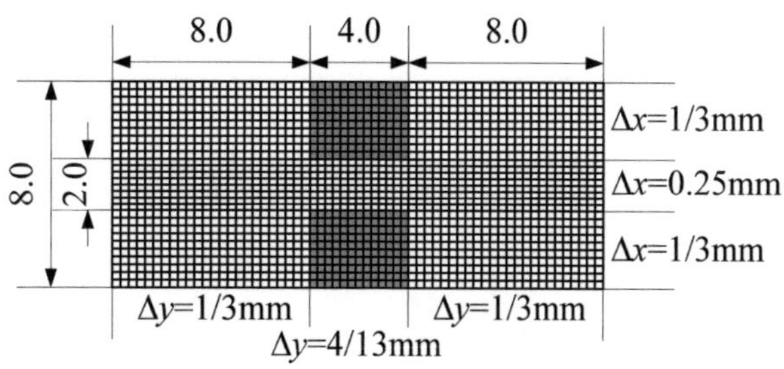

Fig. 13. Calculation meshes in channel cross section for steam-water fluid mixing test.

Inlet mass flow rate (kg/s)		Inlet quality (%)	
Ch.1	Ch.2	Ch.1	Ch.2
0.44	0.23	0.0	0.47

Table 4. Steam-water flow calculation condition.

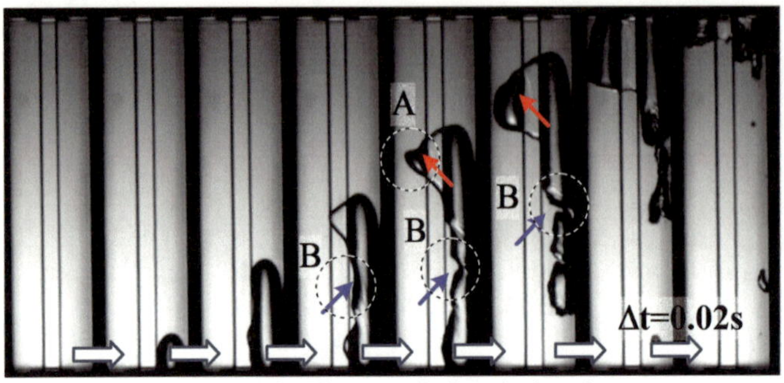

(a) Observed slug behavior

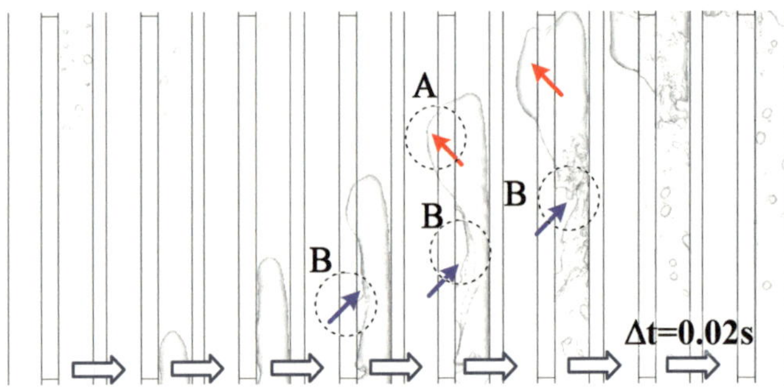

(b) Calculated results

Fig. 14. Observed and calculated slug behavior of steam-water fluid mixing test around the interconnection.

The slug behaviors observed and calculated around the interconnection is shown in Fig.14. As shown in Fig.14 (a), a part of single steam slug in Ch.2 intrudes to the Ch.1 through the interconnection. Averaged slug length is about 56 mm, and observed major slug characteristic behavior is as follows.

- Steam intrusion from Ch.2 to Ch.1 is firstly occurred at the upper part of the steam slug ("A" in the Fig.14).
- Constriction is generated at the center part of the steam slug by water flow from Ch1 to Ch.2, and the steam slug break up ("B" in the Fig.14).

As shown in Fig.14 (b), the occurrence of intrusion of steam from the Ch.2 to the Ch.1 can be effectively calculated, and the calculated amount of steam penetration into the interconnection looks quite similar to the observed one. Predicted slug length is about 59 mm, and almost same as the observed one. As shown in Fig.14 (b), the major slug characteristic behavior observed in the experiment was reproduced in the numerical simulation by TPFIT code.

The measured and calculated differential pressure and cross flow rate between Ch.1 and Ch.2 for steam-water flow are shown in Figs.15 and 16 respectively. The calculated values of the differential pressure and the cross flow rate agreed well with the measured values.

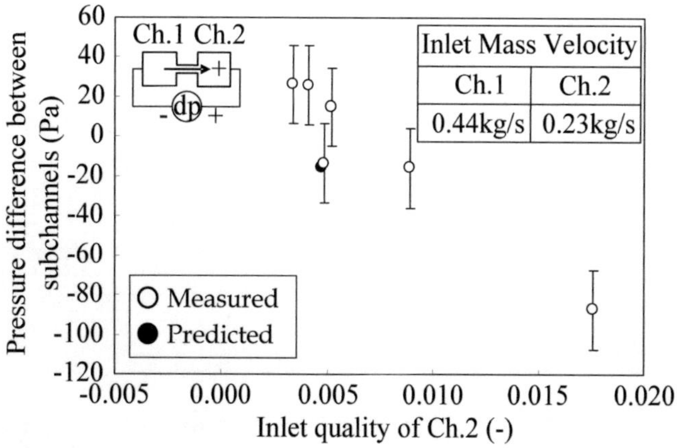

Fig. 15. Measured and calculated pressure difference between subchannels.

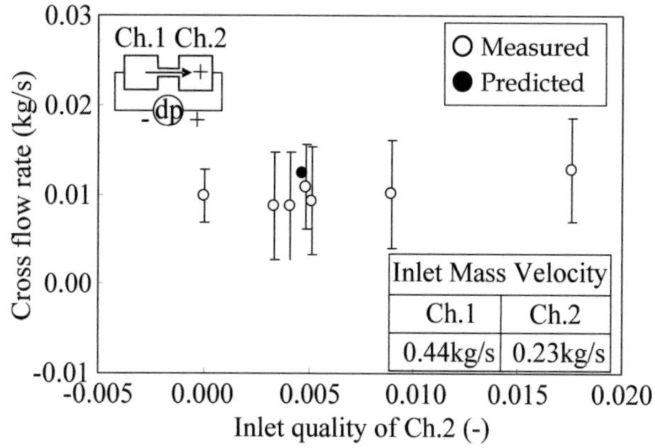

Fig. 16. Measured and calculated pressure difference between subchannels.

3.2.3 Numerical simulation of air-water two-phase flow in modeled 2 subchannels

The TPFIT code was applied to experimental analyses of the existing 2-channel fluid mixing experiments (Sumida, 1995), and comparisons between measured and calculated results were carried. In the experiments, the differential pressure between the subchannel at the center height of the mixing section and the exit air and water flow rate of each subchannel were measured.

Numerical analyses of air-water flow fluid mixing were applied between the length of -100mm and +60mm from the lower edge of the mixing section in the flow direction of the test channel as shown in Fig.17 (a). The flow area is divided into two channels by a flat plate (partition plate). At the upper part of the partition plate, there was a narrow slit, through which the channels were connected. The flow channel was divided into 3 parts, developing section, mixing section and outlet section. The narrow slit was located in the mixing section, and fluid mixing was occurred at this section. The developing section was set up to get developed flow at inlet of the mixing section. The outlet section was located at top of the calculated test channel to let out air-water two-phase flow smoothly.

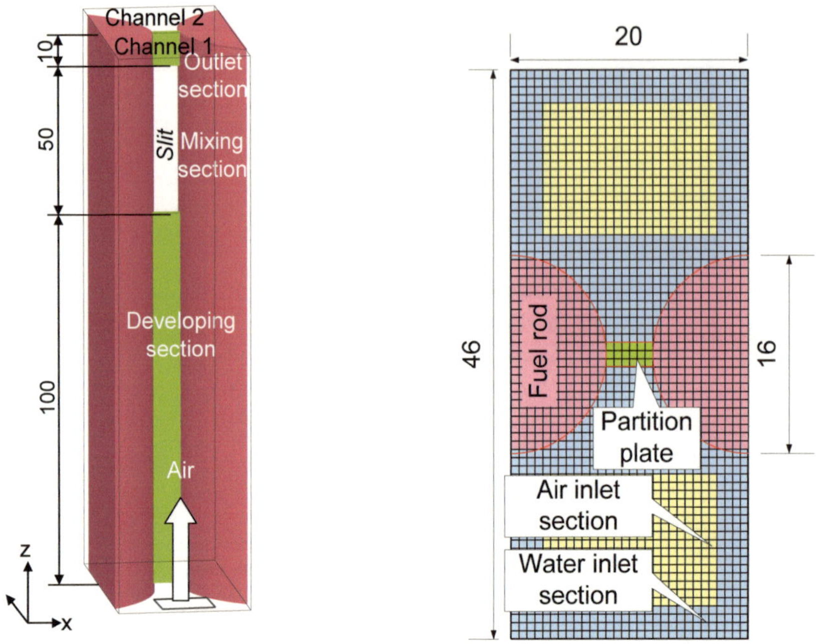

(a) Calculated test channel (b) Calculation mesh

Fig. 17. Dimensions of calculated test channel and calculation meshes in channel cross section for air-water two-phase flow.

Regular mesh division in the Cartesian system was adopted and two subchannels and the interconnection were formed by using obstacles as shown in Fig.17 (b). The calculation mesh size was set to 2/3 mm to satisfy the condition that the number of the calculation meshes of gap region must be more than 6, and the total number of the calculation meshes was 496,800. A non-slip wall, constant exit pressure and constant inlet velocity were selected as boundary conditions for each subchannel. The effects of the contact angle of the water on the channel walls were set to 15 degree.

<table>
<tr><th rowspan="2">Case</th><th colspan="2">Inlet liquid mass flux (kg/m^{2}s)</th><th colspan="2">Inlet quality (%)</th></tr>
<tr><th>Ch.1</th><th>Ch.2</th><th>Ch.1</th><th>Ch.2</th></tr>
<tr><td>L1</td><td colspan="2" rowspan="4">370</td><td rowspan="4">0.0013</td><td>0.0007</td></tr>
<tr><td>L2</td><td>0.0013</td></tr>
<tr><td>L3</td><td>0.0019</td></tr>
<tr><td>L4</td><td>0.0026</td></tr>
<tr><td>H1</td><td colspan="2" rowspan="4">277</td><td rowspan="4">0.0022</td><td>0.0011</td></tr>
<tr><td>H2</td><td>0.0022</td></tr>
<tr><td>H3</td><td>0.0033</td></tr>
<tr><td>H4</td><td>0.0044</td></tr>
</table>

Table 5. Air-water flow calculation condition.

Air and water were injected through the air and water inlet section located at lower part of the modeled test channel (see Fig.17 (a)). The area of the air and water inlet section was constant, and the inlet air and water velocities were varied to simulate experimental conditions. Eight cases of air-water two-phase flow simulations were performed and calculation conditions were summarized in Table 5. In the simulation, inlet liquid mass flux for 2 subchannels was same. Outlet pressure and inlet temperature of air and water is set to atmospheric pressure and room temperature respectively. In the case H1 to H4, inlet liquid mass flux was set to 370 (kg/s), and inlet quality was relatively low. In the case H1 to 4, inlet liquid mass flux was set to 277 (kg/s), and inlet quality was relatively high. Then, we describe case L1 to L4 with "low quality cases", and case H1 to H4 with "high quality cases".

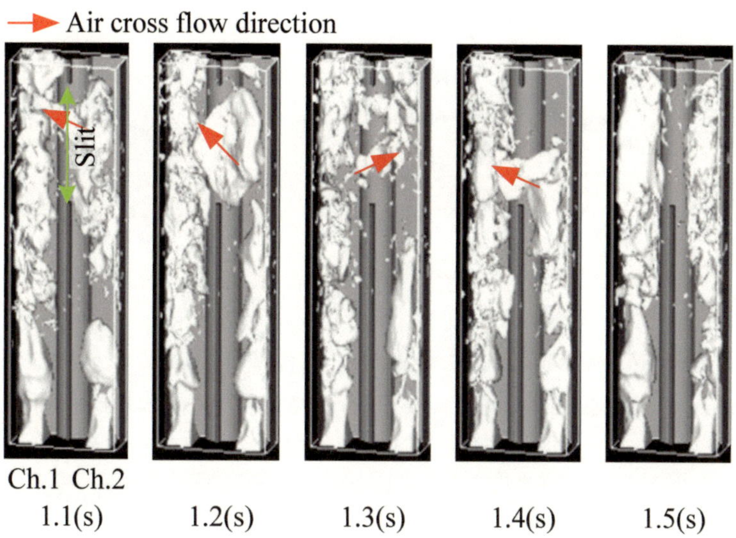

Fig. 18. Observed and calculated slug behavior of case H1.

Example of the calculated slug behaviors in the test channel are shown in Fig.18. As shown in Fig.18, the fluid mixing was observed at the gap between the subchannels. The measured and calculated differential pressure between the 2 subchannels is shown in Fig.19. The pressure differences at the longitudinal center of the mixing section were measured and calculated. In the figure, time averaged values ("Average") and standard deviation of fluctuating values ("Fluctuation" in the figure) of differential pressure are shown. The degree of fluctuation of values was evaluated by the following equation:

$$\sigma_{\Delta p} = \sqrt{\left(\Delta p_T - \Delta p_S\right)^2} \tag{18}$$

where,

$$\Delta p_S = \overline{\Delta p_T} \tag{19}$$

Δp_t: instantaneous value of differential pressure.
Δp_s: time averaged value of differential pressure
Underestimations tended to be made in cases of low inlet quality, but the numerical results agreed well with the experimental results, both qualitatively and quantitatively.

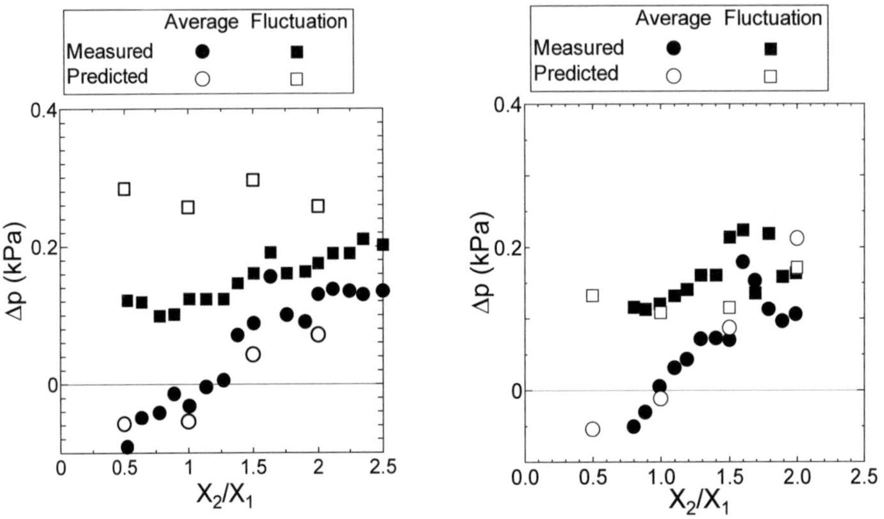

(a) Low quality case (Case L1~L4) (b) High quality case (Case H1~H4)

Fig. 19. Measured and calculated pressure difference between subchannels.

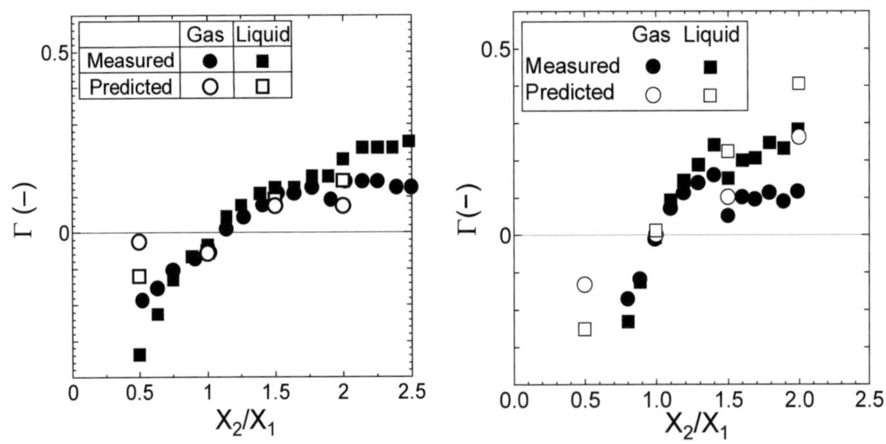

(a) Low quality case (Case L1~L4) (b) High quality case (Case H1~H4)

Fig. 20. Measured and calculated mixing coefficient.

The measured and calculated mixing coefficients of both phases for air-water cases are shown in Fig.20. The mixing coefficients of gas and liquid are defined as below (Sumida, 1995):

$$\Gamma_m = \frac{w_m}{W_{m1} + W_{m2}} \tag{20}$$

where,
W_{m1}: Inlet mass flow rate of m phase for channel 1
W_{m2}: Inlet mass flow rate of m phase for channel 2
w_m: Moved mass flow rate from channel 1 to channel 2
Underestimations tended to be made in cases of low inlet quality, but the numerical results agreed well the experimental results. These underestimations of mixing coefficients corresponded to those of differential pressure. It seems that a main cause of underestimations was overestimation of the flow resistance in the gap region due to insufficient spatial resolution when gas velocity is relatively low.

4. Development of two-phase flow correlation for fluid mixing phenomena

4.1 Evaluation of existing correlations for fluid mixing phenomena

Innovative water reactor for flexible fuel cycle (FLWR) is one of new generation light water reactor and has been developed at Japan Atomic Energy Agency (Uchikawa, 2007). In order to achieve a conversion ratio higher than unity, a hexagonal tight-lattice rod bundle with about 1mm of gap width was adopted. Due to narrower rod gaps and the channels being surrounded by rods, bubble/slug-to-bubble/slug and bubble/slug-to-wall interactions may occur more frequently within the FLWRs core than in those of current BWRs, and these may affect the two-fluid mixing characteristics by way of the deformation, separation and coalescence of bubbles/slugs caused by the interactions.

4.1.1 Analytical conditions

In this section, to evaluate the existing two-phase flow correlation for fluid mixing phenomena, two-phase flow in 2 modeled subchannels for BWRs and FLWRs fuel bundles were performed ("BWR cases" and "FLWR cases"). For this, 16 cases of two-phase flow simulations were performed (see table 6 and 7).

Case	Inlet liquid mass flux (kg/m^{2}s)		Inlet quality (%)	
	Ch.1	Ch.2	Ch.1	Ch.2
B1	1400		0.0067	0.0264
B2			0.0134	
B3			0.0264	
B4			0.0513	
B5			0.0184	0.0362
B6			0.0362	
B7			0.0533	
B8			0.0699	

Table 6. Calculation conditions for fluid mixing phenomena in BWRs fuel bundle.

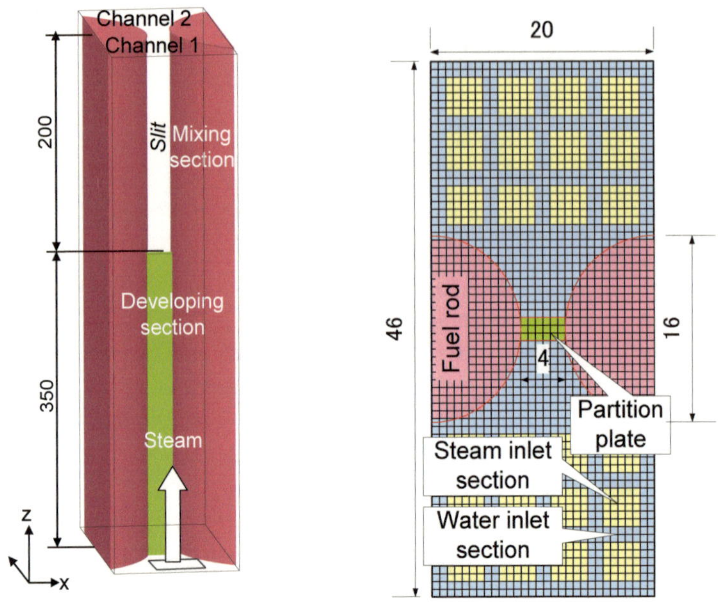

(a) Calculated test channel (b) Calculation mesh

Fig. 21. Dimensions of calculated test channel and calculation meshes for BWR cases.

The calculated test channel is shown in Fig.21 (a) and Fig.22 (a). The flow area is divided into two channels by a flat plate (partition plate) as same as the air-water cases. The flow channel is divided into 2 parts, developing section and mixing section. Liquid phase velocity in the BWR cases and the FLWR cases is relatively higher than that in air-water cases. To remove the effects on flow development and fluid mixing, length of the developing section and the mixing section were extended and the outlet section was removed.

<table>
<tr><th rowspan="2">Case</th><th rowspan="2">Gap width (mm)</th><th colspan="2">Inlet liquid mass flux (kg/m²s)</th><th colspan="2">Inlet quality (%)</th></tr>
<tr><th>Ch.1</th><th>Ch.2</th><th>Ch.1</th><th>Ch.2</th></tr>
<tr><td>F1</td><td rowspan="4">1.3</td><td rowspan="4">600</td><td>150</td><td rowspan="4">0.05</td><td>0.21</td></tr>
<tr><td>F2</td><td rowspan="3">600</td><td>0.002</td></tr>
<tr><td>F3</td><td>0.03</td></tr>
<tr><td>F4</td><td>0.08</td></tr>
<tr><td>F5</td><td rowspan="4">1.0</td><td rowspan="4">600</td><td rowspan="4">600</td><td rowspan="4">0.05</td><td>0.05</td></tr>
<tr><td>F6</td><td>0.03</td></tr>
<tr><td>F7</td><td>0.08</td></tr>
<tr><td>F8</td><td>0.12</td></tr>
</table>

Table 7. Calculation conditions for fluid mixing phenomena in FLWRs fuel bundle.

Regular mesh division in the Cartesian system was adopted except for lower part of the developing section. In the lower part of developing section (z=0~350 mm for BWR cases, z=0~200 mm for FLWR cases), to save computational resources, a relatively coarse computational meshes were used (Δz=2mm). The other region, Δz equals to 1mm. Two subchannels and the interconnection were formed by using obstacles. The calculation mesh size was set to 2/3 mm for BWR cases and 0.21mm or 0.16mm for FLWR cases to satisfy the condition that the number of the calculation meshes of gap region must be more than 6. A non-slip wall, constant exit pressure and constant inlet velocity were selected as boundary conditions for each subchannel.

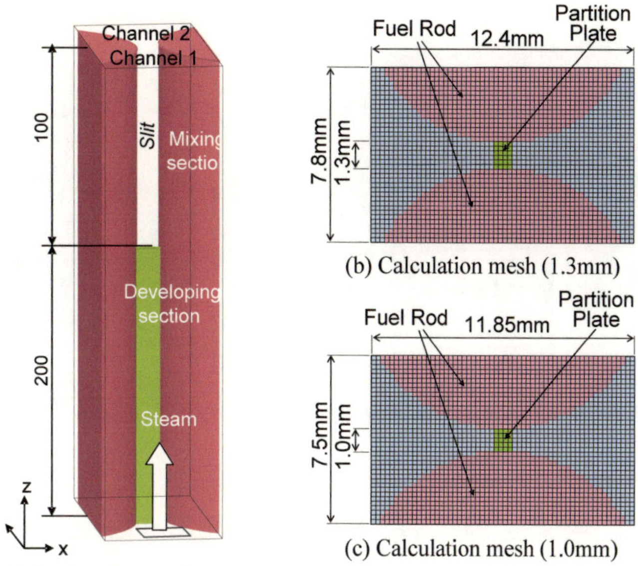

(a) Calculated test channel
(b) Calculation mesh (1.3mm)
(c) Calculation mesh (1.0mm)

Fig. 22. Dimensions of calculated test channel and calculation meshes for FLWR cases.

To simulate the operating conditions of the BWR and the FLWR, outlet pressure and inlet temperature of steam and water is set to 7 MPa and saturation temperature at 7 MPa respectively. Steam and water were injected through the steam and water inlet section located at lower part of the modeled test channel. The steam and water inlet sections were optimized to get a developed flow at inlet of test section, and divided into twelve small sections for BWR cases.

4.1.2 Evaluation of existing correlations

Example of the calculated behaviors in the test channel and detail of slug behavior of are shown in Fig.23. As shown in Fig.23, the fluid mixing between Ch.1 and Ch.2 was observed at a gap between the subchannels. Though inlet quality of both subchannels were equivalent in this case (inlet quality ratio (X_2/X_1) was equal to 1.0), fluid mixing occurred between 2 subchannels.

The existing two-phase flow correlation for fluid mixing (fluctuating pressure model (Takemoto, 1997) was evaluated using detailed numerical simulation data. The fluctuating pressure model is expressed as follows:

$$|w_T| = \sqrt{\frac{2\rho_l |\Delta p_T|}{K(1-x)^2\left[1+Bx\left(\frac{\rho_l}{\rho_g}-1\right)\right]}} = f(x)\sqrt{|\Delta p_T|} \tag{21}$$

where,
w_T: evaluated moved mass flow rate by the fluctuating pressure model [kg/s]
K : time averaged pressure loss coefficient [-]
x : time averaged quality [-]
B : time averaged two-phase flow pressure loss coefficient [-]

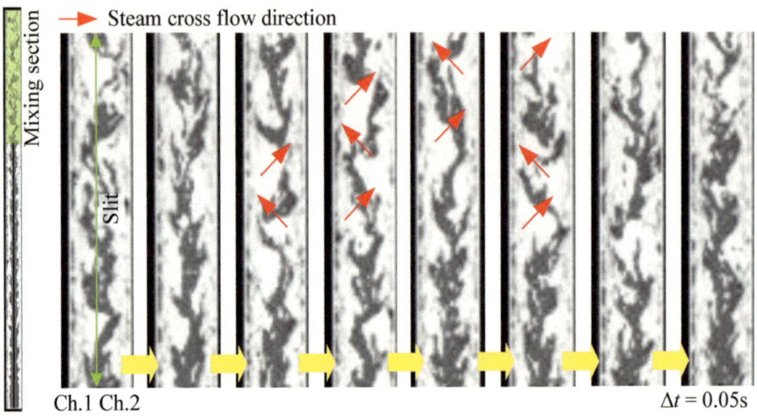

Fig. 23. Calculated slug behavior of case F5 in mixing section.

By the fluctuating pressure difference model, mixing coefficients for both phases are evaluated by following equations.

$$\Gamma_{m,T} = \frac{\overline{w_{m,T}}}{W_{m1} + W_{m2}} \tag{22}$$

where,

$$w_{l,T} = -(1-x)f(x)\frac{\Delta p_T}{\sqrt{|\Delta p_T|}},\ w_{g,T} = -xf(x)\frac{\Delta p_T}{\sqrt{|\Delta p_T|}} \tag{23}$$

In above equations, instantaneous pressure difference values and time averaged values (pressure loss coefficient, quality and two-phase flow pressure loss coefficient) are evaluated by numerical results.
To estimate effects of fluctuating pressure on the mixing coefficients, the mixing coefficients using time averaged pressure difference were also evaluated for BWR cases:

$$\Gamma_{m,S} = \frac{w_{m,S}}{W_{m1} + W_{m2}} \tag{24}$$

where,

$$w_{l,S} = -(1-x)f(x)\frac{\Delta p_S}{\sqrt{|\Delta p_S|}},\ w_{g,S} = -xf(x)\frac{\Delta p_S}{\sqrt{|\Delta p_S|}} \tag{25}$$

Evaluated mixing coefficients by fluctuating pressure model, $\Gamma_{m,T}$ are shown in Fig.24. Predicted mixing coefficients by TPFIT code and $\Gamma_{m,S}$ are also shown in figures. The evaluated mixing coefficients, $\Gamma_{m,T}$ were in reasonable agreement with the predicted results. Evaluated mixing coefficients by use of time averaged pressure difference, $\Gamma_{m,S}$ overestimated the predicted results in almost all cases, and it is understood that the fluctuating component of pressure difference restrains the fluid mixing between subchannels.

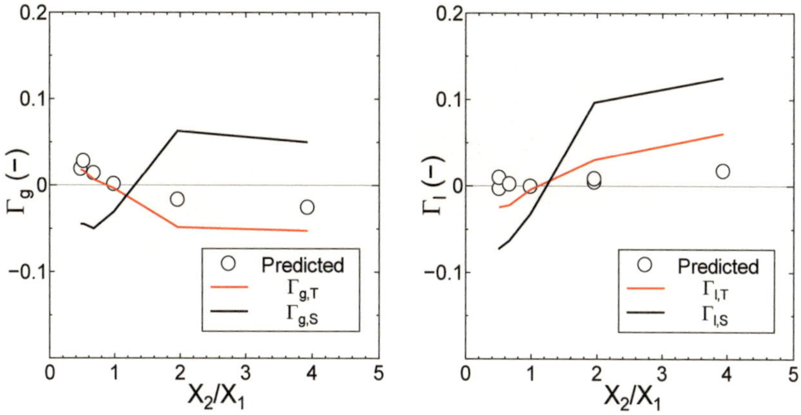

(a) Gas (b) Liquid

Fig. 24. Evaluation of the fluctuating pressure model for BWR cases (Case B1~B8).

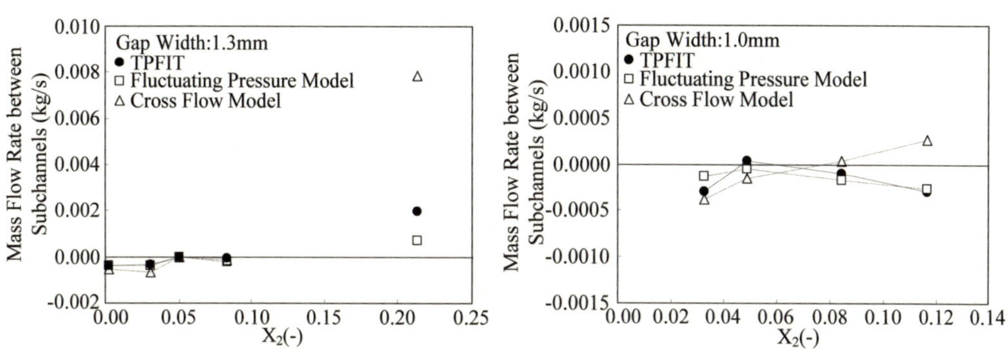

(a) 1.3mm gap spacing (Case F1~F4) (b) 1.0mm gap spacing (Case F5~F8)

Fig. 25. Evaluation of the existing correlations for FLWR cases (Case F1~F8).

Evaluated mixing coefficients by fluctuating pressure model and conventional fluid mixing model (Kelly and Kazimi, 1980) for FLWR cases are shown in Fig.25. Predicted mixing coefficients by the TPFIT are also shown in figures. The evaluated mixing coefficients by fluctuating pressure model for relatively low inlet quality cases were in reasonable agreement with the predicted results for both 1.3 mm and 1.0 mm gap spacing. However, evaluated mixing coefficients by conventional fluid mixing model were different from predicted mixing coefficients by the TPFIT code both qualitatively and quantitatively. Evaluated mixing coefficients for relatively high inlet quality cases (inlet quality ratio (X_2/X_1) is large) by fluctuating pressure model and conventional fluid mixing model showed underestimation and overestimation respectively.

4.2 Development of correlation base on detailed numerical simulation results

In section 4.1, existing correlations for the two-phase flow fluid mixing phenomena were examined. However, enough results were not obtained. Then, we try to develop new correlation for fluid mixing phenomena in tight lattice rod bundle based on numerical results.

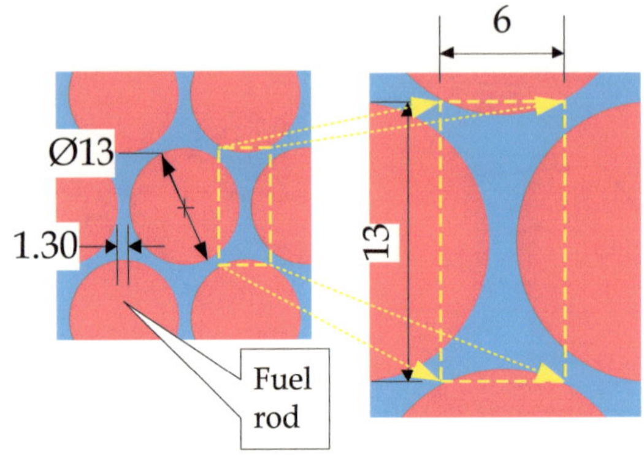

Fig. 26. Simulated region in rod bundle.

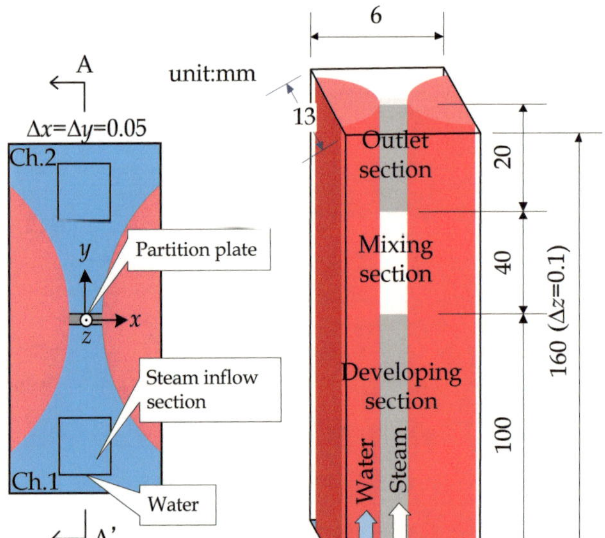

Fig. 27. Modeled two sub-channels.

The simulated region in a tight-lattice rod bundle is schematically shown in Fig.26. The diameter of fuel rods is 13.0mm. The smallest gap spacing between two adjacent fuel rods is 1.3mm. Numerical domain used in this simulation is shown in Fig.27. The length and width of the simulated region are 13.0mm and 6.0mm respectively. The two subchannels are separated by a partition plate with the thickness of 0.2mm, in the upper part of which there is a slit with the height of 40mm. Water and steam flow into the subchannels through the bottom. Gas and liquid flows pass through three sections along the axial direction, i.e. developing, mixing and outlet sections. Grid numbers are 120×260×1600 (49,920,000). Saturated water and steam at 7.2MPa are used as working fluids. Steam and liquid are injected at constant velocities with values tabulated. The total mass flux is set to 400kg/m²s.

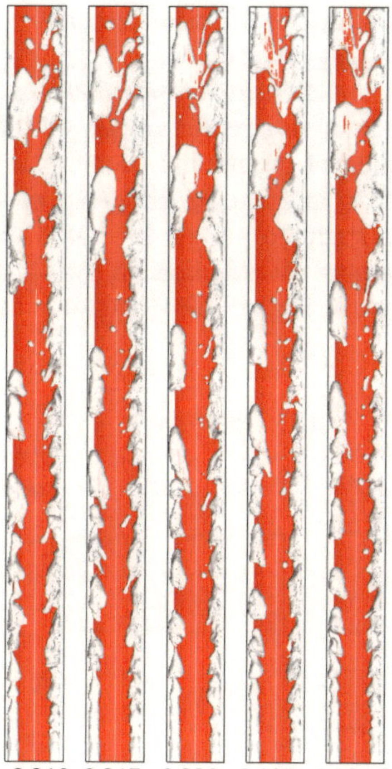

Fig. 28. Examples of simulation results.

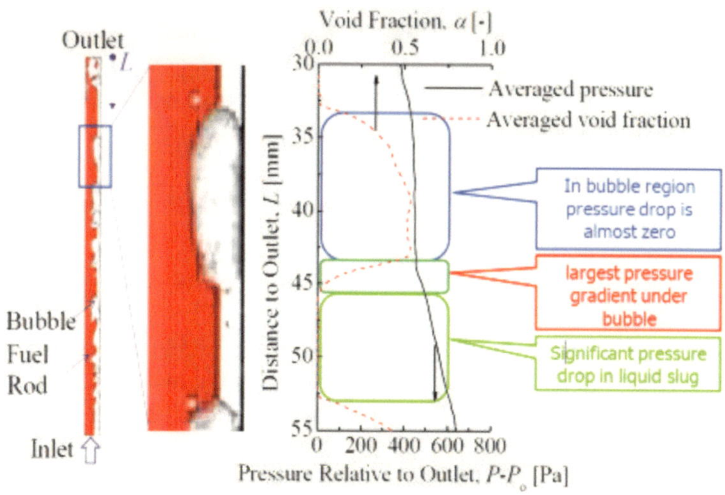

Fig. 29. Axial cross-sectional averaged pressure and void fraction distribution.

Figure 28 shows the time change of void fraction distribution observed from the section A-A′, as indicated in Fig.27. The red color denotes the fuel rod. It can be seen that the gas phases cross the slit mutually. Figure 29 shows the axial cross-sectional pressure and void distributions around a slug bubble. It illustrates that most of pressure gradient takes place in liquid slug zone and the pressure almost keeps constant in large bubble zone. Below the bubble, there exists large pressure gradient. This is reasonable because flow after the bubble is highly disturbed and vortexes may occur there.
In simulation results, strong correlation for liquid phase means that liquid fluid mixing occurs due to local inter-subchannel differential pressure. Then we decided to develop an approximate model for prediction of differential pressure between subchannels. Pressure difference between subchannels is induced by difference of axial pressure distribution in each subchannel. Therefore, to evaluate mixing flow rate between subchannels by fluid mixing phenomena, axial pressure distribution in subchannels must be required. In following section, axial pressure distribution (axial pressure loss) model is developed.

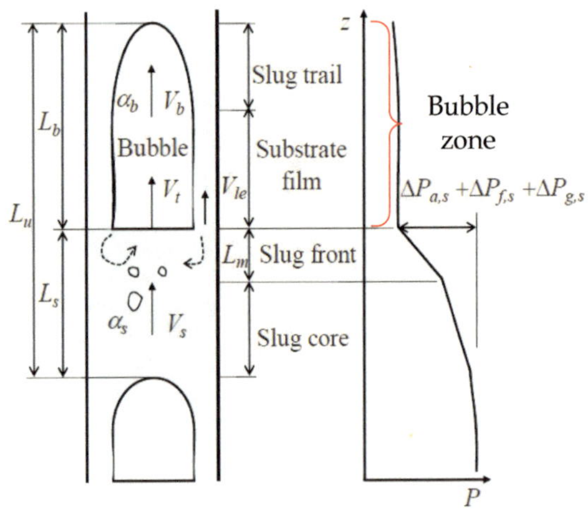

Fig. 30. Physical model for slug flow.

Based on the above-mentioned results of the numerical simulation, we considered pressure distributions in bubble zone, slug front and slug core (see Fig.30). In the bubble zone, the pressure almost keeps constant in this zone. Therefore, pressure drop across a bubble zone is assumed to be zero as follows:

$$\frac{dP_b}{dz} = 0 \tag{26}$$

In slug front and slug core, there are three contributions to the pressure drop across a slug. The first, $dP_{a,s}$, is the pressure drop that results from the acceleration of the slow moving liquid film to slug velocity in the slug front zone. The second, $dP_{f,s}$, is the pressure drop required to overcome wall shear. The third, $dP_{g,s}$, is the static head pressure drop. The total pressure gradient across a liquid slug is thus given by

$$\frac{dP_s}{dz} = \frac{dP_{a,s}}{dz} + \frac{dP_{f,s}}{dz} + \frac{dP_{g,s}}{dz}. \tag{27}$$

In the slug front region, flow after the bubble is highly disturbed and vortexes may occur there. Then additional pressure loss must be considered. A slug that has stabilized in length can be considered as a body receiving and losing mass at equal rates. The velocity of the liquid in the film just before pickup is lower than that in the slug and a force is therefore necessary to accelerate this liquid to slug velocity. This force manifests itself as a pressure drop. If the pressure along the liquid film in the bubble zone can be assumed to be essentially constant, this force can be evaluated by the sum of gravity and wall shear stress in the liquid film zone (Taitel and Barnea, 1990). Here the following equations are employed to evaluate the acceleration pressure drop for vertical flow:

$$\Delta P_a = \frac{W_{le}}{A}\left(V_s - V_{le}\right), \tag{28}$$

where W_{le} is the rate at which mass is picked up by the liquid slug, which can be obtained from the following equation:

$$W_{le} = \rho_l \cdot A \cdot \left(1-\alpha_{le}\right)\cdot\left(V_t - V_{le}\right) \tag{29}$$

where α_{le}, V_{le} are the void fraction and mean velocity of liquid film at font of liquid slug. V_t is the propagation velocity of the slug unit or average translational velocity of the nose of the slug, given by Taitel and Barnea (1990)

$$V_t = 1.2V_s + 0.35\sqrt{gD_b} \tag{30}$$

Here, D_b is the bubble diameter, which may be approximately estimated from the average void fraction of the bubble zone, α_b.

$$D_b = \sqrt{A\cdot\alpha_b} \tag{31}$$

where

$$\alpha_b = \frac{1}{L_b}\int_0^{L_b} \alpha_l dx \tag{32}$$

Here α_l is the local void fraction in the bubble zone. In Eq.(28), the mean velocity of fluid in the slug, V_s, is given as

$$V_s = \frac{1}{A}\left(\frac{W_l}{\rho_l} + \frac{W_g}{\rho_g}\right) \tag{33}$$

The pressure drop due to acceleration takes place in the slug front which penetrates a distances into the body of the slug. The depth of penetration of the liquid film into the slug appears to depend on the relative velocity between slug and film, and may be obtained from the following equation (Dukler and Hubbard, 1975).

$$L_{sf} = 0.3\cdot\frac{\rho_l\left(V_s - V_{ls}\right)^2}{2} \tag{34}$$

And the acceleration gradient in the slug front is given by,

$$\frac{dP_{a,s}}{dz} = \frac{\Delta P_a}{L_{sf}}. \tag{35}$$

In the slug front and slug core region, frictional and gravity pressure drop are acting in subchannels. Frictional pressure drop takes place when liquid slug moves along the channel wall. For the calculation of this term, the similarity analysis for two-phase frictional pressure drop (Dukler et al., 1975) is applied. Within the liquid slug the bubble size is usually small and thus the flow can be deemed as the homogeneous one with negligible two-phase slip. Under this condition, the frictional pressure drop can be calculated as follows:

$$\frac{dP_{f,s}}{dz} = \frac{2f_s}{D_h}\left[\rho_l\left(1-\alpha_s\right)+\rho_g\alpha_s\right]\cdot V_s^2 \tag{36}$$

For "non-slip" conditions f_s could be correlated as a unique function of Re_s

$$f_s = 0.079\cdot Re_s^{-0.025} \tag{37}$$

Here the Reynolds number Re_s is defined in the following manner:

$$Re_s = D_h V_s \frac{\rho_l\left(1-\alpha_s\right)+\rho_g\alpha_s}{\mu_l\left(1-\alpha_s\right)+\mu_g\alpha_s} \tag{38}$$

The static head term for the slug front and slug core can be obtained from the following simple equation:

$$\frac{dP_{g,s}}{dz} = \left[\rho_l\left(1-\alpha_s\right)+\rho_g\alpha_s\right]\cdot g \tag{39}$$

The axial relative pressure in question could be obtained through the integration of differential pressure as follows

$$P = \int_0^z \frac{dP}{dz}dz$$
$$\frac{dP}{dz}\begin{cases}\dfrac{dP_s}{dz} \text{ in slug zone}\\ \dfrac{dP_b}{dz} \text{ in bubble zone}\end{cases} \tag{40}$$

The above equations are incomplete and some parameters are still unknown, such as local void fraction in the bubble zone α_l, the mean velocity of liquid film at front of liquid slug, the bubble length L_b as well as that of slug unit L_u, and instantaneous bubble distribution. These parameters may be predicted by assuming the idealized bubble shape and setting the initial bubble distribution along the channel. We leave them for future study. In this study we aim at exploring the mechanism of differential pressure fluctuation inducing cross flow as a first step, therefore numerical simulation results are used to evaluate these unknown parameters for simplicity. In addition, a criterion to reduce the detailed three-dimensional simulation results is introduced to determine locations and lengths of bubble zones (or slug zones). The regions, where the cross-sectional averaged void fraction is larger than 0.3, are deemed as bubble zones. Other regions are regarded as slug zones.

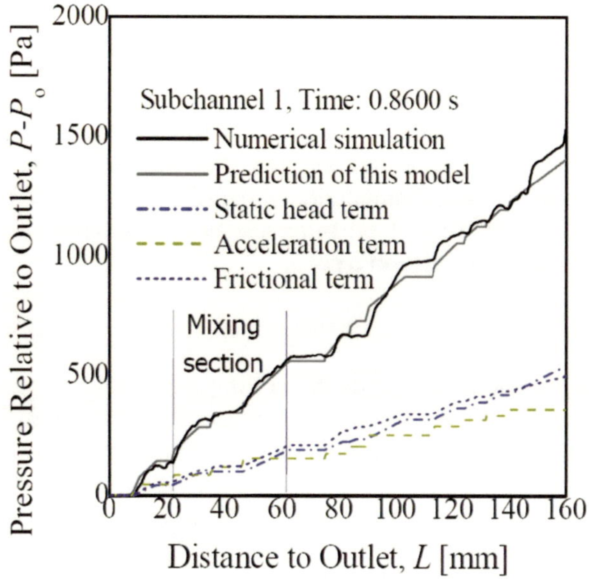

Fig. 31. Instantaneous axial pressure distribution.

Here, the model is evaluated with the axial pressure profile obtained from the numerical simulation for a subchannel with cross flow. Figure 31 shows the evaluation results at an instant with time of 0.8600 s. From the figure, it can be seen that the prediction of the model is generally in agreement with the simulation results, especially for mixing section (abscissa from 20 mm to 60 mm). This means the model may be applicable to subchannels. And furthermore, we can see that the three contributions to pressure drop have almost similar weights in the total pressure drop.

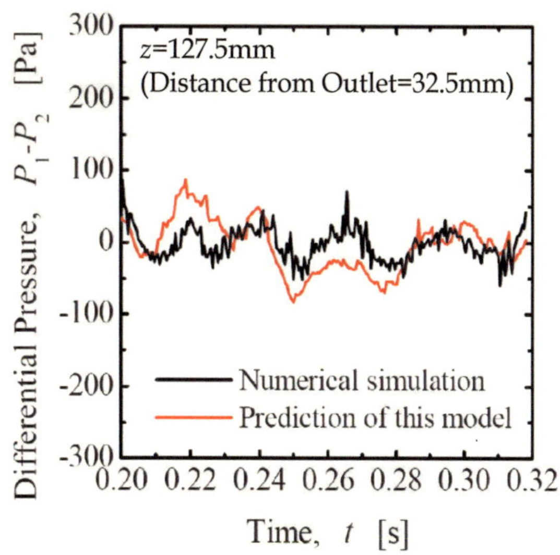

Fig. 32. Fluctuation of differential pressure between two subchannels.

In this study, the way to evaluate the cross-section averaged pressure distribution in a single subchannel has been developed. If we assume that cross flow has minor effect on the pressure distribution in each subchannel, we can evaluate the pressure differences between subchannels by axial pressure distribution for each subchannel. In this way, the prediction of differential pressure by the model is compared to that obtained from the numerical simulation as shown in Fig. 32. It can be seen that the prediction of this model may reproduce the results of numerical simulation generally. For the time of 0.22 or 0.27, cross flow may have not negligible effect on inter-subchannel differential pressures and thus predictions deviate from the simulation results.

5. Conclusion

To perform thermal hydraulic design of the boiling water reactor (BWR) without actual size tests, we have been developed a new design method for BWRs. In this design method, the two-phase flow correlations for fluid mixing phenomena must be modified or created based on results of large scale numerical simulations. Then, we developed an innovative two-phase flow simulation code TPFIT and an advanced interface tracking method. In the advanced interface tracking method, gas and liquid mass conservation equations are solved, to treat compressibility of gas and to keep high volume conservation of gas and liquid.

In the second step, to verify and validate the TPFIT with the advanced interface tracking method, the TPFIT was applied to some experimental analyses including three the 2-channel fluid mixing tests, and comparisons between measured and predicted result were carried out. By these results, it was concluded that the TPFIT can be applied to the two-phase flow fluid mixing phenomena.

In the next step, the TPFIT was applied to the numerical simulation of fluid mixing between subchannels on a current BWR and FLWR that is one of innovative water reactor concept developed in JAEA. The existing two-phase flow correlation for fluid mixing was evaluated using detailed numerical simulation data. When inlet quality ratio of subchannels is relatively large, evaluated mixing coefficients by existing two-phase flow correlations for fluid mixing were different from those of the detailed numerical simulation data. And new correlation based on large scale numerical simulation results are expected.

In the fourth step, we tried to develop new two-phase flow correlations related to the fluid mixing phenomena. Differential pressure fluctuation between subchannels dominates the fluid mixing phenomena. We considered that the differential pressure fluctuation is induced by difference of axial pressure distribution in each subchannel. Then we developed new correlation for axial pressure distribution. In this correlation, a hydrostatic gradient, acceleration and frictional gradients are taken into account in the liquid slug, and no pressure gradient exists in the slug bubble. New correlation was validated by numerical results of the TPFIT, and it was concluded that predicted results of this correlation almost agree with the simulation results. Furthermore, differential pressure fluctuation based on predicted axial pressure distribution in subchannels can predict differential pressure by the TPFIT. We thought that the method to create new two-phase flow correlations by results of large scale numerical simulations is effective. However, there is issue such as required computational resources or validation of prediction accuracy of created correlations.

6. Acknowledgment

This research was conducted using a supercomputer of the Japan Atomic Energy Agency.

7. References

Lahey, Jr, R. T. & Moody, F. J., (1993), *The Thermal-Hydraulics of a Boiling Water Nuclear Reactor*, American Nuclear Society, La Grange Park, Illinois USA.

Kawahara, A., Sadatomi, M. & Tomino, T., (2000), Prediction of Gas and Liquid Turbulent Mixing Rates between Rod Bundle Subchannels in a Two-Phase Slug-Churn Flow, *Trans. JSME, Ser. B*, 66, pp. 1191-1197

Sumida, I,, Yamakita, T., Sakai, S., Iwai, K., & Kondo, T., (1995), Investigation of Two-Phase Flow Mixing between Two Subchannels (1st Report, Fluctuating Pressure Model and its Experimental Verification), *Trans. JSME, Ser. B*, 61, pp. 2662-2668 (in Japanese).

Takemoto, S., Kondo, T., Inatomi, T., Sakai, S., Wakai, K., & Sumida, I., (1997), Investigation of Two-Phase Flow Mixing between Two Subchannels (2nd Report, Verification of Fluctuating Pressure Model without Steady Pressure), *Trans. JSME, Ser. B*, 61, pp. 3107-3113 (in Japanese).

Yabe, T., & Aoki, T., (1991), A Universal Solver for Hyperbolic Equations by Cubic-Polynomial Interpolation I. One-Dimensional Solver, *Comput.Phys.Commun.*, 66, pp. 219-232.

Brackbill, J. U., Kothe, D. B., & Zemach, C., (1992), A Continuum Method for Modeling Surface Tension, *J.* Comput. *Phys.*, 100, pp. 335-354.

Gueyffier, D., Nadim, J. Li, A., Scardovelli, R., & Zaleski, S., (1999), Volume-of-Fluid Interface Tracking with Smoothed Surface Stress Methods for Three-Dimensional Flows, *J. Comput. Phys.*, 152, pp. 423-456.

Rayleigh, L., (1879), On the Capillary Phenomena of Jets, *Proc. R. Soc. London*, 29, p. 71-97.

Moran, K., Inumaru, J., & Kawaji, M., (2002), Instantaneous hydrodynamics of a laminar wavy liquid film, *Int. J of Multiphase Flow*, 28 pp.731-755.

Nusselt, W., (1916), Die oberflachenkondensation des wasserdamphes, *VDI-Zs 60*, 541.

Yoshida, H., Nagayoshi, T., Takase, K., & Akimoto, H., (2007), Development of Design Technology on Thermal-Hydraulic Performance in Tight-Lattice Rod Bundles: IV - Numerical Evaluation of Fluid Mixing Phenomena using Advanced Interface-Tracking Method –, *Proc. of ICONE15 (CD-ROM)*, Nagoya, Japan, September 22-26, 10532.

Uchikawa, S., Okubo, T., Kugo, T., Akie, H., Takeda, R., Nakano, Y., Ohnuki, A., & Iwamura, T., (2007), Conceptual Design of Innovative Water Reactor for Flexible Fuel Cycle (FLWR) and its Recycle Characteristics, *J. Nucl. Sci. Tech.*, 44, 3, pp.277-284.

Taitel, Y., & Barnea, D., (1990), Two-Phase Slug Flow, *Advances in Heat Transfer*, 20, pp. 83-132

Dukler, A. E., & Hubbard, M. G., (1975), A model for gas-liquid slug flow in horizontal and near horizontal tubes, *Ind. Eng. Chem., Fundam.*, 14, pp. 337-347.

Kelly, J.E., & Kazimi, M.S., (1980), Development of the two-fluid multidimensional code THERMIT for LWR analysis, *AIChE Symposium Series*, pp. 149-162.

14

Numerical Simulations of Unsteady Fluid Forces in Heat Exchanger Tube Bundles

H. Omar, M. Hassan and A. Gerber
University of New Brunswick
Canada

1. Introduction

Heat transfer is the main concern in designing shell and tube heat exchangers. Flow-induced vibration (FIV) is also a major concern while designing shell and tube heat exchangers. Fluidelastic instability (FEI), turbulence, periodic instability, and acoustic resonance are the FIV mechanisms that could cause to vibrations in heat exchanger tube bundles. FEI is the most dangers mechanism, since it can cause to tube damage in short time when the flow velocity exceeds the critical flow velocity (U_{cr}). Therefore, intensive researches have been undergoing in the last five decades to predict and under stand this mechanism. Different theories and models are in use to predict the FEI thresholds as function of mass damping parameters (MDP). These theories and models rely on some coefficients and parameters. Experimental approaches are used to predict these parameters for some tube arrays geometries. The experimental approach is expensive and a time consumer. Computational Fluid Dynamics (CFD) is an alternative approach proposed in this study to predict these parameters. This study utilized the CFD model to simulate the unsteady flow and the resulting fluidelastic forces in a tube bundle. Numerical simulations of in-line square tube arrays with a pitch-to-diameter (*P/d*) ratio of 1.33 utilizing a 2-dimensional model are presented. In this model, a single tube was forced to oscillate within an otherwise rigid array. The numerical model solves the Reynolds-Average Navier-Stokes (RANS) equations for unsteady turbulent flow, and is cast in an Arbitrary Lagrangian-Eulerian (ALE) form to handle mesh motion associated with a moving boundary. The fluidelastic instability was predicted for both single and fully flexible tube arrays over a mass damping parameter (MDP) range of 0.1 to 200. Fluid forces acting on the oscillating tube and the surrounding tubes were estimated. The predicted forces were utilized to calculate fluid force coefficients for all tubes.

Fluidelastic instability is the most destructive excitation mechanism leading to rapid failure by fatigue or tube-to-tube clashing if the stability threshold is exceeded. Due to this potential for catastrophic failure intensive research has been ongoing for several decades on the topic of predicting and mitigating FEI effects. This has resulted in a vast amount of literature on the topic. Much of the research has been directed towards obtaining a reliable estimate of the critical flow velocity for the purpose of design. There are several models available to analyse FEI problems and the associated critical velocity. These models range from analytical approaches such as the models of Lever and Weaver (Lever & Weaver, 1982) and Païdoussis and Price (Païdoussis & Price, 1984) to the empirically-based unsteady flow theory models such as those of Chen (Chen, 1991) and Tanaka and Takahara (Tanaka & Takahara, 1981). These approaches provide a good estimate of the critical flow velocity, with models based on the unsteady flow theory being the more general. However, the applicability of the unsteady flow theory is restricted to the availability of the force coefficients they depend on. These force coefficients have to be measured experimentally or alternatively, as is investigated in this paper, can be generated using a comprehensive CFD model.

Several numerical techniques and studies embarked on attempting to simulate unsteady fluid forces (Weber et al, 2001; Omar et al, 2009; Omar, 2010; Hassan et al, 2010). This, in turn, could be used in conjunction with the unsteady flow model. This approach will be presented in this chapter. There has been an attempt to numerically predict the unsteady fluid forces in a tube row by Weber et al (Weber et al, 2001). They utilized a commercial CFD package (STAR-CD) to analyze a tube row with a P/d ratio of 1.35. In this work (Weber et al, 2001), the fluid forces due to the prescribed motion of one tube were predicted. Using these fluid forces, fluid force coefficients equivalent to those of Chen (Chen, 1991) were obtained.

The results obtained via this work (Weber et al, 2001)have good agreement with other experiments. Comprehensive numerical studies to simulate the unsteady fluid forces for In line square and normal triangle tube arrays were conducted by Omar et al (Omar et al, 2009); Omar (Omar, 2010); Hassan et al (Hassan et al, 2010). In these studies (Omar et al, 2009; Omar, 2010; Hassan et al, 2010), the ability to extract fluid force coefficients for the unsteady flow theory was undertaken for two tube array configurations, namely i) in-line square tube array and ii) normal triangle tube array. The ability to predict the tube array FEI from CFD derived coefficients for each configuration and for single and fully flexible tube arrays was assessed. The predicted fluid force coefficients and FEI are then compared to available experimental data. The comparison demonstrates the viability of the proposed model to provide fluid force coefficients for the unsteady flow theory. The effect of the P/d ratio and the Reynolds number on the FEI threshold was also investigated.

In the present study the accuracy of using CFD generated force coefficients in the unsteady flow theory model is tested by comparing against available experimental data for in-line square tube arrays. The base geometry, depicted in Figure 1a, and test conditions, follows the experimental study of Tanaka and Takahara (Tanaka & Takahara, 1981).

2. Fluid dynamics model

The Reynolds averaged Navier-Stokes (RANS) equations describing mass and momentum conservation are solved to obtain the time evolution of velocity and pressure in the tube array. The interactions between fluid motion and moving structures are handled by further casting the governing RANS equations in an Arbitrary Lagrangian-Eulerian (ALE). ALE accommodates moving boundaries and any subsequent deformation of the underlying discrete mesh. The mesh velocity, u_{mj}, is calculated based on the space conservation law:

$$\frac{d}{dt}\int_V dV = \int_S u_{mj} dn_j \tag{1}$$

The left hand term represents the rate of change of a volume V, while the right hand side represents the integral of the surface (S) velocities (where n_j is the surface normal).

2.1 Conservation equations

The RANS equations in ALE form for mass conservation appears as:

$$\frac{\partial \rho}{\partial t}+\frac{\partial \rho(u_j-u_{mj})}{\partial x_j}=0 \tag{2}$$

and momentum equation:

$$\frac{\partial \rho u_i}{\partial t}+\frac{\partial \rho u_i(u_j-u_{mj})}{\partial x_j}=-\frac{\partial P}{\partial x_i}+\frac{\partial}{\partial x_j}\left(\mu_{eff}\frac{\partial u_i}{\partial x_j}\right)+S_i \tag{3}$$

where u_j and u_i are the fluid velocity components, ρ is the fluid density, x_j and x_i are cartesian spatial coordinates, P is the fluid pressure, μ_{eff} is the effective viscosity (includes laminar and turbulent contributions) , and S_i is any additional momentum source contributions. This form allows conservative fluid flow calculations with mesh adaptation in time. The discretization process of the governing equations is similar to that applied for finite-volume/finite-element discretization (Schneider & Raw, 1987; Omar, 2010; Hassan et al, 2010).

The k-ω based Shear Stress Transport (SST) model is used (Menter, 1994) to include the influence of turbulent mixing. The turbulence equations are cast in ALE form :

$$\frac{\partial \rho k}{\partial t}+\frac{\partial \rho k(u_j-u_{mj})}{\partial x_j}=P_k-\beta^* \rho k\omega+\frac{\partial}{\partial x_j}\left[\Gamma_{eff}\frac{\partial k}{\partial x_j}\right] \tag{4a}$$

and the ω-equation:

$$\frac{\partial \rho \omega}{\partial t}+\frac{\partial \rho \omega(u_j-u_{mj})}{\partial x_j}=\alpha\frac{\omega}{k}P_k-\beta\rho\omega^2+\frac{\partial}{\partial x_j}\left[\Gamma_{eff}\frac{\partial \omega}{\partial x_j}\right] \tag{4b}$$

In these equations P_k is the production rate of turbulence. The SST model incorporates a transformation between the k-ε model in the free stream regions of the flow, and the k-ω model in the near wall regions of the flow. Further details on the turbulence model implementation can be found in (Menter, 1994).

Based on the oscillation frequency and amplitude, the nodes on the moving tube surface (shaded tube designated as 1 in Figure 1) are moved to the new position and the remaining nodes in the interior are moved according to a set of Laplacian diffusion equations.

The simulation is first run with a static tube, to obtain a quasi steady-state solution to provide initial flow conditions for the transient simulation. Following this quasi steady-state solution a transient simulation is then started but with tube 1 in motion in the lift direction and then in the drag at a specified frequency and amplitude. Reader is forwarded to (Omar et al, 2009; Omar, 2010; Hassan et al, 2010) for more details.

For each time step convergence is achieved to within an RMS residual of 1×10^{-4} before moving on. The solution of the RANS equations is based on a coupled algebraic multigrid solver (Raw, 1996). Parallel computations are applied in the present case to reduce the solution time required per time step.

3. Unsteady flow model

The unsteady fluid force includes the inertia, the damping, and the stiffness effects.
The inertia effect is assumed to be independent of the flow velocity and can be measured experimentally, or computed using the potential-flow theory. In order to utilize this model, fluid force coefficients are required. The first attempt to obtain these force Coefficients experimentally was done by Tanaka and Takahara (Tanaka & Takahara, 1981). The damping and Stiffness effects were expressed in terms of fluid force amplitudes (C) and phase angles (φ) between fluid forces and tube oscillation. To validate the CFD results with experimental data, a simpler variant of the unsteady flow theory as presented by Tanaka and Takahara (Tanaka & Takahara, 1981) is used. The formulation is presented briefly here, however a complete description and derivation is available in (Tanaka & Takahara, 1981; Omar, 2010).

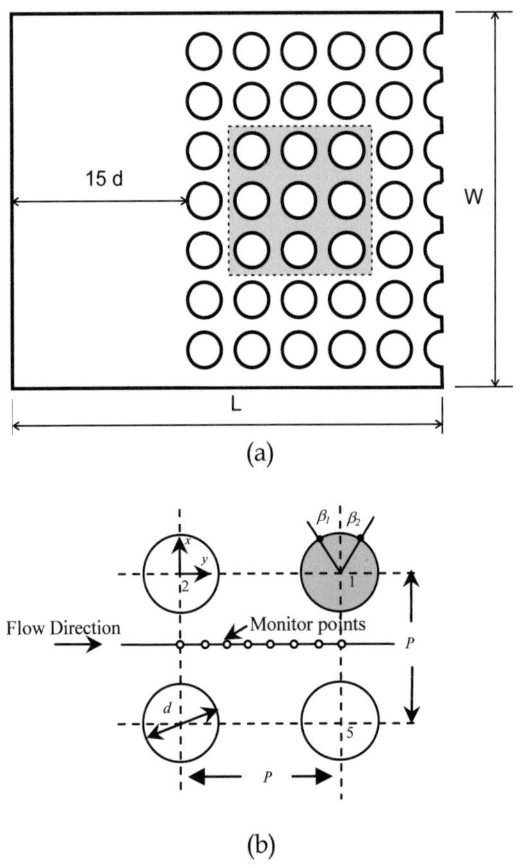

Fig. 1. In-line square tube geometry a) as given in experiments of Tanaka and Takahara (Tanaka & Takahara, 1981; Omar, 2010; Hassan et al, 2010), and b) close-up of moving tube (shaded) and related dimensions.

Referring to the square array in Figure 1a, and considering the forces and displacements in x as well as y, and assuming the effects of all surrounding tubes can be summed linearly (and that only the four tubes immediately adjacent the center tube 1 have significant influence) the total force expected on tube 1 can be expressed as

$$F_x = \frac{1}{2}\rho U_{gap}^2 \sum_{j=1,2,3,4,5} \left(C_{XjX} p_j + C_{XjY} q_j \right) \tag{5a}$$

$$F_y = \frac{1}{2}\rho U_{gap}^2 \sum_{j=1,2,3,4,5} \left(C_{YjX} p_j + C_{YjY} q_j \right) \tag{5b}$$

where C_{X1X} and C_{Y1Y} are fluid force coefficient amplitudes. The fluid forces (F_{X1X}, F_{Y1Y}) acting on tube j lead the displacement of tube j (X_j, Y_j) by phase angles (ϕ_{XjX} and ϕ_{YjY}). The three suffixes of the coefficients represent the direction of the force, the tube index, and the direction of vibration, respectively. For example, the lift fluid force component acting on tube 1 due to the motion of tube 4 in the drag direction (Y) is expressed as F_{X4Y}. Therefore, the total lift fluid forces consists of 10 different components corresponding to the lift motion effect ($C_{X1X} \dots C_{X5X}$) and to the drag motion ($C_{X1X} \dots C_{X5X}$). Similarly, the overall drag force comprises of 10 components ($C_{Y1X} \dots C_{Y5X}$, $C_{Y1Y} \dots C_{Y5Y}$). As the centre tube (1) oscillates in Y direction, F_{XjY} is equal to zero except for F_{X4Y} and F_{X5Y}. Similarly, as the centre tube oscillates in X direction, the F_{YjX} is equal zero except of F_{Y4X} and F_{X5Y}.
The reader can refer to (Tanaka & Takahara, 1981; Omar, 2010) for a description. Based on these simplifications, Eq. 5 can be reduced to:

$$F_X = \frac{1}{2}\rho U_{gap}^2 \Big(C_{X1X} p_1 + C_{X4X}(p_4 + p_5) + C_{X4Y}(q_4 + q_5) + C_{X2X} p_2 + C_{X3X} p_3 \Big) \tag{6a}$$

$$F_y = \frac{1}{2}\rho U_{gap}^2 \Big(C_{Y1Y} q_1 + C_{4LX}(p_4 + p_5) + C_{Y4Y}(q_4 - q_5) + C_{Y2Y} q_2 + C_{Y3Y} q_3 \Big) \tag{6b}$$

4. Results and discussion

The results presented in this section are based on unsteady CFD simulations conducted on a specific tube array geometry over a range of reduced velocities, defined here as $U_r = U_{gap}/fd$ where f is the frequency of oscillation of tube 1 and d the tube diameter. A completed unsteady simulation provided tube forces as a function of time, which, following a FFT of the data, provided the force coefficients and associated phase information. The choice of time step is very important to the accuracy of the calculations, but also for efficient use of computational resources. The optimal simulation time step was chosen based on previous investigations (Williams, 2004; Omar, 2010; Hassan et al, 2010), which indicated that fifty or more time steps per tube oscillation period is needed. In the present computations on average the time step was based on subdividing the tube period by ~90. The total number of tube oscillations simulated, beginning from a quasi-steady initial solution, was 50 and ensured steady statistics could be obtained when applying the FFT process to the force data. The coefficient data as a function of U_r was then processed to obtain an FEI stability map as a function of mass damping parameter, defined here as $mdp = m2\pi\zeta/\rho d^2$ where m is the mass per unit tube length and $2\pi\zeta$ is the log decrement. In generating the stability maps mdp was varied from 0.1 to 200.

An in-line square tube array were considered where the geometry, as given in Figure 1, P/d=1.33 W=0.288 m. A set of force coefficients and phase shift versus U_r curves was created and a stability map generated. For a subset of this data, in particular for the P/d=1.33 case, direct comparison to the force coefficients and phase data of Tanaka and Takahara (Tanaka & Takahara, 1981) could be made as will be discussed subsequently.

4.1 Mesh sensitivity

Before performing the complete set of unsteady simulations a mesh sensitivity study was undertaken to determine the best mesh resolution. This assessment was done using a range of meshes ranging in node count from 18,000 to 220,000. In conducting the simulations changes in predicted C_{X1X} and C_{Y1Y} coefficients were monitored as a function of changing mesh resolution. From this study it was determined that 80,000 nodes was a good compromise between accuracy and computational time. In Figure 2a is shown the mesh topology used in the simulations, while in Figure 2b the near wall mesh resolution is highlighted.

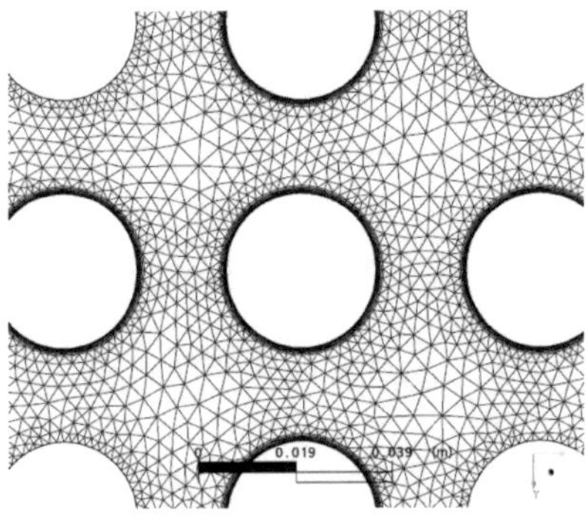

(a)

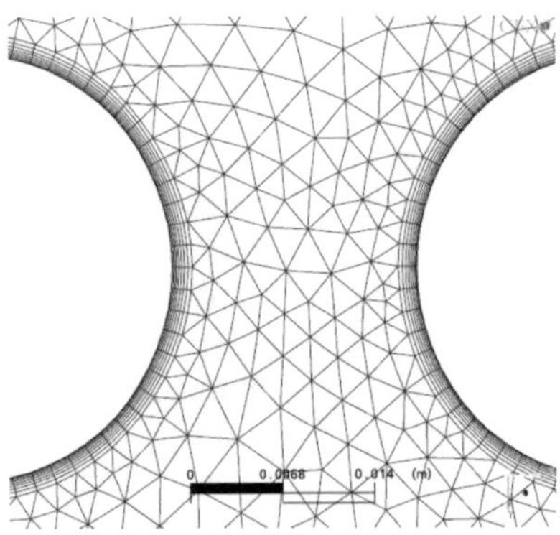

(b)

Fig. 2. Mesh (80,000 node case) with a) view of tubes 1,2,3,4 and 5 intervening mesh topology (Omar, 2010; Hassan et al, 2010), and b) view of near wall mesh.

4.2 Validation of the predicted fluid force coefficients

This study presents samples of the predicted fluid force coefficients (C_{X1X} and C_{Y1Y}) and their phase angles (ϕ_{X1X} and ϕ_{Y1Y}) and compared against the experimental data of Tanaka and Takahara (Tanaka & Takahara, 1981). Figure (3) shows the predicted fluid force coefficients (C_{X1X} and C_{Y1Y}) and Figure (4) shows their phase angles (ϕ_{X1X}, ϕ_{Y1Y}) compared against the experimental data.

As shown in Figure (3), the general behaviour of the fluid force coefficients obtained experimentally and predicted numerically, is similar. All force coefficients decrease sharply from their highest value to a low value in the range of reduced flow velocities between 1.5 and 20, and then become mostly independent of reduced flow velocity. This is because at a low reduced flow velocity, the flow velocity and the tube velocity are comparable. Therefore, the influence of the structural motion on the flow is significant, which in turn causes a high rate of change in the fluid forces.

At reduced flow velocities greater than 20, the flow velocity is much higher than the tube velocity; therefore, the influence of the tube motion on the flow is very small. This causes the fluid forces acting on Tube 1 to be almost independent of the flow velocity.

The predicted phase angles are shown in Figure (4). The trend of the phase angle as a function of the reduced flow velocity can be divided into two groups. In the first group, as depicted by Figures (4a), the phase angle has a trend opposite to that of the fluid force coefficient. For example, the phase angle ϕ_{X1X} increases sharply from a negative value to a positive value over a range of the reduced flow velocities between 1.5 and 5. ϕ_{X1X} approaches a constant value of approximately 150° in the range of reduced flow velocities between 25 and 100. Phase angles with values in the range of 0 to 180° will cause the fluid damping coefficient to have a positive value, which contributes to the instability of the tube array in the lift direction.

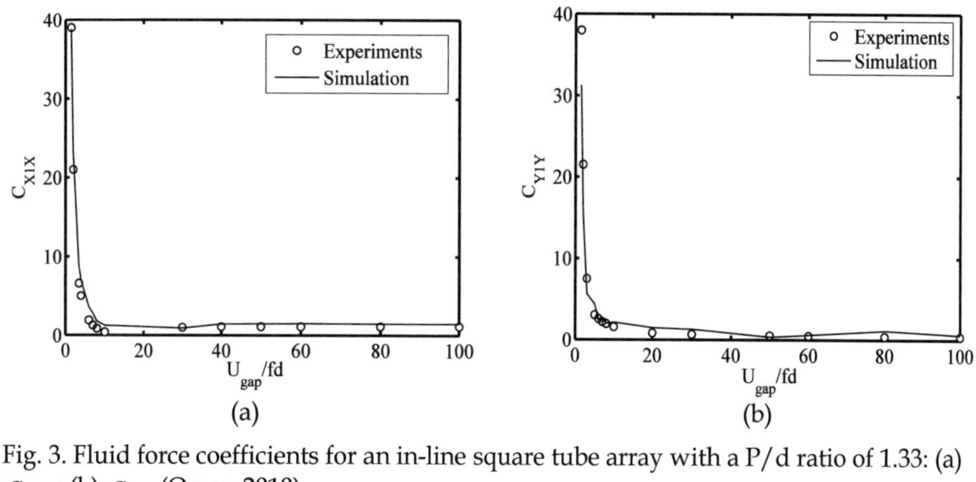

Fig. 3. Fluid force coefficients for an in-line square tube array with a P/d ratio of 1.33: (a) C_{X1X}; (b) C_{Y1Y} (Omar, 2010).

An example of the second group is presented by Figure (4b), where the phase angle ϕ_{Y1Y} decreases to a negative value in the lower ranges of reduced flow velocity, then gradually increases to a value of −20° at a reduced flow velocity of 100. In general, the agreement between the predicted phase angle and the reported experimental results is good especially for ϕ_{X1X}. The largest deviation from the experimental results is found in the case of ϕ_{Y1Y}, especially in the range of reduced flow velocities between 10 and 80.

The rest of the fluid force coefficients and the phase angles due to tube motion in the lift and the drag directions are presented in (Omar, 2010).

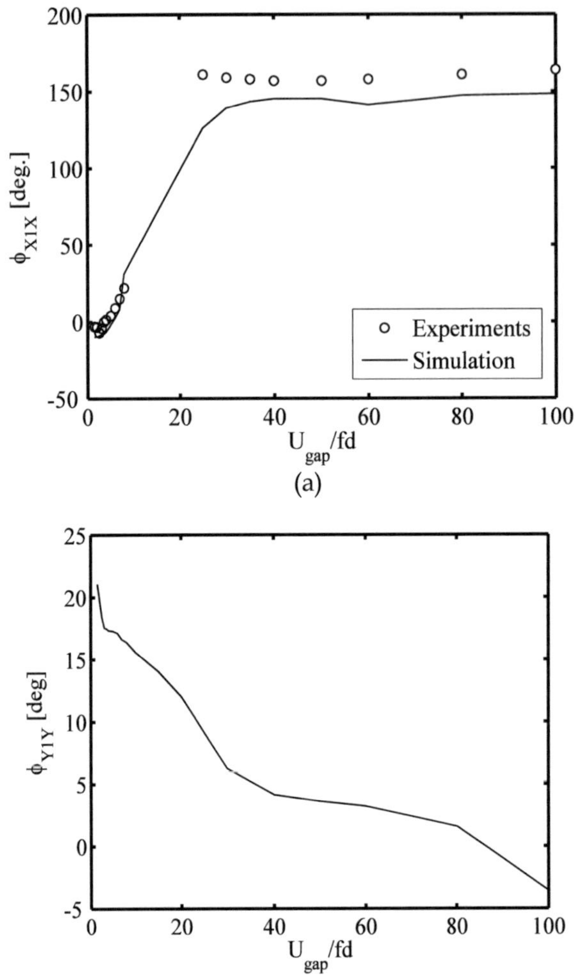

Fig. 4. Fluid force phase angles for an in-line square tube array with a P/d ratio of 1.33: (a) ϕ_{X1X}; (b) ϕ_{Y1Y} (Omar, 2010)

4.3 Prediction of stability map characteristics

In addition to comparison against fluid force coefficients obtained by experiment, the coefficients were used to simulate a fully flexible 3x3 tube array over a *mdp* range of 0.1 to 200. Firstly, the predicted force coefficients were transformed into added stiffness and added damping parameters and incorporated in the system equations of motion. The equation of motion of the tube system is given by:

$$[M_s + M_a]\{\ddot{x}\} + [C_s + C_a]\{\ddot{x}\} + [K_s + K_a]\{\ddot{x}\} = 0$$

where M_s, C_s, and K_s are the structural mass, damping, and stiffness, respectively. M_a, C_a, and K_a are the fluid added mass, damping, and stiffness, respectively. Each individual tube was assumed to have two degrees of freedoms. The size of the system matrices are the same as the total number of degrees of freedoms (18 x 18). The flow added matrices (M_a, C_a, and K_a) are functions of added fluid-damping, fluid stiffness coefficients, flow density, flow velocity and tube diameter. Secondly, the eigenvalue extraction of the above equation was employed to study the stability of the system as a function of the flow velocity. This results in a number of complex eigenvalues and eigen vectors. The reader is forwarded to (Tanaka & Takahara, 1981; Omar, 2010) for more detail. The system is unstable if the real part of the eigenvalue is positive. The critical flow velocity is determined by solving for the flow velocity at which the real part of the eigenvalue becomes zero. Results were located on the stability map and compared to experimental results available in the open literature for the same tube array geometry. The case of Tanaka and Takahara (Tanaka & Takahara, 1981) was selected since it matches the pitch to diameter ratio of the current simulation (*P/d* of 1.33). The predicted reduced critical flow velocity, U_c, as a function of mass damping parameter agrees well with the experimental data sets as shown in Figure 5. The agreement between the simulations and the experimental results is excellent.

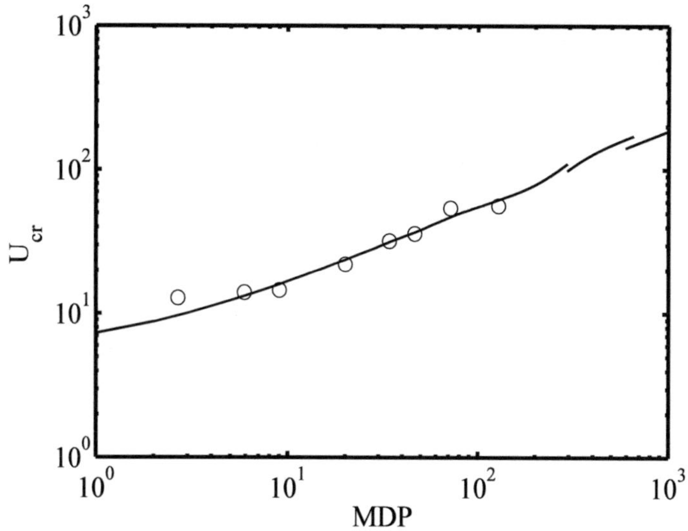

Fig. 5. Comparison of the predicted critical flow velocity with experimental data of Tanaka and Takahara (Tanaka & Takahara, 1981): ◦ experiments, – simulation (Omar, 2010; Hassan et al, 2010).

4.4 Separation and attachment

FEI models such as the unsteady analytical model by Lever and Weaver (Lever & Weaver, 1981) rely on input of separation and attachment angles for their model, shown as β_1 and β_2 respectively in Figure 1. Generally, for either case, an angle of approximately ten degrees is applied. In addition a time delay model is input to account for the delay between stream

lines perturbation and tube motion. The times delay model approximates how quickly flow along the monitoring points shown in Figure 1 is affected by any intervening tube motion.
In models such as that of Lever and Weaver (Lever & Weaver, 1981), it is assumed the flow inside the tube bundle is divided into wake and channel flows. The wake flow appears as large recirculation zones located between tubes in the spaces running transverse to the flow (zones 1 and 2 in Figure 6a). Spaces between tubes aligned with the flow direction allow the flow to proceed relatively freely along lanes (or channels as depicted in Figure 6a). The outer edges of the lanes attach and separate from neighbouring tubes on the basis of β_1 and β_2. Streamlines in the channel regions are assumed not to between intervening recirculation zones. Therefore the mass flow at each gap between tubes remains constant. In the present study the flow patterns are examined in light of these approximations.
Figure 6 shows the streamlines prevalent at three instances during one period (of time T) of tube motion in the lift direction. At time 0 s (Figure 6a) there exists a significant recirculation zone between tubes 2 and 1 (zone 1), while at time 1/3T (Figure 6b), when the tube has just passed it peak downward position, fluid streamlines are redirected from the channel 2 to the channel 1. Conversely when the tube, at 2/3 T (Figure 6c), is nearing its peak upward position, streamlines are diverted from channel 1 to channel 2. The migration of flow back and forth between channels 1 and 2 through zones 1 and 2 is not entirely periodic as other asymmetries exist in the overall flow structure.

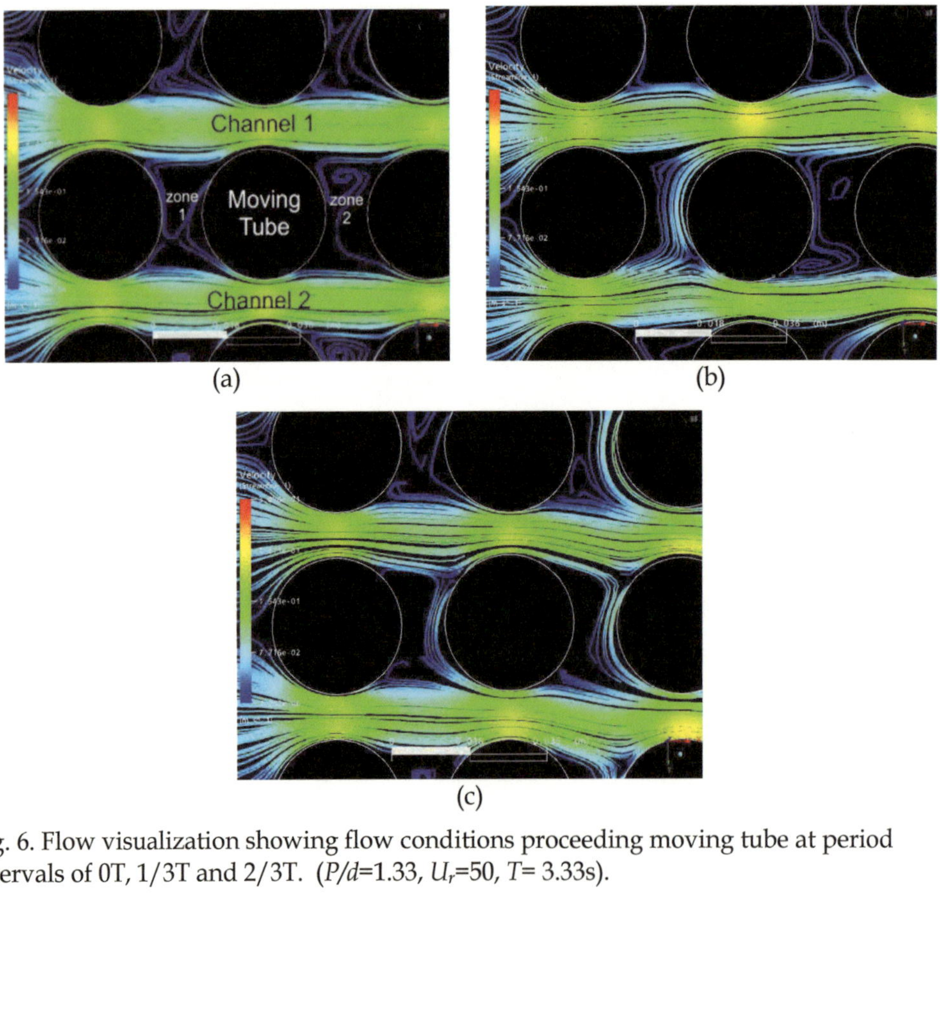

Fig. 6. Flow visualization showing flow conditions proceeding moving tube at period intervals of 0T, 1/3T and 2/3T. (P/d=1.33, U_r=50, T= 3.33s).

5. Conclusions

In this study the use of CFD to generate force coefficients in the unsteady flow models for FEI of Chen (Chen, 1991) and Tanaka and Takahara (Tanaka & Takahara, 1981) has been undertaken. The unsteady CFD simulations, with appropriate care taken for mesh and time step resolution, yield results that enable force coefficients to be well predicted. With comprehensive studies that cover a range of pitch-to-diameter ratios and reduced velocities, a series of FEI stability curves can be generated. The curves generated in this work based on CFD derived data follow the trends of that available in the literature, and reveal expected trends such as increasing critical reduced velocity with increasing *P/d* ratio. The results thus far indicate the CFD based approach for computing stability maps for family of arrays (in this case in-line) is very promising. The use of CFD data also has the added benefit of providing considerable detail on the flow behaviour in the array, and thus enables extracting information that could be used in models such as those of Weaver and Lever (Lever & Weaver, 1981). Along this vein simulations are planned using a larger array in order to isolate the region of interest around the oscillating tube from the downstream vortex shedding. This would allow a more careful investigation of the movement of the stagnation regions on the attachment side, and the degree of mass flow redirected, as a function of pitch-to-diameter ratio and reduced velocity.

6. References

J. Lever and D. S. Weaver (1982). A theoretical model for the fluid-elastic instability in heat exchanger tube bundles, ASME Journal of Pressure Vessel Technology 104, 147-158.

S. J. Price and M. P.Paidoussis (1984). An improved mathematical model for the stability of cylinder rows subject to cross-flow, Journal of Sound and Vibration 97, 615-640.

S.S. Chen (1991). Fluidelastic instabilities in tube bundles exposed to no uniform cross-flow, Journal of Fluids and Structures 5, 299-322.

H. Tanaka and S. Takahara (1981). Fluid elastic vibration of tube array in cross flow, Journal of Sound and Vibration 77, 19-37.

D. Weber, R. Brewster, S. Chen, and T. Wei, (2001). Numerical method for fluidelastic instability evaluation in nuclear reactor system and plant components, Transactions, SMiRT 16, Washington CD, p. Paper number 1194.

H. Omar, M. Hassan, & A. Gerber (2009). Numerical Estimation of Fluidelastic Instability in Staggered Tube Arrays; ASME, PVP conference 2009 -77472, Prague, Czech.

H. Omar (2010). Numerical Simulation of Fluidelastic Instability in Tube Bundles, PhD's thesis, New Brunswick, Canada, 2010, available from http://www.synergiescanada.org/theses/unb/1089

M. Hassan, A. Gerber, H. Omar (2010). Numerical Estimation of Fluidelastic Instability in Tube Arrays, Journal of Pressure Vessel Technology, vol. 132, issue 4, 04130, 2010.

G.E. Schneider and M.J. Raw (1987). Control volume finite-element method for heat transfer and fluid flow using colocated variables - 1. Computational Procedure, Numerical Heat Transfer 11, pp. 363-390.

F.R. Menter (1994). Two-Equation Eddy-Viscosity Turbulence Models for Engineering Applications, AIAA Journal 32, No. 8.

M.J. Raw (1996). Robustness of Coupled Algebraic Multi-grid for the Navier Stokes Equation," AIAA 96-0297, 34th Aerospace and Sciences Meeting & Exhibit, Reno, NV.

E. Williams (2004). A computational fluid dynamics study of unsteady flow theory Coefficients for tube array fluidelastic instability, Master's thesis, New Brunswick, Canada.

15

Large-Eddy Simulation of Turbulent Flow and Plume Dispersion in a Spatially-Developing Turbulent Boundary Layer Flow

Hiromasa Nakayama
Japan Atomic Energy Agency
Japan

1. Introduction

In one of local-scale dispersion problems, we have an important issue in the accurate prediction of airborne contaminant dispersion from industrial or nuclear facilities for safety and consequence assessments of nuclear facilities. For evaluating radiological consequences of radioactive materials, it is need to predict not only the material concentration in the air at the evaluation point for internal dose but also on the three-dimensional distribution of the plume and surface deposition for external dose. In a flat terrain, time-averaged concentration of a plume can be easily predicted by a conventional Gaussian plume model. However, in Japan, most nuclear facilities are located in complex coastal terrain. Therefore, it is important to predict the spatial distribution of concentrations considering effects from terrain and buildings.

Another issue related to atmospheric dispersion in a local-scale is the potential problem that hazardous and flammable materials are accidentally or intentionally released into the atmosphere, either within or close to populated urban areas. For the assessment of human health hazards from such toxic substances, the existence of high concentration peaks in a plume should be considered because it is the instantaneous, not average, concentration that is fatal to humans. In such a situation, it is necessary to accurately predict the unsteady behavior of a plume, considering the effects of individual buildings. For the safety analysis of flammable gases, certain critical threshold levels should be evaluated. Therefore, in such a situation, not only the average levels but also instantaneous magnitudes of concentration should be accurately predicted.

There are various methods for predicting plume dispersion in atmospheric boundary layers, e.g. wind tunnel experiments and Computational Fluid Dynamics (CFD). It is well known that wind tunnel experiments are a rational tool for predicting plume dispersion behavior under local topography and/or building conditions. For the case of accidental or intentional release of contaminated materials within urban areas, many studies using a wind tunnel have been made to investigate the spatial extent of contaminated areas and the characteristics of mean and fluctuating concentrations around an individual building. In the safety assessment for the construction of nuclear facilities, prediction of the spatial distribution of radionuclide concentrations over complex terrain containing buildings is required by using a wind tunnel (*Meteorological Guide for Safety Analysis of Nuclear Power*

Plant Reactor, Nuclear Safety Commission of Japan, 1982). Although reliable data can be obtained on air flow and plume dispersion, wind tunnel experiments are time consuming, costly, and have limited availability for these applications. For example, in the safety assessment, experimental results are only used to derive the effective stack height, which is applied for long term assessment using a Gaussian plume model, and the effective stack height is usually determined lower height than the actual height considering terrain and building effects in a way that provides a conservative evaluation. On the other hand, recently the CFD technique has been proposed for use as an alternative to wind tunnel experiments (Sada *et al.*, 2009) developed a numerical model for atmospheric diffusion analysis and evaluation of effective dose for safety analysis and showed its effectiveness in comparison with wind tunnel experiments.

The CFD technique has been recognized as a helpful tool with the rapid development of computational technology. The CFD technique uses computers to numerically predict fluid flow, heat transfer and mass transfer by solving the governing equations. In particular, there are two different approaches, the Reynolds-Averaged Navier-Stokes (RANS) and Large-Eddy Simulation (LES) models, which are both effective for predicting turbulent flows. In RANS, a mean wind flow is computed, delivering an ensemble- or time-averaged solution, and all turbulent motions are modeled with a turbulence model. The main advantage of the RANS model is its efficiency in computing a mean flow field with relatively low computational cost. Sada *et al.*, (2009) designed a practical numerical model based on the RANS model.

Recently, LES has come to be regarded as an effective prediction method for environmental flows. LES resolves the large-scale turbulent motions and models only the smallest scale motions, which are usually more universal. Although the LES model requires larger computational costs than RANS model, it is no less useful the latter, considering the cost and limited availability of wind tunnels and the experimental time needed. Furthermore, LES can provide accurate predictions and detailed information about turbulence structures, and mean and fluctuating concentrations of a plume as well as wind tunnel experiments can provide them. Therefore, we have developed an LES dispersion model applicable to actual problems of atmospheric dispersion on a local scale. As a first step, we previously performed LES for turbulent flows and plume dispersion over a flat terrain (Nakayama & Nagai, 2009). When compared to experimental results of Fackrell & Robins., (1982), it was shown that turbulence structures, the characteristic mean and r.m.s. (root mean square) concentrations, turbulent concentration flux and peak concentration over a flat terrain are successfully simulated. These findings implied that our LES model could replace wind tunnel experiments for safety assessments of nuclear facilities and also provide detailed information for the consequence assessment of accidental and intentional releases of radioactive materials into the atmosphere.

For the second step, we apply our LES dispersion model to the complex behaviors of separated shear layers and large eddies in the near-wake of a building. First, we propose a scheme to generate a spatially-developing turbulent boundary layer flow with strong velocity fluctuations, which is applicable to various types of wind tunnel flows and perform an LES of plume dispersion around an isolated cubical building. Then, we examine basic performance of the model and scheme by comparing LES data of the turbulent structure and characteristics of mean and r.m.s. concentrations including peak concentration with experimental data.

2. Numerical model

The governing equations for LES of atmospheric flow are the filtered continuity equation, the Navier-Stokes equation,

$$\frac{\partial \overline{u}_i}{\partial x_i} = 0 , \tag{1}$$

$$\frac{\partial \overline{u}_i}{\partial t} + \overline{u}_j \frac{\partial \overline{u}_i}{\partial x_j} = -\frac{1}{\rho}\frac{\partial \overline{p}}{\partial x_i} + \frac{\partial}{\partial x_j} \nu \left(\frac{\partial \overline{u}_i}{\partial x_j} + \frac{\partial \overline{u}_j}{\partial x_i} \right) - \frac{\partial}{\partial x_j}\tau_{ij} + f_i , \tag{2}$$

$$\tau_{ij} = \overline{u_i u_j} - \overline{u}_i \overline{u}_j , \tag{3}$$

$$\tau_{ij} - \frac{1}{3}\delta_{ij}\tau_{kk} = -\nu_{SGS}\overline{S_{ij}} \quad \nu_{SGS} = \left(C_s f_s \overline{\Delta}\right)^2 \left(2\overline{S_{ij}}\,\overline{S_{ij}}\right)^{\frac{1}{2}} , \tag{4}$$

$$\overline{S_{ij}} = \left(\partial \overline{u_i} / \partial x_j + \partial \overline{u_j} / \partial x_i \right) / 2 , \tag{5}$$

and

$$\overline{\Delta} = \left(\overline{\Delta_x}\,\overline{\Delta_y}\,\overline{\Delta_z} \right)^{\frac{1}{3}} , \tag{6}$$

where u_i, t, p, ρ, ν, τ_{ij} and f_i are the wind velocity, time, pressure, density, kinematic viscosity, subgrid-scale Reynolds stress and external force term, respectively. The subscript i stands for coordinates (1, streamwise; 2, spanwise; and 3, vertical direction). Over bars, $(\overline{\ })$ denote application of the spatial filter. δ_{ij}, ν_{SGS}, C_s and f_s are the Kronecker delta, the eddy viscosity coefficient, the model constant of the flow field and Van Driest damping function (Van Driest., 1956), respectively. $\overline{\Delta}$ denotes the grid-filter width. In this LES model, the external force term proposed by Goldstein *et al.*, (1993) is applied because of its computational stability for turbulent flow around a bluff body. The force term, f_i is incorporated into the Navier-Stokes equation to consider the building effects and can be assumed as the following expression;

$$f_i = \alpha \int_0^t u_i(t')dt' + \beta u_i(t), \quad \alpha < 0,\ \beta < 0 \tag{7}$$

where α and β are negative constants. The stability limit is given by $\Delta t < \dfrac{-\beta - \sqrt{\left(\beta^2 - 2\alpha k\right)}}{\alpha}$ where k is a constant of order 1. The most commonly used sub-grid scale models are the standard and dynamic type Smagorinsky models (Smagorinsky., 1963; Germano *et al.*, 1991; Lilly *et al.*, 1992; Meneveau *et al.*, 1996). Although C_s should be estimated depending on the flow type, the standard Smagorinsky model (Smagorinsky., 1963) with the Van Driest damping function is used instead in our LES model because of its simplicity and low computational cost. C_s is set to 0.12 (Shirasawa *et al.*, 2008).

The LES of plume dispersion is also computed by using the standard Smagorinsky model. The spatially filtered scalar conservation equations are presented by

$$\frac{\partial \overline{c}}{\partial t} + \overline{u}_j \frac{\partial \overline{c}}{\partial x_j} = -\frac{\partial}{\partial x_j} s_j \,, \tag{8}$$

$$s_j = \overline{u_j c} - \overline{u}_j \overline{c} \tag{9}$$

and

$$s_j = -\frac{\nu_{SGS}}{Sc_{SGS}} \frac{\partial \overline{c}}{\partial x_j} \,, \tag{10}$$

where s_j is the subgrid-scale scalar flux which is also parameterized by an eddy viscosity model. The model constant, Sc_{SGS}, is the turbulent Schmidt number and it is set to a constant value of 0.5 (Sada & Sato., 2002).

The coupling algorithm of the velocity and pressure fields is based on the Marker and Cell (Harlow & Welch, 1965) method with the Adams-Bashforth scheme for time integration. The Poisson equation is solved by the Successive Over-Relaxation method that is an iterative method for solving a Poisson equation for pressure. For the spatial discretization in the governing equation of flow and the tracer transport, a second-order accurate central difference is used. For only the advection term in the dispersion field, the Cubic Interpolated Pseudo-particle (CIP) method (Takewaki *et al.*, 1985; Yabe & Takei., 1988) is imposed in order to prevent a numerical instability. The CIP is a very stable scheme that can solve generalized hyperbolic equations in space. The Reynolds number based on the cubical building height and wind speed at the building height is almost 5,000.

3. Wind tunnel experiments for evaluating the model performance

Over the past few decades many wind tunnel experiments have been conducted on the dispersion characteristics of a plume in the near-wake of a cubical building. For example, Sada & Sato., (2002) conducted experiments under neutral atmospheric stratification in the wind tunnel of Central Research Institute of Electric Power Industry. The wind tunnel test section was 20m long, 3m wide and 1.5m high. An approaching flow with strong velocity fluctuations was generated using roughness elements with L-shaped cross sections placed on the floor at the entrance of the wind tunnel. It was shown that spanwise and vertical spreads of a plume corresponded to the Pasquill-Gifford stability class D. A plume was released from an elevated point source located upstream from the cubical building and concentration of the plume is measured by a fast-response flame ionization detector. The vertical profiles of mean wind velocity, turbulence intensity, mean and r.m.s. concentrations and peak concentration in the near-wake region of the cubical building were all obtained from the experiments. In this wind tunnel experiment, the building Reynolds numbers based on the cubical building height and wind speed at the building height is about 13,000.

In the present paper, in order to evaluate the model performance, we compare our LES results of turbulent flow and plume dispersion in the near-wake region of a cubical building with the wind tunnel experimental data of Sada & Sato., (2002).

4. Computational settings

In wind tunnel experiments, a neutral atmospheric turbulent boundary layer is simulated mainly using various types of obstacle, such as spires, tripping fences and roughness blocks. Therefore, various wind tunnel flows that have different turbulence characteristics can be obtained depending on the wind tunnel facility. In an LES study of turbulent flow in the atmosphere, an approach flow with turbulent fluctuations as the inlet boundary condition of the model domain should be generated depending on the target wind tunnel flow by a certain method.

In our LES model, the driver region for generating a spatially-developing turbulent boundary layer flow and the main region for simulating of plume dispersion around a cubical building immersed in a fully-developed turbulent boundary layer are set up. In this scheme, first a thick turbulent boundary layer flow is generated by incorporating the existing inflow turbulence generation method, that is, the method of Kataoka & Mizuno., (2002) into an upstream small fraction of the driver region as shown in Figure 1(a). Then, a strong wind velocity fluctuation is produced by a tripping fence placed downstream from the recycle station as shown in Figure 1(b).

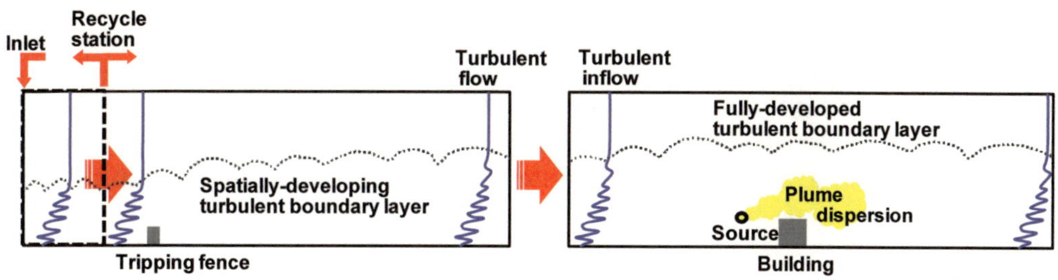

(a) (b)

Fig. 1. Schematic of numerical model. (a) Driver region for generating turbulent boundary layer flow. (b) Main region for turbulent flow and plume dispersion around a cubical building.

In the method of Kataoka & Mizuno., (2002), the fluctuating part of the velocity at the recycle station is recycled and added to the specified mean wind velocity at each time interval by assuming that boundary layer thickness is constant within the driver section. This method requires a driver section with a length of about 1.0δ. The formulation of the method of Kataoka & Mizuno., (2002) is as follows.

$$u_{inlt}(y,z,t) = \langle u \rangle_{inlt}(z) + \phi(\theta)\{u_{recy}(y,z,t) - [u](z)\}, \tag{11}$$

$$v_{inlt}(y,z,t) = \phi(\theta)\, v_{recy}(y,z,t), \tag{12}$$

$$w_{inlt}(y,z,t) = \phi(\theta)\, \{w_{recy}(y,z,t) - [w](z)\}, \tag{13}$$

$$\phi(\theta) = \frac{1}{2}\left\{1 - \tanh\left[\frac{a(\theta - b)}{(1-2b)\theta + b}\right] \Big/ \tanh a\right\}, \tag{14}$$

Here, u_{inlt} and u_{recy} are the instantaneous wind velocity at the inlet and the downstream position (the recycle station), respectively. $\langle u \rangle_{inlt}$ is the specified mean wind velocity at the inlet. $[u_i]$ is the averaged wind velocity in the horizontal plane. $\phi(\theta)$ is a damping function to control the transport of turbulent fluctuation into the free stream. a and b are constants.
Calculations of both driver and main regions are done by the same model with different computational settings. As boundary conditions, the Sommerfeld radiation condition (Gresho., 1992) is imposed at the exit, a free-slip condition for streamwise and spanwise velocity components is imposed and the vertical velocity component is 0 at the top, a periodic condition is imposed at the side, and a non-slip condition for each velocity component is imposed at the ground surface. Here, in our LES model, we do not use wall functions as the boundary condition of the ground surface. Therefore, the resolution of a vertically stretched grid above the ground surface is set to 1.7 in order to resolve the viscous layer.
The size and the number of grid points for the driver region is 32.8H×10.0H×9.5H (H: height of the cubical building) and 410×120×70 in streamwise, spanwise and vertical directions, respectively. A tripping fence has a height of 0.45H.
The size and number of grid points for the main region are 18.9H×10.0H×9.5H and 400×120×70 in streamwise, spanwise and vertical directions, respectively. The cubical building is resolved by 20×20×30 grids in the streamwise, spanwise and vertical directions, respectively. According to numerical experiments of Xie *et al.*, (2006) and Santiago *et al.*, (2008), a building should be resolved by at least 15-20 grid points in each dimension in order to capture complex turbulent behaviors. The mesh number of the building set up in our LES model is enough to accurately simulate turbulent flows around a building. At the inlet of the main region, the inflow turbulence data obtained near the exit of the driver region is imposed at each time interval. In a concentration field, zero gradient is imposed at all the boundaries. The release point of a tracer gas is located 1.5H upstream from the center of the building and elevated at height, H. According to the above-mentioned coordinates, the location of the release point of a plume corresponds to x/H=0.0 and z/H=1.0 as seen in Figure 2.

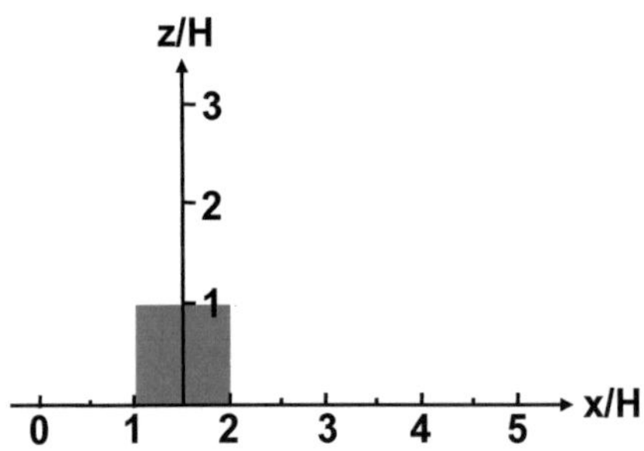

Fig. 2. Coordinate system.

5. Results

5.1 Approach flow

Figure 3 compares the LES model results with wind tunnel experimental data (Sada & Sato., 2002) of the vertical profiles of mean wind velocity (U), each component of turbulence intensities (u', v', w') and Reynolds stress in the driver region. The turbulence statistics is normalized by a free-stream velocity (U_∞). We see that the mean wind velocity profile obtained by our LES model is consistent with the experimental data. Strong turbulent fluctuations are produced from the ground surface to the upper part of the boundary layer and each component of the LES-generated turbulent intensity profiles is found to be in good agreement with the experimental data. The Reynolds stress profile obtained by our LES model is also in good agreement with the experimental data.

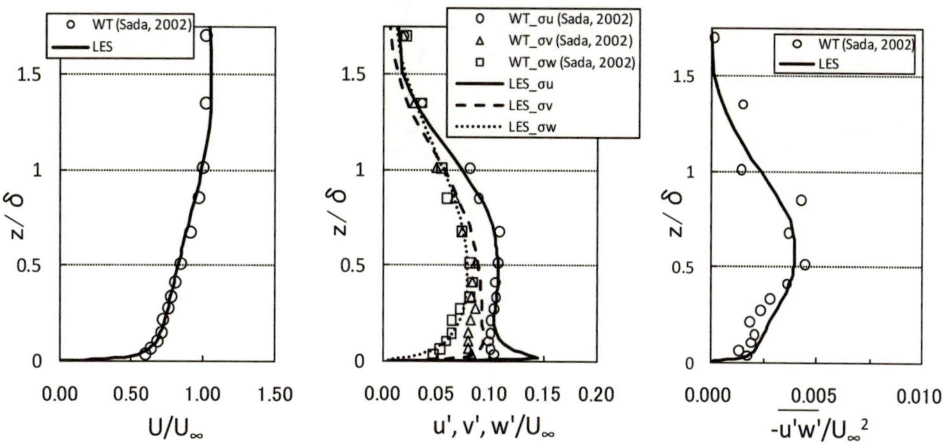

Fig. 3. Turbulence characteristics of approach flow.

5.2 Turbulent flow field

Figure 4 shows mean velocity vectors by LES around a building. The reattachment lengths of recirculating flow behind the building normalized by the building height of the experiments and the LES model is L/H=1.2 and 1.35 (L: reattachment length), respectively; the latter is slightly larger. Figure 5 shows a comparison of our LES model results with the experimental data (Sada & Sato., 2002) of the vertical profiles of mean wind velocity obtained downstream at x/H=0.0, 1.5, 2.5 and 3.5. The LES model results of mean wind velocity are consistent with the wind tunnel experimental data at each downwind position.

Fig. 4. Mean velocity vectors around a building.

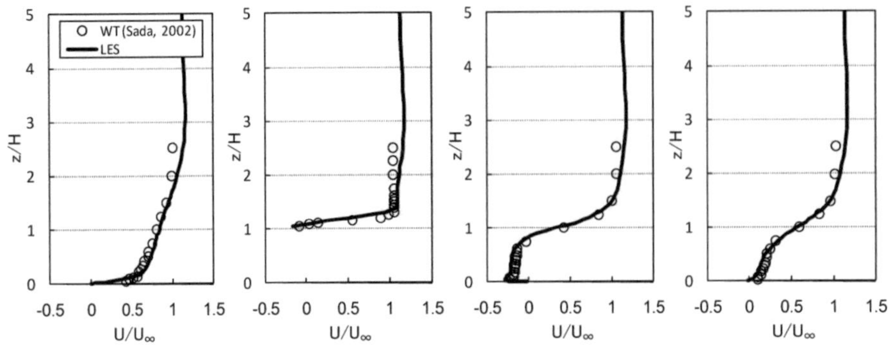

Fig. 5. Streamwise variation of vertical profiles of mean wind velocity.

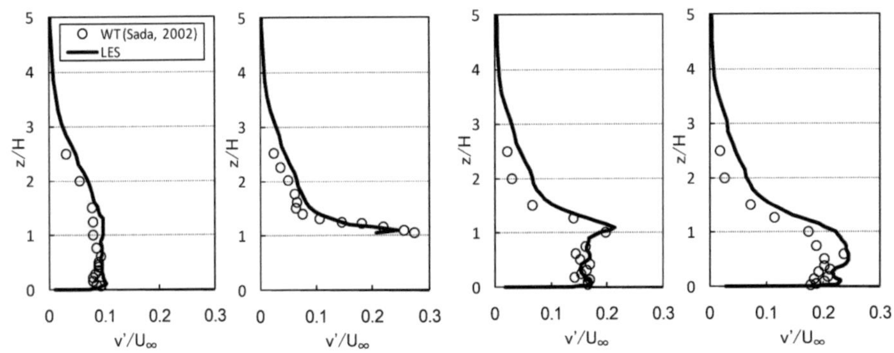

(a)

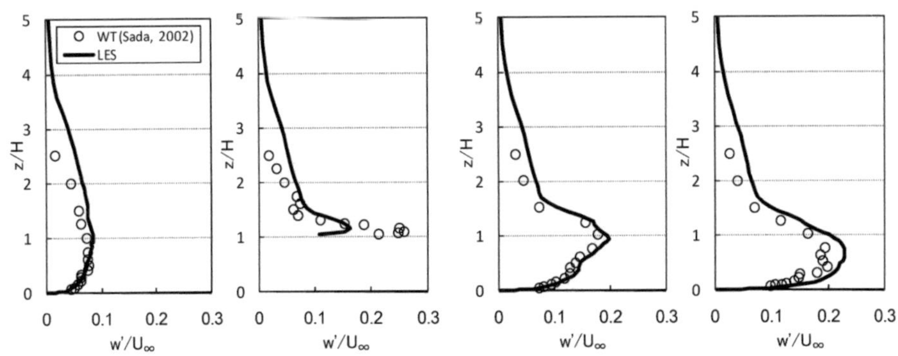

(b)

Fig. 6. Streamwise variation of turbulence intensities. (a) Horizontal turbulence intensity. (b) Vertical turbulence intensity.

Figure 6 shows a comparison of our LES model results with the wind tunnel experimental data of the vertical profiles of (a) horizontal and (b) vertical turbulence intensities normalized by free-stream velocity obtained downstream at x/H=0.0, 1.5, 2.5 and 3.5. Just above the roof of the building at x/H=0.0, the LES model results of both horizontal and vertical turbulence intensities are underestimated. At the position located away from the

building, x/H=3.5, the LES model results of both horizontal and vertical turbulence intensities around the building height are a little overestimated. Mochida *et al.*, (1991) reported that the LES results of turbulence kinetic energy using the standard Smagorinsky model were overestimated around the upper edge of the recirculation zone of an obstacle in comparison with the wind tunnel experimental data. The overestimation of turbulence intensities of LES behind a building is due to the use of the standard Smagorinsky model.
Although the standard Smagorinsky model has the above problems, the main characteristics are obtained in our simulation. They include a sharp peak behind the building due to the strong instability of separated shear layers and the formation of a uniform turbulent flow field with downstream distance due to the active turbulent motions almost the same as in the experimental data of Sada & Sato., (2002). The slight overestimation of the reattachment length has also been reported in other LES calculations (Murakami *et al.*, 1986). Therefore, our LES model with the conventional Smagorinsky model shows reasonable accuracy and satisfactorily results.

5.3 Dispersion field

Figure 7(a), (b) and (c) shows instantaneous plume dispersion fields around a building at times t^* ($=tU_\infty/H$) = 15, 45 and 90 after the plume release. The yellow areas on iso-surface indicate 0.01% of initial concentration. It shows that the plume is passed above the building roof at first, and then the plume is entrained into the wake region of a building. After enough time passing, the plume is found to be widely dispersed behind a building due to the active turbulent motions.
Figure 8 shows a comparison of our LES model results and the wind tunnel experimental data (Sada & Sato., 2002) of the vertical profiles of mean (C) and r.m.s. (c') concentrations obtained downstream at x/H=1.5, 2.5, 3.5 and 5.0 in the near-wake region of the cubical building. The mean and r.m.s. concentrations are normalized by free-stream velocity, the building height and the source strength (Q). In both mean and r.m.s. concentration fields, the peak values of the LES model near the point source are about 50% smaller than the wind tunnel experimental results, while the model results are in good agreement with the experimental data, particularly at the position x/H=5.0, located away from the point source. These large discrepancies near the point source are possibly due to a coarse grid resolution for the plume source.
In our LES model, a plume source is provided in one grid-cell. Thus, the size of the point source is determined by the grid resolution. Michioka *et al.*, (2003) examined the sensitivity of the grid resolution for the point source by LES of a plume dispersion released from the point sources corresponding to 1.0 and 10 times the real diameters of the point source. As a result, they found that the peak values of mean and r.m.s. concentrations near the point source in a coarse grid resolution were 80% smaller than the wind tunnel experimental data, while those in a fine grid resolution were consistent with the experimental data. The plume source diameter in our LES model is about 5.5 times that of the real one. Considering the discrepancy of the plume source diameter between the LES model and the wind tunnel experiments, our results have the same tendency to underestimate near the point source as the LES results by Michioka *et al.* Therefore, if the plume source size corresponding to the real one is properly set in our LES model, the model results near the point source should be improved. However, a fine grid resolution is not appropriate for our purpose and target scale considering its computational cost. Except for this discrepancy, the basic characteristics, such as a sharp peak just behind the cubical building and the formation of

uniform profiles of mean and r.m.s. concentrations with downstream distance are similar to the experimental data.

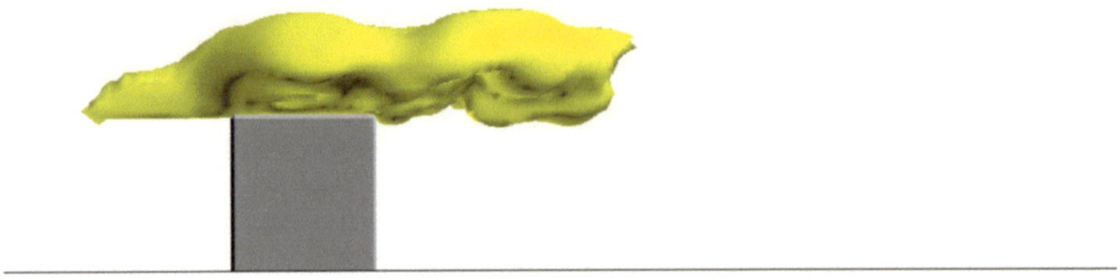

(a) t* =15

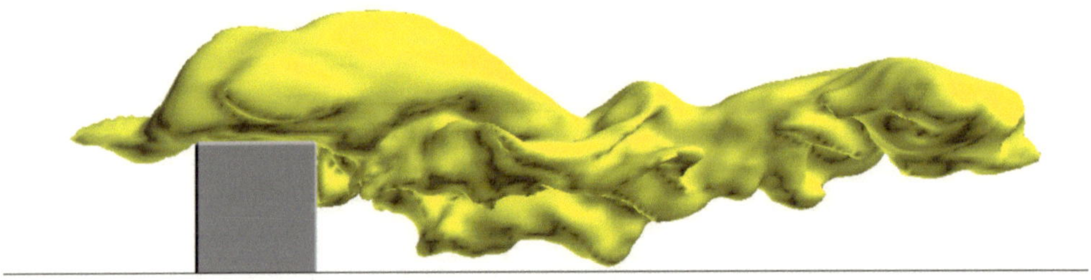

(b) t* =45

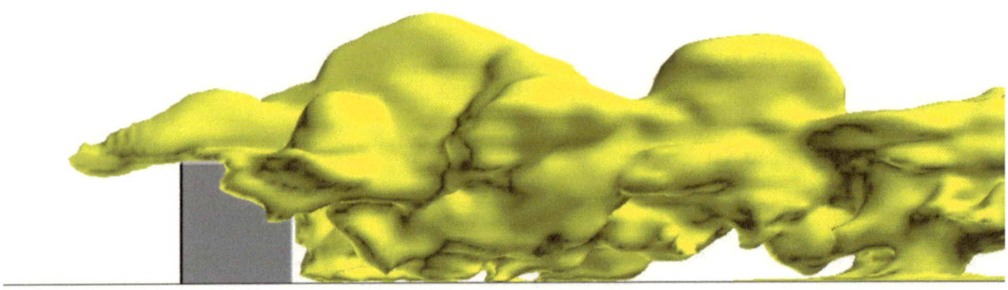

(c) t* =90

Fig. 7. Instantaneous plume dispersion field. The yellow areas on the isosurface indicate 0.01% of initial concentration.

In the present LES model, the point source diameter is larger than the real one because a numerical simulation with a fine grid resolution requires large computational time. However, as we explain above, our LES model presents almost the same patterns of concentration distributions as the wind tunnel experiments. This fact indicates that our LES model gives satisfacotoly results.

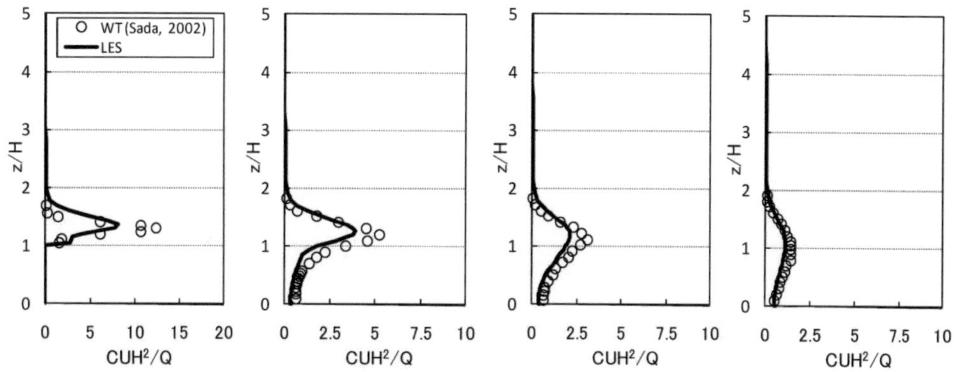

(a)

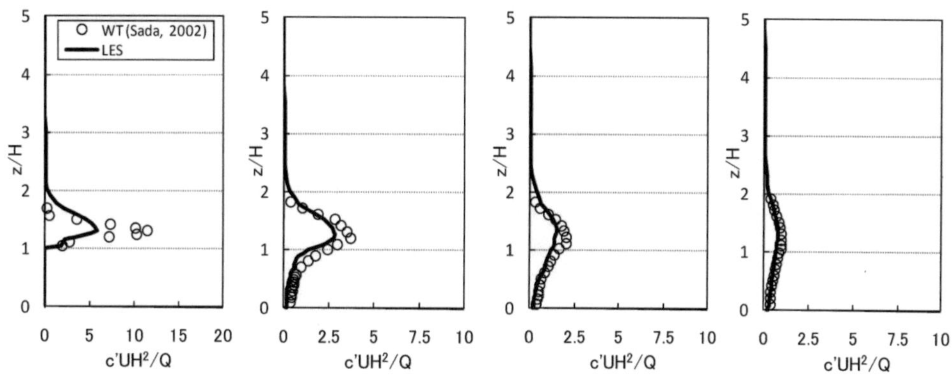

(b)

Fig. 8. Streamwise variation of vertical profiles of mean concentrations in the near-wake of the cubical building. (a) Mean concentration. (b) R.m.s. concentration.

5.4 Characteristics of the peak concentration

In case of accidental or intentional release of toxic or flammable gases into the atmosphere, it is important to estimate not only the mean but also the instantaneous and local peak concentrations near the surface of the ground. For example, Li & Meroney (1983) conducted wind tunnel experiments of gas dispersion of a plume released from the center roof vent of a cubical building and investigated the streamwise variation of vertical profiles of mean and r.m.s. concentrations, and various peak concentrations (c_{99}, c_{95}, c_{90}) defined as the values that are not exceeded for 99, 95, 90% of the cumulative probability density function in the near-wake region. In the theoretical studies of the probability distributions of concentration fluctuation have been studied by many researchers, Csanady (1973), Hanna (1984), and Lewellen & Sykes (1986) proposed theoretical models of the log-normal, exponential and clipped normal distributions for predicting concentration fluctuations of a plume in the atmosphere as follows.

Log-normal distribution function:

$$P(c) = \frac{1}{2}\left[1 + erf\left\{\frac{\ln(c/n_c)}{\sqrt{2}\sigma_l}\right\}\right], \tag{15}$$

Exponential distribution function:

$$P(c) = 1 - I\exp\left(-I\frac{c}{C}\right), \tag{16}$$

Clipped normal distribution function:

$$P(c) = \frac{1}{2}\left\{1 + erf\left(\frac{c - \mu_0}{\sqrt{2}\sigma_0}\right)\right\}, \tag{17}$$

Here, erf, n_c, σ_l, μ_0 and σ_0 are error function, the median concentration, the logarithmic standard deviation, the specified mean and the specified variance. According to Hanna (1984), I can be expressed as follows using C_i which is the concentration fluctuation intensity defined as the ratio of r.m.s. concentration to mean concentration.

$$I = \frac{2}{C_i^2 + 1}, \tag{18}$$

These theoretical models cannot predict the spatial distribution of concentration but can estimate peak concentrations at a stationary point. Sato and Sato., (2002) compared the log-normal, exponential and clipped normal probability distributions of concentration fluctuation in the near-wake region of a cubical building with those for wind tunnel experiments using concentration statistics of n_c, σ_l, C_i, μ_0 and σ_0 obtained in the experiments. They showed that a peak concentration of c_{99} could be predicted using the log-normal type for $0.3<C_i<1.0$, the log-normal or the exponential types for $1.0<C_i<1.5$, and the exponential type for $C_i>1.5$, while peak concentration of the clipped-normal type was entirely underestimated.

Here, we first compare the probability distributions of concentration fluctuation of the LES model with those of the theoretical models and assess the prediction accuracy of the occurrences of instantaneous high concentrations in our LES model. Then, we examine the characteristics of not only peak concentration ratios of c_{99} but also c_{95} and c_{90} in the near-wake region of the cubical building.

Figure 9 shows a comparison of probability distribution functions (1-p(c)) of concentration fluctuation of the LES model at the heights of z/H=0.1, 1.6 and 2.0 at the downstream position of x/H=3.5 with theoretical model. Concentration is normalized with the r.m.s. concentration. Concentration fluctuation intensity, C_i, has values of 0.57, 1.3 and 2.2 at the heights of z/H=0.1, 1.6 and 2.0, respectively. For evaluating probability distributions of concentration fluctuation of each theoretical model, we use concentration statistics of n_c, σ_l, C_i, μ_0 and σ_0 obtained by the LES model. c_{99}, c_{95} and c_{90} are determined from 1-p(c)=0.99, 0.95 and 0.90, respectively. At z/H=0.1, the probability distribution of the LES model is almost the same as that of the log-normal type, while the model result of c_{99}/c' is much smaller than the exponential one. At z/H=1.6, the probability distribution of the LES model is similar to that of both the log-normal and exponential types. At z/H=2.0, the probability distribution of the LES model is consistent with that of the exponential type. Furthermore, the model results of c_{99}/c' are almost the same as those of the exponential one, while the log-normal probability distribution is different from that of the LES model. c_{99}/c' values obtained from the clipped-normal type are underestimated at each height. These facts indicate that the characteristics of probability distributions of the LES model depending on the values of C_i are consistent with those reported by Sato & Sada., (2002). Therefore, the occurrences of instantaneous high concentrations are captured by LES and we conclude that the basic performance of the LES model for plume dispersion around the cubical building is nearly comparable to that for the wind tunnel experiments.

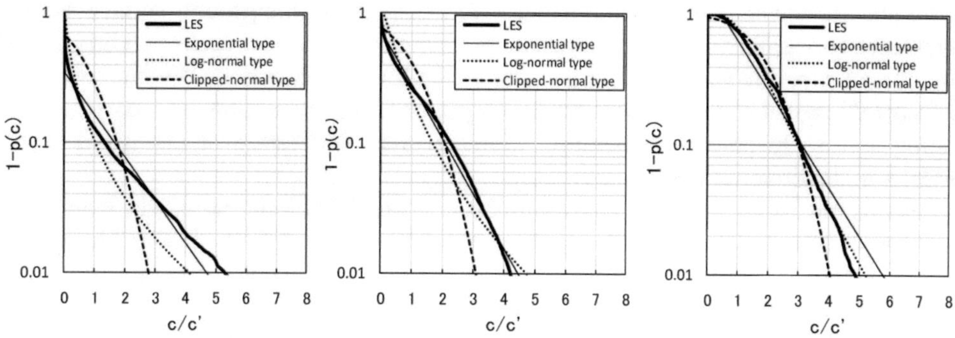

Fig. 9. Probability distribution functions of concentration fluctuation. (a)z/H=0.1, (b)z/H=0.16 and (c)z/H=2.0.

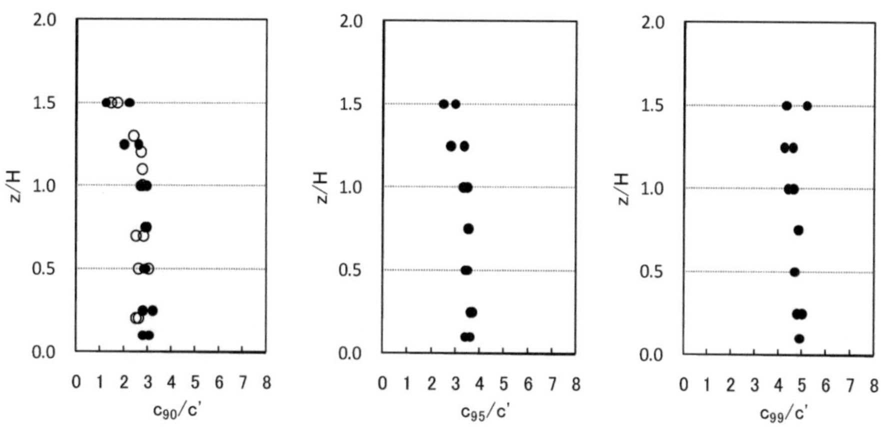

Fig. 10. Vertical profiles of various peak concentration ratios of (a)c_{90}/c', (b)c_{95}/c' and (c)c_{99}/c'.

Next, we examine various peak concentrations of c_{99}, c_{95}, and c_{90} obtained by the LES model. Figure 10 shows vertical profiles of various peak concentration ratios at x/H=2.5 and 3.5. c_{90}/c' values of the LES model have uniform distributions with a constant value of about 3.0 within the building height and gradually decrease above the building height. These tendencies are similar to the experimental data (Sada & Sato., 2002). c_{95}/c' of the LES model also shows a constant value of about 4.0 within the building height and slightly decreases above the building height. c_{99}/c' of the LES model provides uniform distributions with a constant value of about 5.0 at any position. This tendency is the same as the experimental data of Sato and Sato., 2002.

6. Conclusion

In this study, we performed LES of turbulent flow and plume dispersion around a cubical building and investigated the basic performance of the LES model in comparison with experimental data of Sada & Sato., (2002), Sato and Sato., (2002). The scheme to generate a spatially-developing turbulent boundary layer flow in the driver region was proposed by incorporating an existing inflow turbulence generation method into an upstream small fraction of the driver region with a tripping fence placed at the ground surface. With this scheme, we successfully simulated a turbulent boundary layer flow corresponding to that in wind tunnel experiments of Sada & Sato., (2002) in the driver section. The findings implied that our LES model could simulate various types of wind tunnel flow by incorporating the existing inflow turbulence generation method and moderately setting up roughness obstacles in the driver region.

Turbulence intensities behind a cubical building around the building height were slightly overestimated in comparison with experimental data of Sada & Sato., (2002). However, the main characteristics of turbulent flow such as a sharp peak behind the building and the formation of a uniform turbulent flow field with downstream distance, corresponding to the wind tunnel experiment, are obtained. Also, dispersion characteristics such as a sharp peak close to the point source and the formation of concentration profiles with downstream distance were successfully simulated in comparison with the experimental data. These indicated that the difference in turbulence characteristics between the experiments and our LES model was not significant. The basic performance of our LES model for turbulent flow and dispersion fields could be recognized as comparable to the wind tunnel experiment.

Dependence of the patterns of probability distributions of concentration fluctuation of the LES model on the values of concentration fluctuation intensity were consistent with those of the wind tunnel experimental results of Sato & Sada., (2002). Focusing on various peak concentration ratios, we saw c_{90}/c' and c_{99}/c' values of the LES model were in good agreement with the experimental data. From these facts, we considered that the occurrences of high concentrations were captured by our LES model. From the above results, we considered that the basic performance of our LES model was almost comparable level to that obtained by the wind tunnel experimental techniques.

Here, we discuss the applicability of the present LES model for flow and dispersion around an isolated building to the problem of plume dispersion within a group of buildings. Within an urban canopy, three typical flow patterns, isolated flow, wake interference flow and skimming flow within building arrays are formed depending on the ratio of the buildings height to the street width and the flow filed is highly complex (Oke., 1998). Considering a surface geometry of urban canopy is composed of a group of isolated buildings and obstacles, numerical simulation with moderate grid points for each building and obstacle can capture such complex flow patterns with reasonable accuracy. Therefore, from the validation of our LES model for turbulent flow and plume dispersion around an isolated building, it is considered that the present model with moderate grid points for each building can apply to a simulation of plume dispersion within urban canopy.

7. References

Csanady, G.T. (1973). *Turbulent Diffusion in the Environment,* D.Reidel Publishing Co., Dordrecht, Holland, 222-248

Fackrell, J.E. & Robins, A.G. (1982). Concentration fluctuation and fluxes in plumes from point sources in a turbulent boundary layer, *J. Fluid Mech.*, 117, 1-26

Germano, M.; Piomelli, U., Moin, P. & Cabot, W.H. (1991). A dynamic subgrid-scale eddy viscosity model, *Phys. Fluids.*, A3, 7, 1760-1765

Goldstein, D.; Handler, R. & Sirovich, L. (1993). Modeling a no-slip flow boundary with an external force field, *J. Comput. Phys.*, 105, 354-366

Gresho, P.M. (1992). Some interesting issues in incompressible fluid dynamics, both in the continuum and in numerical simulation, *Advances in Appl. Mech.*, 28, 45–140

Hanna, S.R. (1984). The exponential probability density function and concentration fluctuation in smoke plumes, *Bound.-Layer Meteor.*, 29, 361-375

Harlow, F. and Welch, J. E. (1965). Numerical calculation of time dependent viscous incompressible flow of fluid with a free surface, *Phys. Fluids.*, 8, 2182–2189

Kataoka, H. & Mizuno, M. (2002). Numerical flow computation around aeroelastic 3D square cylinder using inflow turbulence, *Wind and Struct.*, 5, 379-392

Lewellen, W.S. & Sykes, R.I. (1986). Analysis of concentration fluctuations from lidar observations of atmospheric plumes, *J. Appl. Meteor. Climatol.*, 25, 1145-1154

Li, W. & Meroney, R. (1983). Gas dispersion near a cubical model building. Part1. Mean concentration measurements, *J. Wind. Eng. Indust. Aero*, 12, 15-33

Li, W. & Meroney, R. (1983). Gas dispersion near a cubical model building. Part2. Concentration fluctuation measurements", *J. Wind. Eng. Indust. Aero.*, 12, 35-47

Lilly, D.K. (1992). A proposed modification of the Germano subgrid-scale closure method, *Phys. Fluids.*, A4, 3, 633-635

Meneveau, C.; Lund, T.S. & Cabot, W.H. (1996). A Lagrangian dynamic subgrid-scale model for turbulence, *J. Fluid Mech.*, 319, 353-385

Meteorological Guide for Safety Analysis of Nuclear Power Plant Reactor, Nuclear Safety Commission of Japan (1982).

Michioka, T.; Sato, A. & Sada, K. (2003). Large-Eddy Simulation for the tracer gas concentration fluctuation in atmospheric boundary layer, *Jpn. Soc. Mechanical Engineers, B*, 69 [680], 116-123

Mochida, A.; Murakami, S. & Hayashi, Y. (1991). Comparison between k-ε model and LES for turbulence structure around cube, *J. Environ. Eng.*, AIJ, 423, 23-31 (1991), [in Japanese]

Murakami, S.; Mochida, A. & Hibi, K. (1986). Three dimensional numerical simulation for air flow and building Part1 -Correspondence between prediction by large eddy simulation and wind tunnel experiment, *J. Architecture, Planning and Environ. Engi.*, AIJ, 360, 174-184[in Japanese]

Nakayama, H & Nagai, H. (2009). Development of local-scale high-resolution atmospheric dispersion model using Large-Eddy Simulation Part1: Turbulent flow and plume dispersion over a flat terrain, *J. Nuc Sci and Tech*, 46, 12, 1170-1177

Oke, T.R. (1998). Street design and urban canopy climate, *Energy and Buildings*, 11, 103-113

Sada, K. & Sato, A. (2002). Numerical calculation of flow and stack-gas concentration fluctuation around a cubical building, *Atmos. Environ.*, 36, 5527-5534

Sada, K.; Komiyama, S.; Michioka, T. & Ichikawa, Y. (2009). Numerical model for atmospheric diffusion analysis and evaluation of effective dose for safety analysis, *Trans. At. Energy Soc. Jpn.*, 8[2], 184-196

Santiago, J.L.; Coceal, O., Martilli, A. & Belcher, S, E. (2008). Variation of the Sectioanl Drag Coefficient of a Group of Buildings with Packing Density, *Bound.-Layer Meteor*, 128, 445-457.

Sato, A. & Sada, K. (2002). A wind tunnel experiment on tracer gas concentration fluctuation near a cubical model building, *J. Soc. Civil Engi.*, 706, 41-49, [in Japanese]

Shirasawa, T.; Endo, Y., Yoshie, R., Mochida, A. & Tanaka, H. (2008). Comparison of LES and Durbin type k-ε model for gas diffusion in weak wind region behind a building, *J. Environ. Eng.*, AIJ, 73 [627], 615-622[in Japanese].

Smagorinsky, J. (1963). General circulation experiments with the primitive equations, *Monthly Weather Review*, 91[3], 99-164

Takewaki, H.; Nishiguchi, A. & Yabe, T. (1985). Cubic Interpolated Pseudo-particle method (CIP) for solving hyperbolic-type equations, *J. Comput. Phys.*, 61, 261-268

Yabe, T. & Takei, E. (1988). A new higher-order Godunov method for general hyperbolic equations, *J. Phys. Soc. Jpn.*, 57[8], 2598-2601

Van Driest, E.R. (1956). On turbulent flow near a wall, *J. Aerospace Sci.*, 23, 1007-1011

Xie, Z.T.; Coceal, O. & Castro, I.P. (2008). Large-eddy simulation of flows over random urban-like obstacles, *Bound.-Layer Meteor.*, 129, 1-23

16

Computations of Flowfield over Reentry Modules at High Speed

R. C. Mehta[1,2]
[1]*Noorul Islam University, Kumaracoil,*
[2]*Formally, Nanyang Technological University*
[1]*India*
[2]*Singapore*

1. Introduction

A high-speed flow-past a reentry capsule generates a bow shock wave which causes a rather high surface pressure and as a result the development of high aerodynamic drag which is require for aero-braking purposes. Highly blunt configurations are generally preferred to decelerate space-capsule for safe returning on the Earth after performing the experiments. The bow shock wave is detached from the blunt fore-body and is having a mixed subsonic-supersonic region between them. The wall pressure distribution, the location of the sonic line and shock stand-off distance on the spherical cap region have been analytically calculated at very high speeds with an adiabatic index near to unity which gives a singular point at 60 deg from the stagnation point (Chester, 1956; Freeman 1956). The analytical approach for the high-speed flow over the blunt-body is considerably difficult and complex (Lighthill 1957). The flow-field over the reentry capsule becomes further complicated due to the presence of corner at the shoulder and the base shell of the reentry module.

Reentry capsule configurations significantly differ from each other due to entry conditions, trajectory, and a number of aerodynamic factors such as aerodynamic axial force, normal force, static moment, damping coefficients. This leads to the necessity to investigate the influence of the shape of blunted bodied on the flow field and aerodynamic characteristics. (Bedin et al., 1992) have presented aerodynamic characteristics and geometrical parameters for the sixteen different reentry modules using experimental data of ballistic test facility. Aero-assist flight experiment (AFE) configurations have been analyzed using two different Navier-Stokes flow solvers by (Venkatapathy et al., 1991). Aerodynamic heating and pressure along with the fore-body and wake-flow structure during atmospheric entry of the Mars Pathfinder spacecraft have been computed by (Hass & Venkatapathy, 1995) using the commercially available general atmospheric simulation program (GASP 2.2). An aerodynamic analysis of the commercial experiment transport (COMET) reentry capsule has been carried out by (Wood et al., 1996) solving the laminar thin layer Navier-Stokes LAURA code for low supersonic to hypersonic speeds. The LAURA code is an upwind, point implicit, second-order accurate fluid dynamics solver based on an extension of the Roe flux-difference splitting scheme. (Yamomoto & Yoshioka, 1995) carried out flow field computation over the OREX (orbital reentry experiments) using computational fluid dynamics approach coupled with the thermal response of the heat shield material using finite element method in conjunction with the aerodynamic flight data. (Tam, 1992) has computed flow field at hypersonic Mach numbers over Viking, Biconic and AFE reentry capsules employing IEC3D (Inviscid Equilibrium Computation in 3-Dimension). (Menne, 1994) has computed flow field over Viking similar to the Apollo type module and Biconic configurations for freestream Mach numbers 2.0 and 3.0 by solving compressible Euler equations. The inviscid analysis is unable to show the flow separation in the back shell region of the reentry capsule. The aerodynamic characterization of the CARINA reentry module in the low supersonic Mach regimes has been performed employing numerical and experimental methods (Solazzo et al., 1994). The flow field simulation over the ARD (ESA's atmospheric reentry demonstrator) module has been computed numerically by (Walpot, 2001) at hypersonic speeds. Developments relating to the base pressure and the base heating prediction for wide range of cone and wedge have been reviewed for supersonic and hypersonic Mach numbers by (Lamb & Oberkampf, 1995). The flow field simulations over the Beagle-2 spacecraft have been carried out by (Liever et al., 2003) using CFD-FASTRAN code for low supersonic to hypersonic speeds. A numerical simulation code has been applied for super orbital reentry flow and has been used to the flow field prediction around the MUSES-C reentry module (Osu et al., 2002). Supersonic and hypersonic flow past a slender cone (Tai & Kao, 1994) has been numerically simulated by solving Navier-Strokes using an explicit multi-stage Roe's method. The flow fields around blunt reentry modules (Teramoto et al., 2001) were numerically analyzed in order to investigate the mechanism of dynamic instability of the capsule at freestream Mach number of 1.3. The blunt and short reentry capsule tends to be dynamically unstable at low supersonic Mach number attributed primarily to the delay in base pressure (Teramoto & Fujii, 2001). Numerical studies have been done by (Ottens, 2001) employing a laminar Navier-stokes flow solver for two different types of Delft aerospace reentry test (DART) demonstrators reentry capsules.

The frontal shape of the reentry body can be classified either employing as a spherical cap as in the case of the Apollo and the ARD, or combination of the spherical nose or blunted-body with cone as in the case of the OREX and the Beagle-2, or a spherical blunt-cone/flare configuration as proposed by DART. The flow field features over the reentry capsule can be delineated through the experimental and numerical flow simulations (Mehta, 2006) at high speeds. Figure 1 shows schematic flow field features over the OREX and the DART capsules. The significant flow features are described by the following. In the fore-body region, the fluid decelerates through the bow shock wave depending on the cruise speed and altitude. As the shoulder of the capsule, the flow turns and expands rapidly and boundary layer detached, forming a free shear layer that separates the inner re-circulating flow region behind the base from the outer flow field. The latter is recompressed and turned back to the freestream direction, first by the so-called lip shock, and further downstream by recompression shock. At the end of the re-circulating flow past the neck, the shear layer develops in the wake trail. A complex inviscid wave structure often includes a lip shock wave (associates with the corner expansion) and wake trail (adjacent to the shear layer confluence). The corner expansion process is a modified Prandtl-Meyer patter distorted by the presence of the approaching boundary layer. An excellent review of the thermodynamic and chemical-kinetic models used for computational fluid dynamics simulations of a non-equilibrium flow field is reported by (Gnoffo & Pettnelli, 1995). Another review of the after body aero-thermal flight data and thermal protection system design for Mercury, Gemini, Project Fire, Apollo, Reentry F, Mars Viking, Galileo, Mars Pathfinder, MIRKA, Atmospheric Reentry Demonstrator (ARD) is given by (Wright et al., 2006). The flight data analysis of the various reentry capsules will be very useful for the numerical simulation purposes.

Aerodynamic performance of Commercial Experiment Transport (COMET) reentry capsule (Allen & Cheng, 1970) is carried out using both the Euler and the laminar thin-layer Navier-Stokes solver LAURA code based on upwind point implicit, and Roe flux difference splitting scheme for supersonic speed range. The small shoulder radius causes a strong compression and acceleration of the flow around the edge of the heat shield, thinning the boundary layer producing locally high heating on the shoulder. (Weinbaum, 1966, & Wood et al. 1996) have analyzed the wake flow field of the capsules.

The conservatism of the after body thermal protection system (TPS) heat shield design of the reentry module will shift the centre of gravity, which reduces the static stability. Wind tunnel test data are usually having the sting interference effects; however shock tunnel having short duration of testing time and free flight (ballistic range) data exist. In the free flight experiments, a scaled model is shot inside a range and orthogonal shadowgraphs are taken as the capsule flies by each shadow graph station. There is no sting in the free flight test. The base flow features observed from the shadow graphs show several known wake features such as shear layers, neck region and recompression shocks. The reentry capsule is usually having a high drag shape with good static stability margin, a simple generic shape to take maximum advantage of available aerodynamic data, nose radius selection for minimum structural mass with maximum drag, leading to a maximum radius limited by the range of bluntness ratios, corner radii minimized for maximum drag, but constrained by structural/ thermal requirements. Figure 2 shows the geometrical details of the various reentry capsules (Mehta, 2006). The large nose radius produces large drag, and the short body length reduces the total weight, resulting in a small ballistic coefficient. To ensure the deployment of the parachute in the transonic region, the attitude of the capsule must be maintained within the limit in the whole speed range. Most of the basic configuration parameters such as nose radii or body lengths are decided mainly from the thermal protection requirement. The centre of gravity of the capsule is located in-forward of the centre of pressure, to get statically stable. (Hiraki et al., 1998) measured the unsteady surface pressure of the oscillating MUSES-C reentry capsule and found that the base pressure is responsible for the dynamic instability. One oscillation cycle corresponds to approximately 150 in non-dimensional time. The dynamic instability occurs at very low reduced frequencies by numerical simulation (Teramoto et al. 2001, & Toramoto & Fujii, 2000) of thin layer RANS using lower-upper alternating direction implicit factorization implicit algorithm in conjunction with higher order by the MUSCL interpolation of primitive variables. Unsteady flow is carried out employing multistage time stepping method (Mehta, 2006).

Table 1(a) shows the dimensional detail of the reentry capsule. The sonic line is located on the OREX-type configuration on the shoulder whereas in the case of the DART's reentry capsule as descried in the schematic sketch in Figure 1. The location of the sonic line is at the junction of the spherical blunt cone. Thus, it is noticed from the figure that the flow field over the reentry capsule needs a high aerodynamic drag with good static stability margin which leads to the selection of an axisymmetric shape of large angle sphere-cone combination. The fore-body geometry of the ARD module is having a spherical cap; the OREX capsule is having combination of the spherical cap with cone. The outer capsule consists of spherically blunted cone/fare. These capsules cover most of the existing reentry modules. Geometrical details of the ARD, Apollo, Apollo-II, MUSES-C, OREX and spherically blunted cone are displayed in Fig. 2. Table 1(b) summarized the geometrical parameters used in various spherically blunted-cone/flare reentry vehicles. (Fujimoto & Fujii, 2006) have numerically found that the shoulder radius has a great influence on the pressure

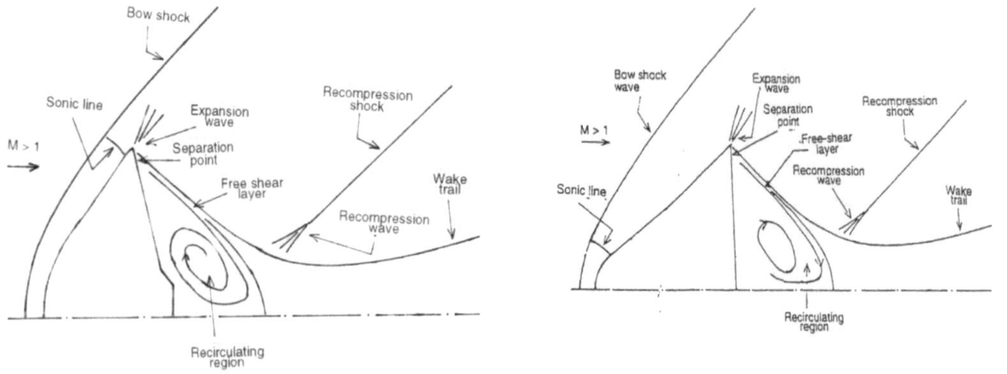

(a) flowfield over OREX capsule (b) flowfield over spherical blunt cone

Fig. 1. Representation of flow features on blunted body at supersonic speeds.

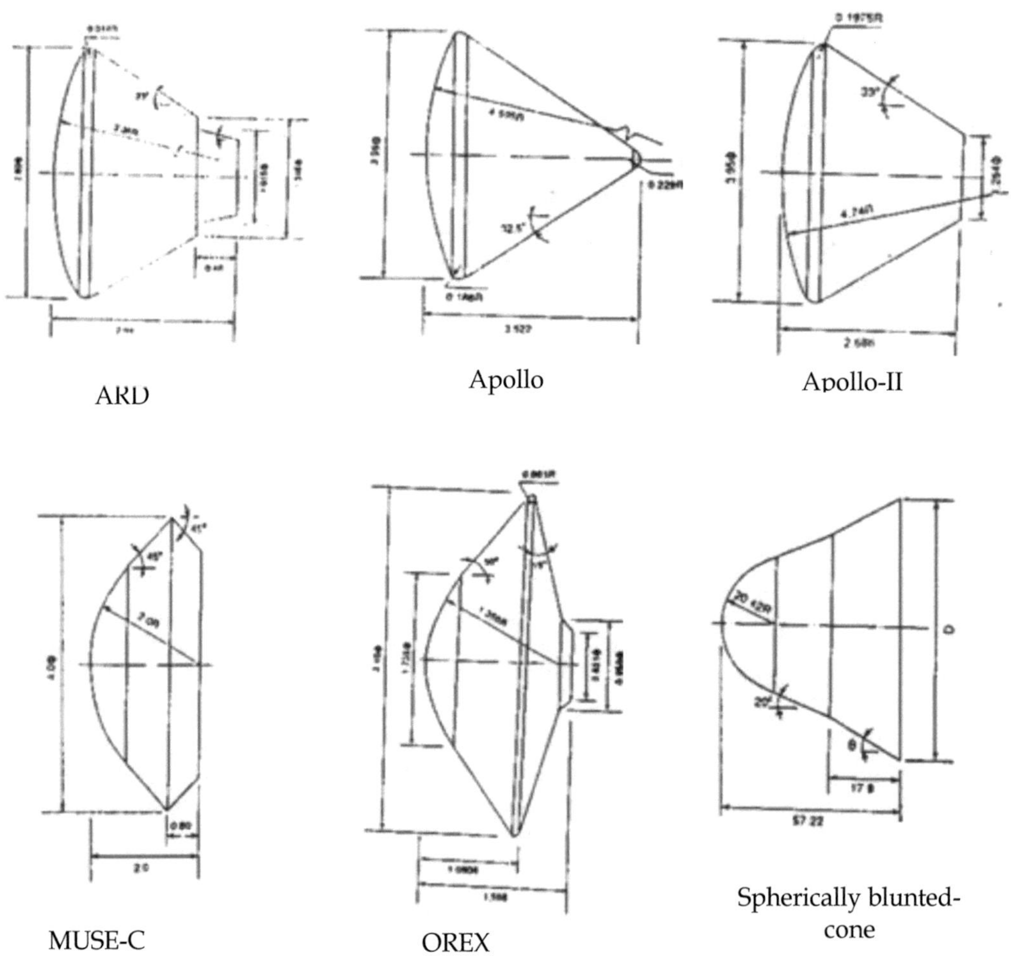

Fig. 2. Geometrical details of various reentry capsules.

Capsule	Spherical radius, R_N	Frontal diameter, D	Corner radius, R_C	Overall length, L	Semi-cone angle, α_N deg	Back-shell angle, α_B deg
ARD	3.36	2.80	0.014	2.04	-	33.0
Apollo	4.595	3.95	0.186	3.522	-	32.5
Beagle - 2	2.8	3.0	0.21	3.5	30	43
COMET	1.22	1.32	-	1.22	-	5
Apollo-II	4.74	3.95	0.1975	2.686	-	33.0
OREX smooth shoulder	1.35	3.40	0.001	1.508	50.0	15.0
OREX sharp shoulder	1.35	3.457	-	1.508	50.0	15.0
CARINA	1.97	1.0	0.25	1.172	-	13.0
Gemini	-	90.0	-	70.2	-	20
Project fire	70.2	58.79	-	38.86		33
Mars path finder	0.6638	2.6492	0.0662	70.19		46.63
Mercury	30	74.50	-	58.38	-	20
Viking	0.912	1.875	0.0914	2.0964	20	33.6
MUSES-C	2.0	4.0	-	2.0	45.0	45.0

Table 1. (a) Geometrical parameters of reentry capsules.

Base diameter, D	Semi-cone angle, θ
73.91	25
77.89	30
82.29	35

Table 1. (b) Geometrical parameters of spherically blunted cone reentry bodies.

level behind the body and separation position. Gnoffo et al. have found that laminar, wind-side heating levels may decrease with increasing angle of attack resulting from an increase in the effective radius of curvature with sonic line movement from the hemispherical nose to the aft shoulder of the blunt cone. Numerical simulation of the flow field is required over various geometrical parameters of the capsules in order to meet the aerodynamic and mission requirements. The numerical simulation of axisymmetric laminar compressible time dependent Navier-Stokes is carried out using a multi-stage Runge-Kutta time stepping scheme. A local time-step is used to simulate the flow over various reentry configurations.

2. Numerical schemes

Hypersonic calculations about complex geometries require large amounts of computer sources, but solution adaptive grids, convergence, acceleration, parallel processing may make run time manageable. The thin-layer approximation (Edwards 1992) is invoked, because viscous effects are generally present boundary layer near the wall. This approximation neglects viscous derivatives in the directions tangent to the body surface, simplifying the equations somewhat alleviating grid resolution requirements. Numerical solution (Mehta et al., 1991) of the Navier-Stokes equations is obtained using Galerkin spatial discretiztion with multistage time integration. Table 2 depicts the various numerical schemes available to simulate the reentry flow field. Figure 3 shows the interlinking of computational fluid dynamics with the interaction of different discipline of sciences and engineering.

2.1 Algorithms

In the flux-splitting approach, the flux vector is separated into the sum of two vectors, one associated with the positive eigenvalues of the flux Jacobian, and the other with the negative values. Then appropriate one-sides differences can be used on the split terms. The main requirement being that the eigenvalues of the split flux Jacobian be positive or negative definite. The split fluxes are discretized with a one-sided difference scheme. This is analogous to adding dissipation to a central difference scheme where the dissipation increases near flow discontinuities such as shock waves, yielding improved stability.

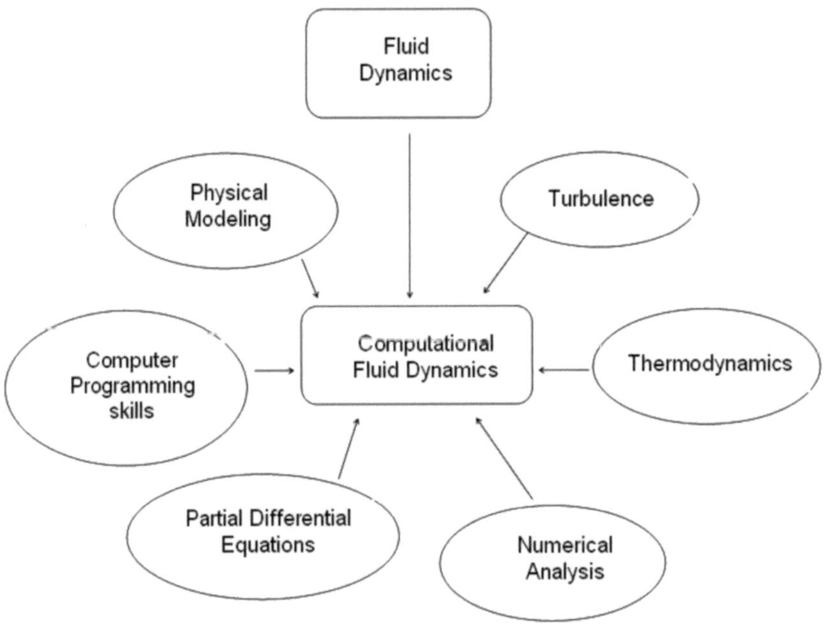

Fig. 3. Interaction of different area with CFD.

Riemann solvers are a class of schemes that propagate flow information according to solutions of Riemann problems. These schemes have the attributes of monotonicity, enabling sharp resolution of discontinuities, and robustness for capturing strong shocks. The one-dimensional inviscid problem can be solved exactly, but needs an expansive iterative approach, so most schemes are linearized, solve an approximate Riemann problem. The implicit numerical is allowed to have much higher time-step and having quadratic convergence. However the implicit algorithm needs computation of the Jacobian matrices of numerical fluxes, and having iterative solution of linear system. The implicit code is more

complicated as compared to explicit code. The numerical solution can be accelerated employing local time step, multi-grid, and preconditioning scheme.
CFD-FASTRAN code (Liever et al., 2003) is based on compressible finite volume solver for thermo-chemical non-equilibrium flow analysis. Roe's flux difference upwind scheme is used with the Van Leer flux limiter to provide higher-order spatial accuracy.

2.2 Air chemistry equations

The chemical behaviour of air depends on the trajectory points. Below about 2000 K, deviations from perfect gas behaviour are negligible. In the atmosphere, this temperature is first reached behind normal shocks at a Mach number of about six. Most of the test facilities are operated at low freestream temperatures and so real gas effects are difficult to obtain, even at high Mach numbers. The perfect gas equation of state is thus sufficient for many hypersonic speeds when the peak temperature is below the above limit. When the temperature in the flow is high enough to cause air to dissociate, the density of the fluid determines the character of the fluid/chemistry interaction. At relative high densities, the intermolecular collision rate is very high, and reactions proceed to equilibrium rapidly. The flow can be considered to be chemical equilibrium at all points in the flow field at all times as in the limit of infinite reaction rates. As the density is lowered, the chemical relaxation time increases and eventually becomes significant compared to the flow convection time. Air chemistry with numerical simulation is explained in details by (Edwards, 1992; and Gnoffo et al. 1989). (Rusanov, 1976) has reviewed fluid dynamics over reentry capsules. For a given thermodynamic state, the equilibrium composition of air is uniquely determined. Tables can be generated for the composition and properties of air in chemical equilibrium.
These tables with a linear interpolation or store the coefficients are used with flow solver. The perfect gas equation of state is modified by an effective specific heats ratio that is evaluated by table interpolation or curve evaluation. In the case of non-equilibrium air chemistry, the concentration of all the species should be known at all points in the flow field determined the properties of air undergoing chemical reactions. This requires solving additional transport equations for each species present in the flow. A source terms presents in the transport equations, accounts for the net production of the species arising in the chemical reactions. This term depends on the forward and backward rates of the reactions being modelled, which will differ with the gas species and reaction set of the gas model. The non-equilibrium gas model requires solving an additional set of partial differential equations, the number of equations being dependent on the number of species in the model.
In the frozen flow approximation (Hansen, 1959; Bailey 1967; & Srinivasan & Weilmuenster, 1987) individual species do not react with one another, but their effect is felt on the fluid dynamics because of variable thermodynamic properties and non-uniform concentration. Thus the species continuity equations are required. The computation time is saved due to not evaluating the production and destruction associated with chemical reactions. The flow is considered as a mixture of thermally perfect gases, with the specific heats and enthalpy of each species of the mixture determined as a function of temperature from a molecular data base.

A catalyst reduces the necessary activation energy of a reaction, hence more collisions level to reactions. The fully catalyst is equivalent to equilibrium of gases (thermal load). Poor catalyst reduces the release of reaction.

Numerical method	Combined space-time Discretization	Separate space discretization and time integration
Space-centered method	Explicit method (Lax & Friedrich, 1954) – First order (Lax & Wendroff, 1954) - second order Two-step method (Richtmyer & Mortan, 1967) (MacCormack, 1969) Implicit method (MacCormack, 1981)	Implicit method (Briley & McDonald, 1975) (Beam & Warming, 1976) Explicit method Multistage Runge-Kutta schme (Jameson, Schmidt & Turkel, 1981)
Upwind schemes	Flux vector splitting method (Moretti , 1979) - shock capturing (Steger & Warming, 1981) Exact Riemann problem solution (Godunov, 1959) – First order (Van Leer, 1979) – Second order Approximate Riemann solvers (Roe, 1981)	
High-resolution (non-linear schemes)	Explicit TVD upwind schemes (Boris & Book, 1973) (Harten, 1984) (Osher, 1984), (Oscher & Chakravarthy, 1984) Implicit TVD upwind schemes (Yee, 1985) Central TVD scheme (Implicit or Explicit) (Davis, 1984), (Roe, 1995)	

Table 2. Numerical method for Fluid Dynamics Equations.

3. Axisymmetric flow solver

The axisymmetric time-dependent compressible Navier-Stokes equations can be written in the following conservation form. The analysis is carried out under the assumption of laminar flow. The coefficient of molecular viscosity is calculated according to Sutherland's law. The temperature is related to pressure and density by the perfect gas equation of state. The ratio of the specific heats is assumed constant.

3.1 Finite volume method

To facilitate the spatial discretization in the numerical scheme, the governing equations are be written in the integral form over a finite volume of the computational domain with the boundary domain. The contour integration around the boundary of the cell is divided in the anticlockwise sense. The computational domain is divided into a finite number of non-overlapping quadrilateral grids. The conservation variables within the computational cell are represented by their average values at the cell centre. When the integral governing equation is applied separately to each cell in the computational domain, we obtain a set of coupled ordinary differential equation.

3.1.1 Inviscid fluxes

The convective fluxes are calculated at the centre of the grid, resulting in cell-centre flux balances. The contour integration of the inviscid flux vector is approximated at the side of the computational grid. The summation is carried out over the four edges of the grid.

3.1.2 Viscous fluxes

The viscous terms are defined at the centre of the cell. The above procedure is repeated to approximate the contour integration of the viscous flux vector. The inclusion of diffusive transport terms requires a choice of the locations at which the derivatives of the primitive variables should be integrated. The grid used for gradient evaluation forms a second grid that is shifted a half cell in the axial and radial directions in relation to the original computational grid. The viscous flux vectors are approximated in such a manner to preserve cell conservations and maintain algorithm simplicity. The derivatives of primitive variables at the vertices of the cell are evaluated by discrete application of the divergence theorem (Peyret & Vivind, 1993) to the auxiliary cell of the secondary grid. The net convective flux is computed by summing the inviscid and viscous terms.

3.1.3 Artificial dissipation

In the cell-centered spatial discretization schemes, such as the one described above which is non-dissipative, therefore, artificial dissipation terms are added. The approach of (Jameson et al., 1981) is adopted to construct the dissipative terms consisting of blend of second and fourth differences of the vector conserved variables. Fourth differences are added everywhere in the flow domain where the solution is smooth, but are 'switched off' in the region of shock waves. A term involving second differences is then 'switched on' to damp oscillations near shock waves. This switching is achieved by means of a shock sensor based on the local second differences of pressure. Since the computational domain is structured. The scaling quantity confirms the inclusion of the cell volume in the dependent variable. The blend of second and fourth differences provides third-order back ground dissipation in smooth region of the flow and first-order dissipation in shock waves.

3.1.4 Time marching scheme

The spatial discretization described above reduces the governing flow equations to semi-discrete ordinary differential equations. The integration is performed employing an efficient multistage scheme (Jameson et al., 1981). The following three-stage, time-stepping method is adopted. A conservative choice of the Courant-Friedritchs-Lewy number (1.4) was made to achieve a stable numerical solution. The numerical algorithm is second-order accurate in space and time discretization. A global time step was used rather than the grid-varying time step to simulate time-accurate solution and is calculated as mentioned (Mehta, 2001).

3.1.5 Initial and boundary conditions

The freestream conditions for each trajectory point are enumerated in Table 3, which are used as initial conditions. The subscript ∞ represents freestream value in Table 3.

M_∞	U_∞, m/s	P_∞, Pa	T_∞, K
1.2	351	4519	210
1.4	409	3952	213
2.0	596	2891	219
3.0	903	2073	224
5.0	1532	1238	232
6.0	1890	1064	234

Table 3. Trajectory points and initial conditions.

Four types of boundary conditions are required for the computation of flow field, i.e. wall, inflow, outflow and symmetric conditions. They are prescribed as follows. At the solid wall, no-slip condition is enforced together with an isothermal wall condition. At the centre line of the symmetric reentry capsule are prescribed For the supersonic outflow case, all flow variables are extrapolated at the outer and wake region of the computational region.

3.2 Reentry capsule geometry

3.2.1 ARD capsule

The dimensional detail of the ARD capsule is having an axisymmetric design with a spherical blunt nose diameter, D = 2.8 m, spherical cap radius, R_N = 3.36 m and a shoulder radius, R_C = 0.014 m. The back shell has inclination angle α_N = 33 deg relative to the capsule's axis of symmetry. A frustum of cone of radius 0.0507 m with a 12 deg half angle cone is attached to the base region. The overall length of the capsule L = 2.04 m. The ARD resembles a 70% scaled version of the Apollo capsule (Liever et al. 2003).

3.2.2 OREX capsule

The OREX geometry is depicted in Fig. 2 with the detailed dimension. The fore-body shape consists of R_N = 1.35 m, a half-angle cone of α_N = 50 deg, D = 3.4 m, L = 1.508 m, and R_C = 0.01 m. The OREX geometry incorporates a rear cover with a small backward facing step at the junction between back cover and heat shield. The aft body is having α_B = 15 deg, half-angle cone relative to the plane of symmetry.

3.2.3 Beagle-2 capsule

The dimensional detail of the Beagle-2 in Table 1(a) is of axisymmetric designs. The fore-body of the Beagle has a 60 deg half cone with a maximum diameter, D = 0.9 m. The Beagle-2 capsule has a spherical blunt nose radius of R = 0.417 m, and a shoulder radius of R_C = 0.029m. The back shell has an inclination angle, α_B = 43.75 deg relative to the vehicle's axis of symmetry. The overall length of the module is L = 0.4995 m and the length to the diameter ratio is 0.555.

3.2.4 Apollo capsule

The dimensional detail of the Apollo is shown in Fig. 2 are of axisymmetric designs. The Apollo capsule has a spherical blunt nose diameter of D = 3.95 m, spherical nose radius of α_N = 4.595 m and a shoulder radius of R_C = 0.186 m. The back shell has an inclination angle, α_B = 32.5 deg relative to the vehicle's axis of symmetry. The overall length of the module is L = 3.522 m.

3.2.5 Spherically blunted-cone/flare capsule

The spherically blunted-cone/flare configuration is illustrated in Fig. 2. The conical fore-body has R_N = 0.51 m, D = 2.03 m, L = 1.67 m and α_N = 20 deg. The flare has a half-angle cone of 25 deg and is terminated with a right circular cylinder and a geometrically similar to the REV of the DART demonstrator. Table 1(b) gives the semi-cone angle of various reentry vehicles.

3.3 Computational grid

One of the controlling factors for the numerical simulation is the proper grid arrangement. The following procedure is used to generate grid in the computational region of the blunted-body. The computational domain is divided into number of non-overlapping zone. The mesh points are generated in each zone using finite element method (Mehta, 2011) in conjunction with the homotopy scheme (Shang, 1984). The spiked blunt nosed body is defined by a number of grid points in the cylindrical coordinate system. Using these surface points as the reference nodes, the normal coordinate is then described by the exponentially stretched grid points extending outwards up to an outer computational boundary.
Grid independence tests (Mehta, 2006; and Mehta 2008) were carried out, taking into consideration the effect of the computational domain, the stretching factor to control the grid intensity near the wall, and the number of grid points in the axial and normal directions. The outer boundary of the computational domain is varied from 2.5 to 3.0 times the maximum diameter D and the grid-stretching factor in the radial direction is varied from 1.5 to 5. These stretched grids are generated in an orderly manner.

Fig. 4. Comparison between density contour and schlieren picture.

To verify the chosen grid delivers an accurate solution, the number of grid cells was increased until a steady-state solution occurred, that is, the resulting axial force on the investigated shape did not change anymore. Several test runs were made with a total doubled grid cell number. Therefore, the grid was highly refined in both directions. Grids are chosen with the number of grid points in the axial direction ranging from 187 for the shortest capsule to up to 220 for the longest reentry configuration, and the number in the radial direction ranging from 52 to 82. The present numerical analysis was performed on 187x62 grid points. The downstream boundary of the computational domain is maintained at 4 to 6 times the maximum diameter, D. This grid arrangement is found to give a relative difference of about ±1.5% for the drag coefficient. The convergence criterion less than the 10^{-5} is based on the difference in the density values at any grid point between two successive iterations. The minimum spacing for the fine mesh is dependent upon the Reynolds number. The finer mesh near the wall helps to resolve the viscous effects. The coarse-mesh helps reducing the computer time. It is important that the grid have sufficient points in the shoulder region of the reentry module in order to capture the rapid expansion and accurately predict the flow separation point and the angle of the resulting shear layer. A close-up view of the computational grid over the various reentry capsules is shown in Reference (Mehta, 2010). The structured grid generation and the mono block are suitable to accommodate spike shape. As seen in the figures of (Mehta, 2006; Mehta 2010), these types of grid use quadrilateral cells in 2-D in the computational array. The quadrilateral cells, which are very efficient at filling space, support a high amount of skew and stretching before the solution will be significantly affected. Additionally, the grid can be aligned with the flow, thereby yielding greater accuracy within the solver. Several grid arrangements are take check the grid independency check.

3.4 Flow characteristics

The flow field features over various capsules have been shown by (Mehta, 2010). Figure 4 shows the comparison between the density contour and schlieren picture for spherical blunted-cone at $\theta = 25$ deg configuration at $M_\infty = 6.0$. All the essential flow field features are well captured and compared well with the schlieren picture. Figure 4 depicts the velocity vector plots for Apollo, Apollo-II and ARD reentry modules. It can be visualized from the vector plots that all the significant flow field behaviors such as bow shock wave, rapid expansion fans and the flow at the shoulder, flow recirculation region with converging free shear layer and formation of the vortex flow in the aft region of the capsules. The wake flow field immediately behind the vehicle base, exhibits complex flow characteristics. The formation of the bow shock wave on the fore body depends on R_N and α_N and M_∞. The bow shock wave moves close to the fore body with the increasing M_∞ and the stand off distance between the bow shock wave and the fore body decreases with the increasing M_∞.

The pressure, density and Mach contour plots show the enlarged view of the computed vector field over the OREX, ARD, Apollo at various freestream Mach number M_∞. It can be visualized from the vector plots that all the significant flow field features such as bow shock wave, rapid expansion fans on the shoulder of the capsule, flow recirculation region with converging free shear layer and formation of the vortex flow in the aft region of the capsules. The wake flow field, immediately behind the capsule base, exhibits complex flow characteristics. The formation of the bow shock wave on the fore body depends on R_N and α_N and M_∞. In the case of spherically blunted-cone/flare (SRE) capsule, the bow shock wave does not follow the body contour, which is attributed to small values of R_N and α_N as compared to the OREX, the ARD and the Apollo.

Computed vector velocity plot around the various vehicles are depicted in Fig. 5. The Mach contour plots show the formation of vortices at the corner region of the capsule for $M_\infty \leq 3$. Characteristics flow features around the blunt body at supersonic speeds is observed. The high surface pressure on the fore-body results the development of high aerodynamic drag which is required for the aerobraking application. Table 4 shows the fore body aerodynamic drag for various reentry modules. It is important to mention here that the aerodynamic drag is highly influenced by the fore body shape.

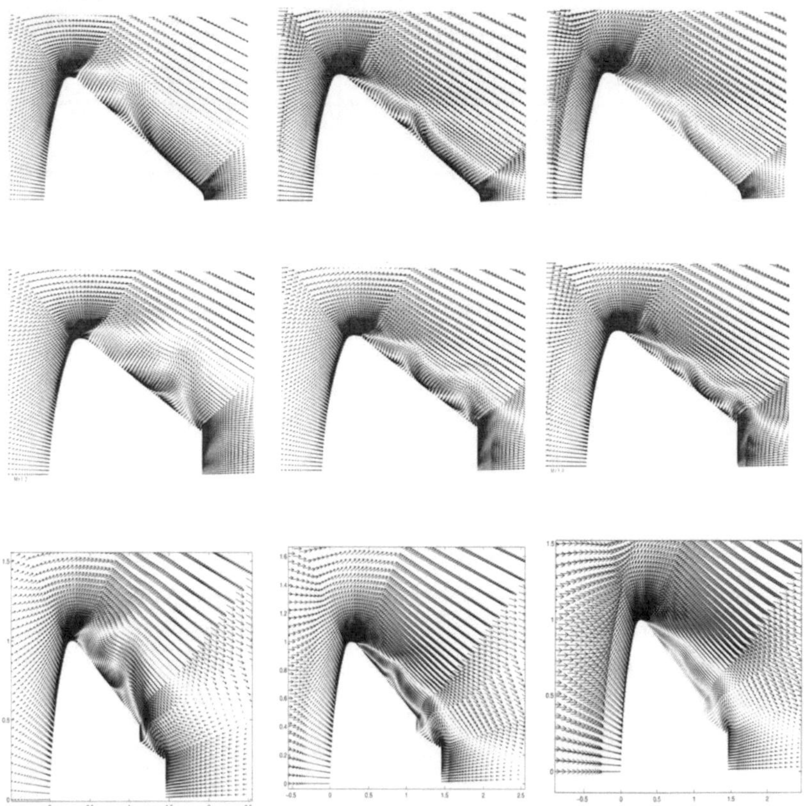

Fig. 5. Enlarged view of velocity vector field over Apollo, Apollo-II and ARD.

3.5 Shock stand-off distance

The computed velocity vector plots are shown in Fig. 6. Close-up views of the velocity vector plot over fore-body of the capsules and schematic shock location are depicted in the figure. The separated shear layer and the recompression shock from the reattachment point on the shoulder of the hemispherical cap are visible in the vector plot. The shock wave in front of the cap will increase the aerodynamic drag due to high pressure region. In the fore region of the spherical cap, the fluid decelerates through the bow shock wave. At the shoulder of the disk or hemispherical cap, the flow turns and expands rapidly, the boundary layer detaches, forming a free shear layer that separates the inner recirculating flow region behind the base from the outer flow field. The corner expansion over disk process is a modified Prandtl-Mayer pattern distorted by the presence of the approaching boundary layer.

Capsules	M_∞ =1.2	M_∞=1.4	M_∞=2.0	M_∞=3.0	M_∞=5.0	M_∞=6.0
ARD	1.41	-	1.43	1.40	1.38	-
Apollo	1.30	-	1.50	1.43	1.40	-
Apollo - II	1.32	-	1.47	1.43	1.05	-
OREX (with smooth shoulder)	1.79	1.77	1.50	1.30	1.16	-
OREX (with sharp shoulder)	1.80	1.66	1.36	1.17	1.05	-
CARINA	1.40	-	1.50	1.45	1.45	-
MUSSES - C	1.27	-	1.24	1.36	1.38	-
Beagle - 2	1.58	1.59	1.54	1.47	1.42	-
Spherically blunted cone, θ=25 deg	0.40	-	0.43	0.44	-	0.42
Spherically blunted cone, θ=30 deg	0.51	-	0.49	0.46	-	0.42
Spherically blunted cone, θ=35 deg	0.58	-	0.56	0.51	-	0.47

Table 4. Fore-body aerodynamic drag.

For the case of flat-nosed capsule flying at hypersonic speeds, a detached bow wave is formed in front of the nose which is practically normal at the body axis (Truit, 1959; Liepmann & Roshko 2007). Since the flow behind the normal shock is always subsonic, simple continuity considerations show that the shock-detachment distance and stagnation-velocity gradient are essentially a function of the density ratio across the shock. The flow behind the shock wave is subsonic, the shock is no longer independent of the far-downstream conditions. A change of the spike shape (geometry) in the subsonic region affects the complete flow field up to the shock. The shock-detachment distance becomes smaller with increasing density ratio. (Hayer & Probstein 1959) gives expression for the shock detachment distance Δ_F with diameter of the flat-disk D_S ratio as

$$\frac{\Delta_F}{D_S} = 2.8\sqrt{\frac{\rho_\infty}{\rho_0}} \tag{1}$$

where the density ratio across the normal shock (Ames Research Staff, 1953) is

$$\varepsilon = \frac{\rho_\infty}{\rho_0} = \frac{(\gamma - 1)M_\infty^2 + 2}{(\gamma + 1)M_\infty^2} \tag{2}$$

The ratio of shock stand-off distance Δ_S with hemispherical cap of diameter, D_S is

$$\frac{\Delta_S}{D_S} = \frac{2\varepsilon}{1 + \sqrt{\frac{8\varepsilon}{3}}} \tag{3}$$

The values of Δ_F/D_S and Δ_S/D_S are found 0.1898 and 0.1109, respectively. The numerical values of the ratio of shock stand-off to cap diameter are calculated from the velocity vector and pressure contour plot and they are 0.19 and 0.11 which show good agreement with the analytical values. The spherical spike shows the greatest change in velocity gradient as compared to the flat disk. The flow is compressed to subsonic condition, which appears as inviscid and incompressible (Truit, 1959; Liepmann & Roshko 2007) . The shock wave stands in front of the blunt body and forms a region of subsonic flow around the stagnation region.

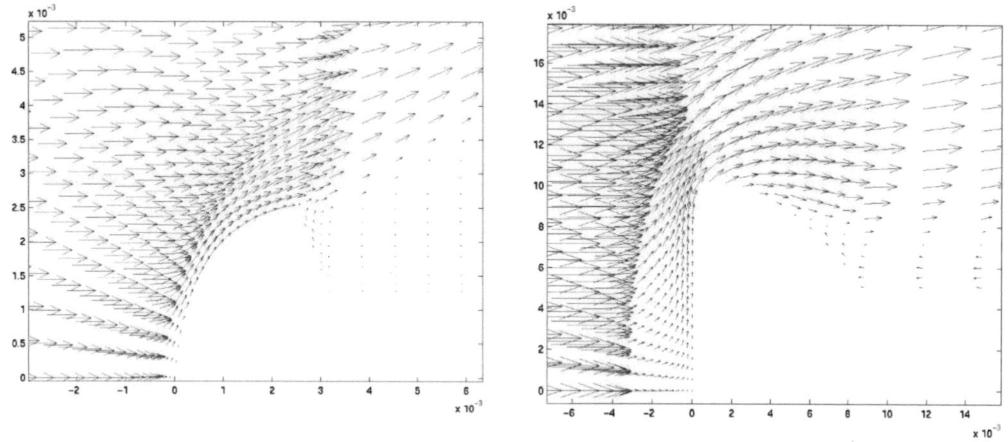

(a) Hemispherical forebody (b) Flat-disc forebody

Fig. 6. Close-up view of Velocity vector plot over fore body of the capsules.

3.6 Wall heat flux

The inviscid flow field in the vicinity of the stagnation point is described in a fluid dynamics sense as the conversion of a unidirectional high velocity stream by a normal shock wave into a high temperature subsonic layer, which is taken to be inviscid and incompressible (Truit, 1959). The stagnation point of a blunt body, the incoming hypersonic flow brought to rest by a normal shock and adiabatic compression. The heat transfer rate is directly proportional to the enthalpy gradient at the wall and square root of the tangential velocity gradient at the edge of the boundary layer. The inviscid flow field in the vicinity of the stagnation point is described as the conversion of the uni-directional, high velocity stream by a normal shock wave into a high temperature subsonic layer. The enthalpy gradient is determined by the shape of the velocity profile in the boundary layer and by the variation of the air properties with temperature. Heat flux at the stagnation point can be calculated using following expression of (Fay & Riddle, 1958)

$$q_w = 0.763 \, \mathrm{Pr}^{-0.6} \sqrt{(\rho_\infty \mu_\infty K)} \sqrt{\left(\frac{\rho_w \mu_w}{\rho_\infty \mu_\infty}\right)} (h_\infty - h_w) \tag{4}$$

where the subscripts ∞ and w are freestream and wall, respectively. Pr is Prandtl number, K stagnation point velocity gradient and h enthalpy of air. The value of stagnation point velocity gradient K is taken as 0.3 (White, 1991). The hemispherical spike shows the greatest changes in the velocity gradient as compared to the flat disk spike. The magnitude of the stagnation-velocity gradient indicates the maximum heat transfer over the hemispherical spike. The computed values of the stagnation point heat flux are 0. 556×10^7 W/m^2 and 1.45x10^7 W/m^2 for the flat-disk and the hemispherical disk spike, respectively. The stagnation point calculated using Eq. (4) is 0. 831x10^7 W/m^2 and 1.55×10^7 W/m^2 for the flat-disk and the hemispherical disk spike, respectively. The discrepancy is due to value of the K. The value of K is difficult to calculate for the flat disk (Bertin, 1994). The results show reasonably good agreement between them. Close-up view of velocity vector plot over the blunt body gives a comparative velocity gradient. The velocity vector is turning in the stream line fashion on the hemispherical spike where as on the flat-disk of the reentry modules as appears that the flow is impinging.

3.7 Oscillation flow field characteristics

The oscillation motion is noticed in the numerical simulations. The flow field can be visualized in the instantaneous velocity vector plots. One oscillation cycle is corresponding to approximately 0.12s for the Apollo and 0.96s for the OREX capsule. For the sake of brevity we are displaying one flow cycle in the six time intervals of 0.002s and 0.16s for the Apollo and the OREX capsules, respectively. Figures 6 and 7 show the close-up view of the computed instantaneous velocity vector field over the Apollo and the OREX modules at $M_\infty = 1.2$. It can be observed from the vector plots that all the significant flow field features such as bow shock wave ahead of the capsule, rapid expansion fans on the corner, flow recirculation region with converging free shear layer and formation of the vortex flow in the aft region of the capsule.

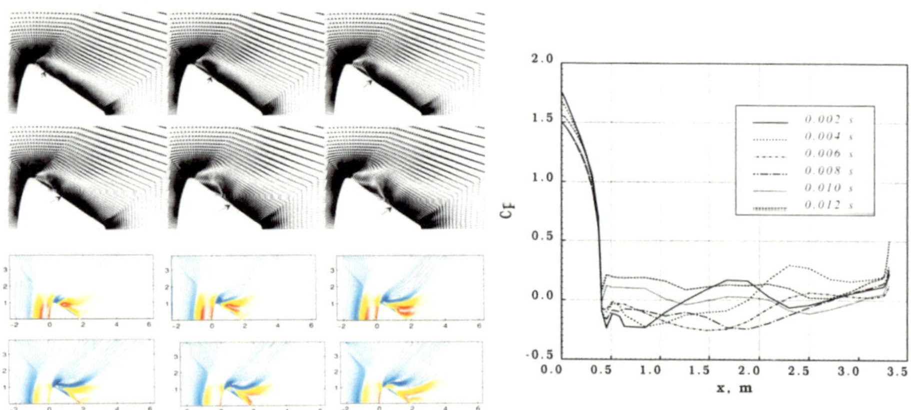

Fig. 7. Instantaneous vector field, pressure contour plots and wall pressure distribution over Apollo capsule.

The wake flow field immediately behind the capsule base exhibits complex flow characteristics. It is also seen that the formation of the bow shock wave on the fore-body of the capsules and which depends on the R_N, R_C and α_B. A gradual flow turning can be observed in Fig. 7 for the case of Apollo which is having smooth shoulder of radius $R_C = 0.01$ m. The approaching supersonic boundary layer separates at the corner and free shear layer is formed in the wake region. The wake flow features also depicts vortex attached to the corner with a large recirculating flow behind the capsule adjacent to the axis of symmetry which depends on back shell cone angle. The separation point moves downstream zone and location of vortex depend on time as can be visualized from the vector and density contour plots.

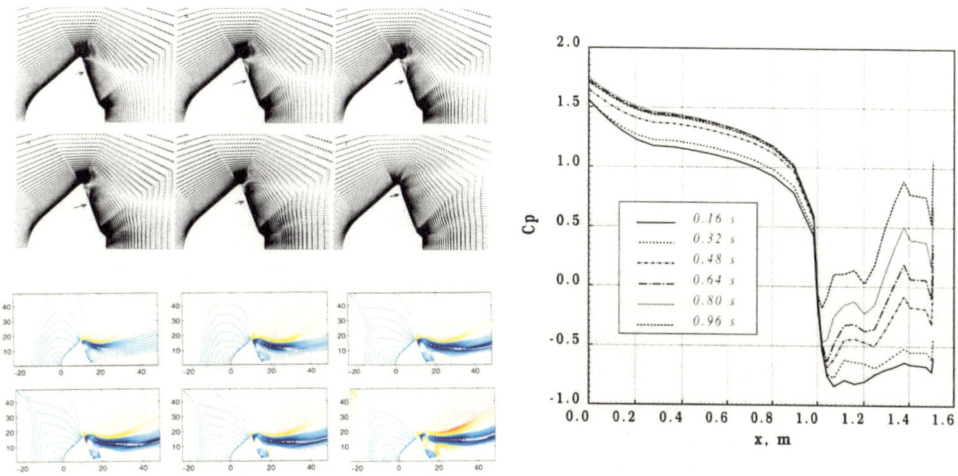

Fig. 8. Instantaneous vector field, pressure contour plots and wall pressure distribution over OREX capsule.

Computed instantaneous Mach contour plots over the Apollo and the OREX capsules are also depicted in Figs. 7 - 8. It can be observed from the contour plots that the oscillatory motion of the flow field in the base region of the flow capsules. Vortices are generated at the capsules and are changing location as a function of time. The flow structure inside the recirculating region is influenced by the periodic motion of the separation bubble and the vorticity of the flow.

The periodic phenomenon is analyzed using the surface pressure variation over the capsules. The figures also show the pressure coefficient Cp variation over the Apollo and the OREX modules. The x = 0 location is the stagnation point. The sonic point moves to the corner of the blunt bodies and affects the pressure distribution throughout the subsonic flow. The pressure coefficient shows over expanded flow in the case of the OREX module. These types of flow field features are also explained by (Bertin, 1994) in conjunction with the flow past reentry capsule. A sudden drop of Cp is noticed on the shoulder of the module followed by a negative pressure variation in the base region. A low pressure is formed immediately downstream of the base which is characterized by a low speed recirculation flow region which can be attributed to fill-up the growing space between the shock wave and body. In the base region, the Cp is increasing with time interval of the cycle. The effect of the shoulder radius of the capsule on the Cp can be seen in the figures. The Apollo capsule is having small conical angle at the base-shell as compared to the OREX base-shell geometry of semi-angle cone of 75 deg. The pressure over the fore body of the capsules is varied with time. Thus, the cyclic of the flow field in the base region is influenced the fore body flow. The different base-shell cone angles give significant effects in the time period. A wavy pattern is seen in the pressure distribution in the base region which may be attributed to complex geometry in the base region. The periodicity of the flow field in the base region are 0.12s (8.33 Hz) and 0.096s (1.04 Hz) for the Apollo and the OREX modules, respectively. It is important to say that the cycle of the flow field over the OREX is 8 times slower than the Apollo. Comparing the computed base-pressure with a common engineering formula (Bonner et al., (1989).

$$\Delta C_{D,base} = \frac{1}{M_\infty^2} - \frac{0.57}{M_\infty^4} \tag{5}$$

The relation is useful to determine the base drag of the capsule as well as to validate the numerical results.

4. Three-dimensional Navier-Stokes equations

The reentry capsule considered here is typified by the Apollo command module. This shape encompasses most of the problems that arises from both viscous and inviscid flow field considerations. The module is at an arbitrary angle of attack that achieved by an offset centre of gravity relative to the free-stream flow. Thus, though the body is axisymmetrical, the geometry of the flow field is not. The only plane of symmetry is the pitch plane, which contains the free-stream velocity vector and the body axis. The bow shock wave in front of the body is fully detached; a subsonic region exists behind the shock wave on the front side of the capsule. As the flow expands around the body, a sonic surface is created (Mach = 1); since the flow continues to increase in speed, it becomes supersonic downstream of this surface. At the downstream the boundary layer tends to separate. The details of the flow vary with geometry and freestream conditions, the general flow features remain the same. The fore body flow field is dominated by a strong bow shock wave. As the flow turns around the shoulder of the reentry module it rapidly expands and can separate. The leeward side flow separates just after the shoulder, whereas the windward side flow remains attached until the rear apex. A shear layer separates the outer flow from the recirculating inner core, which contains multiple counter rotating vortices. The separation shear layer eventually coalesces, forming the neck or narrowest point in the wake. A wake shock is formed at that point, which compresses the flow, leading to local maxima in pressure and temperature. Further away from the neck is far wake region, which extends for many body diameters downstream as the momentum deficit created by the passing module is slowly recovered. Emanating from the separation regions the dividing stream surface, that defines the boundary of the recirculation region - an area in which the flow is trapped. The flow field outside the dividing stream lines proceeds to a single flow stream at the neck of the wake. Oblique shocks are generated near the neck because of the flow external to the wake is turned supersonically. The surrounding inviscid flow and the viscous mixing layer flow build up in the wake much like a boundary layer and develop into the far wake downstream of the base flow field.

4.1 Three-dimensional Euler equations

The flow field analysis over various reentry configurations is studied numerically by solving time-dependent compressible Euler equations. The governing fluid flow equations are discretized in spatial coordinates employing a finite volume approach, which reduces the equations to semi-discretized ordinary differential equations. Temporal integration is performed using multi-stage Runge-Kutta time stepping scheme. A local time step is used to achieve steady state solution. The numerical computation is carried out for freestream Mach number of 10.0 and angle of attack of 10.0 degree. The flow features around the blunt body are characterized by a bow shock wave, expansion wave and base flow region. The numerical scheme captures all the flow field features well. Comparisons of the flow field and surface pressure distribution results are made between different configurations of the blunt body capsules such as ARD (ESA's Atmospheric Reentry Demonstrator), Apollo II, MUSES-C, OREX (Orbital Reentry EXperiments) with and without shoulder curvature and spherically blunted cone with flare angle of 30 and 35 degree. The inviscid analysis takes into consideration centrifugal force and expansion fan at the shoulder of the reentry capsules. The effects of the capsule geometry on the flow field may be useful for optimization of the reentry capsule. The Newtonian flow assumptions are used to calculate forebody aerodynamic drag for various blunt-bodies in conjunction with the NISA software. A comparison between CFD and the Newtonian flow assumptions for various reentry modules are made, and comparison shows an agreement between them. The numerical scheme is described in detail in References (Mehta & Tiwari, 2008; Mehta, 2007).

A finite volume cell is specified by eight corners, which are connected by straight lines. Figure 9 shows hexahedral cell in the computational domain. The discrete values of the flow quantities are calculated at the centre of the cell. The surface integral) over the convective part of the flux density tensor is evaluated for each component cell using an arithmetic average of the flux quantities at the vertices to determine the values on each of the cell faces. Then, the resultant convective inflow of mass, momentum, energy associated with cell centre point is computed by summing the contributions of the component cells. Any open-surface element for a given boundary has a unique, effective surface vector S that is independent of the shape of the surface. This is because, by applying the divergence theorem to a constant vector, the integral of the outward-oriented surface normal over a closed surface vanishes. For instance, the surface vector S-5678 is independent of the choice of which partitioning surface diagonal is used to define the cell volume with vertices 1 to 8. Whether the four vertices are on a plane or not, the surface vector is equal to one-half the cross product of its diagonal line segment. Given eight arbitrary corner points prescribing a general hexahedral, a simple way to define a shape whose volume can be precisely calculated is to partition each face into two planar triangles. The volume is then dependent on which diagonal is used on each face. The volume is the dependent on which diagonal is based on each face, since the diagonal of four non-planar points do not intersect. (Kordulla & Vinokur, 1983) had been used here to calculate cell volume.

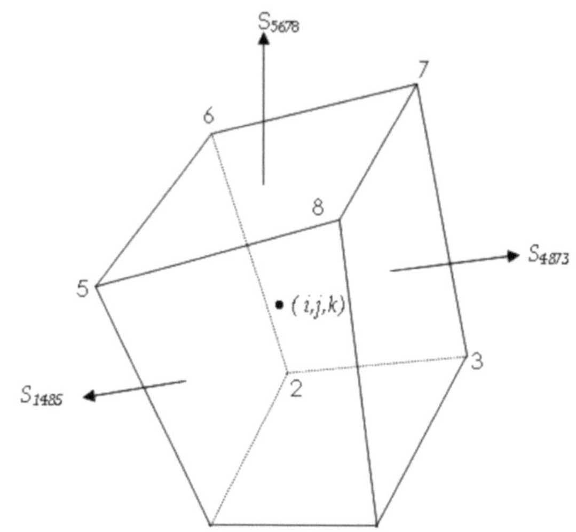

Fig. 9. A hexahedral computational grid of point (i,j,k).

4.2 Flow field over vehicle at angle of attack

Figure 10 shows the Mach contour plots over the OREX and Apollo modules. For the sake of brevity we are presenting windward and leeward sides flow field over OREX with smooth and without smooth shoulder, ARD, Apollo II and spherical-cone configurations are shown at M = 10.0 and at angle of attack 10.0 degree in Fig. 10. The Mach contour plots display the flow field in the windward and the leeward side of the capsules. A shock wave stands in front of the reentry blunt body and forms a region of subsonic flow around the stagnation region. Characteristic features of the flow field around the blunt body at high speed, such as bow shock wave ahead of the capsule and the expansion waves on the shoulder of the capsules. The bow shock wave follows the body contour and the fore body is entirely subsonic up to the corner tangency point of the ARD, the Apollo and the OREX where the sonic line is located. In the case of the spherically blunted cone-flare module, the sonic line is located at the junction of the sphere cone as seen in the Mach contour plots. The flow expands at the base corner. The flow field over the reentry modules became complicated due to the presence of corner at the shoulder and the base shell of the capsule as delineated in the Mach contour plots. Detailed flow field analysis is presented in (Mehta 2007). It is found at the transonic flow cases that a steady state solution could not be achieved due to unsteady nature of the base flow. Table 5 shows the aerodynamic drag numerically computed for COMET and Beagle-2 reentry modules.

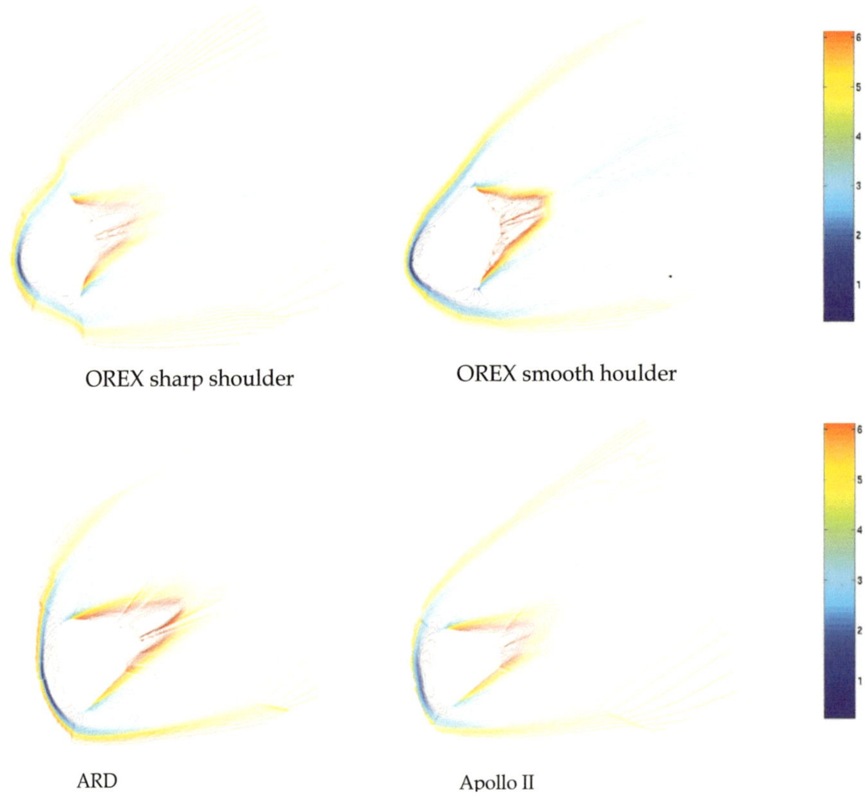

Fig. 10. Mach contour plots over reentry capsules at M = 6.0 and angle of attack 5 deg.

Capsules	M_∞=1.5	M_∞=2.0	M_∞=3.0	M_∞=5.0	M_∞=7.0
COMET	1.56	1.55		1.49	-
Beagle - 2	1.48	1.50	1.502	1.508	1.482

Table 5. Numerically computed aerodynamic drag coefficient.

4.3 Newtonian impact theory

In the Newtonian flow concept the shock wave is assumed to coincide with the body surface. It is also assumed that the freestream maintain its speed and direction unchanged until it strike the surface exposed to the flow. The impact theory does not specify the pressure on surface that do not "visualize" the flow, that is, the surfaces on which gas dynamics would predict Prandtl-Mayer flow. When the flow is curved in the direction of freestream, the difference in pressure from the shock wave to the body surface equals the centrifugal force, due to the curvature of the flow.

A computer program is written to compute the aerodynamic coefficients using the modified Newtonian sine-squared law $C_p = C_{p,max} \sin^2\theta$, where θ is the angle between the freestream velocity vector, and $C_{p,\ max}$ maximum pressure coefficient, which is calculated at a stagnation point behind a normal shock using the Rayleigh pitot tube formula for frozen gas chemistry (constant specific ratio of heats). (Lees, 1955) proposed a modified Newtonian theory, which consists in scaling down so as to be exact at stagnation point, where the correct value is known. The forebody aerodynamic drag is also computed using Newtonian flow assumptions. The numerical simulation can be validated with the post flight data of the Gemini, Apollo and Star dust flights data (Griffith, 1967; Griffith & Boylan, 1968; Lockman, 1970; & Wood, 1997).

5. Conclusion

The aerodynamic characteristics of the reentry capsules are studied experimentally employing the shock tube, the high enthalpy tunnel, wind-tunnel, and free-flight testing. The experimental set up has to design to meet the specific requirements and conditions for the reentry probes. The post flights test data are available for many reentry modules. The flow fields over many reentry modules are generated using computational fluid dynamics for various test conditions. The computational fluid dynamics can be used to analyze and understand the complex flow field features in the wake region of the modules. Numerical simulation can be used to get aerodynamic characteristics, wall heat flux, and stability margin for the optimization of the trajectory of the capsules.

6. Acknowledgment

The author is indebted to his parents and Vikram Sarabhai Space Centre, Trivandrum, India for their valuable encouragement, help and contributions to build the research career.

7. References

Allen, J. S. and Cheng, S. I. (1970). Numerical solution of the compressible Navier-Stokes equations for the near wake, Physics of Fluids, Vol. 13, No. 1, pp. 37-52

Ames Research Staff (1953). Equations, tables and charts for compressible flow, NACA report 1135

Beam, R. M., and Warming, R. F. (1976). An implicit finite-difference algorithm for hyperbolic systems in conservation law form, Journal of Computational Physics, Vol. 22, pp. 87-110.

Bedin, A. P., Mishin, G. I., and Chistyakove, M. V. (1992). Experimental investigation of the aerodynamic characteristics and geometric parameters of flows about various molecular structures, in "Gas Dynamics" edited by Yu. I. Koptev, Nova Science Publishers, N.Y., pp. 39-67

Bertin, J. J. (1994). *Hypersonic Aerothermodynamics*, AIAA Education Series, AIAA Press, VA, USA

Bonner, E., Clever, W., and Dunn, K. (1989). Aerodynamic preliminary analysis system II, part I - theory, NASA CR 165627

Briley, W. R., and McDonald, H. (1975). Solution of the tree-dimensional compressible Navier-Stokes equations by an implicit technique, Proceedings of Fourth International Conference on Numerical Methods in Fluid Dynamics, Lecture Notes in Physics, Vol. 35, Springer-Verlag, Berlin

Bailey, H. E.(1967). Programs for computing equilibrium thermodynamic properties of gases, NASA TN D-3921

Boris, J. P., and Book, D. L. (1973) Flux corrected transport 1, SHASTA, a finite transport algorithm that works, Journal of Computational Physics, Vol. 11, pp. 38-69

Chester, W. (1956). Supersonic flow past a bluff body with a detached shock, Journal of Fluid Mechanics, Vol. 1, pp. 353-365

Davis, S. F. (1984) TVD finite difference schemes and artificial viscosity, NASA CR-172373.

Edwards, T. A. (1992). Fluid/chemistry modeling for hypersonic flight analysis, Computers Mathematical Applications, Vol. 24, No. 5/6, pp. 25-36

Fay, J. A., and Riddle, F. R. (1958). Theory of stagnation point heat transfer in dissociated air, Journal of Aeronautical Sciences, Vol. 25, pp. 73-85

Freeman, N. C. (1956). On the theory of hypersonic flow past plane and axially symmetric bluff bodies, Journal of Fluid Mechanics, Vol. 1, pp. 366-387

Fujimoto, K., and Fujii, K. (2006). Computational aerodynamic analysis of capsule configurations toward the development of reusable rockets, Journal of Spacecraft and Rockets, Vol. 43, No. 1, pp. 77-83

Gnoffo, P. A., Weilmuenster, K. J. (1996). Braun, R. D., Cruz, C. I., Influence of sonic-line location on Mars Pathfinder probe aerothermodynamics, Journal of Spacecraft and Rockets, Vol. 33, No. 2, pp. 169-173

Gnoffo, P., Gupta, R., and Shinn, J. (1989). Conservation equations and physical models for hypersonic air flows in thermal and chemical non-equilibrium, NASA TP-267

Godunov, S. K. (1959). A difference scheme for numerical computation of discontinuous .solution of hyperbolic equations, Math. Sb., Vol. 47, pp. 271-306

Grasso, F. and Pettinelli, C. (1995). Analysis of laminar near wake hypersonic flow, Journal of Spacecraft and Rockets, Vol. 32, No. 6, pp. 970-980

Griffith, B. J. (1967). Comparison of aerodynamic data from the Gemini flights and AEDC-VKF wind tunnels, Journal of Spacecraft and Rockets, Vol. 4, No. 7, pp. 919-924

Griffith, B. J., and Boylan, D. E. (1968). Post flight Apollo command module aerodynamic simulation tests, Journal of Spacecraft and Rockets, Vol. 5, No. 7, pp. 843-848

Haas, B. L. and Venkatapathy, E. (1995). Mars path finder computations including base heating predictions, AIAA 95-2086

Harten, A. (1984). On a class of high resolution total variation stable finite difference schemes, SIAM Journal of Numerical Analysis, Vol. 21, pp. 1-23

Hansen, C.F. (1959). Approximations for the thermodynamic and transport properties of high temperature air, NASA TR R-50

Hiraki, K., Inatani, Y., Ishii, N., Nakajima, T., and Shimoda, T. (1998). Dynamic stability of MUSES-C capsule, 21st International Symposium on Space Technology and Science, Report ISTS-98-d-33

Hayer, W. D. and Probstein, R. F. (1959). *Hypersonic Flow Theory*, Academic Press, New York

Jameson, A., Schmidt, W., Turkel, E. (1981). Numerical solution of Euler equations by finite volume methods using Runge-Kutta time stepping schemes, AIAA paper 81-1259

Kordulla, W. and Vinokur, M. (1983). Efficient computation of volume in flow predictions, AIAA Journal, Vol. 21, No. 6, pp. 917-918

Lamb, J. P. and Oberkampf, W. L. (1995). Review and development of base pressure and base heating correlations in supersonic flow, Journal of Spacecraft & Rockets, Vol. 32, No. 1, pp. 8-23

Lax, P. D., (1954). Weak solutions of nonlinear hyperbolic equations and their numerical computation, Communications in Pure and Applied Mathematics, Vol. 7, pp. 159-193

Lax, P. D., and Wendroff, B. (1954). Systems of conservation laws, Communications in Pure and Applied Mathematics, Vol. 15, pp. 363-388

Lees, L. (1955). *Hypersonic flow*, Institute Aeronautical Science, Preprint No. 554

Liever, P. A., Habchi, S. D., Burnell, S. I. and Lingard, J. S. (2003). Computational fluid dynamics prediction of the Beagle 2 aerodynamic data base, Journal of Spacecraft and Rockets, Vol. 40, No. 5, 2003, pp. 632-638

Liepmann, H. W., and Roshko, A. (2007). *Elements of Gas Dynamics,* 1st South Asian Edition, Dover Publications Inc, New Delhi

Lighthill, M. J. (1957). Dynamics of a dissociating gas, Part 1: Equilibrium flow, Journal of Fluid Mechanics, Vol. 2, pp. 1-32

Lockman, W. K. (1970). Base-heating measurements on Apollo block II command module, Journal of Spacecraft and Rockets, Vol. 7, No. 1, pp. 93-94

MacCormack, R. W., (1969). The effect of viscosity in hyper-velocity impact cratering, AIAA paper 66-354

MacCormack, R. W., (1981). A numerical method for solving the equations of compressible viscous flow, AIAA paper 81-0110

Menne, S. (1994). computation of non-winged vehicle aerodynamics in the low supersonic range, in the proceedings of the 2nd European Symposium on Aerothermodynamics for Space Vehicles, ESTEC, Noordwiik, The Netherlkands, 21-25 November, pp. 73-78

Mehta, R. C. (2006). Computational investigation of flow oscillation over reentry capsules, Computational Fluid Dynamics JOURNAL, Vol. 15, No. 2, pp. 247-260

Mehta, R. C. (2006). Numerical simulation of supersonic flow past reentry capsules, Shock Waves, Vol. 15, No. 1, pp. 31-41

Mehta, R. C., Jayachandran, T., and Sastri, V. M. K. (1991). Numerical solution of the Navier-Stokes equations using a finite element method, International Journal for Numerical Methods in Fluids, Vol. 13, pp. 481-489

Mehta, R. C. (2001). Comparative study of surface pressure fluctuations over bulbous heat shield at Mach 0.95, Computers & Fluids, Vol. 30, No. 6, pp. 689-709

Mehta, R. C. (2011). Block Structured Finite Element Grid Generation Method, paper accepted for publication in Computational Fluid Dynamics Journal

Mehta, R. C. (2006).Aerodynamic Drag Coefficient for Various Reentry Configurations at High Speed, AIAA paper 2006-3179

Mehta, R. C. (2004). Computation of flow field over reentry capsules at supersonic Mach numbers, Computational Fluid Dynamics JOURNAL, Vol. 13, No. 3, pp. 585-596

Mehta, R. C. (2008). Computations of flow field over Apollo and OREX reentry modules at high speed, Indian Journal of Engineering and Materials Sciences, Vol. 15, pp. 459-466

Mehta, R. C. (2010). Flow field simulations over reentry modules at high speed, Journal of Aerospace Sciences and Technologies, Vol. 62 , No. 1, pp. 55-65

Mehta, R. C. (2007). Three-dimensional inviscid flow field computation over various reentry configurations, AIAA paper 2007-133

Mehta, R. C. and Tiwari, S. B. (2008). Comparative studies of aerodynamic drag using inviscid flow computation and Newtonian method at high speed, Journal of Aerospace Sciences and Technologies, Vol. 60, No. 1, pp. 35-44

Moretti, G. (1979). Conformal mapping for the computation of steady three-dimensional supersonic flows, Numerical/Laboratory for Computer Methods in Fluid Mechanics , edis.- A. A. Pouring and V. I. Shah, ASME New York, pp. 13-28

Osu, H., Abe, T., Ohnishi, Y. Sasoh, A. and Takayama, K., (2002).Numerical investigation of high enthalpy flow generated by expansion tube, AIAA Journal, Vol. 40, No. 12, pp. 2423-2430

Otten, H. B. A. (2001). Preliminary computational investigation on aerodynamic phenomena DELFT aerospace reentry test vehicle, , in the proceedings of the 4th European Symposium on Aerothermodynamics for Space Applications, ESA, Capua, Italy, 15-18 October, pp. 207-213

Osher, S. (1984). Riemann solvers, the entropy condition and difference approximations, SIAM Journal of Numerical Analysis, Vol. 21, 1984, pp. 217-235

Osher, S., and Chakravarthy (1984). S. R., High resolution schemes and the entropy condition, SIAM Journal of Numerical Analysis, Vol. 21, pp. 955-984

Peyret, R., and Vivind, H. (1993). *Computational Methods for Fluid Flows,* Springer-Verlag, Berlin, pp. 109-111

Ritchtmyer, R. D., and Morton, K. W. (1967). *Difference Methods for Initial-Value Problems,* 2nd Edition, New York, Wiley, Interscience Publishers

Roe, P. L. (1981). Approximate Riemann solvers, parameter vectors and difference schemes, Journal of Computational Physics, Vol. 43, pp. 357-372

Roe, P. L. (1995). Upwind schemes using various formulations of the Euler equations in Numerical Methods for the Euler Equations of Fluid Dynamics, Philadelphia, PA, SIAM Publications

Rusanov, V. V. (1996). A blunt body in a supersonic stream, Annual Review of Fluid Mechanics, Vol. 8, pp. 377-404

Shang, J. S. (1984). Numerical Simulation of Wing-fuselage Aerodynamic Interference, AIAA Journal, Vol. 22, No. 10, pp. 1345-1353

Solazzo, M. A., Sansoner, A., Gasbarri, P. (1994). Aerodynamic characterization of the Carnia reentry module in the low supersonic regimes, in the proceedings of the 2nd European Symposium on Aerothermodynamics for Space Vehicles, ESTEC, Noordwiik, The Netherlkands, 21-25 November, pp. 41-47

Srinivasan, S. and Weilmuenster, K. J. (1987). Simplified curve fits for the thermodynamic properties of equilibrium air, NASA TP 1181

Steger, J. L., and Warming, R. F. (1981). Flux vector splitting of the inviscid gas dynamics equations with applications to finite difference methods, Journal of Computational Physics, Vol. 40, pp. 263-293

Tam, L. T. (1992). LU-SGS implicit scheme for entry vehicle flow computation and comparison with aerodynamic data, AIAA 92-2671 CP

Tai, C-S. and Kao, A. F. (1994). Navier-Stokes solver for hypersonic flow over a slender cone, Journal of Spacecraft and Rockets, Vol. 31, No. 1, pp. 215-222

Teramoto, S., Hiraki, K., Fujii, K. (2001). Numerical analysis of dynamic stability of a reentry capsule at transonic speeds, AIAA Journal, Vol. 39, No. 4, pp. 646-653

Teramoto, S., and Fujii, K. (2002) Mechanism of dynamic instability of a reentry capsule at transonic speeds, AIAA Journal, Vol. 40, No. 12, pp. 2467-2476

Truit, R. W. (1959). *Hypersonic Aerodynamics,* The Ronald Press Co., New York

Venkatapathy, E., Palmer, G., and Prabhu, D. K. (1991). AFE base computations, AIAA paper 91-1372

Van Leer, B., (1979). Towards the ultimate conservative difference scheme, V A second orders equal to Godunov's method, Journal of Computational Physics, Vol. 32, pp. 101-136

Walpot, I. (2001). Numerical analysis of the ARD capsule in S4 wind tunnel, in the proceedings of the 4th European Symposium on Aerothermodynamics for Space Applications, ESA, Capua, Italy, 15-18 October, pp. 523-527

Weinbaum, S. (1966). Rapid expansion of a supersonic boundary layer and its applications to the near wake, AIAA Journal, Vol. 4, No. 2, pp. 217-226

White, F. M. (1991). *Viscous Fluid Flow*, 2nd Edition, McGraw Hill International Edition, Singapore

Wood, W. A., Gnoffo, P. A., and Rault, D. F. G. (1996). Aerothermodynamic analysis of commercial experiment transporter (COMET) reentry capsule, AIAA paper 96-0316

Wood, A. W., Gnoffo, P. A. and Rault, D.F.G. (1996). Aerodynamic analysis of commercial experiment transport reentry capsule, Journal of Spacecraft & Rockets, Vol. 33, No. 5, 1996, pp. 643-646

Wood, W. A. (1997). Hypersonic pitching-moment shift for star dust reentry capsule fore body, NASA TM 97-206266

Wright, J. M., Milos, F. S., and Tran, P. (2006), Afterbody aero-heating flight data for planetary probe thermal protection system design, Journal of Spacecraft and Rockets, Vol. 43, No. 5, pp. 929-943

Yamamoto, Y. and Yoshioka, M. (1995). CFD and FEM coupling analysis of OREX aero-thermodynamic flight data, AIAA 95-2087

Yee, H. C. (1985). On symmetric and upwind TVD schemes, Proceedings of the 6th GAMM Conference on Numerical Methods in Fluid Mechanics, Braunschweig, Vieweg, pp. 399-407

17

Numerical Simulation of Dense Phase Pneumatic Conveying in Long-Distance Pipe

Zongming LIU, Guangbin DUAN and Kun WANG
University of JINAN
China P.R

1. Introduction

Computational Fluid Dynamics is now a new ramification of the numerical discretization method based on high-performance electronic computers, which focuses on fluid mechanics simulation. Fluid mechanics has two main braches that one is theoretical analysis and another is experimental research. Therefore, theoretical and experimental fluid mechanics were created as most important constituents in early days. Although the theoretical method could give the quantum results of the solving problem, it was still little used for its complicated solution procedure.

Computational fluid mechanics has developed rapidly to cover the shortage of theoretical method. It has been involved each fluid field though its development history is short. Many numerical solution methods were formed according to different simulation purpose. Finite difference calculus and finite element method were mainly involved. In the application, Finite difference calculus was usually used in resolving fluid problem, while finite element method was exploited to research solid mechanics themes.

Gas-solids two phase flow means solid particles are conveyed by compressed gas phase. The particles' traces are irregular, which caused by the dispersion action and coupling force between gas and solids phase. The interaction process leads to the irregular motion of gas solid two phase flow and the flow characteristic parameter altering greatly. Nowadays, the recognization and analysis of gas solid two phase flow was not enough with limitation of test technique, which restricted the application development and system optimization of gas solid flow. So some fresh technique must be appeared to suit the application situation.

Until now, the research technique in gas solid two phase flow focus on experiment cases because of the complexity of gas solid flow. Te gas solid two phase flow theory became more and more sophisticated with the development of particle dynamics and aerodynamics. Both had some deficiency. For example, in experimental research, calculation of some conveying parameters mostly depends on empirical equations based on experiments which leads to the limitation, and which are the same with its experimental condition commonly and generalized hardly. Theoretical studies are mostly short of accuracy because of lots of hypothesis in the process of deduction. Therefore, in this thesis, simulation study on the process of dense-phase gas-solid two phase flow was carried on based on experimental and theoretical investigations in order to cover the shortage of experimental and theoretical investigations.

Numerical simulation technique improves rapidly with the advance of computer hardware. And it plays more and more important role in the research of dense-phase gas solid flow. This article gave the numerical simulation conclusions based on the experimental and theoretical research. By associating with experimental condition and the applicability of experimental equations, transport equation of Reynolds was deduced by using time averaged method based on instantaneous equation of gas and solid. The control equations of turbulent energy and turbulent dissipative ratio were formed, which considered reciprocity between gas and solid, collision of particles and interaction between particle and wall. The model included continuity equation, momentum equation, turbulent kinetic energy equation and turbulent kinetic energy ratio equation. Physical meaning of primary item of control equation was discussed too.

Two-fluid model of gas-solid turbulence in process of dense-phase gas solid two phase flow was founded, so did the corresponding numerical solution and calculating flow. The model could mention reciprocity between gas and solid, collision of particles and interaction between particle and wall.

The process of dense phase gas solid two phase flow in pipeline under experimental conditions was simulated with FLUENT software by founded model and corresponding arithmetic. Pressure distribution diagram, density distribution diagram and velocity vectogram etc. were given which displayed the flow alternation of dense-phase pneumatic conveying. And comparison between simulated result and experimental case showed good suitable which illuminated the model had good accuracy and forecasting capacity.

In all, in this study, fluid mechanics characteristics of dense-phase gas solid two phase flow in pipeline were discussed by computational fluid dynamics method based on flow theory of gas-solid, and a series of significative results were obtained. The research showed that the numerical simulation of dense-phase pneumatic conveying can complement experimental and theoretical studies which had promoted effect on the application and development of dense-phase gas solid flow in pipeline technique.

2. Experiment

The technique of dense-phase pneumatic conveying has been widespread applied in industry. Investigations on dense-phase pneumatic conveying usually include experimental research and theoretical research because of the complexity of flow in pneumatic conveying. But, both of the methods have limitation. In experimental research, calculation of some conveying parameters mostly depends on empirical equation based on experiments which leads to the limitation, and which are the same with its experimental condition commonly and generalized hardly.

Experimental research were carried on by changing feeding pressure on the positive pressure style pneumatic conveying pilot-scale experiment table. The conveying characteristics along pipeline were studied primarily.

Pneumatic conveying system in this paper was a circulating experiment system with long-distance pipeline, which consisted of an air compressor, a feeder, a conveying pipeline, and a set of measurement/control system, as shown in Fig.1.

The pipeline was made of seamless steel pipe with a length of 203 m and pipe diameter of 80 mm. Weight balance was installed to measure the fly ash discharge rate of the feeding bin. Gas mass flow meter was adopted to measure the mass flow ratio of the compressed air.

GP/DP transmitters were used to measure pressure of the feeder, setting points along pipeline and pressure drop of test segments.

Fly ash was transported from the feeder vessel into the receiver in dense phase. The material properties were shown in Table 1.

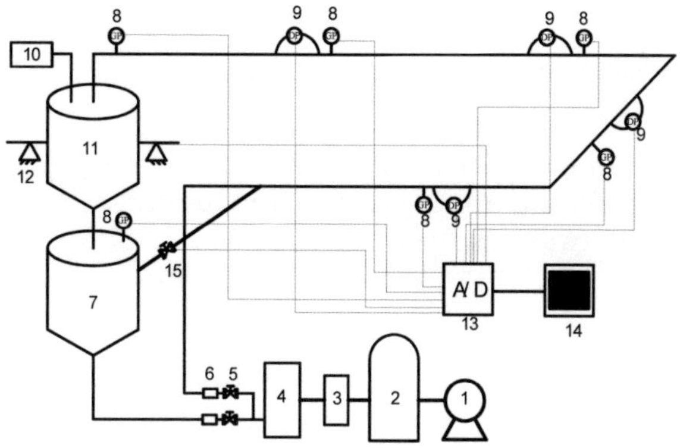

Fig. 1. Schematic diagram of experimental system. 1. air compressor 2. gas storage pot 3.oil-water segregator and air drier 4. gas adapter 5. gas inlet valve 6. gas flow meter 7. feeder 8. static pressure gauge 9. differential pressure gauge 10 dust catcher 11. collecting bin 12. weighing-appliance 13 data acquisition equipment 14. micro-computer 15. bleeder valve.

After being put into the feeder, fly ash was fluidized by compressed air. Then at a preset transporting pressure in the feeder, fly ash passed through the conveying pipeline and reached the collecting bin finally. Five test segments along horizontal pipeline were employed averagely to analyze the tendency of pressure drop along the pipeline. A differential pressure transmitter and a gauge pressure transmitter were assembled in the segments of 52.2 -53.4 m, 90.5 -91.7 m, 126.5 -127.7 m, 176-177.2 m. Gauge pressure transmitters were also installed at the terminal of pipeline (6) as well as the vent of feeder. In this experiment, operating condition was mainly controlled by changing the pressure of feeder The experiments under different operating conditions and each with several repetitions were carried out in total.

Material	Equivalent spherical diameter (μm)	Bulk density (kg m-3)	Sphericity
Fly ash	60	770	0.96

Table 1. Experimental material properties.

3. Experimental results

3.1 Gas velocity along the pipe

The gas velocity along the pipe is an important parameter, and it can be expressed by the following equation.

$$u_g = \frac{M_g}{A\varepsilon\rho_g} = \frac{M_g}{A\varepsilon}\frac{RT}{p} \tag{1}$$

Where, M_g is the gas mass flow ratio. A is the cross section of pipeline. *T* stands for Kelvin temperature. P is static pressure in the pipe. ε is porosity, and it can be achieved by the following equation.

$$\varepsilon = \frac{\rho_s}{k\rho_g + \rho_s} \tag{2}$$

In this equation, ρ_s is solid density. ρ_g is gas density. k is solids loading ratio, the ratio of solids mass versus gas mass in total.

Fig. 2 shows the trend of gas velocity along the pipeline under different feeder pressure. Gas velocity increases gradually with the increase of feed pressure. While under the same feed pressure, gas velocity increases gradually along pipeline, which is caused by gas volume expansion.

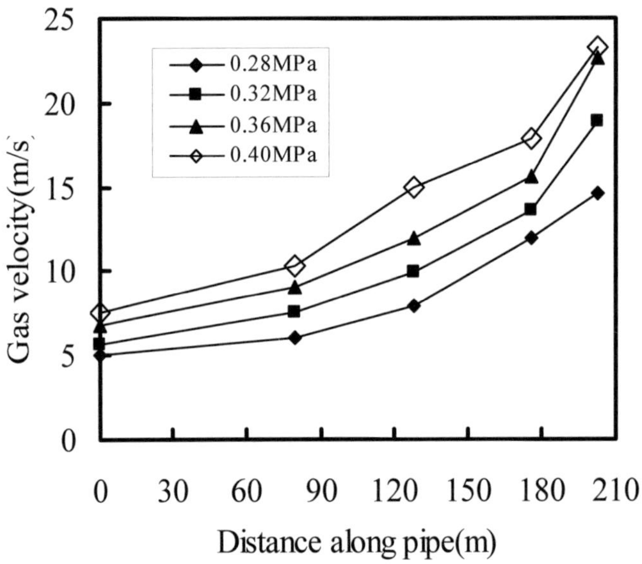

Fig. 2. Experimental values of gas velocity along pipeline.

3.2 Solid velocity along the pipe

In this paper, the solid velocity along the pipe can be given by the following equations.

$$u_{ij} = \frac{L_{ij}}{t_{ij}} \tag{3}$$

Where Lij means the distance between the transmitter of NO. i and NO. j. and tij stands for the time interval of the pressure signal appearance between NO. i and NO. j transmitters.

The relationship between pressure drop and transport distance along pipeline in different feed pressure was obtained based on the measured data from the four differential pressure transmitters in the experiment process, as shown in Fig. 3.

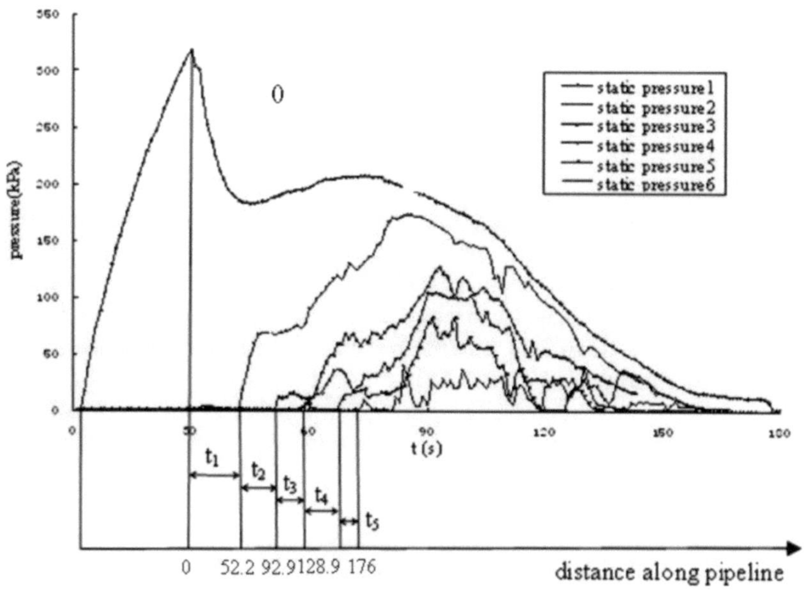

Fig. 3. Variable curve of static pressures with the feed pressure 0.32Mpa.

Fig. 4 shows the trend of solid velocity along the pipeline under different feeder pressure. solid velocity increased gradually with the increase of feed pressure. And under the same feed pressure, solid velocity increases gradually along pipeline, which is caused by the increasing of gas velocity.

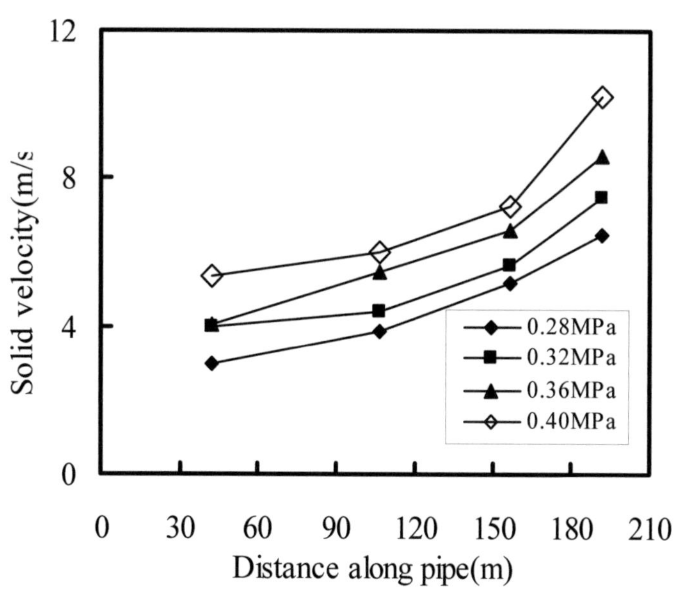

Fig. 4. Experimental values of solid velocity along pipeline.

4. Numerical simulation of gas solid flow in pipe

4.1 Mathematical models

As we all know, the physical aspects of fluid flow are governed by three fundamental principles (1) mass is conserved; (2) Newton's second law; (3) energy is conserved. So N-S equations are formed.

To this paper, the suitable mathematical models were selected according to experimental conclusions. As we all know, the Reynolds Number values of gas and granule in dense phase gas solid flow are both high than that of lean phase, which lead to more turbulent motion. Therefore, the addition of solid particles greatly changed gas phase turbulent construction and meanwhile gas fluctuation affect particle motions. So the interaction between the two phases leads to the mass, momentum and energy transmission.

When the solid concentration is high enough, interaction among particles affect solid flow characteristics greatly. Consequently, the interaction among particles should be given in simulation process in addition to gas solid interaction and turbulent as the gas solid two phase flow turbulent model being set up.

Two-fluid model which based on granule dynamics theory was adapted in the study. Flow parameters such as macroscopic granule transport equations, solid pressure, viscous coefficient, diffusion coefficient, heat conductivity coefficient, granule temperature etc can be obtained through the model. This model was used comprehensively in several fields because it mentioned interation action of gas solid flow, granule turbulent viscosity and particle collision roundly.

In this study, by using k-ε two phase model, granule dynamics model and gas solid two phase coupled, the gas solid two phase turbulent model were built up. Some reasonable assumptions about the flow process must be given as following.

1. The particles were composed of smooth rigid sphere with the same diameter. And during the flow process, two sphere collisions were mentioned while collision among lots of solid particles must be ignored.
2. Gas solid two phase existed in the flow pipe homogeneously with defined physical parameter. Each phase was continuous while the time averaged velocity and volume ratio was different.
3. The acting force of solid phase involved gravity and resistance force. Other kind of force such as buoyancy, false-mass-force, Basset force, thermophoretic force etc was ignored according to experimental cases.
4. The turbulent impulse of gas solid two phase was isotropy. Diffusion and Brownian movement effect could be neglected. The change of gas phase turbulent energy showed the influence of particle to gas phase.

4.1.1 Instantaneous equation setup of gas solid flow

According to mass conservation and momentum conservation law, gas and solid phase instantaneous volume averaged conservation equations can be given as following.

Gas continuity equation:

$$\frac{\partial\left(\alpha_g\rho_g\right)}{\partial t}+\frac{\partial\left(\alpha_g\rho_g u_{gj}\right)}{\partial x_j}=0 \tag{4}$$

Solid continuity equation:

$$\frac{\partial(\alpha_s\rho_s)}{\partial t}+\frac{\partial(\alpha_s\rho_s u_{sj})}{\partial x_j}=0 \tag{5}$$

Gas momentum equation:

$$\frac{\partial(\alpha_g\rho_g u_{gi})}{\partial t}+\frac{\partial(\alpha_g\rho_g u_{gi}u_{gj})}{\partial x_j}=-\alpha_g\frac{\partial p}{\partial x_i}+\alpha_g\rho_g g_i+\frac{\partial\tau_{ij}}{\partial x_j}+F_i^{cd} \tag{6}$$

Solid momentum equation:

$$\frac{\partial(\alpha_s\rho_s u_{si})}{\partial t}+\frac{\partial(\alpha_s\rho_s u_{si}u_{sj})}{\partial x_j}=-\alpha_s\frac{\partial p_s}{\partial x_i}+\alpha_s\rho_s g_i+\frac{\partial\tau_{sij}}{\partial x_j}-F_i^{cd} \tag{7}$$

Where, α_g, α_s are gas, solid volume rate, $\alpha_g+\alpha_s=1$; ρ_g, ρ_s are gas density and solid density respectively ; u_{gi}, u_{gj}, u_{si}, u_{sj} are instantaneous velocity component of gas, solid in i, j direction. p_g、p_s are pressure of gas, solid; g_i is component of gravitation in i direction; F_i^{cd} is interaction between gas and solid, which includes the inter-phase resistance, false mass force, and pressure gradient force. In horizontal pipe, drag force is the dominant factor. So here

$$F_i^{cd}=\beta(u_{gi}-u_{pi}) \tag{8}$$

Where β is drag force coefficient between the two phase.
As $a_g \geq 0.8$, according to experiment results, the expression of β can be given as below.

$$\beta=0.75C_D\alpha_s\frac{|u_g-u_s|}{d_p}\rho_g\alpha_g^{-2.65} \tag{9}$$

C_D is single particle drag force coefficient, the calculation equations are given as following.

$$\begin{array}{l} \mathrm{Re}_p>1000 \\ 1000\geq \mathrm{Re}_p>1 \\ \mathrm{Re}_p\leq 1 \end{array} \begin{cases} C_D=0.44 \\ C_D=\dfrac{24}{\mathrm{Re}_p}(1+0.15\mathrm{Re}_p^{0.68}) \\ C_D=\dfrac{24}{\mathrm{Re}_p} \end{cases} \tag{10}$$

$$\text{Here, } C_D=\frac{24}{\mathrm{Re}_p}\left(1+0.15\mathrm{Re}_p^{0.68}\right) \tag{11}$$

Re_p is defined as particle Reynolds number,

$$\mathrm{Re}_p = \frac{\alpha_g \rho_g d_p \left| u_g - u_s \right|}{\mu_g} \tag{12}$$

τ_{ij} is gas viscosity stress.

$$\tau_{ij} = \alpha_g \mu_g \left[\left(\frac{\partial u_{gi}}{\partial x_j} + \frac{\partial u_{gi}}{\partial x_i} \right) - \frac{2}{3} \delta_{ij} \frac{\partial u_{gk}}{\partial x_k} \right] \tag{13}$$

Where, μ_g is gas phase kinetic viscosity coefficient.

δ_{ij} is Kronecker delta,

$$\delta_{ij} = \begin{cases} 1 & \mathrm{i = j} \\ 0 & \mathrm{i \neq j} \end{cases},$$

4.1.2 Time averaged equation setup of gas solid flow

Gas continuity equation:

$$\frac{\partial \left(\alpha_g \rho_g \right)}{\partial t} + \frac{\partial \left(\alpha_g \rho_g u_{gj} \right)}{\partial x_j} + \frac{\partial \left(\rho_g \overline{\alpha_g u_{gj}} \right)}{\partial x_j} = 0 \tag{14}$$

Solid continuity equation:

$$\frac{\partial \left(\alpha_s \rho_s \right)}{\partial t} + \frac{\partial \left(\alpha_s \rho_s u_{sj} \right)}{\partial x_j} + \frac{\partial \left(\rho_s \overline{\alpha_s u_{sj}} \right)}{\partial x_j} = 0 \tag{15}$$

Gas momentum equation:

$$\frac{\partial}{\partial t}\left(\alpha_g \rho_g u_{gi} \right) + \frac{\partial}{\partial x_j}\left(\alpha_g \rho_g u_{gi} u_{gj} \right) = -\alpha_g \frac{\partial p}{\partial x_i} - \frac{2}{3} \frac{\partial}{\partial x_j} \left[\mu_g \alpha_g \frac{\partial u_{gk}}{\partial x_k} + \mu_g \overline{\alpha_g^{'} \frac{\partial u_{gk}^{'}}{\partial x_k}} \right] + \tag{16}$$

$$\frac{\partial}{\partial x_j} \left[\mu_g \alpha_g \left(\frac{\partial u_{gi}}{\partial x_\mathrm{j}} + \frac{\partial u_{gj}}{\partial x_i} \right) + \mu_g \overline{\alpha_g^{'} \left(\frac{\partial u_{gi}^{'}}{\partial x_\mathrm{j}} + \frac{\partial u_{gj}^{'}}{\partial x_i} \right)} \right] + \alpha_g \rho_g g_i + \beta \left(u_{si} - u_{gi} \right) + \overline{\beta^{'} \left(u_{si}^{'} - u_{gi}^{'} \right)}$$

$$-\frac{\partial}{\partial x_j} \left(\alpha_g \rho_g \overline{u_{gi}^{'} u_{gj}^{'}} + \rho_g u_{gi} \overline{\alpha_g^{'} u_{gj}^{'}} + \rho_g u_{gj} \overline{\alpha_g^{'} u_{gi}^{'}} + \rho_g \overline{\alpha_g^{'} u_{gi}^{'} u_{gj}^{'}} \right)$$

Solid momentum equation:

$$\frac{\partial}{\partial t}\left(\alpha_s\rho_s u_{si}\right)+\frac{\partial}{\partial x_j}\left(\alpha_s\rho_s u_{si}u_{sj}\right)=-\alpha_s\frac{\partial p}{\partial x_i}+\alpha_s\rho_s g_i+\frac{\partial}{\partial x_j}\left(\overline{\tau_{sij}+\tau_{dij}^{'}}\right)+\beta\left(u_{gi}-u_{si}\right)$$
$$+\overline{\beta^{'}\left(u_{gi}^{'}-u_{si}^{'}\right)}-\frac{\partial}{\partial x_j}\left(\alpha_s\rho_s\overline{u_{si}^{'}u_{sj}^{'}}+\rho_s u_{si}\overline{\alpha_s^{'}u_{sj}^{'}}+\rho_s u_{sj}\overline{\alpha_s^{'}u_{si}^{'}}+\rho_s\overline{\alpha_s^{'}u_{si}^{'}u_{sj}^{'}}\right) \quad (17)$$

From equations above, time averaged equation setup provided several unknown quantity. Above all factors, turbulent stress played a dominant role to the governing equations. So some assumption or new turbulent model equations must be introduced to accomplish the equations set. Nowadays, Reynolds stress model and vortex model were often employed to agree with different suitable cases. In the study, by contrast to all occasions, Reynolds stress model was selected.

4.1.3 Turbulent kinetic energy and turbulent dissipation rate equation

1. Reynolds stress transport equation

According to Boussines assumption and some mathematical operation, Reynolds stress transport equation can be given as below.

$$\frac{\partial}{\partial t}\left(\rho\overline{u_i^{'}u_j^{'}}\right)+\frac{\partial}{\partial x_k}\left(\rho u_k\overline{u_i^{'}u_j^{'}}\right)=\frac{\partial}{\partial x_k}\left(\frac{\mu_t}{\sigma_k}\frac{\partial\overline{u_i^{'}u_j^{'}}}{\partial x_k}+\mu\frac{\partial\overline{u_i^{'}u_j^{'}}}{\partial x_k}\right)-\rho\left(\overline{u_i^{'}u_k^{'}}\frac{\partial u_j}{\partial x_k}+\overline{u_j^{'}u_k^{'}}\frac{\partial u_j}{\partial x_k}\right)$$
$$-\frac{\mu_t}{\rho \mathrm{Pr}_t}\left(g_i\frac{\partial\rho}{\partial x_j}+g_j\frac{\partial\rho}{\partial x_i}\right)-C_1\rho\frac{\varepsilon}{k}\left(\overline{u_i^{'}u_j^{'}}-\frac{2}{3}k\delta_{ij}\right)$$
$$-C_2\left[\rho\left(\overline{u_i^{'}u_k^{'}}\frac{\partial u_j}{\partial x_k}+\overline{u_j^{'}u_k^{'}}\frac{\partial u_i}{\partial x_k}\right)-\frac{1}{3}P_{kk}\delta_{ij}\right]+C_1^{'}\rho\frac{\varepsilon}{k}\left(\overline{u_k^{'}u_m^{'}}n_k n_m\delta_{ij}-\frac{2}{3}\overline{u_i^{'}u_k^{'}}n_i n_k\right)\frac{k^{3/2}}{C_l\varepsilon d}$$
$$+C_2^{'}\left(\Phi_{km,2}n_k n_m\delta_{ij}-\frac{3}{2}\Phi_{ik,2}n_j n_k-\frac{3}{2}\Phi_{ik,2}n_i n_k\right)\frac{k^{3/2}}{C_l\varepsilon d}-\frac{2}{3}\rho\varepsilon\delta_{ij} \quad (18)$$

To this study, the buoyant force and revolution effect were neglected. So the equation above can be rewritten as below.

$$\frac{\partial}{\partial t}\left(\rho\overline{u_i^{'}u_j^{'}}\right)+\frac{\partial}{\partial x_k}\left(\rho u_k\overline{u_i^{'}u_j^{'}}\right)=\frac{\partial}{\partial x_k}\left(\frac{\mu_t}{\sigma_k}\frac{\partial\overline{u_i^{'}u_j^{'}}}{\partial x_k}+\mu\frac{\partial\overline{u_i^{'}u_j^{'}}}{\partial x_k}\right)-\rho\left(\overline{u_i^{'}u_j^{'}}\frac{\partial u_j}{\partial x_k}+\overline{u_j^{'}u_k^{'}}\frac{\partial u_j}{\partial x_k}\right)$$
$$-C_1\rho\frac{\varepsilon}{k}\left(\overline{u_i^{'}u_j^{'}}-\frac{2}{3}k\delta_{ij}\right)-C_2\left[\rho\left(\overline{u_i^{'}u_k^{'}}\frac{\partial u_j}{\partial x_k}+\overline{u_j^{'}u_k^{'}}\frac{\partial u_i}{\partial x_k}\right)-\frac{1}{3}P_{kk}\delta_{ij}\right]-\frac{2}{3}\rho\varepsilon\delta_{ij} \quad (19)$$

2. Gas Turbulent Kinetic Energy Equation and Turbulent Dissipation Rate Equation

By analogy single flow theory and Boussinesq vortex assumption, the relationship of gas Reynolds stress and averaged velocity gradient was shown as below.

$$g_0=\left[1-\left(\alpha_s/\alpha_{s,\max}\right)^{1/3}\right]^{-1} \quad (20)$$

Where p_t is addition pressure which is caused by pulsed velocity.

$$P_t = \frac{2}{3}\alpha_g \rho_g k \tag{21}$$

k is turbulent kinetic energy.

$$k = \frac{\overline{u_i^{'} u_j^{'}}}{2} = \frac{1}{2}\left(\overline{u_{gi}^{'2}} + \overline{u_{gj}^{'2}} + \overline{u_{gk}^{'2}}\right) \tag{22}$$

μ_{gt} is turbulent viscosity, which depends on flowage.

Then, turbulent dissipation rate ε is introduced.

$$\varepsilon = \frac{\mu_{gt}}{\rho_g}\overline{\left(\frac{\partial u_i^{'}}{\partial x_k}\right)\left(\frac{\partial u_i^{'}}{\partial x_k}\right)} \tag{23}$$

The transport expression of k and ε can be given when the addition drag source caused by adding the solid phase. Therefore, the gas turbulent kinetic energy and turbulent dissipation rate in the gas solid flow can be given.

Gas phase turbulent kinetic energy equation:

$$\frac{\partial\left(\alpha_g \rho_g k\right)}{\partial t} + \frac{\partial\left(\alpha_g \rho_g u_{gj} k\right)}{\partial x_j} = \frac{\partial}{\partial x_j}\left(\frac{\mu_e}{\sigma_k}\frac{\partial k}{\partial x_j}\right) + G_{kg} + G_{sg} - \alpha_g \rho_g \varepsilon \tag{24}$$

Gas phase turbulent dissipation rate equation:

$$\frac{\partial\left(\alpha_g \rho_g \varepsilon\right)}{\partial t} + \frac{\partial\left(\alpha_g \rho_g \varepsilon u_{gj}\right)}{\partial x_j} = \frac{\partial}{\partial x_j}\left(\frac{\mu_e}{\sigma_\varepsilon}\frac{\partial \varepsilon}{\partial x_j}\right) + \frac{\varepsilon}{k}\left[C_{1\varepsilon}\left(G_{kg} + G_{sg}\right) - C_{2\varepsilon}\alpha_g \rho_g \varepsilon\right] \tag{25}$$

G_{kg} is the generation of gas turbulent kinetic energy.

$$G_{kg} = \mu_{gt}\frac{\partial u_{gj}}{\partial x_i}\left(\frac{\partial u_{gj}}{\partial x_i} + \frac{\partial u_{gj}}{\partial x_j}\right) - \mu_{gt}\delta_{ij}\frac{\partial u_{gi}}{\partial x_i}\frac{\partial u_{gk}}{\partial x_k} - \frac{2}{3}\mu_e\left(\frac{\partial u_{gk}}{\partial x_k}\right)^2 \tag{26}$$

G_{sg} is additional source caused by granule adding to gas phase turbulent kinetic energy.

$$G_{sg} = 2\beta\left(k_s - k\right) \tag{27}$$

Where $C_{1\varepsilon}$=1.44，$C_{2\varepsilon}$=1.92，σ_k=0.82，σ_ε=1.0。

3. Solid turbulent kinetic energy equation and turbulent dissipation rate equation

By using the same processing method, Solid turbulent kinetic energy equation can be given as following.

$$\frac{\partial\left(\alpha_s \rho_s k_s\right)}{\partial_t} + \frac{\partial\left(\alpha_s \rho_s u_{sj} k_s\right)}{\partial x_j} = \frac{\partial}{\partial x_j}\left(\frac{\mu_p}{\sigma_k}\frac{\partial k_s}{\partial x_j}\right) + G_{ks} + G_{gs} - \alpha_s \rho_s \varepsilon_s \tag{28}$$

Solid Turbulent Dissipation Rate Equation

$$\frac{\partial(\alpha_s\rho_s\varepsilon)}{\partial t}+\frac{\partial(\alpha_s\rho_s\varepsilon u_{si})}{\partial x_i}=\frac{\partial}{\partial x_j}\left(\frac{\mu_p}{\sigma_\varepsilon}\frac{\partial\varepsilon}{\partial x_j}\right)+\frac{\varepsilon_s}{k_s}\left[C_1\left(G_{ks}+G_{gs}\right)-C_2\alpha_s\rho_s\varepsilon_s\right] \tag{29}$$

G_{ks} is the generation of solid turbulent kinetic energy.

$$G_{ks}=\mu_{st}\frac{\partial u_{sj}}{\partial x_i}\left(\frac{\partial u_{sj}}{\partial x_i}+\frac{\partial u_{sj}}{\partial x_j}\right)-\mu_{st}\delta_{ij}\frac{\partial u_{sj}}{\partial x_i}\frac{\partial u_{sk}}{\partial x_k}-\frac{2}{3}\mu_p\left(\frac{\partial u_{sk}}{\partial x_k}\right)^2 \tag{30}$$

G_{gs} is additional source caused by granule adding to gas phase.

$$G_{gs}=2\beta\left(ck-k_s\right) \tag{31}$$

Thereinto, $c=1/\left(1+10\alpha_s/\alpha_{s,\max}\cdot\tau/T_L\right)$
Lagrangian time scale of gas turbulent can be written as below.

$$T_L=0165k/\varepsilon$$

Particle relaxation time, $\tau=\alpha_s\rho_s/\beta$
When the mathematical model is built up, the key step of the simulation is how to identify turbulent viscosity μ_t. In this paper, by comparing to the pure flow, gas and granule phase turbulent viscosity μ_{gt}, μ_{st} can be achieved as following equations respectively.

$$\mu_{gt}=C_\mu\alpha_g\rho_g\frac{k^2}{\varepsilon} \tag{32}$$

$$\mu_{st}=C_\mu\alpha_p\rho_p\frac{k_s^2}{\varepsilon_s} \tag{33}$$

The expression of gas effective viscosity coefficient is given as below.

$$\mu_e=\alpha_g\mu_g+\mu_{gt} \tag{34}$$

The granule effective viscosity coefficient is the following equation.

$$\mu_p=\mu_s+\mu_{st} \tag{35}$$

The granule phase shear viscosity can be gained by the next equation.

$$\mu_s=\frac{4}{5}\alpha_s^2\rho_s g_0 d_s(1+e)\sqrt{\frac{\Theta}{\pi}}+\frac{\frac{5\sqrt{\pi}}{48}\rho_s d_s\sqrt{\Theta}}{(1+e)g_0}\left(1+\frac{4}{5}\alpha_s g_0(1+e)\right)^2 \tag{36}$$

Where g_0 stands for granule radial distribution function, which can reflect the effect of solid concentration

$$g_0 = \left[1 - \left(\alpha_s / \alpha_{s,\max}\right)^{1/3}\right]^{-1} \tag{37}$$

The expression of granule phase pressure is given as below.

$$p_s = \alpha_s \rho_s \Theta\left[1 + 2(1+e)\alpha_s g_0\right] \tag{38}$$

The total viscosity of granule phase is the below equation.

$$\xi_s = \frac{4}{3}\alpha_s^2 \rho_s d_p g_0 (1+e)\sqrt{\frac{\Theta}{\pi}} \tag{39}$$

It must be noted that, in the equations above, the symbol of e stands for granule collision recovery coefficient. And it obeys the following rule.

$$\begin{cases} e = 0 \\ e = 1 \\ 0 < e < 1 \end{cases} \tag{40}$$

When e= 1, it means elastic collision, which is in case of no energy loss.
When e=0, it means complete inelastic collision.
When $0 < e < 1$, it means energy will diffuse in form of elastic collision.

4.2 Simulation conditions

4.2.1 Geometric model and grid

As we all know, in numerical simulation process, the grid structure has a greatly effect on the calculation precision. Mesh with bad structure may lead to the enlargement of relative error and stability degradation or even simulation procedure divergent.

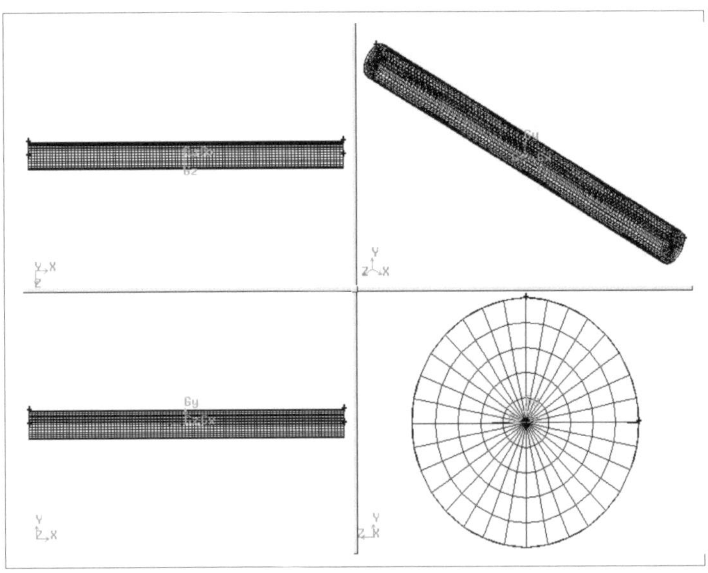

Fig. 5. Diagram of grid for geometric model.

Meanwhile, the grid formation technique has become a critical part in modern computational fluid dynamics. The mesh formation method can be divided two ways. One is algebraic method and the other is differential method. Thereinto, differential method can be used to produce smooth grid to suit complex flow domain. Of course, we can adjust the mesh degree of closeness by changing the control function. And if more accurate solution needed, mash must be thicker.

In this study, horizontal pipe section with 1 meter length, 0.08 meter diameter and range from 127.7 to 128.7m were chosen as research object. In this pipe section, fly ash was conveyed by compressed gas. Fig.5 gave the pipe geometric model with full grid.

4.2.2 Boundary conditions

1. Boundary condition for gas phase
   - Inlet boundary for gas

There are the assumptions that the gas axial velocity cross-section of the entrance with the fully developed turbulent flow of smooth pipe, radial velocity is zero, given the pressure of the entrance, turbulent kinetic energy expression is

$$k = \frac{3}{2}\left(u_g I_g\right)^2 \tag{41}$$

Turbulent dissipation rate can be expressed by

$$\varepsilon = C_\mu^{0.75}\frac{k^{1.5}}{l} \tag{42}$$

Where Ig is gas turbulent intensity, to the fully arisen turbulent flow, then,

$$I_g = 0.16\left(\mathrm{Re}_{gD_H}\right)^{1/8} \tag{43}$$

To the equation, D_H is hydraulic diameter. From the equation above, it can be concluded, the Reynolds number in the gas turbulent intensity equation is regard hydraulic diameter as characteristic length.

L is length dimension, to circle pipe,

$$l = 0.07L\,,$$

L is pipe diameter.

The gas velocity of inlet is set 9.9m/s.

- Outlet boundary for gas

The assumption that the fully developed conditions of the pipe flow, namely the normal derivative of the variables solved is zero, given the export pressure.

$$\frac{\partial \phi}{\partial x_i} = 0 \quad (\phi_g = u_{gi}, k, \varepsilon) \tag{44}$$

- Pipe wall surface

In the study, no-slip condition was adapted. Each parameter near the pipe wall was considered as zero. And wall function method was applied. So

$$\tau_w = \begin{cases} \dfrac{\overline{u_{gi}} k C_\mu^{0.25} \rho_g k^{0.5}}{\ln\left(EY^+\right)} & Y^+ \geq 11.63 \\ \dfrac{\overline{u_{gi}} \mu_g}{\delta_y} & Y^+ \leq 11.63 \end{cases} \tag{45}$$

Where $\overline{u_{gi}}$ stands for the gas velocity which is parallel to the pipe axis near the pipe wall. $Y^+ = \rho_g C_\mu^{0.25} k^{0.5} \delta_y / \mu$, δ_y is the distance between calculated nodes and pipe wall. E=9.793.

2. Boundary condition for solid phase
   - Inlet boundary for solid

Homogeneous inlet conditions are set and the volume fraction of particles is given. The expressions of turbulent kinetic energy and turbulent dissipation rate are set as following.

$$k_s = \frac{3}{2}\left(u_s I_s\right)^2, \varepsilon_s = C_\mu^{3/4} \frac{k_s^{3/2}}{l} \tag{46}$$

Where

$$I_s = 0.16\left(\mathrm{Re}_{sD_H}\right)^{1/8} \tag{47}$$

The solid velocity is set 4.3 m/s based on experiment data.

- Outlet boundary for solid

The assumption that the solid phase was the fully developed conditions of the pipe flow, namely the normal derivative of the variables solved is zero.

$$\frac{\partial \phi_s}{\partial x_i} = 0\left(\phi_s = u_{si}, k_s, \varepsilon_s\right) \tag{48}$$

- Pipe wall surface

To granule phase, the velocity doesn't agree with no-slip condition, thus the velocity value can't be equal to zero. According to particles collision near pipe wall research, the granule phase normal velocity can be given as following.

$$\left(\lambda_1 - \lambda_2\right)\left(u_{si}\right)_w + \lambda_1 h Kn \left(\frac{\partial u_{si}}{\partial x_i}\right)_w = 0 \tag{49}$$

where,

$$\lambda_1 = \left(1 - \frac{e^2}{2}\right)^{1/2}, \lambda_2 = \left[\frac{e(1-e)}{1+e}\right]^{1/2}$$

h means the distance between the center point of the first control bulk and the pipe wall. Kn is Knudsen number, which can be given as following.

$$Kn = \tau_s \left|u_{gi} - u_{si}\right|_w = \tau_s \left|u_{si}\right|_w \tag{50}$$

It must be noted that, in this paper, the turbulent kinetic energy and turbulent dissipation rate near the pipe wall were defined zero.

4.2.3 Basic parameter in process of simulation

Table 2 gave the basic parameter in process of numerical simulation

Solid phase	gas phase	pipe
$\rho_s=770kg\ m^{-3}$	$\rho_g=2.03kg\ m^{-3}$	D=0.08m
$d_s=60\mu m$	$\mu_g=1.85\times10^{-5}$	L=1m

Table 2. Basic parameter used for simulation.

4.3 Numerical simulation process

4.3.1 Equation discretization

In this paper, Finite Volume Method was utilized to discrete the governing equations above. The selected pipe section was divided into many non-concurrent domains which was called calculating grid. And then, each nodal point of stationary divided domain and its controlled volume were confirmed. In the process of discretization, the physical quantity of this controlled volume were defined and stored in the determined nodal point.

4.3.2 Numerical calculation method

In this study, we used SIMPLE method to carry out two phase flow simulation. And the gas solid two phase flow were coupled each other. First of all, on the basis of initial condition and boundary condition, pure gas phase governing equation can be solved. And then, we can resolve granule phase governing equations which are based on gas flow characteristics. The last step was to gain the gas and solid flow field respectively by combining with this two single flow and coupling effect between two phases.

4.3.3 Numerical calculation circuitry

The numerical calculation circuitry is shown as below.

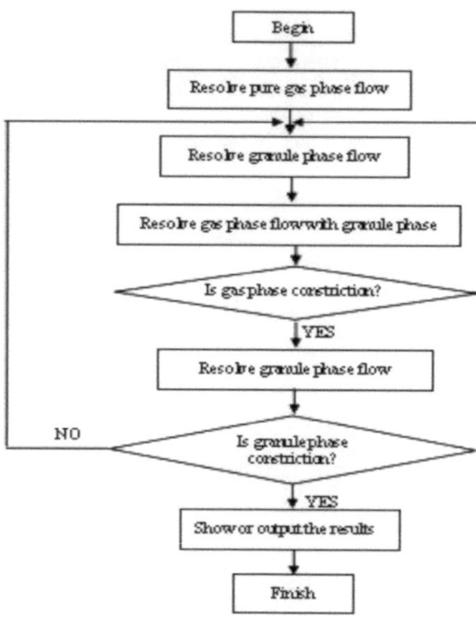

4.3.4 Relaxation factor

Because of the existence of inter phase coupled and nonlinear, the governing equations of gas solid two phase flow became more complex. So sometimes, low relaxation interation may be adopted to ensure the stable constriction during the simulation process.
The relaxation factors of this study can be given as the following table.

Pressure, p	Turbulent kinetic energy k	Turbulent dissipation rate, ε	Gas velocity, u_g	Solid velocity u_s	Granule volume ratio,α_s
0.5	0.4	0.4	0.3	0.3	0.2

Table 3. Relaxation factor.

4.4 Simulation result and analysis

On the basis of simulation analysis above, high concentration gas solid flow in horizontal pipe sufficient development was simulated. Flow information such as pressure, solid concentration, gas and granule velocity can be achieved.

4.4.1 Pressure distribution along the pipe

Fig.6 gives the static pressure distribution along the pipe. From this figure, it can be seen that the static pressure and differential pressure gradient decreases along the pipe. That is to say, the differential pressure reduces with the decreasing of static pressure. It is because, with the gas solid flow moving in pipeline, more static pressure transit to dynamic power to impel and accelerate particles. This conclusion agrees with experimental results well.

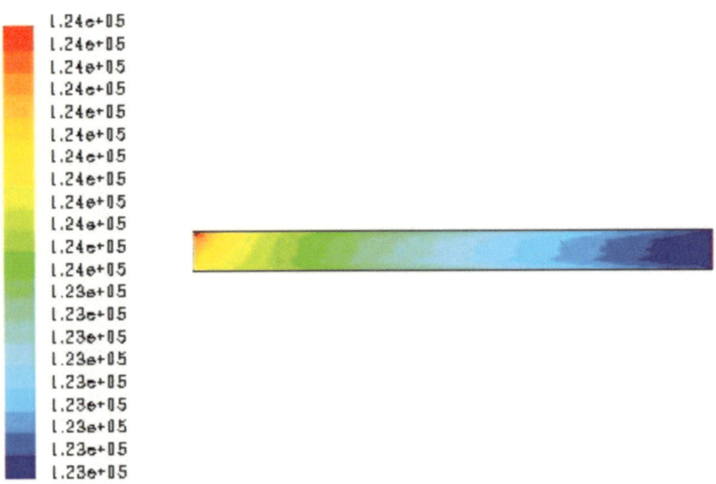

Fig. 6. Distribution diagram of static pressure.

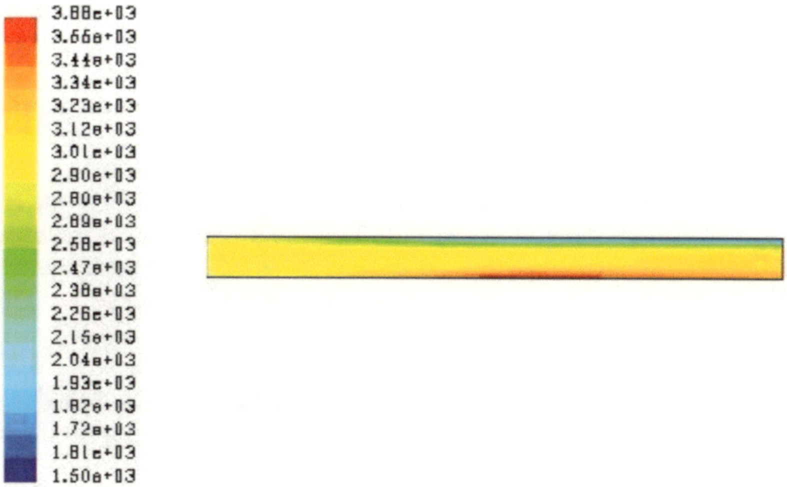

Fig. 7. Distribution diagram of dynamic pressure.

Fig.7 shows dynamic pressure distribution along the pipe. From the diagram, we can know that the dynamic pressure decreased gradually in the upper of the pipe, while at the bottom of pipe the dynamic pressure increased on the contrary. The reason for the phenomenon is the increasing of particle concentration at the bottom of pipe.

4.4.2 Solid concentration distribution along the pipe

Solid concentration can reflect the solid motion style directly in process of pneumatic conveying. But in the experiment research, it's hard to measure this parameter accurately. In this study, we use numerical simulation method to gain the solid concentration in pipeline, as shown in Fig.8.

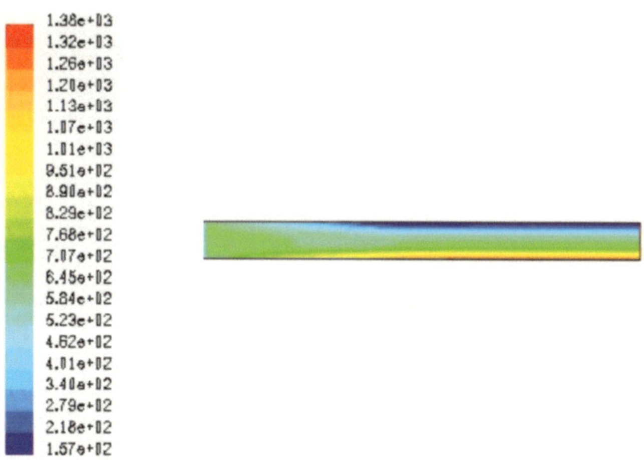

Fig. 8. Graph of concentration distribution.

Fig.9 shows that the particle is accelerated by gas phase along the axial direction, so the concentration becomes lower. But at the same time, the turbulent kinetic energy of two phase flow increases at the tube center, which lead to more pressure difference.
The particles near pipe center diffuse to upper or bottom of pipeline under high pressure gradient. Meanwhile, with the action of gravity force, the solid particles continue moving to the bottom of pipe, which result in the concentration increasing of pipe bottom.
As in all, particle concentration decreased in the upper of the pipe, while at the bottom of the pipe the particle concentration was growing. This illuminated that particles were not homogeneous suspension in conveying process, but the settlement of particles, so particle concentration at the bottom of the pipe was greater than that of the upper part.

4.4.3 Velocity distribution along the pipe

In the pneumatic conveying of horizontal pipe, the original pure gas flow style doesn't exist any more. The largest gas velocity value position will deviate from the pipe centre and rise to upper parts of the pipe. By contraries, the gas velocity reduces under the pipe centre.

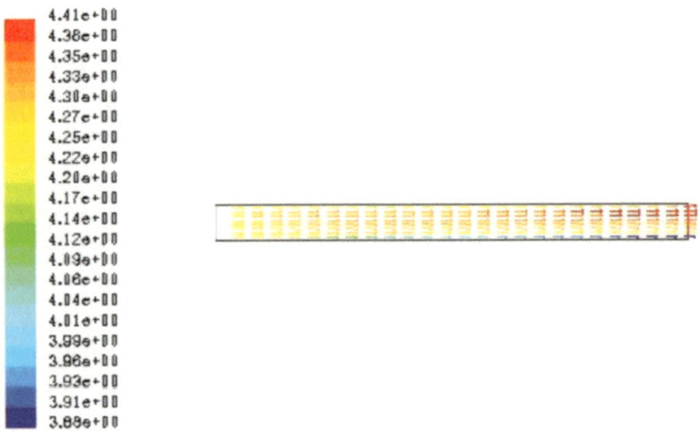

Fig. 9. Vector graph of gas velocity.

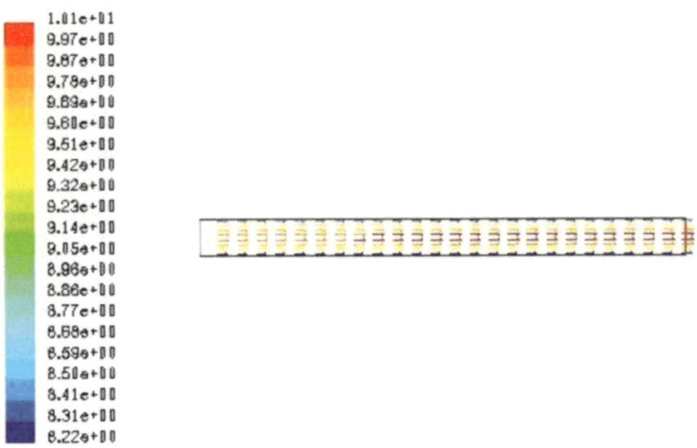

Fig. 10. Vector graph of particle velocity.

In all, the gas velocity distribution is more unstable, and the value is much higher near pipe center, while lower near the pipe boundary, which is chiefly because no slip of gas phase.
Fig.9 and 10 show gas and particle velocity vector along pipe respectively. As can be seen from the diagrams, gas and particle velocity increased gradually along pipe, as expected, near the pipeline wall velocity is less, and the velocity upper part is larger than the velocity of the bottom. The particle velocity at the inlet is 4.3 m/s, and which at the outlet is 4.6 m/s. The gas velocity of inlet is set as 9.9 m/s, while the velocity at the outlet is 10.3 m/s. then all this is approximately consistent

4.5 Comparison of experimental data and simulation result

4.5.1 Comparison of gas velocity

Fig.11 gives the contrast of experiment data and simulation result for gas velocity in the selected pipe section under a set conveying pressure. From the figure, the trend of the two results is similar. And its relative error is less.

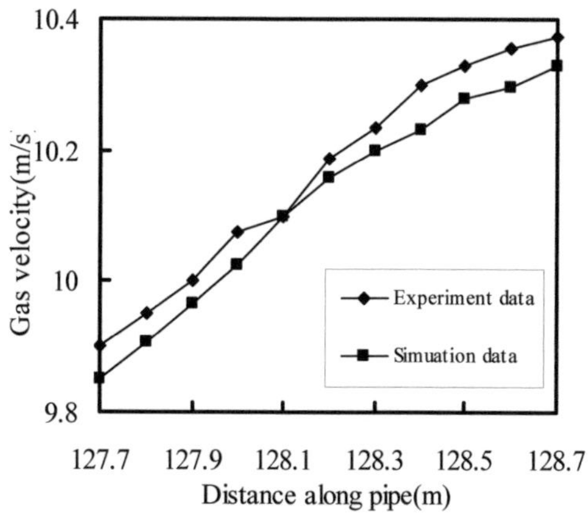

Fig. 11. Relationship of gas velocity between simulated and experimental value.

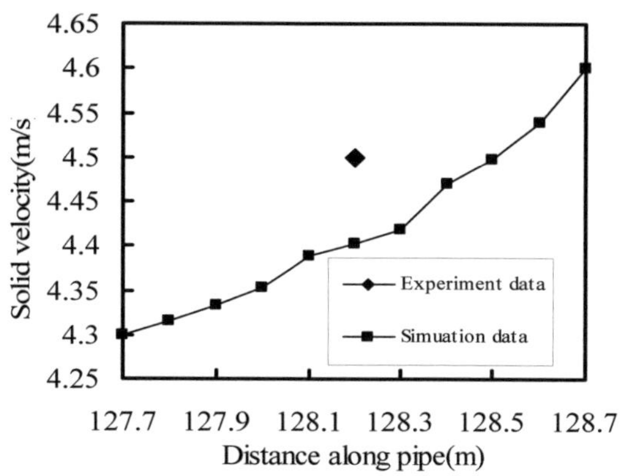

Fig. 12. Relationship of solid velocity between simulated and experimental value.

4.5.2 Comparison of solid velocity

Actually, the experimental solid velocity in selected pipe section concentrates a point velocity which stands for the average velocity in this segment.

Fig 12 gives the contrast of experiment data and simulation result for solid velocity in the selected pipe section under a stationary pressure. From the figure, we can conclude that the simulation data is approximately equal to the average value of experiment value. So, numerical simulation can be used to predict the gas solid flow parameter precisely.

4.5.3 Comparison of pressure drop

Similar to the solid velocity distribution, the experimental value of pressure drop is to be regarded as the average value along the pipe.

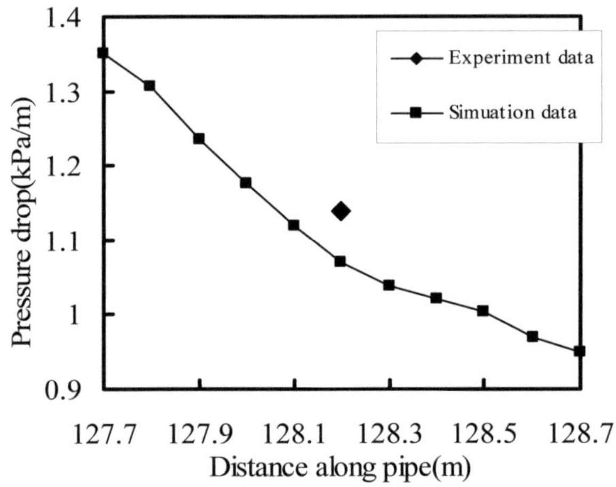

Fig. 13. Relationship of pressure drop between simulated and experimental value.

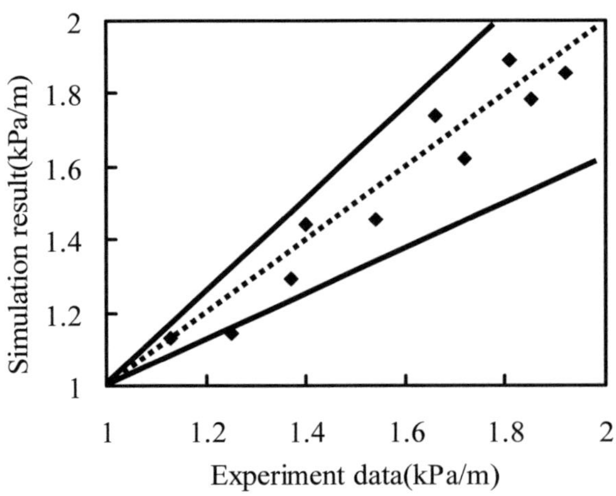

Fig. 14. Relationship between experiment data and simulation result.

Fig.13 gives the contrast case of experiment data and simulation result for pressure drop. From the figure, we can gain that the experiment data point lie in the simulation average value dot.

In this work, we also set another several set of boundary conditions to simulate corresponding experiment cases in the selected pipe section. Figure 14 shows the comparison of the experimental data and simulation results. From this figure, we can know, the relative error between the experiment and simulation range from -8.48% to 4.70%, which illustrate good agreement and accuracy.

5. Conclusions

In this paper, dense phase pneumatic conveying is carried out. The trend of flow characteristic along the pipe is given in different cases. And based the experimental results, the k-ε-kp-εp two-fluid model was established with the consideration of gas-solid turbulent flow and taking into account the issue of gas-solid two-way coupling. Numerical simulation of fly ash flow for dense-phase pneumatic conveying was carried out by using Fluent software. The numerical simulation and experimental results were compared. The simulated conclusions are given as below.

1. Along pipe axial direction, pressure and pressure gradient decreased, dynamic pressure increased gently. Meanwhile the dynamic pressure in the upper part of pipe decreased, while at the bottom of pipe dynamic pressure enlarged gradually. It can be seen that gas and particle velocity increase along the pipeline, the velocity in the upper pipe part was larger than that of the bottom of pipe. Particle concentration is different along pipe radial direction. The solid consistency is larger at the bottom of pipe.
2. The results of numerical simulation were compared with experimental results. The simulation results were validated by the experimental data, which indicate that the model and the corresponding algorithm have higher accuracy and better prediction. So it can reveal the basic characteristics of dense phase pneumatic conveying in horizontal pipe.

6. Acknowledgment

The authors gratefully acknowledgements the financial support from the National Natural Science Foundation of China (No. 50946032) and Shandong Provincial .Education Department of China (No. J10LD05)

7. References

Examples of fluid engineering and application of computer simulation. (Han zhan-zhong, 2005).

Modeling of the Gas-Solid Turbulent Flow in a Riser Reactor. (ZHENG Yu, WAN Xiao-tao, WEI Fei, etl., 2001).

Numerical study on the I nfluence of various physical parameters over the gas-solid two-phase flow in the 2D riser of a circulating fluidized bed.(Luben Cabezas-Gomez, Fernando Eduardo Milioli. 2003).

Numerical simulation of the gas-particle turbulent flow in riser reactor based on k-ε-k_p-ε_p-Θ two-fluid model. (Zheng Y, Wan X T, Qian Z, et al., 2001).

Velocity Analysis of Fly Ash Solid Particles Conveyed by Dense-phase Pneumatic Force. (YI Hua ,LIU Zong-ming ,DU Bin, et al., 2007).

Effects of an electrostatic field in pneumatic conveying of granular materials through inclined and vertical pipes. (EldinWee Chuan Lim, Yan Zhang, Chi-HwaWang, 2006).

Evaluation of models and correlations for pressure drop estimation in dense phase pneumatic conveying and an experimental analysis. (Luis Sancheza, Nestor A. Vasqueza, George E. Klinzinga, et al, 2005).

Dilute gas–solid two-phase flows in a curved 90° duct bend: CFD simulation with experimental validation(B. Kuan, W.Yang, M.P. Schwarz., 2007).

Analytical prediction of pressure loss through a sudden-expansion in two-phase pneumatic conveying lines. (Mehmet Yasar Gundogdu, Ahmet Ihsan Kutlar, Hasan Duz, 2009)

Numerical simulation on dense phase pneumatic conveying of pulverized coal in horizontal pipe at high pressure. (Wenhao Pu , Changsui Zhao , Yuanquan Xiong , et al., 2010).

18

A Three-Dimensional Numerical Simulation of the Free Surface Flow Around a Ship Hull

J. B. V. Wanderley, M. Vitola, S. H. Sphaier and C. Levi
LabOceano - COPPE/UFRJ
Brazil

1. Introduction

Offshore oil and gas production is advancing fast towards water depth deeper and deeper. In the last couple of years, offshore oil production depth world records have been successively superseded. Oil industry is about to achieve production in fields approaching 2000m water depth while keeping on exploring new oil reservoirs in ocean depths close to 3000m. As water depth increases, the distance from oil field to mainland depots increases at similar rates and more hostile the ocean environment becomes. In such operational conditions the use of VLCC ship tanker, as a production unit, has been proved to be technically and economically appealing.

Good hydrodynamic characteristics in severe sea environments, adequate storage capability and possibly the low prices of used tanker hulls in the ship market are the main reasons to justify the increasing popularity of tanker hull as production units (Floating Storage and Offloading - FSO and Floating Production Storage and Offloading - FPSO) among offshore oil producer companies. The complete assessment of the dynamic behavior of moored tankers depends very much on the accuracy of the hydrodynamic loading and response evaluation that need to be performed. Potential and viscous effects on the FSO/FPSO come into play equally important role on the acting flow around the ship hull. Furthermore, translational and rotational motions of the hull have to be incorporated all together into the analysis to produce a realistic picture of the physical problem.

Recently, Computational Fluid Dynamics (CFD) has been experiencing rapid advances due to both computer technology progress and efficient algorithms that have been developed to solve the Navier-Stokes (N-S) equations used in the flow analysis around ship hulls. The present work is a contribution to the numerical solution of the viscous flow around ship-like bodies.

In the present work, the slightly compressible Navier-Stokes equations (Wanderley et al. [1]) are solved through the conservative upwind TVD scheme of Roe [2] and Sweby [3]. This finite difference method is second order accurate in space and time. The physical domain is discretized using a Cartesian mesh and the no-slip boundary condition on the body surface is imposed through the Immersed Boundary Method (IBM), Marcelo et al. [4]. The Cartesian mesh is not conformed to the body contour and the IBM is used to inform the fluid flow the presence of a body through a force field added to the momentum equations. The code was implemented using the message passing interface (MPI) and can be run in a cluster with an arbitrary number of computers. Numerical results were obtained for the flows around a sphere without free surface and around a series-60 ship hull in order to verify the implemented code. The agreement between the numerical results and the experimental and numerical data from the literature indicates that the implemented code is able to reproduce correctly the drag coefficient, pressure field, velocity field, and the free-surface elevation around a ship hull.

2. Mathematical formulation

The slightly compressible Navier-Stokes equations written in 3-D Cartesian coordinates are given below in the conservative form with the volume fraction equation included.

$$Q_t + (E_e - E_v)_x + (F_e - F_v)_y + (G_e - G_v)_z = H \tag{1}$$

$$\rho = \rho_w c + \rho_{air}(1-c) \tag{2}$$

where

$$Q = \begin{Bmatrix} p \\ \rho u \\ \rho v \\ \rho w \\ c \end{Bmatrix}, \quad H = \begin{Bmatrix} 0 \\ \rho\left(\frac{M_\infty}{F_n}\right)^2 h_x \\ \rho\left(\frac{M_\infty}{F_n}\right)^2 h_y \\ 0 \\ 0 \end{Bmatrix} \tag{3}$$

$$E_e = \begin{Bmatrix} pu \\ \rho u^2 + p \\ \rho vu \\ \rho wu \\ cu \end{Bmatrix} \quad G_e = \begin{Bmatrix} pw \\ \rho uw \\ \rho vw \\ \rho w^2 + p \\ cw \end{Bmatrix} \quad F_e = \begin{Bmatrix} pv \\ \rho uv \\ \rho v^2 + p \\ \rho wv \\ cv \end{Bmatrix} \tag{4}$$

$$E_v = \frac{M_\infty}{R_L}\begin{Bmatrix} 0 \\ u_x \\ v_x \\ w_x \\ 0 \end{Bmatrix} \quad G_v = \frac{M_\infty}{R_L}\begin{Bmatrix} 0 \\ u_z \\ v_z \\ w_z \\ 0 \end{Bmatrix} \quad F_v = \frac{M_\infty}{R_L}\begin{Bmatrix} 0 \\ u_y \\ v_y \\ w_y \\ 0 \end{Bmatrix} \tag{5}$$

Equation (1) is solved numerically together with the initial conditions (6), boundary conditions on the body surface (7), and free-stream boundary conditions (8), where M_∞=0.2 for incompressible flows, and β=1 (water) and β=0 (air).

Initial conditions:

$$\begin{cases} p = 1 \\ u = M_\infty \\ v = 0 \\ w = 0 \\ c = \beta \end{cases} \quad (6)$$

Boundary conditions on the body surface:

$$\begin{cases} \partial p / \partial n = 0 \\ u = 0 \\ v = 0 \\ w = 0 \\ \partial c / \partial n = 0 \end{cases} \quad (7)$$

Free stream boundary conditions:

$$\begin{cases} p = 1 \\ u = M_\infty \\ v = 0 \\ w = 0 \\ c = \beta \end{cases} \quad (8)$$

3. Numerical formulation

Equation (9) shows the conservative scheme used to solve the governing equations. The second order Lax-Wendroff method is used for the time integration, and the spatial derivatives are approximated using second order finite differences.

$$\begin{aligned} Q_{i,j}^{n+1} = Q_{i,j}^{n} - \Delta t \big[& \delta_\xi E_e + \delta_\eta F_e + \delta_\varsigma G_e - \\ & \nabla_\xi E_v - \nabla_\eta F_v - \nabla_\varsigma G_v - \\ & \nabla_\xi E_{RS} - \nabla_\eta F_{RS} - \nabla_\varsigma G_{RS} - H \big]^n \end{aligned} \quad (9)$$

The Roe - Sweby fluxes are responsible for the upwinding and TVD of the scheme, see Eq. (10). For more details about the application of the upwind TVD scheme of Roe -Sweby to the slightly compressible Navier-Stokes equations, refer to Wanderley et al. (2008).

$$\left(E_{RS}\right)_{i+1/2,j} = \frac{1}{2} \tilde{A}_{i+1/2,j} \left(Q_{i+1,j}^{n} - Q_{i,j}^{n} \right) \quad (10)$$

where

$$\tilde{A} = T \tilde{\Lambda} T^{-1} \quad (11)$$

In Eq. (11), the matrix $\tilde{\Lambda}$ is a diagonal matrix with terms shown in Eq. (12) and the matrix T is defined in Eq. (13).

$$\tilde{\lambda}_k = |\lambda_k| + \psi_k \left[\frac{\Delta t}{\Delta x} |\lambda_k|^2 - |\lambda_k| \right] \tag{12}$$

$$T = \left[\vec{x}_1, \vec{x}_2, \vec{x}_3, \ldots, \vec{x}_k \right] \tag{13}$$

where $(\lambda_k, \vec{x}_k)$ are the eigenvectors and eigenvalues of the Jacobian matrix A defined in Eq. (14).

$$A = \frac{\partial E_e}{\partial Q} \tag{14}$$

The van Leer [5] flux limiter defined in Eq. (15) is a function of the coefficient r defined in Eq. (16) in the wave domain.

$$\psi_k = \begin{cases} 0 & r_k \le 0 \\ \dfrac{2r_k}{1+r_k} & r_k > 0 \end{cases} \tag{15}$$

$$r_k = \begin{cases} \dfrac{w^k_{i+2,j} - w^k_{i+1,j}}{w^k_{i+1,j} - w^k_{i,j}} & \lambda_k \le 0 \\ \dfrac{w^k_{i,j} - w^k_{i-1,j}}{w^k_{i+1,j} - w^k_{i,j}} & \lambda_k > 0 \end{cases} \tag{16}$$

where

$$\vec{w} = T^{-1} \vec{Q} \tag{17}$$

The no-slip boundary condition on the body surface is imposed using the Immersed Boundary Method (IBM), Marcelo et al. [4]. In this method, the flow field is informed of the body presence through a force field added to the momentum equations. These forces are computed such that the no-slip condition on the body surface is satisfied. The forces are applied only on the grid points close to the body surface through the reconstruction of the flow properties by linear interpolation. Fig. 1 illustrates the geometry of interpolation.

The properties of the flow field at the pyramid base (grid points 1, 2, and 3) are known because those are computed by the solver. The property at the pyramid pick (point 0 at the body surface) is imposed such that the no-slip condition on the body surface is satisfied. For example, the force added to the x-momentum equation (at point R) is computed as shown in Eq. (18). In this equation, u_R is the reconstructed velocity and u is the velocity obtained by the solver in the iterative process.

$$F_x = \rho \frac{u_R - u}{\Delta t} \tag{18}$$

where

$$u_R = ax_R + by_R + cz_R + d \tag{19}$$

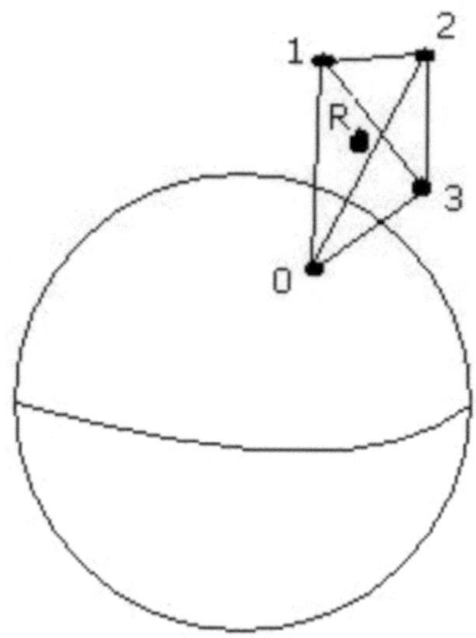

Fig. 1. Reconstruction geometry.

The coefficients *a*, *b*, *c* and *d* in Eq. (19) are obtained by the solution of the system of linear equations shown in Eq. (20).

$$\begin{aligned} ax_1 + by_1 + cz_1 + d &= u_1 \\ ax_2 + by_2 + cz_2 + d &= u_2 \\ ax_3 + by_3 + cz_3 + d &= u_3 \\ ax_0 + by_0 + cz_0 + d &= u_0 \end{aligned} \tag{20}$$

where u_0=0 is the no-slip condition on the body surface.

4. Grid generation

A Cartesian computational mesh generator is used to discretize the three-dimensional physical domain. The grid is refined in the region close to the body to allow the capturing of viscous effects close to the body surface. An exponential stretching is used to concentrate grid points close to the body surface and to coarsening the computational mesh in regions away from the body, where the variation of the flow properties is small. The Cartesian computational mesh does not fit the body surface and the no-slip boundary condition is imposed using the Immersed Boundary Method (IBM). Fig. 2 shows a computational mesh plane at the level of the undisturbed free surface. The grid is divided in slices and each slice is superimposed to the neighbors such that the boundary of one side corresponds to interior points of the other. Each slice is solved by different nodes in the computer cluster using the message passing interface (MPI). Between successive iterations, the slices communicate to the neighbors for boundary condition update.

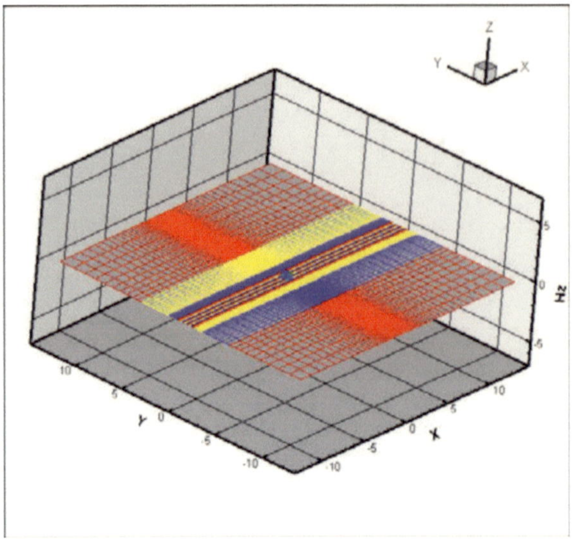

Fig. 2. Computational mesh.

5. Flow field around a sphere without free surface

The results obtained for the flow field around a sphere without free surface are presented below.

Figure 3 presents the pressure field and stream lines around a sphere. The figure shows two vortices attached to the trailing edge of the body, the stagnation point (in red) at the leading edge, and two regions of low pressure (in blue) at the top and bottom of the sphere. This result agrees with what is observed experimentally. For Reynolds number equal to 200, two vortices attached to the trailing edge of the sphere are observed experimentally.

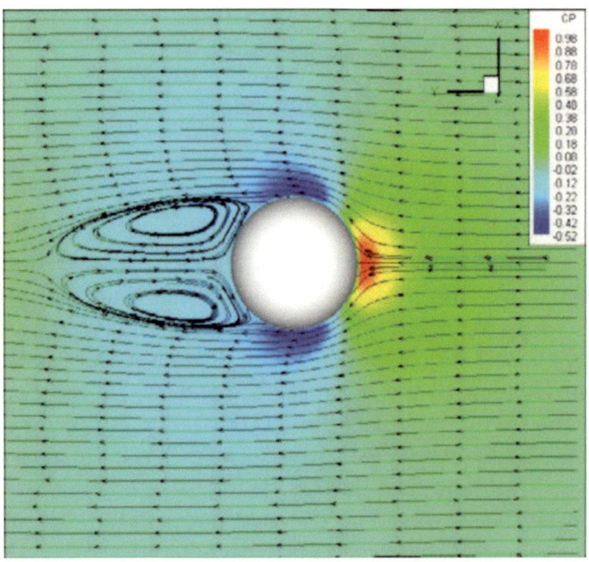

Fig. 3. Pressure field and stream lines around a sphere for *Re*=200.

Figure 4 presents the temporal series of the total drag (in black), frictional drag (in blue), and pressure drag (in red) coefficients for the sphere for Reynolds number equal to 200. Table 1 presents a comparison between the total drag coefficient obtained in the present work and other experimental and numerical data obtained from the literature. The agreement among the three results is remarkable.

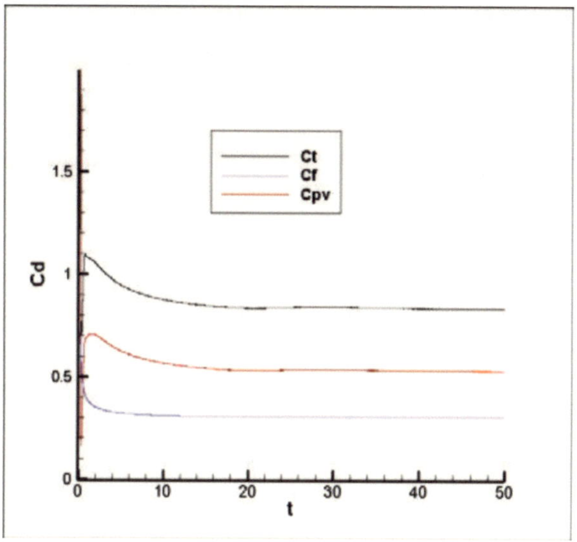

Fig. 4. Frictional, pressure, and total drag coefficients for *Re*=200.

Reference	*Re*	*Ct*	Comment
Schlichting [10]	100 200	1.100 0.800	Experimental
Campregher [2]	100 200	1.178 0.815	Numerical
Present study	100 200	1.200 0.832	Numerical

Table 1. Comparison of drag coefficient comparison.

6. Flow field around a series-60 hull

Additional verification of the numerical code is presented for the Series-60 hull for a low Reynolds number of 1.0×10^3. Figures 5, 6, and 7 show a plane of the computational grid generated around the hull at the level of the undisturbed free surface. The grid has 240x160x160 points and the smallest element is a cube with dimension of 0.0075Lpp. The grid has 11Lpp in the y direction, and 7.2 Lpp in the *x* and *z* directions.

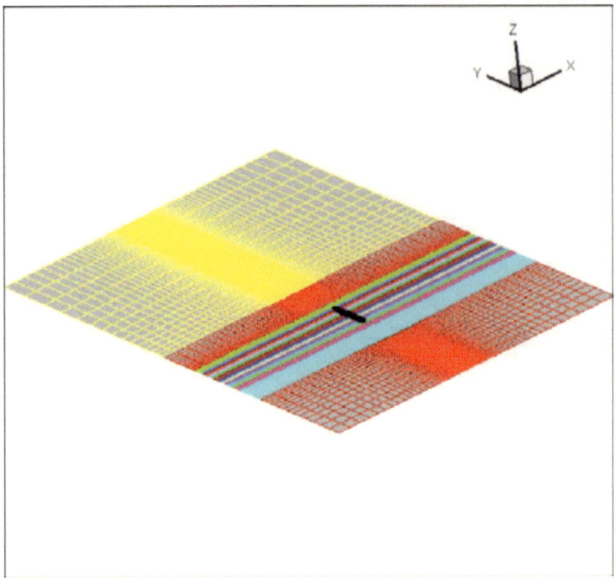

Fig. 5. Grid generated around the Series-60 hull.

A top view and a bottom view of the hull can be seen in Fig. 6 and Fig. 7, respectively. Close to the body, the grid is uniform and sufficiently refined to capture the viscous effects close to the hull surface. An exponential stretching is used to increase the size of the grid elements away from the body, where property gradients are small.

Fig. 6. Grid generated around the Series-60 hull (top view).

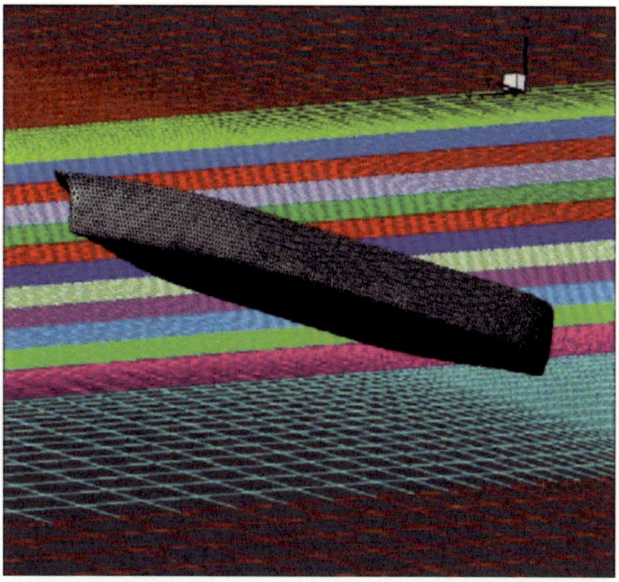

Fig. 7. Grid generated around the Series-60 hull (bottom view).

Figure 8 illustrates the pressure contour around the Series-60 hull at the same plane of the undisturbed free-surface. In this simulation, the free-surface is not allowed to deform. A stagnation point (in red) is observed at the bow of the hull and a low pressure region (in blue) is observed at the side walls of the body.

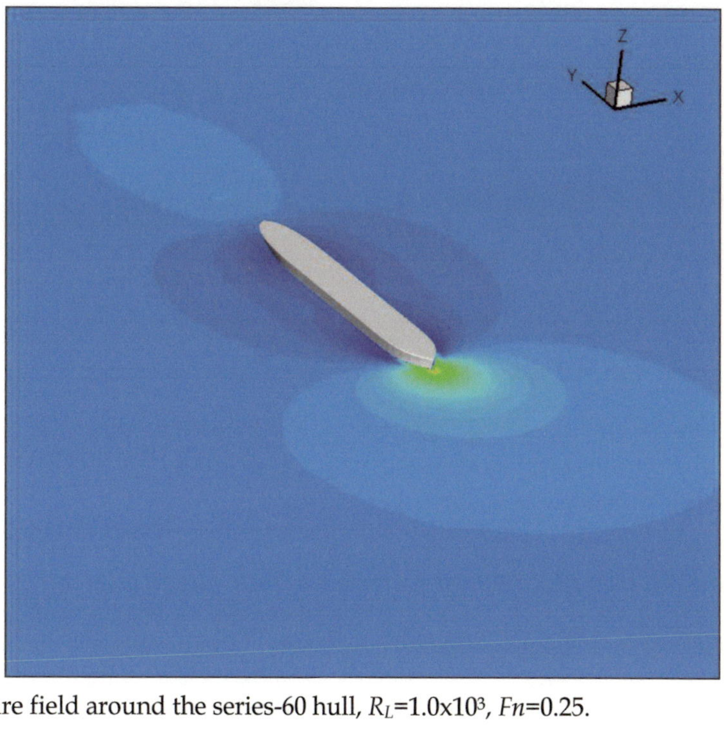

Fig. 8. Pressure field around the series-60 hull, R_L=1.0x10^3, Fn=0.25.

Figure 9 illustrates the pressure contour and the velocity field around the hull. The velocity profile inside the boundary layer and at the wake can be observed at the body surface and behind the hull, respectively.

Fig. 9. Pressure and velocity fields around the Series-60 hull, R_L=1.0x10^3, *Fn*=0.25.

Figure 10 shows the free surface elevation after allowing the free surface to deform and after the steady state is obtained. The diverging wave formation can be observed at the port and starboard of the ship hull. Figure 11 shows the velocity field around the hull and at the level of the free surface. The velocity profile inside the boundary layer along the side walls of the hull and at the wake of the body can be observed in yellow arrows.

Fig. 10. Free-surface elevation around the Series-60 hull, R_L=1.0x10^3, Fn=0.25.

Fig. 11. Free-surface elevation around the Series-60 hull, R_L=1.0x10^3, Fn=0.25 and velocity field.

Figure 12 presents the pressure coefficient contour around the ship hull at the level of the free surface. The low pressure regions can be seen in blue at the wave crests of the divergence wave and the high pressure regions can be seen in red at the bow of the ship and at the wave trough.

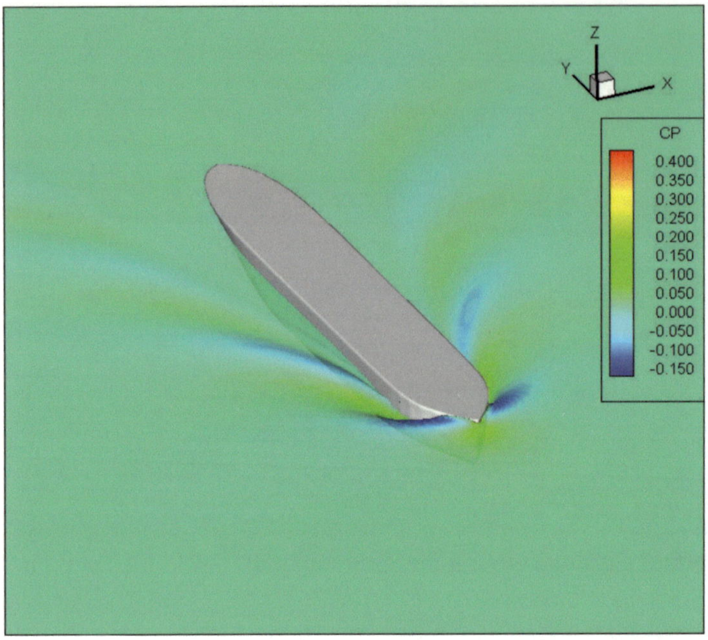

Fig. 12. Free-surface elevation around the Series-60 hull, R_L=1.0x10^3, Fn=0.25 and pressure field.

Figure 13 shows the total (in red), frictional (in black), and pressure (in blue) drag coefficients on the ship hull. After time=4, the steady state is obtained and the drag coefficients are constant.

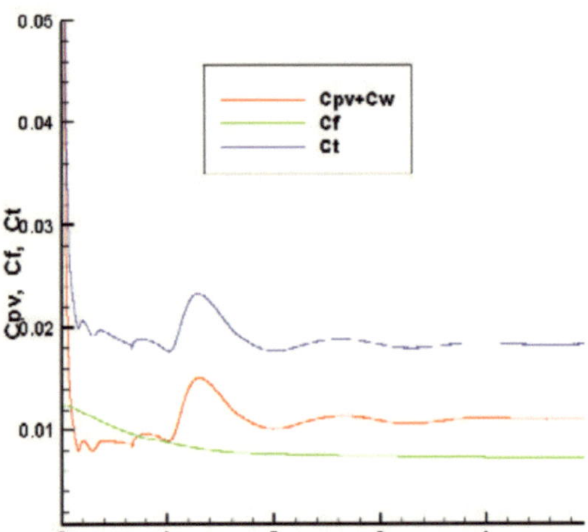

Fig. 13. Drag coefficient on the Series-60 hull, R_L=1.0x10^3, Fn=0.25.

7. Conclusions

An upwind and TVD numerical scheme was implemented to solve the unsteady slightly compressible Navier-Stokes equations for the free-surface flow around ship hulls. The physical domain is discretized in a Cartesian grid and the boundary condition on the body surface is implemented using the Immersed Boundary Method (IBM).

The implemented code is parallelized using MPI to be run in an arbitrary number of computers of a cluster. The numerical code was verified for the flow around a sphere, and a Series-60 hull.

The results obtained for the sphere were compared to numerical and experimental data from literature showing the good quality of the numerical results. The numerical results obtained for the ship hull were not compared to other numerical and experimental data because of the difficulty to find those data for lower Reynolds number. However, the numerical results agree qualitatively well to experiments.

Next phase of development will include the implementation of the k-ε turbulence model and validation of the numerical code for higher Reynolds numbers and configurations of practical interest, such as, resistance to motion, moonpool - free decay and forced motion, wave run-up and air gap, and wake and shadow flows.

8. Acknowledgments

This research was sponsored by the Brazilian Innovation Agency - FINEP under Grant 0106067200.

9. References

[1] Alessandrini, B., and Delhommeau, G., 1994, "Simulation of Three-Dimensional Unsteady Viscous Free Surface Flow around a Ship Model", International Journal for Numerical Methods in Fluids, Vol. 19, pp.321-342.

[2] Campregher, R., Mansur, S. S., and Silveira-Neto, A., 2005, "Numerical Simulation of the Flow Around a Sphere Using the Immersed Boundary Method for Low Reynolds Number", Proceedings of the Sixth International ERCOFTAC Workshop on Direct and Large-Eddy Simulation, held at the University of Poitiers, September, 12-14.

[3] Ciortan, C., Wanderley, J., and Guedes, C., 2007, "Turbulent Free-surface Flow around a Wigley Hull Using the Slightly Compressible Formulation", Ocean Engineering, V. 34, pp. 1383-1392.

[4] Ciortan, C., Guedes, C., and Wanderley, J., 2007, "Assessment of Free Surface Treatment Techniques and Turbulence Models Influence Using the Slightly Compressible Flow Simulation", Proceedings of the 26th International Conference on Offshore Mechanics and Arctic Engineering, June 10-15, San Diego, California, USA.

[5] Hino, T., 1987, "Numerical Simulation of a Viscous Flow with a Free Surface around a Ship Model", Journal of the Society of Naval Architects of Japan, Vol. 161.

[6] Ratcliffe, T., 1998, "Validation of the Free Surface Reynolds-Averaged navier-Stokes and Potential Flow Codes", Proceedings of the 22nd ONR Symposium on Naval Hydrodynamics.

[7] Rider, W.J., and Kothe, D. B., 1997, "Reconstructing Volume Tracking", Journal of Computational Physics, Vol. 141, 112-152.

[8] Roe, P. L., 1984, "Generalized Formulation of TVD Lax-Wendroff Scheme, ICASE Report 84-53.

[9] Rudman, M., 1997, "Volume-Tracking Methods for Interfacial Flow Calculations", International Journal for Numerical methods in Fluids, Vol. 24, 671-691.

[10] Schlichting, H., 1979, "Boundary Layer Theory". McGraw-Hill, New York.

[11] Sweby, P. K., 1984, "High Resolution Scheme Using Flux Limiter for Hyperbolic Conservation Laws, SIAM J. Num. Anal., vol. 21, pp. 995-1011.

[12] van Leer, B., 1979, "Towards the Ultimate Conservative Difference Scheme, V: A Second-Order Sequel to Godunov's Method, J. Comput. Phys., vol. 32, pp. 101-136.

[13] Vitola, M. A., Schettini, E. B. C., and Silvestrini, J. H., 2006, "Three Dimensional Wake Structure of Free Planar Shear Flow Around Horizontal Cylinder". In: Eric Lamballais, Rainer Friedrich, Bernard J. Geurts and Olivier Métais. (Org.). Direct and Large-Eddy Simulation VI. : Springer Netherlands, 2006, p. 669-676.

[14] Wanderley, J. B. V., and Levi, C., 2006, "Free Surface Viscous Flow around a Ship Model", Proceedings of the 25th International Conference on Offshore Mechanics and Arctic Engineering, June 4-9, Hamburg, Germany.

[15] Wanderley, J. B. V., Souza, G. H. B., Sphaier, S. H., and Levi, C. A., 2008, "Vortex-Induced Vibration of an Elastically Mounted Circular Cylinder using an Upwind TVD Two-Dimensional Numerical Scheme", Ocean Engineering, V. 35, pp. 1533-1544.

19

Hydrodynamic Analysis of Electrochemical Cells

Cesar Augusto Real-Ramirez and Jesus Isidro Gonzalez-Trejo
Universidad Autonoma Metropolitana - Azcapotzalco
Mexico

1. Introduction

The systems in which an electrode immersed in a solution causes a chemical reaction have been studied for over a hundred years. It has long been known that the behavior of these systems is determined by two main factors: the rate with which the substance comes into contact with the electrode and the rate of the electrochemical reactions at the electrode.
During the first four decades of the twentieth century, many works were devoted to this subject; however, most of them were experimental works. Those works found that the limiting current increases with increasing the rate of stirring (Bircumshaw & Riddiford, 1952). Usually, the results were expressed by means of a power relation of the form:

$$j_{\mathrm{lim}} \propto \omega^{a} \tag{1}$$

where j_{lim} is the limiting current, ω is the rotation speed and a is the power such that $0 < a \leq 1$.
The earliest theoretical studies of electrochemical cells with a rotating disk were reported by Nernst (Nernst, 1904; Nernst & Merriam, 1905). In that works, Nernst introduced the concept of diffusion layer. According to Nernst, the thickness of the diffusion layer is extremely small and the movement of fluid within it may be neglected.
In 1932, Eucken (Eucken, 1932) presented another theoretical study of electrochemical cells. The aim of that work was to provide an exact hydrodynamics theory of the diffusion towards a plane electrode submerged in a solution moving with a relatively high velocity.
Following a similar approach to that employed by Eucken, Levich (Levich, 1942) presented a theory describing accurately the hydrodynamics generated by an electrode with the shape of a flat disk of a sufficiently large area, rotating about an axis perpendicular to the plane of the disc with a constant angular velocity. The theory of Levich is restricted to the case of sufficiently small Reynolds numbers, so that the motion of the fluid might be considered as laminar. Levich used the transformation proposed by von Kármán (von Kármán, 1921), which allows writing the Navier-Stokes equations as a system of ordinary differential equations. Levich also used the solution proposed by Cochran (Cochran, 1934) to the resulting system of ordinary differential equations.
Although the theory developed by Levich was in a good agreement with most experimental results reported previously, at the end of his work Levich pointed out that: "… a precise experimental study of the phenomena of concentration polarization in a wide range of

Reynolds numbers and simple geometrical conditions, allowing to establish decisively the quantitative agreement between the theory and the experiment, is highly desirable" (Levich, 1942).

Several authors have analyzed experimentally some of the geometrical features of systems typically used in electrochemical studies in order to verify if these systems meet the basic theoretical requirements of the Levich theory.

The electrode shape, the electrode immersion depth and the cell volume were considered among the main sources of discrepancy between ideal and existent experimental systems. In accordance with Riddiford (Riddiford, 1966), a cylindrical shape for the electrode promotes an adverse fluid flow pattern and other electrode shapes should be used instead. Azim and Riddiford (Azim & Riddiford, 1962) recommended conical or bell-shaped electrode designs. The effect of the electrode shape upon the rate of mass transfer was widely analyzed by Blurton and Riddiford (Blurton & Riddiford, 1965) and by Prater and Adams (Prater & Adams, 1966). However, in accordance with Prater and Adams: "... the difficulty of fabricating the bell-shaped electrode probably outweighs its advantages...".

Prater and Adams (Prater & Adams, 1966) also studied the effect of electrode immersion depth upon limiting currents, but only a bell-shaped electrode was employed. In accordance with these authors: "... identical results may be obtained whether the electrode is immersed to a depth of 1.85 cm. or barely touching the solution...".

An accurate experimental determination of the velocity field near the electrode becomes difficult due to cell geometry and electrode dimensions. This task is hard to accomplish even using modern non-intrusive techniques such as Particle Imaging Velocimetry (PIV). Nevertheless, recently the flow field inside a confined electrochemical cell configuration was measured through Laser Doppler Anemometry (Mandin, Pauporte, Fanouillere, & Lincot, 2004).

Another alternative to obtain an accurate approximation of the velocity and pressure profiles due to a rotating disk electrode is to use the Computer Fluid Dynamics (CFD) technique in which, the three-dimensional Navier-Stokes equations are solved numerically.

The aim of this chapter is to review some of the works recently published in which the CFD technique has been used to characterize the hydrodynamic behavior of the liquid inside electrochemical cells with a rotating disk electrode (RDE). This chapter also discusses the assumptions stated in the revised works as well as the accurateness of their results. In addition, this paper discusses some of the implications of the results obtained with the CFD technique on the geometric characteristics of the electrochemical cell, the electrode geometry and the operating conditions.

This chapter is organized as follows. The properties as well as the main features of the ideal system considered in the theory developed by Levich (Levich, 1942) are discussed in Section 2. This section also presents a comparison between two approximate solutions to the problem stated by von Kármán (von Kármán, 1921). The main features of several works recently published in which the CFD technique has been used to characterize the hydrodynamics of electrochemical cells with a RDE are presented in Section 3. Based on the results obtained with CFD technique, Section 4 discusses some simple modifications that can be implemented in electrochemical cells that can significantly improve the accuracy of measurements made on these devices.

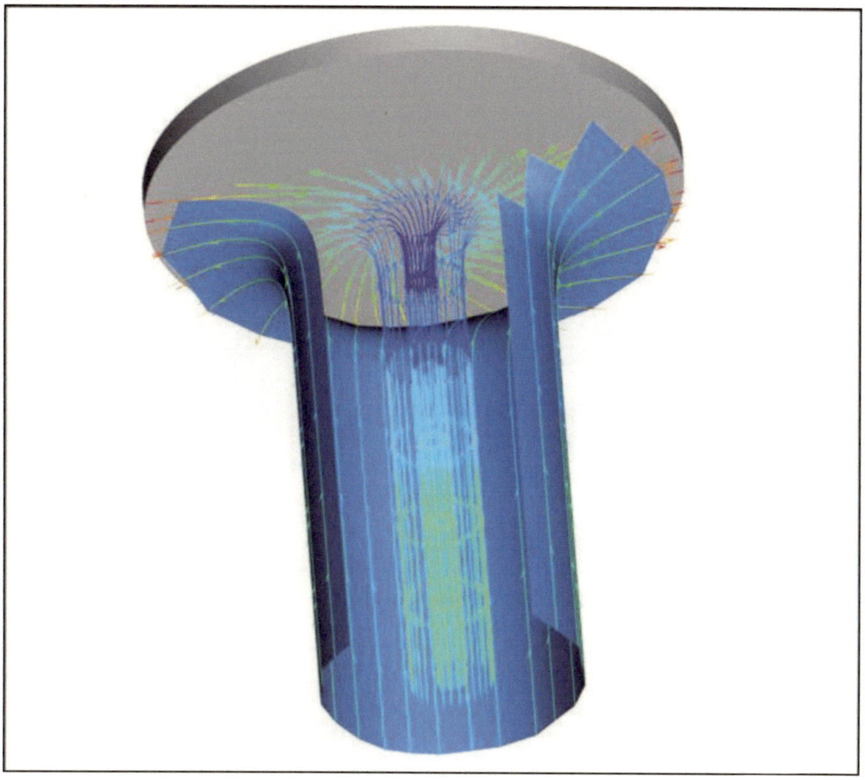

Fig. 1. Typical fluid flow pattern of the ideal system.

2. Ideal system model

2.1 System description

In the model of the ideal system considered by Levich (Levich, 1942), the analytical expressions describing the hydrodynamic behavior of the fluid in the vicinity of the electrode active surface is in accordance with the behavior described by von Kármán (von Kármán, 1921). Levich considered that the fluid velocity field inside the cell can be modeled as the steady-state motion of an incompressible Newtonian viscous fluid due to an infinite rotating plane disk whose thickness is equal to zero. A system like this was originally proposed by von Kármán (von Kármán, 1921). This model assumes that the fluid density and viscosity remain constant. Additionally, the fluid is infinite in extent and is located above the disc.

Figure 1 shows the typical fluid flow pattern of the ideal system. To create this figure, a small value for the electrode rotation speed was employed. Several stream lines were included in this figure. The stream lines were colored in accordance with its radius value. Given that the rotating disc acts as a centrifugal fan, the fluid moves radially outwards near the disc. Therefore, to preserve continuity, an axial motion towards the lamina is generated (Cochran, 1934). Figure 1 shows that far from the disk the radial and angular velocity components are zero. On the contrary, near the disk, the behaviour of the fluid resembles logarithmic spirals. Figure 2 shows the fluid velocity field on a plane parallel to the disk. This figure also shows that a stagnation point is formed at the center of the disk.

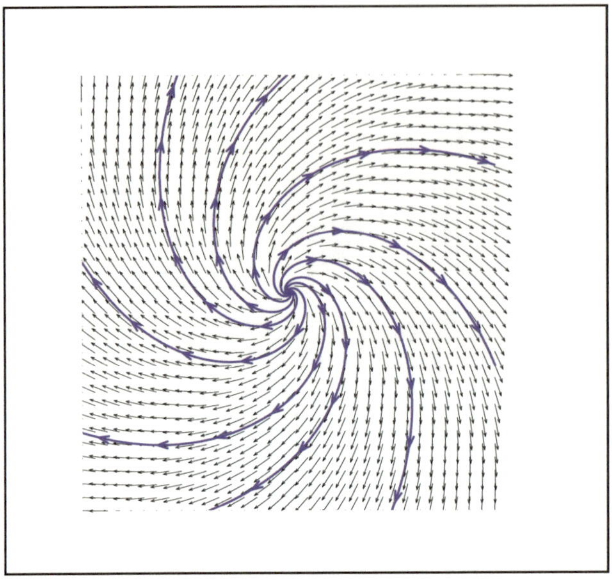

Fig. 2. Fluid velocity field on a plane parallel to the disk which resembles logarithmic spirals.

2.2 Mathematical equations

The mathematical equations of the ideal model are the continuity and the Navier-Stokes equations in cylindrical coordinates at the steady-state:

$$u + r\frac{\partial u}{\partial r} + r\frac{\partial w}{\partial z} = 0 \tag{2}$$

$$\begin{aligned} u\frac{\partial u}{\partial r} - \frac{v^2}{r} + w\frac{\partial u}{\partial z} &= -\frac{1}{\rho}\frac{\partial p}{\partial r} + \nu\left\{\frac{\partial^2 u}{\partial r^2} + \frac{\partial}{\partial r}\left(\frac{u}{r}\right) + \frac{\partial^2 u}{\partial z^2}\right\} \\ u\frac{\partial v}{\partial r} - \frac{uv}{r} + w\frac{\partial v}{\partial z} &= \nu\left\{\frac{\partial^2 v}{\partial r^2} + \frac{\partial}{\partial r}\left(\frac{v}{r}\right) + \frac{\partial^2 v}{\partial z^2}\right\} \\ u\frac{\partial w}{\partial r} + w\frac{\partial w}{\partial z} &= -\frac{1}{\rho}\frac{\partial p}{\partial z} + \nu\left\{\frac{\partial^2 w}{\partial r^2} + \frac{1}{r}\frac{\partial w}{\partial r} + \frac{\partial^2 w}{\partial z^2}\right\} \end{aligned} \tag{3}$$

This model assumes that the fluid flow pattern is axisymmetric respect the axial axis. In this equations, r and z are the radial and axial coordinates, p is the pressure, ρ is the density of the fluid and ν is the kinematic viscosity of the fluid. In (2) and (3), u, v and w are the radial, the angular and the axial velocity components respectively. This model also assumes that the flow regime is laminar.

The boundary conditions for (2) and (3) are as follows: At the disc surface $(z=0)$, a non-slip condition is assumed, that is, $u=0$, $w=0$ and $v=\omega r$, where ω is the electrode rotation speed. Far from the disc $(z\to\infty)$, it is assumed that there is no flow in the radial and the angular directions, which can be expressed as $u=0$ and $v=0$. In addition, the axial velocity reaches its limiting velocity U_0, that is, $w=U_0$.

2.3 Approximate solutions

von Kármán (von Kármán, 1921), introduced the following dimensionless independent (Equation 4) and dependent variables (Equation 5):

$$\xi = z\sqrt{\frac{\omega}{\nu}} \tag{4}$$

$$F(\xi) = \frac{u}{r\omega}, \quad G(\xi) = \frac{v}{r\omega}, \quad H(\xi) = \frac{w}{\sqrt{\nu\omega}} \quad \text{and} \quad P(\xi) = \frac{p}{\rho\nu\omega} \tag{5}$$

After applying the variable change, Equations (2) and (3) can be rewritten as a set of four ordinary differential equations:

$$2F + H' = 0 \tag{6}$$

$$F'' - HF' - F^2 + G^2 = 0 \tag{7}$$

$$G'' - HG' - 2FG = 0 \tag{8}$$

$$H'' - HH' - P' = 0 \tag{9}$$

The boundary conditions for the system are:

$$H = F = P = 0, \quad G = 1 \quad \text{at} \quad \xi = 0, \tag{10}$$

and

$$F = G = 0 \quad \text{at} \quad \xi = \infty \tag{11}$$

Several authors have developed approximate solutions to the equations system (6)-(8) subject to boundary conditions given by Equations (10) and (11). The most famous approximate solution was obtained by Cochran (Cochran, 1934), which is composed by two infinite series, one a power series near the disk and the other a series in exponential functions away from the disk.

The first set of equations is valid only near the disk $(\xi \to 0)$:

$$F = a\xi - \frac{1}{2}\xi^2 - \frac{b}{3}\xi^3 + \cdots \tag{12}$$

$$G = 1 + b\xi + \frac{1}{3}a\xi^3 + \cdots \tag{13}$$

$$H = -a\xi^2 + \frac{1}{3}\xi^3 + \frac{b}{6}\xi^4 + \cdots \tag{14}$$

The second set is valid far from the disk $(\xi \to \infty)$:

$$F = Ae^{-\alpha\xi} - \frac{\left(A^2 + B^2\right)}{2\alpha^2}e^{-2\alpha\xi} + \frac{A\left(A^2 + B^2\right)}{4\alpha^4}e^{-3\alpha\xi} + \cdots \tag{15}$$

$$G = Be^{-\alpha\xi} - \frac{B\left(A^2+B^2\right)}{12\alpha^4}e^{-3\alpha\xi} + \cdots \quad (16)$$

$$H = -\alpha + \frac{2A}{\alpha}e^{-\alpha\xi} - \frac{\left(A^2+B^2\right)}{2\alpha^3}e^{-2\alpha\xi} + \frac{A\left(A^2+B^2\right)}{6\alpha^5}e^{-3\alpha\xi} + \cdots \quad (17)$$

Where in both sets, a, b, A, B and α are constants.

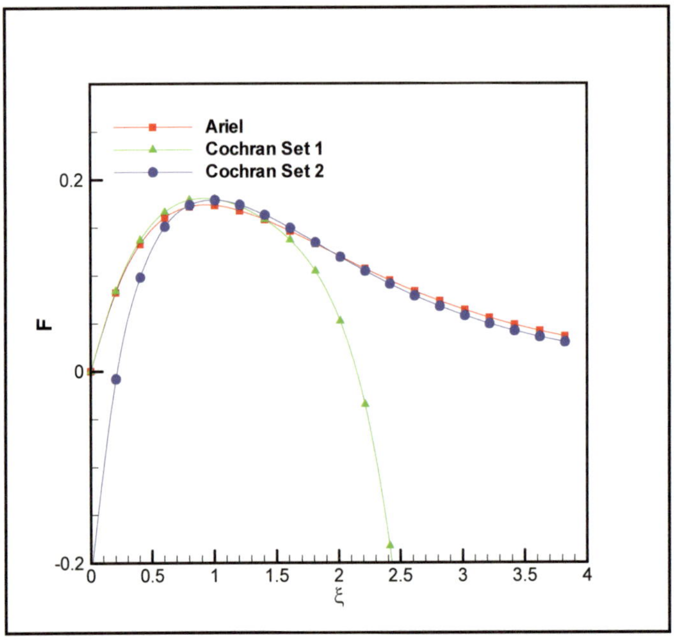

Fig. 3. Comparison of the solutions developed by Cochran and Ariel for the radial velocity component.

Contrary to the approach stated by Cochran, Ackroyd (Ackroyd, 1978) developed a solution composed by only one set of infinite series of exponential terms with negative exponents. Following Arckroy approach, Ariel (Ariel, 1996) presented an approximate solution in which is possible to obtain better results than that obtained with other approximate methods. The solution developed by Ariel is given by the following equations:

$$F = \beta^2\left(\frac{1}{8}\left(2e^{-\beta\xi} - e^{-2\beta\xi}\right)\ln\left(\frac{4e^{\beta\xi}-1}{3}\right) + \frac{1}{2}\left(e^{-\beta\xi} - e^{-2\beta\xi}\right)\right) \quad (18)$$

$$G = \frac{1}{3}\left(4e^{-\beta\xi} - e^{-2\beta\xi}\right) \quad (19)$$

$$H = \beta\left(\frac{1}{8}\left(4e^{-\beta\xi} - e^{-2\beta\xi}\right)\ln\left(\frac{4e^{\beta\xi}-1}{3}\right) - \frac{1}{2}\left(2 - 3e^{-\beta\xi} + e^{-2\beta\xi}\right)\right) \quad (20)$$

Where ξ is defined as in Equation (4) and $\beta = 0.9130294741$. The main advantage of the solution proposed by Ariel over that obtained by Cochran is that Equations (18)-(20) can be evaluated for any value of ξ such that $0 \le \xi < \infty$.

Figures 3, 4 and 5 show a comparison of the solutions obtained by Cochran and Ariel for the radial, angular and axial velocity components, respectively. Roughly speaking, these figures show that the first of functions of the solution proposed by Cochran are valid when $\xi \le 1$. These figures also shows that the trend of the two sets of functions that comprises the solution proposed by Cochran are completely distinct for $\xi \ge 1.5$.

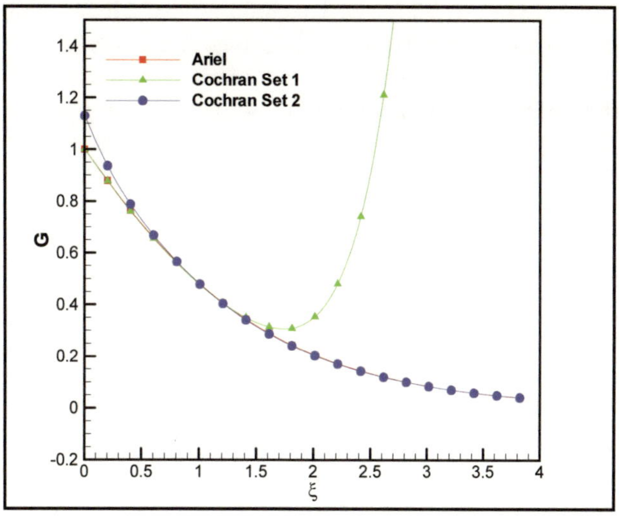

Fig. 4. Comparison of the solutions developed by Cochran and Ariel for the angular velocity component.

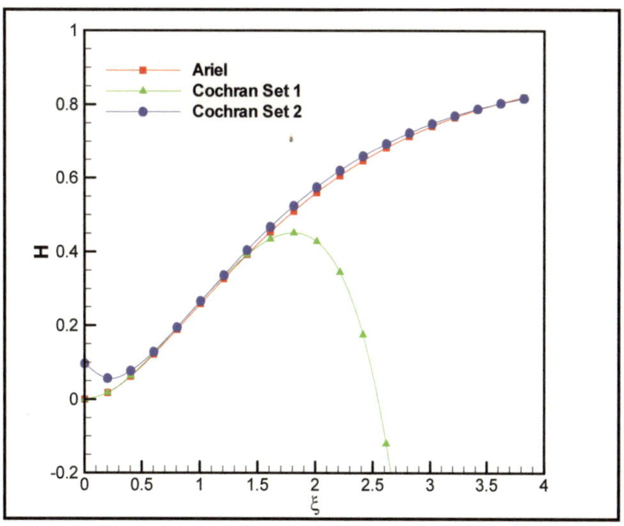

Fig. 5. Comparison of the solutions developed by Cochran and Ariel for the axial velocity component.

Figures 3, 4 and 5 show that the results of the approximate solutions developed by Cochran and by Ariel are very similar. Volgin and Davydov (Volgin & Davydov, 2007) shown that the error associated to the available approximate equations to calculate the velocity field range from 1 to 0.01%. In addition, they found that to provide an accuracy of about 0.1%, the length of computational region should be approximately twice the diffusion layer thickness. To reach higher accuracy, the extension of the computational region must be increased.

3. Simulation with CFD

Computational Fluid Dynamics (CFD) is a technique that allows generating fluid flow simulations with by means of computers. CFD solves numerically the governing laws of fluid dynamics. The set of partial differential equations associated with the system under study are solved in a geometrical domain divided into small volumes, commonly known as a mesh (or grid). The accuracy and validity of simulation results depends on the choice of the CFD model, the physical features incorporated in the governing equations and the boundary conditions (Ferziger & Peric, 1996; Tu, Yeoh, & Liu, 2008).

3.1 Two-dimensional models

Almost all the numerical simulations of the hydrodynamic behavior inside electrochemical cells with a RDE have used axisymmetric two-dimensional models, but there are significant differences in the extent of the electrochemical cell volume of the systems reported in literature. The entire cell volume was simulated by Mandin et al. (Mandin, et al., 2004) whereas only a small amount of liquid below a rotating disc ring electrode was considered by Dong et al. (Dong, Santhanagopalan, & White, 2007). In those works, only the electrode active face is in contact with the fluid. Nevertheless, a common practice of submerge the working electrode into the cell liquid was not considered in those works. Mandin et al. (Mandin, Fabian, & Lincot, 2006) show the significance of the submerged electrode side wall by means of two-dimensional numerical simulations of an electrochemical cell with a rotating cylinder electrode.

Dong et al. (Dong, Santhanagopalan, & White, 2008) carried out two-dimensional axisymmetric numerical simulations of a entire electrochemical cell with a RDE, where the electrode is partially submerged into the electrolyte. To include the existence of an air-liquid interface present in actual electrochemical cells, a slip wall was employed as boundary condition for the cell upper wall to represent numerically this interface. The system modeled by Dong et al. (Dong, et al., 2008) is schematically represented in Figure 6. In accordance with these authors, the simulated fluid velocity field and that obtained with the theoretical model proposed by von Kármán (von Kármán, 1921) and Cochran (Cochran, 1934) are in good agreement.

Mandin et al. (Mandin, et al., 2004) also carried out two-dimensional axisymmetric numerical simulations of a entire electrochemical cell with a RDE. The system studied by these authors is schematically represented in Figure 7. Their results were compared with the fluid flow pattern calculated with the analytical expressions obtained by Cochran (Cochran, 1934). These authors found that the velocity profiles calculated with these expressions are in accordance with their numerical simulations only in a narrow region close to the electrode active face. However, apparently these authors only made use of one of the two sets of equations that comprises the solution obtained by Cochran.

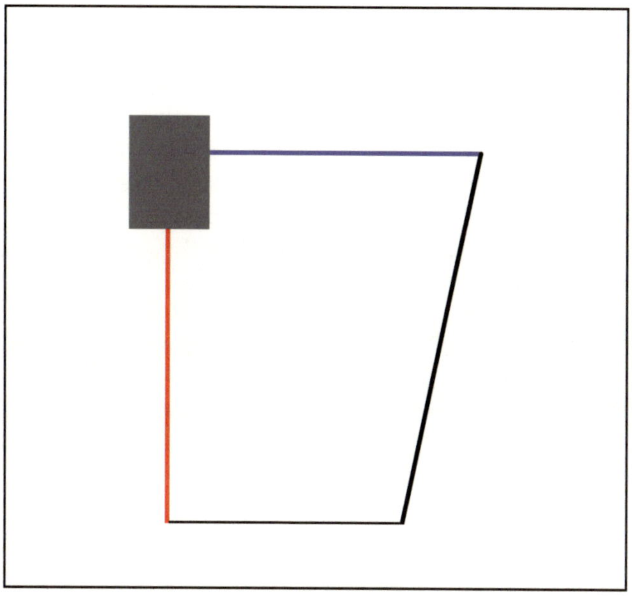

Fig. 6. Schematic representation of the cell simulated by Dong et al. (Dong, et al., 2008). The line in blue represents a slip wall. The line in red represents symmetry axis.

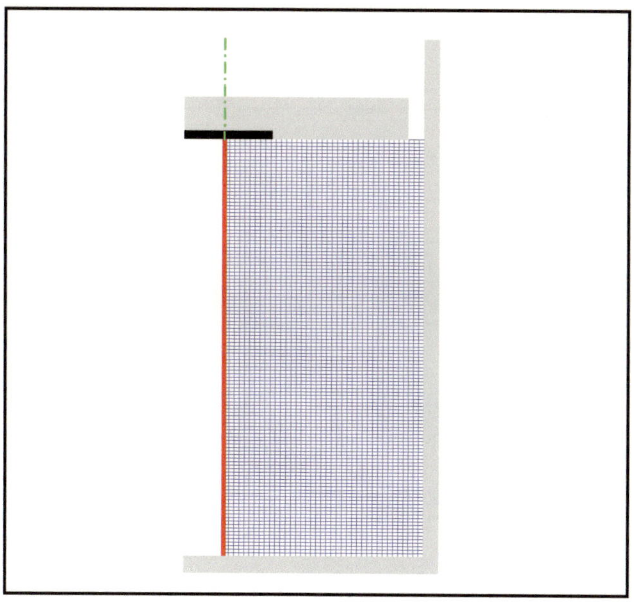

Fig. 7. Schematic representation of the cell simulated by Mandin et al. (Mandin, et al., 2004). The line in red represents symmetry axis. The line in black represents the electroactive zone.

3.2 Three-dimensional models

All the two-dimensional mathematical models of electrochemical cells with a RDE assumed that the fluid velocity field is axisymmetric. Nevertheless, the asymmetry of the fluid flow was observed in informal experiments reported by Adams (Adams, 1969) (see Figure 4-3 in that work). Despite the asymmetry is evident, no comments regarding this fact were raised; maybe because in accordance with the author, those experiments were done only to illustrate the general behavior of an electrochemical cell with a RDE.

Due to the size and inner geometry of most of the electrochemical cells, scarce measurements of the liquid velocities inside the cell are reported. However, measurements of liquid velocities inside a cell with a rotating disc electrode through the Doppler Laser Anemometry (DLA) technique were performed by Mandin, et al. (Mandin, et al., 2004). In that work, reproducible high amplitude oscillations that increased substantially with the electrode rotation speed were observed. These authors also compared their experimental measurements with the results of a two-dimensional axisymmetric mathematical model, but liquid velocities oscillations were not reproduced.

By using a three-dimensional model, the symmetry constraint can be avoided and therefore, it is possible to reproduce the hydrodynamic behavior of the internal flow of electrochemical cells under more realistic conditions. The correctness of this assumption can be evaluated by comparing the results of the numerical simulations against the physical experiments measurements.

Real, et al. (Real, et al., 2008) characterized the hydrodynamics inside electrochemical cells with several geometric features using three-dimensional models. These authors studied how the fluid flow pattern is affected by the electrode rotation speed, the cell volume, the electrode submergence depth and the distance between the electrode active face and the cell bottom wall. In that work, the authors found that the fluid flow pattern inside the electrochemical cell is not symmetric. Nonetheless, the asymmetry grade strongly depends on the geometrical configuration of the system.

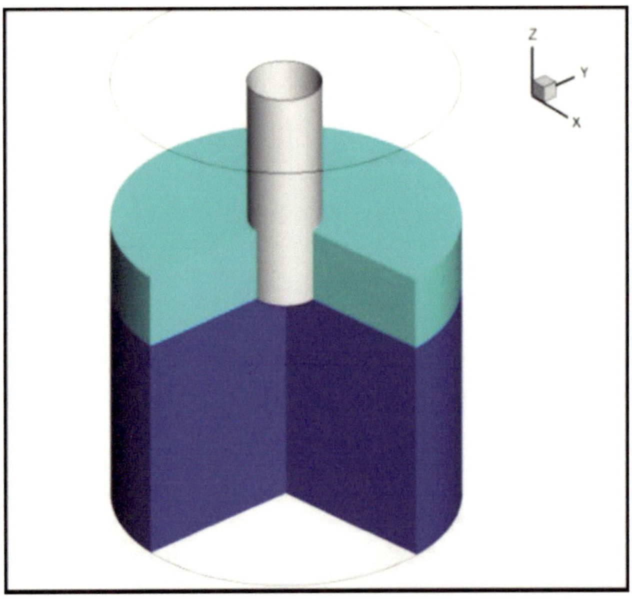

Fig. 8. Example of the biphasic three-dimensional models employed by Gonzalez, et al. (Gonzalez, Real, Hoyos, Miranda, & Cervantes, 2011), Real-Ramirez, et al. (Real-Ramirez, Miranda-Tello, Hoyos-Reyes, & Gonzalez-Trejo, 2010) and Real, et al. (Real, et al., 2008).

In the work of Real, et al. (Real, et al., 2008) only the hydrodynamic behavior of the electrolyte inside the cell was simulated. This means that the effect of the interface electrolyte-air in actual electrochemical cells is neglected. However, the significance of the free surface on the flow pattern inside a stationary cylinder with a rotating bottom has been recognized by several authors (Brøns, Shen, Sørensen, & Zhu, 2007). By comparing the flow inside two different container geometries, one with a rigid cover and the other with a free surface, significant differences in the resulting behavior were observed experimentally (Spohn, Mory, & Hopfinger, 1998). This result was reproduced numerically through three-dimensional numerical simulations (Serre & Bontoux, 2007).

The effect of the liquid phase free surface on the flow pattern inside the electrochemical cell with a RDE has been studied recently by Real, et al. (Real, et al., 2008), Real-Ramirez, et al. (Real-Ramirez, et al., 2010) and Gonzalez, et al. (Gonzalez, et al., 2011). These works conducted several three-dimensional unsteady-state numerical simulations using biphasic systems. An example of the biphasic three-dimensional models employed in those works is presented in Figure 8. In this example, the volume occupied by the electrolyte was colored in blue and the electrode was colored in grey. The electrode submergence depth is equal to the electrode external diameter. The distance between the electrode active face and the cell bottom wall is equal to four times the electrode external diameter.

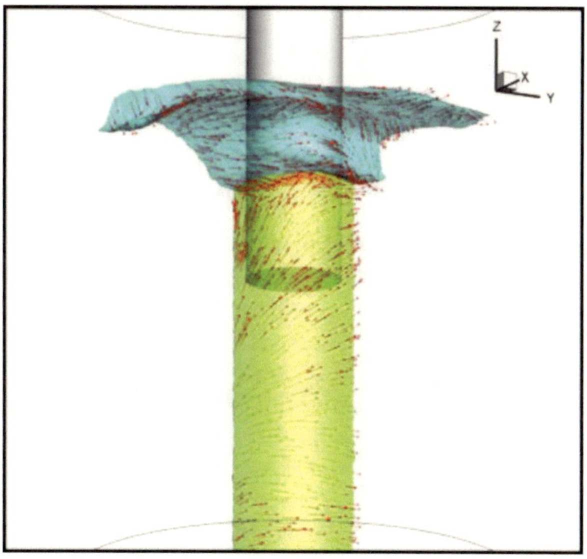

Fig. 9. Liquid velocity vectors near and below the electrode. A section of the liquid free-surface colored in blue is also presented.

Through the biphasic three-dimensional numerical simulations, the authors found that the fluid flow pattern inside the electrochemical cell is not symmetric respect the electrode rotation axis. Figure 9 presents the liquid velocity vectors near and below the electrode. This figure also shows a section of the liquid free-surface, which is colored in blue. A big value for the electrode rotation speed was employed to generate the results shown in Figure 9.

By comparing Figures 1 and 9 it is clear that there is a difference between the behaviors of an actual electrochemical cell and the ideal model stated by von Kármán (von Kármán, 1921).

The asymmetry of the fluid flow pattern about the axis of rotation of the electrode causes a displacement of the stagnation point on the electrode active face. This displacement is shown in Figure 10.

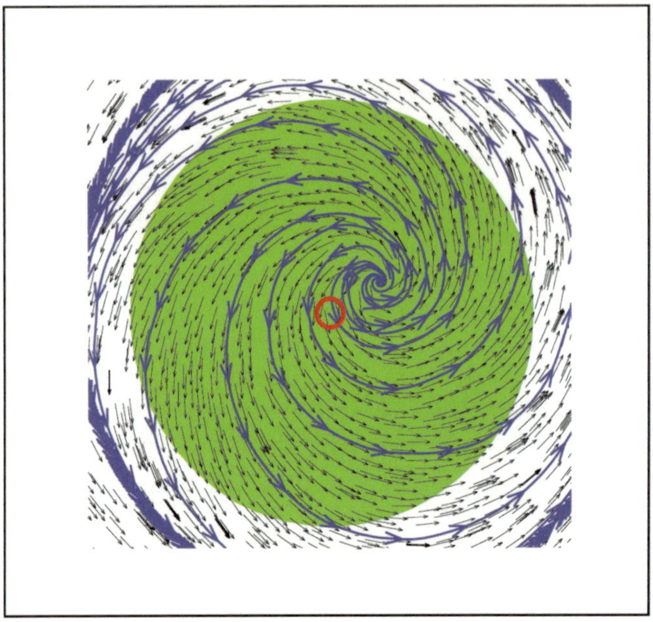

Fig. 10. Displacement of the stagnation point on the electrode active face originated by the asymmetry of the fluid flow pattern. The red circle denotes the centre of the electrode.

The biphasic three-dimensional numerical simulations confirm that the asymmetry grade strongly depends on the geometrical configuration of the system. By analyzing the results of several physical and numerical simulations at different electrode rotation speeds and several cell sizes, those works found that there exist a synergetic effect of the cell internal walls, the submerged electrode side wall and the liquid free surface (Real-Ramirez, et al., 2010). Their numerical simulations showed that the asymmetry of the electrochemical cell flow pattern is intensified by the free surface asymmetry, which depends directly on the electrode rotation speed and the electrode submergence depth (Gonzalez, et al., 2011).

Several fluid stream lines below the electrode for two distinct values of the distance between the electrode active face and the cell bottom wall are shown in Figures 11 and 12. This distance for the cell shown in Figure 11 is small, whereas a large value for the distance between the electrode active face and the cell bottom wall was employed for the cell shown in Figure 12. The same value of the electrode rotation speed was used for the simulations shown in Figures 12 and 13.

Figures 11 and 12 clearly show that the offset from the center of the electrode of the stagnation point depends strongly on the distance between the electrode active face and the cell bottom wall. Based on the results of their numerical simulations, Real-Ramirez, et al. (Real-Ramirez, et al., 2010) stated as rule of thumb that the distance between the electrode active face and the cell bottom wall must be at least three times the electrode external diameter.

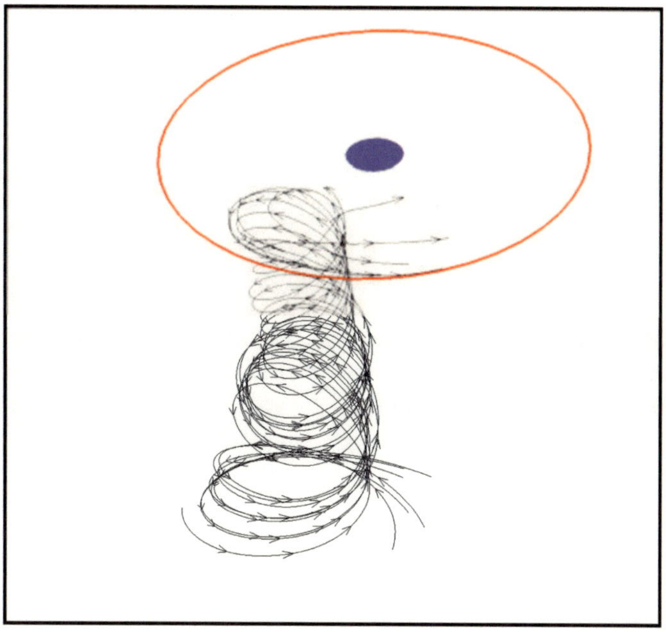

Fig. 11. Fluid stream lines below the electrode when the distance between the electrode active face and the cell bottom wall is small. The blue circle defines the centre of the electrode.

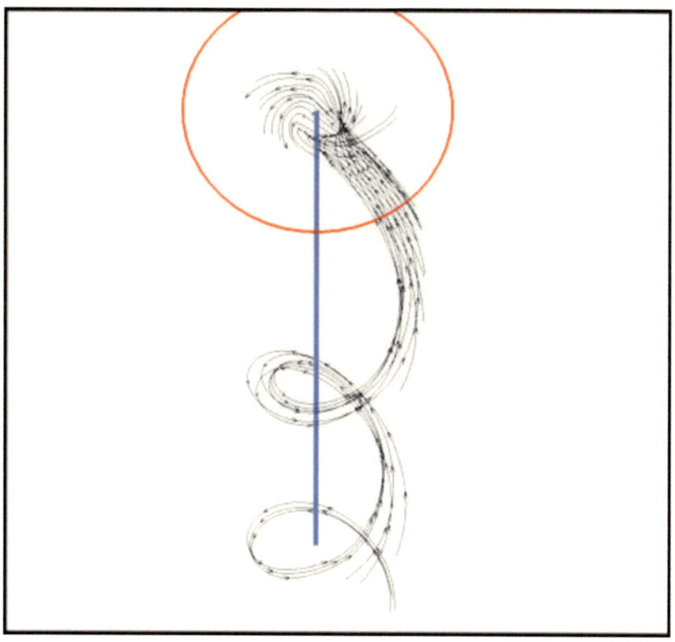

Fig. 12. Fluid stream lines below the electrode when the distance between the electrode active face and the cell bottom wall is large. The blue line coincides with the axis of rotation of the electrode.

3.3 Comparison between mathematical and physical experiments

Based on the results of their numerical simulations and following the functional form of the solutions proposed by Ackroyd (Ackroyd, 1978) and Ariel (Ariel, 1996), Gonzalez, et al. (Gonzalez, et al., 2011) argued that the fluid velocity component orthogonal to the electrode active face decreases almost exponentially with the square root of the electrode rotation speed. Gonzalez, et al. (Gonzalez, et al., 2011) proposed an empirical correction to the Levich equation as follows:

$$i_L = \psi \, \omega^{1/2} e^{-\gamma \omega^{1/2}} \tag{21}$$

where $\psi > 0$ has the usual interpretation and γ is a constant such that $0 < \gamma \ll 1$. The smaller the value of γ, the closer will be the system to the ideal one. The previous equation implies that $i_L \to 0$ as $\omega^{1/2} \to 0$, nevertheless, the value of ω cannot be as large as desired because beyond a certain threshold, the Levich equation is no longer valid.

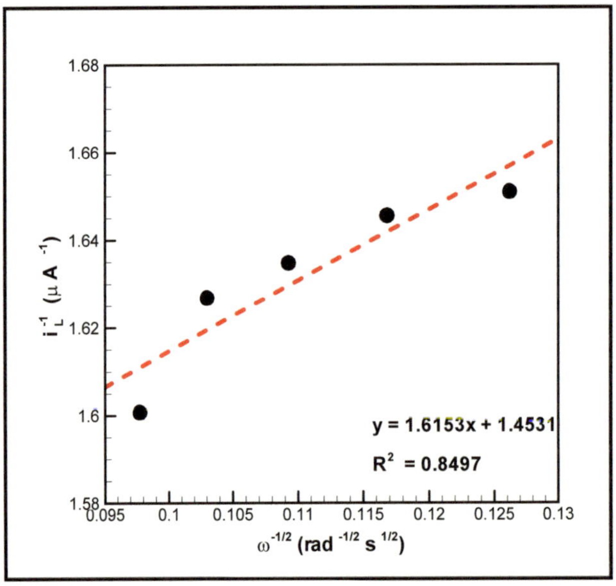

Fig. 13. Koutecky-Levich plot of data reported by Unguresan & Gligor (Unguresan & Gligor, 2009) for a concentration of NADH of 1.2 m*M*.

Gonzalez, et al. evaluated the validity of Equation (21) using the experimental results reported by Unguresan & Gligor (Unguresan & Gligor, 2009). The experiments correspond with the electrocatalytic NADH oxidation process taking place at graphite electrodes modified with a polymer of phenothiazine formaldehyde at various concentrations of NADH and for an electrolyte pH value of 6.0.

Figure 13 shows the traditional Koutecky-Levich plot of data reported by Unguresan & Gligor for a concentration of NADH of 1.2 m*M*. Figure 14 shows the fitting of the same experimental data by using Equation (21). The equations of the linear adjustment was included these figures. Similar values for the Levich constants ψ are obtained with the model proposed by Gonzalez, et al. (Gonzalez, et al., 2011) and the Koutecky-Levich equation, but the goodness of the fit is significantly improved.

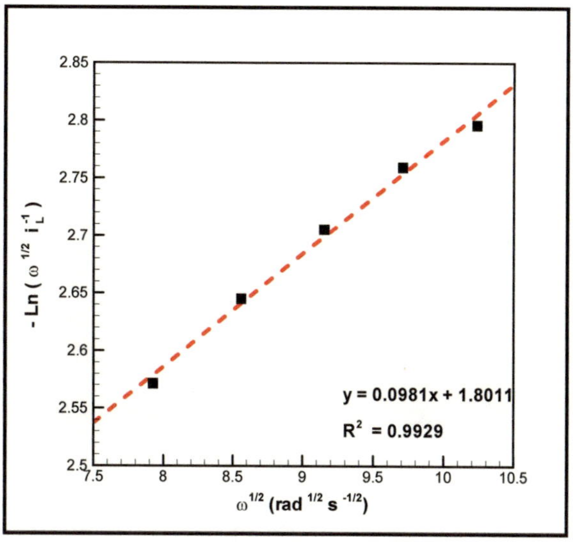

Fig. 14. Fitting of the experimental data reported by Unguresan & Gligor (Unguresan & Gligor, 2009) for a concentration of NADH of 1.2 m*M* by using Equation (21).

The same analysis to that previously described but now for a concentration of NADH of 1.6 m*M* is presented in Figures 15 and 16. As in the as in the previous case, the goodness of the fit is superior by using the model proposed by Gonzalez, et al. (Gonzalez, et al., 2011).

4. Effect of the electrode shape and future trends

The importance of electrode shape on the behavior of the electrochemical cell has been recognized for a long time. For instance, the inaccuracies caused by the geometry of the electrode are discussed in detail in Section 6 of the Levich work (Levich, 1942).

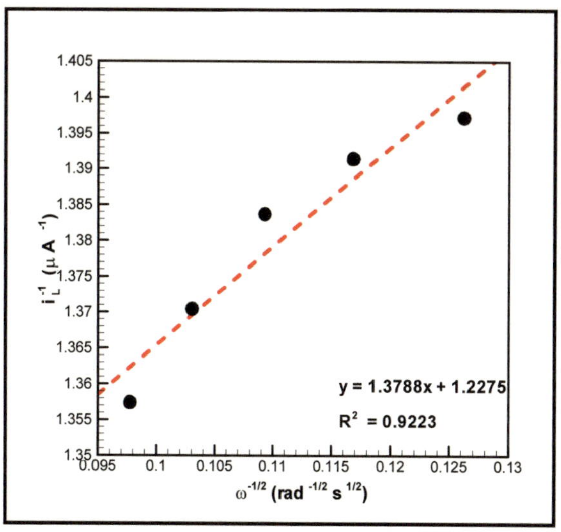

Fig. 15. Koutecky-Levich plot of data reported by Unguresan & Gligor (Unguresan & Gligor, 2009) for a concentration of NADH of 1.6 m*M*.

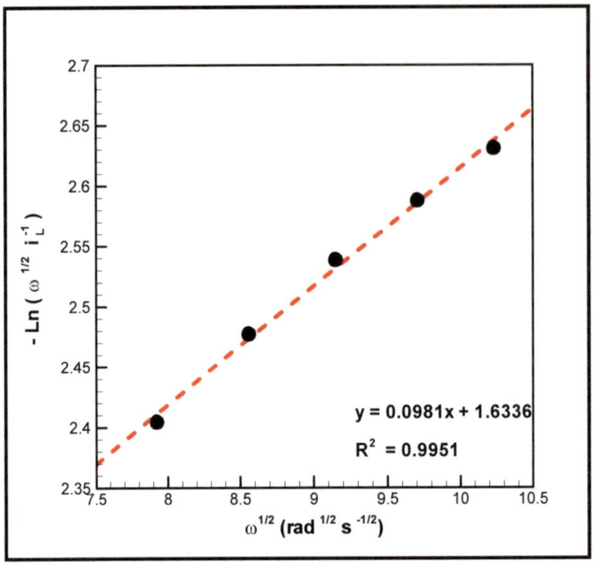

Fig. 16. Fitting of the experimental data reported by Unguresan & Gligor (Unguresan & Gligor, 2009) for a concentration of NADH of 1.6 m*M* by using Equation (21).

By analyzing the results of biphasic three-dimensional numerical simulations of an electrochemical cell with a cylindrical electrode, several authors found that the submerged electrode side wall along with its right angle shape induces that the liquid velocities in the vicinity of the electrode active face were lower than that predicted with the ideal model (Gonzalez, et al., 2011; Real-Ramirez, et al., 2010). To obtain a liquid velocities field as close as possible to the ideal one, those authors suggest using electrodes with rounded border shape.

The cylindrical electrodes are the ones mostly used for the characterization of electrochemical reactions. However, some authors still using bell-shaped electrodes. According to the authors of this chapter, the results of numerical simulations suggest that this type of electrodes may have a better performance than the cylindrical electrodes. Therefore, it is strongly recommended to conduct numerical simulations to characterize the hydrodynamics of an electrochemical cell with a bell-shaped electrode.

5. Acknowledgements

The authors are grateful to the support by Universidad Autonoma Metropolitana (Nos.2231207 and 2270303) and to Sistema Nacional de Investigadores (SNI-CONACYT).

6. References

Ackroyd, J. A. D. (1978). Steady flow produced by a rotating-disk with either surface suction or injection. *Journal of Engineering Mathematics, 12*(3), 207-220.

Adams, R. N. (1969). *Electrochemistry at solid electrodes*. New York,: M. Dekker.

Ariel, P. D. (1996). The flow near a rotating disk: An approximate solution. *Journal of Applied Mechanics-Transactions of the ASME, 63*(2), 436-438.

Azim, S., & Riddiford, A. C. (1962). A new type of rotating disk electrode. *Analytical Chemistry, 34*(8), 1023-1025

Bircumshaw, L. L., & Riddiford, A. C. (1952). Transport control in heterogeneous reactions. *Quarterly Reviews, Chemical Society, 6*(2), 157-185.

Blurton, K. F., & Riddiford, A. C. (1965). Shapes of practical rotating disc electrodes. *Journal of Electroanalytical Chemistry, 10*(5-6), 457-464.

Brøns, M., Shen, W. Z., Sørensen, J. N., & Zhu, W. J. (2007). The influence of imperfections on the flow structure of steady vortex breakdown bubbles. *Journal of Fluid Mechanics, 578*, 453.

Cochran, W. G. (1934). The flow due to a rotating disc. *Proceedings of the Cambridge Philosophical Society, 30*, 365-375.

Dong, Q., Santhanagopalan, S., & White, R. E. (2007). Simulation of the oxygen reduction reaction at an RDE in 0.5 m H2SO4 including an adsorption mechanism. *Journal of the Electrochemical Society, 154*(9), A888-A899.

Dong, Q., Santhanagopalan, S., & White, R. E. (2008). A comparison of numerical solutions for the fluid motion generated by a rotating disk electrode. *Journal of the Electrochemical Society, 155*(9), B963-B968.

Eucken, A. (1932). Die Ermittelung der absoluten Grösse des Diffusionsstromes in Bewegten Elektrolyten. *Zeitschrift für Elektrochemie und angewandte physikalische Chemie, 38*(6), 341-345.

Ferziger, J. H., & Peric, M. (1996). *Computational methods for fluid dynamics*. Berlin ; New York: Springer.

Gonzalez, J., Real, C., Hoyos, L., Miranda, R., & Cervantes, F. (2011). Characterization of the hydrodynamics inside a practical cell with a rotating disk electrode. *Journal of Electroanalytical Chemistry, 651*(2), 150-159.

Levich, B. (1942). The theory of concentration polarization. *Acta Physicochimica URSS, 17*, 257-307.

Mandin, P., Fabian, C., & Lincot, D. (2006). Importance of the density gradient effects in modelling electro deposition process at a rotating cylinder electrode. *Electrochimica Acta, 51*(19), 4067-4079.

Mandin, P., Pauporte, T., Fanouillere, P., & Lincot, D. (2004). Modelling and numerical simulation of hydrodynamical processes in a confined rotating electrode configuration. *Journal of Electroanalytical Chemistry, 565*(2), 159-173.

Nernst, W. (1904). Theory on the reaction rate in heterogenous systems. *Zeitschrift Fur Physikalische Chemie--Stochiometrie Und Verwandtschaftslehre, 47*(1), 52-55.

Nernst, W., & Merriam, E. S. (1905). On the theory of residual current. (According to experiments by Mr. Merriam.). *Zeitschrift Fur Physikalische Chemie--Stochiometrie Und Verwandtschaftslehre, 53*(2), 235-244.

Prater, K. B., & Adams, R. N. (1966). A critical evaluation of practical rotated disk electrodes. *Analytical Chemistry, 38*(1), 153-155.

Real-Ramirez, C. A., Miranda-Tello, R., Hoyos-Reyes, L. F., & Gonzalez-Trejo, J. I. (2010). Hydrodynamic characterization of an electrochemical cell with rotating disc electrode: A three dimensional biphasic model. *International Journal of Chemical Reactor Engineering, 8*, 1-37.

Real, C., González, J., Palomar-Pardavé, M., Romero-Romo, M., Aguilar, M., & Hoyos, L. (2008). *A CFD hydrodinamics condition simulation of electrochemical cells with rotating electrodes*. Paper presented at the International Materials Research Congress, Cancun.

Riddiford, A. C. (1966). The rotating disk system. In P. Delahay (Ed.), *Advances in electrochemistry and electrochemical engineering* (Vol. 4, pp. 47-116). New York: Wiley.

Serre, E., & Bontoux, P. (2007). Vortex breakdown in a cylinder with a rotating bottom and a flat stress-free surface. *International Journal of Heat and Fluid Flow, 28*, 229-248.

Spohn, A., Mory, M., & Hopfinger, E. J. (1998). Experiments on vortex breakdown in a confined flow generated by a rotating disc. *Journal of Fluid Mechanics, 370*, 73-99.

Tu, J., Yeoh, G. H., & Liu, C. (2008). *Computational fluid dynamics: A practical approach* (1st Ed.) Amsterdam ; Boston: Butterworth-Heinemann.

Unguresan, M. L., & Gligor, D. M. (2009). Numerical modelling and simulation of Koutecky-Levich equation for NADH electrocatalytic oxidation at graphite electrodes modified with a new polymeric phenothiazine. *Indian Journal of Chemistry, Section A, 48A*(02), 206-210.

Volgin, V. M., & Davydov, A. D. (2007). Numerical simulation of steady-state ion transfer to rotating disk electrode: Accuracy and computational efficiency. *Journal of Electroanalytical Chemistry, 600*(1), 171-179.

von Kármán, T. (1921). Über laminare und turbulente reibung. *Zeitschrift für Angewandte Mathematik und Mechanik, 1*, 486.

Part 3

Other Applications of Computational Simulations

20

Upper Burst Error Bound for Atmospheric Correlated Optical Communications Using an Alternative Matrix Decomposition

Antonio Jurado-Navas, José María Garrido-Balsells, Miguel Castillo-Vázquez and Antonio Puerta-Notario
Communications Engineering Department, University of Málaga
Campus de Teatinos
Málaga, Spain

1. Introduction

Atmospheric optical communication has been receiving considerable attention recently for use in high data rate wireless links (Arnon, 2003; Haas et al., 2002; Juarez et al., 2006; Zhu & Kahn, 2002). Considering their narrow beamwidths and lack of licensing requirements as compared to microwave systems, atmospheric optical systems are appropriate candidates for secure, high data rate, cost-effective, wide bandwidth communications. Furthermore, the atmospheric optical communications are less susceptible to the radio interference than radio-wireless communications. Moreover, free space optical (FSO) communication systems represent a promising alternative to solve the "last mile" problem, above all in densely populated urban areas. However, even in clear sky conditions, wireless optical links may experience fading due to the turbulent atmosphere. In this respect, inhomogeneities in the temperature and pressure of the atmosphere lead to variations of the refractive index along the transmission path. These random refractive index variations produce fluctuations in both the intensity and the phase of an optical wave propagating through this medium. Such fluctuations can lead to an increase in the link error probability limiting the performance of communication systems. In this particular scenario, the turbulence-induced fading is called scintillation.

If the receiving aperture size in these optical systems, D_0, can be made larger than the correlation length, d_0, then the received irradiance becomes a spatial average over the aperture area and the scintillation level measured by the detector begins to decrease. This effect is known as aperture averaging (Andrews & Phillips, 1998). Unfortunately, it could be neither practical nor desirable to satisfy this condition, especially in diversity receivers, so we will assume that $D_0 < d_0$ throughout this chapter.

Finally, weather-induced attenuation caused by rain, snow and fog can also degrade the performance of atmospheric optical communication systems in the way shown in (Al Naboulsi & Sizun, 2004; Muhammad et al., 2005), but are not considered in this chapter.

Spatial diversity reception is a good proposal in order to mitigate the adverse effect of the scintillation on the transmitted signal. Nevertheless, many researchers assume in a first approach that turbulence-induced fading is uncorrelated at each of the optical receivers

(Ibrahim & Ibrahim, 1996; Lee & Chan, 2004; Razavi & Shapiro, 2005). In order for this assumption to hold true, the spacing between receivers should be greater than the fading correlation length, what may be difficult to satisfy in practice because of the available physical space or due to the fact that the receiver spacing required for uncorrelated fading may exceed the beam diameter in power-limited links with well-collimated beams. For instance, with a propagation path length, L, of 1 km and an optical wavelength, λ, of 830 nm, the fading correlation length, approximated by $d_0 = (\lambda L)^{1/2}$ (Zhu & Kahn, 2002), would be of 2.89 cm. But, if $\lambda = 1550$ nm and $L = 10$ km, then the receiver spacing required for uncorrelated scintillation should be greater than 12.45 cm. In this respect, the spatial correlation is studied in detail in (Anguita et al., 2007), presenting a dependence on the turbulence parameter C_n^2 and, above all, a more remarkable dependence on the propagation distance and on the receiver aperture.

Thus, in (Jurado-Navas & Puerta-Notario, 2009), a complete model using an autorregresive (AR) model was presented to include correlated scintillations in simulations of free space optical links using multiple receivers. Obtained results showed a diversity gain penalty due to the impact of the spatial coherence which should not be ignored in many practical scenarios. Hence, the method proposed in (Jurado-Navas & Puerta-Notario, 2009) extended the applicability of the existing techniques (Beaulieu, 1999; Ertel & Reed, 1998), including the effect of the atmospheric dynamics in order to break the uniformity of the frozen-in hypothesis (Zhu & Kahn, 2002). This latter effect was incorporated by defining a factor, ρ_l, as follows:

$$\rho_l = \tau_0 / \tau_e \tag{1}$$

which represents the degree of randomness as effect of the dynamic evolution of the turbulence, with

$$\tau_0 = \frac{\sqrt{\lambda L}}{u_\perp} \tag{2}$$

being the turbulence correlation time, where λ is the optical wavelength, L is the propagation distance and $u_\perp$ the component of the wind velocity transverse to the propagation direction. Finally, τ_e is seen as the lifetime of turbulent eddies and it is directly depending on the turbulent kinetic energy dissipation rate, ϵ, that represents the atmospheric dynamics. as the rate of energy cascading from larger eddies to smaller ones.

The method is focused on a multichannel generalization of the autoregressive (AR) variate generation method in a way similar to (Baddour & Beaulieu, 2002) in order to satisfy Taylor's hypothesis of frozen turbulence. Therefore, m lognormal scintillation sequences are generated with specified second-order statistics: concretely, the cross-correlation function and the autocorrelation function between different sequences that let spatial and temporal correlations be interrelated.

2. Upper error bound in a simpler channel model

The AR model presented in (Jurado-Navas & Puerta-Notario, 2009) and commented above is computationally complex due to its inherent numerically ill-conditioned covariance matrix (Baddour & Beaulieu, 2002). In this chapter, we propose a space-time separable statistics model, extremely simple, to avoid such a problem, providing an excellent accurate upper burst error bound and with the advantage of a reduced computational time, for correlated atmospheric terrestrial links operating at optical wavelengths. This limit is heuristically corroborated after comparing the obtained performance using scintillation sequences derived from (Jurado-Navas & Puerta-Notario, 2009) with different cross-correlation (CC) coefficient in terms of burst error rate, for an atmospheric optical link in the following two extreme situations: first, when a full accomplishment of the frozen turbulence hypothesis is assumed ($\rho_l \to 0$, $\tau_e \to \infty$); and second, when an unrealistic scenario is supposed owing to using only a space-time separable statistics model ($\rho_l \to 1$, $\tau_e \to \tau_0$), so that it can be assumed that the frozen-in turbulence is not incorporated to the system. Naturally, this latter situation is not corresponding to a real scenario, but it is presented in this paper as a benchmark in order to compare the obtained performance in burst error rate. In view of the results obtained by this latter scenario (shown through section 6 in this proposal of chapter) in comparison to the ones derived by using the first model (incorporating the frozen turbulence), it is concluded that a realistic upper error limit can be easily achieved with a high simplicity by using a space-time separable statistics model.

We must remark, however, that the space-time separable statistics model proposed here is an efficient approach that accomplishes more realistic performances when higher wind velocities are considered. In fact, this approach is based on coloring independent Gaussian sequences first between them and then in time in order to generate m log-normal random processes of scintillation. Evidently, such method is restricted to have cross-correlation functions that have the same time-dependencies as the autocorrelation functions, i.e., the obtained sequences have statistics that are space-time separable. Due to this fact, Taylor's hypothesis (Tatarskii, 1971) is not fully satisfied. For such a case, we must redirect readers to (Jurado-Navas & Puerta-Notario, 2009), where Taylor's frozen turbulence hypothesis is properly taken into account. Conversely, the frozen-in hypothesis is unquestionably an approximation and must fail as distance between receivers becomes large or in especial situations when there are both strong velocity fluctuations of the wind or long-range spatial correlations (Burghelea et al., 2005; Moore et al., 2005), or even in urban atmospheres, especially near or among roughness elements, where strong wind shear is expected to create high turbulent kinetic energy (Christen et al., 2007). Furthermore, in urban canopies and cloud streets up to $2-5$ times the average building height of such particular streets (Christen et al., 2007), the strong wind shear creates turbulence intensities that are tipically near the threshold where the hypothesis of frozen turbulence becomes inapplicable (Christen et al., 2007; Willis & Deardorff, 1976). In this fashion, difference in performance obtained from the realistic model presented in (Jurado-Navas & Puerta-Notario, 2009) and the upper bound performance proposed in this chapter are even closer to each other. Thus, the separable statistics model proposed here may be seen as a highly accurate upper error bound of the complete model detailed in (Jurado-Navas & Puerta-Notario, 2009), with the advantage of a reduced computational complexity in comparison to an AR method.

3. Turbulent atmospheric channel model

There is an extensive literature on the subject of the theory of line-of-sight propagation through the atmosphere (Andrews & Phillips, 1998; Andrews et al., 2000; Fante, 1975; Ishimaru, 1997; Strohbehn, 1978; Tatarskii, 1971). One of the most important works was developed by Tatarskii (Tatarskii, 1971). He supposed a plane wave that is incident upon the random medium (the atmosphere in this particular case). It is assumed an atmosphere having no free charges with a constant magnetic permeability. In addition, it is suppossed that the electromagnetic field has a sinusoidal time dependence (a monochromatic wave). Under these circumstances, the vector wave equation becomes

$$\nabla^2 \mathbf{E} + k^2 n^2(\mathbf{r})\mathbf{E} + 2\nabla(\mathbf{E} \cdot \nabla \log n(\mathbf{r})) = 0, \tag{3}$$

where $\mathbf{E}$ is the vector amplitude of the electric field, $k{=}2\pi/\lambda$ is the wave number of the electromagnetic wave with λ being the optical wavelength; whereas n is the atmospheric refractive index whose time variations have been suppressed, and being a random function of position, $\mathbf{r} = (x, y, z)$. The ∇ operator is the well-known vector derivative $(\partial/\partial x, \partial/\partial y, \partial/\partial z)$. Equation (3) can be simplified by imposing certain characteristics of the propagation wave. In particular, since the wavelength λ for optical radiation is much smaller than the smallest scale of turbulence, l_0, (Strohbehn, 1968) the maximum scattering angle is roughly $\lambda/l_0 \approx 10^{-4}$ rad. As a consequence, the last term on the left-hand side of Eq. (3) is negligible. Such a term is related to the change in polarization of the wave as it propagates (Strohbehn, 1971; Strohbehn & Clifford, 1967). This conclusion permit us to drop the last term and Eq. (3) then reduces to

$$\nabla^2 \mathbf{E} + k^2 n^2(\mathbf{r})\mathbf{E} = 0. \tag{4}$$

Because Eq. (4) is easily decomposed into three scalar equations, one for each component of the electric field, $\mathbf{E}$, we may solve one scalar equation and ignore the vector character of the wave until the final solution. Therefore if we let $U(\mathbf{r})$ denote one of the scalar components that is transverse to the direction of propagation along the positive x-axis (Andrews & Phillips, 1998), then Eq. (4) may be replaced by the scalar stochastic differential equation

$$\nabla^2 U + k^2 n^2(\mathbf{r}) U = 0. \tag{5}$$

The index of refraction, $n(\mathbf{r}){=}n_0 + n_1(\mathbf{r})$, fluctuates about the average value $n_0 = E[n(\mathbf{r})] \cong 1$, whereas $n_1(\mathbf{r}) \ll 1$ is the fluctuation of the refractive index from its free space value. Thus

$$\nabla^2 U + k^2 (n_0 + n_1(\mathbf{r}))^2 U = 0. \tag{6}$$

For weak fluctuation, it is necessary to obtain an approximate solution of Eq. (6) for small n_1. Most of the literature since 1960 has followed the approach of using the so-called Rytov method, which substitutes U in a series:

$$U = \exp(\psi_0 + \psi_1 + \psi_2 + ...) = \exp(\psi). \tag{7}$$

In Eq. (7), ψ_1, ψ_2 are the first and second order complex phase perturbations, respectively, whereas ψ_0 is the phase of the optical wave in free space. The Rytov solution is widely used in line-of-sight propagation problems because it simplifies the procedure of obtaining both amplitude and phase fluctuations. From the Rytov solution, the wave equation becomes:

$$\nabla^2 \psi + (\nabla \psi)^2 + k^2 (n_0 + n_1(\mathbf{r}))^2 = 0. \tag{8}$$

This is a nonlinear first order differential equation for $\nabla \psi$ and is known as the Riccati equation. Consider now a first order perturbation, then

$$\psi(L, \mathbf{r}) = \psi_0(L, \mathbf{r}) + \psi_1(L, \mathbf{r}); \tag{9a}$$

$$n(\mathbf{r}) = n_0 + n_1(\mathbf{r}); \qquad n_0 \cong 1. \tag{9b}$$

Operating, assuming that $|\nabla\psi_1| \ll |\nabla\psi_0|$, due to $n_1(\mathbf{r}) \ll 1$, neglecting $n_1^2(\mathbf{r})$ in comparison to $2n_1(\mathbf{r})$, and equating the terms with the same order of perturbation, then the following expressions are obtained:

$$\nabla^2\psi_0 + (\nabla\psi_0)^2 + k^2 n_0^2(\mathbf{r}) = 0; \tag{10a}$$

$$\nabla^2\psi_1 + 2\nabla\psi_0\nabla\psi_1 + 2k^2 n_1(\mathbf{r}) = 0. \tag{10b}$$

The first one is the differential equation for $\nabla\psi$ in the absence of the fluctuation whereas turbulent atmosphere induced perturbation are found in the second expression. The resolution of Eq. (10b) is detailed in (Fante, 1975; Ishimaru, 1997). For the particular case of a monochromatic optical plane wave propagating along the positive x-axis, i.e., $U_0(L,\mathbf{r}) = \exp(jkx)$, this solution can be written as:

$$\psi_1(L,\mathbf{r}) = \frac{k^2}{2\pi}\iiint_V n_1(\mathbf{r}')\frac{\exp\left(jk\left[|\mathbf{r}-\mathbf{r}'| - |L-x'|\right]\right)}{|\mathbf{r}-\mathbf{r}'|}d^3\mathbf{r}', \tag{11}$$

where the position $(L,\mathbf{r})$ denotes a position in the receiver plane (at $x = L$) whereas $(x',\mathbf{r}')$ represents any position at an arbitrary plane along the propagation path. The mathematical development needed to solve Eq. (11) can be consulted in (Andrews & Phillips, 1998; Ishimaru, 1997). Furthermore, the statistical nature of $\psi_1(L,\mathbf{r})$ can be deduced in an easy way. Equation (11) has the physical interpretation that the first-order Rytov perturbation, $\psi_1(L,\mathbf{r})$ is a sum of spherical waves generated at various points $\mathbf{r}'$ throughout the scattering volume V, the strength of each sum wave being proportional to the product of the unperturbed field term U_0 and the refractive-index perturbation, n_1, at the point $\mathbf{r}'$ (Andrews & Phillips, 1998). Thus it is possible to apply the central limit theorem. According to such a theorem, the distribution of a random variable which is a sum of N independent random variables approaches normal as $N \to \infty$ regardless of the distribution of each random variable. Application of the central limit theorem to this integral equation leads to the prediction of a normal probability distribution for ψ. Since we can substitute $\Psi = \chi + jS$, where χ and S are called the log-amplitude and phase, respectively, of the field, then application of the central limit theorem also leads to the prediction of a Gaussian (normal) probability distribution for both χ and S, at least up to first order corrections (χ_1 and S_1).
Accordingly, under this first-order Rytov approximation, the field of a propagating optical wave at distance L from the source is represented by:

$$U = \exp(\psi) = U_0(L,\mathbf{r})\exp(\psi_1), \tag{12}$$

with $U_0(L,\mathbf{r})$ being the unperturbed portion of the field in the absence of turbulence. Hence, the irradiance of the random field shown in Eq. (12) takes the form:

$$I = |U_0(L,\mathbf{r})|^2\exp(\psi_1 + \psi_1^*) = I_0\exp(2\chi_1), \qquad [w/m^2] \tag{13}$$

where, from now onwards, we denote χ_1 as χ for simplicity in the notation. Hence,

$$I = I_0\exp(2\chi), \qquad [w/m^2]. \tag{14}$$

In Eq. (13), operator $*$ denotes the complex conjugate, $|U_0|$ is the amplitude of the unperturbed field and I_0 is the level of irradiance fluctuation in the absence of air turbulence that ensures that the fading does not attenuate or amplify the average power, i.e., $E[I] = |U_0|^2$. This may be thought of as a conservation of energy consideration and requires the choice of $E[\chi] = -\sigma_\chi^2$, as was explained in (Fried, 1967; Strohbehn, 1978), where $E[\chi]$ is the ensemble average of log-amplitude, whereas σ_χ^2 is its variance depending on the structure parameter, C_n^2. With all of these expressions, we have modeled the irradiance of the random field, I, in the space at a single instant in time. Now, because the state of the atmospheric turbulence varies with time, the intensity fluctuations is also temporally correlated. Then, Eq. (14) can be expressed as:

$$I = \alpha_{sc}(t) \cdot I_0, \tag{15}$$

whereas $\alpha_{sc}(t) = \exp(2\chi(t))$ is the temporal behavior of the scintillation sequence and represents the effect of the intensity fluctuations on the transmitted signal. In Eq. (15), a space-to-time statistical conversion has been assumed by employing the well-known Taylor's hypothesis of frozen turbulence (Tatarskii, 1971; Taylor, 1938).

As analyzed before, and by the central limit theorem, the marginal distribution of the log-amplitude, χ, is Gaussian. Thus,

$$f_\chi(\chi) = \left(\frac{1}{2\pi\sigma_\chi^2}\right)^{1/2} \exp\left[-\frac{(\chi - E[\chi])^2}{2\sigma_\chi^2}\right]. \tag{16}$$

Hence, from the Jacobian statistical transformation (Papoulis, 1991),

$$f_I(I) = \frac{f_\chi(\chi)}{\left|\frac{dI}{d\chi}\right|}, \tag{17}$$

the probability density function of the intensity, I, can be identified to have a lognormal distribution typical of weak turbulence regime. Then:

$$f_I(I) = \left(\frac{1}{2I}\right)\left(\frac{1}{2\pi\sigma_\chi^2}\right)^{1/2} \exp\left[-\frac{(\ln I - \ln I_0)^2}{8\sigma_\chi^2}\right]. \tag{18}$$

Theoretical and experimental studies of irradiance fluctuations generally center around the scintillation index. It was evaluated in (Mercier, 1962) and it is defined as the normalized variance of irradiance fluctuations:

$$\sigma_I^2 = \frac{E[I^2]}{(E[I])^2} - 1. \tag{19}$$

Hence it is possible to define the weak turbulence regimes as those regimes for which the scintillation index given in Eq. (19) is less than unity.

With all these considerations taken into account, an efficient channel model for FSO communications using intensity modulation and direct detection (IM/DD) was presented in (Jurado-Navas et al., 2007; 2011a) under the assumption of weak turbulence regime. For these systems, the received optical power, $Y(t)$, can be written as

$$Y(t) = \alpha_{sc}(t)X(t) + N(t), \tag{20}$$

being $X(t)$ the received optical power without scintillation; whereas $\alpha_{sc}(t) = \exp[2\chi(t)]$ is the temporal behavior of the scintillation sequence and represent the effect of the intensity fluctuations on the transmitted signal. To generate $\alpha_{sc}(t)$, a scheme based on a lowpass filtering of a random Gaussian signal, $z(t)$, is implemented as in (Jurado-Navas et al., 2007; 2011a). $\chi(t)$ is, as was explained above, the log-amplitude of the optical wave governed by Gaussian statistics with ensemble average $E[\chi]$ and variance σ_χ^2. Finally, the additive white Gaussian noise, $N(t)$, is assumed to include any front-end receiver thermal noise as well as shot noise caused by ambient light much stronger than the desired signal. In the following section, we complete the scheme presented in (Jurado-Navas et al., 2007) to afford the inclusion of m correlated scintillation sequences approximating to the model introduced in (Jurado-Navas & Puerta-Notario, 2009).

4. Proposed approximation: space-time separable statistics channel model

As indicated in the last section, we can simplify the model proposed in (Jurado-Navas & Puerta-Notario, 2009) by an unrealistic but reasonably accurate space-time separable statistics model with a reduced computational load if it is compared with the complete model. Through this section, we develop the space-time separable statistics model.

4.1 Spatial diversity reception

When multiple receivers are considered, then, as shown in (Zhu & Kahn, 2002), the real symmetric auto-covariance matrix of the log-amplitude, $\mathbf{C}_\chi=\{c_\chi(i,j)\}_{i,j=1}^{m}$, at m receivers in a plane transverse to the direction of propagation is given by:

$$\mathbf{C}_\chi = \begin{pmatrix} \sigma_\chi^2 & \sigma_\chi^2\rho_{d_{12}} & \cdots & \sigma_\chi^2\rho_{d_{1m}} \\ \sigma_\chi^2\rho_{d_{21}} & \sigma_\chi^2 & \cdots & \sigma_\chi^2\rho_{d_{2m}} \\ \cdots & \cdots & \cdots & \cdots \\ \sigma_\chi^2\rho_{d_{m1}} & \sigma_\chi^2\rho_{d_{n2}} & \cdots & \sigma_\chi^2 \end{pmatrix}_{m\times m} \tag{21}$$

where d_{ij} and $\rho_{d_{ij}}$ are the distance and its normalized CC coefficient respectively between points i and j in the receiver plane. In (Jurado-Navas & Puerta-Notario, 2009; Zhu & Kahn, 2002), a Gaussian spatial covariance function for the log-amplitude fluctuations is employed that approximates the theoretical covariance function resulting from Rytov theory.
In order to satisfy the hypothesis of frozen turbulence, we can adopt an AR model as in (Baddour & Beaulieu, 2002; Jurado-Navas & Puerta-Notario, 2009) as a possible solution. By doing so, the multichannel Yule-Walker equations are expressed as (Jurado-Navas & Puerta-Notario, 2009):

$$\begin{pmatrix} \mathbf{C}_\chi[0]_{m\times m} & \mathbf{C}_\chi[-1]_{m\times m} & \cdots & \mathbf{C}_\chi[-p+1]_{m\times m} \\ \mathbf{C}_\chi[1]_{m\times m} & \mathbf{C}_\chi[0]_{m\times m} & \cdots & \mathbf{C}_\chi[-p+2]_{m\times m} \\ \cdots & \cdots & \cdots & \cdots \\ \mathbf{C}_\chi[p-1]_{m\times m} & \mathbf{C}_\chi[p-2]_{m\times m} & \cdots & \mathbf{C}_\chi[0]_{m\times m} \end{pmatrix} \begin{pmatrix} \mathbf{A^H}[1]_{m\times m} \\ \mathbf{A^H}[2]_{m\times m} \\ \cdots \\ \mathbf{A^H}[p]_{m\times m} \end{pmatrix} = - \begin{pmatrix} \mathbf{C}_\chi[1]_{m\times m} \\ \mathbf{C}_\chi[2]_{m\times m} \\ \cdots \\ \mathbf{C}_\chi[p]_{m\times m} \end{pmatrix}. \tag{22}$$

where $\mathbf{A}^H[k]$, $k = 1, 2, ...p$ are $m \times m$ matrices containing the multichannel AR model coefficients; whereas $\mathbf{C}_\chi[j]$ is the covariance matrix evaluated in the 'j'-time instant. Then, the system of equations in Eq. (22) can be solved efficiently via the Levinson-Wiggins-Robinson algorithm (Kay, 1988). Once the $\mathbf{A}^H[k]$ coefficient matrices have been determined, we can obtain the $m \times m$ covariance matrix of the driving noise vector process of the AR model from:

$$\mathbf{C}_w = \mathbf{C}_\chi[0] + \sum_{k=1}^{p} \mathbf{C}_\chi[-k]\mathbf{A}^H[k]. \tag{23}$$

Thus, after obtaining $\mathbf{C}_w = E\{\boldsymbol{\omega}[n]\boldsymbol{\omega}[n]^T\}$, where the hermitian operator has been substituted by a transpose operator due to all the samples are real; the driving noise process, $\boldsymbol{\omega}[n]$, can be accomplished as was indicated in (Baddour & Beaulieu, 2002). But first we need to compute the factorization $\mathbf{C}_{w} = \mathbf{L}\mathbf{L}^{T}$. If $\mathbf{C}_{w}$ is positive definite, a Cholesky decomposition is performable using the interval Cholesky method proposed in (Alefeld & Mayer, 1993) in order to include the desired correlation among scintillation sequences, with $\mathbf{L}$ being a lower triangular matrix (Beaulieu & Merani, 2000; Ertel & Reed, 1998). So, the driving process is then generated by the product $\boldsymbol{\omega}[n] = \mathbf{L}\mathbf{z}[n]$, where $\mathbf{z}[n]$ is an $m \times 1$ vector of independent zero mean Gaussian variates with unit variance and a autocorrelation function expressed as:

$$\mathbf{R}_{zz} = E\{\mathbf{z}[n]\mathbf{z}^{T}[n]\} = \mathbf{I}_{\mathbf{m}}, \tag{24}$$

where $\mathbf{I}_{\mathbf{m}}$ is the 'm'-element identity matrix. Finally,

$$\chi[n] = -\sum_{k=1}^{p} \mathbf{A}[k]\chi[n-k] + \mathbf{w}[n]. \tag{25}$$

But if $\mathbf{C}_{w}$ is not positive definite, then an alternative efficient decomposition algorithm that let the matrix be factorized was proposed in (Jurado-Navas & Puerta-Notario, 2009).

In addition, as said in the introduction, we can simplify the model proposed in (Jurado-Navas & Puerta-Notario, 2009) by an unrealistic but reasonably accurate space-time separable statistics model with a reduced computational load if it is compared with the complete model. Hence, we work directly with the covariance matrix, $\mathbf{C}_{\chi}$, unlike the work proposed in (Jurado-Navas & Puerta-Notario, 2009), where the matrix to be decomposed is $\mathbf{C}_{w}$.

Thus, when $\mathbf{C}_{\chi}$ is positive definite, as in the Gaussian approximation employed in (Zhu & Kahn, 2002), a Cholesky decomposition is performable using the interval Cholesky method proposed in (Alefeld & Mayer, 1993) in order to include the desired correlation among scintillation sequences. Hence we find a lower triangular matrix $\mathbf{L}$ such that $\mathbf{C}_{\chi} = \mathbf{L}\mathbf{L}^{H}$ in a similar way as in (Beaulieu & Merani, 2000; Ertel & Reed, 1998).

4.2 Constructing the coloring matrix

As we have already said, the AR model presented in (Jurado-Navas & Puerta-Notario, 2009) can be simplified by directly coloring independent Gaussian sequences first between them and then in time (space-time separable statistical model), avoiding the realization of the AR model. Obviously, this procedure is unrealistic because it implies that Taylor's hypothesis is not considered. However, numerical results obtained (and included through this chapter) show that this simplification behaves as a good approximation in terms of burst error rate.

Thus, we can directly consider the auto-covariance matrix of the log-amplitude, $\mathbf{C}_{\chi}$. As commented before, when $\mathbf{C}_{\chi}$ is positive definite, a Cholesky decomposition is performable by using the interval Cholesky method proposed (Alefeld & Mayer, 1993) in order to include the desired correlation among scintillation sequences. Hence we find a lower triangular matrix, $\mathbf{L}$, as a coloring matrix such that $\mathbf{C}_{\chi} = \mathbf{L}\mathbf{L}^{H}$ in a similar way as in (Ertel & Reed, 1998).

Nevertheless, $\mathbf{C}_{\chi}$ may not be positive definite so the Cholesky decomposition is not always feasible. Although any theoretical covariance matrix must be positive or, at least, semipositive definite, when such matrices are processed on a computer, small deviations from theory are introduced by the limits of floating point computations, inducing numeric inconsistencies. In this respect, there are no guarantees that the finite precision representation of the matrix can ensure positive definiteness, even more when the Cholesky algorithm is unstable for positive definite matrices that have one or more eigenvalues close to 0, as it is explained in

(Holton, 2004). In (Abramovich et al., 2001), the particular problem of non-positive definite matrices that arise from characterizing a realistic system is investigated in detail, showing that in 988 outcomes of their 1000 Monte Carlo trials, gave rise to a non-positive definite covariance matrix, although the corresponding "contracted" matrix may well be positive definite. In addition, in most practical situations the covariance matrix must be estimated from scintillation measurements (Monserrat et al., 2007; Moore et al., 2005) and outliers and other special situations as urban canopies may induce that correlation matrices derived from measurements are not always guaranteed to be positive definite, although a theoretical correlation matrix must always be.

In such cases, a real Schur decomposition is proposed (Golub & van Loan, 1996). Since the symmetric matrix $\mathbf{C}_\chi \in \Re^{mxm}$, then there exists an orthogonal matrix, $\mathbf{Q} \in \Re^{mxm}$, such that

$$\mathbf{Q}^T\mathbf{C}_\chi\mathbf{Q} = \mathbf{\Lambda} = \text{diag}(\lambda_1, ...\lambda_m) \tag{26}$$

as was shown in (Golub & van Loan, 1996), where superscript T denotes the transpose and $\lambda_i, \forall i = 1...m$, are the eigenvalues of $\mathbf{C}_\chi$. In this case, we allow $\mathbf{C}_\chi$ to have zero-eigenvalues. But however, as we will explain later, all the eigenvalues must be either zeros or positives. Unluckily, there will exist particular cases where $\mathbf{C}_\chi$ might have any negative eigenvalue, as was indicated above. When this circumstance occurs, an adjustment of the Schur decomposition will be accomplished in order to obtain a positive semi-definite approximation, $\widetilde{\mathbf{C}}_\chi$={$\widetilde{c}_\chi$(i,j)}, to the original auto-covariance matrix of the log-amplitude, $\mathbf{C}_\chi$, by minimizing the distance (Halmos, 1972):

$$\delta(\mathbf{C}_\chi) = \min_{\widetilde{\mathbf{C}}_\chi = \widetilde{\mathbf{C}}_\chi^T \geq 0} \|\mathbf{C}_\chi - \widetilde{\mathbf{C}}_\chi\|, \tag{27}$$

where $\|\cdot\|$ represents the norm of the matrix $\mathbf{C}_\chi - \widetilde{\mathbf{C}}_\chi$. We distinguish two main situations (Jurado-Navas & Puerta-Notario, 2009) corresponding to minimize the Frobenius norm (Golub & van Loan, 1996) or the the p-norms (with $p = 1, 2, \infty$), respectively. In both cases, we can substitute the diagonal matrix $\mathbf{\Lambda}$ by a resulting matrix written as $\mathbf{R} = \mathbf{\Lambda} + \mathbf{Y}$, where $\mathbf{Y}$ is a perturbation matrix obtained after minimizing Eq. (27) in any of the two situations mentioned above. After that, and for any of these two scenarios, we can form the coloring matrix, $\mathbf{K}$, as $\mathbf{K} = \mathbf{Q}(\mathbf{R})^{1/2}$ in order to generate the correlated log-normal scintillation samples. Here it is shown why we need that $\mathbf{C}_\chi$ were approximated by a positive semi-definite matrix if any eigenvalue of $\mathbf{C}_\chi$ is negative. In this case,

$$\widetilde{\mathbf{C}}_\chi = \mathbf{K}\mathbf{K}^T = \left(\mathbf{Q}\left(\mathbf{\Lambda}+\mathbf{Y}\right)^{1/2}\right)\left(\mathbf{Q}\left(\mathbf{\Lambda}+\mathbf{Y}\right)^{1/2}\right)^T = \mathbf{Q}\mathbf{R}\mathbf{Q}^T; \tag{28}$$

however, if all eigenvalues of $\mathbf{C}_\chi$ are positive, then

$$\mathbf{C}_\chi = \mathbf{K}\mathbf{K}^T = \left(\mathbf{Q}\mathbf{\Lambda}^{1/2}\right)\left(\mathbf{Q}\mathbf{\Lambda}^{1/2}\right)^T = \mathbf{Q}\mathbf{\Lambda}\mathbf{Q}^T. \tag{29}$$

Let us see these two scenarios in detail:

4.2.1 General scenario

If any λ_i in $\mathbf{\Lambda}$ is negative, then we can approximate the matrix $\mathbf{\Lambda}$ substituting every negative eigenvalue for 0. The resulting matrix may be written as

$$\mathbf{R} = \mathbf{\Lambda} + \mathbf{Y}, \tag{30}$$

where $\mathbf{Y}$ is a diagonal perturbation matrix with diagonal elements, $\{v_i\}_{i=1}^{m}$, of

$$v_i = \begin{cases} -\lambda_i, & \text{if } \lambda_i < 0; \\ 0, & \text{if } \lambda_i \geq 0; \end{cases} \qquad \forall \text{i} = 1,2...\text{m}. \tag{31}$$

In this case, the approximation $\widetilde{\mathbf{C}}_{\mathcal{X}} = \mathbf{QRQ}^T$ is proven to optimize the Frobenius norm if $(v_i + \lambda_i) \to 0$, and with the constraint of having a positive semi-definite solution matrix, $\widetilde{\mathbf{C}}_{\mathcal{X}}$; where the Frobenius norm is detailed in (Golub & van Loan, 1996) and represented by

$$\|\mathbf{A}\|_F = \sqrt{\sum_{i=1}^{m} \sum_{j=1}^{m} |c_{\mathcal{X}}(\text{i,j}) - \widetilde{c}_{\mathcal{X}}(\text{i,j})|^2}. \tag{32}$$

4.2.2 Specific scenario

If instead of employing the Frobenius norm, the expression (27) is optimized for the relevant 2−norm matrix defined as:

$$\|\mathbf{C}_{\mathcal{X}} - \widetilde{\mathbf{C}}_{\mathcal{X}}\|_2 = \sqrt{\rho\left\{(\mathbf{C}_{\mathcal{X}} - \widetilde{\mathbf{C}}_{\mathcal{X}})^H (\mathbf{C}_{\mathcal{X}} - \widetilde{\mathbf{C}}_{\mathcal{X}})\right\}}, \tag{33}$$

then we can obtain a new and different solution for the same problem. In equation (33), $\rho\left\{(\mathbf{C}_{\mathcal{X}} - \widetilde{\mathbf{C}}_{\mathcal{X}})^H (\mathbf{C}_{\mathcal{X}} - \widetilde{\mathbf{C}}_{\mathcal{X}})\right\}$ is the spectral radius of the matrix $(\mathbf{C}_{\mathcal{X}} - \widetilde{\mathbf{C}}_{\mathcal{X}})^H (\mathbf{C}_{\mathcal{X}} - \widetilde{\mathbf{C}}_{\mathcal{X}})$, defined as the supremum among the absolute values of its eigenvalues. Obviously, the hermitian operator can be substituted by a transpose operator since the samples are all real. As a characteristic feature, optimizing the 2−norm entails, in general, multiple solutions for $\widetilde{\mathbf{C}}_{\mathcal{X}}$, as a main difference with respect to the previous situation.

Again, we define $\mathbf{R} = \mathbf{\Lambda} + \mathbf{Y}$, being $\mathbf{Y}$ the perturbation matrix. One of the possible solutions for $\mathbf{Y}$ that let $\mathbf{R}$ be a semi-definite positive matrix is obtained by constructing $\mathbf{Y}$ as a diagonal matrix whose elements are defined as $\{v_i = -\lambda \ \ \forall \, \text{i} = 1...m\}$, being λ the highest among the absolute values of the negative eigenvalues of the matrix $\mathbf{C}_{\mathcal{X}}$. Obviously, as in the above scenario, we obtain greater accuracies when smaller magnitudes were summed to $\mathbf{\Lambda}$. The limit, again, is the necessary magnitude that let the negative eigenvalue be canceled and so, $\mathbf{C}_{\mathcal{X}}$ were approximated to the closest positive semi-definite matrix. In this way, this second scenario is proven to minimize the p-norms (with $p = 1, 2, \infty$) since $\mathbf{Y}$ is a diagonal matrix in which all its entries have the same value. These norms can be consulted in (Golub & van Loan, 1996).

As final comment to this second scenario, we can remark that the great resemblance obtained between $\mathbf{C}_{\mathcal{X}}$ and $\widetilde{\mathbf{C}}_{\mathcal{X}}$ is based on the orthogonality of the rows of the matrix $\mathbf{Q}$. For example, suppose that the covariance matrix is non-positive definite expressed as

$$\mathbf{C}_{\mathcal{X}} = \begin{pmatrix} 0.100 & 0.079 & 0.010 \\ 0.079 & 0.100 & 0.079 \\ 0.010 & 0.079 & 0.100 \end{pmatrix}_{3\times 3}. \tag{34}$$

Hence, applying the decomposition shown in scenario 2, we obtain that $\widetilde{\mathbf{C}}_{\mathcal{X}} = \mathbf{C}_{\mathcal{X}}$, except for the principal diagonal, that now is $\widetilde{c}_{\mathcal{X}}(i,i) = 0.106 \ \forall i = 1...3$, i.e.:

$$\mathbf{C}_{\mathcal{X}} = \begin{pmatrix} 0.106 & 0.079 & 0.010 \\ 0.079 & 0.106 & 0.079 \\ 0.010 & 0.079 & 0.106 \end{pmatrix}_{3\times 3}. \tag{35}$$

Finally, if the original auto-covariance matrix is not symmetric, then the Schur decomposition is written as

$$\mathbf{C}_{\chi} = \mathbf{QUQ}^{T}, \tag{36}$$

where $\mathbf{U} \in \Re^{nxn}$ is upper triangular as was shown in (Golub & van Loan, 1996). In these circumstances, we can form the matrix $\mathbf{\Lambda}$ taking into account solely the diagonal elements of $\mathbf{U}$ before applying any of the two approximations proposed in this paper.

4.3 Generation of turbulent spatially-correlated channels

Now we can form the coloring matrix, $\mathbf{K} \in \Re^{mxm}$

$$\mathbf{K} = \mathbf{Q}\left(\mathbf{\Lambda} + \mathbf{Y}\right)^{1/2}, \tag{37}$$

in order to generate the correlated log-normal scintillation samples. Then, it follows that (Jurado-Navas & Puerta-Notario, 2009)

$$\mathbf{KK}^{T} = \left(\mathbf{Q}\left(\mathbf{\Lambda} + \mathbf{Y}\right)^{\frac{1}{2}}\right)\left(\mathbf{Q}\left(\mathbf{\Lambda} + \mathbf{Y}\right)^{\frac{1}{2}}\right)^{T} = \mathbf{Q}\left(\mathbf{\Lambda} + \mathbf{Y}\right)^{\frac{1}{2}}\left(\left(\mathbf{\Lambda} + \mathbf{Y}\right)^{\frac{1}{2}}\right)^{T}\mathbf{Q}^{T} = \mathbf{Q}(\mathbf{\Lambda} + \mathbf{Y})\mathbf{Q}^{T} = \widetilde{\mathbf{C}}_{\chi}, \tag{38}$$

as was shown in Eq. (28), where $\widetilde{\mathbf{C}}_{\chi} = \mathbf{C}_{\chi}$ if there does not exist any negative element in diagonal matrix $\mathbf{\Lambda}$ written in (26). Equation (37) shows why we need that $\mathbf{C}_{\chi}$ were approximated by a positive semi-definite matrix if any eigenvalue of $\mathbf{C}_{\chi}$ is negative even when a Schur decomposition could be always accomplished if the starting matrix is squared.
Next, define $\mathbf{Z} = \left[z^{(1)}[n], z^{(2)}[n], \ldots z^{(m)}[n]\right]^{T}$ as a set of uncorrelated white Gaussian signals. Its correlation matrix, R_{ZZ}, is given by

$$\mathbf{R_{ZZ}} = E\{\mathbf{z}[n]\mathbf{z}^{T}[n]\} = \mathbf{I_m}, \tag{39}$$

where $\mathbf{I_m}$ is the 'm'-element identity matrix. By calculating $\mathbf{w}[n] = \mathbf{Kz}[n]$, being

$$\mathbf{w}[n] = \left[w^{(1)}[n], w^{(2)}[n], \ldots w^{(m)}[n]\right]^{T}, \tag{40}$$

the desired auto-covariance matrix of the log-amplitude fluctuations is obtained since

$$E\{\mathbf{w}[n] \cdot \mathbf{w}^{T}[n]\} = E\{\mathbf{K} \cdot \mathbf{z}[n] \cdot \mathbf{z}[n]^{T} \cdot \mathbf{K}^{T}\} = \mathbf{KK}^{T} = \widetilde{\mathbf{C}}_{\chi}. \tag{41}$$

Furthermore, every $w^{(i)}[n], \forall i = 1...m$ in Eq. (40) remains statistically Gaussian so it is possible to filter them in the way proposed in (Jurado-Navas et al., 2007) in order to obtain $\alpha_{sc}^{(i)}(t)$ for each of the m receivers. The filter employed in each branch is the Gaussian filter shown in (Jurado-Navas et al., 2007). Therefore, the output signal of these filters is the log-amplitude fluctuations, $\chi^{(i)}(t)$ $\forall i = 1...m$, for each receiver. These outputs exhibit a Gaussian probability density function and have the desired covariance matrix, $\mathbf{C}_{\chi}$, among sequences but without its inherent time-dependencies that would be enforced by the frozen-in hypothesis, according to the space-time separable statistics approximation imposed in this chapter. Next, its probability density function is converted from Gaussian to lognormally distributed, generally accepted for the irradiance fluctuations under weak turbulence conditions. Figure 1 shows clearly the overall process.
In this respect, it is possible to employ the same procedure explained in this paper but knowing that, instead of the log-normal employed here, a Beckman probability density much

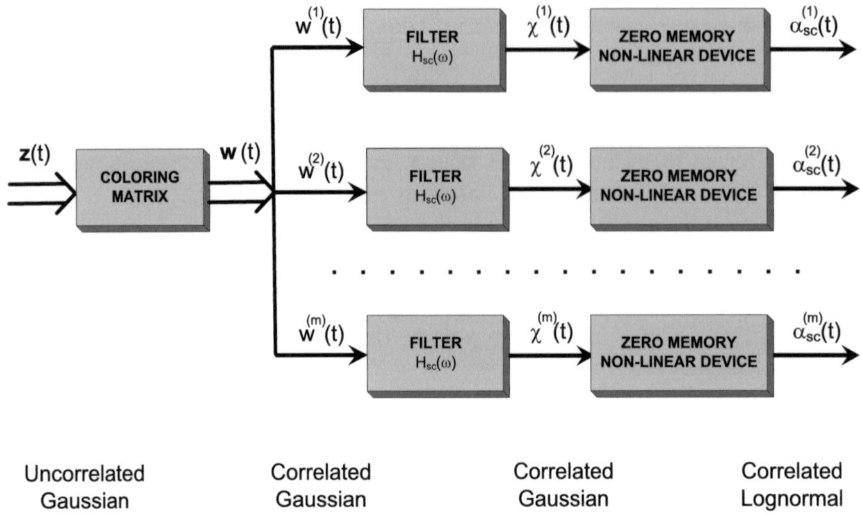

Fig. 1. Block diagram representing the generation of 'm' equal power log-normal scintillation sequences with a space-time separable statistics approximation.

more accurately reflects the statistics of the intensity scintillations (Hill & Frehlich, 1997) if Rytov variance increases even beyond the limits of the weak turbulence regime; or even the recently discovered Málaga probability density function (Jurado-Navas et al., 2011b), also very accurate with the statistics of the intensity scintillations.

5. System model

To study the performance of different values of spatial CC coefficients, ρ_{ij}, between points i and j in the receiver plane, intensity modulation and direct detection (IM/DD) links are assumed operating at a laser wavelength of 830 nm through a 250 m horizontal path at a bit rate of 50 Mbps. Assume three receivers in the system, where a conventional equal-gain combining (EGC) of diversity branches is implemented. Figure 2 shows the temporal behavior of correlated scintillation sequences for these three different receivers with a CC coefficient of $\rho_{12} = 0.56$ and $\rho_{13} = 0.1$ respectively, for this two extreme scenarios: an AR model, as in (Jurado-Navas & Puerta-Notario, 2009), and the space-time separable statistics approximation employed in this chapter. The component of the wind velocity, $u_{\perp}$, transverse to the propagation direction is fixed to $u_{\perp} = 20$ m/s, where ρ_{ij} is the normalized CC coefficient between points i and j in the receiver plane. Clearly, the election of a 20 m/s wind speed in this chapter will not be by far the typical operational scenario unless one of the terminals is in motion or the optical link is settled in particular geographical locations specifically affected by strong wind (Campins et al., 2007); but, however, such value is selected for numerical convenience so that we can work with a lower computational cost, because the total amount of samples needed to obtain a scintillation sequence with the desired lognormal statistics is smaller than using more conventional values for $u_{\perp}$, but letting us extract the same conclusions than employing a standard velocity.

Hence, a different temporal variability is shown in Figure 2 (a) and (b) for the EGC-combined scintillation sequence, being faster for the obtained sequence from a space-time separable statistics model. This different variability must have a different repercussion in the associated burst error rate curves, as shown below, where we followed Deutsch and Miller's

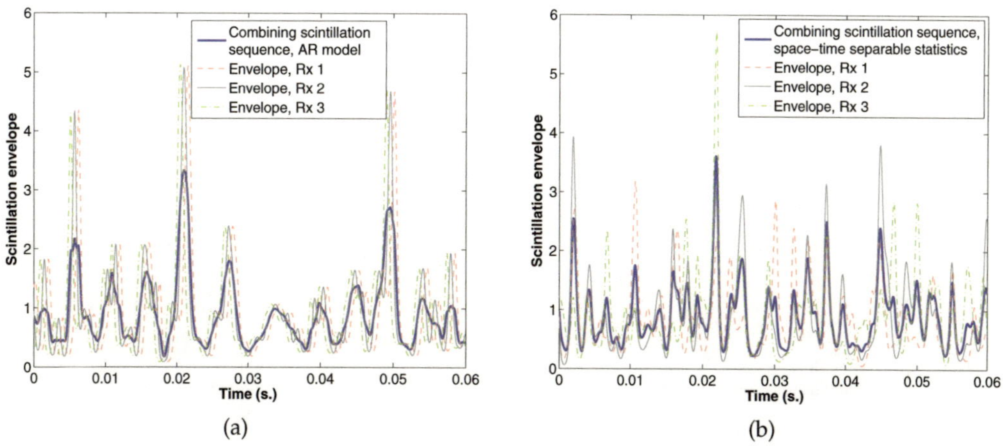

Fig. 2. Scintillation sequences generated from (a) an AR model; (b) a space-time separable statistics model, for a 3-receivers system. The EGC sequence is displayed in thicker solid line.

(Deutsch & Miller, 1981) definition of a burst error with lengths of 192, and 64 bits, not containing more than 4 consecutive correct bits ($L_b = 5$, as explained in (Deutsch & Miller, 1981)) any sequence of burst error.

Then, pulses with on-off keying format (OOK) and Gaussian shape (OOK-GS) with a duty cycle (d.c.) of 100% are adopted, where identical average optical power is transmitted for every simulated case representing the reference condition to establish the comparative analysis (Jurado-Navas et al., 2010). All these features are included in the system model, where its remarkable elements are: first, the channel model presented in (Jurado-Navas et al., 2007) corresponding to a turbulent atmospheric environment, but included in a m-branch reception as in (Jurado-Navas & Puerta-Notario, 2009), which represent the m different correlated turbulence-induced fadings at each of the optical receivers; secondly, a 500 kHz three-pole Bessel highpass filter for natural and artificial light adverse effects suppression; and, thirdly, a five-pole, Bessel, lowpass filter employed as a matched filter. As said above, a conventional EGC is implemented whereas the detection procedure considered is a maximum likelihood (ML) detection. The receivers employed in this paper are point receivers whereas the weather-induced attenuation is neglected so that we concentrate our attention on turbulence effects. Furthermore, the atmospheric-induced beam spreading that causes a power reduction at the receiver is also neglected because, in our specific case, we are considering a terrestrial link where beam divergence is typically on the order of 10 μRad. This temporal spreading may be considered at high data rate, as in (Jurado-Navas et al., 2009), particularly when operating in special scenarios where dust particles are likely present.

6. Numerical results

The first set of results are displayed in Figure 3 for a three-receivers system and for $\sigma_\chi^2 = 0.25$ and $\sigma_\chi^2 = 0.1$, where the CC coefficients between scintillation sequences are:

- $\rho_{12}=\rho_{21}=\rho_{23}=\rho_{32}=0.30$ and $\rho_{13}=\rho_{31}=0.008$
- $\rho_{12}=\rho_{21}=\rho_{23}=\rho_{32}=0.56$ and $\rho_{13}=\rho_{31}=0.1$
- $\rho_{12}=\rho_{21}=\rho_{23}=\rho_{32}=0.79$ and $\rho_{13}=\rho_{31}=0.1$

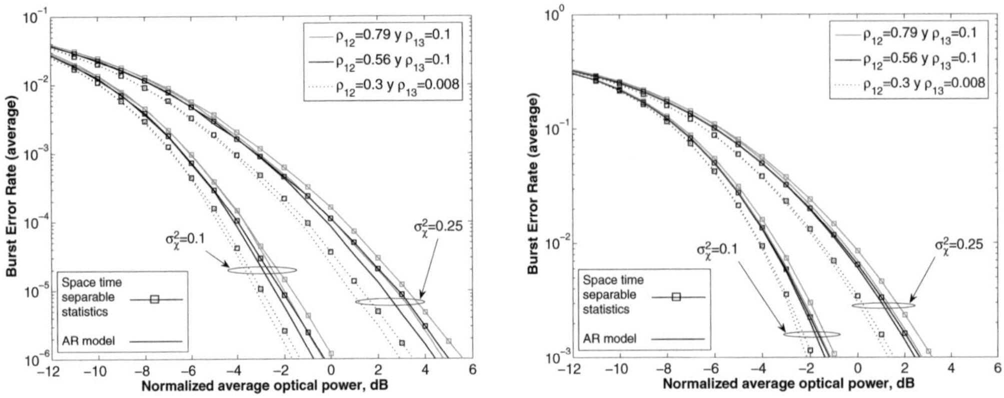

(a) (b)

Fig. 3. Burst error rate of a system with 3 receivers versus normalized average optical power using OOK and ML detection, for different values of ρ_{ij} and σ_χ^2, with a wind velocity of $u_\perp = 20$ m/s. The burst error length is established to (a) 192 bits, (b) 64 bits.

where, for the last case, we need to calculate the positive semidefinite approximation to the original autocovariance matrix of the log-amplitude, as was explained in this chapter for a space-time separable statistics model and in (Jurado-Navas & Puerta-Notario, 2009) for an AR model, because the original autocovariance matrix is not positive definite and can not be factorized by a classical Cholesky decomposition method. Anyway, the obtainment of the covariance matrix involving the process in both scenarios must be factored to finally build the set of Gaussian log-amplitude sequences measured at the different receivers in the system. As shown in Figure 3, there only exists a slight difference (approx. 1–2 optical dB at a burst error rate of 10^{-6} for a length of burst of 192 bits) between the obtained performance from the AR model ($\rho_l \to 0$) and the one obtained from the space-time separable statistics model ($\rho_l \to 1$) proposed in this paper. In fact, this latter model offers an accurate upper error bound for the link performance in terms of burst error rate. Similar conclusions may be deduced from the curves simulated with a length of burst of 64 bits. Nevertheless, from this Figure 3, we can observe that diversity reception can improve the performance of the link, but a gain penalty is shown when the CC coefficient between two receivers is high, especially if the log-amplitude variance, σ_χ^2, is larger. This fact can be a plausible reason to include the consideration of the spatial channel coherence as a key factor to fully evaluate the performance of atmospheric optical communication systems.

Furthermore, Figure 4 shows some obtained results when the CC coefficient has been established to ρ_{12}=ρ_{21}=ρ_{23}=ρ_{32}=0.56 and ρ_{13}=ρ_{31}=0.1, for a length of burst of 192 bits. Figure 4 (a) represents the behavior of an OOK-GS format with a 100% d.c. for different intensities of turbulence. As in Figure 3, the difference in performance is not significant for the two extreme scenarios studied in this chapter. Only when the log-amplitude variance, σ_χ^2, is getting stronger, such difference between scenarios gets higher, for instance, from 0.17 to 1.2 optical dB for $\sigma_\chi^2 = 0.01$ and $\sigma_\chi^2 = 0.5$ respectively at a burst error rate of 10^{-6}.

Next, the pair of curves displayed for $\sigma_\chi^2 = 0.15$ are taken as a reference in Figure 4 (b). To show the superiority of the different pulse, we analyze the performance of Gaussian pulse shapes in terms of the peak-to-average optical power ratio (PAOPR) and burst error rate. Note that the PAOPR is a favorable characteristic in IM/DD infrared links due to

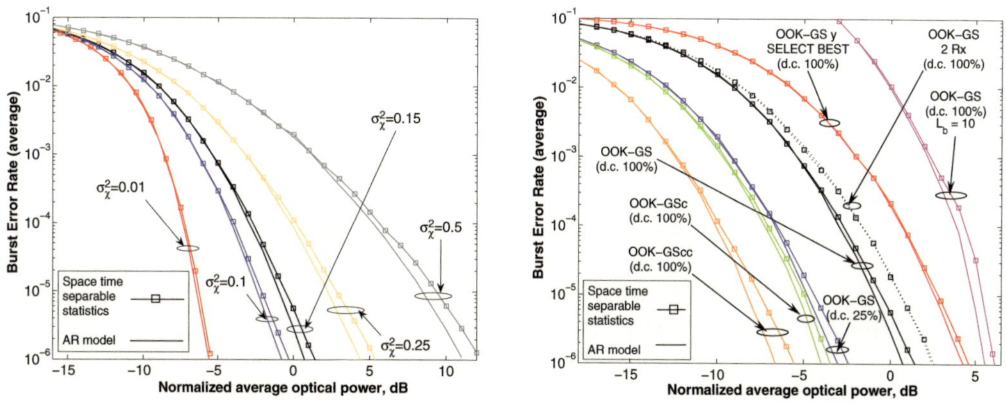

(a) (b)

Fig. 4. Burst error rate of a system with 3 receivers versus normalized average optical power using OOK format, EGC and ML detection, assuming $\rho_{12} = 0.56$ and $\rho_{13} = 0.1$, being $u_{\perp} = 20$ m/s, whereas the burst error length is established to 192 bits. An OOK-GS format with d.c. of 100% is represented in (a), for different values of σ_{χ}^2. Different transmission formats have been displayed in (b) for $\sigma_{\chi}^2 = 0.15$.

the inherent cuadratic response of the optical detector and the average power constraints previously mentioned (Jurado-Navas et al., 2010). For this reason, we use the increase in PAOPR as a figure of merit to compare the different pulses performance, taking into account that a burst error rate analysis must be performed to take into account the temporal variability of different combined sequences and verify that the increase in distortion of shorter pulses does not counteract the PAOPR benefits. In this sense, pulses have been modified by varying their statistics of the amplitude sequence with the purpose of increasing this PAOPR, for example with a reduced d.c. of 25%; or even using OOK-GS formats with memory to avoid the appearance of more than one pulse in sets of two (OOK-GSc) and three (OOK-GScc) consecutive symbol periods (Jurado-Navas et al., 2010) but maintaining the average optical power at the same constant level in all cases. The inclusion of memory on OOK formats allows to increase the separation in burst error rate between the AR model and space-time separable statistics one. The same conclusion may be deduced when different combining techniques are employed (an EGC technique offers more distant results than a select best scheme); or when a different number of receivers make part of the system, or even when the definition of a burst error is modified allowing to contain, for instance, up to 9 consecutive correct bits any sequence of burst error, as displayed in Figure 4 (b). Thus, when we get more complicated the transmission format with the aim of obtaining a better performance, then the difference in burst error rate between considering (AR model) or not (separable statistics model) the frozen-in hypothesis is getting increased in a more meaningful way, but offering this separable statistics model a reasonably accurate upper error limit in terms of burst error rate in all simulated cases with a reduced computational load.

7. Concluding remarks

When technical specifications may not permit sufficient receiver spacing, scintillation sequences may be spatially correlated. For these cases, an efficient method for generating an accurate approximation of 'm' equal power log-normal scintillation sequences with any CC coefficient is proposed in this paper, overcoming the restrictions of a Cholesky decomposition. Hence, the AR-model proposed in (Jurado-Navas & Puerta-Notario, 2009) and its inherent numerically ill-conditioned covariance matrix (Baddour & Beaulieu, 2002) may be avoided in many cases when calculating burst error rate curves due to the difference between the two extreme scenarios studied in this chapter is usually limited to approximately 2 dB at a burst rate of 10^{-6}. In this sense, the space-time separable statistics model proposed here can be used to consider spatial correlations among scintillation sequences without fear of making big mistakes and with the advantage of a reduced computational time. Thus, such separable statistics model may be seen as a highly accurate upper error bound of the whole model detailed in (Jurado-Navas & Puerta-Notario, 2009).

8. Acknowledgment

This work was supported by the Spanish Ministerio de Ciencia e Innovación, Project TEC2008-06598.

9. Nomenclature

$\mathbf{A}[k]$	$m \times m$ matrices containing the multichannel AR model coefficients.
C_n^2	Refractive-index structure parameter.
$\mathbf{C}_w$	Covariance matrix of the driving noise vector process of an AR model.
$\mathbf{C}_\chi$	Covariance matrix of the log-amplitude scintillation.
$\mathbf{C}_\chi[j]$	Covariance matrix of the log-amplitude scintillation evaluated in the j-time instant.
$\widetilde{\mathbf{C}}_\chi$	Positive semi-definite approximation of $\mathbf{C}_\chi$.
d_0	Correlation length of intensity fluctuations.
d_{ij}	Distance between points i and j in the receiver plane (m).
$\mathbf{E}$	Vector amplitude of the electric field.
$f_\chi(\chi)$	Probability density function of random log-amplitude scintillation.
$f_I(I)$	Probability density function of intensity fluctuations ($=f_{\alpha_{sc}}(\alpha_{sc})$).
I	Irradiance of the random field.
I_0	Level of irradiance fluctuation in the absence of air turbulence.
$\mathbf{I_m}$	m-element identity matrix.
k	Wave number of beam wave ($=2\pi/\lambda$).
$\mathbf{K}$	Coloring matrix.
L	Propagation path length.
$\mathbf{L}$	Lower triangular matrix obtained after applying a Cholesky decomposition.
l_0	Inner scale of turbulence.
$n(\mathbf{r})$	Index of refraction.
n_0	Average value of index of refraction.
n_1	Fluctuations of the refractive index.
$\mathbf{Q}$	Orthogonal matrix.
$\mathbf{r}$	Transverse position of observation point.
$U(\mathbf{r}, z)$	Complex amplitude of the field in random medium.
$u_\perp$	Component of the wind velocity transverse to the propagation direction.
$\mathbf{w}[n]$	Coloring Gaussian vector ($= \mathbf{Kz}[n]$).

$\mathbf{z}[n]$	Vector of independent zero mean Gaussian variates with unit variance.
$\alpha_{sc}(t)$	Time-varying atmospheric scintillation sequence.
$\chi(t)$	Log-amplitude fluctuation of scintillation.
$\mathbf{\Lambda}$	Diagonal matrix containing the eigenvalues of $\mathbf{C}_\chi$.
ϵ	Turbulent kinetic energy dissipation rate (m^2/s^3).
λ	Wavelength.
$\psi(\mathbf{r}, L)$	Phase perturbations of Rytov approximation.
ρ_{ij}	Normalized cross-correlation coefficient between points i and j in the receiver plane (m).
ρ_l	Degree of randomness as effect of the dynamic evolution of the turbulence (=$\rho_l = \tau_0/\tau_e$).
σ_I^2	Scintillation index (normalized irradiance variance).
σ_χ^2	Log-amplitude variance.
τ_0	Turbulence correlation time.
τ_e	Lifetime of turbulent eddies.
$\boldsymbol{\omega}[n]$	Driving noise vector process of an AR model.
$\mathbf{Y}$	Perturbation matrix employed to obtain $\widetilde{\mathbf{C}}_\chi$.

10. References

Abramovich, Y. I.; Spencer, N.K. & Gorokhov, A. Y. (2001). Detection-estimation of more uncorrelated Gaussian sources than sensors in nonuniform linear antenna arrays - part I: fully augmentable arrays. *IEEE Transactions on Signal Processing,* Vol. 49, No. 5 (May 2001), pp. 959–971, ISSN 1053-587X.

Alefeld, G. & Mayer, G. (1993). The Cholesky method for interval data. *Linear Algebra and its Applications,* Vol. 194, No.22, (November 1993), pp. 161-182, ISSN 0024-3795.

Al Naboulsi, M. & Sizun, H. (2004). Fog attenuation prediction for optical and infrared waves. *SPIE Optical Engineering,* Vol. 43, No. 2 (February 2004), pp. 319–329, ISSN 091-3286.

Andrews, L. C. & Phillips, R. L. (1998). *Laser Beam Propagation Through Random Media*, SPIE - The International Society for Optical Engineering, ISBN 081942787x, Bellingham, Washington, USA.

Andrews, L. C.; Phillips, R. L. & Hopen, C. Y. (2000). Aperture Averaging of Optical Scintillations: Power Fluctuations and the Temporal Spectrum. *Waves in Random Media,* Vol. 10, No. 1 (2000), pp. 53 – 70, ISSN 1745-5049.

Anguita, J. A.; Neifeld, M. A. & Vasic, B. V. (2007). Spatial correlation and irradiance statistics in a multiple-beam terrestrial free-space optical communication link. *OSA Applied Optics*, Vol. 46, No. 26 (September 2007), pp. 6561–6571, ISSN 1559-128X.

Arnon, S. (2003). Effects of atmospheric turbulence and building sway on optical wireless-communication systems. *Optics Letters,* Vol. 28, No. 2 (January 2003), pp. 129–131, ISSN 0146-9592.

Baddour, K.E.. & Beaulieu, N.C. (2002). Accurate simulation of multiple cross-correlated fading Channels. *IEEE International Conference on Communications (ICC) 2002,* pp. 267–271, ISBN 0-7803-7400-2, New York, NY, USA, April 28 - May 2, 2002.

Beaulieu, N. C. (1999). Generation of correlated Rayleigh fading envelopes. *IEEE Communication Letters*, Vol. 3, No. 6 (June 1999), pp. 172–174, ISSN 1089-7798.

Beaulieu, N. C. & Merani, M. L. (2000). Efficient simulation of correlated diversity channels. *IEEE Wireless Communications and Networking Conference (WCNC 2000),* Vol. 1, pp. 207–210, ISBN 0-7803-6596-8, Chicago, IL September 2000.

Burghelea, T.; Segre, E. & Steinberg, V. (2005). Validity of the Taylor hypothesis in a random spatially smooth flow. *Physics of Fluids*, Vol. 17, No. 10 (October 2005), art. no. 103101, pp. 103101–103101-8, ISSN 1070-6631.

Campins, J.; Aran, M.; Genovés, A. & Jansà, A. (2007). High impact weather and cyclones simultaneity in Catalonia. *Advances in Geosciences*, Vol. 12, (September 2007), pp. 115–120, ISSN 1680-7340.

Christen, A.; van Gorsel, E. & Vogt, R. (2007). Coherent Structures in Urban Roughness Sublayer Turbulence. *International Journal of Climatology*, Vol. 27, No. 14 (November 2007), pp. 1955–1968, ISSN 1097-0088.

Deutsch, L. J. & Miller, R. L. (1981). Burst Statistics of Viterbi Decoding, In: *The Telecommunications and Data Acquisition Progress Report*, TDA PR 42-64 (May and June 1981), pp. 187-193, Jet Propulsion Laboratory, California Institute of Technology, Pasadena, California.

Ertel, R.B. & Reed, J.H.. (1998). Generation of two equal power correlated Rayleigh fading envelopes. *IEEE Communications Letters*, Vol.2, No.10, (October 1998), pp. 276-278, ISSN 1089-7798.

Fante, R. L. (1975). Electromagnetic Beam Propagation in Turbulent Media. *Proceedings of the IEEE*, Vol. 63, No. 12 (December 1975), pp. 1669–1692, ISSN 0018-9219.

Fried, D.L. (1967). Aperture Averaging of Scintillation. *Journal Optical Society of America*, Vol. 57, No. 2 (February 1967), pp. 169–175, ISSN 0030-3941.

Golub, G.H. & van Loan, C.F. (1996). *Matrix Computations*, The John Hopkins U. Press, ISBN 0-8018-5414-8, Baltimore and London

Haas, S. M.; Shapiro, J. H. & Tarokh, V. (2002). Space-time codes for wireless optical communications. *EURASIP Journal on Applied Signal Processing*, vol. 2002, No. 3 (March 2002), pp. 211–220, ISSN 1110-8657.

Halmos, P.R. (1972). Positive Approximants of Operators. *Indiana University Mathematics Journal*, Vol.21, No.10, (October 1972), pp. 951-960, ISSN 0022-2518.

Hill, R. J. & Frehlich, R. G. (1997). Probability distribution of irradiance for the onset of strong scintillation. *Journal of the Optical Society of America A*, Vol. 14, No. 7 (July 1997), pp. 1530–1540, ISSN 0740-3232.

Holton, G.A. (2004). *Value at Risk: Theory and Practice*, Academic Press, ISBN 978-0123540102, San Diego, USA.

Ibrahim, M.M. & Ibrahim A.M. (1996). Performance analysis of optical receivers with space diversity reception. *IEE Proceedings on Communications*, Vol. 143, No. 6 (December 1996), pp. 369–372, ISSN 1350-2425.

Ishimaru, A. (1997) *Wave Propagation and Scattering in Random Media*, IEEE Press and Oxford University Press, Inc. vol. 1-2, ISBN 0-7803-4717-X, New York, USA.

Juarez, J. C.; Dwivedi, A.; Hammons, A. R.; Jones, S. D.; Weerackody, V. & Nichols, R.A. (2006). Free-Space Optical Communications for Next-Generation Military Networks. *IEEE Communications Magazine*, Vol. 44, No. 11 (November 2006), pp. 46–51, ISSN 0163-6804.

Jurado-Navas, A.; García-Zambrana, A. & Puerta-Notario A. (2007). Efficient lognormal channel model for turbulent FSO communications. *IEE Electronics Letters*, Vol. 43, No. 3 (February 2007), pp. 178 – 180, ISSN 0013-5194.

Jurado-Navas, A. & Puerta-Notario A. (2009). Generation of correlated scintillations on atmospheric optical communications. *OSA Journal of Optical Communications and Networking*, Vol. 1, No. 5 (October 2009), pp. 452–462, ISSN 1943-0620.

Jurado-Navas, A.; Garrido-Balsells, J.M..; Castillo-Vázquez, M. & Puerta-Notario A. (2009). Numerical Model for the Temporal Broadening of Optical Pulses Propagating through Weak Atmospheric Turbulence. *OSA Optics Letters,* Vol. 34, No. 23 (December 2009), pp. 3662 – 3664, ISSN 0146-9592.

Jurado-Navas, A.; Garrido-Balsells, J.M.; Castillo-Vázquez, M. & Puerta-Notario A. (2010). An efficient rate-adaptive transmission technique using shortened pulses for atmospheric optical communications. *OSA Optics Express,* Vol. 18, No. 16 (August 2010), pp. 17346–17363, ISSN 1094-4087.

Jurado-Navas, A.; Garrido-Balsells, J.M.; Castillo-Vázquez, M. & Puerta-Notario A. (2011). A computationally efficient numerical simulation for generating atmospheric optical scintillations, In: Numerical Simulations / Book 2, Editor Dr. Jan Awrejcewicz, InTech, ISBN 978-953-307-1423-5, Vienna, Austria.

Jurado-Navas, A.; Garrido-Balsells, J.M.; Paris, J. F. & Puerta-Notario A. (2011). A unifying statistical model for atmospheric optical scintillation, In: *arXiv:1102.1915v1 [physics.optics]*, February 2011, Available from: http://arxiv.org/abs/1102.1915. An extended version to appear in: Numerical Simulations / Book 2, Editor Dr. Jan Awrejcewicz, InTech, ISBN 978-953-307-1423-5, Vienna, Austria.

Kay, S. M. (1988). *Modern Spectral Estimation: Theory and Application*, Prentice-Hall, ISBN 013598582x, Englewood Cliffs, NJ.

Lee, E. J. & Chan, V. W. S. (2004). Part I: Optical communication over the clear turbulent atmospheric channel using diversity. *IEEE Journal on Selected Areas in Communicactions*, Vol. 22, No. 9 (November 2004), pp. 1896–1906, ISSN 0733-8716.

Mercier, F.P. (1962). Diffraction by a Screen Causing Large Random Phase Fluctuations. *Mathematical Proceedings of the Cambridge Philosophical Society,* Vol. 58, No. 2 (April 1962), pp. 382–400, ISSN 0305-0041.

Monserrat, J.F.; Fraile, R. & Rubio, L. (2007). Application of alternating projection method to ensure feasibility of shadowing cross-correlation Models. *IET Electronics Letters,* Vol. 43, No. 13 (June 2007), pp. 724–725, ISSN 0013-5194.

Moore, C. I.; Barris, H. R.; Stell, M. F.; Wasiczko, L.; Suite, M. R.; Mahon, R.; Rabinovich, W. S.; Gilbreath, G. C. & Scharpf, W. J. (2005). Atmospheric turbulence studies of a 16 km maritime path. *Proceedings of SPIE: Atmospheric Propagation II*, SPIE, Vol. 5793, Orlando, FL, pp. 78–88, ISSN 9780819457783.

Muhammad, S.S.; Kohldorfer, P. & Leitgeb, E. (2005). Channel modeling for terrestrial free space optical links. *Proceedings of 2005 7th International Conference on Transparent Optical Networks*, IEEE, Barcelona, Spain, pp. 407–410, ISBN 0-7803-9236-1.

Papoulis, A. (1991). *Probability, Random Variables, and Stochastic Processes* (3rd edition), McGraw-Hill, ISBN 0070484775, New York, USA.

Razavi, M. & Shapiro J.H. (2005). Wireless optical communications via diversity reception and optical preamplification. *IEEE Transactions on Wireless Communications,* Vol. 4, No. 3 (May 2005), pp. 975–983, ISSN 1536-1276.

Strohbehn, J.W. (1968) Line-of-Sight Wave Propagation through the Turbulent Atmosphere. *Proceedings of the IEEE*, Vol. 56, No. 8, (August 1968), pp. 1301–1318, ISSN 0018-9219.

Strohbehn, J.W. (1971) Optical Propagation through the Turbulent Atmosphere. in *Progress in Optics*, Vol. 9, pp. 73 – 122, ISBN 0720415098, edited by E. Wolf (North-Holland, Amsterdam, 1971).

Strohbehn, J.W. (1978)*Laser Beam Propagation in the Atmosphere*, Springer, Topics in Applied Physics Vol. 25, ISBN 3-540-08812-1, New York, USA.

Strohbehn, J.W. & Clifford, S.F. (1967) Polarization and Angle-of-Arrival Fluctuations for a Plane Wave Propagated through a Turbulent Medium. *IEEE Transactions on Antennas and Propagation*, Vol. 15, No. 3 , (May 1967), pp. 416–421, ISSN 0018-926X.

Tatarskii, V. I. (1971). *The Effects of the Turbulent Atmosphere on Wave Propagation*, McGraw-Hill, ISBN 0 7065 06804, New York, USA.

Taylor, G.I. (1938). The Spectrum of Turbulence. *Proceeding of the Royal Society of London. Series A, Mathematical and Physical Sciences,* Vol. 164, No. 919 (February 1938), pp. 476–490.

Willis, G.E. & Deardorff, J. W. (1976). On the use of Taylor's hypothesis for diffusion in the mixed layer. *Quarterly Journal of the Royal Meteorological Society,* Vol. 102, No. 434 (October 1976), pp. 817 – 822, ISSN 0035-9009.

Zhu, X. & Kahn, J.M. (2002). Free-space optical communication through atmospheric turbulence channels. *IEEE Transactions on Communications,* Vol. 50, No.8, (August 2002), pp. 1293-1300, ISSN 0090-6778.

21

Climate System Simulations: An Integrated, Multi-Scale Approach for Research and Decision-Making

Ángel G. Muñoz, Alfredo Nuñez and Ramón J. Cova
Centro de Modelado Científico (CMC). Universidad del Zulia. Venezuela

1. Introduction

Climate physicists define the Climate System in terms of the different interactions taking place between hydrosphere, atmosphere, cryosphere, biosphere and lithosphere. Being the associated general thermo-hydrodynamic partial differential equation system so complex for analytical solving, it is usually integrated numerically involving a good deal of computational resources.

Moreover, today different spatial scales involve different physical parametrisations, and each forecast horizon (few days, seasonal, annual, decadal and climate change periods) of interest deserves a special treatment, mostly defined by the predictability of the Climate System and the characteristic response time of the interacting components at the corresponding temporal scale. Thus, it is presently customary to distinguish between large-, meso- and micro-scale numerical models, their descriptions ranging from global climate state to basin availability of hydrological resources. An integrated, multi-scale approach considering the output of the various models is of vital to understand at the different levels the behaviour of the Climate System, and thus offer useful tools for decision makers and stake holders.

In this chapter, after introducing a few fundamental concepts and equations in Section 2, and a hierarchy flux of information among the models for different scales in Section 3, the methodologies involving downscaling executions are discussed in detail, regarding both scientific research and policy-making applications. In section 4 we explain the usefulness of conducting several simulations (realisations) to partially reduce the inherent uncertainties. Later, in Section 5 we offer a plausible way to put into operation all the components, presenting several examples based on the experience acquired through a regional initiative known as the *Latin-American Observatory for Climate Events*. Some concluding remarks and suggestions for future research are presented in Section 6.

2. Fundamentals

In this section several fundamental aspects related to the definition of the Climate System, its temporal scales and the governing equations of the atmosphere and the oceans are discussed. While the formal definition in terms of the Climate Subsystems is standard, it is important to remark that different models tend to write the corresponding system of thermo-hydrodynamical equations in different ways, due to the employment of particular numerical methods, simplifications, coordinate systems or physical assumptions.

Nonetheless, for the sake of simplicity, we follow here an approach suggested by (Marshal et al., 2004), which enables a mathematical representation of both atmosphere and ocean dynamics via isomorphisms. This methodology has the advantage of providing an elegant way to better understand the underlying similarities between these subsystems by coupling physical quantities at the boundaries in a clear manner.

2.1 The Climate System and its scales

The Climate System (S) can be defined in terms of five subsystems, namely the atmosphere (A), hydrosphere (H), cryosphere (C), biosphere (B) and lithosphere (L) , and their complex, nonlinear interactions. These components can be described as non isolated, open and heterogeneous thermo-hydrodynamical systems, which are physically characterized by their corresponding mechanical (e.g. forces) and thermodynamical states (e.g. pressure, temperature, salinity). Actually A, H, C and B act as a cascading system involving mass, momentum and energy fluxes through their boundaries (Peixoto & Oort, 1992).
There is a general consensus in defining S as

$$S \equiv A \cup H \cup C \cup B \cup L \tag{1}$$

Due to the great complexity in the different interactions among the climate subsystems and taking into consideration the timescales of the involved phenomena, it is useful to define a hierarchy of internal systems in terms of the characteristic response time to stable state perturbations. First we consider the systems with shortest typical times, and the other components are considered to be part of the external systems. For example, the characteristic times associated to perturbations in the planetary boundary layer are in the order of minutes to hours, while for tectonic dynamic the timescale is in the order of tens of millons of years (Peixoto & Oort, 1992).
This hierarchy gives the possibility of defining the Climate System for a particular timescale in a simplified way without losing any important physical phenomena. If one is interested in weather forecast with timescales from a few hours to 1-2 weeks, then the only internal component is the atmosphere:

$$S \equiv A \tag{2}$$

considering in the boundary conditions the effects of the oceans, sea ice, land surface processess and other phenomena like being part of the external system. In a similar way, for studying the Climate System from months to decades, it is possible to write

$$S \equiv A \cup O \cup B \tag{3}$$

where the oceans O belong to the hydrosphere subsystem.
Basically, equations 2 and 3 are normally used today for hindcast simulations, weather and seasonal forecasts and climate change scenarios.

2.2 Coordinate systems

It is customary to use latitude and longitude as rectangular coordinates on a tangent plane located at a certain point on Earth's surface or above it. However, the real world is better described through non-orthogonal, *terrain-following* coordinate systems, especially if we need high resolution domains and to consider the local orography. As one should expect from this discussion, the selection of the vertical coordinate is one of the most important issues in modern numerical models. In this section a general approach is presented, reviewing briefly some typical vertical coordinates.

The altitude z (or the radial distance) is not the most convenient vertical coordinate for most applications (cf (Haltiner & Williams, 1980)). There is a general tendency to employ the pressure coordinates p or $\ln p/p_0$, being p_0 a reference level pressure (e.g. at sea level). Other common vertical coordinates are $\sigma = p/p_0$, a close modification called *eta* coordinate, the potential temperature θ and the isoentropic vertical coordinate. For details the reader can consult (Haltiner & Williams, 1980) and references therein.
It is possible to generalise the discussion considering a vertical coordinate ξ, which is a single-valued, monotonic function of the altitude. In general, ξ is a function x, y, z and t:

$$\xi \equiv \xi(x,y,z,t) \tag{4}$$

where x and y are horizontal cartesian coordinates. Thus, a scalar field A can be written as

$$A(x,y,\xi,t) \equiv A(x,y,z(x,y,\xi,t),t) \tag{5}$$

Now, the partial derivative with respect s (a dummy parameter denoting x, y or t), reads

$$(\partial_s A)_\xi = (\partial_s A)_z + \partial_z A\,(\partial_s z)_\xi \tag{6}$$

where the subscript z or ξ denotes the corresponding vertical coordinate. Since the vertical derivatives correspond to

$$\partial_z A = \partial_\xi A \partial_z \xi, \tag{7}$$

so that equation (6) becomes

$$(\partial_s A)_\xi = (\partial_s A)_z + \partial_\xi A \partial_z \xi\,(\partial_s z)_\xi \tag{8}$$

This expression can iteratively be used with $s = x$ and $s = y$ to construct the gradient of A and the bidimensional divergence of the vector field $\mathbf{B}$:

$$\nabla_\xi A = \nabla_z A + \partial_\xi A \partial_z \xi \nabla_\xi z \tag{9}$$

$$\nabla_\xi \cdot \mathbf{B} = \nabla_z \cdot \mathbf{B} + \partial_\xi \mathbf{B} \partial_z \xi \cdot \nabla_\xi z \tag{10}$$

For $s = t$,

$$(\partial_t A)_\xi = (\partial_t A)_z + \partial_\xi A \partial_z \xi\,(\partial_t z)_\xi\,. \tag{11}$$

The total derivative in terms of ξ is

$$D_t A = (\partial_t A)_\xi + \mathbf{V} \cdot \nabla_\xi A + \dot{\xi} \partial_\xi A \tag{12}$$

where $\mathbf{V}$ is the horizontal velocity and $\dot{\xi} = d\xi/dt$ is the vertical velocity.
Naturally, we also have to calculate the elements of Jacobian matrices, as we usually need to go from the rectangular coordinate system used for the computational domain, to the the real-world terrain-following coordinate system, and viceversa. The general curvilinear models are becoming more common today for they lead to better results at regional and microscale levels.

2.3 Atmosphere equations

As mentioned before, here we follow the approach advanced in (Marshal et al., 2004). The equations representing a compressible and hydrostatic atmosphere (for the non-hydrostatic

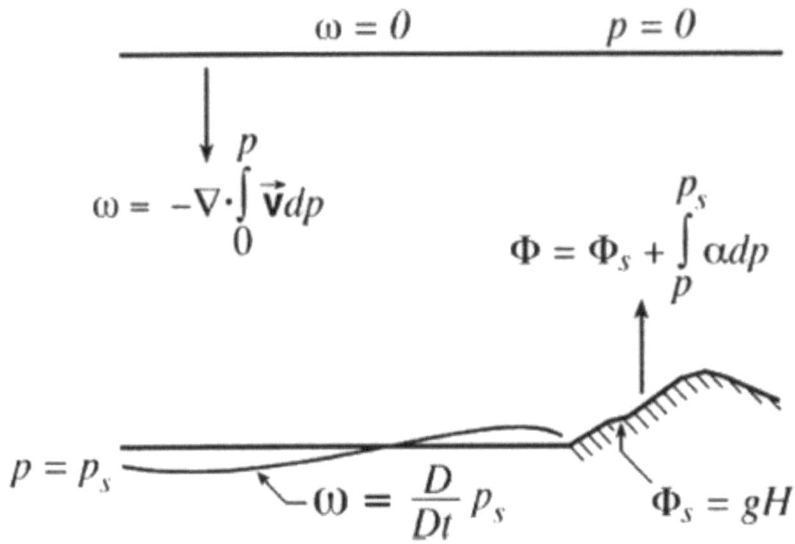

Fig. 1. Mathematical description of the atmosphere boundary conditions. Source: (Marshal et al., 2004)

case see (Adcroft et al., 2011)) in pressure coordinates are

$$D_t\mathbf{V} + f\mathbf{k} \times \mathbf{V} + \nabla_p\Phi = \mathbf{F} \tag{13}$$

$$\partial_p\Phi + \alpha = 0 \tag{14}$$

$$\nabla_p \cdot \mathbf{V} + \partial_p\omega = 0 \tag{15}$$

$$\alpha = \alpha(\theta, p) = \theta\partial_p\Pi \tag{16}$$

$$D_t\theta = \frac{Q_\theta}{\Pi} \tag{17}$$

$$D_t q = Q_q \tag{18}$$

where $\omega = D_t p$ denotes the vertical velocity in pressure coordinates, f the Coriolis parameter, $\mathbf{k}$ a versor along the vertical coordinate, $\Phi = gz$ the geopotential, α the specific volume, T the temperature, $\theta = c_p T/\Pi$ the potential temperature, $\Pi = c_p(p/p_0)^\kappa$ the Exner function and q the especific humidity. c_p corresponds to the especific heat at constant pressure, $\kappa = R/c_p$, with R the Rydberg's constant and $D_t = \partial_t + \mathbf{V} \cdot \nabla_p + \omega(\partial_p)$ is equivalent to (12) in pressure coordinates.

The terms $\mathbf{F}$, Q_θ and Q_q represent sources and sinks of momentum, heat and humidity, respectively, and are parametrised in the numerical models.

The boundary conditions are written as

$$\omega = \begin{cases} 0, & p = 0 \\ D_t p_s, & p = p_s(x, y, t) \end{cases} \tag{19}$$

The boundary condition for integrating the hydrostatic equation (14) is

$$\Phi = \Phi_s = gH, \tag{20}$$

valid for $p = p_s$, where p_s is the sea surface level pressure and H stands for a scalar field describing the terrain altitude in the lower boundary.
The surface pressure evolves according to

$$\partial_t p_s = \nabla \cdot (p_s < \mathbf{V} >) = 0 \tag{21}$$

where

$$< \mathbf{V} >= \frac{1}{p_s} \int_0^{p_s} dp\mathbf{V} \tag{22}$$

is the horizontal mean wind velocity. Figure 1 illustrates the case.

2.4 Ocean equations

The hydrostatic equations describing the dynamics of an incompressible ocean in the Boussinesq approximation and using depth coordinates are (Marshal et al., 2004)

$$D_t\mathbf{V} + f\mathbf{k} \times \mathbf{V} + \nabla_z \frac{p}{\rho_0} = \mathbf{F} \tag{23}$$

$$\partial_z \frac{p}{\rho_0} + g\frac{p}{\rho_0} = 0 \tag{24}$$

$$\nabla_z \cdot \mathbf{V} + \partial_z \omega = 0 \tag{25}$$

$$\rho = \rho(\theta, S, p) \tag{26}$$

$$D_t\theta = \frac{Q_\theta}{\Pi} \tag{27}$$

$$D_t S = Q_s \tag{28}$$

where $\omega = D_t z$ is the vertical velocity, p denotes pressure, ρ the density, ρ_0 a constant density reference, S the salinity and $D_t = \partial_t + \mathbf{V} \cdot \nabla_z + \omega(\partial_z)$ corresponds to (12) but in depth coordinates.
Again, $\mathbf{F}$, Q_θ and Q_s represent sources and sinks of momentum, heat and salinity, respectively, and are parametrised in the numerical models.
The boundary conditions are

$$\omega = \begin{cases} -\mathbf{V} \cdot \nabla H, & z = -H \\ D_t\eta = -(P - E), & z = \eta \end{cases} \tag{29}$$

with H being a scalar field describing the bathymetry ($-H$ is the sea bottom), η being the ocean surface and $(P - E)$ being the net difference between precipitation and evaporation. The boundary condition for the hydrostatic equation in this case reads

$$p = p_s \tag{30}$$

at $z = \eta$, where we recall that p_s is the sea level pressure.
The surface elevation evolves following

$$\partial_t \eta + \nabla \cdot (H + \eta) < \mathbf{V} >= P - E \tag{31}$$

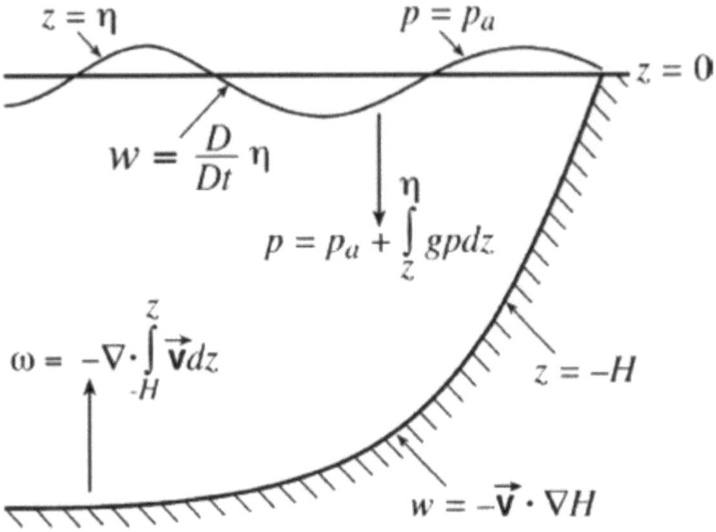

Fig. 2. Mathematical description of the ocean boundary conditions. Source: (Marshal et al., 2004)

where

$$< \mathbf{V} >= \frac{1}{H+\eta}\int_{-H}^{\eta} dz\mathbf{V} \tag{32}$$

is the horizontal mean wind velocity. See figure 2 for illustration.

2.5 Isomorphisms and physical coupling

By taking a look at the previous subsections it is easy to recognize the change in variables for writing the isomorphism. Choosing r as the new isomorphic variable, such that (Marshal et al., 2004)

$$\begin{array}{ccc} ocean \longleftrightarrow & isomorphism & \longleftrightarrow atmosphere \\ z & r & p \\ \omega & \dot{r} & \omega \\ \frac{p}{\rho_0} & \phi & \Phi \\ -g\frac{\rho}{\rho_0} & b & -\alpha \\ \theta & \theta & \theta \\ S & s & q \\ \eta & r_s^{'} & p_s \\ P-E & P_r & 0 \end{array} \tag{33}$$

the boundary conditions (19,20,29,30) automatically remain isomorphic too. An illustration is depicted in Figure 3.
Then, the general equations are

$$D_t\mathbf{V} + f\mathbf{k}\times\mathbf{V} + \nabla_r\phi = \mathbf{F} \tag{34}$$

$$\partial_r\phi - b = 0 \tag{35}$$

$$\nabla_r\cdot\mathbf{V} + \partial_r\dot{r} = 0 \tag{36}$$

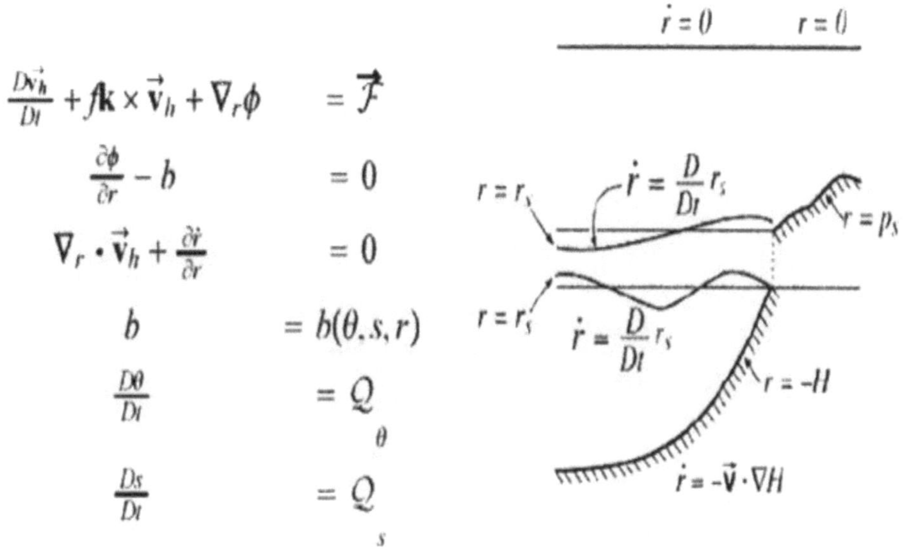

Fig. 3. Isomorphic relations and coupling. Source: (Marshal et al., 2004)

$$b = b(\theta, s, r) \tag{37}$$

$$D_t\theta = Q_\theta \tag{38}$$

$$D_t s = Q_s \tag{39}$$

where r is the vertical, isomorphic coordinate. The total derivative takes the form

$$D_t = \partial_t + \mathbf{V} \cdot \nabla A + \dot{r}\partial_r, \tag{40}$$

and

$$\nabla = \nabla_h + \mathbf{k}\partial_r, \tag{41}$$

with ∇_h being applied on the horizontal surfaces (constant r) and $\mathbf{k}\partial_r$ acting along the vertical coordinate. ϕ is associated with pressure or geopotential, b is the buoyancy, s is the especific humidity for the atmosphere or the salinity for the ocean, $\mathbf{F}$ represents the external forcings and dissipation on $\mathbf{V}$, Q_θ the external forcings and dissipation on θ and Q_s the ones on s.
The terms $\mathbf{F}$, Q_θ and Q_s are provided by physical parameterizations of the subgrid scale atmosphere and ocean fluxes.
The corresponding boundary conditions are

$$\dot{r} = \begin{cases} -\mathbf{V} \cdot \nabla R_{fixed}, & z = R_{fixed} \\ D_t r_s - P_r, & r = R_s \end{cases} \tag{42}$$

where

$$R_{fixed} = \begin{cases} -H, & \text{at sea bottom} \\ 0, & \text{at atmosphere top} \end{cases} \tag{43}$$

defines the location of the fixed boundary surface, while

$$R_s = R_0 + r_s \tag{44}$$

defines the location of the moving boundary surface, being

$$R_0 = \begin{cases} 0, & \text{at sea surface} \\ R_0(x,y) = p_s(x,y), & \text{at terrain surface} \end{cases} \tag{45}$$

The reference location of the moving boundary surface and its deviations are described by

$$r_s = \begin{cases} \eta, & \text{at sea surface} \\ p_s, & \text{at terrain surface} \end{cases} \tag{46}$$

Moreover,

$$P_r = \begin{cases} P - E, & \text{at sea surface} \\ 0, & \text{in the atmosphere} \end{cases} \tag{47}$$

is the volumetric flux through r_s.
It is important to remark at this level how the system of equations presented are so complex that they need to be solved numerically in the general case. The last section shows a natural way to couple the needed quantities at the boundaries (see figure 3), which sketchs the coupling between ocean and atmosphere, the two most dynamic components of the Climate System. Bearing this review of the fundamental equations in mind, it will be easy to consider the particular expressions used in the different numerical models.

3. An integrated, multi-scale approach

The rationale behind climate modeling is to mathematically express the different interactions present in the Climate System. This is ussually accomplished by means of

- Dynamical climate models
- Statistical climate models.
- Hybrid climate models.

The dynamical approach tries to describe the observed phenomenology using physics (Anderson, 2008), with sets of equations like the ones presented in the previous section. On the other hand, the statistical approach looks for the same goal, but it tries to recognize spatio-temporal patterns in the historical dataset of at least two different variables (usually known as the *predictor* and the *predictand*); it employs these patterns to build a mathematical model (Mason & Baddour, 2008), capable of reproducing the historical behaviour and to forecast the future, in analogous way to the dynamical approach. Finally, mixtures of both methodologies are also possible, entailing different kinds of hybrid models. The climate numerical simulations are the execution of these models. Executions reproducing the past are called *retrospective simulations* or *hindcasts*. Weather and seasonal forecasts, and climate change scenarios are examples of climate simulations looking at the future.
Each of the aforementioned approaches has its own pros and cons. For instance, the dynamical models need to solve the set of equations for each cell in the selected spatial domain, and thus they consume a lot of computational resources and are slow compared with the common statistical models. The latter, in turn, need homogeneous and quality datasets for the variables under study, an important issue in several regions of the planet. However, once the temporal

domain has been selected, the speed of the computations for all the methods is strongly dominated by the spatial resolution, even when in general the statistical methods will run many times faster than the dynamical ones. A coarse resolution implies less cells where to compute the models (physical, statistical or hybrid). The coarser the domain, the faster the computations, but the less the ability to accurately represent in a point the state of the Climate System.

In this section we review some of these aspects and discuss how to construct a multi-scale approach for climate research and decision-making.

3.1 General Circulation Models: Coupled vs non-coupled

The planetary-scale, dynamical numerical models are called General Circulation Models (GCMs), and they can be coupled (CGCMs) or non coupled (e.g. atmospheric GCMs - AGCMs, and oceanic GCMs - OGCMs), with typical spatial resolutions in the order of 2.5^o to 1°. The coupling makes reference to linking different models for mimetizing the various interactions of the Climate System components, following the ideas presented in section 2.1. Nonetheless, as it has been discussed previously, S can be simplified (see equation (2)) when considering certain temporal and spatial scales. Such cases are usually simulated by means of non-coupled GCMs, and due to their shorter execution times and some key advantages (see Mason (2008) and references therein), they have been the global dynamical models most widely utilised.

Coupled and non-coupled models may or may not coincide in their results, depending on several aspects. One of the main differences, as can be deduced from the previous discussion, is the inclusion or not of the various feedbacks. As an example, consider the simulation of the interactions between the atmosphere and the ocean on a seasonal (e.g. 3 months) scale. The coupled models are designed to guarantee the feedbacks, but the stand-alone atmospheric models consider the ocean effects via the boundary conditions (which in general evolve in time), without permiting any updates to the sea surface coming from the new atmospheric states. In other words, for these non-coupled atmospheric models to run it is first necessary to subscribe the evolution of the boundaries in a separate tier. This is why sometimes the stand-alone models are also called *two-tiered* models. One way to account for the differences among one-tiered and two-tiered simulations is to look at the energy balance between the surface and the top of the atmosphere. The radiative imbalance is usually less than 0.5 Wm^{-2}, which is considered acceptable for seasonal timescales. However, the Climate System's slow component interactions can provide severe bias that must be considered in detail (Hazeleger et al., 2010).

Amongst the main CGCMs used today are the CCSM-CESM (National Center for Atmospheric Research-NCAR Community Earth System Model (Blackmon et al., 2001)), COSMOS (Max Planck Institute-MPI Community Earth System Models (Roeckner et al., 2006)), HadGEM (Hadley Centre Global Environmental Model (Johns et al., 2006)) and CFS (NCEP Climate Forecast System (Saha et al., 2006)). Older and newer versions are available at a number of research and forecast centers around the world.

3.2 Seasonal forecast methodologies for GCMs

Both hindcast and forecast are important for climate simulations in research and decision-making. Retrospective simulations make use of grids filled with observations (e.g. gauge stations, satellite) for providing the GCMs' boundary conditions along the past period of interest while, obviously, there is no direct analog for a simulation of the future. The key idea here is that the GCM integrates exactly the same set of equations for the past or the future, the difference being on how the boundary evolves: in a hindcast, the observations are used for describing its evolution, while in a forecast there are several ways of predicting the behaviour of the boundaries.

Clearly, the sea surface temperature (SST) is one of the main modulators of the Climate System (see for example Peixoto & Oort (1992) and references therein). Indeed, modern GCMs need both the SST and the ice cover as boundary conditions, whose spatial patterns are known to vary on a monthly to seasonal basis. The way they are constructed to evolve defines the forecast methodology.

In the case of modern CGCMs, atmosphere, ocean and land-surface models run synchronously and interactively to describe not only the different component states, but also the boundary conditions evolution, simultaneously.

On the other hand, in two-tiered forecasts the tier-1 is associated to the SST and ice cover forecast, whereas the tier-2 is the AGCM. There are different ways to forecast in the tier-1. Here we study some principal methodologies for SST.

The simplest method -but not very reliable- is to prescribe the SST to behave as its climatological value, i.e. its monthly mean value over the last 30 to 50 years. Thus, the climatological January corresponds to all the 30 to 50 January values averaged over. This is done for each ocean cell (or ocean basin cell) each month. Naturally, this prescription is most probably destined to fail whenever years or seasons exhibit extreme events, like ENSO for instance.

The method most widely used is called *persistence* (Li et al., 2008). Also known as 'serial dependence' (Wilks, 2006), it assumes that the SST anomalies (aSST, from now on) in the preceding month or season will persist along the forecast period. Thus the *persisted SST* or *pSST* forecast for the following months is constructed as their corresponding climatological value plus the preceding ($t = 0$) month observed anomaly $aSST_0$. Over the extratropical oceans, it is customary to include a damping coefficient with an e-folding time of 3 months,

$$aSST(t) = aSST_0 e^{-t/3}, \qquad t = 0, ..., 3 \tag{48}$$

Another methodology is called *constructed analogues* or *caSST* (Van den Dool, 1994). Suggested in 1994, the rationale is to write the preceding month (base) aSST as a linear combination of the same month aSST for a long past period (at least 30 years, excluding the year in course). The coefficients of the linear combination are computed via classical least-squares minimization; the resulting weights are used to forecast the target months in terms of the subsequent base months in the past period. It is important to note that the constructed analogue is the same linear combination for all leads, i.e the weights persist.

Finally, we may find the aSST as tier-1, forecasted by a CGCM (see (Li et al., 2008)). For example, the Andean Observatory (Muñoz et al., 2010), a regional initiative which produces seasonal forecasts in the Andean countries, employs aSST from the CFS. Let us refer to this case as *cfsSST*.

Figure 4 compares two of the foresaid *cfsSST* and *pSST* methods.

Similar approaches can be followed for the ice cover, but very frequently it is prescribed to follow the climatological monthly variation. Figure 4 compares two of the foresaid cfsSST and pSST methods. Both realisations provide similar distributions and magnitudes of the accumulated seasonal precipitation. However, the differences between them are important, for they allow probable alternative precipitation behaviours in the final ensemble product (see Section 4).

Once the tier-1 is provided, the AGCM (tier-2) integrates the associated equations and gives all the required atmospheric variables.

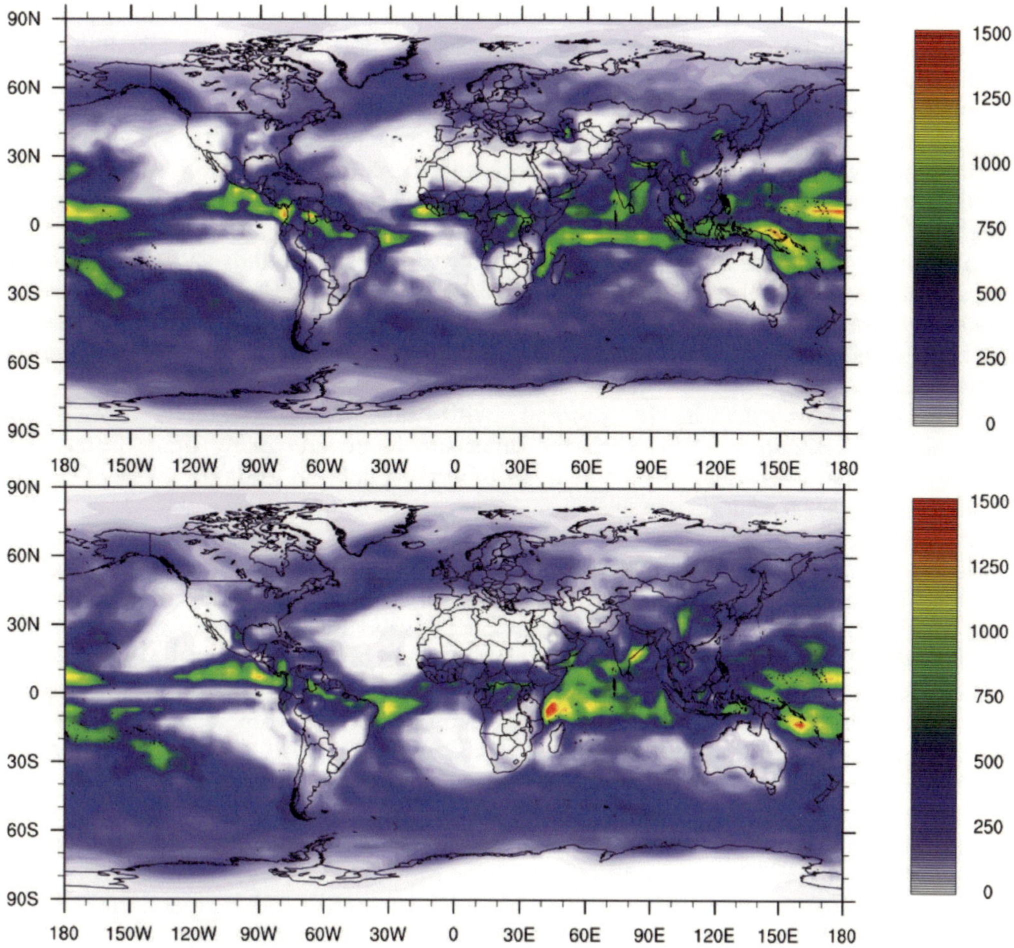

Fig. 4. Accumulated precipitation (in mm) for Apr-May-Jun 2011 using CAM and two forecast methodologies discussed for two-tiered models: *cfsSST* (above) and *caSST* (below). See main text.

3.3 Interpolation and Downscaling

Normally, the GCM output does not describe all the physical processes in one especific region of the planet. As pointed out before, different physical mechanisms are associated to different spatio-temporal scales, and so we normally need to increase either the spatial or the temporal resolution of the GCM output, or both. This resolution increase can be achieved by means of interpolations, statistical estimators or downscaling.

Interpolations change the resolution using a wide variety of mathematical expressions to provide new points on an array already in existence. For example, if the GCM output grid possesses a spatial resolution of 1°, this means that the mean distance between the main node points (i.e. the intersection of latitude and longitude lines) is about 111.11 km at the equator. An interpolation will provide more new node points to the grid, say each one at 56 km, thus increasing the spatial resolution. The main concern is that at this new resolution, different interpolation rules provide different values of the physical variable at the new points. Which rule is better? In addition, there is no guarantee that the interpolated fields will satisfy the original set of physical equations that provided the variables (Haltiner & Williams, 1980). A common interpolation rule nowadays is the bilinear interpolator, a 2D generalization of the standard linear interpolator.

Commonly included as interpolators (the difference is not always clear in the literature), the estimators use statistics (e.g. variance/covariance matrix, stochastic models with spatial dependence, variograms, unbiased linear regressions, see (Cressie, 1993)) to increase the spatial resolution of the fields. One of the most employed statistical estimators is the Krigging method (Cressie, 1993).

Finally, there are downscaling methods. In this case the spatial and temporal resolution increase is done through physical equations (dynamic downscaling, see for example (Murphy, 1999)) or statistical methods like principal component analysis or canonical correlation analysis (statistical downscaling, see (Mason & Baddour, 2008; Murphy, 1999) and references thererin).

The general consensus is to proceed with downscaling methods instead of interpolations/estimators, even when the latter are in general many times faster than the former. The downscaling needs analysis (observed data on grids) or GCMs fields to produce the higher resolution variables.

In statistical downscaling, models are constructed recognizing relationships between sets of variables through statistical analyses of time series, from historical observations or GCM output. For example, one can downscale the precipitation provided by a global model (the predictor) using the historical precipitation reported by rainfall gauge stations (the predictand). This process is accomplished, for instance, by constructing statistical models with principal component regressions or, more often, canonical correlation analysis (for details see (Mason & Baddour, 2008)). Sometimes this particular downscaling aimed at correcting the dynamical model output using observed data is known as Model Output Statistics (MOS), but indeed the MOS involves a more general set of processess (Wilks, 2006).

Another possibility is to downscale GCM outputs using higher resolution dynamical models, known as Regional Climate Models (RCMs). In this case, the physical equations are solved using as boundary and initial conditions the fields provided by the global model, ensuring physical consistency among the variables at the new spatial and temporal resolutions. However, it is important to bear in mind that at different scales the dynamical models require different *physical parametrisations* in order to represent sub-grid scale phenomena. There are often several parametrisations for the same spatial scale, and several possible configurations for the dynamical downscaling models, aimed at resolving the physics for the region of interest.

In the case of multi-scalar phenomena, a nesting procedure is used for RCMs, where the mother (or father) domain is fed by the GCM output, provides the necessary information for their sons and so on. Due to scarcity of computational resources, in the past a one-way nesting approach has been used. This means that the information flux goes only from mother to son. Today, a two-way nesting feeds back the mothers with the information of higher resolution fields. Several technical issues (e.g. the domain's location and size and its *buffering zone* configuration) must be taken into account in all these cases to ensure that the mass and energy fluxes through the lateral boundaries are adequately considered. For details see (Liang & Kunkel, 2001).

To illustrate the differences among the precipitation spatial patterns provided by the CAM (approximately at 2.5^o resolution) and the WRF (Skamarock et al., 2005) at 0.27^o resolution, see Figure 5. Here, their specific configurations correspond to those in operation at the Andean Observatory (Muñoz et al., 2010). The RCMs seem to be more adequate than the GCMs to simulate and forecast climate events because they recognise multi-scale patterns and higher

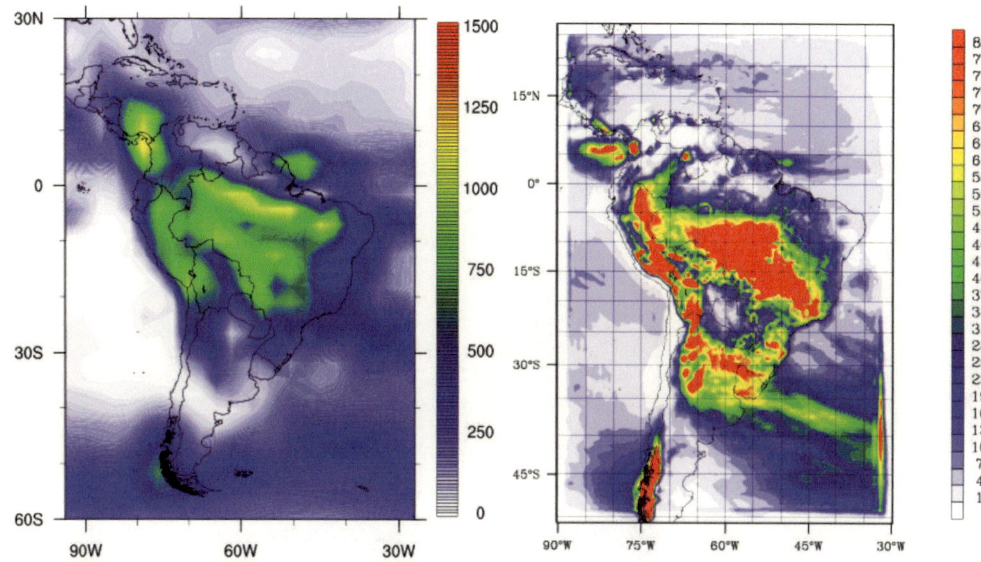

Fig. 5. Mean rainfall fields for season Jan-Feb-Mar 2011 provided by CAM (left) and the downscaling model WRF in its climate version (right). Source: the Andean Observatory (Muñoz et al., 2010)

resolution, but especial care must be exercised since the downscaling process may increase the inherent uncertainties.

3.4 Hierarchical flux approach

Hitherto, we have discussed how to perform climate simulations and forecasts using different tools, and how they can be related with each other. It is clear that in order to have an integrated, multi-scale approach for research and decision-making, especially if dealing with basin scale applications or the atmospheric dynamics over complex terrain, we need a system that considers all the representative interactions. Such a technique is described below.

The simplest way to take into account the different phenomena at the various scales in the Climate System is through a unified, fully coupled GCM at very high resolutions, such that there is no need to use any parametrisations because the physics can be resolved explicitly by the model equations. Despite some good efforts (Hazeleger et al., 2010), the computational (e.g. time execution and infrastructure) costs for such a seamless Earth System Model are so high that it will take several years before it becomes an operational standard. This is why it is necessary to stablish a hierarchical flux of information between the different models, and to execute them in a sequential mode to built up a multi-scale simulation system.

A three-level hierarchy can thus be defined (see Figure 6). Level I involves the various GCMs that can be used, at a coarse resolution, to provide the initial and boundary conditions for the RCMs and the predictors for the statistical downscaling models that make up the Level II. Tailored application models (e.g. Malaria (MacDonald, 1957; Recalde, 2010), ecodynamical (Tapias, 2010), fire (Chandler et al., 1983), drought (Palmer, 1968; Svoboda et. al, 2002) or off-line hydrological models (Liang & Xie, 2001)) using the Level II output as part of their own input, belongs to the hierarchy's Level III.

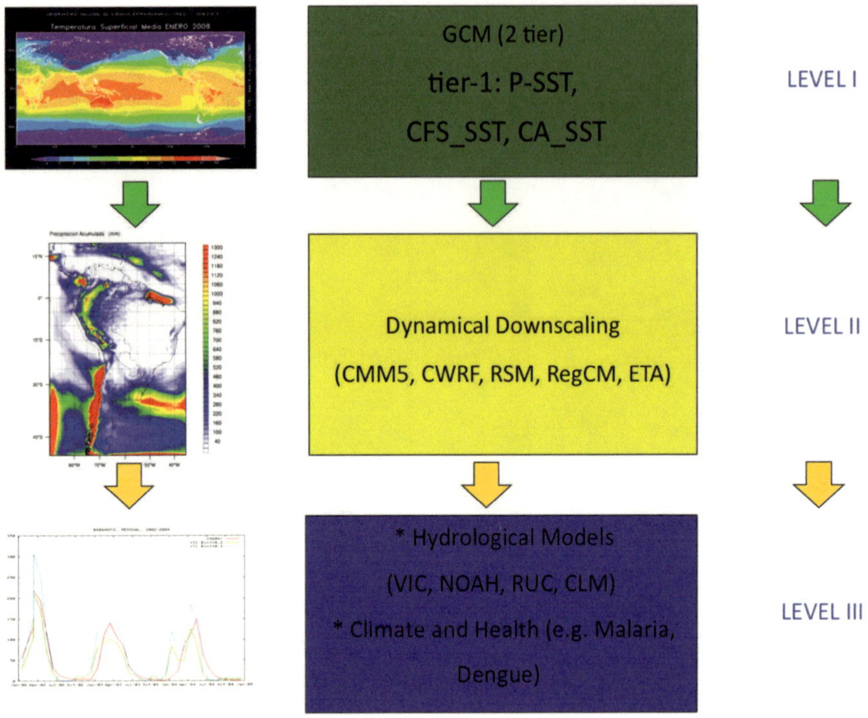

Fig. 6. The three level, two-way hierarchical information flux between climate related models. Source: (Muñoz et al., 2010)

We emphasise that the same hierarchical information flux works for both weather (short-term) and climate (seasonal to long-term) simulations. Statistical, dynamical or hybrid models can be present at any level.
This simple and efficient structure allows higher-level (i.e. levels II and III) models to run using as *first guess* the output of the preceding level, but the opposite must be also considered. Lower-level models should also be updated as in *upscaling* applications, providing a two-way flux that enables a feedback among the different models.

4. Multiple feasible futures

Clearly, forecasts are model dependent. Different models and parametrisations will determine different probable futures, all of them physically acceptable if using dynamical models. Some will behave better than others when compared with observations, depending on several factors (e.g. the adequacy of the physical phenomena description in a dynamical model or the boundary conditions employed). Therefore, useful products for decision-makers should include, aside from the forecast maps themselves, additional information about their confidence and uncertainty.
The uncertainty of the final products can be decreased if several *realizations* are used, each one corresponding to a different and independent model execution (i.e. a feasible future). The idea is to *ensemble* in a final product as many independent realizations as possible, using statistical weights for each member that are defined in terms of how well each one represents the observed values in a certain period. It is a common practice, however, to

employ equally weighted members in the final ensemble. For weather applications of the ensemble methodology the reader can review (Toth & Kalnay, 1993), and for seasonal forecast applications (Li et al., 2008) and references therein.
The different realizations can be produced in several ways. For example, they can be constructed in terms of perturbations to some initial state, using different methodologies (like the ones explained in section 3.2) for the tier-1 in seasonal forecast, or even employing diverse combinations of physical parametrisations. Figure 7 sketches a two member behaviour for the SST evolution in an AGCM equatorial grid cell. Each member originally differed in the SST cell by only 10^{-3} K. Due to the *butterfly effect*, after a few weeks we will likely see important differences in the temporal behaviour of the variable, and not only for that cell. Climate models fed with these two SST fields as boundary conditions will provide different members in the ensemble forecast.
For climate simulations, it has been shown (Li et al., 2008) that the use of different methodologies for the tier-1 offers better results (fewer uncertainties) in the final ensemble than the simulations associated with only one methodology.

5. The Latin American Observatory: An operational research and forecast system

To illustrate an operational research and forecast system which provides useful tools for decision-makers and stake-holders, in this section the *Latin America Observatory for Climate Events* structure will be discussed briefly. Its goals are similar to those of the Andean Observatory (Muñoz et al., 2010), but in this case the participation of all interested institutions in the Latin American countries is fully brought forth and supported. The idea is to facilitate scientific tools for the decision-makers, thus enabling the continuous interaction between research (universities and centers in the region) and operational activities (basically the National Weather Services and related institutions). The present coordinator of this project is the Centre for Scientific Modelling (Centro de Modelado Científico - CMC, in Spanish) at the University of Zulia, Venezuela.
The Observatory, known as OLE^2, currently has got a number of methodologies:

- Dynamical Weather Forecast

  At present, OLE^2 offers 72-hour weather forecasts on a daily basis using the high resolution downscaling models MM5 (Michalakes, 2000) and WRF (Skamarock et al., 2005). The GFS (Kalnay et. al, 1990) 3-hourly outputs and assimilation of SYNOP, METAR and TEMP reports are used as initial conditions. Each country determines the best set of model parametrisations, typically running at resolutions of 30 km and higher. The model outputs are valuable for the forecasting processes in countries where the Andes Mountain Chain provides complex disturbances that frequently GFS and other global models cannot resolve.

- Dynamical Seasonal Forecast

  The NCAR Community Atmospheric Model version 3.1 (CAM3) (Collins et al., 2006) has been configured at T42L26 resolution at CMC by the Atmospheric Model Intercomparison Project (AMIP); it runs through the Green House Gases (GHGs) with monthly variability from 1966 to present. The first 5 years have been discarded for spin-up reasons. The selected climatology corresponds to the 1971-2000 period.

  The current seasonal forecast methodology is sketched in Figure 8. On a monthly basis, the CAM runs 6 ensemble members, where as tier-1: (a) two of them follow the persisted SST e-folding methodology (psst, see for example, (Li et al., 2008)), (b) two members use the SST forecast of the CFS model (cfssst, (Saha et al., 2006)), and (c) two realizations are

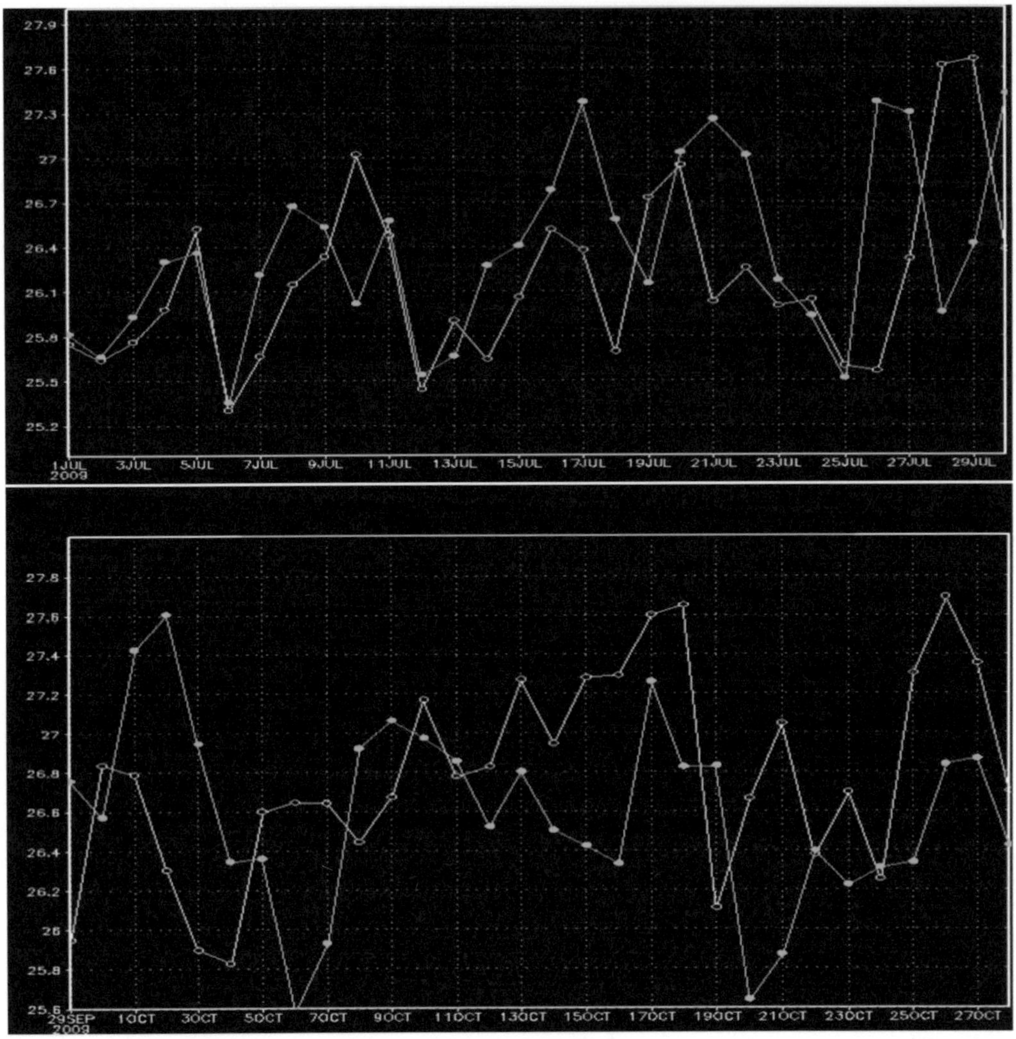

Fig. 7. SST behaviour for Jul 2009 (above) and Oct 2009 (below) using two CAM members for a cell located in the equator and the dateline (180W). The green lines corresponds to a 10^{-3} K perturbation of the climatological value (in white). After three months the differences are notable.

obtained following the constructed analog (casst, (Van den Dool, 1994)) methodology. For all members the lead's monthly ice fraction coverage is described by the climatological values. For each member's output, the necessary initial and boundary conditions are extracted and written in the special (intermediate) format requested by the climatic versions of MM5 and WRF (CMM5 and CWRF, from now on), and are then available for the Andean NWSs through the OLE[2] web portal (`http://ole2.org`), which has been totally built with Open Source resources by CMC developers.

Each NWS downloads the required files to execute the models in their own computational infrastructures and, since January 2010, using two different sets of physical parametrisations per model. Thus, a multi-parametric multi-model ensemble is produced

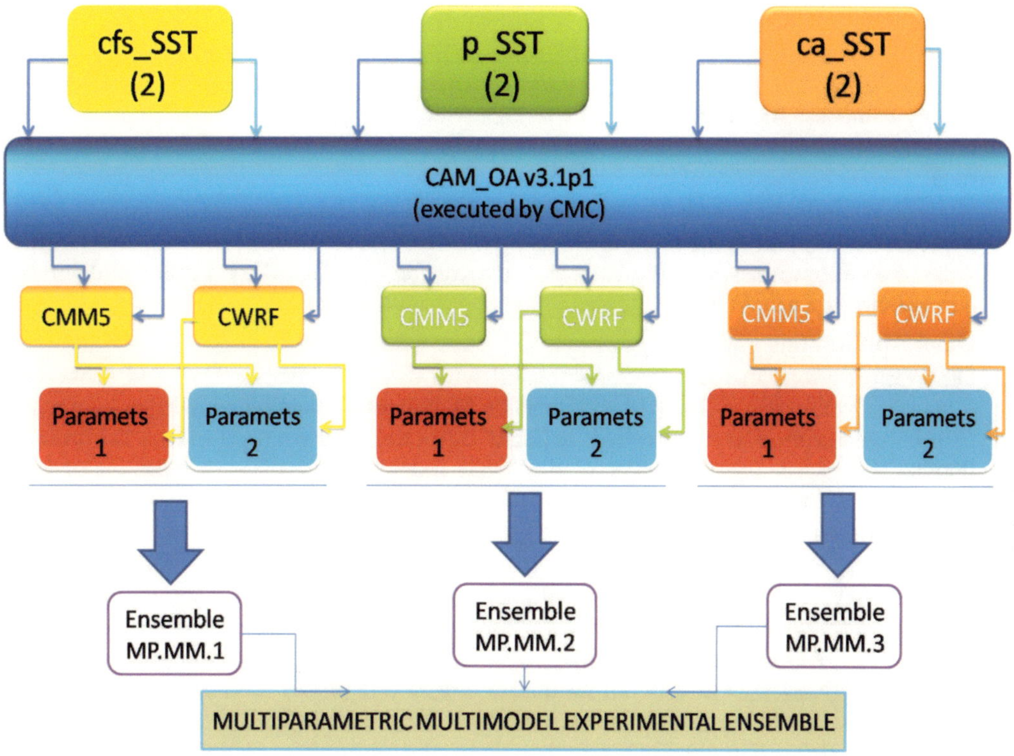

Fig. 8. Multi-parametric, multi-model ensemble employed for the seasonal forecast in the Latin American Observatory.

for each country, and then uploaded to the OLE^2 web portal for its publication after internal filters and discussion. Figure 2 depicts an OLE^2 seasonal precipitation anomaly map for South America, with the corresponding observed rainfall anomaly for comparison. These products are also used in each NWS for the generation of agricultural risk maps as well as products and tools for decision makers.

- Oceanographic High Resolution Forecast

  The Regional Oceanic Modeling System (ROMS-AGRIF, (Penven et al, 2007)) has been configured for a computational domain in the Eastern Pacific. At present, the boundary and initial conditions are provided by the ECCO Consortium (Estimating the Circulation and Climate of the Ocean, (Stammer et al., 1999)) and the GFS (Kalnay et. al, 1990). The OLE^2 runs daily ROMS for a 5-day high resolution (30 km) forecast, sharing in the web portal products like SST, surface salinity, vertical velocities (upwelling and downwelling) and marine currents. This kind of product is very useful as a basis for fishery maps, indicating locations of nutrient-rich areas due to upwelling processes.

  This OLE^2 component has been developed at CMC in collaboration with the *Comisión Permanente del Pacífico Sur* (CPPS) in order to set up the same methodology developed by the NWS for the Marine and Coastal Services of Colombia, Ecuador, Peru, and Chile.

- Dynamical Hydrological Forecast

  The Dynamical Hydrological Forecast (Level III) process is carried out at OLE^2 by coupling the NOAH Land Surface Model (Schaake et al., 1996) with the Level II models, or directly using the latter's forecast precipitation, temperatures and wind outputs into the Variable Infiltration Capacity (VIC) Model of (Liang & Xie, 2001). VIC is a macroscale (typical cell resolution > 1 km), semi-distributed hydrologic model that solves full water and energy balances. At OLE^2 the VIC is specifically configured for each basin of interest (the resolution depends on the selected basin) with the corresponding soil and vegetation type data.

For both procedures (coupled LSMs or uncoupled VIC Model), a bias correcting calibration procedure is applied to the raw output using historical, local streamflow data as reference. After the calibration stage, the final outputs can be considered as a main tool for the corresponding Early Warning System in the countries involved.

- Other Applications

  Other applications include products related with droughts, floods, fires and ecosystem dynamics. In the case of droughts (Palmer, 1968), indices are employed, while a composite map between runoff and hydrologic capacity of model cells are used to forecast possible floods. Likewise, the (Chandler et al., 1983) index is utilised as a measure of joint probability of fire occurrence and propagation.

  Climate and Health applications are focused mainly on malaria seasonal predictability for northwestern South America using the model studied in (MacDonald, 1957). Given the necessary entomological and epidemiological parameters, the high resolution output at OLE^2 supplies the climate information for running this epidemiological tool.

  Finally, a new framework is related to Ecosystem Dynamics, especially Lemna (duckweed) population dynamics. In 2004 an important duckweed bloom took place in Maracaibo Lake (Tapias, 2010), the South American largest lake, bringing economic (e.g. fisheries) and health related (e.g. necrotic Lemna at lake shores produce an increase of diseases) problems to human populations in those coastal zones. Recently, the CMC provided an application known as CAVEL ((Tapias, 2010)) that makes use of MODIS VIS and IR data (Barnes et al., 2002) for providing normalized vegetation index (NDVI) maps, and time series of total surface coverage.

6. Concluding remarks and future research

In this article we have studied a general methodology for research and forecasting. It utilises a hierarchical flux of information between different models, aimed at providing useful, easy to understand scientific tools for decision makers and stake-holders. It can be decomposed into three levels. The first involves either coupled or non-coupled General Circulation Models which supply the initial and boundary conditions for the second level, namely, Regional Models, which employ statistical or dynamical downscaling. The third level feeds on the information given by level 1, offering tailor-made applications for decision makers, ranging from hydrological resources availability in a basin to ecosystem dynamics or vector borne diseases related to climate.

The various applications take into consideration different climate phenomena occurring at several spatial and temporal scales. The goal is to develop really useful tools for policy making, where high spatial resolutions are often needed for short-term, seasonal, decadal and climate-change scales. These efforts require heavy computational resources which, fortunately, are becoming more commonly available nowadays in Climate Centres, and sometimes through regional collaborations like the Latin American Observatory of Climate Events, as has been stressed throughout this article.

In the near future the present methodology is likely to change through the use of a seamless Earth System Simulator, capable of executing hundreds of petaflops which support the numerous time scales and integrate the physical equations resorting to new meshes and more powerful numericall schemes. With the help of such systems, climate science should advance significantly over the next few years.

7. References

Anderson, D. (2008). Overview of Seasonal Forecasting, in *Seasonal Climate: Forecasting and Managing Risk*, Springer Science+Business Media B.V., pp 45-66.

Adcroft, A.; Campin, J.M.; Dutkiewicz, S.; et al. (2011). MITGCM USer Manual. Available at `http://mitgcm.org/public/r2_manual/latest/online_documents/manual.pdf`

Barnes, W. L., and V. V. Salomonson, 1992: A global imaging spectroradiometer for the Earth Observing System. Critical Review, *Optical Technologies for Aerospace Sensing*, Vol. CR 47, 1?23.

Blackmon, M. B., Boville, B., Bryan, F. et al. (2001) The Community Climate System Model. *BAMS*, 82, 11, 2357-2376.

Chandler C., P. Cheney, P. Thomas, L. Trabaud & D. Williams (1983) Fire in Forestry, in Vol. I: *Forest Fire Behavior and Effects*. Jhon Wiley & Sons, New York, NY. 450 pp.

Cressie, N. (1993) *Statistics for Spatial Data*, Wiley, New York.

Collins, W. D., and Coauthors, 2006: The formulation and atmospheric simulation of the Community Atmosphere Model Version 3 (CAM3). *J. Climate*, 19, 2144?2161.

Haltiner, G. & Williams, R. (1980) *Numerical Prediction and Dynamic Meteorology*, 2nd Edition, John Wiley & Sons, NY.

Hazeleger, W., Severijns, C., Semmler, T., et al., 2010: EC-Earth: A seamless Earth System Prediction Approach in Action, *BAMS*, 9, 10, 1357-1363.

Johns, T.C, Durman, C.F., Banks, H.T. et al. (2006) The new Hadley Centre climate model HadGEM1: Evaluation of coupled simulations. *Journal of Climate*, 19, pp. 1327-1353

Kalnay, E., M. Kanamitsu, and W. E. Baker, 1990: Global numerical weather prediction at the National Meteorological *Center. Bull. Amer. Meteor. Soc.*, 71, 1410 - 1428.

Li, Sh., Goddard, L., Dewitt, D. (2008). Predictive Skill of AGCM Seasonal Climate Forecasts Subject to Different SST Prediction Methodologies, *Journal of Climate*, 21, 10, 2169.

Liang, X-Z & Kunkel, K. (2001). Development of a Regional Climate Model for U.S. Midwest Applications. Part I: Sensitivity to Buffer Zone Treatment, *Journal of Climate*, 14, pp. 4363-4378.

Liang, X., & Xie, Z. (2001) A new surface runoff parameterization with subgrid-scale soil heterogeneity for land surface models, *Advances in Water Resources*, 24(9-10), pp. 1173-1193.

Marshall, J.; Adcroft, A.; Campin, J. M.; Hill, C. & White, A. (2004). Atmosphere Ocean Modeling Exploiting Fluid Isomorphisms. *Monthly Weather Review*. 132, 2882-2894.

Mason, S. (2008). From Dynamical Model Predictions to Seasonal Climate Forecasts, in *Seasonal Climate: Forecasting and Managing Risk*, Springer Science+Business Media B.V., pp 163-201.

Mason, S. and O. Baddour (2008). Statistical Modelling, in *Seasonal Climate: Forecasting and Managing Risk*, Springer Science+Business Media B.V., pp 163-201.

MacDonald, G. (1957) The Epidemiology and Control of Malaria. London, U.K. Oxford University Press.

Michalakes, J. (2000) The same-source parallel MM5. in *Sci. Comput.*, 8, 5?12

Muï£¡oz, ï£¡. G., Lï£¡pez, P., Velï£¡squez, R., et al., 2010: An Environmental Watch System for the Andes Countries: El Observatorio Andino. *BAMS*, 91, 1645?1652.

Murphy, J. (1999). An evaluation of statistical and dynamical techniques for downscaling local climate, *Journal of Climate*, 12, pp. 2256-2284.

Palmer, W. C. (1968) Keeping track of crop moisture conditions nationwide: The new crop moisture index. *Weatherwise*, 21, pp. 156-161.

Peixoto, J. & Oort, A. (1992) *Physics of Climate*, American Institute of Physics, NY.

Penven, P., P. Marchesiello, L. Debreu, and J. Lefevre, 2007: Software tools for pre- and post-processing of oceanic regional simulations. *Environ. Modell. Software*, 23, 660?662.

Recalde, G. C. (2010). Malaria predictability experiment for the Ecuadorian coast using dynamical models (Thesis). Environmental Enginering. Universidad Agraria del Ecuador. 72 pp. Available at `http://cmc.org.ve/descargas/Recalde2010.pdf`

Roeckner, E., R. Brokopf, M. Esch, et al. (2006). Sensitivity of simulated climate to horizontal and vertical resolution in the ECHAM5 atmosphere model, *Journal of Climate*, 19, 3771-3791.

Saha, S., Nadiga, S., Thiaw, C. et al. (2006). The NCEP Climate Forecast System. *Journal of Climate*, 19, 15, 3483-3517.

Schaake, J. C., V. I. Koren, Q.-Y. Duan, K. Mitchell, and F. Chen, 1996: Simple water balance model for estimat- ing runoff at different spatial and temporal scales. J. Geophys. Res., 101 (D3), 7461?7475.

Skamarock, W. C., J. B. Klemp, J. Dudhia, D. O. Gill, D. M. Barker, W. Wang and J. G. Powers (2005). A Description of the Advanced Research WRF Version 2, NCAR Tech. Note NCAR/TN-468&STR, 88 pp.

Stammer, D., and Coauthors, 1999: The consortium for estimating the circulation and climate of the ocean (ECCO)?Science goals and task plan. ECCO Consortium Rep. 1, 24 pp.

Svoboda, M. D., et al. (2002) The Drought Monitor, *BAMS*, 83, pp. 1181-1190.

Tapias, E. (2010) CAVEL: An automated system for Lemna recognition and analysis in the Lake Maracaibo.(Thesis). Facultad de Ciencias. La Universidad del Zulia, 104 pp. Available at `http://cmc.org.ve/descargas/Tapias2010.pdf`

Toth, Z. & Kalnay, E. (1993) Ensemble Forecasting at NMC: The generation of perturbations, *BAMS*, 74, pp. 2317-2330

Van Den Dool, H. (1994). Searching for analogues, how long must we wait?, *Tellus*, 46 A, 314-324.

Wilks, D., (2006). *Statistical Methods in the Atmospheric Sciences*, 2nd Edition, Elsevier, Amsterdam.

22

The Effect of Tomography Imaging Artefacts on Structural Analysis and Numerical Permeability Simulations

Viivi Koivu and Tuomas Turpeinen
University of Jyväskylä, Department of Physics
Finland

1. Introduction

Fluid flow phenomena in porous materials can be found in many important processes in nature and in society. In particular, fluid flow through a porous medium contribute to several technological problems, e.g. extraction of oil or gas from porous rocks, spreading of contaminants in fluid-saturated soils and certain separation processes, such as filtration (Torquato, 2001). In paper and wood industry single and multi phase fluid flow properties in porous media play important roles related to manufacturing process and product development.

The general laws describing creeping fluid flows are well known. However, a detailed study of fluid flow in porous heterogeneous media is complicated. This is a direct consequence of the often very complex, internal micro-scale structures of these materials. That is, the interplay between fluid flow and complex internal structure at the micro-scale gives rise to the effective fluid flow properties at the macro-scale. Traditionally, efforts for analysing fluid flow properties by means of modelling are based on using regular pore geometries that may possess the bulk properties of the actual medium and are simple enough to allow for analytic solution of the relevant transport equations. However, the development of imaging techniques based on computerised x-ray micro-tomography (CXμT) together with advanced numerical techniques have made it possible to analyse structural and transport properties of complex materials based on 3D digitalisation of their real microstructures (Coles et al., 1998; Samuelsen et al., 2001; Goel et al., 2002; Thibault & Bloch, 2002; Holmstad et al., 2003; Rolland et al., 2005; Goel et al., 2006; Stock, 2009). X-ray tomography is a non-invasive and non-destructive imaging method where individual x-ray images recorded from different viewing directions are used for reconstructing the internal 3D structure of the object of interest (Stock, 2009). Although a great opportunity to materials research, CXμT also poses new challenges. The imaging method produces noise, edge blurring, and various other artefacts that may distort the 3D reconstruction of the sample structure and thus result in unrealistic analysis results.

In various industrial and scientific applications an effective material property, permeability, is used for describing the ability of porous materials to transmit fluids. Permeability coefficient for single phase creeping fluid flow through a porous media is defined by the phenomenological law by Henry Darcy as the proportionality constant between the average fluid velocity and applied pressure gradient (Darcy, 1856). The analytical approaches to analyse permeability are often confined to simplified sample geometries. Some of the numerical permeability studies are based on analysis made for computationally generated models of porous media (Rasi et al., 1999; Aaltosalmi et. al., 2004; Belov et al., 2004; Holmstad et al. 2005; Lundstrom et al., 2004; Verleye et al., 2005; Verleye et al., 2007). Tomographic reconstructions are increasingly utilised in combination with numerical methods to analyse permeability of porous materials (Manwart et al., 2002; Martys & Hagedorn, 2002; Aaltosalmi et al., 2004; Kutay et al., 2006; Fourie et al., 2007). According to our knowledge, only a few studies are based on analysing the effect of tomographic image properties on numerical permeability results (Aaltosalmi et al., 2004; Holmstad, 2005)

The effects of imaging noise, imaging artefacts and the quality of image segmentation on flow permeability found by using direct numerical flow simulation by a specific implementation of finite-difference method (FDM) (Wiegmann, 2007) are studied. The specific surface area of the samples and the features of pore geometry are also analysed. The analyses are done for four different sample types. First, an artificial sample geometry, comprised of hexagonal array of cylinders with known analytical permeability result, is used to analyse the effect of added random noise and edge blurring on the analysis results. Second, CXμT reconstructions of wool fibre web, packaging board and sandstone samples are used to illustrate the effects of different artefact removal and image segmentation methods on permeability results. Finally, the numerically simulated values of flow permeability are compared with experimental results for the same material.

2. Tomography and image processing

CXμT is a non-destructive technique for analysing interior features within solid objects and for obtaining digital information of their 3D structure and properties. During the recent decade, the precision of x-ray tomographic imaging techniques have reached the sub-micrometre resolution and enables analyses of statistical properties of various materials.

2.1 Tomography imaging of porous samples

Authentic simulation geometries were obtained by utilising CXμT. Both synchrotron -based x-ray beams and conventional x-ray tubes were used as the radiation sources. The adequate resolution and the overall quality of the images depend on the techniques used. In this study, two laboratory scale devices (Sky-Scan 1172 and Xradia Micro XCT-400) based on x-ray tubes, and a tomographic imaging facility ID19 of the European Synchrotron Radiation Facility (ESRF) were used.

The voxel resolution of the laboratory scale devices can be varied from a few micrometres up to few tens of micrometres. The wool fibre web sample was imaged by SkyScan 1172 device with the voxel resolution of 4.48 μm and the sand stone sample with Xradia Micro XCT-400 with the voxel resolution of 2.10 μm. The packaging board sample was scanned at ESRF beam-line ID19. The imaging set-up used at ID19 facility had the voxel resolution fixed to 0.7 μm.

2.2 Imaging artefacts and image processing

CXμT imaging is a two phased process. First, a tomographic scanner is utilised to acquire a series of 2D shadowgraphs of a sample from multiple angles. Then, the 3D reconstruction of the sample is computed from the shadowgraphs using special algorithms (Kak & Slaney, 1988). The process involves many sources of artefacts.

Typical CXμT imaging system is comprised of a light source, optical elements and a camera which all pose certain imaging artefacts (Gonzales & Woods, 2002). Basically, the main imaging artefacts are noise and edge blurring caused by optics or the non-optimal light source of laboratory scale devices. In addition, the reconstruction procedure can add more artefacts to the tomographic reconstructions (Stock, 2009). The main reconstruction -based artefacts are rings, streaks and shadows caused by hardening of x-rays (Stock, 2009) or mechanical inaccuracy of the system.

Many image processing tools have been developed in order to overcome the problems related to the imaging artefacts, see e.g. Stock (2009) and references therein. However, most of the artefacts cannot be fully removed algorithmically and they thus require either removal by hardware optimisation or robust analysis software.

2.2.1 Sample geometry preparation

Representative elementary volumes (REVs) of the sample geometries were cropped out of the full CXμT reconstructions. In this study the REVs were determined in a deterministic way by evaluating the porosity of larger and larger sample volumes always centred on the same image voxel (Drugan & Willis, 1996; Rolland du Roscoat et al., 2007). A REV size thus obtained for the wool fibre web sample was (in XxYxZ -directions, see Fig. 1) 300x300x360 voxels, for the sand stone sample 500x500x500 voxels and for the packaging board sample 450x450x420 voxels.

The sample REVs were filtered by variance-weighted mean filter (Gonzales & Woods, 2002) and later thresholded to yield binary images including the solid material and the pore space. Visualisations of the REVs are presented in Fig. 1.

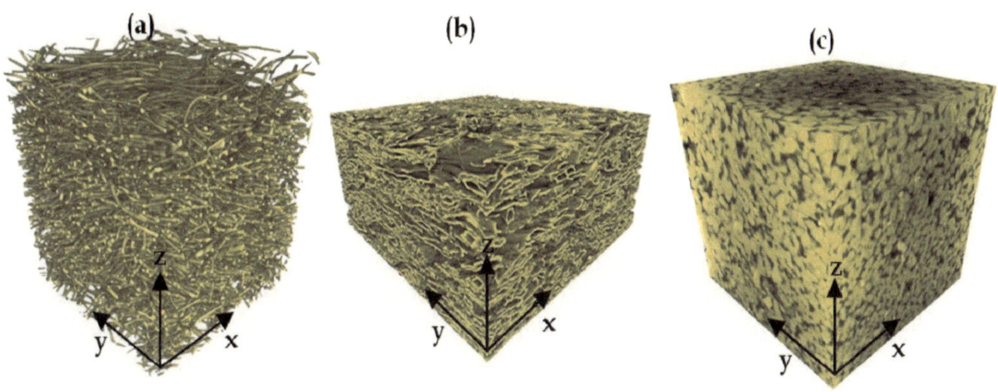

Fig. 1. Tomographic reconstructions of (a) the wool fibre web, (b) the packaging board and (c) the sandstone samples.

2.2.2 Edge blurring and imaging noise

Especially in laboratory scale CXμT systems, like SkyScan and Xradia, the image quality of the material edges in the reconstructed geometry is limited by optical properties of the system. The edge spreading is caused by the non-zero aperture diameter of the x-ray source, the optics in between the source and detector, and scintillator, i.e. the component that converts the x-rays into visible light. Thus, instead of sharp transition between different material phases, there is a smooth curve called edge spread function (ESF). In Fig. 2, the edge smoothness can be seen in the intensity profile plot. The width of the ESF in this case is around 7 pixels.

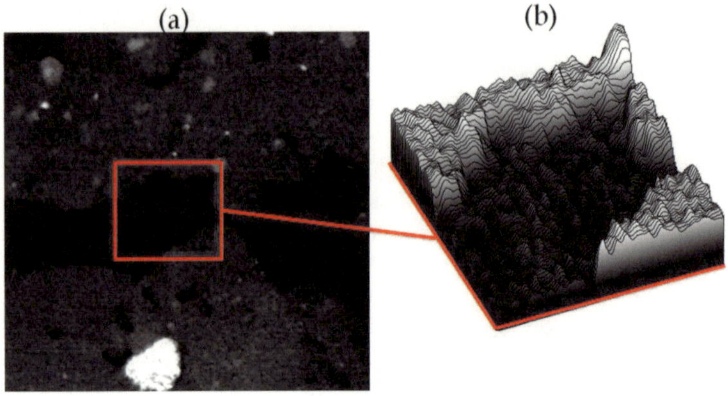

Fig. 2. An example of a noisy CXμT image (a) and the intensity profile plot for the area marked on the CXμT image (b).

In addition to ESF, the tomographic reconstructions are often contaminated by imaging noise. Collecting photons with Charge-Coupled Device (CCD) is a time-dependent discrete procedure that presents Poisson noise into the collected data. Utilisation of an analogue-to-digital -converter such as in CCD causes Gaussian -type of noise into the images. In the final 3D representation of the tomographic sample, noise can be seen as random variation of grey values. This effect causes edge blurring. Furthermore, when binarised by thresholding procedure, falsely labelled voxels can appear.
Many algorithms have been developed to decrease the noise, e.g. anisotropic diffusion (Perona & Malik, 1987), bilateral filtering (Tomasi & Manduchi, 1998) and SUSAN filtering (Smith & Brady, 1997). However, none of the filtering methods is perfect and post processing is often necessary to reduce the artefacts from the binarised images.

2.2.3 Image segmentation

Segmentation means separation of the image into interesting sub-regions for further analyses. For segmentation of 3D reconstructions, there is a large variety of algorithms. To mention few the most commonly used, are global algorithms like thresholding, spatially aware algorithms like region grow and watershed (Gonzales & Woods, 2002), optimisation -based algorithms like level sets (Osher &, Sethian, 1988) or active contours (Kass et al, 1987), shape -based methods like LOG or DOG (Gonzales & Woods, 2002), texture -based methods like local binary patterns (Ojala et al, 1994), and combinations of these. Often the complexity of the required algorithm is directly proportional to the signal-to-noise ratio of the original image.
A typical task in segmentation procedure is to separate the image of a porous media to solid and void phase. In optimal conditions, the phases can be distinguished by the difference in their grey value distributions. However, the grey value distributions are often overlapping due to imaging noise. In many cases, thresholding combined with post processing gives satisfactory results. The post processing procedures aim to remove the non-connected parts, i.e. the "levitating" solid objects from the images or to fill the small non-effective (isolated) pores. In the cases where the overlapping regions of the grey value distributions are wide, more sophisticated algorithms are needed.

We have developed a so-called forest fire algorithm to separate the material phases when their grey value distributions are overlapping too much for simpler methods. As an input, a user will give the limits for the overlapping area in the grey value histogram. The algorithm processes the grey values in between the given limits and decides whether it is solid or void by adding more voxels to each phase iteratively. In addition to grey value information, spatial information is incorporated. The voxels are added into the group if there are enough members of the same group around it. By adjusting the number of required neighbours, the sensitivity of the method can be adjusted individually for each phase. In practice, the method is closely related to region grow method, but it enhances the traditional region grow by adding a weak "surface tension" to it. The benefits of the method are smooth surfaces and possibility to alter the volume of selected phase by allowing either solid or void to conquer its area easier. The disadvantage of the method is that some of the smallest details can be lost. The name forest fire comes from simple forest fire simulations where forest is divided into cells which will catch fire if certain amounts of its neighbouring cells are already burning.

3. Fluid flow permeability analysis

Permeability κ is a tensor valued measure of the ability of a porous material to transmit fluids. It is defined for slow, steady-state, isothermal, Newtonian fluid flow through a porous medium by Darcys's law (Darcy, 1856; Bear, 1972)

$$\vec{q} = -\frac{1}{\mu}\kappa \times \tilde{N}\psi, \tag{1}$$

where $\vec{q}$ is the superficial volume flux vector and μ is the dynamic viscosity of the fluid. The pietsometric head ψ is defined by equation $\nabla\psi = \nabla p - \rho\vec{g}$ where p is the pressure and ρ is the density of the fluid, and $\vec{g}$ is the acceleration due to a body force. In general, permeability is a symmetric second-order tensor (Liakopoulos, 1965):

$$\kappa = \begin{bmatrix} k_{xx} & k_{xy} & k_{xz} \\ k_{yx} & k_{yy} & k_{yz} \\ k_{zx} & k_{zy} & k_{zz} \end{bmatrix} \tag{2}$$

Several theoretical results for permeability coefficients have been reported in the literature. Perhaps the most common formula which can be derived analytically for simplified capillary model is the Kozeny-Carman relation

$$k = \frac{1}{c\tau^2 S_0^2}\frac{\phi^3}{(1-\phi)^2} \tag{3}$$

where c is a constant that depends on the cross section of the capillaries (being $c = 2$ for circular cross section), s_0 is the specific surface area of the sample, τ is the tortuosity of the flow and ϕ is the porosity of the media (Bear, 1972; Dullien, 1979).

3.1 Numerical method

Numerical permeability analyses were done directly on the voxel model of the samples. The diagonal elements of permeability tensor κ (in Eq. (2)) were obtained within FDM by first solving over a periodic REV the following boundary value problem arising from the homogenisation process:

$$\begin{aligned} &\mu\nabla^2\vec{v} - \nabla\delta p - \nabla\psi = 0, && \text{in } \Omega_f \\ &\nabla\cdot\vec{v} = 0 && \text{in } \Omega_f, \\ &\vec{v} = 0 && \text{on } \Gamma \end{aligned} \tag{4}$$

where Ω_f and Γ represent the fluid volume and the fluid-solid interface, respectively. These three equations are the conservation of momentum, conservation of mass and the no-slip condition on the fluid-solid interface. Here $\vec{v}$ stands for the periodic microscopic velocity field, $\nabla\psi$ is the pietsometric head and δp is the first order periodic fluctuation of the pressure p.

The boundary value problem Eq. (4) was solved by using FDM implemented in GeoDict2010 R1 (64 bit Linux) software. In the method, the velocity $\vec{v}$ and the pressure p are discretised on a staggered grid: velocities are defined on their respective voxel faces and the pressure is defined in the centre of the voxel. Then the partial differential equations are solved by using the FFF-Stokes solver based on Fast Fourier Transform. This solver appears to be fast and memory efficient for large computations dedicated to 3D images (Wiegmann, 2007). Finally, the permeability coefficients of the samples can be deduced from equations (1) and (2) by calculating the volume average of the velocity field over the REV ($\langle\vec{v}\rangle = \vec{q}$) for a given macroscopic gradient of pressure $\nabla\psi$.

During the permeability analysis, periodic boundary condition was enforced on all the sample faces. For tomographic samples, ten extra fluid layers were added in flow direction on both sides of the sample volume. This was done in order to mimic the experimental measurement conditions, see Koivu et al., (2009a) and Koivu et al., (2009b).

3.2 Experimental method

Permeability coefficients k_{zz} of the samples were measured experimentally using the permeability measurement device (PMD) presented in refs (Koivu et al., 2009a; Koivu et al., 2009b). The PMD can be utilised for measuring permeability of porous materials using both liquids and gases as permeating fluids.

For the purpose of this work, the PMD was modified such that the sample was compressed only at its peripheral part to prevent any flow on that region, and the central part was left fully open for flow; see a schematic illustration of the measurement set-up in Fig. 3a. The measured sample size for the wool fibre web and the packaging board had 90 mm diameter. For the measurements, the sand stone samples with diameter of 35 mm and thickness 10 mm was attached with silicone glue into a special sample holder, see Fig. 3b.

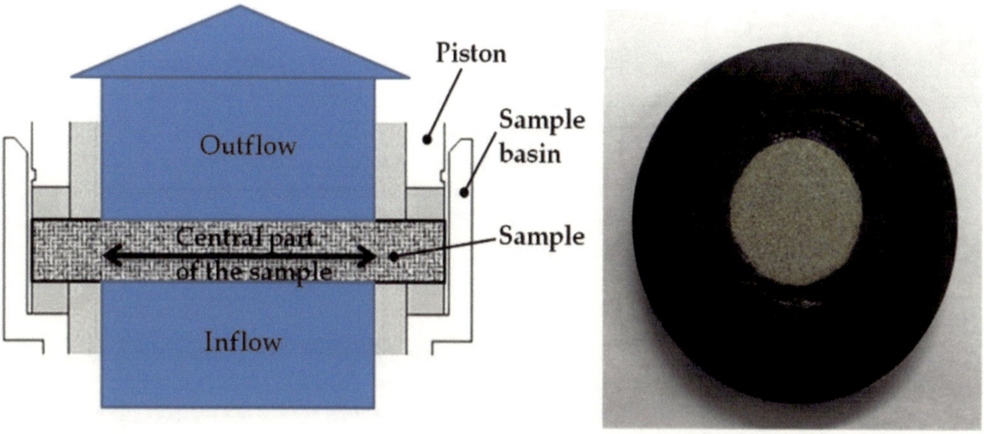

Fig. 3. Schematic illustration of the measurement set-up (a) and a sandstone sample attached in the sample holder (b).

In the experimental method, the diagonal values of the permeability tensor in the case dependent coordinate system (see e.g. Fig. 1) are found using the integrated form of Darcy's law

$$k_{ii} = -\frac{\mu q_i}{\Delta P / \Delta L_i} = \frac{\mu Q \Delta L_i}{A(P_{out} - P_{in})} \tag{5}$$

where Q is the volumetric flow rate through the sample, A is the cross-sectional flow area, $\Delta P = P_{out} - P_{in}$ is the pressure drop and ΔL_i is the length over which the pressure drop takes place.

Experiments were conducted with air flow in order to prevent structural changes due to swelling of sample material. This is important in order to obtain similar structure of materials in experiments and in numerical flow solution based on the pore geometry given by tomographic images of dry material samples. Equation (5) is valid for the incompressible fluid flows. For gas flows through porous medium, Darcy's law must be slightly modified to account for compressibility effects. For isothermal compressible flow the permeability coefficient is thus given by

$$k_{ii} = -\frac{\mu q_i}{\Delta P / \Delta L_i}\frac{P_{out}}{P_{ave}} = \frac{\mu Q \Delta L_i}{A(P_{out} - P_{in})}\frac{P_{out}}{P_{ave}} \tag{6}$$

where P_{out} is the pressure, Q is the volumetric flow rate at the downstream side of the medium, and $P_{ave} = P_{out} + 1/2(P_{in} - P_{out})$ (Bear, 1972; Leskelä & Simula, 1998).

In the experimental approach, the values of the permeability coefficient in z-direction (k_{zz}) were calculated using Darcy's law for compressible fluid flow by Eq. (6). The coordinate conventions for the sample types are shown in Fig. 1. Measurements were repeated for five macroscopically identical samples in order to obtain an estimate of the statistical uncertainty of the results. The statistical uncertainty of the experimental results was 20%.

4. Results

We proceeded in two steps. First, we used a numerical method to find values of permeability for fibrous porous media based on regular hexagonal array of cylinders. The numerical results thus obtained were compared with the analytical results found in the literature. In the second step, we used the numerical method to find values of permeability coefficient for the wool fibre web, packaging board and sandstone samples. These results were compared with the experimental results obtained by using the PMD (Koivu et al., 2009a; Koivu et al., 2009b).

4.1 Regular arrays

Artificial sample geometries of hexagonal arrays of cylinders were prepared to test and demonstrate the effect of different imaging artefacts on structure and numerical fluid flow analysis. The volume size of the simulation geometries were 693 x 400 x 100 pixels and the porosity of the cylinder arrays was selected to be 50 %.

4.1.1 Effect of noise

Visualisations of flow speed field of four hexagonal arrays of cylinders having different levels of noise are shown in Fig. 4. The noise levels are defined as percentage of the faulty voxels of the total volume of the sample.

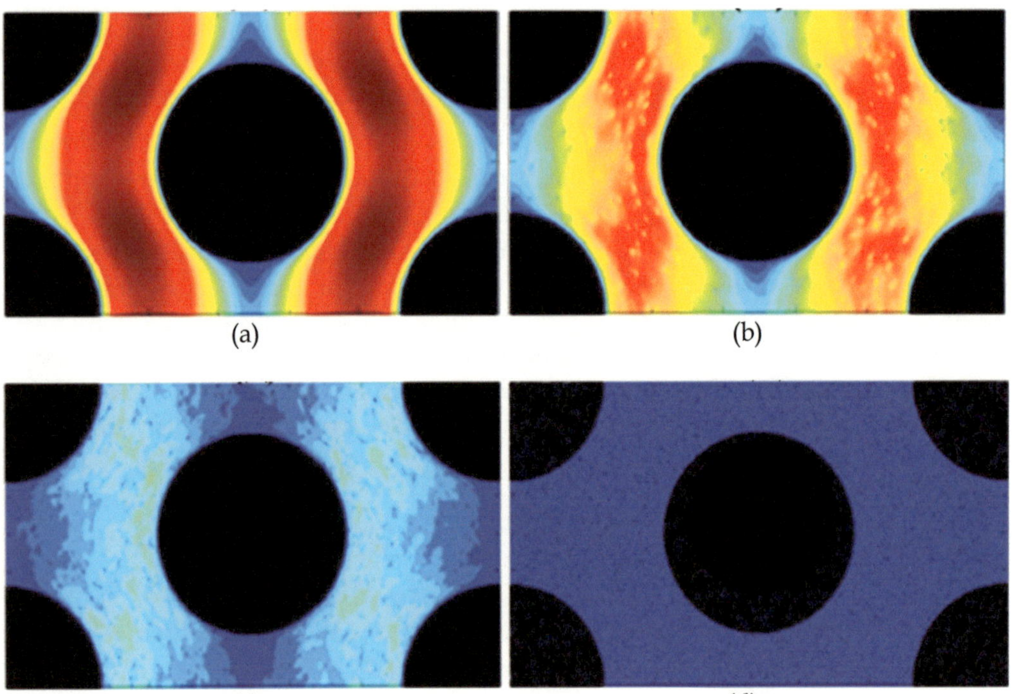

(a) (b) (c) (d)

Fig. 4. Visualisation of flow speed field of four hexagonal arrays of cylinders having different levels of noise: (a) 0 %, (b) 0.05 %, (c) 0.3 % and (d) 5 %. Flow direction is in these cases from top to bottom. Red and yellow colours represent high flow speed and green and blue low flow speed.

Numerically analysed permeability values and corresponding (noise free) analytical value by Drummont & Tahir (1984) are shown in Fig. 5. According to the results, even a small amount of noise has a drastic influence on fluid flow permeability.

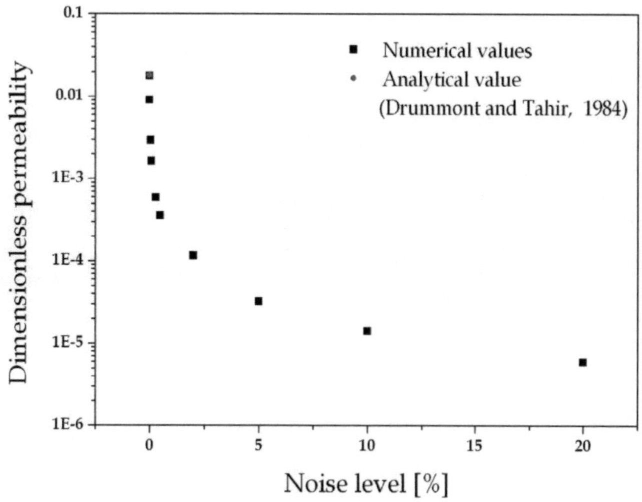

Fig. 5. Numerically solved permeability values for the hexagonal array of cylinders as a function of noise level. For comparison, analytical value for noise free geometry is also given (Drummont & Tahir, 1984).

The effect of noise on specific surface area was evaluated as a function of noise level, see Fig. 6. The specific surface areas were analysed utilising the marching cubes algorithm (Lorensen & Clive, 1987a; Lorensen & Clive, 1987b). Increase in the amount of noise increases the specific surface area of the simulation geometry and thus decreases the permeability value, see Eq. (3).

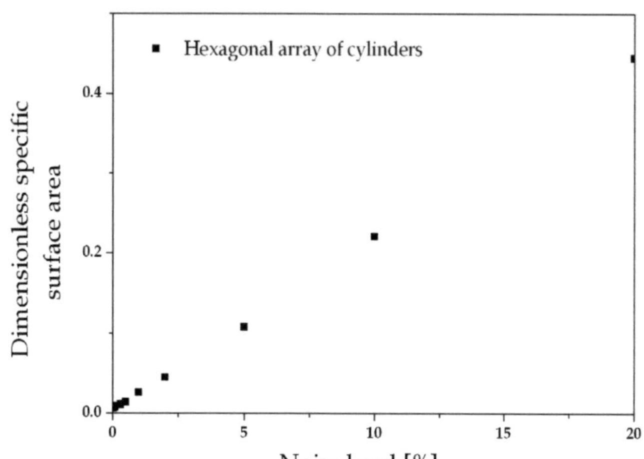

Fig. 6. Dimensionless specific surface area as a function of noise level for the hexagonal array of cylinders.

The effect of noise on pore size distribution was evaluated as a function of noise level, see Fig. 7. The pore size distributions were determined with the so-called sphere fitting algorithm. In the sphere fitting method, the pore space is filled by non-overlapping spheres. The distribution of the radii gives estimation for the pore size distribution (Wu et al., 2007). The pore size distribution was found to change dramatically as a function of noise level. The mode value of the distribution of the geometry with the noise level of 0.01 % was approximately one third of the mode value for the noise free geometry.

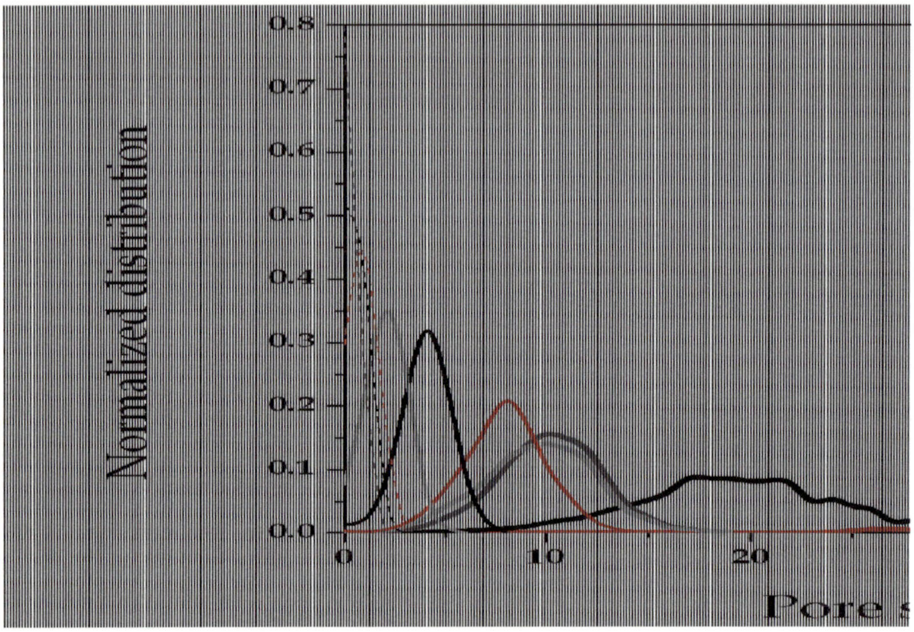

Fig. 7. Normalized pore size distribution for the hexagonal array of cylinders as a function of pore size in pixels with different noise levels.

4.1.2 Effect of edge blurring

Grey scale profiles on solid-void boundaries of a material in tomographic images are often blurred due to ESF. Imaging noise combined with blurred boundaries can cause the thresholded solid-void boundary of the final reconstruction to look rough, see visualisation in Fig. 8b. Without noise, the pure edge spreading causes changes mainly in the porosity value of the sample geometry and thus changes in the permeability value, see e.g. the results published by Koivu et al. (2010). When noise is incorporated, the surface roughness will have an effect to the fluid flow close to the surfaces.

Artificial edge roughness was generated into the geometries of the hexagonal arrays of cylinders, see visualisations of the rough edges in Fig. 8a. To generate the simulation geometries the original geometry was blurred using standard 3D Gaussian blur. Gaussian distributed noise with known standard deviation was added to the blurred image. The image was then thresholded using 128 as the threshold value (in the original image void is 0 and solid is 256). Finally, all the particles not touching the solid phase were removed. The number of the edge roughness level corresponds to the standard deviation of the Gaussian distributed noise.

Fig. 8. Visualisations of artificially generated edge roughness on the hexagonal array of cylinders (a) and edge roughness on reconstruction of wool fibre web caused by CXμT and image processing methods (b).

Edge roughness on solid-void boundary increases the specific surface area of the sample and therefore decreases the permeability value, see Figs 9 and 10. Edge roughness has only small effect on the pore size distribution, see Fig. 11.

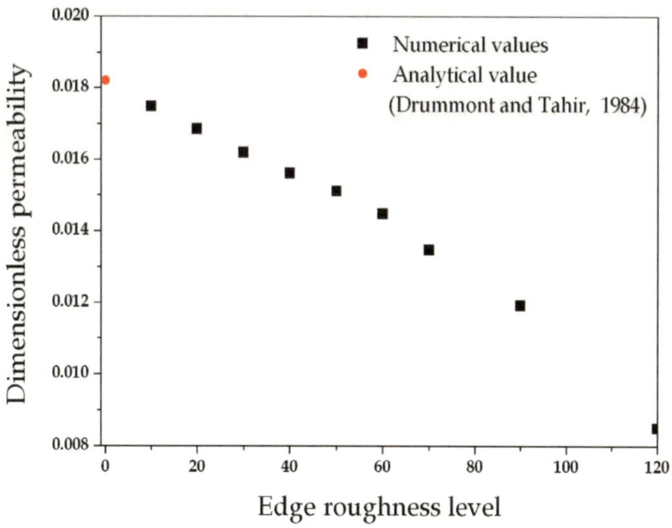

Fig. 9. Numerically solved permeability values for the hexagonal array of cylinders as a function of edge roughness level. Analytical value for noise free geometry is also given (Drummont & Tahir, 1984).

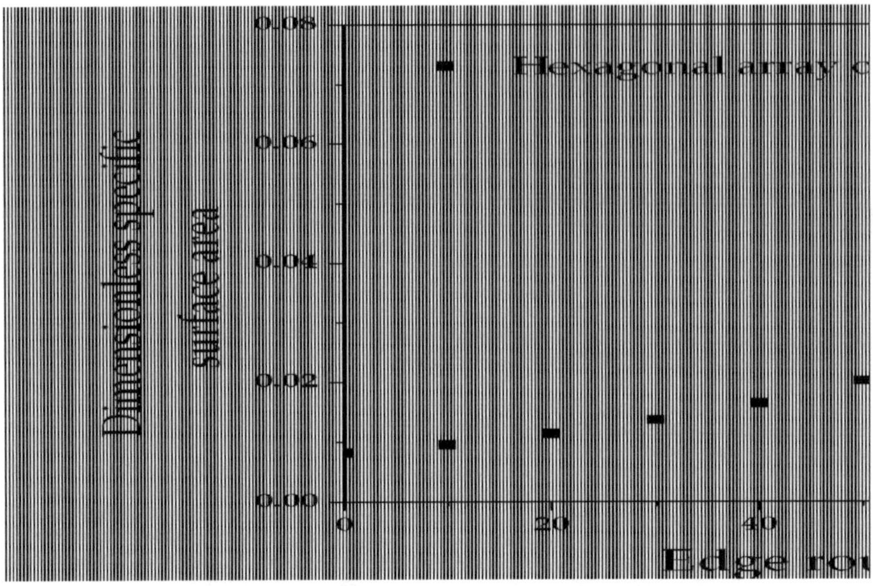

Fig. 10. Dimensionless specific surface area as a function of edge roughness level for the hexagonal array of cylinders.

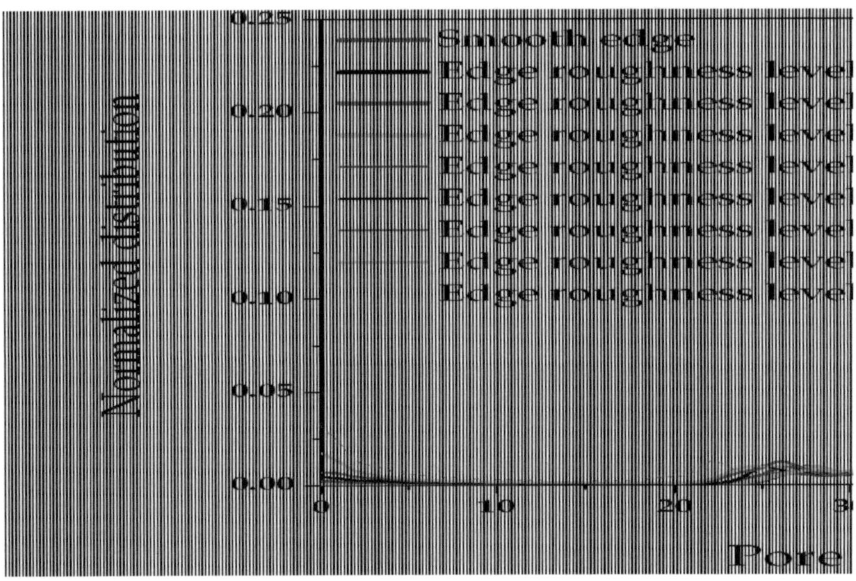

Fig. 11. Normalized pore size distribution as a function of pore size in pixels for the hexagonal array of cylinders with different edge roughness levels.

4.2 Tomographic geometries

Tomographic sample geometries were obtained with three different imaging methods. This was done in order to demonstrate the effects of very common imaging artefacts, which are produced by most of the tomographic imaging methods.

4.2.1 Effect of artefacts on fluid flow permeability

Visualisations of wool fibre web sample with different threshold values are shown in Fig. 12. The sample geometries in (a) - (c) were denoised and then binarised using grey value - based threshold (Gonzales & Woods, 2002). At the lowest threshold levels (a) and (b), the noise is clearly visible in the void space. While threshold value was gradually increased, the noise became less evident and the thickness of the fibres (or size of the solid particles) diminished. The sample geometry in Fig. 12d was segmented utilising the forest fire method. The forest fire method was found to give noise free pore space and a fibre radius that corresponded well with the mean value obtained from scanning electron microscope images, 20 μm.

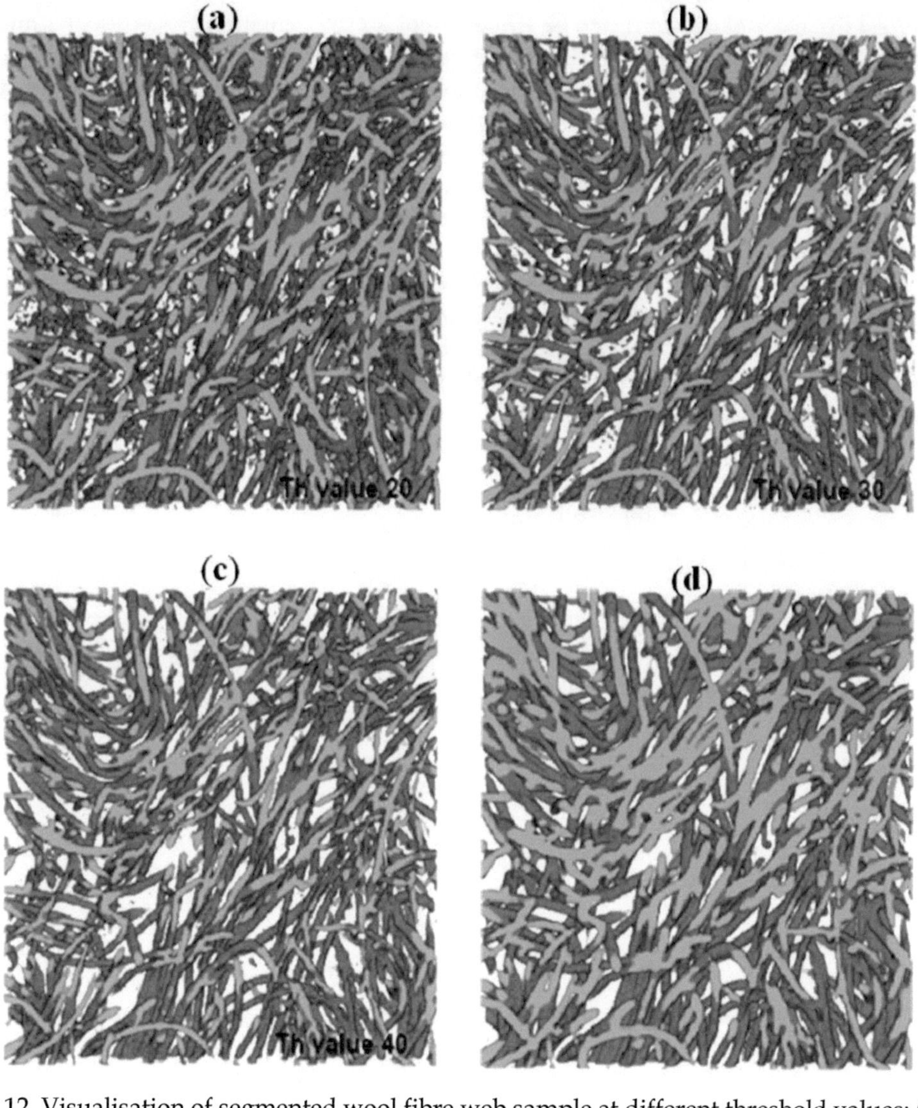

Fig. 12. Visualisation of segmented wool fibre web sample at different threshold values: (a) 20, (b) 30 and (c) 40, and with the forest fire method (d).

Grey value -based thresholding procedure with different threshold values were conducted for all the three tomographic sample types. Numerical fluid flow permeability analyses were conducted for all the geometries and the obtained values were compared with experimental results, see Fig. 13.

As an example, for the wool fibre web, the "optimal" threshold value would have been between 20 and 30, see Fig. 13a. By visually examining the corresponding images, it was found that there was still noise left in flow channels at threshold value 30. Permeability at the optimal threshold value would not have been result of the realistic sample geometry, but combination of noise causing higher specific surface area and thinner fibres increasing the porosity of the geometry. The results were found qualitatively similar for the packaging board and the sand stone samples.

The forest fire method was found to be efficient tool for segmentation procedure. Numerical permeability values for the geometries segmented by the forest fire method were 2.5E-11 m^2, 4.8E-14 m^2 and 2.5E-12 m^2 for the wool fibre web, the packaging board and the sand stone samples, respectively. Corresponding experimental measurement results for the samples were 2.5E-11 m^2, 5.1E-14 m^2 and 2.5E-12 m^2. The maximum difference between the experimental results and the numerical permeability values found by using the forest fire segmented sample geometries was in these cases less than 6.5 %. The statistical uncertainty of the experimental results was 20%.

The numerical permeability results for the samples with different added noise levels (proportion of false voxels) are shown in Fig. 14. Artificial noise levels were generated into the sample geometries which were segmented by the forest fire method. The effect of noise on permeability was found to be qualitatively similar as for the hexagonal cylinder array. Increase in noise level caused decrease in fluid flow permeability value.

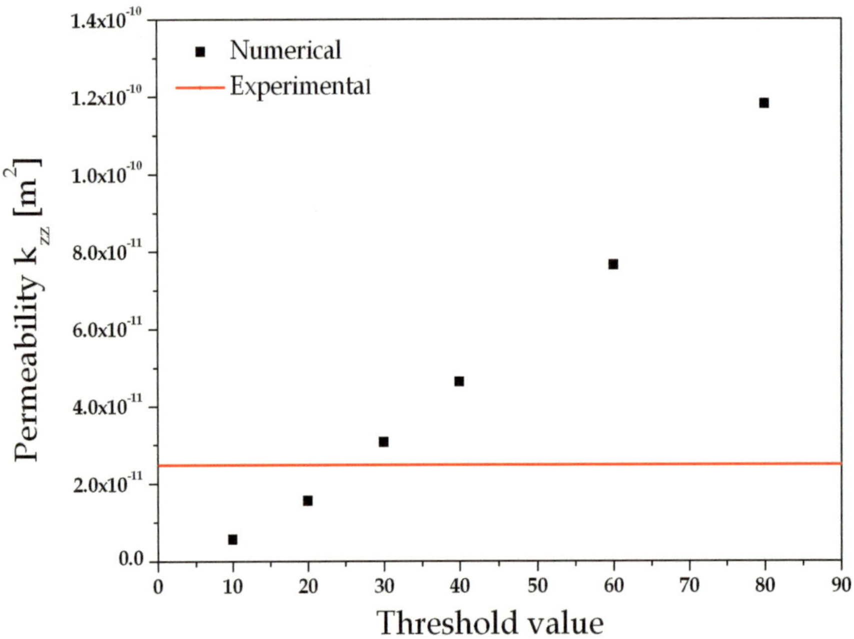

Fig. 13. (a)

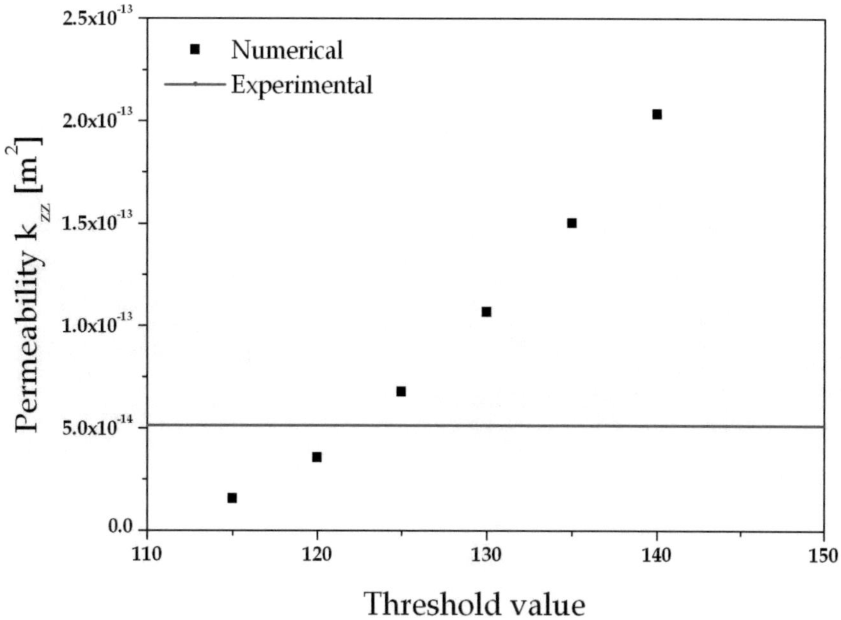

Fig. 13. (b)

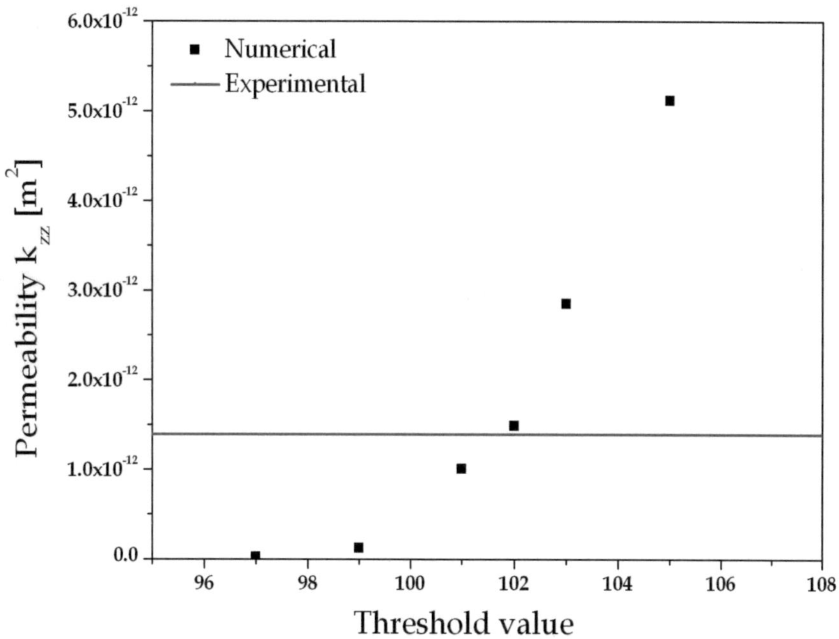

(c)

Fig. 13. Numerically solved permeability coefficients for the wool fibre web (a), the packaging board (b) and the sand stone (c) as a function of threshold value. Experimental results are given as an average of the five measurements for each sample types.

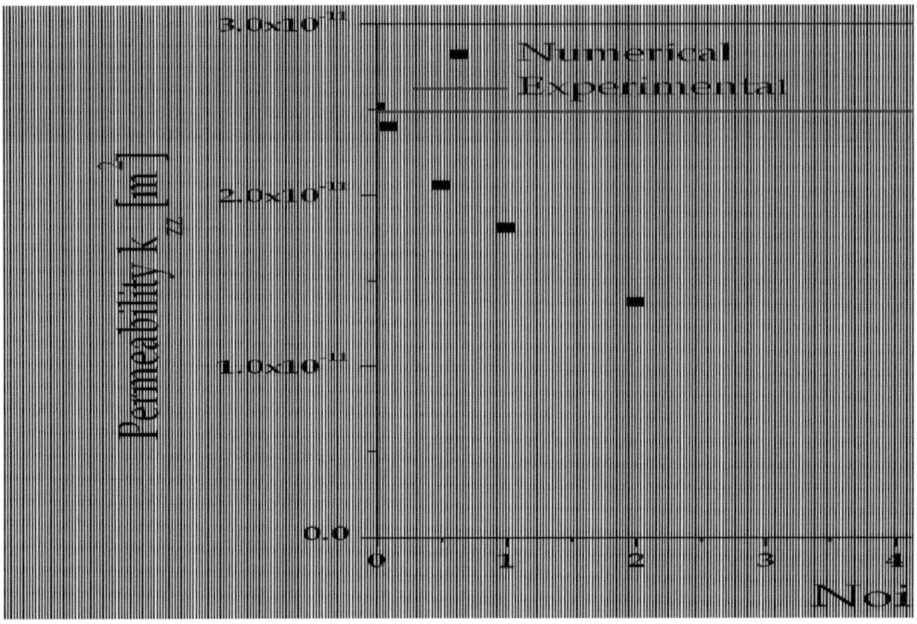

Fig. 14. (a)

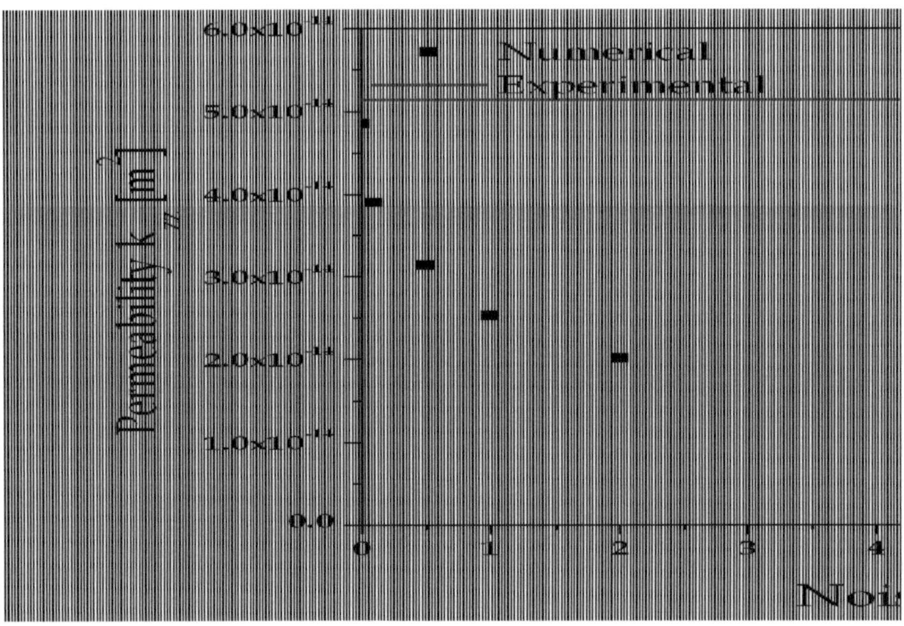

Fig. 14. (b)

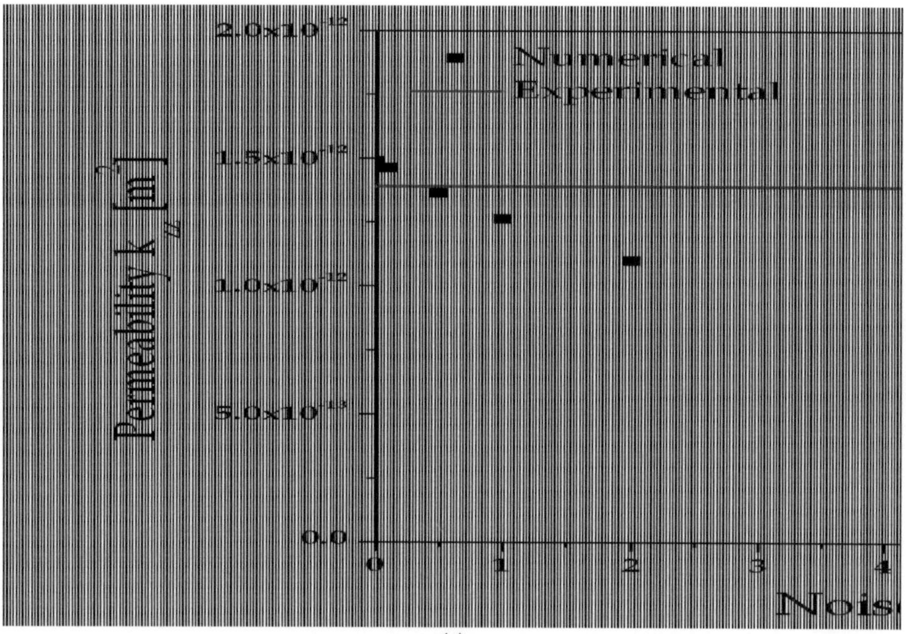

(c)

Fig. 14. Numerically solved permeability coefficients for the wool fibre web (a), the packaging board (b) and the sand stone (c) as a function of noise level. Experimental results are given as an average of the five measurements for each sample types.

4.2.2 Effect of artefacts on specific surface area and pore size distribution

Specific surface area of the wool fibre web sample was analysed as a function of threshold value and noise level, see the results in Fig. 15. The specific surface area of the geometry thresholded by the forest fire method had a value of 0.175 m^{-1}. The value of specific surface area of the sample geometry decreased as a function of increasing threshold value and increased as a function of increasing noise level. According to Eq. (3), when a sample geometry has a high specific surface area, it has a small permeability value. This could also be seen from the results in Fig. 15 and in Figs 13a and 14a.

Pore size distribution of the wool fibre web sample geometry was analysed as a function of threshold value, see the results in Fig. 16a. When compared to the experimental permeability results, the optimal threshold value was found to be between 20 and 30, see Fig. 13a. The results in Fig. 16a clearly show that with the threshold values of 20 or 30 the pore size distribution differs highly from the pore size distribution of the geometry that was segmented using the forest fire method. These results support the interpretation related to the permeability values obtained using the geometries segmented by conventional grey value -based thresholding. Combination of too high specific surface area and too thin fibres (high porosity) resulted to the permeability values very close to the experimental results. These interpretations were found to be similar for the packaging board and for the sand stone samples also.

Pore size distribution as a function of noise level for the wool fibre web sample is presented in Fig. 16b. The effect of added noise was found to be not as high as for the hexagonal array of cylinders, see Fig. 7. For noise level of 2 %, the mode value of the distribution was approximately a half of the mode value of the noise free geometry.

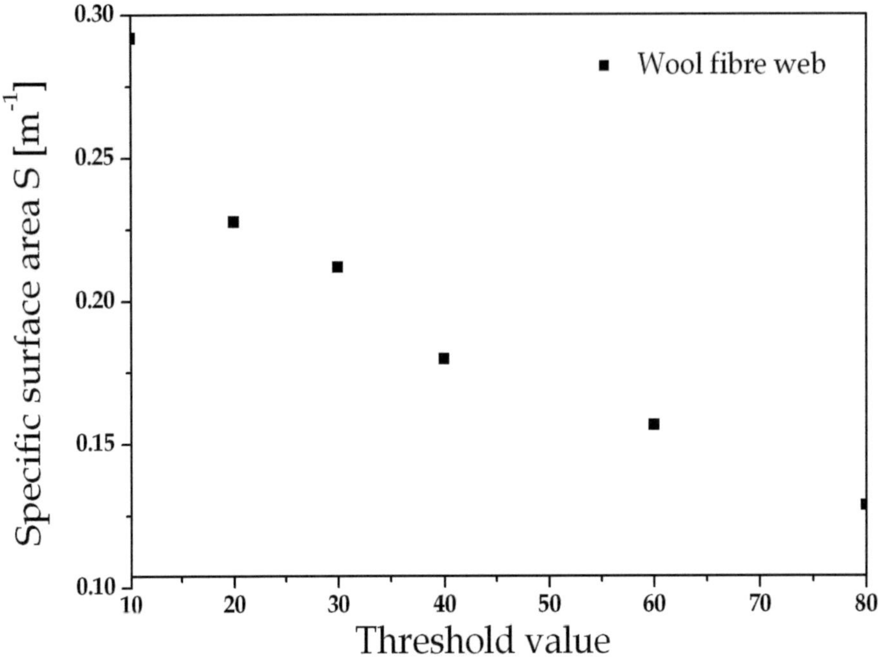

Fig. 15. (a)

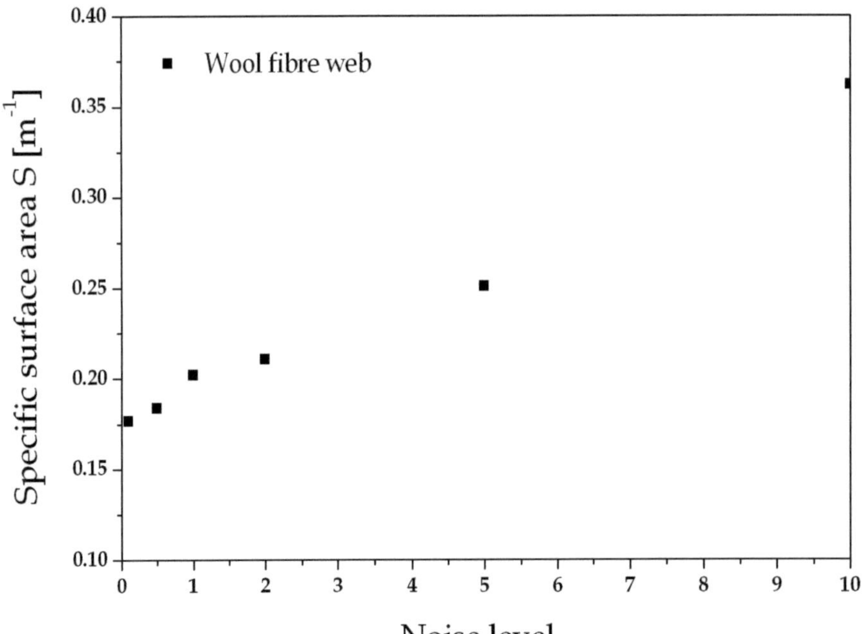

(b)

Fig. 15. Specific surface area of the wool fibre web sample as a function of threshold value (a) and noise level (b).

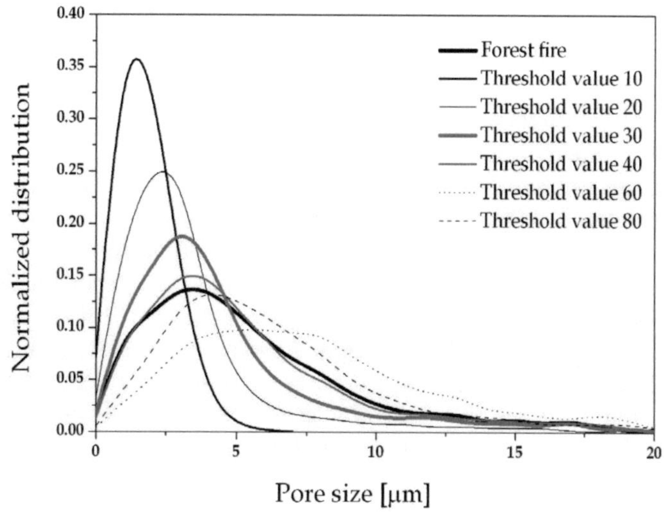

Fig. 16. (a)

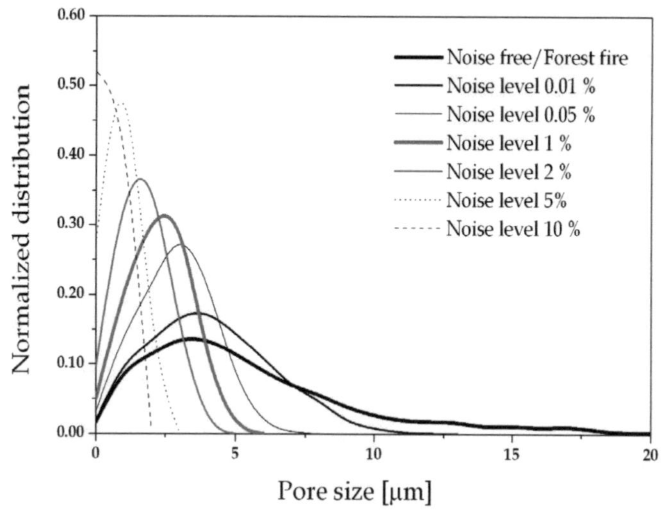

(b)

Fig. 16. Normalized pore size distribution for the wool fibre web sample as a function of pore size with different threshold values (a) and with different noise levels (b).

5. Conclusions

Approximate factors of how certain levels of noise and edge roughness effect on permeability value, mode value of pore size distribution and specific surface area of the hexagonal array of cylinders are summarised in Table 1. According to the results, even a small amount (0.01 % of sample volume) of noise in the void space has a drastic influence on the permeability values. The noise level of few percent caused magnitudes decrease in the permeability values. Increase in the amount of noise increases the specific surface area of the simulation geometry and thus decreases the permeability value. Also the pore size

distributions of the simulation geometries were found to change dramatically as a function of noise level. The mode value of the pore size distribution with the noise level of 0.01 % is approximately one third of the mode value of the noise free geometry.
Edge roughness on solid-void boundaries increases the specific surface area of the hexagonal cylinder geometry and therefore decreases the flow permeability value. The effect is, however, moderate compared to the effect of noise. Edge roughness was found to have only a small effect on the pore size distribution of the geometry.
Approximate factors of how certain levels of threshold value and noise effect on permeability value, mode value of pore size distribution and specific surface area of the wool fibre web sample are given in Table 2. The factors are given as values compared to the analysis results based on the forest fire segmented geometry that gives values very close to the experimental results. The results obtained using the forest fire method were compared to the data obtained from the scanning electron microscope images. Agreement with the sizes of characteristic solid objects was found to be good. The numerical permeability analyses for the sample geometries segmented using the forest fire method provided good agreement with the experimental results. The difference between the experimental results and the numerical permeability values found by using the forest fire segmented simulation geometries was less than 6.5 % for all the sample types.

	Noise level 0.01 %	Noise level 1 %	Noise level 10 %
Permeability	0.5	0.01	0.001
Mode value of pore size distribution	0.3	0.2	0.1
Specific surface area	1.1	3	30
	Edge roughness level 10	Edge roughness level 50	Edge roughness level 120
Permeability	1	0.9	0.5
Mode value of pore size distribution	1	0.9	0.8
Specific surface area	1.2	2.5	9

Table 1. Approximate factors of how certain levels of noise and edge roughness effect on permeability value, mode value of pore size distribution and specific surface area of the hexagonal array of cylinders. Factors are given as values compared to the results for the noise free geometry.

The permeability results were found to be very sensitive for the threshold value used in segmenting the 3D geometries. Faulty selection of the threshold value can cause an error for the permeability value by a factor of approximately 2-5. By using grey value -based threshold method, the permeability value might by chance have approximately correct values (compared to the experimental results). However, the permeability value with selected threshold value would not necessarily be result of the realistic sample geometry, but combination of noise causing higher specific surface area and too thin fibres increasing the porosity value of the geometry. This result was found to be qualitatively similar for all the three sample types and the imaging methods used here.

Pore size distributions of the tomographic geometries were analysed as a function of threshold value. Although fluid flow analyses based on geometries segmented by grey value -based segmentation method might result in approximately correct permeability values, the structure of the pore geometry does not necessarily correspond with the realistic case. According to the results, the pore size distributions based on the grey value segmented geometries differ from the distributions based on geometries which were segmented using the forest fire method.

The forest fire segmented tomographic reconstructions were used in studying the effect of noise on tomographic geometries. Results in these cases indicate that the permeability results of tomographic geometries are not as sensitive to noise as in the case of regular hexagonal cylinder arrays. By increasing the noise level to 2 %, the permeability results decreased approximately by a factor of 0.5.

The effect of noise level on pore size distribution was analysed. The effect of added noise on tomographic reconstructions is not as drastic as in the case of the hexagonal cylinder arrays. With the noise level of 2 %, the mode value of the distribution is approximately a half of the mode value for the noise free geometry.

The results indicate that effective methods for handling imaging artefact removal and segmentation are essential for obtaining reliable results for structural and transport properties by means of direct numerical analyses based on CXμT reconstructions of the 3D structure of complex porous materials. According to our studies, the most essential factor for successful structural analysis and flow simulation is the quality of the tomographic reconstruction, i.e. noiseless and realistic structure. To achieve this requirement, a well controlled image acquisition and a good segmentation algorithm together with a verification based on a characteristic parameter, e.g. the mode value of pore size distribution measured by an independent method like mercury intrusion porosimetry or average characteristic dimension from a 2D microscopic image of the material, is required.

	Error in threshold value + 10 grey values	Error in threshold value + 20 grey values	Error in threshold value + 30 grey values
Permeability	2	3	5
Mode value of pore size distribution	1.1	1.4	2
Specific surface area	0.9	0.8	0.7
	Noise level 2 %	Noise level 5 %	Noise level 10 %
Permeability	0.5	0.3	0.2
Mode value of pore size distribution	0.5	0.2	0.1
Specific surface area	1.2	1.2	2

Table 2. Approximate factors of how certain levels of threshold value and noise effect on permeability values, mode value of pore size distribution and specific surface area of the wool fibre web. The factors are given as values compared to the analysis results based on the forest fire segmented geometry.

6. Acknowledgement

The authors thank Dr. Keijo Mattila for fruitful discussions related to the project and M.Sc. Jarno Alaraudanjoki for the support related to the experimental permeability measurements. The authors express their gratitude to the ID19's team of ESRF for help with the acquisition of the images.

7. References

Aaltosalmi, U.; Kataja, M.; Koponen, A.; Timonen, J.; Goel, A.; Lee, G. & Ramaswamy, S. (2004). Numerical analysis of fluid flow through fibrous porous materials, *Journal of Pulp Paper Science*, Vol.30, No.9, pp. 251–255

Bear, J. (1972). *Dynamics of Fluid in Porous Media*, Dover Publications inc., pp. 151–173

Belov, E. B.; Lomov, S. V.; Verpoest, I.; Peters, T.; Roose, D.; Parnas, R. S.; Hoes, K. & Sol, H. (2004). Modelling of permeability of textile reinforcements: lattice boltzmann method, *Composites science and techology*, Vol64, pp. 1069–1080

Coles, M. E., D.; Hazlett, R., P.; Spanne, E.; Soll,W. & Jones, E. L. K. W. (1998). Pore level imaging of fluid transport using synchrotron x-ray microtomography, *Journal of Petroleum Science and Engineering*, Vol.19, No.1, pp. 55–63

Darcy, H. (1856). *Les fontaines publiques de la ville de dijon*. Dalmont, Paris Drummont, M. I. & Tahir, J. E. (1984). The permeability of fibrous porous media. *International Journal of Multiphase Flow*, Vol.10, No.5, pp. 515–525

Drugan, W. & Willis, J. A. (1996). A micromechanics-based nonlocal constitutive equation and estimates of representative volume element size for elastic composites, *Journal of the mechanics and physics of solids*, Vol.44, No.4, pp.497-524

Dullien, F. A. L. (1979). *Porous Media: Fluid Transport and Pore Structure*, Academic Press Inc. San Diego, pp. 269–324

Fourie, W.; Said, R.; Young, P. & Barnes, D. L. (2007). The simulation of pore scale fluid flow with real world geometries obtained from x-ray computed tomography, *Proceedings of European COMSOL Multiphysics Conference*, Boston, COMSOL inc.

Goel, A.; Tzanakakis, M.; Huang, S.; Ramaswamy, S.; Choi, D. & Ramarao., B. (2002). Characterization of three-dimensional structure of paper using X-ray microtomography, *Tappi Journal*. Vol.84, No.5, pp. 111-122

Goel, A.; Arns, C. H.; Holmstad, R.; Gregersen, O. W.; Bauget, F., Averdunk, H.; Sok, R. M.;

Sheppard, A. P. & Knackstedt, M. A. (2006). Analysis of the Impact of Papermaking Variables on the Structure and Transport Properties of Paper Samples by X-ray Microtomography, *Journal of Pulp and Paper Science*, Vol.32, No.2, pp. 111-122

Gonzales, R. C. & Woods R. E. (2002). Digital Image Processing, second edition, Prentice Hall

Holmstad, R.; Aaltosalmi, U.; Ramaswamy, S.; Kataja, M.; Koponen, A.; Goel, A. & Gregersen, O. W. (2005). Comparison of 3D structural characteristics of high and low resolution x-ray microtomographic images of paper, Nordic Pulp and Paper Research Journal, Vol.20, No.3, pp. 283-288

Holmstad, R.; Antonie, C.; Nygård P. & Helle, T. (2003). Quantification of the three-dimensional paper structure: Methods and potential. Pulp & Paper C*anada*, Vol.42, No.7, pp. 86–189

Kak, A. C. & Slaney, M. (1988). *Principles of Computerized Tomographic Imaging,* IEEE Press
Kass, M; Witkin, A. & Terzopoulos, D. (1987). Snakes - Active Contour Models. *International Journal of Computer Vision*, Vol.1, No.4, pp.321-331

Koivu V.; Mattila K. & Kataja M. (2009a). A method for measuring Darcian flow permeability. *Nordic Pulp and Paper Research Journal*, Vol.24, No.4, pp. 395–402

Koivu V.; Decain M.; Geindreau C.; Mattila K., Alaraudanjoki, J.; Bloch J.-F. & Kataja M. (2009b). Flow permeability of fibrous porous materials. Micro-tomography and numerical simulations. *Proceedings in the 14th Fundamental Research Symposium*, Oxford, pp. 437–454.

Koivu V.; Decain M.; Geindreau C.; Mattila K.; Bloch J.-F. & Kataja M. (2010) Transport properties of heterogeneous materials. Combining computerised X-ray micro-tomography and direct numerical simulations, *International Journal of Computational Fluid Dynamics*, Vol. 23, No.10, pp. 713–721

Kutay, M. E.; Aydilek, A. H. & Masad, E. (2006). Laboratory validation of lattice Boltzmann method for modeling pore-scale flow in granular materials. *Computers and Geotechnics*, Vol.33, No.8, pp. 381–395

Leskelä, M. and Simula, S. (1998). *Papermaking Science and Technology, Paper Physics, Transport phenomena*, ISBN952-5216-16-0, Fapet Oy, Helsinki, pp. 284–317

Liakopoulos, A. C. (1965). Darcy's coefficient of permeability as symmetric tensor of second rank. *Hydrolocical Sciences Journal*, Vol.10, No.3, pp.41–48

Lundström, T. S.; Frishfelds, V. & Jakovics, A. (2004). A statistical approach to permeability of clustered fibre reinforcements, *Journal of Composite and Materials,* Vol.38, No.13, pp. 1137–1149

Lorensen, W. E. & Clive H. E. (1987a). Marching cubes: A high resolution 3D surface construction algorithm, *ACM SIGGRAPH Computer Graphics*, Vol.21, No.4, pp. 163-169

Lorensen, W. E. & Clive H. E. (1987b). Marching cubes: A high resolution 3D surface construction algorithm, *Proceedings of the 14th annual conference on computer graphics and interactive techniques*, New York, USA

Manwart, C.; Aaltosalmi, U.; Koponen, A.; Hilfer, R. & Timonen, J. (2002). Lattice-Boltzmann and finite-difference simulations for the permeability for three-dimensional porous media, *Physical Review. E.*, Vol.66, No.1, 016702.

Martys, N. S. & Hagedorn, J. G. (2002). Multiscale modeling of fluid transport in heterogeneous materials using discrete Boltzmann methods, Journal of Materials and Structures, Vol.35, No.10, pp. 650–659

Ojala, T.; Pietikäinen, M. & Harwood, D. (1994). Performance evaluation of texture measures with classification based on Kullback discrimination of distributions, *Proceedings of the 12th IAPR International Conference on Pattern Recognition (ICPR 1994)*, vol.1, pp. 582-585

Osher, S.; Sethian, J. A. (1988). Fronts propagating with curvature-dependent speed: Algorithms based on Hamilton-Jacobi formulations, *Journal of Computational Physics*, Vol.79, pp. 12–49

Perona, P. & Malik J. (1987). Scale-space and edge detection using anisotropic diffusion. *Proceedings of IEEE Computer Society Workshop on Computer Vision*, pp. 16–22.

Rasi, M., Koponen, A., Aaltosalmi, U., Timonen, J., Kataja, M., & Niskanen, K. J. (1999). Permeability of paper: Experiments and numerical simulations. TAPPI, International Paper Physics Conference, pp. 297–306

Rolland du Roscoat, S.; Bloch, J.-F. & Thibault, X. (2005). Synchrotron Radiation microtomography applied to paper investigation, *Journal of Physics D: Applied Physics*, Vol.38, pp. A78-A84

Rolland du Roscoat, S.; Decain, M.; Thibault, X.; Geindreau, C. & Bloch, J.-F. (2007). Estimation of microstructural properties from synchrotron X-ray micro tomography and determination of the REV in paper materials. *Acta Materiala*, Vol.55, No.8, pp. 2841–2850.

Samuelsen, E. J.; Houen, P.-J.; Gregersen, O. W.; Helle, T. & Raven C. (2001). Three Dimensional Imaging of Paper by Use of Synchrotron X-ray Microtomography, *Journal of Pulp and Paper Science*, Vol.27, No.2, pp. 50-53

Smith, S.M.; Brady, J.M. (1997). SUSAN - a new approach to low level image processing. *Int. Journal of Computer Vision*, Vol. 23, No.1, pp. 45-78

Stock, S. R. (2009). *Micro Computed Tomography, Methodology and Applications*, CRC press Taylor and Francis Group, Boca Raton

Thibault, X. & Bloch, J.-F. (2002). Structural Analysis of X-ray Microtomography of a Strained Nonwoven Papermaker Felt, *Textile Research Journal*, Vol.72, No.6, pp. 480-485

Tomasi, C. & Manduchi, R. (1998). Bilateral Filtering for Gray and Color Images, *Proceedings of the 1998 IEEE International Conference on Computer Vision*, Bombay, IndiaTorquato, S. (2001). *Heterogeneous Materials, Microstructure and Macroscopic Properties*, Springer-Verlag New York Inc., New York, pp. 1-19

Verleye, B.; Croce, R.; Griebel, M.; Klitz, M.; Lomov, S.; Morren, G.; Sol, H.; Verpoest, I. & Roose, D. (2007). Permeability of textile reinforcements: Simulation, influence of shear and validation, *Composite Science and Technology*, Vol.68, No.1, pp. 2804–2810.

Verleye, B.; Klitz, M.; Croce, R.; Roose, D.; Lomov, S. & Verpoest, I. (2005). Computation of permeability of textile reinforcements. *Proceedings in Scientific Computation IMACS 2005*, Paris, France

Wiegman, A. (2007). Computation of the permeability of porous materials from their microstructure by fft-Stokes, Report of the Fraunhofer ITWM 129, Fraunhofer Institute

Wu, K.; Jiang, Z.; Couples, G. D.; Van Dijke, M. I. J. & Sorbie, K. S. (2007). Reconstruction of multi-scale heterpogeneous porous media and their flow prediction, *Proceedings in the International Symposium of the Society of Core Analysts*, Calgary, Canada

23

Nongray EWB and WSGG Radiation Modeling in Oxy-Fuel Environments

Osama A. Marzouk[1] and E. David Huckaby[2]
[1]*U.S. Department of Energy, National Energy Technology Laboratory; and West Virginia University Research Corporation*
[2]*U.S. Department of Energy, National Energy Technology Laboratory*
USA

1. Introduction

According to a recent U.S. Greenhouse Gas Emissions Inventory (1), about 42% of 2008 CO_2 (a greenhouse gas) emissions in the U.S were from burning fossil fuels (especially coal) to generate electricity. The 2010 U.S. International Energy Outlook (2) predicts that the world energy generation using coal and natural gas will continue to increase steadily in the future. This results in increased concentrations of atmospheric CO_2, and calls for serious efforts to control its emissions from power plants through *carbon capture* technologies. Oxy-fuel combustion is a *carbon capture* technology in which the fossil fuel is burned in an atmosphere free from nitrogen, thereby reducing significantly the relative amount of N_2 in the flue-gas and increasing the mole fractions of H_2O and CO_2. This low concentration of N_2 facilitates the capture of CO_2. The dramatic change in the flue composition results in changes in its thermal, chemical, and radiative properties. From the modeling point of view, existing transport, combustion, and radiation models that have parameters tuned for air-fuel combustion (where N_2 is the dominant gaseous species in the flue) may need revision to improve the predictions of numerical simulations of oxy-fuel combustion.

In this chapter, we consider recent efforts done to revise radiation modeling for oxy-fuel combustion, where five new radiative-property models were proposed to be used in oxy-fuel environments. All these models use the weighted-sum-of-gray-gases model (WSGGM). We apply and compare their performance in two oxy-fuel environments. Both environments consist of only H_2O and CO_2 as mixture species, and thus there is no N_2 dilution, but the environments vary in the mole fractions of these two species. The first case has a CO_2 mole fraction of 65%, whereas the second has a CO_2 mole fraction of 90%. The former case is more relevant to what is referred to as *wet flue gas recycle (wet FGR)* where some flue gas is still recirculated into the furnace, but after to act as coal carrier or diluent (to temper the flame temperature). On the other hand, the second case is more relevant to what is referred to as *dry flue gas recycle (dry FGR)* where some flue gas is still recirculated into the furnace but after a stage of H_2O condensation. This increases the CO_2 fraction in the recycled flue gas (RFG) and consequently in the final flue gas leaving the furnace and the boiler of the plant.

To highlight the influence of using an air-fuel WSGGM (a model with parameters were developed for use in air-fuel combustion) in oxy-fuel environments, the air-fuel WSGGM of

Smith et al. (1982) is included as the sixth WSGGM. The WSGG solutions are accompanied by solutions using the more-rigorous exponential wide band model (EWBM) approach and the spectral line-base weighted-sum-of-gray-gases model (SLW) approach. All the solutions presented here are nongray, meaning that the radiative properties of the emitting/absorbing mixture vary across the spectrum and multiple radiative transfer equations (RTEs) are solved per spectrum. The total pressure is 1 atm (101 325 N/m^2).

2. Mathematical description

The spectral radiative transfer equation (RTE) along a path s (with a unit vector $\hat{s}$) in an emitting/absorbing medium is (3; 4)

$$\frac{d\,I_\eta(s,\eta)}{d\,s} = \hat{s} \bullet \nabla I_\eta = k_\eta(s,\eta)\left(I_{b,\eta}(s,\eta) - I_\eta(s,\eta)\right) \tag{1}$$

where η is the wavenumber (its SI unit is 1/m), I_η is the spectral radiative intensity (its SI unit is $\frac{\mathrm{W/m^2}}{\frac{1}{\mathrm{m}}\ \mathrm{steradian}}$), $I_{b,\eta}$ is the blackbody radiative intensity, and k_η is the spectral linear radiative absorption coefficient (its SI unit is 1/m). From a molecular view, when k_η is uniform along a path, $1/k_\eta$ is the mean free path traveled by a photon until it is absorbed by an electron (3; 4). From a continuum view, and from Equation (1), it can also be viewed as simply the fraction of radiation pencil absorbed over a distance of 1 meter (5). The blackbody radiative intensity, or the Planck function, ($I_{b,\eta}$) depends on the wavenumber (or wavelength), local temperature, and the refractive index of the medium. This dependence has the following form:

$$I_{b,\eta}(s,\eta) = \frac{2\,h\,c_0^2\,\eta^3}{n^2\left(\exp\left(\frac{h\,c_0\,\eta}{k_B\,T}\right) - 1\right)} \tag{2}$$

where n is the refractive index of the medium (being unity for vacuum), h is the Planck constant (in SI units, $h = 6.6261 \times 10^{-34}$ J-s), c_0 is the speed of light in vacuum (in SI units, c_0= 299 792 458 m/s), k_B is the Boltzmann constant (in SI units, $k_B = 1.3807 \times 10^{-32}$ J/K), and T is the temperature. When Equation (2) is integrated over the entire spectrum, we obtain the total blackbody radiation intensity, which depends only on the medium type (through its refractive index) and the local temperature, as follows:

$$I_{b,tot}(n,T) = n^2\,\sigma\,T^4/\pi \tag{3}$$

where σ is the Stefan-Boltzmann constant (in SI units, $\sigma = 5.67 \times 10^{-8}$ W/m^2-K^4).
In modeling, the thermal effect of radiation appears in the energy equation through a radiative source term (its SI unit is W/m^3), which takes the following form:

$$\text{source} = \int_{\eta=0}^{\infty} \left(\int_{4\pi} k_\eta\, I_\eta d\Omega - 4\pi\, k_\eta\, I_{b,\eta}\right) d\eta \tag{4}$$

where Ω is the solid angle (in steradian). This source term is negative when the radiation has cooling effect on the medium, as in flames and reacting flows (6; 7).
Defining the spectral direction-integrated incident radiation

$$G_\eta \equiv \int_{4\pi} I_\eta d\Omega \tag{5}$$

then Equation (4) can be re-written as

$$\text{source} = \int_{\eta=0}^{\infty} \left(k_\eta \, G_\eta - 4\pi \, k_\eta \, I_{b,\eta} \right) d\eta \tag{6}$$

In the most comprehensive approach, known as the line-by-line (LBL) approach (4), the spectrum is divided into high-resolution intervals where k_η is approximately constant over each interval, and an RTE per direction is solved for each interval. Then, the total radiative intensity and the total radiative source term are obtained from spectral integration of the respective spectral quantities.

The spectral absorption coefficient for gaseous species is known to vary rapidly and it is far from being a smooth function of η. This is due to the fact that radiation from a hot gas (e.g., a flame) is absorbed by combustion gases only at wavenumbers at which electrons can be excited to the next discrete energy level. Therefore these gases are radiatively-transparent at certain portions of the spectrum, but become radiatively-active at other portions (8). The LBL approach for solving the radiation problem is not practical in real combustion simulations, where such approach would involve hundreds of thousands of RTEs. Alternative approaches exist where much fewer RTEs are solved to resolve the spectrum.

Of course the extreme case is to solve a single RTE per direction for the entire spectrum, assuming constant properties over the entire spectrum. This approach is referred to as *gray*. This simplifies the calculations greatly, but completely loses the spectral character of radiation through its full-spectrum averaging. In that approach, the RTE becomes

$$\frac{d\, I_{tot}}{d\, s} = \hat{s} \bullet \nabla I_{tot} = k_{gray} \left(I_{b,tot} - I_{tot} \right) \tag{7}$$

and the radiative source becomes

$$\text{source} = k_{gray} \left(G_{tot} - 4\,\pi\, I_{b,tot} \right) \tag{8}$$

As a compromise between the formidable LBL approach and the too-coarse gray approach, we apply two other approaches where spectral variation is accounted for, but with a much lower resolution than the LBL. These approaches are the nongray WSGGM and the box model based on the EWBM. In either approach, for each direction a small number of RTEs solved, each of which covers a fraction of the spectrum where the linear absorption coefficient is considered to be constant, and where the fraction of the total blackbody radiation over that spectral portion is what acts to augment the radiation. Therefore, the RTE of the ith fraction is

$$\frac{d\, I_i}{d\, s} = \hat{s} \bullet \nabla I_i = k_i \left(a_i \, I_{b,tot} - I_i \right) \tag{9}$$

where the quantity a_i is the fraction of the total (i.e., spectrally-integrated) blackbody radiation that belongs to the ith spectral fraction. The source term is

$$\text{source} = \sum_i k_i \left(\, G_i - a_i \, 4\, \pi \, I_{b,tot} \right) \tag{10}$$

In the box/EWB, the spectrum partitioning is based on modeled band structure that reflects the presence of the vibration-rotation or pure-rotation bands of the emitting/absorbing species. In the nongray WSGGM, no direct partitioning of the spectrum is done, and each of the so-called fractions is a hypothetical collection of noncontiguous intervals of the spectrum having the same value of the spectral absorption coefficient. In the following subsections, we describe further the box/EWB model and the nongray WSGG model.

2.1 Box/EWB model

In the general box model, the erratic spectral profile of k_η is idealized as a piecewise-constant function, with constant k_η values over a range of η. This value can be zero over intervals of spectrum where no absorption is occurring (called the *windows*). In the present work, a piecewise-constant function of k_η is calculated using the exponential wide band model, which idealizes each vibration-rotation band of H_2O or CO_2 as well as the far-infrared pure-rotation band of H_2O according to the block approximation (9). A block is formed between the edges of each idealized band. There are 6 vibration-rotation bands of CO_2, four vibration-rotation bands of H_2O, and a pure-rotation band of H_2O. The number of blocks varies depending on the width of each idealized band; which in turn depends on the fractions of H_2O and CO_2 in the medium, its temperature, and its total pressure.

We have used a model with 22 blocks that cover the wavenumbers from η=0 to 100 000 1/cm. This corresponds to wavelengths from λ=0.1 μ m to ∞. Such range is wide enough to handle thermal radiation (10). Consequently, 22 RTEs per direction are solved to resolve the spectrum. This range covers more than 99.99% of the area under the Planck function at 1 500 K. The band equivalent widths are computed using the Edwards-Menard 3-regime expressions (11; 12) for the vibration-rotation bands, and using the Fleske-Tien theoretical expression (13; 15) for the pure-rotation band. The parameters for the vibration-rotation bands are those in (14) and for the pure-rotation bands are those in (15). Relating this approach to Equation (9), each k_i is a block value and each a_i is the fraction of the Planck function over that block. The box/EWB approach requires the specification of a mean pathlength (some characteristic length for radiation) for the problem, which is approximated as 3.6 times the volume divided by the surface areas (3). For the 12×12×40 m rectangular enclosure we consider here, this value is 9.3913 m. This length was also used to obtain k_i for each block from its calculated emissivity.

Figure 1 shows the idealized spectra of k_η for the two gas compositions studied in this work (i.e., 65% CO_2 with 35% H_2O, and 90% CO_2 and 10% H_2O) at a constant temperature of 1 500 K. The corresponding blackbody emissive power ($E_{b,\eta} = \pi I_{b,\eta}$) is superimposed in each plot. The corresponding spectra using the wavelength λ as the spectral variable are given in Figure 2.

Whereas both CO_2 and H_2O are radiatively-active, as some H_2O is replaced by CO_2 (moving from wet recycle to dry recycle), the absorption/emission of the mixture decreases (17; 18). The full listing of the linear absorption coefficients and blackbody weights of each block for both oxy-fuel environments are given in Appendix 7, Tables 9 and 10.

2.2 WSGGM

Despite the large reduction in the number of calculations when switching from the LBL approach to the box/EWB approach, it is still desirable to attain further reduction in the number of RTEs to be solved for the entire spectrum when performing complex combustion simulations as they involve many physical and chemical phenomena other than radiation. The WSGGM has enjoyed great popularity (4) and is utilized here as a *more-practical* approach for complex combustion modeling, whereas the aforementioned more-expensive

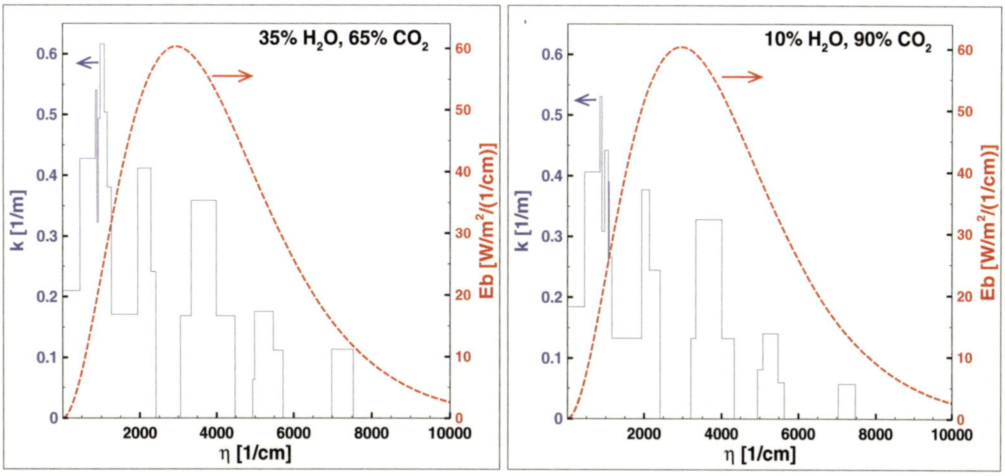

Fig. 1. Spectra (versus wavenumber) of the blackbody emissive power and the box/EWB linear absorption coefficient and at 1 500 K for two oxy-fuel environments

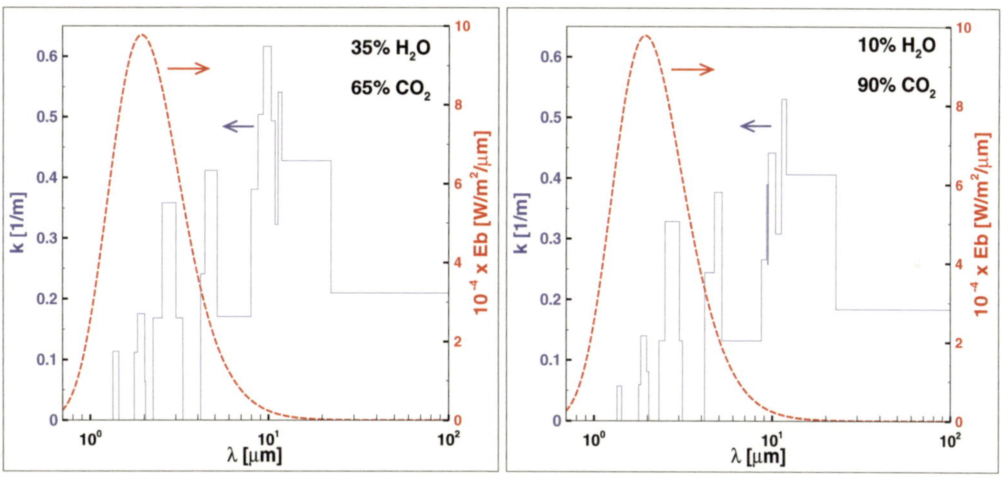

Fig. 2. Spectra (versus wavelength) of the blackbody emissive power and the box/EWB linear absorption coefficient and at 1 500 K for two oxy-fuel environments

box/EWB approach serves to provide a benchmark solution to compare with. In the nongray WSGG approach, Equation (9) is still solved as was the case in the box model, but the physical interpretation and the evaluation of the k_i and a_i are very different. The WSGG approach (5; 16; 19–21) is based on the presence of N hypothetical gray gases; $N-1$ are absorbing/emitting, and one is clear (no radiative emission or absorption) to represent the presence of spectral windows. Each absorbing/emitting gray gas has a constant k_i, and the clear gas has k_0=0. The fractions a_i are cast as a polynomial of temperature only. The parameters of a WSGGM are the k_i and the polynomial coefficients for each absorbing/emitting gray gas. There are $(N-1) \times (M+1)$ model parameters for N gray gases and a polynomial order M. The parameters for a single total pressure and a single gas composition (H_2O and CO_2 partial pressures) are calculated through an optimization process.

The optimization requires a set of emissivities for a range of temperatures and pathlengths at these total pressure and gas composition.
When used to calculate the total emissivity (either during the model coefficient optimization process or for evaluating the total emissivity with fixed model coefficients), the WSGGM returns a weighted sum of individual emissivities of the hypothetical absorbing/emitting gray gases, i.e.

$$\epsilon_{tot} = \sum_{i=1}^{N-1} a_i(T)\left(1 - \exp\left[-K_{p,i}\,PL\right]\right) \tag{11a}$$

$$\text{where}\quad a_i(T) = \sum_{j=1}^{M+1} b_{ij}\ (T/\hat{T})^{j-1} \tag{11b}$$

where ϵ_{tot} is the total emissivity (dimensionless), PL is pressure-pathlength, L is the mean pathlength, $K_{p,i}$ are the pressure absorption coefficients for the $N-1$ absorbing/emitting gray gases, a_i are the blackbody weights for these absorbing/emitting gray gases, b_{ij} are the coefficients for a polynomial of degree M in $T/\hat{T}$, and $\hat{T}$ is a scaling temperature that aids in the minimization process.
When the WSGGM is used to perform nongray calculations for use in Equation (9), the weights a_i are also evaluated from the temperature polynomial in Equation (11b); the ith linear absorption coefficient is evaluated as

$$k_i = K_{p,i}\,P \tag{12}$$

where P is the sum of the partial pressures of H_2O and CO_2 (in units consistent with those of $K_{p,i}$). A total of N RTEs are solved per direction to resolve the spectrum. In the WSGG models considered here, N takes the value of 4 or 5, which is a considerable reduction in computations compared to the box/EWB procedure described in subsection 2.1.
Table 1 compares the characteristics of the WSGG models which we consider. The first five WSGG models have been optimized for oxy-fuel combustion, whereas the last was developed for air-fuel combustion. Its inclusion in the study is a method to estimate the errors in radiation modeling when applying air-fuel WSGG models in oxy-fuel combustion simulations.
All models shown in Table 1 have mode parameters at finite sets of gas compositions, except for the 2011 model of Johansson et al. (24) where the model parameters are expressed as continuous functions of the molar ratio H_2O/CO_2. We perform piecewise-linear interpolation/extrapolation using the molar ratio $H_2O/(H_2O+CO_2)$ as an independent variable to apply the model at arbitrary gas compositions (18; 26). Marzouk and Huckaby (18) compared this technique to the piecewise-constant technique and recommended the former based on gray radiation modeling of non-isothermal media. The full listing of the linear absorption coefficients and blackbody weights for the gray gases of the 6 WSGG models for both oxy-fuel environments is given in Appendix 7, Tables 11-16. Notice that for either oxy-fuel environment, the clear-gas weight (a_0) in the air-fuel WSGGM (28) is higher than its counterpart in all the oxy-fuel WSGG models. This acts to reduce the radiative participation of the gaseous mixture.

Ref.	N	T-poly	Num. sets	$\hat{T}(K)$	T range (K)	PL range	Training data
(22)	4	quadratic	2	1 200	500–2 500	0.01–60 bar-m	SNBM (23)
(22)	5	quadratic	2	1 200	500–2 500	0.01–60 bar-m	SNBM (23)
(24)	5	quadratic	N/A	1 200	500–2 500	0.01–60 bar-m	SNBM (23)
(25)	4	linear	3	1	1 000–2 000	0.005–10 atm-m	empirical correlation (26)
(27)	5	cubic	7	1 200	500–3 000	0.001–60 atm-m	EWBM (9; 14; 15)
(28)	4	cubic	5	1	300–3 000	0.001–10atm-m	EWBM (9; 14; 15)

[a] at compositions: H_2O:CO_2 = 11.1%:88.9% and 50%:50% by mole
[b] *SNBM* is statistical narrow band model
[c] $K_{p,i}$ are expressed as linear functions of the H_2O/CO_2 molar ratio, and b_{ij} as quadratic functions of it
[d] at compositions: H_2O:CO_2 = 10%:10% (80% N_2), 33%:66%, and 10%:90% by mole
[e] implied from the empirical correlation used for the training data
[f] at compositions: H_2O:CO_2 = 11.1%:88.9%, 20%:80%, 33.3%:66.7%, 42.9%:57.1%, 50%:50%, 66.7%:33.3, 80%:20 by mole (3 others sets are given but not for oxy-fuel environments)
[g] at compositions: H_2O:CO_2 = $\rightarrow$ 0:0 (diluent is N_2), 10%:10% (80% N_2), 20%:10% (70% N_2), 0:$\rightarrow$ 0, 0%:100% (diluent is N_2) by mole.

Table 1. Summary of the 6 WSGG models considered here (5 oxy-fuel and 1 air-fuel)

3. Test cases

In coupled combustion simulations, different sub-models interact and thus it becomes difficult to examine the independent response of a particular sub-model. It is advantageous to isolate the radiation modeling when examining different solution approaches, which is what we have followed here. The two test problems to be presented in this section correspond to a stagnant homogeneous isothermal gas mixture. Only the radiative intensity is allowed to vary, thereby eliminating cross-model interactions which could make it difficult to judge the performance of the performance of the particular radiation model from the simulation results. Since our primary goal is to study the performance of the different oxy-fuel WSGG models when used in oxy-fuel environments, we considered two idealized oxy-fuel product gas compositions. Both environments have an atmospheric total pressure, which is also the sum of the partial pressures of H_2O and CO_2 (thus, no N_2 dilution, which is relevant to oxy-fuel operations). The only difference between the two environments is the gaseous composition, which is summarized in Table 2. In both environments, the CO_2 mole fraction is higher than the fraction of the H_2O. However, the second environment features dominance of CO_2 (9 times H_2O), which is more relevant to dry-recycle oxy-fuel operations.

Test case	H_2O mole fraction	CO_2 mole fraction	Total pressure (atm)	Temperature (K)
case 1	35%	65%	1	1 500
case 2	10%	90%	1	1 500

Table 2. Summary of the 2 studied oxy-fuel environments

The geometry of both problems is a large rectangular enclosure, with dimensions $12\times12\times40$ m. The medium temperature is 1 500 K. The temperature of the walls is kept at 750 K, with an emissivity of 0.725. This configuration was proposed by Krishnamoorthy et al. (25) to roughly represent the dimensions of a full-scale 300 MW front-wall-fired, pulverized-coal, utility boiler (29). The domain is discretized with a uniform mesh of $27\times27\times82$ cells, resulting in a total of 59 778 hexahedral cells.

4. Results

4.1 Numerical settings

The box/EWB model and each of the 6 WSGG models are applied to each of the 2 oxy-fuel environments. As mentioned in subsections 2.1 and 2.2, there are 22 RTEs per direction to resolve the spectrum for the box/EWB approach, and either 4 or 5 RTEs per direction to resolve the spectrum for the WSGG approach. We use the finite-volume method for the both the spatial and directional discretizations. As mentioned earlier in section 3, the enclosure is discretized into 59 778 cells. In each cell, the 3D angular space of 4π is divided into 128 angular divisions. A coarse representation of such angular discretization for a hemisphere (angular space of 2π) is shown in Figure 3. We have performed sensitivity analyses to check the suitability of both linear and angular resolutions by comparing a solution obtained using the aforementioned ones with a solution obtained using a finer linear resolution ($33\times33\times110$ = 119 790 cells) while keeping the angular resolution unchanged; and with a solutions obtained using a finer angular resolution (200 divisions) while keeping the linear resolution unchanged. In both situations, the solutions are nearly identical, and thus the adopted resolutions are considered sufficient. The nongray radiation simulation is performed iteratively using the computational fluid dynamics software ANSYS FLUENT 13.0 (30). None of the radiative-property models described here are available in the standard release. We implemented each method through a user-defined function that is complied and linked to the software for run-time access.

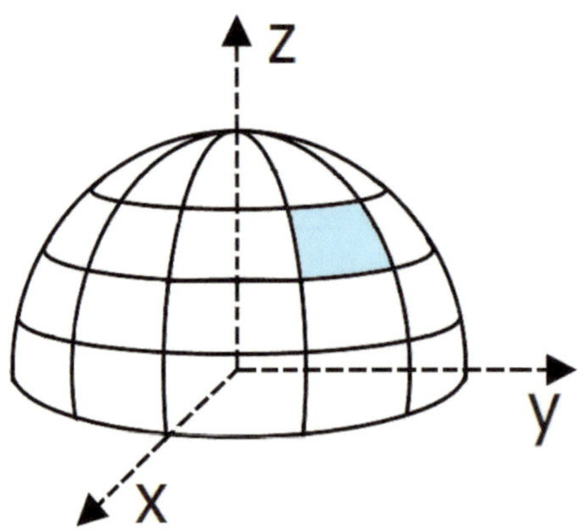

Fig. 3. Sketch illustrating the angular finite-volume discretization in a hemisphere

4.2 Order of presentation

In the four subsequent subsections, the solutions of the radiative solution for the two oxy-fuel environments are presented. We first start in subsection 4.3 with 2D flooded contours of the radiative source term (in kW/m^3) along the 12×40 vertical midplane (the symmetry plane midway between the two vertical side walls separated by a distance of 12 m). Due to the symmetry of the problem, this plane should be identical to the horizontal symmetry plane. Next, the 1D profiles of this radiative source term along the centerline of the enclosure (i.e., the 40-m longitudinal line passing through the geometric center of the 12×12 cross-section of the enclosure) are presented in subsection 4.4. In these profiles, we also include published results (25) using the SLW approach.

The SLW approach (originally proposed by Denison and Webb (31)) is a more-rigorous implementation of the WSGGM. The individual gray gases now have a physical meaning and direct mathematical relationship with the absorption spectrum (in terms of the absorption cross-section, whose SI unit is m^2/mol). The range of the absorption coefficient is divided into segments, each of which represents an absorbing/emitting gray gas. In addition, there is one clear gas (as in the WSGG approach). The segmentation of the range of absorption coefficient is typically done such that their logarithmic values are equally spaced. For each segment (i.e., each absorbing/emitting gray gas), a logarithmic average absorption cross-section C_i is assigned, and the corresponding blackbody weight a_i is evaluated to be the fraction of the Planck function that belongs to the range of absorption coefficient of the segment represented by the ith gray gas. The linear absorption coefficient for a species is related to the absorption cross-section by the species molar concentration (its SI units is $kmol/m^3$). The exact implementation of this method would require the processing of a high-resolution spectrum (which incurs the processing of millions of spectral data points at high combustion or flue temperatures), the computations are highly simplified by utilizing a fitted hyperbolic tangent function for the cumulative distribution of the absorption cross-section, which is known as the absorption-line blackbody distribution function (ALBDF) (32; 33).

Several different approaches have been developed to apply the SLW method to multicomponent gas mixtures. The approaches are derived using different assumptions and vary in computational cost and accuracy. For the SLW solution we include here, the absorption cross-section domains of H_2O and CO_2 were individually discretized into 20 logarithmically-spaced intervals between 3×10^{-5} m^2/mol and 120 m^2/mol for H_2O, and between 3×10^{-5} m^2/mol and 600 m^2/mol for CO_2. The analytical expressions for the absorption-line blackbody distribution functions of H_2O (32) and CO_2 (33) were used to compute the blackbody weights of each gray gas. The multiplication method (34) was used to handle the presence of a mixture. Implied in this method, is the assumption that the absorption cross-sections of H_2O and CO_2 are statistically independent. The number of RTEs per direction was 21 (one RTE per each of the 20 gray gases plus an RTE for the clear gas). The SLW calculations were performed using the T4 angular quadrature (35), and using the same spatial resolution we employed for the other two approaches (namely $27\times27\times82$) and using a similar angular resolution (128 directions).

Unlike the box/EWB and WSGG solutions, in which we use the angular finite-volume method for treating the angular dependence of radiation, the SLW solutions were obtained using the discrete-ordinate method. Whereas both methods have some similarity, the angular finite-volume method conserves the radiative energy (4) and thus is considered a more accurate method for handling the directional dependence of radiation. In addition, the analytical fits for ALBDF of H_2O and CO_2 are based on an extension of an old version (1991/1992) of the spectral database HITRAN (36). This database was assembled for a (low) temperature of 296 K and thus when applied at high temperatures the absorption of the medium will be underpredicted because many *hot lines* (i.e., transitions from excited vibration levels) are missing (4; 32; 37). Whereas a procedure (37) was followed to extend the original database by generating *hot-line* estimates from *cold-lines* (i.e., transitions from the ground level), Modest (4) showed that these analytical expressions result in nontrivial deviations from LBL calculations at 2 000 K. However, at 1 000 K, they are in good agreement with the LBL solution. On the other hand, the SLW approach does not require the specification of a pathlength as the EWB approach.

In the legends, the different WSGG models are designated by the total number of radiating and clear gases (either 4 or 5) and the temperature-polynomial order (linear, quadratic, or cubic). Since the WSGGM in reference (22) and the one in reference (24) have the same number of gray gases and the same polynomial order (5 gases and quadratic polynomials), we add a suffix *(cont)* to the WSGGM in reference (24) to highlight that its parameters are continuous functions of the H_2O/CO_2 molar ratio. Also, the air-fuel WSGGM here (28) is further distinguished by adding the suffix *(air)* to its legend entry.

The following subsection, number 4.5, shows also 1D profiles, but for the to-wall radiative flux (in kW/m^2) along the 40-m longitudinal midline of the top 12×40 wall of the enclosure. Due to the symmetry of the problem, this should be identical to any midline on the other three 12×40 walls.

The final subsection, number 4.6, is dedicated to the area-integrated radiative heat transfer rate to the walls (in MW). This subsection provides a quantitative measure of the variation among the different solutions with regard to the total radiative heat transfer rate (in MW) to the walls of the enclosure. The area-integrated heat transfer is an important quantity when we are concerned about the operation of the furnace unit within the boiler, as this effects steam generation rate. The average radiative heat flux is calculated from this quantity by dividing area-integrated heat transfer rate by the total surface area of the walls (2 208 m^2), and is also included in the comparison tables. This quantity provides a geometry-independent measure of the radiative heat load in oxy-fuel furnaces. The deviations from the benchmark box/EWB solution are also included. One table is provided per oxy-fuel environment.

4.3 Radiative-source contours

Slices of the radiative source term along the 12×40 plane of symmetry are shown in Figure 4. Each figure corresponds to a different model, with a plot for each of the two oxy-fuel environments. The number and values of the contour levels are the same for the plots. The double-symmetric pattern in all plots is expected. The calculated negative value of the radiative heat source would *drive* the temperature field to lower values in a coupled simulation. The radiative source is smallest near the colder-than-medium walls; it increases steeply and becomes nearly flat over a large portion of the plane. Notice that this value is very similar for both environments. The box/EWB solution exhibits a smaller decrease of the radiative source near the walls than the WSGG solutions. For both environments, the air-fuel WSGGM (28) and the 5-gas/cubic WSGGM (27) show noticeable overprediction of the radiative source, which indicates a weaker influence of radiation on the thermal field.

4.4 Radiative-source profiles

Profiles of the radiative source term along the longitudinal centerline of the 3D enclosure are compared in Figure 5 for the two oxy-fuel environments. As mentioned in subsection 4.2, we also add published profiles (25) predicted using the SLW approach. For both environments,

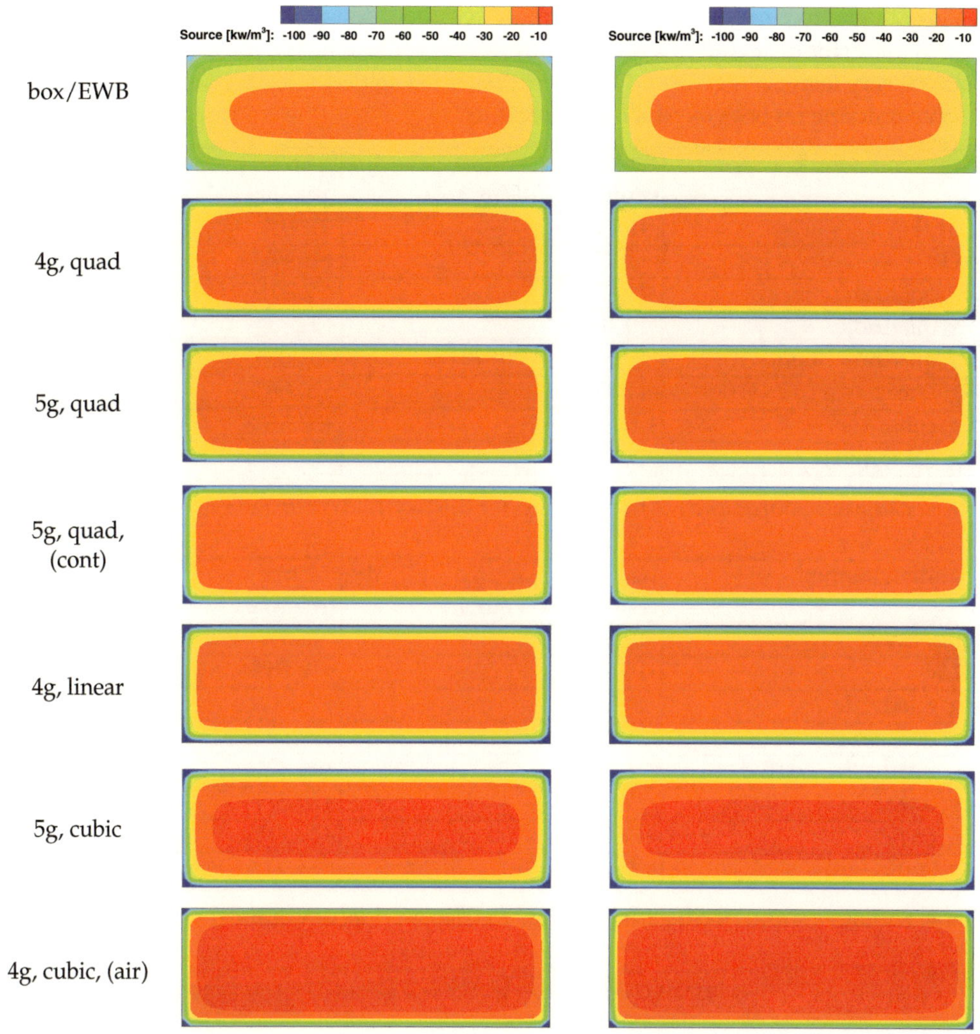

Fig. 4. Midplane radiative source (left: 65%CO_2; right: 90%CO_2)

the flat portion of the radiative-source curve is smallest in the case of the box/EWB solution. As suggested from the 2D contours in the previous subsection, the air-fuel and the 5-gas/cubic WSGGM solutions show noticeable overprediction of the radiative source, with the air-fuel solution being the worst.

Tables 5 and 6 list the values of the radiative source at the middle of the profiles (which corresponds to the centroid of the 3D enclosure) for the various solutions, with the relative deviation from the box/EWB solution, computed as

$$\text{Percent error} = \frac{\text{SLW/WSGG} - \text{box/EWB}}{\text{box/EWB}} \times 100\% \tag{13}$$

For the SLW and oxy-fuel WSGGM, the errors have decreased for the high-CO_2-fraction case, whereas this error increased in the case of the air-fuel solution. For the air-fuel solution, the errors are very large, being around 80%. Further, if the solutions are ranked by error, we get the same ordering for both oxy-fuel environments.

Solution method	Radiative source at the centroid (kW/m^3)	%Error (relative to box/EWB)
box/EWB	-15.91	0.00%
SLW	-13.24	+16.80 %
4g, quadratic	-14.67	+ 7.80%
5g, quadratic	-10.70	+32.73%
5g, quadratic, (cont)	-10.96	+31.09%
4g, linear	-11.95	+24.88%
5g, cubic	- 7.53	+52.66%
4g, cubic, (air)	- 3.22	+79.73%

Table 3. Radiative source term at the centroid for the oxy-fuel environment with 65%CO_2

Solution method	Radiative source at the centroid (kW/m^3)	%Error (relative to box/EWB)
box/EWB	-15.15	0.00%
SLW	-13.53	+10.75%
4g, quadratic	-14.64	+ 3.37%
5g, quadratic	-11.05	+27.09%
5g, quadratic, (cont)	-11.47	+24.32%
4g, linear	-11.61	+23.37%
5g, cubic	- 7.62	+49.71%
4g, cubic, (air)	- 2.52	+83.40%

Table 4. Radiative source term at the centroid for the oxy-fuel environment with 90%CO_2

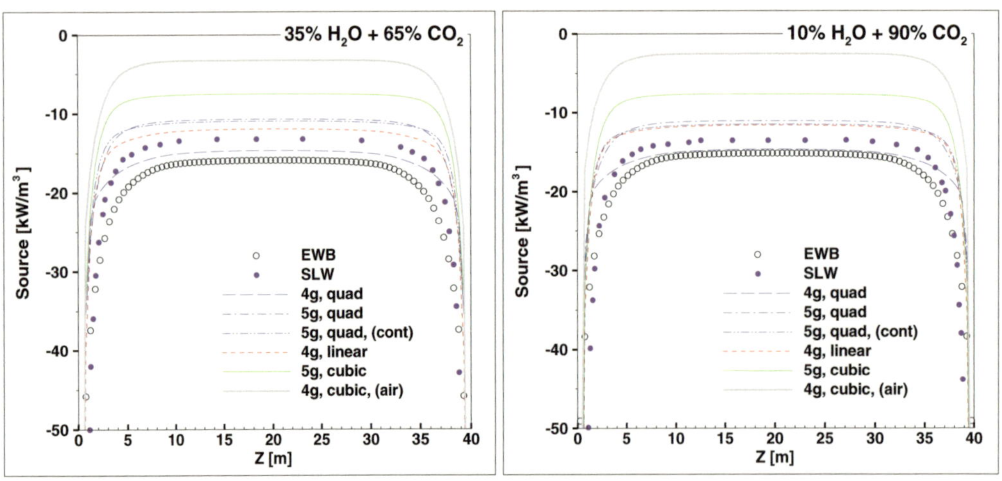

Fig. 5. Centerline radiative source for 2 oxy-fuel environments

4.5 Radiative-flux profiles

The profiles of the radiative flux along the symmetry line of the 12×40 top wall for the two oxy-fuel environments are shown in Figure 6. We notice that the wall radiative flux is significantly more sensitive to the change in mixture composition than the centerline radiative source (see Figure 5). When the CO_2 content increased, the radiative flux decreased. This is consistent with the decrease in total emissivity (18) and the changes in the idealized spectra of the linear absorption coefficient shown in Figure 1. We also notice that the relative deviations between the various WSGG models and the box/EWB predictions for the radiative flux differ from the deviations reported for the centerline radiative source. In particular, the 5-gas/cubic WSGGM (27) that showed noticeable error in the radiative source, has excellent agreement (-0.70%) with the box/EWB solution in the wet-recycle oxy-fuel environment and good agreement (-2.67%) in the dry-recycle environment. The radiative flux at the center point (Z=20 m) of the profiles in Figure 6 and their relative errors with respect to the box/EWB are compared in Tables 5 and 6 for the wet-recycle and dry-recycle oxy-fuel environments, respectively. All the WSGGM solutions are within 6.1% error (some underpredict and others overpredict) for both oxy-fuel environments, whereas the air-fuel WSGGM exhibits underprediction of 19.9% for the wet-recycle environment. For the dry-recycle environment, this underprediction jumps to 33.9%.

Solution method	Wall-center's radiative flux (kW/m^2)	%Error (relative to box/EWB)
box/EWB	113.98	0.00%
4g, quadratic	119.94	+ 5.23%
5g, quadratic	119.96	+ 5.25%
5g, quadratic, (cont)	113.85	−0.12%
4g, linear	116.33	+ 2.06%
5g, cubic	113.19	− 0.70%
4g, cubic, (air)	91.32	−19.88%

Table 5. Radiative flux at top-wall center for the oxy-fuel environment with 65%CO_2

Solution method	Wall-center's radiative flux (kW/m^2)	%Error (relative to box/EWB)
box/EWB	97.22	0.00%
4g, quadratic	99.67	+ 2.52%
5g, quadratic	95.83	−1.43%
5g, quadratic, (cont)	94.37	−2.93%
4g, linear	103.11	+ 6.05%
5g, cubic	94.63	−2.67%
4g, cubic, (air)	64.30	−33.87%

Table 6. Radiative flux at top-wall center for the oxy-fuel environment with 90%CO_2

4.6 Wall radiative heat transfer

The area-integrated wall radiative heat flux results are compared for all the solutions in Table 7 for the wet-recycle environment and in Table 8 for the dry-recycle environment. Consistent with the profiles in the preceding subsection, the air-fuel WSGGM underpredicts the heat

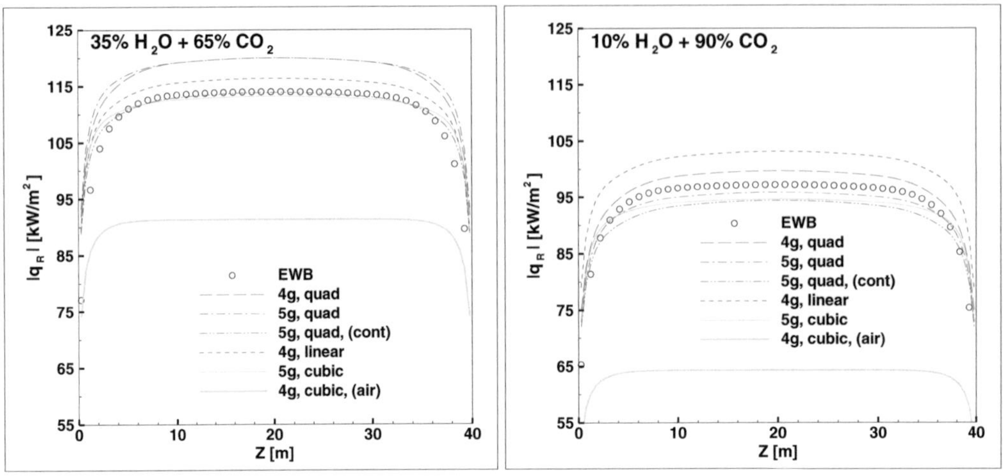

Fig. 6. Radiative flux along the midline of the 12×40 top wall

transfer for both environments. Although the relative error with respect to the box/EWB is smaller than the error recorded for the 1D flux profile, the relative error for the dry-recycle environment is larger than the relative error for the wet-recycle environment. All the oxy-fuel WSGG models overpredict the heat transfer, but the error is within 10.4%.

Solution method	Wall radiative heat transfer (MW)	Average wall radiative flux (kW/m^2)	%Error (relative to box/EWB)
box/EWB	224.74	101.78	0.00%
4g, quadratic	244.18	110.59	+ 8.65%
5g, quadratic	246.48	111.63	+ 9.67%
5g, quadratic, (cont)	233.99	105.97	+ 4.12%
4g, linear	238.15	107.86	+ 5.97%
5g, cubic	235.43	106.62	+ 4.76%
4g, cubic, (air)	191.63	86.79	−14.73%

Table 7. Wall radiative heat transfer for the oxy-fuel environment with 65%CO_2

5. Conclusions

We performed nongray radiation calculations of two radiation problems in homogeneous isothermal media. The first medium is typical of wet-recycle oxy-fuel combustion environment, with a molar composition of 65% CO_2 and 35% H_2O; whereas the second approximates a dry-recycle environment, with a molar composition of 90% CO_2 and 10% H_2O. The domain was a 12×12×40 m rectangular enclosure at 1 500 K. For each environment, we generated reference solutions using the box model based on the exponential wide band approach. We also calculated solutions using five (recent) oxy-fuel and one (older) air-fuel weighted-sum-of-gray-gases models that were proposed in the literature. Comparing

Solution method	Wall radiative heat transfer (MW)	Average wall radiative flux (kW/m^2)	%Error (relative to box/EWB)
box/EWB	190.54	86.30	0.00%
4g, quadratic	200.62	90.86	+ 5.29%
5g, quadratic	194.48	88.08	+ 2.06%
5g, quadratic, (cont)	191.72	86.83	+ 0.62%
4g, linear	210.34	95.26	+10.39%
5g, cubic	194.76	88.21	+ 2.21%
4g, cubic, (air)	134.70	61.00	−29.31%

Table 8. Wall radiative heat transfer for the oxy-fuel environment with 90%CO_2

different qualitative and quantitative radiative characteristics from the obtained solutions, we see that significant improvements in predictive capability can be obtained using an oxy-WSGGM. Using the air-fuel model would result in appreciable underprediction of the local and area-integrated radiative heat flux to the wall, and in an overprediction of temperatures due to the underprediction of the heat loss due to radiation. The errors become more pronounced for the high-CO_2-concentration case, which is relevant to dry-recycle oxy-fuel combustion. The radiative heat flux was much more sensitive to the gas composition than the radiative source term. For the oxy-fuel WSGG models, no particular model was clearly superior. This suggests that the model used for a particular combustion problem should be selected based on the simplicity of the model and the consistency between the operating regime of the target system and the regime of the training data.

6. Acknowledgments

This technical effort was performed in support of the National Energy Technology Laboratory's ongoing research in CO_2 Capture in the Existing Plants Emissions and Capture (EPEC) Technology Program. Dr. Marzouk activities were funded under the RES contract DE-FE0004000. The authors appreciate the help of Dr. Chungen Yin (Aalborg University, Denmark) in implementing the EWBM.

7. Appendix

A. Idealized spectra for the box/EWB approach

This appendix presents numerically the idealized spectra of the linear absorption coefficients k_i and the corresponding blackbody weights a_i that were computed from the EWB approach for each of the two oxy-fuel environments. The values are used when solving the RTEs given in Equation (9).

B. WSGG linear absorption coefficients and blackbody weights

Analogous to the tabulation in Appendix 7, the computed linear absorption coefficients and the corresponding weights for the gray gases are given in this appendix for all the 6 WSGG models for each of the two oxy-fuel environments. These values are used when solving the

i	η (1/cm)	$k_i(1/m)$	a_i	i	η (1/cm)	$k_i(1/m)$	a_i
1	0.00 – 448.47	0.2097897	0.00346421	12	2 410.00 – 3 048.95	0.0000000	0.13252660
2	448.47 – 845.47	0.4276537	0.01647795	13	3 048.95 – 3 334.04	0.1683664	0.05929771
3	845.47 – 885.53	0.5403818	0.00261648	14	3 334.04 – 3 985.96	0.3584664	0.12793486
4	885.53 – 921.00	0.3225178	0.00247182	15	3 985.96 – 4 471.05	0.1683664	0.08419003
5	921.00 – 969.29	0.4931395	0.00360145	16	4 471.05 – 4 929.89	0.0000000	0.06916402
6	969.29 – 1 074.53	0.6162794	0.00879137	17	4 929.89 – 4 982.64	0.0633557	0.00727657
7	1 074.53 – 1 150.71	0.5035513	0.00716945	18	4 982.64 – 5 470.11	0.1754496	0.06076172
8	1 150.71 – 1 258.43	0.3804114	0.01127985	19	5 470.11 – 5 717.36	0.1120939	0.02650485
9	1 258.43 – 1 944.35	0.1706217	0.09986805	20	5 717.36 – 6 975.54	0.0000000	0.09647500
10	1 944.35 – 2 279.00	0.4116662	0.06230296	21	6 975.54 – 7 524.46	0.1135142	0.02613845
11	2 279.00 – 2 410.00	0.2410445	0.02595104	22	7 524.46 – 100 000	0.0000000	0.06573557

Table 9. Idealized box/EWB spectrum for the oxy-fuel environment with 65% CO_2

i	η (1/cm)	$k_i(1/m)$	a_i	i	η (1/cm)	$k_i(1/m)$	a_i
1	0.00 – 440.64	0.1841169	0.00329548	12	2 410.00 – 3 193.84	0.0000000	0.16280362
2	440.64 – 839.06	0.4063678	0.01624495	13	3 193.84 – 3 319.79	0.1324004	0.02608835
3	839.06 – 893.36	0.5304856	0.00355165	14	3 319.79 – 4 000.21	0.3281601	0.13349028
4	893.36 – 964.10	0.3082347	0.00513915	15	4 000.21 – 4 326.16	0.1324004	0.05756875
5	964.10 – 1 059.44	0.4417534	0.00785136	16	4 326.16 – 4 931.64	0.0000000	0.09340562
6	1 059.44 – 1 067.07	0.2576366	0.00067467	17	4 931.64 – 5 073.92	0.0809341	0.01929669
7	1 067.07 – 1 080.94	0.3902864	0.00124357	18	5 073.92 – 5 468.36	0.1404420	0.04830074
8	1 080.94 – 1 155.90	0.2661685	0.00710566	19	5 468.36 – 5 626.08	0.0595080	0.01724289
9	1 155.90 – 1 930.42	0.1326498	0.10819446	20	5 626.08 – 7 033.12	0.0000000	0.10905531
10	1 930.42 – 2 132.93	0.3772371	0.03674431	21	7 033.12 – 7 466.88	0.0571616	0.02063116
11	2 132.93 – 2 410.00	0.2445874	0.05394936	22	7 466.88 – 100 000	0.0000000	0.06812197

Table 10. Idealized box/EWB spectrum for the oxy-fuel environment with 90% CO_2

RTEs given in Equation (9). The linear absorption coefficient for the clear gas is k_0=0; its blackbody weight (a_0) is obtained from the requirement that $a_0 = 1 - \sum_{i=1}^{N-1} a_i$.

	65% CO_2		90% CO_2	
i	$k_i(1/m)$	a_i	$k_i(1/m)$	a_i
0	0	0.29433	0	0.37459
1	0.11695	0.41272	0.09837	0.41704
2	2.51559	0.23307	2.66557	0.15639
3	70.56945	0.05988	88.92354	0.05198

Table 11. Linear absorption coefficients and blackbody weights for the 4-gas/quadratic WSGGM in (22) – Two oxy-fuel environments

	65% CO_2		90% CO_2	
i	$k_i(1/m)$	a_i	$k_i(1/m)$	a_i
0	0	0.26177	0	0.31687
1	0.05677	0.30533	0.04006	0.33408
2	0.58148	0.25560	0.41427	0.20004
3	5.64642	0.13281	5.18028	0.10602
4	100.07946	0.04449	123.52189	0.04298

Table 12. Linear absorption coefficients and blackbody weights for the 5-gas/quadratic WSGGM in (22) – Two oxy-fuel environments

	65% CO_2		90% CO_2	
i	$k_i(1/m)$	a_i	$k_i(1/m)$	a_i
0	0	0.28678	0	0.34849
1	0.06146	0.33543	0.05633	0.36697
2	0.86869	0.23910	0.87767	0.17687
3	9.13846	0.10048	9.82222	0.07032
4	116.15385	0.03822	131.11111	0.03734

Table 13. Linear absorption coefficients and blackbody weights for the 5-gas/quadratic WSGGM in (24) – Two oxy-fuel environments

	65% CO_2		90% CO_2	
i	$k_i(1/m)$	a_i	$k_i(1/m)$	a_i
0	0	0.31064	0	0.32763
1	0.09370	0.33218	0.06288	0.35561
2	1.08144	0.25582	1.02333	0.22449
3	99.99991	0.10136	100.00000	0.09227

Table 14. Linear absorption coefficients and blackbody weights for the 4-gas/linear WSGGM in (25) – Two oxy-fuel environments

	65% CO_2		90% CO_2	
i	$k_i(1/m)$	a_i	$k_i(1/m)$	a_i
0	0	0.31812	0	0.39788
1	0.05225	0.22831	0.05105	0.23703
2	0.69574	0.26925	0.68033	0.25810
3	7.71486	0.15584	14.04069	0.08263
4	188.01466	0.02849	294.45477	0.02436

Table 15. Linear absorption coefficients and blackbody weights for the 5-gas/cubic WSGGM in (27) – Two oxy-fuel environments

	65% CO_2		90% CO_2	
i	$k_i(1/m)$	a_i	$k_i(1/m)$	a_i
0	0	0.52282	0	0.66567
1	0.42019	0.28898	0.40334	0.20536
2	9.63050	0.16303	13.92300	0.10516
3	242.96000	0.02517	351.06000	0.02381

Table 16. Linear absorption coefficients and blackbody weights for the 4-gas/cubic WSGGM in (28) – Two oxy-fuel environments

8. References

[1] "Inventory of U.S. Greenhouse Gas Emissions and Sinks: 1990 -Ű 2008," The United States Environmental Protection Agency (EPA), Washington, DC, 2010.

[2] "International Energy Outlook 2010," The United States Energy Information Administration (EIA), Office of Integrated Analysis and Forecasting, U.S. Department of Energy, Washington, DC, 2010.

[3] R. Siegel, J. R. Howell, *Thermal Radiation Heat Transfer* ed. 4. USA: Taylor & Francis, 2002.

[4] M. F. Modest, *Radiative Heat Transfer* ed. 2. USA: Academic Press, 2003.

[5] H. C. Hottel, A. F. Sarofim, *Radiative Transfer*. New York: McGraw-Hill, 1967.

[6] A. Wang, M. F. Modest, D. C. Haworth, L. Wang, "Monte Carlo Simulation of Radiative Heat Transfer and Turbulence Interactions in Methane/Air Jet Flames," *Journal of Quantitative Spectroscopy & Radiative Transfer*, vol. 109, pp. 269Ű-279, 2008.

[7] D. C. Haworth, "Progress in Probability Density Function Methods for Turbulent Reacting Flows," *Progress in Energy and Combustion Science*, vol. 36, pp. 168-Ű259, 2010.

[8] L. D. Smoot, Ed., *Fundamentals of Coal Combustion: For Clean and Efficient Use* The Netherlands: Elsevier, 1993.

[9] D. K. Edwards, "Molecular Gas Band Radiation," *Advances in Heat Transfer*, vol. 12, pp. 115–193, 1976.

[10] W. L. Grosshandler, "RADCAL: a Narrow-Band Model for Radiation Calculations in a Combustion Environment," Technical Note 1402, The United States National Institute of Standards and Technology (NIST), 1993.

[11] D. K. Edwards, W. A. Menard, "Comparison of Models for Correlation of Total Band Absorption," *Applied Optics*, vol. 3, pp. 621–625, 1964.

[12] D. K. Edwards, W. A. Menard, "Correlations for Absorption by Methane and Carbon Dioxide Gases," *Applied Optics*, vol. 3, pp. 847–852, 1964.

[13] J. D. Felske, C. L. Tien, "A Theoretical Closed Form Expression for Total Band Absorptance of Infrared-Radiating Gases," *International Journal of Heat and Mass Transfer*, vol. 17, pp. 155–158, 1974.

[14] D. K. Edwards, A. Balakrishnan, "Thermal Radiation by Combustion Gases," *International Journal of Heat and Mass Transfer*, vol. 16, pp. 25–40, 1973.

[15] A. T. Modak, "Exponential Wide Band Parameters for the Pure Rotational Band of Water Vapor," *Journal of Quantitative Spectroscopy & Radiative Transfer*, vol. 21, pp. 131–142, 1978.

[16] H. C. Hottel, Chapter 4: Radiant Heat Transmission, in *Heat Transmission* (W. H. McAdams, Ed.) ed. 3. New York: McGraw-Hill, 1954.

[17] L. C. R. Johansen, "RANS Simulation of Oxy-Natural Gas Combustion,", M.S. Thesis, Aalborg University, Denmark, 2010.

[18] O. A. Marzouk, E. D. Huckaby, "New Weighted Sum of Gray Gases (WSGG) Models for Radiation Calculation in Carbon Capture Simulations: Evaluation and Different Implementation Techniques," in *7th U.S. National Combustion Meeting of the Combustion Institute*, Georgia-USA, 2011, paper OT08.

[19] H. C. Hottel, "The Melchett Lecture for 1960; Radiative Transfer in Combustion Chambers," *Journal of the Institute of Fuel*, vol. 34, pp. 220–234, 1961.

[20] A. F. Sarofim, "Radiant Heat Transmission in Enclosures," Sc.D. Dissertation, Massachusetts Institute of Technology, Cambridge, USA, 1962.

[21] M. F. Modest, "The Weighted-Sum-of-Gray-Gases Model for Arbitrary Solution Methods in Radiative Transfer," *Journal of Heat Transfer*, vol. 113, pp. 650-Ű656, 1991.

[22] R. Johansson, K. Andersson, B. Leckner, H. Thunman, "Models for Gaseous Radiative Heat Transfer Applied to Oxy-fuel Conditions in Boilers," *International Journal of Heat and Mass Transfer*, vol. 53, pp. 220–230, 2010.

[23] A. Soufiani, J. Taine, "High Temperature Gas Radiative Property Parameters of Statistical Narrow-band Model for H_2O, CO_2 and CO, and Correlated-K Model for H_2O and CO_2," *International Journal of Heat and Mass Transfer*, vol. 40, pp. 987–991, 1997.

[24] R. Johansson, B. Leckner, K. Andersson, F. Johnsson, "Account for Variations in the H_2O to CO_2 Molar Ratio When Modelling Gaseous Radiative Heat Transfer with the Weighted-Sum-of-Grey-Gases Model," *Combustion and Flame*, vol. 158, pp. 893–901, 2011.

[25] G. Krishnamoorthy, M. Sami, S. Orsino, A. Perera, M. Shahnam, E. D. Huckaby, "Radiation Modelling in Oxy-fuel Combustion Scenarios," *International Journal of Computational Fluid Dynamics*, vol. 24, pp. 69–82, 2010.

[26] H. C. Hottel, J. J. Noble, A. F. Sarofim, G. D. Silcox, P. C. Wankat, K. S. Knaebel, Section 5: Heat and Mass Transfer, in *Perry's Chemical Engineers' Handbook* (D. W. Green, R. H. Perry, Eds.) ed. 8. New York: McGraw-Hill, 2007.

[27] C. Yin, L. C. R. Johansen, L. A. Rosendahl, S. K. Kær, "New Weighted Sum of Gray Gases Model Applicable to Computational Fluid Dynamics (CFD) Modeling of Oxy-fuel Combustion: Derivation, Validation, and Implementation," *Energy & Fuels*, vol. 24, pp. 6275-Ű6282, 2010.

[28] T. F. Smith, Z. F. Shen, J. N. Friedman, "Evaluation of Coefficients for the Weighted Sum of Gray Gases Model," *Journal of Heat Transfer*, vol. 104, pp. 602–608, 1982.

[29] M. Costa, J. L. T. Azevedo, "Experimental Characterization of an Industrial Pulverized Coal-fired Furnace Under Deep Staging Conditions," *Combustion Science and Technology*, vol. 179, pp. 1923-Ű1935, 2007.

[30] ANSYS FLUENT User's Guide, Release 13.0, November 2010, Canonsburg, Pennsylvania, USA.

[31] M. K. Denison, B. W. Webb, "A Spectral Line-based Weighted-sum-of-gray-gases Model for Arbitrary RTE Solvers," *Journal of Heat Transfer*, vol. 115, pp. 1004–1012, 1993.

[32] M. K. Denison, B. W. Webb, "An Absorption-line Blackbody Distribution Function for Efficient Calculation of Total Gas Radiative Transfer," *Journal of Quantitative Spectroscopy & Radiative Transfer*, vol. 50, pp. 499–510, 1993.

[33] M. K. Denison, B. W. Webb, "Development and Application of an Absorption-line Blackbody Distribution Function for CO_2," *International Journal of Heat and Mass Transfer*, vol. 38, pp. 1813–1821, 1995.

[34] V. P. Solovjov, B. W. Webb, "SLW Modeling of Radiative Transfer in Multicomponent Gas Mixtures," *Journal of Quantitative Spectroscopy & Radiative Transfer*, vol. 65, pp. 655–672, 2000.

[35] C. P. Thurgood, A. Pollard, A. B. Becker, "The TN Quadrature Set for the Discrete Ordinates Method," *Journal of Heat Transfer*, vol. 117, pp. 1068–1070, 1995.

[36] L. S. Rothman, R. R. Gamache, R. H. Tipping, C. P. Rinsland, M. A. H. Smith, D. C. Benner, V. M. Devi, J. M. Flaud, C. Camy-Peyret, A. Perrin, A. Goldman, S. T. Massie, L. R. Brown, "The HITRAN Molecular Database: Editions of 1991 and 1992," *Journal of Quantitative Spectroscopy & Radiative Transfer*, vol. 48, pp. 469–507, 1992.

[37] J. M. Hartmann, R. Levi Di Leon, J. Taine, "Line-by-line and Narrow-band Statistical Model Calculations for H_2O," *Journal of Quantitative Spectroscopy & Radiative Transfer*, vol. 32, pp. 119–127, 1984.

24

Numerical Modeling of Solidification Process

Bohdan Mochnacki
Czestochowa University of Technology
Institute of Mathematics
Poland

1. Introduction

This chapter is devoted to the problems connected with numerical modeling of moving boundary ones. In particular the solidification and cooling processes proceeding in the system casting-mould are considered. The subject matter of solidification process modeling is very extensive and only the selected problems from this scope will be here discussed. From the mathematical point of view the thermal processes proceeding in the domain considered (both in macro and micro/macro scale) are described by a system of partial differential equations (energy equations) supplemented by the geometrical, physical, boundary and initial conditions. The typical solidification model bases on the Fourier-Kirchhoff type equations, but one can formulate the more complex (coupled with the basic model) ones concerning the heat convection in a molten metal sub-domain, the changes of local chemical constitution of solidifying alloy (segregation process) etc. Here we limit oneself only to the tasks connected with the predominant heat conduction process, and (as the examples of various problems) the macro models of alloys solidification and the micro/macro models of pure metals crystallization will be presented, at the same time the direct and inverse problems will be discussed.

In order to construct a numerical model and an adequate computer program simulating the course of problem considered, one must accept a certain mathematical description of the process (the governing equations). The next step is the transformation of this mathematical model into a form called the re-solving system constructed on the basis of a selected numerical method.

After transformation of the algorithm developed into a computer program and supplementing it with suitable pre- and post-processing procedures (input data loading, graphic presentation of results, print-outs etc.), and carrying out of computations, one obtains the results including information concerning the transient temperature field, kinetics of solidification process, the temporary shapes of sub-domains etc. They may have a form of numerical print-outs, e.g., giving the temperature field at distinguished set of points or the volumetric fraction of solid state at the neighbourhood of these points.

Numerical modeling of the heat and mass transfer in solidifying metal is a typical interdisciplinary problem and requires particular knowledge in the field of foundry practice, mathematics (a course in mathematical analysis offered in technical schools is quite sufficient here), thermodynamics (in particular heat transfer), numerical methods and, in the final stage, also programming and operation of computer equipment.

2. Heat transfer in the system casting – mould

2.1 Description of the process

At first, we will consider the heat transfer processes in a system casting-mould-environment The solidification and cooling of casting material (alloy or pure metal) can be described by the following energy equation

$$c(T)\frac{\partial T(x,t)}{\partial t} = \nabla\left[\lambda(T)\nabla T(x,t)\right] + L\frac{\partial f_S(x,t)}{\partial t} \tag{1}$$

where $c(T)$ is a volumetric specific heat of casting material, $\lambda(T)$ is a thermal conductivity, L is a volumetric latent heat, $T = T(x, t)$, $f_S = f_S(x, t)$ denote the temperature and the local volumetric fraction of solid state, x denotes the spatial co-ordinates, t is a time. One can see, that only heat conduction in a casting volume is considered. The energy equation can constitute a base both in a case of macro-scale modeling and micro/macro one (Stefanescu, 1999; Mochnacki & Majchrzak, 2007a; Mochnacki & Suchy, 1995). The differences appear on a stage of solidification rate $\partial f_S/\partial t$ computations.

The equation determining the course of thermal processes in a mould sub-domain is of the form

$$c_m(T)\frac{\partial T_m(x,t)}{\partial t} = \nabla\left[\lambda_m(T)\nabla T_m(x,t)\right] \tag{2}$$

where the index m identifies the mould sub-domain, the non-homogeneous mould can be also considered.

On the external surface of mould the continuity condition (3rd type of boundary condition)

$$-\lambda_m\frac{\partial T_m(x,t)}{\partial n} = \alpha\left[T_m(x,t) - T_a\right] \tag{3}$$

is, as a rule, accepted. Here α is a heat transfer coefficient, T_a is an ambient temperature, $\partial/\partial n$ denotes a normal derivative.

On the contact surface between casting and mould the continuity condition is given

$$-\lambda\frac{\partial T(x,t)}{\partial n} = \frac{T(x,t) - T_m(x,t)}{R(x,t)} = -\lambda_m\frac{\partial T_m(x,t)}{\partial n} \tag{4}$$

where R is a thermal resistance. For $R = 0$ (a such assumption can be done in the case of sand mix mould) the last equation takes a form

$$\begin{cases} -\lambda\dfrac{\partial T(x,t)}{\partial n} = -\lambda_m\dfrac{\partial T_m(x,t)}{\partial n} \\ T(x,t) = T_m(x,t) \end{cases} \tag{5}$$

The initial temperature distribution for $t = 0$ is also known

$$t = 0: \; T(x,0) = T_0(x), \; T_m(x,0) = T_{m0}(x) \tag{6}$$

The mathematical model presented above can be more complicated. One can consider the convectional component of heat transfer which appear in the molten metal sub-domain. In the case of alloys solidification the segregation effects can be also taken into account, etc.

2.2 Macro models of solidification

In this sub-chapter the model called the one domain approach will be discussed (Mochnacki & Suchy, 1995). Let us denote the temperatures corresponding to the beginning and the end of solidification process as T_L and T_S . If one considers the solidification of pure metals or eutectic alloys then the border temperatures can be introduced in an artificial way substituting the solidification point T^* by a certain temperature interval $[T^* - \Delta T, T^* + \Delta T]$. Numerical experiments show that the assumed values of ΔT (in reasonable limits) are not very essential, and the results of numerical simulations of solidification process are similar.
One assumes the knowledge of temperature-dependent function f_S for interval $[T_S, T_L]$ and then

$$\frac{\partial f_S(x,t)}{\partial t} = \frac{\mathrm{d} f_S}{\mathrm{d} T} \frac{\partial T(x,t)}{\partial t} \tag{7}$$

Introducing this formula to equation (1) one obtains

$$C(T)\frac{\partial T(x,t)}{\partial t} = \nabla\left[\lambda(T)\nabla T(x,t)\right] \tag{8}$$

where $C(T) = c(T) - L\,\mathrm{d}f_S/\mathrm{d}T$ is called 'a substitute thermal capacity'. This parameter can be defined in the different ways.
Introducing the following definition of substitute thermal capacity

$$C(T) = \begin{cases} c_L & T > T_L \\ c_P - L\dfrac{\mathrm{d} f_S}{\mathrm{d} T} & T_S \le T \le T_L \\ c_S & T < T_S \end{cases} \tag{9}$$

where c_L, c_P, c_S are the volumetric specific heats of molten metal, mushy zone and solid state sub-domains, one can use the equation (9) as the model of thermal processes proceeding in the whole, conventionally homogeneous, casting domain. It is the reason that the approach presented is called 'a one domain method'.
The function f_S must fulfill the conditions $f_S(T_L) = 0$ and $f_S(T_S) = 1$, additionally for $T < T_S$: $f_S = 0$, for $T > T_L$: $f_S = 0$.
The integral

$$\int_{T_S}^{T_L} C(T)\,\mathrm{d}T = c_P(T_L - T_S) + L \tag{10}$$

corresponds to the change of volumetric physical enthalpy for $[T_S, T_L]$ gives the additional information assuring the proper choice of f_S.
As an example the following function can be considered

$$f_S(T)=\left(\frac{T_L-T}{T_L-T_S}\right)^n \tag{11}$$

and then

$$\frac{\mathrm{d}\,f_S(T)}{\mathrm{d}T}=-\frac{n}{T_L-T_S}\left(\frac{T_L-T}{T_L-T_S}\right)^{n-1} \tag{12}$$

Finally

$$C(T)=c_P+\frac{L}{T_L-T_S}\,n\left(\frac{T_L-T}{T_L-T_S}\right)^{n-1} \tag{13}$$

The quotient $L/(T_L-T_S)=c_{sp}$ is called 'a spectral latent heat'. Introducing this parameter one has

$$C(T)=c_P+c_{sp}\,n\left(\frac{T_L-T}{T_L-T_S}\right)^{n-1} \tag{14}$$

It is easy to check that

$$\int_{T_S}^{T_L}\left[c_P+c_{sp}\,n\left(\frac{T_L-T}{T_L-T_S}\right)^{n-1}\right]\mathrm{d}T=c_P(T_L-T_S)+L \tag{15}$$

Above formulas are very often used for exponent $n=1$ and then

$$C(T)=c_P+\frac{L}{T_L-T_S}=c_P+c_{sp}\,,\quad T\in[T_S,T_L] \tag{16}$$

So, the linear course of f_S leads to the constant value of mushy zone thermal capacity. Assuming additionally the constant values of c_S and c_L one obtains the staircase function as an approximation of $C(T)$. In Figure 1 this type of function is shown. If the changes of border temperatures are taken into account (macrosegregation effect) then the families of functions $C(T)$ should be considered (Szopa, 1999).

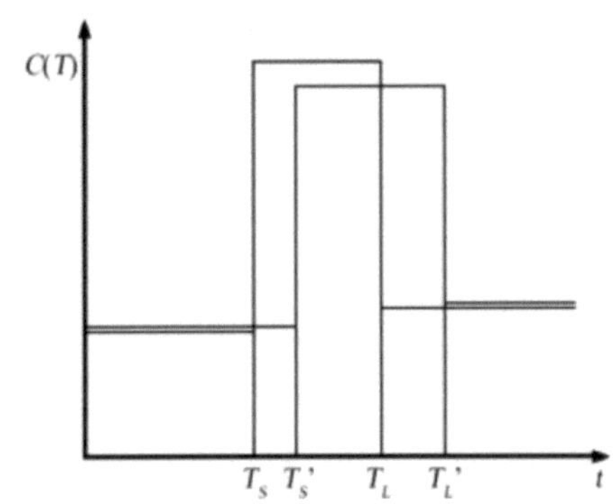

Fig. 1. Substitute thermal capacity

2.3 Introduction of enthalpy function and Kirchhoff transformation

Let us introduce the physical enthalpy of alloy defined in the following way

$$H(T) = \int_{T_r}^{T} C(\mu)\, \mathrm{d}\mu \tag{17}$$

where the lower limit of integration corresponds to the optional reference level.
The energy equation (8) written using the function (17) takes a form

$$\frac{\partial H(x,t)}{\partial t} = \nabla\left[a(T)\nabla H(x,t)\right], \qquad a(T) = \frac{\lambda(T)}{C(T)} \tag{18}$$

In Figure 2 the course of enthalpy function for carbon steel (0.44%C) under the assumption that the substitute thermal capacity $C\,(T)$ is approximated by piece-wise constant function (equation (16)) is shown.

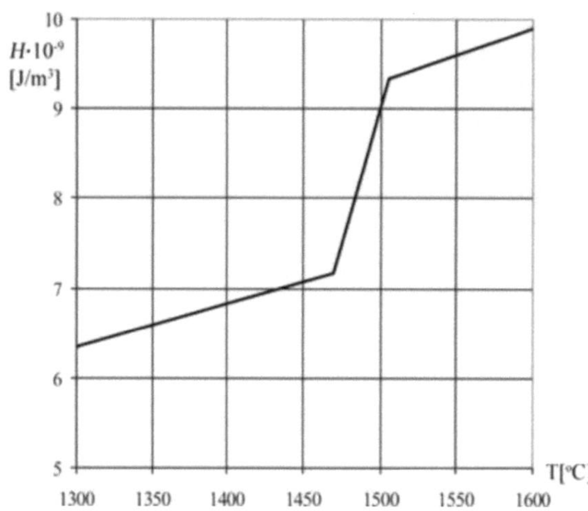

Fig. 2. Enthalpy function.

The transformation of typical boundary and initial conditions supplementing the equation (18) can be found, among others, in (Mochnacki & Suchy, 1995).
The mathematical model of solidification basing on the enthalpy function is often used at the stage of numerical modeling. In particular, the approach discussed seems to be very effective in a case of more complex courses of phase changes (e.g. solidification of cast iron, the process proceeds partially at the constant temperature and partially at the interval of temperature and then the introduction of enthalpy function and the application of numerical procedure called the Alternating Phase Truncation Method (Mochnacki & Suchy, 1995; Majchrzak & Mochnacki, 1995; Majchrzak & Mendakiewicz, 1993) leads to the simple and effective numerical algorithm).
The other form of energy equation determining the thermal processes in domain of solidifying alloy can be obtained using the Kirchhoff transformation, this means

$$U(T) = \int_{T_r}^{T} \lambda(\mu)\, \mathrm{d}\mu \tag{19}$$

It is easy to check that the introduction of function (19) Leeds to the following form of equation (8)

$$\phi\,[T(U)]\frac{\partial U(x,t)}{\partial t}=\nabla^2 U(x,t)\ , \qquad \phi\,(U)=\frac{C\,[T(U)]}{\lambda\,[T(U)]} \tag{20}$$

One can see, that the right hand side of energy equation (20) becomes a linear one and it can be essential at the stage of numerical modeling. The details concerning this approach and also the transformed form of typical boundary and initial conditions can be found in (Mochnacki & Suchy, 1995; Szopa, 1999).

3. Micro/macro models of solidification

A generalized form of solidification model belonging to the second generation ones (Stefanescu, 1999) will be here discussed. The equation describing the thermal processes proceeding in domain of solidifying metal contains the term (source function) controlling the course of latent heat evolution. A capacity of internal heat sources is proportional to crystallization rate, more precisely, to time derivative of function $f_S(x, t)$ corresponding to the local and temporary volumetric fraction of solid state at the point considered (Majchrzak et al., 2006; Mochnacki & Szopa, 2007; Fraś et al., 1993; Lupa et al. 2004) see: equation (1). If the micro/macro approach is taken into account, then the changes of f_S result from the crystallization laws in a micro scale (nucleation and nuclei growth). In this way the macro model basing on the Kirchhoff-Fourier-type equation is coupled with the model describing the processes proceeding on the level of single grains.
In literature one can find two basic models determining the mutual connections between f_S and temporary volume of grains. In particular, the following function is introduced

$$\omega(x,t)=N(x,t)\,V(x,t) \tag{21}$$

where N is a nuclei density [nuclei/m^3], V is a single grain volume. If one assumes $f_S(x, t) = \omega(x, t)$ then the linear model is considered (Majchrzak et al., 2006), while if $f_S(x, t) = 1 - \exp[-\omega(x, t)]$ then the exponential one is taken into account (Fraś et al., 1993; Lupa et al. 2004). In this place one can see that for the small values of ω, both models lead to the same results because $\exp(-\omega) \Rightarrow 1-\omega$ and $1 - \exp(-\omega) \Rightarrow \omega$. During the final stages of solidification the models discussed give the different results. The assumption of exponential changes of ω allows, in a certain way, to take into account the mutual geometrical interactions between the grains.
In this sub-chapter the generalization of the models previously presented will be shown. The differential equation from which linear and exponential models result, will be modified and in this way the new possibilities of f_S definition will appear.
As was mentioned, the micro/macro models of solidification discussed below require the introduction of function being the product of nuclei density and single grain volume. In a practical realization the exponent ω (equation (21)) is determined by the following formula (Mochnacki & Szopa, 2007; Fraś et al., 1993)

$$\omega(x,t)=\frac{4}{3}\pi\,v\,N(x,t)\left[\int_0^t u(\tau)\,\mathrm{d}\tau\right]^3 \tag{22}$$

where $u = \partial R / \partial t$ is a crystallization rate (R is a grain radius), N is nuclei density, v is a coefficient which equals 1 in case of spherical grains or $v < 1$ (e.g. dendritic growth, as in Figure 3 (Majchrzak & Piasecka, 1997)).

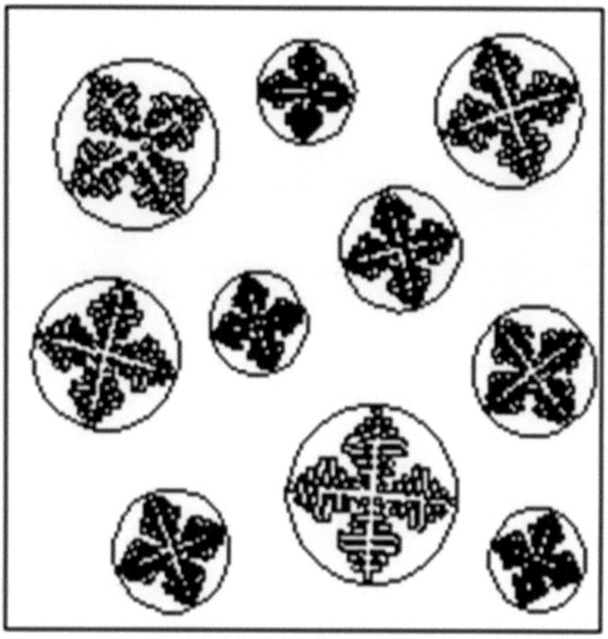

Fig. 3. Dendritic growth.

In the case of so-called linear model we have

$$f_S(x, t) = \omega(x,t) \tag{23}$$

and if $f_S = 1$ then the crystallization process stops.
The derivative of f_S with respect to time equals

$$\frac{\partial f_S(x, t)}{\partial t} = \frac{\partial \omega(x,t)}{\partial t} \tag{24}$$

The model above discussed determines the geometrical volume (volume fraction) and it is the correct assumption on the first stages of crystallization.
In order to take into account the limitations of growth in the final stages of the process one introduces the following modification of equation (24)

$$\frac{\partial f_S(x, t)}{\partial t} = \frac{\partial \omega (x,t)}{\partial t}[1 - f_S(x, t)] \tag{25}$$

Then

$$\frac{\mathrm{d} f_S(\omega)}{1 - f_S(\omega)} = \mathrm{d}\,\omega \tag{26}$$

next

$$f_S(\omega) = 1 + C\exp(-\omega) \tag{27}$$

Because for $\omega = 0$: $f_S = 0$ therefore $C = -1$ and finally

$$f_S(\omega) = 1 - \exp(-\omega) \tag{28}$$

The last equation corresponds to the well known exponential model (the Kolmogoroff formula).
Here, the following modification of equation (24) can be proposed (Mochnacki & Szopa, 2007; Mochnacki & Szopa, 2010)

$$\frac{\partial f_S(x,t)}{\partial t} = \frac{\partial \omega(x,t)}{\partial t}\left[1 - f_S(x,t)\right]^n \tag{29}$$

where $n \geq 0$. From the physical point of view the same conditions as in previous case are fulfilled and the component $1 - f_S$ changes from 0 to 1.
So, we have

$$\frac{\mathrm{d} f_S(\omega)}{\left[1 - f_S(\omega)\right]^n} = \mathrm{d}\omega \tag{30}$$

It is easy to check that the solution fulfilling the condition $\omega = 0$: $f_S = 0$ is of the form

$$f_S(\omega) = 1 - \left[(n-1)\omega + 1\right]^{\frac{1}{1-n}} \tag{31}$$

One can see that the last power-type formula constitutes the generalization of linear and exponential models. For $n = 0$ one obtains the linear one, while for $n = 1$ one has

$$\lim_{n \to 1} 1 - \left[(n-1)\omega + 1\right]^{\frac{1}{1-n}} = 1 - \exp(-\omega) \tag{32}$$

The others values of n can be also introduced. For example

$$\begin{aligned} n = 2: \quad & f_S = 1 - \frac{1}{\omega + 1} \\ n = 3: \quad & f_S = 1 - \frac{1}{\sqrt{2\omega + 1}} \\ n = \frac{1}{2}: \quad & f_S = 1 - \left(1 - \frac{\omega}{2}\right)^2 \end{aligned} \tag{33}$$

It should be pointed out that if $n \geq 1$ then for $\omega \to \infty$: $f_S \to 1$. This property is not fulfilled for $n < 1$ and it must be taken into account on the stage of numerical simulation. For example if $n = 1/2$ then solidification process takes place only for $\omega \leq 2$, the values $\omega > 2$ are not physically correct.
Now, the way of function ω modeling will be discussed.
A driving force of nucleation and nuclei growth is an undercooling below solidification point T^*. We assume that a local and temporary number of nuclei is proportional to the

second power of undercooling below the solidification point T^* (Mochnacki & Szopa, 2007; Fraś et al., 1993; Lupa et al. 2004)

$$N(x,t) = \eta\, \Delta T(x,t)^2 = \eta \left[T^* - T(x,t)\right]^2 \tag{34}$$

where η is the nucleation coefficient. The nucleation stops when $\Delta T(x, t + \Delta t) < \Delta T(x, t)$, additionally for $T(x, t) > T^*$: $N(x, t) = 0$ (Figure 4).

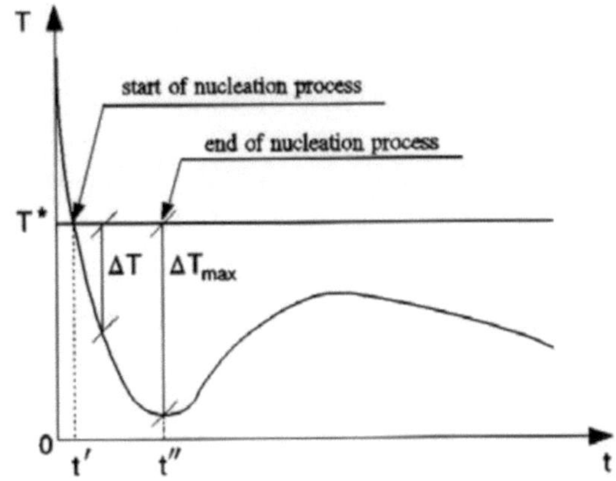

Fig. 4. Undercooling below point T^*

The solid phase growth (equiaxial grains) is determined by

$$\frac{\mathrm{d}R(x,t)}{\mathrm{d}t} = \mu\, \Delta T(x,t)^m \tag{35}$$

where μ is the growth coefficient, $m \in [1, 2]$. In literature one can also find the following equation

$$u(x,t) = \frac{\mathrm{d}R(x,t)}{\mathrm{d}t} = \mu_1\, \Delta T(x,t)^2 + \mu_2\, \Delta T(x,t)^3 \tag{36}$$

where μ_1, μ_2 are the growth coefficients.
Now, the certain aspects of function ω modelling will be discussed.
Because the problem considered is non-steady one, so one introduces the time grid defined as follows

$$0 = t^0 < t^1 < t^1 < \ldots < t^{s-1} < t^s < \ldots < t^S\,, \quad \Delta t = t^s - t^{s-1} \tag{37}$$

while the metal domain is divided into m control volumes .
Let us consider the control volume ΔV_i from casting domain. During a certain interval of time the temperature at central point of ΔV_i decreases below the solidification point and the crystallization process starts.
We find a number of the first 'portion' of nuclei $N_i^{(1)}$ (using equation(34)) and the final radius of grains (formula (35)).
The first value of ω is equal to

$$\omega_i^{(1)} = \frac{4}{3}\pi v N_i^{(1)} \Delta R_i^{(1)} \tag{38}$$

This value is introduced into the macro model for transition corresponding to the next time interval.
In the second stage of crystallization process modeling we find the quantity N_i using the equation (34) and next we can estimate the size of the second generation, this means $N_i^{(2)} = N_i - N_i^{(1)}$. We can also find the new increment of the grains radius $\Delta R_i^{(2)}$. It should be pointed out that the current radii of the first generation are equal to $\Delta R_i^{(1)} + \Delta R_i^{(2)}$, while for the second generation: $\Delta R_i^{(2)}$.
The new value of function ω is determined by the formula

$$\omega_i^{(2)} = \frac{4}{3}\pi v\left[N_i^{(1)}\left(\Delta R_i^{(1)} + \Delta R_i^{(2)}\right)^3 + N_i^{(2)}\Delta R_i^{(2)3}\right] \tag{39}$$

The next steps of crystallization process modeling result from the generalization of considerations above presented. It should be pointed out that after the transition by the maximum undercooling, the number of nuclei at control volume ΔV_i is constant and this fact must be taken into account in adequate numerical procedure. The knowledge of two successive values of $\omega_i^{(k)}$ allows to estimate the source term in equation (1) using the differential quotient, in particular

$$L\frac{\partial f_S(x,t)}{\partial t} = L\frac{\mathrm{d} f_S}{\mathrm{d}\omega}\frac{\partial \omega(x,t)}{\partial t} \approx L[(n-1)\omega + 1]^{\frac{n}{1-n}}\frac{\Delta\omega}{\Delta t} \tag{40}$$

4. Examples of numerical methods application

In this sub-chapter only the selected problems connected with numerical modelling of solidification process will be discussed. In particular a certain version of control volume method and next the algorithms basing on the boundary element method will be here presented.
So, the first part of considerations is devoted to the application of control volume method (CVM) for numerical simulation of solidification process both in the macro and micro/macro scale. The control volume method (Mochnacki & Suchy, 1995; Domański et al., 2009a; Domański et al., 2009b; Mochnacki & Ciesielski, 2007) constitutes an effective tool for numerical computations of the heat transfer processes. The domain analyzed is divided into N volumes. The CVM algorithm allows to find the transient temperature field at the set of nodes corresponding to the central points of the control volumes. The nodal temperatures can be found on the basis of energy balances for the successive volumes. In order to assure the correctness and exactness of the algorithm proposed the control volumes are generated in the shape of the Voronoi polygons (see: Fig. 5).
Let us consider the control volume ΔV_0 with the central node x_0. It is assumed here that the thermal capacities and capacities of the internal heat sources are concentrated in the nodes representing elements, while thermal resistances are concentrated in the sectors joining the nodes

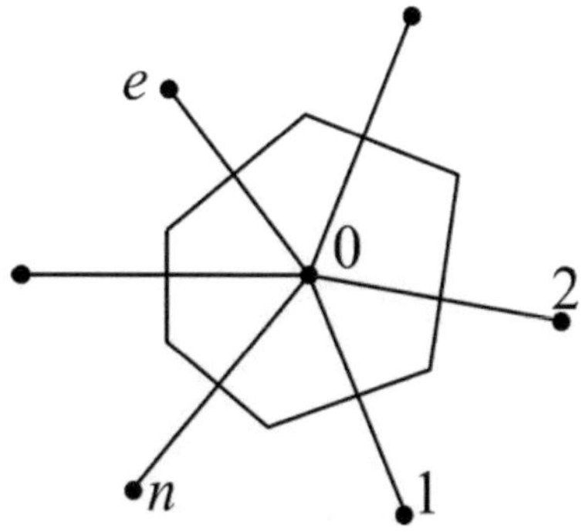

Fig. 5. Control volume ΔV_0

The energy balance for the control volume ΔV_0 can be written in the form

$$\Delta H_0 = \sum_e Q_e + |\Delta V_0| q_V \Delta t \tag{41}$$

where ΔH_0 is a change of control volume enthalpy during the time interval Δt, Q_e is a heat conducted at the time Δt from the adjoining nodes to the node x_0, q_V is a mean capacity of internal heat sources resulting from the evolution of latent heat in the control volume ΔV_0.
If one assumes that the heat fluxes flowing to the element ΔV_0 are proportional to the temperature differences at the moment $t = t^f$, then we shall obtain a solving system of the type 'explicit scheme'. So

$$Q_e = \frac{T_e^f - T_0^f}{R_{0e}^f} \Delta A_e \Delta t \tag{42}$$

where R_{0e}^f is the thermal resistance between points x_0 and x_e (Majchrzak & Mendakiewicz, 1993), ΔA_e surface limiting the domain ΔV_0 in the direction e. If we denote by h_e the distance between the nodes x_0, x_e then

$$R_{0e}^f = \frac{h_e}{2\lambda_0^f} + \frac{h_e}{2\lambda_e^f} \tag{43}$$

where λ_0^f and λ_e^f are the thermal conductivities in the control volumes ΔV_0 and ΔV_e at the moment $t = t^f$. The other definition of thermal resistance should be introduced for the boundary volumes (Mochnacki & Suchy, 1995). In a case of no-flux boundary condition (see: example presented) one assumes $R_{0e}^f = \infty$ (in numerical realization e.g. $R_{0e}^f = 10^{10}$) if the surface limiting the domain ΔV_0 in direction e is a part of 'adiabatic' boundary.
The change of enthalpy of the control volume ΔV_0 during the time Δt equals (Domański et al., 2009a; Domański et al., 2009b; Mochnacki & Ciesielski, 2007)

$$\Delta H_0 = C_0^f \left(T_0^{f+1} - T_0^f \right) |\Delta V_0| \tag{44}$$

where $C_0{}^f$ is the volumetric specific heat (substitute thermal capacity), f, f+1 denotes two successive time levels.
Let us write the balance equation using the explicit scheme

$$C_0^f\left(T_0^{f+1}-T_0^f\right)|\Delta V_0|=\sum_e \frac{T_e^f-T_0^f}{R_{0e}^f}\Delta A_e\,\Delta t+|\Delta V_0|q_V\,\Delta t \tag{45}$$

or

$$T_0^{f+1}=\sum_{e=0}^{n} W_e T_e^f+\frac{q_V\,\Delta t}{C_0^f} \tag{46}$$

where

$$W_e=\frac{\Delta t\,\Delta A_e}{C_0^f R_{0e}^f|\Delta V_0|},\quad e=1,\dots,n \tag{47}$$

$$W_0=1-\sum_{e=1}^{n} W_e \tag{48}$$

In order to assure the stability of the above explicit scheme the coefficient W_0 must be positive.

It was mentioned above that the control volumes have been constructed in the form of Voronoi polygons (Thiessen cells). A single polygon is defined by the lines that bisect the lines between the central point and its surrounding points. The bisecting lines and the connection lines are perpendicular to each other and this property is very essential when the control volume method is used.

Many algorithms to construct the Voronoi polygons can be found in literature. One popular method is based on the Delaunay triangulation (Domański et al., 2009b; Mochnacki & Ciesielski, 2007) and this method has been used at the stage of 'in house' computer program construction. The aim of computations was the analysis of thermal processes in domain of solidifying cast composite made from Al-Si alloy (metal matrix) and silicon (fibres). In particular the problem of 'spontaneous' solidification of matrix due to presence of fibres has been analyzed.

In Figure 6 an example of the structure of cast composite with 40% fibres is shown. The geometrical parameters of a matrix-fibres system are chosen on the basis of the optical micrographs presented in (Domański et al., 2009b). It can be seen that the fibres diameters are different, and also their mutual positions are rather incidental. The only unquestionable information concerning the geometry of the system results from the volumetric fraction of the fibres in the domain analyzed. So, the numerical procedure realizing the mesh generation, fibres localization, values of fibres radii bases on the application of random numbers generation. The sub-domain presented in Figure 6 corresponds to the central part of composite (side of square equals 100 μm) and on the external surface the no-flux conditions have been assumed. It turned out that the spontaneous solidification takes place for 55% fraction of fibres. The kinetics of solidification in this case is shown in Figure 7. The input data concerning the parameters of cast composite components can be found in (Domański et al., 2009b).

A similar algorithm basing on the control volume method can be used also in a case of macro/micro modelling of solidification. One can see that the shapes of Thiessen cells are similar to the primary structure of casting and it was a reason of investigations connected with the application of presented version of CVM in a scope of macro/micro problems.

As an example the results of computations concerning the solidification of aluminium casting (2D problem) are presented. The macro control volume shown in Figure 8 (Mochnacki & Ciesielski, 2007) has been divided into micro control volumes. The heat fluxes (the Neumann boundary conditions) given on the periphery of macro control volume result from the solution of macroscopic problem (here the finite difference method has been applied). The micro model has been solved using the CVM under the assumption that the nuclei density is a constant value (this assumption is often used), the nuclei growth results from equation (35) for $m = 2$, while the changes of solid state fraction are determined by the Kolmogoroff formula. The result (cooling curve) shown in Figure 9 concerns the central point of macro control volume being in the direct thermal contact with sand mould sub-domain. The micro/macro approach allows one to observe the undercooling below the solidification point and next, the growth of local temperature. This effect cannot be observed when the numerical solution bases on the macro approach.

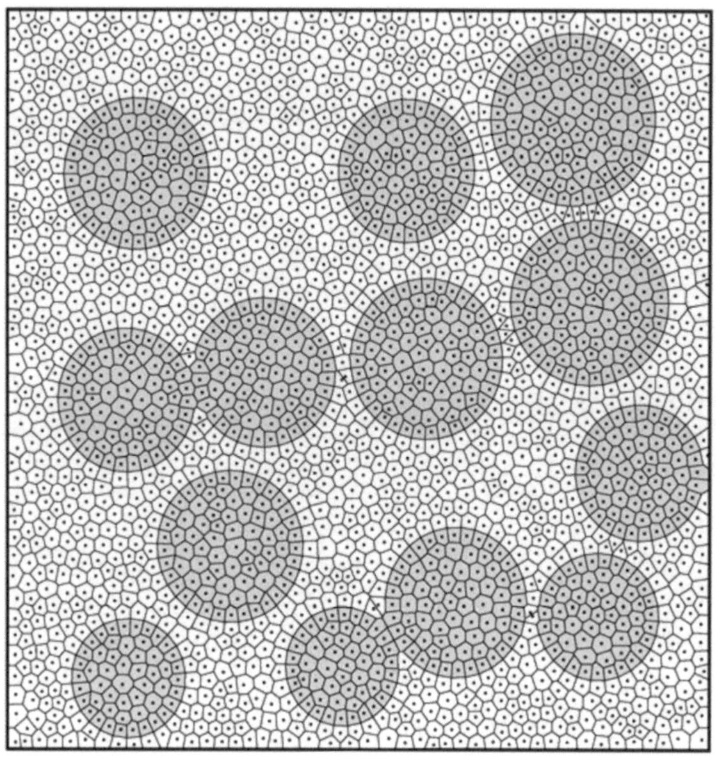

Fig. 6. Example of structure and its discretization.

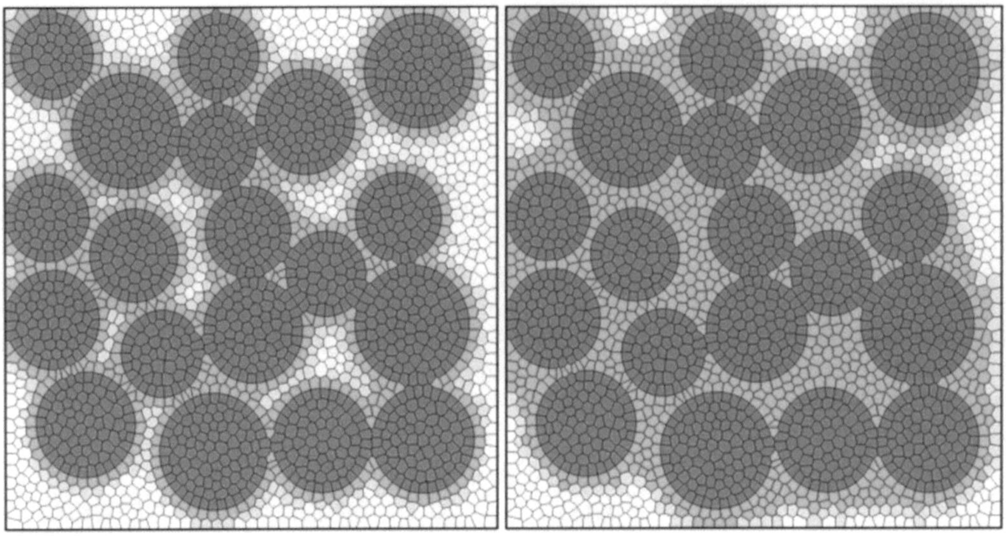

Fig. 7. Kinetics of composite solidification.

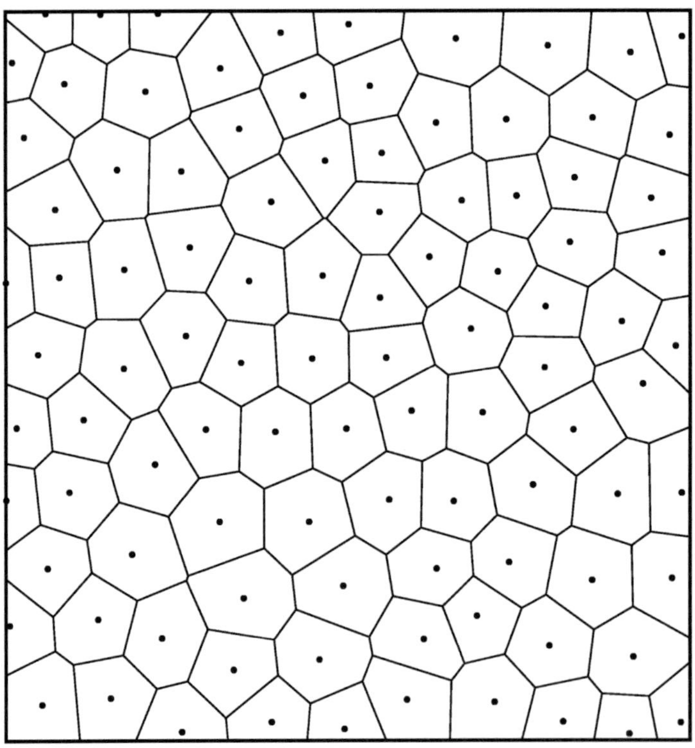

Fig. 8. The inner structure of macro control volume.

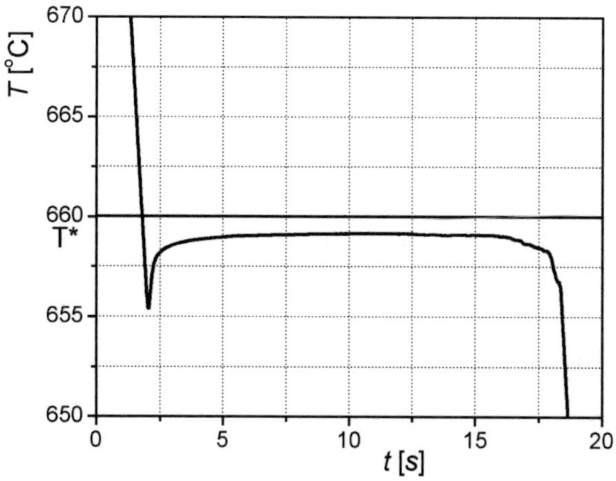

Fig. 9. Temperature history at the central point of macro control volume.

Now, the problems connected with the boundary element method (Brebbia et al., 1984; Brebbia & Dominguez, 1992; Majchrzak, 2001) application in the scope of solidification process modeling will be discussed. So, the boundary element method constitutes the effective tool for numerical simulation of solidification processes (Majchrzak & Mochnacki, 1995; Majchrzak & Mochnacki, 1996; Majchrzak & Szopa, 2001; Mochnacki & Majchrzak, 2007b). The method assures the exact approximation of real shapes of the boundaries and also the very good exactness of boundary conditions approximation (Brebbia et al., 1984; Brebbia & Dominguez, 1992). These features of the BEM are very essential in the case of solidification processes modeling because the big gradients of temperature near the boundary require the adequate exact method of temperature field computations. The main disadvantage of the method is the fact that it can be used only for linear tasks (the constant values of metal and mould thermophysical parameters) because the fundamental solutions are only available for linear equations. Nevertheless, several techniques have been developed for the numerical solution of nonlinear problems. In the case of solidification problem the basic BEM algorithm for linear Fourier's equation should be coupled with procedures correcting the temporary solutions for successive levels of time. These procedures are called the temperature field correction method (Mochnacki & Suchy, 1995; Mochnacki & Szopa, 2008), the alternating phase truncation method (Mochnacki & Suchy, 1995; Majchrzak & Mochnacki, 1995; Majchrzak & Mendakiewicz, 1993) and the artificial heat source method (Mochnacki & Majchrzak, 2010; Mochnacki & Szopa, 1998).

The basic idea of the BEM can be realized in different ways. In the case of parabolic equations the I and II scheme of the BEM, the dual reciprocity BEM, the BEM using discretization in time etc. are used. The detailed information concerning the BEM application in the scope of heat transfer problems can be found in the numerous books and papers published by Ewa Majchrzak from the Silesian University of Technology (Poland). Below, the short discussion of the BEM using discretization in time taken from (Majchrzak & Szopa, 2001; Mochnacki & Szopa, 1998; Mochnacki & Szopa, 2002) (it is not very popular but quite effective version of the BEM) will be presented.

Let us consider the following parabolic equation

$$\frac{\partial T(x,t)}{\partial t} = a \nabla^2 T(x,t) + \frac{Q(x,t)}{c} \tag{49}$$

where a is a thermal diffusivity, c is a volumetric specific heat, Q is a capacity of internal heat sources. The equation (49) is supplemented by the assumed boundary and initial conditions. At first the time grid

$$0=t^0<t^1<\ldots<t^{f-2}<t^{f-1}<t^f<\ldots<t^F<\infty \tag{50}$$

with constant step $\Delta t = t^f - t^{f-1}$ is introduced.
We substitute the energy equation (10) for time $t \in [t^{f-1}, t^f]$ by the equation in which the time derivative is approximated by the differential quotient, in particular

$$\frac{T(x,t^f) - T(x,t^{f-1})}{\Delta t} = a\, \nabla^2 T(x,t^f) + \frac{Q(x,t^f)}{c} \tag{51}$$

The last equation can be written in the form

$$\begin{gathered}\nabla^2 T(x,t^f) - \frac{1}{a\,\Delta t} T(x,t^f) + \\ \frac{1}{a\,\Delta t} T(x,t^{f-1}) + \frac{Q(x,t^f)}{\lambda} = 0\end{gathered} \tag{52}$$

Using the weighted residual method criterion (WRM) (Stefanescu, 1999; Szopa, 1999) one obtains

$$\begin{gathered}\int_\Omega \left[\nabla^2 T(x,t^f) - \frac{1}{a\,\Delta t} T(x,t^f) + \right. \\ \left. \frac{1}{a\,\Delta t} T(x,t^{f-1}) + \frac{Q(x,t^f)}{\lambda} \right] T^*(\xi,x)\, \mathrm{d}\Omega = 0\end{gathered} \tag{53}$$

where $T^*(\xi, x)$ is the fundamental solution and for the objects oriented in rectangular co-ordinate system it is a function of the form

$$T^*(\xi, x) = \begin{cases} \dfrac{\sqrt{a\,\Delta t}}{2} \exp\left(-\dfrac{r}{\sqrt{a\,\Delta t}} \right), & \text{for 1 D problem} \\ \dfrac{1}{2\pi} \mathrm{K}_0 \left(\dfrac{r}{\sqrt{a\,\Delta t}} \right), & \text{for 2 D problem} \\ \dfrac{1}{4\pi r} \exp\left(-\dfrac{r}{\sqrt{a\,\Delta t}} \right), & \text{for 3 D problem} \end{cases} \tag{54}$$

where $\mathrm{K}_0(\cdot)$ is the modified Bessel function of zero order, r is the distance between the points x and ξ.
The fundamental solution fulfills the following equation

$$\nabla^2 T^*(\xi,x) - \frac{1}{a\,\Delta t} T^*(\xi,x) = -\delta(\xi,x) \tag{55}$$

Additionally, on a basis of formula (54) the heat flux resulting from the fundamental solution

$$q^*(\xi,x)=-\lambda n\cdot\nabla T^*(\xi,x) \tag{56}$$

can be calculated in analytical way.

Applying the second Green formula to the first component of criterion (53) and taking into account the property (55) of fundamental solution one obtains the following boundary integral equation ($\xi \in \Gamma$)

$$\begin{aligned}T(\xi,t^f)+\frac{1}{\lambda}\int_\Gamma T^*(\xi,x)q(x,t^f)\,\mathrm{d}\Gamma=\\ \frac{1}{\lambda}\int_\Gamma q^*(\xi,x)T(x,t^f)\,\mathrm{d}\Gamma+\\ \frac{1}{a\Delta t}\int_\Omega T(x,t^{f-1})\,T^*(\xi,x)\,\mathrm{d}\Omega+\\ \frac{1}{\lambda}\int_\Omega Q(x,t^f)T^*(\xi,x)\,\mathrm{d}\Omega\end{aligned} \tag{57}$$

For example, in a case of 1D problem (plate of thickness L) the last equation takes a form

$$\begin{aligned}T(\xi,t^f)+\left[\frac{1}{\lambda}T^*(\xi,x)q(x,t^f)\right]_0^L=\\ \left[\frac{1}{\lambda}q^*(\xi,x)T(x,t^f)\right]_0^L+p(\xi)+z(\xi)\end{aligned} \tag{58}$$

where

$$p(\xi)=\frac{1}{a\Delta t}\int_0^L T^*(\xi,x)\,T(x,t^{f-1})\,\mathrm{d}x \tag{59}$$

and

$$z(\xi)=\frac{1}{\lambda}\int_0^L Q(x,t^f)\,T^*(\xi,x)\,\mathrm{d}x \tag{60}$$

For $\xi\to 0^+$ and for $\xi\to L^-$ one obtains the system of equations which can be written in the matrix form

$$\begin{aligned}\begin{bmatrix} g_{11} & g_{12}\\ g_{21} & g_{22}\end{bmatrix}\begin{bmatrix} q(0,t^f)\\ q(L,t^f)\end{bmatrix}=\\ \begin{bmatrix} h_{11} & h_{12}\\ h_{21} & h_{22}\end{bmatrix}\begin{bmatrix} T(0,t^f)\\ T(L,t^f)\end{bmatrix}+\begin{bmatrix} p(0)\\ p(L)\end{bmatrix}+\begin{bmatrix} z(0)\\ z(L)\end{bmatrix}\end{aligned} \tag{61}$$

where

$$g_{11} = -g_{22} = -\frac{\sqrt{\Delta t}}{2\sqrt{\lambda c}} \quad g_{12} = -g_{21} = \frac{\sqrt{\Delta t}}{2\sqrt{\lambda c}} exp\left(-\frac{L}{\sqrt{a\Delta t}}\right) \tag{62}$$

while

$$h_{11} = h_{22} = -\frac{1}{2} \quad h_{12} = h_{21} = \frac{1}{2} exp\left(-\frac{L}{\sqrt{a\Delta t}}\right) \tag{63}$$

Equation (61) allows to determine the 'missing' boundary values (temperatures and heat fluxes for $x = 0$ and $x = L$), while in the second step of computations the temporary temperatures in the set of internal points $\xi \in (0, L)$ can be found on the basis of equation (58).
As the example of 1D solution concerning the solidification process (micro/macro approach) a problem of heat transfer in domain of aluminium plate ($L = 0.02$ [m]) is discussed. On the outer surface of the plate the boundary temperature $T_B = 655$°C, while for the axis of symmetry $q_B = 0$ are assumed. The growth coefficient is equal to $\mu = 3 \cdot 10^{-6}$ [m/sK^2], at the same time the nucleation coefficient: $\psi = 10^{10}$ [m^{-3} K^{-2}], exponent $n = 1.5$ (equation (31)). Pouring temperature: $T_0 = 700$°C, solidification point: $T_c = 660$°C. The thermophysical parameters of Al are assumed to be constant. The solidification model corresponds to description previously presented (see: formulas (38), (39), (40)). In domain of plate 20 internal points has been distinguished and in Figure 10 the cooling curves at points 10, 14 and 18 are presented, while in Figure 11 the evolution of source function at the same points are shown.

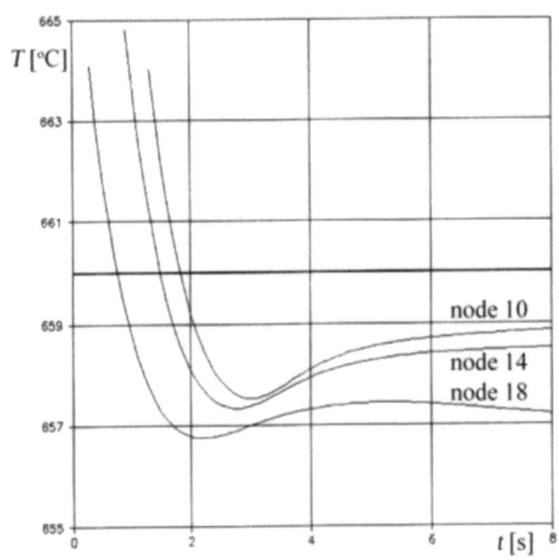

Fig. 10. Cooling curves.

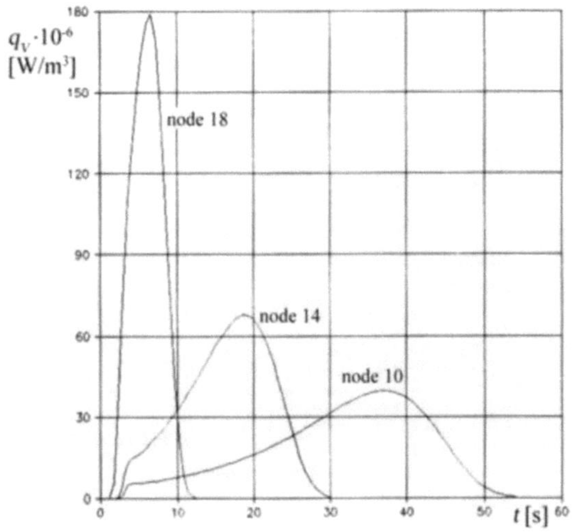

Fig. 11. Source function evolution.

The second example concerns the 3D problem solution (Szopa, 1999). Figure 12 shows the shape of considered steel casting domain (dimensions are marked in mm).
The boundary surface was divided into constant boundary elements (squares), whereas the interior was divided into constant internal cells (cubes). The boundary condition of the form $x \in \Gamma$: $T(x, t) = 1465°C$ was assumed (this value results from well known Schwarz's solution and was treated as a constant one). The initial temperature $T(x, 0) = 1550°C$ whereas the thermophysical parameters correspond to the cast steel 0.35%C. The solidification process was taken into account by the correction of temperature field for successive levels of time (Temperature Field Correction Method). In Figure 13 the temporary temperature field for $t = 180$s and two selected vertical sections is shown.

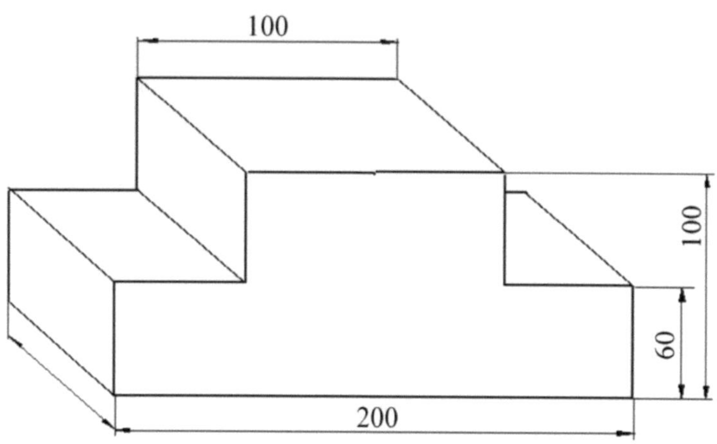

Fig. 12. Temperature field in domain considered.

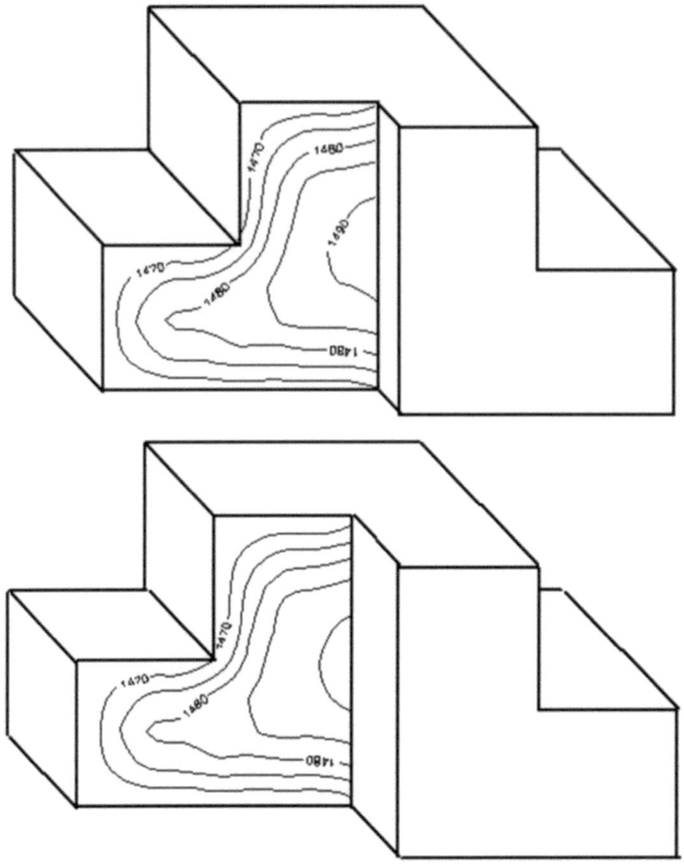

Fig. 13. Temperature field in domain considered.

5. Sensitivity analysis

In this sub-chapter the selected problems from the scope of sensitivity analysis application in the thermal theory of solidification processes are discussed. It should be pointed out that the sensitivity models are the essential part of inverse problems solutions, they allow to rebuilt the solution obtained for assumed input data on the other one (see: considerations and examples presented below), sensitivity methods can be also used on a stage of measurements in order to determine the optimum positions of sensors.

The examples of applications here discussed concern the sensitivity of temperature field in a system solidifying metal-mould with respect to perturbations of external, boundary and initial parameters appearing in the mathematical model of process discussed, at the same time the approach called 'a direct sensitivity analysis' is presented. Both the macro models and macro/micro ones are considered

Let us assume that the searched solution of boundary-initial problem (e.g. transient temperature field in the system metal - mould), is the function of parameters z_1 , z_2 ,..., z_n . They can correspond, among others, to thermophysical parameters of sub-domains, heat transfer coefficient on the outer surface of the system, pouring temperature, initial temperature of mould, geometrical parameters etc. The sensitivity U_k of boundary-initial problem solution with respect to parameter z_k is defined as a partial derivative $U_k(x,t) = \partial T(x,t,z_1,\dots z_n)/\partial z_k$ (Kleiber, 1997; Dems & Rousselet, 1999). As it was mentioned below the methods of sensitivity analysis allows one 'to rebuilt' the solution of problem considered to the solution concerning the other value of parameter z_k. So, the set of parameters introduced to the computer program as the input data we denote by z_1^0, z_2^0, ..., z_n^0. Additionally we are interested in the others solutions corresponding to changed input data (e.g. new pouring temperature). The methods of sensitivity analysis give the possibilities to transform the basic solution on the solution for disturbed initial parameters. The transformation results from the Taylor formula, namely

$$\begin{gathered} T(x,\, t,\, z_1^0, z_2^0, \dots, z_k^0 \pm \Delta z_k, \dots, z_n^0) = \\ T(x,\, t,\, z_1^0, z_2^0, \dots, z_k^0, \dots, z_n^0) \pm U_k^0\, \Delta z_k + V_k^0 \frac{\Delta z_k^0}{2} + \dots \end{gathered} \tag{64}$$

where T is a searched function (e.g. temperature), x is a spatial coordinate, t is a time, U_k^0 denotes the derivative $\partial T/\partial z_k$ at the start point 0, whereas V_k^0 is the second derivative with respect to z_k at the same point. The equations determining the values of U_i^0 (the first order sensitivity) and V_i^0 (the second order sensitivity) result from the differentiation of equations and conditions describing the physical process considered with respect to parameter z_k (direct approach) We can notice that formula (64) concerns to the disturbance of distinguished parameter, but one can analyze also the disturbance of the certain set of parameters z_k, simultaneously.

5.1 Sensitivity analysis of macro models

Sensitivity analysis with respect to boundary and initial conditions (e.g. heat transfer coefficient α, ambient temperature T_a , initial temperatures T_0, T_{m0}) or mould parameters (c_m, λ_m) will be discussed, at the same time the direct approach will be applied. The problem is more complicated in comparison with the others ones, because the mathematical model of solidification is strongly non-linear (Szopa, 2005; Szopa & Wojciechowska, 2003; Szopa et al., 2004; Mochnacki & Szopa, 2009).

At first, the energy equation (8) should be differentiated with respect to parameter z_k, this means

$$\frac{\partial}{\partial z_k}\left[C(T)\frac{\partial T(x,t)}{\partial t} \right] = \nabla\left[\frac{\partial}{\partial z_k}[\lambda(T)\nabla T(x,t)] \right] \tag{65}$$

Because

$$\frac{\partial C(T)}{\partial z_k} = \frac{\mathrm{d}C(T)}{\mathrm{d}T}\frac{\partial T}{\partial z_k}, \qquad \frac{\partial \lambda(T)}{\partial z_k} = \frac{\mathrm{d}\lambda(T)}{\mathrm{d}T}\frac{\partial T}{\partial z_k} \tag{66}$$

therefore (using additionally Schwarz theorem)

$$\begin{gathered} C(T)\frac{\partial U(x,t)}{\partial t} = \nabla[\lambda(T)\nabla U(x,t)] + \\ \nabla[\lambda'(T)U(x,t)\nabla T(x,t)] - C'(T)U(x,t)\frac{\partial T(x,t)}{\partial t} \end{gathered} \tag{67}$$

where $U = \partial T / \partial z_k$ is the sensitivity of temperature field in a solidifying metal domain with respect to perturbations of parameter z_k.
Now, the equation concerning a mould sub-domain is differentiated with respect to z_k under the assumption that c_m and λ_m are the constant values (this assumption is not necessary)

$$\begin{aligned} &\frac{\partial c_m}{\partial z_k}\frac{\partial T_m(x,t)}{\partial t}+c_m\frac{\partial U_m(x,t)}{\partial t}= \\ &\frac{\partial \lambda_m}{\partial z_k}\nabla^2 T_m(x,t)+\lambda_m \nabla^2 U_m(x,t) \end{aligned} \qquad (68)$$

where $U_m = \partial T_m / \partial z_k$. Taking into account the equation (2) one can write

$$\begin{aligned} &c_m\frac{\partial U_m(x,t)}{\partial t}=\lambda_m \nabla^2 U_m(x,t)+ \\ &\left(\frac{\partial \lambda_m}{\partial z_k}\frac{c_m}{\lambda_m}-\frac{\partial c_m}{\partial z_k}\right)\frac{\partial T_m(x,t)}{\partial t} \end{aligned} \qquad (69)$$

The sensitivity equations become simpler when in place of z_k the actual parameters (e.g. initial casting temperature, initial mould temperature, heat transfer coefficient or ambient temperature) are introduced.
The following boundary conditions should be considered

- Robin condition (e.g. external surface of mould):

$$\begin{aligned} &-\frac{\partial \lambda_m}{\partial z_k}\frac{\partial T_m(x,t)}{\partial n}-\lambda_m\frac{\partial U_m(x,t)}{\partial n}= \\ &\frac{\partial \alpha}{\partial z_k}\left[T_m(x,t)-T_a\right]+\alpha\left[U_m(x,t)-\frac{\partial T_a}{\partial z_k}\right] \end{aligned} \qquad (70)$$

- metal-mould contact surface:

$$\begin{cases} -\lambda'(T)U(x,t)\dfrac{\partial T(x,t)}{\partial n}-\lambda(T)\dfrac{\partial U(x,t)}{\partial n}= \\ \quad -\dfrac{\partial \lambda_m}{\partial z_k}\dfrac{\partial T_m(x,t)}{\partial n}-\lambda_m\dfrac{\partial U_m(x,t)}{\partial n} \\ \qquad U(x,t)=U_m(x,t) \end{cases} \qquad (71)$$

One can see that for the constant values of metal and mould thermal conductivities the conditions (70) and (71) are similar to conditions (3) and (5).
The initial conditions takes a form

$$t=0: \quad U=\frac{\partial T_0}{\partial z_k}=U_0, \quad U_m=\frac{\partial T_{m0}}{\partial z_k}=U_{m0} \qquad (72)$$

If the sensitivity analysis does not concern the initial temperatures then the initial conditions are uniform

$$t=0: \quad U=\frac{\partial T_0}{\partial z_k}=0, \qquad U_m=\frac{\partial T_{m0}}{\partial z_k}=0 \tag{73}$$

Below, as an example, the sensitivity method is applied to the analysis of dependence between the pouring temperature and the course of solidification and cooling proceeding in the casting domain. The equation describing the heat diffusion in the casting is non-linear one, whereas the thermophysical parameters of mould are assumed to be the constant.

The equation describing the thermal processes proceeding in the metal domain oriented in rectangular co-ordinate system $\{x, y\}$ (2D problem) is of the form (c.f. equation (1))

$$C(T)\frac{\partial T(x,y,t)}{\partial t}= \frac{\partial}{\partial x}\left[\lambda(T)\frac{\partial T(x,y,t)}{\partial x}\right]+\frac{\partial}{\partial y}\left[\lambda(T)\frac{\partial T(x,y,t)}{\partial y}\right] \tag{74}$$

The energy equation for the mould domain is the following

$$c_m\frac{\partial T_m(x,y,t)}{\partial t}=\lambda_m\left(\frac{\partial^2 T_m(x,y,t)}{\partial x^2}+\frac{\partial^2 T_m(x,y,t)}{\partial y^2}\right) \tag{75}$$

The boundary conditions on the outer surface of the mould determine the continuity of heat flux between the mould and the environment (the Robin condition), but in practice one can assume in this place the no-flux condition (especially in the case of sand mould). On the contact surface between casting and the condition (5) is given.

The mathematical model is supplemented by the initial conditions:

$$t=0: \quad T=T_0, \quad T_m=T_{m0} \tag{76}$$

In order to analyze the influence of the pouring temperature on the course of casting solidification the direct variant of sensitivity analysis has been used and the solidification model is differentiated with respect to pouring temperature T_0. So, for $(x, y) \in \Omega$

$$C_T\, U\frac{\partial T}{\partial t}+C\frac{\partial U}{\partial t}=\frac{\partial}{\partial x}\left(\lambda\,\frac{\partial U}{\partial x}\right)+\frac{\partial}{\partial y}\left(\lambda\,\frac{\partial U}{\partial y}\right)+ \frac{\partial}{\partial x}\left(\lambda_T\, U\frac{\partial T}{\partial x}\right)+\frac{\partial}{\partial y}\left(\lambda_T\, U\frac{\partial T}{\partial y}\right) \tag{77}$$

where $U = \partial T/\partial T_0$, $C_T = \mathrm{d}C/\mathrm{d}T$, $\lambda_T = \mathrm{d}\lambda/\mathrm{d}T$. Next

$$(x,y)\in\Omega_m: \quad c_m\frac{\partial U_m}{\partial t}=\lambda_m\left(\frac{\partial^2 U_m}{\partial x^2}+\frac{\partial^2 U_m}{\partial y^2}\right) \tag{78}$$

where $U_m = \partial T_m/\partial T_0$.

If on the outer surface Γ_0 of the system we assume the no-flux condition then the adequate boundary condition takes a form, $\partial U_m/\partial n = 0$. On the contact surface (for λ = const) one has

$$(x,y) \in \Gamma_m: \quad \begin{cases} -\lambda \dfrac{\partial U}{\partial n} = -\lambda_m \dfrac{\partial U_m}{\partial n} \\ U = U_m \end{cases} \tag{79}$$

The problem is supplemented by the initial condition for $t = 0$: $U = 1$, $U_m = 0$.

As an example the bar of rectangular section (10×14 cm) made from Cu-Sn alloy (10% Sn) is considered. The casting is produced in the sand mix which parameters are equal $\lambda_m = 2.28$ [W/mK], $c_m = 2.320 \cdot 10^6$ [J/m^{3}K]. The thermal conductivity of the casting material equals $\lambda = 50$ [W/mK]. According to literature (e.g. [3]) the substitute thermal capacity can be approximated by the piece-wise constant function $T > 990$°C: $C = 3.678 \cdot 10^6$ [J/m^{3}K], $T < 825$°C: $C = 3.678 \cdot 10^6$ [J/m^{3}K], $T \in [825, 990]$: $C = 14.558 \cdot 10^6$ [J/m^{3}K]. In order to assure the differentiation of function C, the smoothing procedure has been applied (Mochnacki & Suchy, 1995). The initial temperatures are equal to $T(0) = 1000$°C, $T_m(0) = 30$°C. The quarter of domain is taken into account and its shape is marked in Figure14. In this Figure the temperature field for time $t = 6$ minutes is shown.

The sensitivity analysis shows that the influence of pouring temperature on the temperature field is the most essential in the metal sub-domain (in particular at the initial stages of cooling process) and sand mix layer close to contact surface. In other words, the change of $T_0 = 1000$°C to the value from interval $[T_0 - \Delta T_0, T_0 + \Delta T_0]$ determines the essential fluctuations of temporary temperature field in these sub-domains.

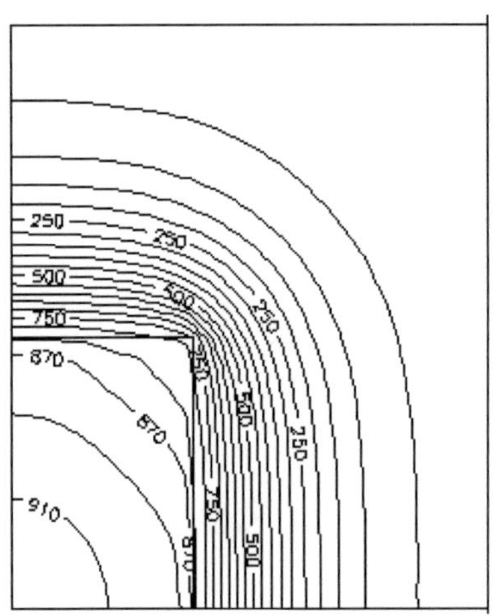

Fig. 14. Temperature field.

Figure 15 illustrates the isolines of function U for the same time.

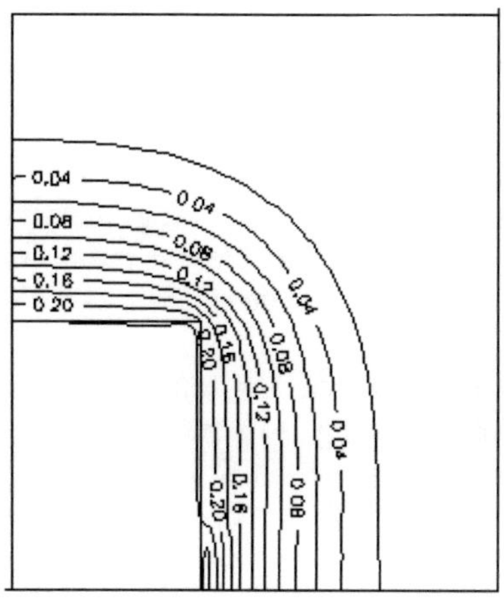

Fig. 15. Distribution of function U for time 6 minutes.

Now, the considerations concerning the continuous casting process will be presented. The goal of work is to apply the sensitivity analysis tool in order to observe the perturbations of casting solidification due to the perturbations of substitute heat transfer coefficient in primary cooling zone of CCT installation. The basic energy equation describing the thermal processes in the domain of vertical, rectangular cast slab can be written in the form

$$C(T)\left[\frac{\partial T}{\partial t} + w\frac{\partial T}{\partial z}\right] = \frac{\partial}{\partial x}\left[\lambda(T)\frac{\partial T}{\partial x}\right] + \frac{\partial}{\partial y}\left[\lambda(T)\frac{\partial T}{\partial y}\right] + \frac{\partial}{\partial z}\left[\lambda(T)\frac{\partial T}{\partial z}\right] \tag{80}$$

where $T = T(x, y, z, t)$, w is the pulling rate – the cast slab shifts in z direction (see: Figure 16).

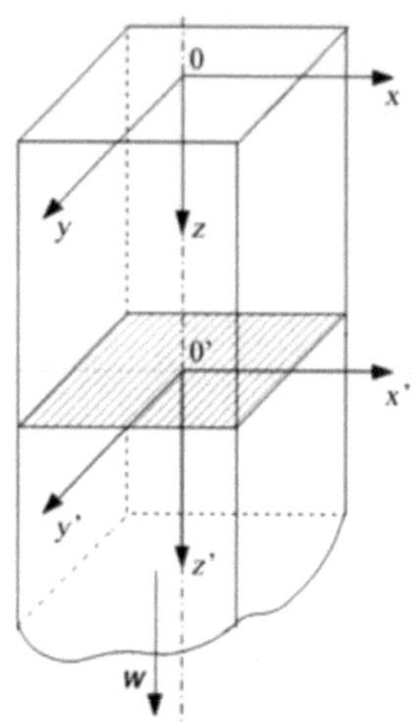

Fig. 16. Vertical continuous casting.

The boundary conditions on the lateral surface of cast slab (the continuous casting mould region) are assumed in the form

$$-\lambda(T)\frac{\partial T}{\partial n} = \alpha(T - T_w) \tag{81}$$

where α is the substitute heat transfer coefficient, T_w is the cooling water temperature. On the upper surface of the casting (free surface of molten metal) the boundary condition of the 1st type (pouring temperature) can be taken into account. On the conventionally assumed bottom surface limiting the domain considered we can put $\partial T/\partial n = 0$, this means the adiabatic condition.

The initial condition resolves itself into the assumption, that a certain layer of molten metal directly over the starter bar has a pouring temperature T_p. The starter bar allows to shut the continuous casting mould during the plant starting.

The numerous experiments show that conductional component of heat transfer corresponding to the direction of cast strand displacement is very small (in the case of steel castings this component constitutes about 5% of the heat conducted from the axis to the lateral surfaces). So, the equation (80) can be simplified to the 2D one. Let we rewrite this equation using the coordinate system 'tied' to a certain section of shifting casting, namely $x' = x,\ y' = y,\ z' = z - wt$. It is easy to check up that we 'lose' in energy equation the component $\partial T/\partial z$ and we obtain

$$C(T)\,\frac{\partial T}{\partial t} = \frac{\partial}{\partial x'}\left[\lambda(T)\frac{\partial T}{\partial x'}\right] + \frac{\partial}{\partial y'}\left[\lambda(T)\,\frac{\partial T}{\partial y'}\right] \tag{82}$$

This approach is called 'a wandering cross section method' (Mochnacki & Suchy, 1995). We consider the lateral section of the cast strand which position at the moment $t = 0$ corresponds to $z = 0$ (the initial condition has a form $T(0) = T_p$), while the boundary conditions on the periphery of this section are the functions of time. If Δt_1 corresponds to the 'hold time' of the section in the continuous casting mould region, then for $0 \le t \le \Delta t_1$ on the casting periphery the boundary condition for the primary cooling zone (e.g., heat flux) is assumed. For the next interval Δt_2 we consider the boundary condition characterizing the heat transfer in the 1st sector of the secondary cooling zone etc.

In order to construct the sensitivity model respect to α we differentiate the governing equations over this parameter (a direct approach is applied)

$$\begin{gathered}\frac{\mathrm{d}C(T)}{\mathrm{d}T}U\frac{\partial T}{\partial t} + C(T)\frac{\partial U}{\partial t} = \\ \frac{\partial}{\partial x}\left[\frac{\mathrm{d}\lambda(T)}{\mathrm{d}T}U\frac{\partial T}{\partial x} + \lambda(T)\frac{\partial U}{\partial x}\right] + \frac{\partial}{\partial y}\left[\frac{\mathrm{d}\lambda(T)}{\mathrm{d}T}U\frac{\partial T}{\partial x} + \lambda(T)\frac{\partial U}{\partial x}\right] +\end{gathered} \tag{83}$$

In equation (83) one substitutes again $x' = x$, $y' = y$, symbol $\partial T/\partial\alpha = U$ denotes the sensitivity function.

Differentiating the condition (81) one has

$$-\lambda\frac{\partial U}{\partial n} = T - T_w + \alpha U \tag{84}$$

The initial condition takes a form: $U(x, y, 0) = 0$.
As an example the following task is presented. The rectangular steel slab (0.44%C) with dimensions 0.6×0.2 m is considered. The pouring temperature equals 1550°C, pulling rate: $w = 0.017$ m/s] The basic heat transfer coefficient in the primary cooling zone equals $\alpha = 1500$ [W/m^{2}K]. The temperature field at the distance 0.6 m from upper surface of the slab has been observed. The precise results will be shown below. For the nodes located near the corner of cast slab the nodal temperatures for $\alpha = 1500$ are collected on the left side of the page. The temperatures found directly for $\alpha = 1700$ are written in the middle of this page, while on the right side one can find the temperatures for $\alpha = 1700$ obtained on the basis of the sensitivity analysis and Taylor series:

925 883 812 812	858 815 741 741	855 814 740 740
1259 1201 1046 812	1216 1155 986 741	1214 1155 987 740
1496 1478 1201 883	1492 1468 1155 816	1493 1471 1155 814
1512 1496 1259 925	1510 1492 1216 858	1510 1493 1215 855

The sensitivity analysis constitutes also the essential tool of inverse problems solution, in particular when the minimum of functional (corresponding to the least squares criterion) is searched using the gradient methods. The problems connected with the inverse methods applications in the thermal theory of foundry processes can be found, among others, in (Majchrzak et al., 2007; Majchrzak et al., 2008a; Majchrzak & Mendakiewicz 2009; Mochnacki & Majchrzak, 2006; Mendakiewicz, 2008; Majchrzak & Mendakiewicz, 2007; Majchrzak et al., 2008b; Majchrzak et al., 2008c).
In this chapter only the part of problems connected with the solidification process modeling has been presented because the subject-matter discussed is very extensive. It also the reason that the references contain mainly the papers prepared by the author of this chapter and his co-workers.

6. References

Stefanescu, D.M. (1999). Critical review of the second generation of solidification models for casting, *Modelling of Casting, Welding and Advanced Solidification Processes VI*. The Minerals, Metals and Materials Society 1999, pp. 3-20.

Mochnacki, B. & Majchrzak, E. (2007a). Identification of macro and micro parameters in solidification model, *Bulletin of the Polish Academy of Sciences, Technical Sciences*, Vol. 55, No. 1, 2007, pp. 107-113.

Mochnacki, B. & Suchy, J. S. (1995). *Numerical methods in computations of foundry processes*, PFTA, Cracow, Poland.

Szopa, R. (1999). Modelling of solidification using the combined variant of the BEM, *Metallurgy, Publ. of the Silesian Univ. of Technology*, Gliwice, Poland.

Mochnacki, B., Majchrzak, E., Szopa, R. & Suchy, J.S. (2006). Inverse problems in the thermal theory of foundry, *Scientific Research of the Institute of Mathematics and Computer Science*, Czestochowa, 1(5), pp. 154-179.

Majchrzak, E. & Mochnacki, B. (2007). Identification of thermal properties of the system casting - mould, *Materials Science Forum*, Vols. 539-543, pp. 2491-2496.

Majchrzak, E. & Mochnacki, B. (1995). Application of the BEM in the thermal theory of foundry, *Engineering Analysis with Boundary Elements*, Vol. 16, pp. 99-121.

Majchrzak, E. & Mendakiewicz, J. (1993). Application of the generalized alternating phase truncation method for numerical modelling of cast iron solidification, *Solidification of Metals and Alloys*, Vol. 18, pp. 103-112.

Majchrzak, E., Suchy, J. S. & Szopa, R. (2006). Linear model of crystallization. Identification of nuclei density, *Giessereiforschung, International Foundry Research*, Vol. 2, pp. 29-32.

Mochnacki, B. & Szopa, R. (2007) Model of pure metal solidification using the power-type function, *Journal of Achievements in Materials and Manufacturing Engineering*, Vol. 22, pp. 65-71.

Fraś, E., Kapturkiewicz, W. & Lopez, H.F. (1993). Macro and micro modelling of the solidification kinetics of casting, *AFS Transactions*, Vol. 48-92, pp. 583-591.

Lupa, M., Szopa, R. & Wojciechowska, W. (2004). Sensitivity analysis of crystallization with respect internal parameters, *Scientific Research of the Institute of Mathematics and Computer Science*, 1(3), pp. 91-98.

Mochnacki, B. & Szopa, R. (2010). Generalized micro/macro model of crystallization and its numerical realization, *Journal for Multiscale Computational Engineering*, 8(3), pp. 259-266.

Majchrzak, E. & Piasecka, A. (1997). Numerical micro/macro model of solidification process, *Journal of Materials Processing Technology*, Vol. 64, pp. 267-276.

Domański, Z., Ciesielski, M. & Mochnacki, B. (2009a). Voronoi tessellations description of cast composite solidification process, *World Congress on Engineering 2009, Lecture Notes in Engineering and Computer Science*, Vol. 2, pp. 1197-1201.

Domański, Z., Ciesielski, M. & Mochnacki, B. (2009b). Applicatiom of CVM using the Voronoi tesselation in numerical modelling of solidification process, *Current Themes in Engineering Science 2009*. Ed. M. Korsunsky, American Institute of Physics, Melville, New York, pp. 17-27.

Mochnacki, B. & Ciesielski, M. (2007). Micro/macro model of solidification. Numerical simulation using the control volume method, *17th International Conference on Computer Methods in Mechanics CMM-2007*, CD ROM Proceedings, ISBN-978-83-923982-3-3.

Brebbia, C.A., Telles, J.C.F. & Wrobel, L.C. (1984). *Boundary Element Techniques*, Springer-Verlag.

Brebbia, C.A. & Dominguez, J. (1992). *Boundary elements, an introductory course*, Computational Mechanics Publications, McGraw-Hill Book Company, London.

Majchrzak, E. (2001). *Boundary element method in heat transfer*, Publication of the Czestochowa University of Technology, Czestochowa, Poland (in Polish).

Majchrzak, E. & Mochnacki, B. (1996). The BEM application for numerical solution of non-steady and non-linear thermal diffusion problems, *Computer Assisted Mechanics and Engineering Sciences*, Vol. 3, No. 4, pp. 327-346.

Majchrzak, E. & Szopa, R. (2001). Analysis of thermal processes in solidifying casting using the combined variant of the BEM, *Journal of Materials Processing Technology*, Vol. 109, pp. 126-132.

Mochnacki, B. & Majchrzak, E. (2007b). Application of the shape sensitivity analysis in numerical modelling of solidification process, *Materials Science Forum*, Vols. 539-543, pp. 2524-2529.

Mochnacki, B. & Szopa, R. (2008). Generalization of temporary temperature field correction method in numerical modelling of solidification, *Archives of Foundry Engineering*, Vol. 8, No. 1, pp. 219-222.

Mochnacki, B. & Majchrzak, E. (2010). Numerical modeling of casting solidification using generalized finite difference method, *Materials Science Forum*, Vols. 638-642, pp. 2676-2681.

Mochnacki, B. & Szopa, R. (1998). Application of the boundary element method in numerical modelling of solidification – Part I. The One Domain Approach, *Journal of Theoretical and Applied Mechanics*, Vol. 2, No. 36, pp. 457-468.

Mochnacki, B. & Szopa, R. (2002). Numerical modelling of heat transfer in spherical domains by mean of the BEM using discretization on time, *Journal of Theoretical and Applied Mechanics*, Vol. 2, No. 40, pp. 357-370.

Kleiber, M. (1997). *Parameter Sensitivity in Nonlinear Mechanics*, J. Wiley & Sons Ltd., Chichester, England.

Dems, K. & Rousselet, B. (1999). *Structural Optimization*, Vol. 17, pp. 36-45.

Szopa, R. (2005). The parametric sensitivity analysis of solidification process, *Archives of Foundry*, Vol. 5, No. 15, pp. 395-404.

Szopa, R. & Wojciechowska, W. (2003). Sensitivity analysis of solidification process with respect to grains geometry, *Archives of Foundry*, Vol. 3, No 10, pp. 255-260.

Szopa, R., Siedlecki, J. & Wojciechowska, W. (2004). The influence of initial conditions on the course of solidification process, *Scientific Research of the Institute of Mathematics and Computer Science*, 1(3), pp. 201-208.

Mochnacki, B. & Szopa, R. (2009). Application of sensitivity analysis in numerical simulation of solidification process, In: *Progress of Foundry Theory and Practice*, Pol. Ac. of Sciences, pp. 271-286.

Majchrzak, E., Dziewonski, M. & Kaluza, G. (2007). Identification of cast steel latent heat by means of gradient method, *Int. J. Computational Materials Science and Surface Engineering*, Vol. 1, No. 5, pp. 555-570.

Majchrzak, E., Mochnacki, B. & Suchy, J.S. (2008a). Identification of substitute thermal capacity of solidifying alloy, *Journal of Theoretical and Applied Mechanics*, Vol. 46, No. 2, pp. 257-268.

Majchrzak, E. & Mendakiewicz, J. (2009). Identification of cast steel latent heat on a basis of thermal and difference analysis, *Computer Methods in Material Science*, Vol. 9, No. 2, pp. 195-199.

Mochnacki, B. & Majchrzak, E. (2006). The methods of inverse problems solution in the thermal theory of foundry processes, In: *Research in Polish Metallurgy at the beginning of XXI century*, Ed. K. Świątkowski, Committee of Metallurgy of the Polish Academy of Sciences, pp. 239-254.

Mendakiewicz, J. (2008). Application of identification methods in solidification process modelling, *Archives of Foundry Engineering*, Vol. 8, No. 1, pp. 203-210.

Majchrzak, E. & Mendakiewicz, J. (2007). Gradient method of cast iron latent heat identification, *Archives of Foundry Engineering*, Vol. 7, No. 4, pp. 121-126.

Majchrzak, E., Mochnacki, B. & Suchy, J.S. (2008b). Estimation of boundary heat flux between casting and mould using the global function specification method, *Archives of Foundry Engineering*, Vol. 8, No. 1, pp. 193-198.

Majchrzak, E., Mochnacki, B., Dziewoński, M. & Jasiński, M. (2008c). Identification of boundary heat flux on the continuous casting surface, *Archives of Foundry Engineering*, Vol. 8, No. 4, pp. 105-110.

25

Performance Evaluation of Adaptive Algorithms for Wave Field Analysis/Synthesis Using Sound Field Simulations

Paolo Peretti, Stefania Cecchi, Laura Romoli and Francesco Piazza
Università Politecnica delle Marche
Italy

1. Introduction

The main objective of a multi-channel sound reproduction system is to give an optimal acoustical sensation to the listener. These systems are designed to produce sounds that are as natural as possible, so that the listener does not realize that they are generated by a loudspeakers system. For this purpose, the knowledge of only audio temporal information is not sufficient: also spatial information is needed. Furthermore, since the invention of stereophony, it is well known that at least two loudspeakers are needed in order to generate a virtual source that is not spatially localized at the speaker position. However, the stereo reproduction is very limited because the optimal source localization is focused on one point, called sweet spot. Starting from this assumption, in the recent literature, research efforts have focused on reproduction techniques that use an extremely high number of loudspeakers in order to reproduce not only a simple audio source but a complete sound field. Various techniques, able to record and to reproduce the entire sound field, have been proposed in the literature (Berkhout et al., 1993; Daniel et al., 2003; Fazi et al., 2008).

One of the most studied techniques is Wave Field Synthesis (WFS) that is directly based on the Huygens' principle. It has been introduced in the late '80s by Berkhout, who showed that audio reproduction can be linked to audio holography concepts (Berkhout, 1988). WFS is based on Kirchhoff-Helmholtz integral which permits the calculation of the pressure field inside a volume by knowing pressure and normal particle velocity on the enclosing surface. The underlying idea of WFS is to generate a sound field inside a volume bounded by an array of loudspeakers. Actually, the surface is reduced to a 2D curve positioned on the ear plane. The number of loudspeakers on this curve depends on the desired localization quality. Similarly, Wave Field Analysis (WFA) implements a sound field recording technique based on microphone arrays (Hulsebos et al., 2002). Therefore, this approach allows to record the entire sound field in the recording room (WFA) and subsequently to reproduce it in the listening room (WFS) more or less accurately depending on loudspeakers/microphones number.

As it happens in traditional reproduction systems, digital algorithms based on adaptation processing have to be applied inside the WFS/WFA in order for these techniques to be used in real applications (music, cinema, theatre, etc.). Examples of adaptive algorithms that are very useful in real applications are Acoustic Echo Cancellation (AEC), Active Noise Control (ANC), room compensation, etc. (Haykin, 1996). A straightforward implementation of these algorithms in WFA/WFS systems is not feasible due to the dramatically high number of inputs/outputs causing an unreasonable computational complexity. This led to the introduction of Wave Domain Adaptive Filtering – WDAF (Buchner, Spors & Rabenstein, 2004). WDAF is an extension of Frequency Domain Adaptive Filtering – FDAF (Shynk, 1992): the filtering is not only performed in temporal frequency domain (as in FDAF), but also in angular frequency domain that takes into account the spatial components of the acoustic field shape. Several WDAF applications can be found in the recent literature (Peretti et al., 2007; 2008; Spors et al., 2005).

In order to evaluate the performance of WDAF-based algorithms, all the points of the sound field have to be analyzed in order to give a complete view of the acoustic scene at several time instants. The main topic of this chapter concerns with a detailed explanation of the steps regarding numerical sound fields simulations during the application of WDAF-based algorithms in order to analyze their performance in terms of sound field reconstruction.

In section 2 the theory of WFS and WFA is summarized and their discrete versions are derived. Then, the basic concepts of WDAF are reviewed and the involved transformations are described in section 3. Therefore, in section 4, the overall simulation processing is described. The discussion starts from the derivation of the sound field of a simple monopole source. Then, the sound field of a static source is virtually reproduced by an array of loudspeakers through the WFS algorithm. In the next step, starting from the simulation of sound field recording with an array of microphones, the PC simulation of the WDAF algorithm is performed. Variations of the whole set of involved parameters are taking into account. Finally, a WDAF application to the attenuation of undesired sources is derived from the well known mono channel approach. The results of the cancellation of the entire sound field of a virtual source through an adaptive algorithm based on WDAF approach is shown. Conclusions are reported in section 5.

2. Wave field analysis/synthesis

WFA and WFS are techniques based on microphones and loudspeakers arrays, arranged in order to shape a closed curve. The process, which permits to obtain the sound field in the area enclosed by the microphones array starting from microphones signals, is called *sound field extrapolation*. Essentially, the sound field extrapolation and its subsequently reproduction can be done in three ways:

- In the reproduction room the loudspeakers are positioned in the same location of the microphones in the recording room (Fig. 1(a)). This technique is called *holophony*, (Nicol & Emerit, 1999);
- The sound field is extrapolated in arbitrary positions starting from the microphones signals. In this way the loudspeakers can not be placed in the same microphones position (Verheijen, 1997);
- The room impulse response is recorded with the microphones array. In the reproduction stage this response is convolved with the desired signal, previously recorded in an anechoic chamber. In this way, any signal can be reproduced with the acoustic characteristics of the recording room (Hulsebos, 2004).

The holophonic technique does not need intermediate processing between recording and reproduction signals. However, its main limitation is given by the fact that the recorded sound field can only be reproduced through loudspeakers exactly placed at microphones positions. For this reason, the holophony technique can not be used in practical applications.

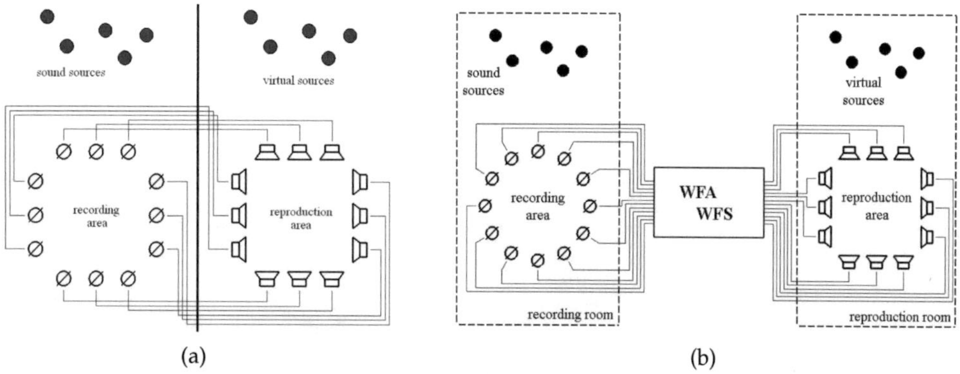

Fig. 1. Schematic representation of audio recording and reproduction techniques. (a) Holophony. (b) WFA/WFS.

On the other hand, the second and the third approaches need a processing of the recorded signals. In these cases the loudspeakers can be positioned in an arbitrary way and the loudspeakers number is not compulsorily equal to the microphones number. Even if their processing needs a higher computational load, these techniques present more flexibility and can be easily used in a real application. Sound field extrapolation can be obtained by the combination of WFA and WFS techniques. These approaches allow to record the entire sound field in the recording room (WFA) and subsequently to reproduce it in the listening room (WFS) more or less accurately depending on loudspeakers/microphones number (Fig. 1(b)). It was found that circular microphone arrays permit a very good sound field extrapolation and the problem can be treated more easily in circular coordinates (Hulsebos et al., 2002), hence in the following this geometry is considered.

2.1 Sound field reproduction

The basic idea of WFS derives from Huygens' Principle (1678). It states that, at any time t, all the points on the wave front due to a point source can be taken as point sources for the production of secondary wavelets. Following this principle, the sound field of an arbitrary primary source p can be reproduced by a series of secondary sources s positioned on the primary wavelet. These sources can be obtained by considering the medium local vibrations on s due to p. Kirchhoff's theorem is the generalization of the Huygens' Principle:

> *Considering a source-free volume V, the sound pressure inside the volume generated by external sources can be calculated if the pressure and the normal particle velocity on the enclosing surface S are known.*

The Kirchhoff-Helmholtz integral is the mathematical formulation of the Kirchoff's theorem. With reference to Fig. 2, considering a sound propagation in a volume V enclosed by a surface S, the Kirchhoff-Helmholtz integral is given by (Williams, 1999)

$$P(\vec{r}_0,\omega) = \frac{1}{4\pi} \oint_S \left(G_{\vec{r}_0}(\vec{r},\omega) \frac{\partial P_{\vec{r}_0}(\vec{r},\omega)}{\partial n} - P(\vec{r},\omega) \frac{\partial G_{\vec{r}_0}(\vec{r},\omega)}{\partial n} \right) dS, \tag{1}$$

where $\vec{r}_0$ and $\vec{r}$ denote the generic position inside V and on S respectively, ω is the angular frequency, $G_{\vec{r}_0}(\vec{r},\omega)$ is the Green function which synthesizes the secondary sources located in $\vec{r}_0$, while P defines the sound pressure level.

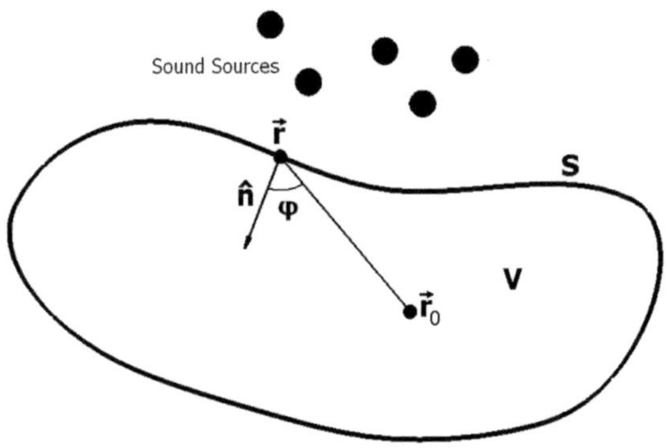

Fig. 2. Geometry used for the Kirchhoff-Helmholtz integral.

It is possible to write (1) in terms of sound pressure P and particle velocity V_n normal to S. From Euler's equation we have that

$$\frac{\partial P_{\vec{r}_0}(\vec{r},\omega)}{\partial n} = j\rho_0 ckV_n(\vec{r},\omega), \tag{2}$$

where c is the sound velocity, $k = \omega/c$ is the wave number, and ρ_0 is the medium density. Therefore, (1) becomes

$$P(\vec{r}_0,\omega) = \frac{1}{4\pi}\oint_S \left(j\rho_0 ckV_n(\vec{r},\omega)G_{\vec{r}_0}(\vec{r},\omega) - P(\vec{r},\omega)\frac{\partial G_{\vec{r}_0}(\vec{r},\omega)}{\partial n} \right) dS. \tag{3}$$

The Green function is not unique. The simplest Green functions are the monopole solutions for a source at the position $\vec{r}_0$

$$G_{\vec{r}_0}(\vec{r},\omega) = \frac{e^{-jk|\vec{r}-\vec{r}_0|}}{|\vec{r}-\vec{r}_0|} \tag{4}$$

$$G_{\vec{r}_0}(\vec{r},\omega) = \frac{e^{jk|\vec{r}-\vec{r}_0|}}{|\vec{r}-\vec{r}_0|}. \tag{5}$$

By inserting (4) in (3), the 3D forward Kirchhoff-Helmholtz integral is obtained

$$P(\vec{r}_0,\omega) = \frac{1}{4\pi}\oint_S \left(jk\rho_0 cV_n(\vec{r},\omega) + P(\vec{r},\omega)\frac{1+jk\,|\vec{r}-\vec{r}_0|}{|\vec{r}-\vec{r}_0|}\cos\varphi \right) \frac{e^{-jk|\vec{r}-\vec{r}_0|}}{|\vec{r}-\vec{r}_0|} dS, \tag{6}$$

where φ is the angle between the vector normal to S and the vector $\vec{r}_0 - \vec{r}$ (Fig. 2). From (6) it can be seen that the sound field inside V is obtained by a distribution of monopole and dipole sources (Berkhout et al., 1993). Equation (6) represents the direct integral and indicates a direct propagation due to the presence of the term $e^{-jk|\vec{r}-\vec{r}_0|}$. Similarly, by inserting (5) in (3), the 3D inverse Kirchhoff-Helmholtz integral is obtained

$$P(\vec{r}_0,\omega) = \frac{1}{4\pi}\oint_S \left(jk\rho_0 cV_n(\vec{r},\omega) + P(\vec{r},\omega)\frac{1-jk\,|\vec{r}-\vec{r}_0|}{|\vec{r}-\vec{r}_0|}\cos\varphi \right) \frac{e^{jk|\vec{r}-\vec{r}_0|}}{|\vec{r}-\vec{r}_0|} dS, \tag{7}$$

where the term $e^{jk|\vec{r}-\vec{r}_0|}$ indicates an inverse propagation (Yon et al., 2003).

In two dimensions, Kirchhoff-Helmholtz integral (3) is also valid considering a closed curve L instead of the surface S (Hulsebos et al., 2002). In this case, the appropriate Green functions are

$$G_{\vec{r}_0}(\vec{r},\omega) = -j\pi H_0^{(2)}(k|\vec{r}-\vec{r}_0|) \tag{8}$$

$$G_{\vec{r}_0}(\vec{r},\omega) = j\pi H_0^{(1)}(k|\vec{r}-\vec{r}_0|), \tag{9}$$

where $H_i^{(j)}$ is the Hankel function of kind j and order i. The Green function (8) leads to 2D forward Kirchhoff-Helmholtz integral

$$P^{(2)}(\vec{r},\omega) = \frac{-jk}{4}\oint_L \left(j\rho_0 c V_n(\vec{r},\omega) H_0^{(2)}(k|\vec{r}-\vec{r}_0|) + P(\vec{r},\omega)\cos\varphi H_1^{(2)}(k|\vec{r}-\vec{r}_0|)\right) dL. \tag{10}$$

Similarly, the Green function (9) leads to 2D inverse Kirchhoff-Helmholtz integral

$$P^{(1)}(\vec{r},\omega) = \frac{-jk}{4}\oint_L \left(j\rho_0 c V_n(\vec{r},\omega) H_0^{(1)}(k|\vec{r}-\vec{r}_0|) + P(\vec{r},\omega)\cos\varphi H_1^{(1)}(k|\vec{r}-\vec{r}_0|)\right) dL. \tag{11}$$

It is worth underlying that the forward Kirchhoff-Helmholtz integral is used for deriving the sound field generated by a source positioned outside S, while the inverse integral is used if the source is located inside S (or L in the 2D case).
In order to obtain Kirchhoff-Helmholtz integrals relative to circular geometry of radius R, (10) and (11) are simplified in (Hulsebos et al., 2002)

$$P^{(2)}(\vec{r},\omega) = \frac{-jk}{4}\oint_0^{2\pi} \left(j\rho_0 c V_n(\theta,\omega) H_0^{(2)}(k|\vec{r}-\vec{r}_0|) + P(\theta,\omega)\cos\varphi H_1^{(2)}(k|\vec{r}-\vec{r}_0|)\right) Rd\theta \tag{12}$$

$$P^{(1)}(\vec{r},\omega) = \frac{-jk}{4}\oint_0^{2\pi} \left(j\rho_0 c V_n(\theta,\omega) H_0^{(1)}(k|\vec{r}-\vec{r}_0|) + P(\theta,\omega)\cos\varphi H_1^{(1)}(k|\vec{r}-\vec{r}_0|)\right) Rd\theta. \tag{13}$$

The discrete forms of (12) and (13), necessary for a practical implementation, are obtained through a sampling operation at the loudspeakers positions

$$P^{(2)}(\vec{r},\omega) = \frac{-jk}{4}\sum_{i=1}^{N_L} \left(P(\theta_i,\omega)\cos\varphi H_1^{(2)}(k|\vec{r}-\vec{r}_i|) + j\rho c V_n(\theta_i,\omega) H_0^{(2)}(k|\vec{r}-\vec{r}_i|)\right) R\Delta\theta \tag{14}$$

$$P^{(1)}(\vec{r},\omega) = \frac{-jk}{4}\sum_{i=1}^{N_L} \left(P(\theta_i,\omega)\cos\varphi H_1^{(1)}(k|\vec{r}-\vec{r}_i|) + j\rho c V_n(\theta_i,\omega) H_0^{(1)}(k|\vec{r}-\vec{r}_i|)\right) R\Delta\theta. \tag{15}$$

Fig. 3 explains the meaning of $\vec{r}_i$, $\vec{r}$, φ and $\Delta\theta$. In section 4 it is shown how to implement (14) and (15) in an experimental configuration.

2.2 Sound field recording

Initially, in (Berkhout et al., 1993) the sound field recording was done through 2D microphones matrices. However, this technique was complicated and its practical realization was very difficult due to the necessity of extremely high performance hardware. In order to reduce the number of signals to be processed, the advantages of Huygens' principle were exploited also in the recording stage and microphones arrays enclosing the area of interest were used as alternative to microphones matrices (Berkhout et al., 1997).

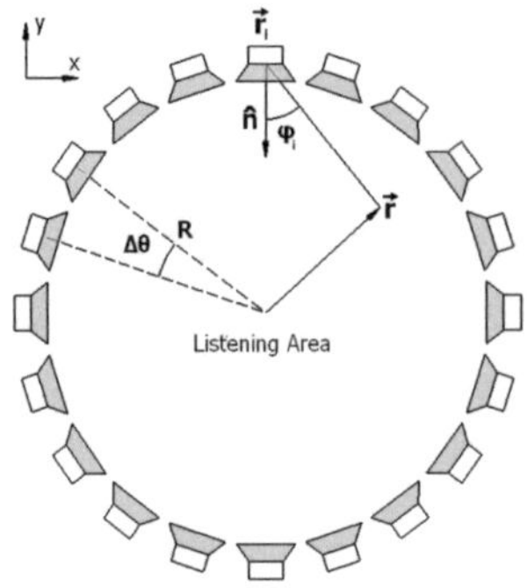

Fig. 3. Geometry used for the driving function calculation relative to circular array.

In section 2.1 we have seen the Kirchhoff-Helmholtz integrals referred to the circular array configuration. The global sound field is given by the sum of $P^{(1)}(\vec{r},\omega)$ and $P^{(2)}(\vec{r},\omega)$ which represent the inverse and forward extrapolated sound field, respectively (Hulsebos et al., 2002). By using Kirchhoff-Helmholtz integrals only the sound field within the closed curve can be extrapolated. To avoid this limitation, the sound field extrapolation through circular microphones array can be performed by using the cylindrical harmonics decomposition (Hulsebos, 2004).

Cylindrical harmonics of order k_θ are defined as solutions of the homogeneous wave equation in terms of cylindrical coordinates (Blackstock, 2000; Williams, 1999)

$$\mathcal{P}^{(1)}(r,\theta,\omega) = H^{(1)}_{k_\theta}(kr)e^{jk_\theta\theta}e^{jk_z z} \tag{16}$$

$$\mathcal{P}^{(2)}(r,\theta,\omega) = H^{(2)}_{k_\theta}(kr)e^{jk_\theta\theta}e^{jk_z z}, \tag{17}$$

where $H^{(1)}_m$ and $H^{(2)}_m$ are the Hankel function of kind 1 and 2, respectively, and m represents its order. k_θ and k_z are the wave numbers along the azimuth and z components of the cylindrical coordinates system defined by (r,θ,z) (Fig. 3). The far field approximation ($kr >> 1$) of the Hankel functions is given by

$$H^{(1)}_{k_\theta}(kr) \approx (-j)^{k_\theta}\frac{1-j}{\sqrt{\pi}}\frac{e^{jkr}}{\sqrt{kr}} \tag{18}$$

$$H^{(2)}_{k_\theta}(kr) \approx j^{k_\theta}\frac{1+j}{\sqrt{\pi}}\frac{e^{-jkr}}{\sqrt{kr}}. \tag{19}$$

In case of planar geometry, we have $k_z = 0$, hence (16) and (17) become

$$\mathcal{P}^{(1)}(\vec{r},\omega) = H^{(1)}_{k_\theta}(kr)e^{jk_\theta\theta} \tag{20}$$

$$\mathcal{P}^{(2)}(\vec{r},\omega) = H^{(2)}_{k_\theta}(kr)e^{jk_\theta\theta}, \tag{21}$$

where $^{(1)}$ and $^{(2)}$ are referred to incoming and outgoing cylindrical harmonics, respectively, while k_θ can be any signed integer number.

The objective is to decompose the entire sound field recorded by circular microphones array in cylindrical harmonics components. It is necessary to know both pressure and normal particle velocity values. The radial velocity can be calculated starting from the second Newton's Law

$$-\nabla P = j\omega\rho\vec{V}. \tag{22}$$

In order to obtain the normal velocity in terms of cylindrical components for a circular configuration, the ∇ operator can be reduced to partial derivative with respect to radial component

$$\frac{\partial P}{\partial r} = j\omega\rho V_n. \tag{23}$$

The application of the second Newton's Law to (20) and (21) results in

$$j\rho c\mathcal{V}_{k_\theta}^{(1)}(r,\theta,\omega) = H_{k_\theta}^{'(1)}(kr)e^{jk_\theta\theta} = \frac{1}{2}\left\{H_{k_\theta-1}^{(1)}(kr) - H_{k_\theta+1}^{(1)}(kr)\right\}e^{jk_\theta\theta} \tag{24}$$

$$j\rho c\mathcal{V}_{k_\theta}^{(2)}(r,\theta,\omega) = H_{k_\theta}^{'(2)}(kr)e^{jk_\theta\theta} = \frac{1}{2}\left\{H_{k_\theta-1}^{(2)}(kr) - H_{k_\theta+1}^{(2)}(kr)\right\}e^{jk_\theta\theta}, \tag{25}$$

taking into account the definition of the derivative of Hankel functions (Abramowitz & Stegun, 1970). Therefore, the sound field can be decomposed in cylindrical harmonics components

$$P(\theta,\omega) = \sum_{k_\theta}\left(M^{(1)}(k_\theta,\omega)\mathcal{P}_{k_\theta}^{(1)}(R,\theta,\omega) + M^{(2)}(k_\theta,\omega)\mathcal{P}_{k_\theta}^{(2)}(R,\theta,\omega)\right) \tag{26}$$

$$V_n(\theta,\omega) = \sum_{k_\theta}\left(M^{(1)}(k_\theta,\omega)\mathcal{V}_{k_\theta}^{(1)}(R,\theta,\omega) + M^{(2)}(k_\theta,\omega)\mathcal{V}_{k_\theta}^{(2)}(R,\theta,\omega)\right), \tag{27}$$

where $M^{(1)}$ and $M^{(2)}$ are the incoming and outgoing expansion coefficients of the sound field in terms of cylindrical harmonics. To find $M^{(1)}$ and $M^{(2)}$ behaviors, a spatial Fourier transform $\mathcal{F}_\theta$ is performed with respect to θ:

$$\tilde{P}(k_\theta,\omega) = \mathcal{F}_\theta(P) = \frac{1}{2\pi}\int_0^{2\pi} P(\theta,\omega)e^{-jk_\theta\theta}d\theta \tag{28}$$

$$\tilde{V}_n(k_\theta,\omega) = \mathcal{F}_\theta(V_n) = \frac{1}{2\pi}\int_0^{2\pi} V_n(\theta,\omega)e^{-jk_\theta\theta}d\theta \tag{29}$$

that are the Fourier coefficients of the series

$$P(\theta,\omega) = \sum_{k_\theta}\tilde{P}(k_\theta,\omega)e^{jk_\theta\theta} \tag{30}$$

$$V_n(\theta,\omega) = \sum_{k_\theta}\tilde{V}_n(k_\theta,\omega)e^{jk_\theta\theta}. \tag{31}$$

By substituting (30) in (26) and (31) in (27), the following relations keep valid for each k_θ

$$\tilde{P}(k_\theta,\omega) = M^{(1)}(k_\theta,\omega)H_{k_\theta}^{(1)}(kR) + M^{(2)}(k_\theta,\omega)H_{k_\theta}^{(2)}(kR) \tag{32}$$

$$j\rho c\tilde{V}_n(k_\theta,\omega) = M^{(1)}(k_\theta,\omega)H_{k_\theta}^{'(1)}(kR) + M^{(2)}(k_\theta,\omega)H_{k_\theta}^{'(2)}(kR). \tag{33}$$

Therefore, it is possible to solve these equations for $M^{(1)}$ and $M^{(2)}$:

$$M^{(1)}(k_\theta,\omega) = \frac{H_{k_\theta}^{'(2)}(kR)\tilde{P}(k_\theta,\omega) - H_{k_\theta}^{(2)}(kR)j\rho c\tilde{V}_n(k_\theta,\omega)}{H_{k_\theta}^{(1)}(kR)H_{k_\theta}^{'(2)}(kR) - H_{k_\theta}^{(2)}(kR)H_{k_\theta}^{'(1)}(kR)} \tag{34}$$

$$M^{(2)}(k_\theta,\omega) = \frac{H_{k_\theta}^{'(1)}(kR)\tilde{P}(k_\theta,\omega) - H_{k_\theta}^{(1)}(kR)j\rho c\tilde{V}_n(k_\theta,\omega)}{H_{k_\theta}^{(2)}(kR)H_{k_\theta}^{'(1)}(kR) - H_{k_\theta}^{(1)}(kR)H_{k_\theta}^{'(2)}(kR)}. \tag{35}$$

Finally, the sound field can be reconstructed:

$$P(r,\theta,\omega) = \sum_{k_\theta} \left(M^{(1)}(k_\theta,\omega)\mathcal{P}^{(1)}_{k_\theta}(r,\theta,\omega) + M^{(2)}(k_\theta,\omega)\mathcal{P}^{(2)}_{k_\theta}(r,\theta,\omega) \right) \tag{36}$$

$$V_n(r,\theta,\omega) = \sum_{k_\theta} \left(M^{(1)}(k_\theta,\omega)\mathcal{V}^{(1)}_{k_\theta}(r,\theta,\omega) + M^{(2)}(k_\theta,\omega)\mathcal{V}^{(2)}_{k_\theta}(r,\theta,\omega) \right). \tag{37}$$

By using cylindrical harmonics decomposition it is possible to extrapolate also the sound field external to the microphones array. Therefore, the sound field extrapolation can be summarized in 4 steps:

1. Signals recording by circular pressure and velocity microphones array to obtain $P(\theta,\omega)$ and $V_n(\theta,\omega)$;
2. Fourier transform with respect to angle θ of $P(\theta,\omega)$ and $V_n(\theta,\omega)$ to obtain $\tilde{P}(k_\theta,\omega)$ and $\tilde{V}(k_\theta,\omega)$;
3. Calculation of the expansion coefficients $M^{(1)}(k_\theta,\omega)$ and $M^{(2)}(k_\theta,\omega)$ in terms of cylindrical harmonics;
4. Sound field extrapolation at each point of the area through (36) and (37).

Moreover, it has been seen that the plane wave decomposition is a flexible format that can be used in order to recreate the sound field at any position (Hulsebos et al., 2002; Spors et al., 2005). The mathematical derivation of this decomposition (exploiting far field approximation of Hankel functions (18) and (19)) is given by

$$s^{(1),(2)}(\theta,\omega) = \frac{1}{2\pi} \sum_{k_\theta} j^{k_\theta} M^{(1),(2)}(k_\theta,\omega) e^{jk_\theta \theta} \tag{38}$$

$$P(r,\theta,\omega) = \int_0^{2\pi} s^{(1),(2)}(\theta',\omega) e^{-jkr\cos(\theta-\theta')} d\theta', \tag{39}$$

where $s^{(1)}$ and $s^{(2)}$ are the incoming and outgoing part of the wave field, respectively. The decomposition into incoming and outgoing waves can be used in order to distinguish between sources inside and outside the recording area.

3. Wave domain adaptive filtering

A practical implementation of digital signal processing algorithms (room equalization, noise reduction, echo cancellation) to WFA/WFS needs efficient solutions with the aim of decreasing the high computational cost due to the extremely high number of microphones/loudspeakers. To this end, Wave Domain Adaptive Filtering (WDAF) has been introduced (Buchner, Spors & Kellermann, 2004) as an extension in the spatial domain of Fast LMS (FLMS) (Haykin, 1996; Shynk, 1992). A more detailed explanation of this technique can also be found in (Buchner, 2008; Buchner & Spors, 2008; Spors, 2005).

It is known that FLMS optimal performance arises from the orthogonality property of the DFT basis functions. Therefore, in order to apply adaptive filtering to WFA/WFS systems, a proper set of orthogonal basis functions has been identified allowing a combined spatio-temporal transform, denoted with $\mathcal{T}$ and $\mathcal{T}^{-1}$, directly based on sound field extrapolation. FLMS has been derived from time-domain block-LMS (Shynk, 1992). However, in the FLMS case, the adaptation process is performed in the temporal frequency domain. By operating in the

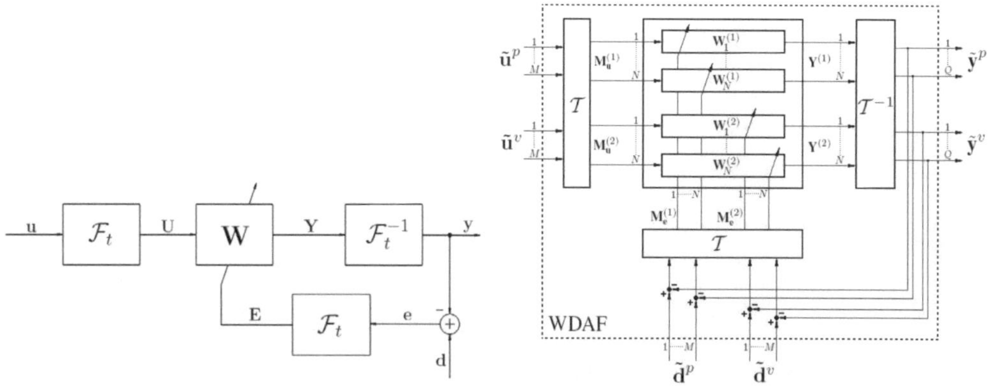

(a) (b)

Fig. 4. Typical configuration of adaptive algorithms. (a) FLMS. (b) WDAF.

transformed domain the computational load is particularly reduced because the convolution operation becomes a simple multiplication. Overlap and Save (OLS) and Overlap and Add (OLA) are used for avoiding circular convolution problems (Oppenheim et al., 1999). The general scheme of FLMS algorithm is shown in Fig. 4(a). Lowercase letters represent time domain signals while uppercase letters represent frequency domain signals. **u** is the input signal, **d** is the reference signal and **y** is the output signal. **W** is the adaptive filter where its coefficients are updated in real-time so that the output signal **y** is equal to **d** as much as possible.

Therefore, WDAF derives directly from FLMS: assuming to record the sound field with a circular array composed of M pressure and M particle velocity microphones (section 2.2), the basic scheme of WDAF is shown in Fig. 4(b), where **u** represents the $2M$ input signals, **d** represents the $2M$ desired signals, **y** represents the $2Q$ outputs relative to microphone positions (in all three cases pressure and particle velocity signals are considered) and **W** represents the adaptive process composed of $2N$ filters and based on least mean square approach. In this case, Fourier transform $\mathcal{F}_t$ has to be replaced by a wave domain transform $\mathcal{T}$. This transform derives directly from sound field extrapolation, just introduced in section 2.2. Therefore, starting from pressure $p(\theta, t)$ and particle velocity $v_n(\theta, t)$ signals, the $\mathcal{T}$-transform can be obtained by two Fourier transforms $\mathcal{F}_t$, $\mathcal{F}_\theta$ (in temporal and spatial frequency domain) followed by cylindrical harmonics decomposition $\mathcal{M}$ (Fig. 5(a)). The first Fourier transform is performed in the temporal frequency domain and it is given by

$$P(\theta, \omega) = \mathcal{F}_t(p) = \int_{-\infty}^{\infty} p(\theta, t) e^{-j\omega t} dt \tag{40}$$

$$V_n(\theta, \omega) = \mathcal{F}_t(v_n) = \int_{-\infty}^{\infty} v_n(\theta, t) e^{-j\omega t} dt \tag{41}$$

As regards the second Fourier transform and the cylindrical harmonics decomposition, they have just been introduced in (28) (29) (34) and (35).

As for the inverse transform ($\mathcal{T}^{-1}$), we can obtain the temporal frequency domain acoustic field at any point by applying $\mathcal{M}^{-1}$ (Fig. 5(b)) given by (36) and (37). Finally, an inverse

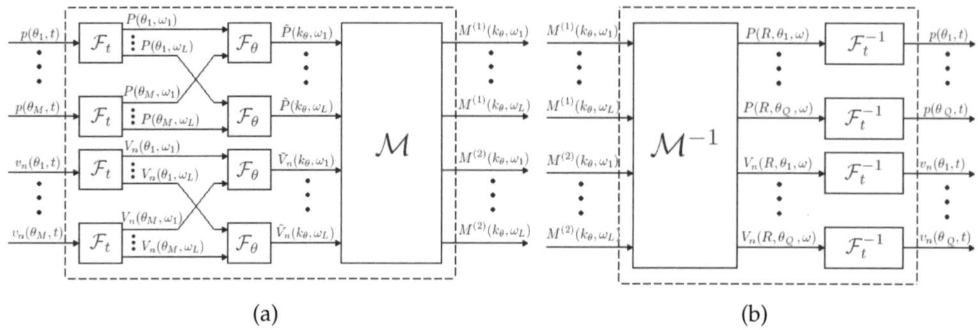

Fig. 5. Schemes of wave domain transforms. (a) Direct transform $\mathcal{T}$. (b) Inverse transform $\mathcal{T}^{-1}$.

Fourier transform $\mathcal{F}_t^{-1}$ is needed to come back to the time domain

$$p(\theta,t) = \mathcal{F}_t^{-1}(p) = \frac{1}{2\pi}\int_{-\infty}^{\infty} P(\theta,\omega)e^{j\omega t}d\omega \tag{42}$$

$$v_n(\theta,t) = \mathcal{F}_t^{-1}(v_n) = \frac{1}{2\pi}\int_{-\infty}^{\infty} V_n(\theta,\omega)e^{j\omega t}d\omega. \tag{43}$$

As stated, loudspeakers number and their positions in the area are totally independent from the number and the positions of the microphones and the generalization is extremely easy by using a $\mathcal{T}^{-1}$ transform at the loudspeakers location.
In (Peretti et al., 2008) a frame-by-frame WDAF implementation for streaming scenarios has been proposed. Furthermore, the computational cost of the WDAF implementation can be reduced taking advantage of filter banks theory. Moreover, the signal decomposition into subbands allows to achieve a faster convergence rate and a lower mean-square error for these adaptive algorithms.

4. Numerical simulations

Adaptive algorithms in WFA/WFS strictly depend on sound field quality that can be obtained through the aforementioned techniques. In fact, transformations $\mathcal{T}$ and $\mathcal{T}^{-1}$, WDAF is based on, have been directly derived from sound field extrapolation steps. Subsequently, the adaptive processing is the same as the mono-channel case, hence its performance depends on the numerical implementations of $\mathcal{T}$ and $\mathcal{T}^{-1}$ and it is necessary to understand how the parameters, introduced in previous sections, weigh on the sound field extrapolation.
The reference is an ideal monopole source pulsing at a certain frequency $f = 2\pi\omega$. Fig. 6 shows the sound field behaviour of an ideal 500 Hz-monopole obtained with PC simulations. It is derived by the evaluation of the sound pressure level through

$$p(\omega,\vec{r}) = A\frac{e^{-jk|\vec{r}-\vec{r}_s|}}{|r-\vec{r}_s|} \tag{44}$$

at the desired position $\vec{r}$ (virtual microphone) on the environment. $\vec{r}_0$ is the monopole position and A is a fixed gain. Therefore, a matrix of virtual microphones is considered in order to obtain the monopole behaviour.

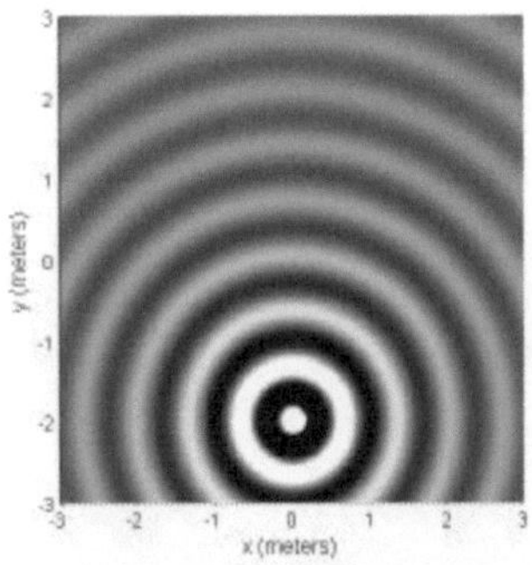

Fig. 6. Sound field of an ideal monopole with reproducing frequency 500 Hz at $[0, -2]$.

4.1 Sound field reproduction

By considering (12) and (13) it is possible to obtain the sound field of Fig. 6 through the knowledge of the sound pressure and the normal particle velocity on the perimeter of a circle of radius R. The sound pressure can be easily evaluated through (44) at positions $\vec{r} = [R, \theta]$ for each θ, while the particle velocity normal to the circumference can be obtained by difference quotient between the sound pressure levels at $\vec{r}_{R-h} = [R - h, \theta]$ and $\vec{r}_{R+h} = [R + h, \theta]$ (circular coordinates)

$$V_n(\omega, \theta) = \frac{p_{R-h}(\omega, \theta) - p_{R+h}(\omega, \theta)}{2jh\omega\rho}. \tag{45}$$

The results of the Kirchhoff-Helmoltz integral application are shown in Fig. 7(a) and Fig. 7(b). A circle of radius 1 m and 48 sensors of sound pressure and 48 sensors of sound velocity have been taking into account, and forward and inverse extrapolation have been performed. Inside the circle the sound field can be reconstructed in a good way. Good performance can be obtained also considering sound source inside the sensors array (Fig. 7(c) and Fig. 7(d)). As stated in section 2.1 it is possible to obtain correct sound fields only inside the circular array. In order to obtain suitable signals for loudspeakers, dipole sources have to be eliminated. Recently, an analytic secondary source selection criterion has been introduced where the selection depends on the sound source position in the area of interest (Spors, 2007): if the local propagation direction of the signal to be reproduced coincides with the loudspeaker axis direction $\hat{n}$ then the loudspeaker is turned on (Fig. 8). Fig. 9 shows results of simulations by considering only monopoles as secondary sources for sound sources either outside and inside the array. As happens in time sampling, there is a minimal distance Δd between two adjacent loudspeakers that permits to prevent the aliasing (in this case, spatial aliasing) (Spors & Rabenstein, 2006). Therefore, the maximum reproducible frequency without artefacts is $c/\Delta d$. Fig. 10 shows sound fields generated by a circular array that does not respect the spatial aliasing condition.

4.2 Wave Domain Transformations

Wave Domain Transformations $\mathcal{T}$ and $\mathcal{T}^{-1}$ are based on sound field extrapolation, i.e., cylindrical harmonics or plane waves components. Sound field reconstruction depends on the maximum order k_θ that is used in (36). Fig. 11 shows how the sound field of a 500 Hz monopole can be extrapolated depending on k_θ. The larger the area the higher the order, but there is a limit for k_θ where the area does not increase anymore. Furthermore, the sound field near the origin of the circle can not be extrapolated because of the considerable floating point error arising for the presence of multiplications between numbers with different orders

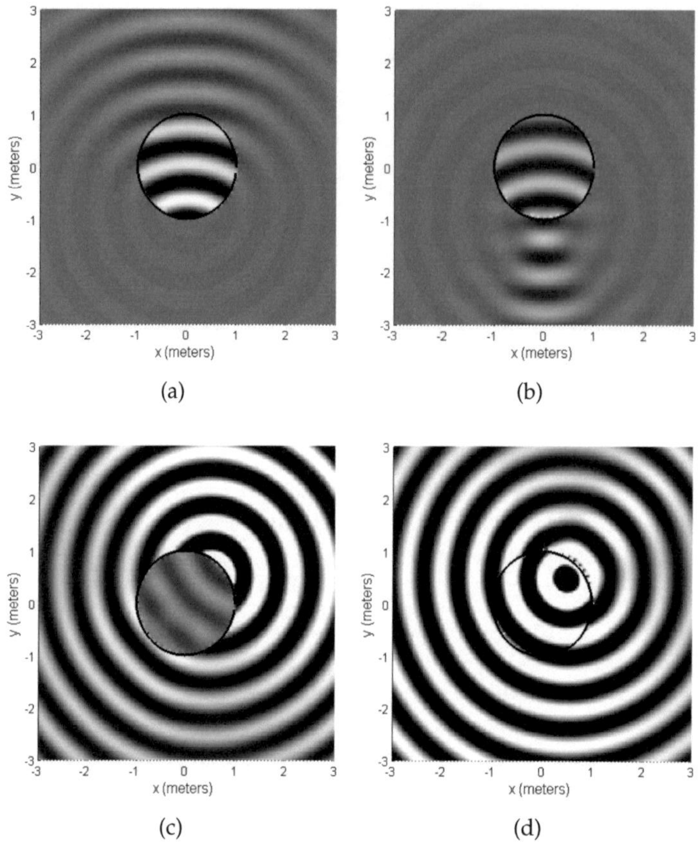

Fig. 7. Sound fields obtained through forward and inverse Kirchhoff-Helmholtz integrals by taking into account a sensors array of 48 elements and radius 1 m. (a) and (b) Forward and inverse sound field referred to a 500 Hz-sound source positioned outside the array $[0, -2]$. (c) and (d) Forward and inverse sound field referred to a 500 Hz-sound source positioned inside the array $[0.5, 0.5]$.

of magnitude. It should be noted that, k_θ being equal, the width of the area is in inverse proportion with respect to frequency (Fig. 12).
By considering plane waves decomposition the problem of floating pointing precision could be avoided and sound field can extrapolated also near the origin. The width of the area to be extrapolated depends on time frequency ω and spatial frequency k_θ as in the cylindrical harmonics decomposition (Fig. 13).

4.3 Application example: Adaptive source cancellation

An application example of WDAF algorithm can be found in (Peretti et al., 2007) with a novel approach to adaptive source cancellation. In a realistic scenario undesired noise sources can be present in the recording room. Therefore, it would be desirable to reduce the negative effect they have on the listener's acoustic experience. The algorithm for WFA/WFS systems can be obtained by using the spatio-temporal transforms $\mathcal{T}$ and $\mathcal{T}^{-1}$ presented in the previous section. Let us first consider an adaptive noise cancellation scheme used in traditional systems

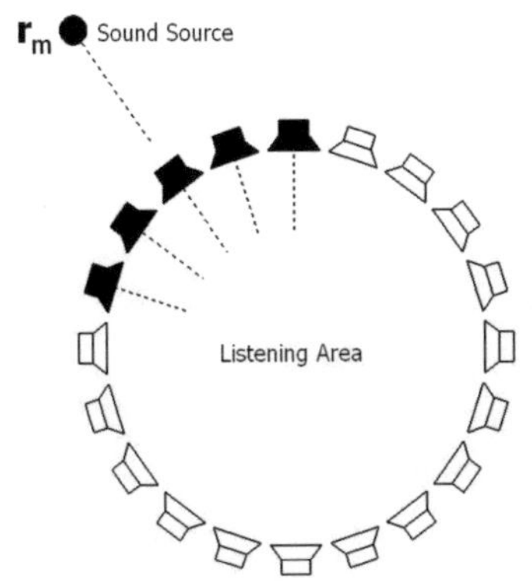

Fig. 8. Application example of the analytic secondary source selection criterion. Filled loudspeakers represent active secondary sources.

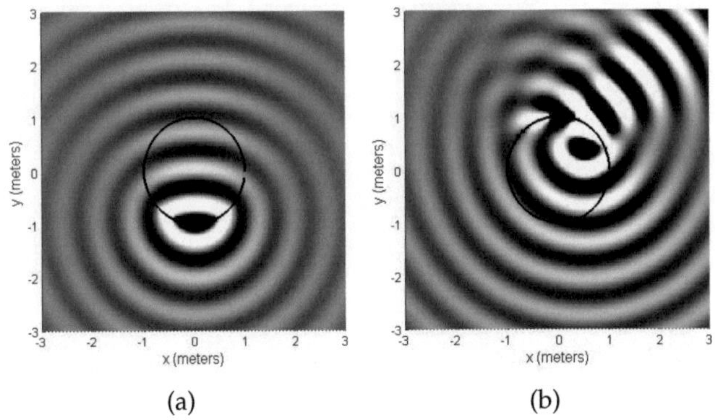

Fig. 9. Sound fields obtained through forward Kirchhoff-Helmholtz integrals by taking into account a sensors array of radius 1 m and 48 monopole sources activated following the secondary source criterion referred to a 500 Hz-sound source. (a) Source positioned outside the array. (b) Source positioned inside the array.

in which the noise signal is denoted with **n**, the global signal (superimposition of noise and desired fields) is denoted with **u**, and the noise free signal is **e** (Fig. 14(a)). The adaptation is carried out in the frequency domain through FLMS algorithm. Therefore, it can be applied to WFS/WFA systems through the introduction of WDAF (by employing transforms $\mathcal{T}$ and $\mathcal{T}^{-1}$) as shown in Fig. 14(b).

Some results of this WDAF application are reported in Fig. 15. Fig. 15(a) shows the desired sound field produced by a 700 Hz-monopole coming from the top with respect to the figure, and the noise field generated by a 400 Hz-monopole coming from bottom-right (denoted by **u** in the figures). In order to analyze the performance of the algorithm (Fig. 14(b)), the sound field related to the expansion coefficients of cylindrical harmonics **e** has been reconstructed. Sound field extrapolation has been carried out using plane waves decomposition (with 32 microphones and 32 loudspeakers arranged in a circular array of radius 1 m) as previously reported. Fig. 15(b) shows the resulting sound field relative to **e** after the steady state condition.

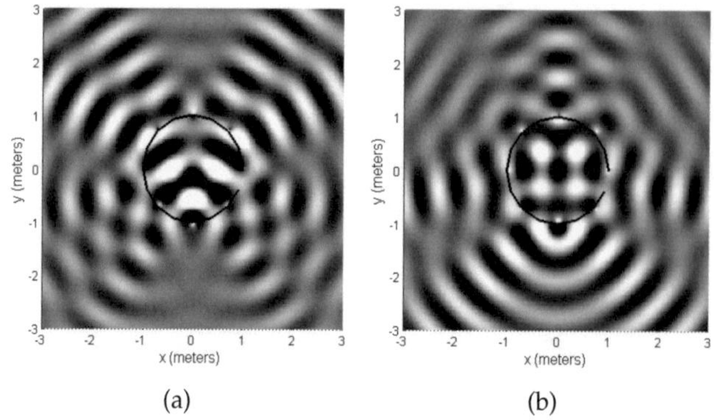

Fig. 10. Sound fields obtained through Kirchhoff-Helmholtz integrals by taking into account a sensors array of 8 elements and radius 1 m. They are referred to 500 Hz-sound source generated outside the array $[0, -2]$. (a) Forward integral. (b) Inverse integral.

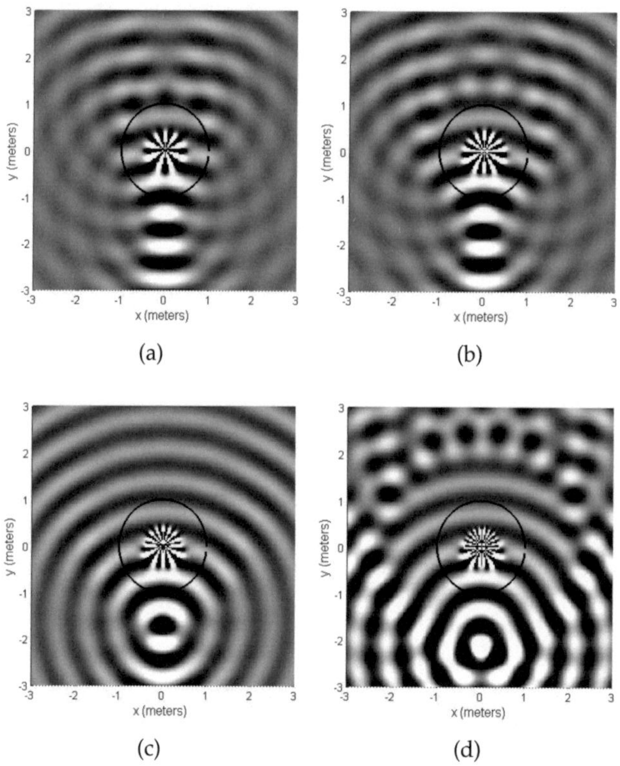

Fig. 11. Sound fields obtained through cylindrical harmonics derivation by taking into account a sensors array of 48 elements and radius 1 m. A 500 Hz-monopole generated at $[0, -2]$ has been considered. Simulations have been performed taking into account different order for k_θ. (a) $k_\theta = -9 : +9$. (b) $k_\theta = -12 : +12$. (c) $k_\theta = -15 : +15$. in (d) $k_\theta = -20 : +20$.

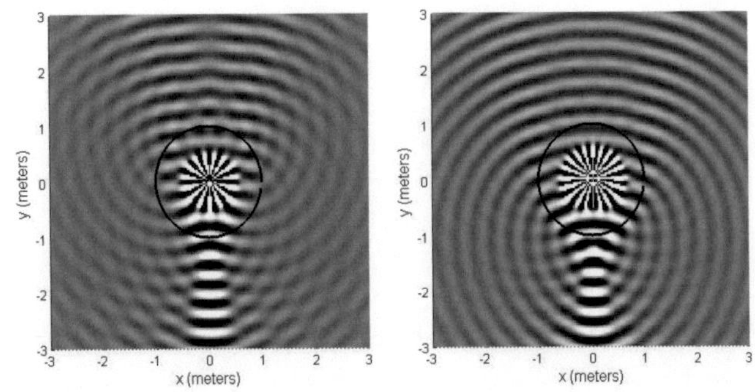

(a) (b)

Fig. 12. Sound fields obtained through cylindrical harmonics derivation by taking into account a sensors array of 48 elements and radius 1 m. A 1000 Hz-monopole generated at $[0, -2]$ has been considered. Simulations have been performed taking into account different order for k_θ. (a) $k_\theta = -15 : +15$. (b) $k_\theta = -20 : +20$.

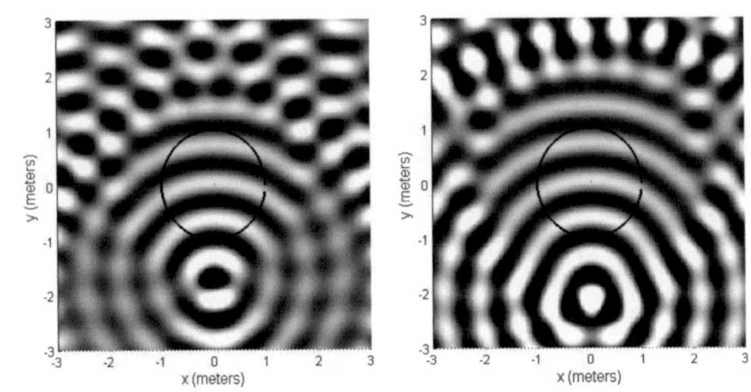

(a) (b)

Fig. 13. Sound fields obtained through plane waves decomposition by taking into account a sensors array of 48 elements and radius 1 m. A 500 Hz-monopole generated at $[0, -2]$ has been considered. Simulations have been performed taking into account different order for k_θ. (a) $k_\theta = -15 : +15$. (b) $k_\theta = -20 : +20$.

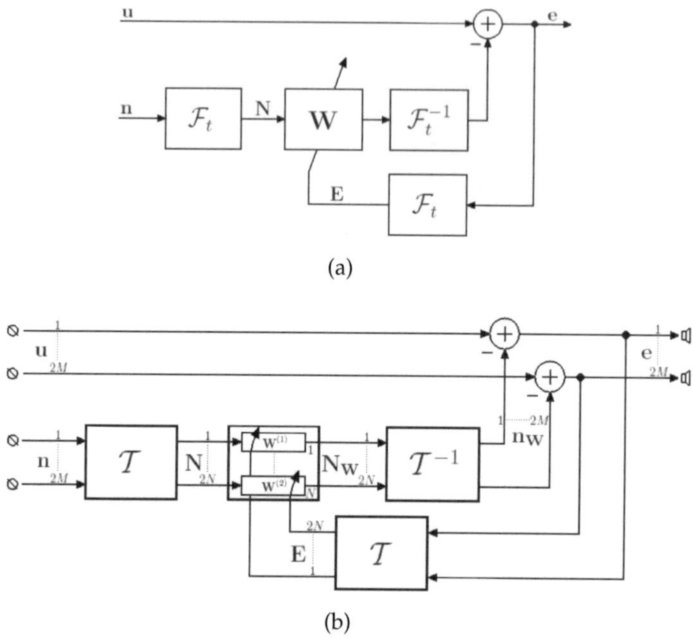

Fig. 14. Adaptive noise cancellation schemes. (a) Traditional mono-channel approach. (b) Wave domain extension for WFA/WFS systems; in case of loudspeakers positions different from microphones positions, a further extrapolation is needed for signal **u**.

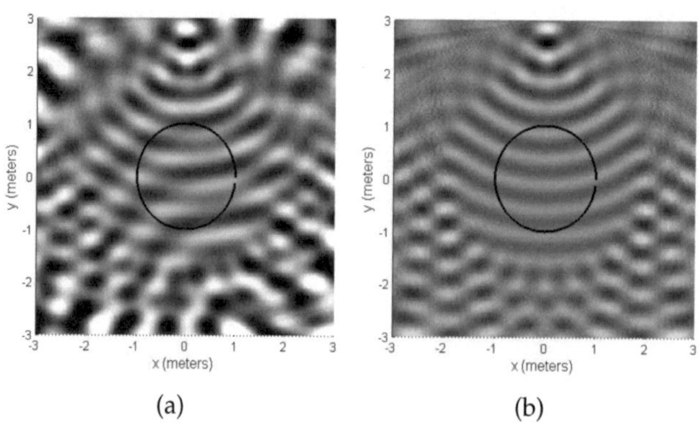

Fig. 15. Adaptive Noise Cancellation with WDAF approach. (a) Corrupted input sound field. (b) Noise-free output sound field.

5. Conclusions

Wave Field Analysis and Synthesis are two techniques that permit direct sound field recording and reproduction using microphones and loudspeakers arrays. In order to use these techniques in real world applications (e.g., cinema, home theatre, teleconferencing), it is necessary to apply multi-channel Digital Signal Processing algorithms, already developed for traditional systems. A straightforward implementation needs an extremely high computational complexity, hence Wave Domain Adaptive Filtering (WDAF) has been introduced extending the well-known Fast LMS algorithm. Since WDAF is derived from transforms related to WFA/WFS, it inherits their strengths: the extension of optimal listening area and a better source localization in the environment. It is based on cylindrical harmonics decomposition. In this chapter, the numerical implementation of WDAF transformations have been described and results of simulations have been presented. In particular, considering circular arrays, the area, the sound field is correctly extrapolated on, becomes larger increasing the maximum order of cylindrical harmonic and decreasing the reproduced frequency. Through the only cylindrical harmonics decomposition, some numerical problems could arise nearby the origin of the circular array. Therefore, plane wave decomposition, based on far field approximations, can be used in order to overcome this problem. Numerical simulations of the application of WDAF to adaptive noise cancellation show the effectiveness of the algorithm.

6. References

Abramowitz, M. & Stegun, I. (1970). *Handbook of Mathematical Functions*, Dover Pubblications Inc., United States.

Berkhout, A. J. (1988). A holographic approach to acoustic control, *J. Audio Eng. Soc.* 36(12): 977–995.

Berkhout, A. J., de Vries, D. & Sonke, J. J. (1997). Array Technology for Acoustic Wave Field Analysis in Enclosures, 102(5): 2757–2770.

Berkhout, A. J., De Vries, D. & Vogel, P. (1993). Acoustic control by wave field synthesis, *J. Acoust. Soc. Amer.* 93(5): 2764–2778.

Blackstock, D. T. (2000). *Fundamentals of Physical Acoustics*, Wiley-Interscience, United States.

Buchner, H. (2008). Acoustic Echo Cancellation for Multiple Reproduction Channels: from first principles to Real-Time Solutions, *Proc. ITG Conference on Speech Communication*, Aachen, Germany.

Buchner, H. & Spors, S. (2008). A general derivation of Wave-Domain Adaptive Filtering and application to Acoustic Echo Cancellation, *Proc. IEEE 42nd Asilomar Conference on Signals, Systems, and Computers*, Pacific Grove, CA, USA, pp. 816–823.

Buchner, H., Spors, S. & Kellermann, W. (2004). Wave-domain adaptive filtering: Acoustic echo cancellation for full- duplex systems based on wave-field synthesis, *Proc. IEEE International Conference on Acoustics, Speech and Signal Processing*, Vol. 4, Montreal, Canada, pp. 117–120.

Buchner, H., Spors, S. & Rabenstein, R. (2004). Efficient active listening room compensation for wave field synthesis, *Proc. 116th AES Conv.*, Berlin, Germany.

Daniel, J., Nicol, N. & Moreau, S. (2003). Further investigations of high order ambisonics and wavefield synthesis for holophonic sound imaging, *Proc. of 114th AES Conv.*, Amsterdam, The Netherlands.

Fazi, F. M., Nelson, P. A., Christensen, J. E. N. & Seo, J. (2008). Surround system based on three dimensional sound field reconstruction, *Proc. of 125th AES Conv.*, San Francisco, CA, USA,.

Haykin, S. (1996). *Adaptive Filter Theory*, Prentice-Hall, Inc., Englewood Cliffs, NJ.

Hulsebos, E. (2004). *Auralization using Wave Field Synthesis*, PhD thesis, Delft University of Technology, Delft, The Netherlands.

Hulsebos, E., de Vries, D. & Bourdillat, E. (2002). Improved microphone array configurations for auralization of sound fields by wave field synthesis, *J. Audio Eng. Soc.* 50(10): 779–790.

Nicol, R. & Emerit, M. (1999). 3d-sound reproduction over an extensive listening area: A hybrid method derived from holophony and ambisonic, *Proc. 16th Audio Engineering Society Conference*, Rovaniemi, Finland.

Oppenheim, A. V., Schafer, R. W. & Buck, J. R. (1999). *Discrete-Time Signal Processing*, Prentice Hall International Inc. pp. 274-279.

Peretti, P., Cecchi, S., Palestini, L. & Piazza, F. (2007). A novel approach to active noise control based on wave domain adaptive filtering, *Proc. IEEE Workshop on Applications of Signal Processing to Audio and Acoustics*, New Paltz, NY, USA, pp. 307–310.

Peretti, P., Palestini, L., Cecchi, S. & Piazza, F. (2008). A subband approach to wave domain adaptive filtering, *Proc. Joint Workshop on Handsfree Speech Communication and Microphone Arrays*, Trento, Italy.

Shynk, J. J. (1992). Frequency-domain and multirate adaptive filtering, *IEEE Signal Process. Mag.* 9(1): 14–37.

Spors, S. (2005). *Active Listening Room Compensation for Spatial Sound Reproduction Systems*, PhD thesis, Friedrich-Alexander-University of Erlangen-Nurnberg, Nurnberg, Germany.

Spors, S. (2007). Extension of an analytic secondary source selection criterion for wave field synthesis, *Proc. 123rd Audio Engineering Society Convention*, New York, NY, USA.

Spors, S. & Rabenstein, R. (2006). Spatial aliasing artifacts produced by linear and circular loudspeaker arrays used for wave field synthesis, *Proc. 120th Audio Engineering Society Convention*, Paris, France.

Spors, S., Renk, M. & Rabenstein, R. (2005). Limiting effects of active room compensation using wave field synthesis, *Proc. 118th AESociety Conv.*, Barcelona, Spain.

Verheijen, E. N. G. (1997). *Sound Reproduction by Wave Field Synthesis*, PhD thesis, Delft University of Technology, Delft, The Netherlands.

Williams, E. G. (1999). *Fourier Acoustics: Sound Radiation and Nearfield Acoustical Holography*, Academic Press, London, UK.

Yon, S., Tanter, M. & Fink, M. (2003). Sound focusing in rooms: The time-reversal approach, *J. Acoust. Soc. Amer.* 113(3): 1533–1543.